SAS® and SPSS® Program Solutions

for use with

Applied Linear Statistical Models

Fifth Edition

Michael H. Kutner
Emory University

Christopher J. Nachtsheim
University of Minnesota

John Neter
University of Georgia

William Li
University of Minnesota

Prepared by
William D. Johnson
William H. Replogle
Both of University of Mississippi Medical Center

McGraw-Hill
Irwin

Boston   Burr Ridge, IL   Dubuque, IA   Madison, WI   New York   San Francisco   St. Louis
Bangkok   Bogotá   Caracas   Kuala Lumpur   Lisbon   London   Madrid   Mexico City
Milan   Montreal   New Delhi   Santiago   Seoul   Singapore   Sydney   Taipei   Toronto

SAS® and SPSS® Program Solutions for use with
APPLIED LINEAR STATISTICAL MODELS
Michael H. Kutner, Christopher J. Nachtsheim, John Neter, William Li

Published by McGraw-Hill/Irwin, an imprint of The McGraw-Hill Companies, Inc., 1221 Avenue of the
Americas, New York, NY 10020. Copyright © 2005 by The McGraw-Hill Companies, Inc. All rights reserved.

2 3 4 5 6 7 8 9 0 QSR/QSR 0 9 8

ISBN 978-0-07-302177-5
MHID 0-07-302177-6

www.mhhe.com

The McGraw-Hill Companies

Preface

The first edition of *Applied Linear Statistical Models* was published in 1974 and immediately became a popular text with both instructors and students. Each edition has brought many improvements while the clarity in presentation and usefulness of examples and exercises have remained consistent. We have used the book as a required text for many years; however, the students in our courses typically have limited statistical programming skills. As a result, many students spend a disproportionate amount of time mastering programming skills rather than statistical concepts. In an effort to minimize the amount of assignment time students spend learning SAS® or SPSS® computer code, we present source programming code and sample output for the most salient chapter examples given in *Applied Linear Statistical Models*, 5th *Edition* by Kutner, Nachtsheim, Neter, and Li (2004). The resulting text is intended to be a supplement to *Applied Linear Statistical Models*, although it also may be a helpful reference for the practicing analyst/statistician.

This book is divided into two sections: SAS® Solutions and SPSS® Solutions. Chapters 1-30 of each section parallel the 30 chapters of *Applied Linear Statistical Models*. In addition, we have added a Chapter 0 that explains how to get started using the SAS and SPSS statistical packages. This chapter includes a brief discussion of how to access SAS or SPSS, enter data, perform computations, and store and retrieve results. Each of the remaining chapters gives specific SAS and SPSS instructions and resulting output for solving the examples presented in *Applied Linear Statistical Models*.

We display illustrative SAS and SPSS syntax almost entirely in *Insert* boxes. Each *Insert* is intended to represent a fully functional program that is not dependent on syntax from preceding *Inserts*. We have taken this approach to simplify the steps for new users. As you become familiar with SAS and SPSS programming, you will be able to combine some *Inserts* to decrease the number of steps needed to complete a specific analysis. Additionally, most programming tasks can be accomplished through many different choices of computer syntax. Some of the more esoteric programming techniques, however, can be difficult for beginners. We have taken a pragmatic approach and presented syntax using strategies that we have found to be fairly easy for first year graduate students to grasp. These strategies can be easily modified to analyze problems similar to the illustrative examples. As you gain experience, you may choose to use more sophisticated and perhaps more efficient programming solutions.

The modules required to perform the analyses in the SAS chapters are Release 8.1 of SAS/STAT™, SAS/IML™, and SAS/GRAPH™. The modules used in the SPSS chapters are Release 11.5.0 of SPSS Base™, SPSS Advanced Models™, and SPSS Regression Models™. Both SAS and SPSS have a variety of other products that may be useful for some applications presented in *Applied Linear Statistical Models*. The products we used are commonly available to students enrolled in statistics courses and can be used to solve almost all of the examples and exercises in *Applied Linear Statistical Models*.

William D. Johnson

William H. Replogle

CONTENTS

SAS Solutions

Chapter 23 SAS®

Chapter 24 SAS®

Chapter 25 SAS®

Chapter 26 SAS®

Chapter 29 SAS®

Chapter 30 SAS®

SPSS Solutions

Chapter 11 SPSS®

Chapter 12 SPSS®

Chapter 13 SPSS®

Chapter 27 SPSS®

Chapter 28 SPSS®

SAS® Solutions

Chapter 0 SAS®

Working with SAS®

The purpose of this chapter is to introduce the requisite methods for entering, creating, and opening the data files provided with *Applied Linear Statistical Models*, *5th Edition* by Kutner, Nachtsheim, Neter, and Li (2004). Although we will work with many of the SAS programs as we progress through *Applied Linear Statistical Models* (ALSM), the present chapter is not intended to be a comprehensive review of SAS capabilities.

SAS is a modular, integrated, product line for the analytical process. The SAS products can be used for:

- Planning
- Data collection
- Data access and management
- Report writing
- Statistical analysis
- File handling

SAS is available for most mainframe and personal computers running under the Windows® or Macintosh® operating systems. The modules required to perform the analyses in the forthcoming chapters are SAS/STAT, SAS/IML, and SAS/GRAPH.

Starting SAS: Most computer systems have a SAS icon on the desktop. We double click the icon to start SAS. When we first start SAS software, the five main SAS windows open: the Explorer, Results, Editor, Log, and Output windows. In this book, we will be working with the Editor, Output, and Log windows. The Editor window allows the user to enter, edit, and submit SAS programs.

The first step in executing a SAS program is to enter the program on the Program Editor screen. If we are in the Program Editor, we can enter a program by clicking the File tab at the top of the screen and then clicking Open on the drop-down menu. We can then identify the folder and name of the program to be opened. Alternatively, we can type a program directly onto the Program Editor. Once we have entered the program onto the Program Editor screen, we can save it to a folder for future use. There is a *run* icon at the top right portion of the screen. When we are ready to execute a program that is entered on the Program Editor screen, we select Run > Submit from the dropdown menu or click the symbol.

When the program is executed, the Output screen will appear on the monitor. The Output screen contains the results that are printed when the submitted program has executed. The Program

Editor, Log, and Output tab bars appear at the bottom of the monitor. If there is a graph in the output, there may also be a Graph tab bar at the bottom of the monitor. We can click on these tab bars to go to the Editor, Log, Output, and Graph screens. Alternatively, we can click on the View tab bar at the top of the monitor and then click on one of the tab bars on the pop-down menu. *Caution*: If nothing happens when we execute the program, we probably have an error in the program. We can click on the Log tab to look for error messages that may be printed by the SAS System. We can scroll down the Log screen to search for errors. Once we discover the errors, we must go back to the Program Editor screen, make corrections, and re-execute the program. When writing a new program, it is not unusual to go through this process several times. We can scroll down the Output screen to see different portions of the output. If applicable, we can click on the Graph bar to inspect graphical output.

At the top of the screen, there is a tab labeled Help. We can click on the Help tab and search for answers to questions about the SAS System. As discussed above, when we submit a SAS program from within the Editor window, SAS creates the Output window, which automatically moves to the front of other windows. The Log window displays messages including error messages regarding the SAS syntax in the submitted program.

The SAS Program: The typical SAS program is made up of two or more steps that are usually specified in the program in the following order:

- Data Step
- Procedure Step

The Data step defines the data file. The Procedure Step identifies the specific SAS programs (Procedures) you want to implement. After we define the data file in a Data Step, we can specify Procedures to be executed. However, once we have specified a Data Step and then one or more Procedures, you cannot alter the data without going through a new Data Step. Thus, a typical organization of a SAS program might be:

- Data a
- Procedure
- Procedure
- Procedure
- Data b
- Procedure
- Procedure
- Data c
- Procedure

Data b and Data c may specify entirely new data sets or they may specify data sets created from results of procedures executed in previous data steps.

The SAS System is made up of many computer programs (software) designed to perform the five functions listed above. As users of the SAS System, we must use SAS instructions to call on the "canned" programs within the SAS System to execute a specific application of a task.

We shall refer to a single SAS instruction as a *statement*. It is essential that all SAS statements end with a semicolon, and the most common SAS programming error is to omit the semicolon. We refer to a set of SAS statements used in an execution of a task as *SAS code* or a *SAS program*. We begin with a basic program to enter data and then to print the data. We then show how to write SAS statements to modify the data using algebraic expressions.

A Basic SAS Program to Input/Output Data: The simple SAS program in Insert 0.1 serves as a starting point for learning SAS syntax:

```
                        INSERT 0.1

options ls = 72 ps = 65 nodate nonumber;
        title 'Chapter 0 Example 1';
        data ch00ex01;
          input firstname $ age gender $ glucose;
        datalines;
        eric     41 male    102
        karen   38 female  93
        ann      43 female 121
        eugene 35 male     109
        frank    47 male    134
        gary     39 male    117
        gloria   42 female  95
        gwen    46 female  99
        robert   37 male    103
        mary     40 female 110
        ;
      proc print;
        var firstname glucose;
      run;
```

In this SAS program the first statement begins with the SAS keyword *options*. This option statement instructs the SAS System to print output according to the specified instructions. The *ls = 72* option specifies that output will have line size with a maximum of 72 printed characters per line. The *ps = 65* option specifies that output will have page size with a maximum of 65 printed lines per page. The *nodate* option specifies that the date is not to be printed on output pages. The *nonumber* option specifies that the page numbers are not to be printed on the output. *ls, ps, nodate,* and *nonumber* are all SAS code or keywords.

The second statement in the program begins with the SAS keyword *title*. This statement instructs the SAS System to print the words that appear in single quotes at the top of all pages of printed output; i.e., *Chapter 0 Example 1* is to be printed at the top of all output pages.

The third statement in the program begins with the SAS keyword *data*. This statement initiates a data step in the program. We have chosen the name *ch00ex01* for this data step. Thus, *ch00ex01* is not a SAS keyword but rather a name we have assigned for convenience. The data defined in this step will be stored under the data file name *ch00ex01* and can be accessed in a future step using this name.

The fourth statement in the program begins with the SAS keyword *input*. This statement assigns variable names to data fields and specifies the type of data that is in the field. We have chosen "firstname" as a name for the first variable, "age" as a name for the second variable, "gender" as a name for the third variable, and "glucose" as a name for the fourth variable. The dollar sign ($) after *firstname* and *gender* specifies that these variables may contain alphanumeric data; if nothing appears after a variable name in an *input* statement, the corresponding data field must contain only numeric data. The variable names must be arranged in order corresponding to the order of the data fields in the input data set.

The fifth statement in the program begins with the SAS keyword *datalines*. This statement indicates that the typed data set follows. The data fields in the typed data set are separated by one or more blank spaces. Each line of data contains data for a single study unit. A semicolon appears after the last line of data. There are many allowable variations in the way the data are entered in a SAS program, but the way described here is probably the simplest.

The sixth statement in the program begins with the SAS keyword *proc*. This keyword initiates a procedure step in the program. Many *procedures* are available in the SAS system. For illustration, we have chosen the *print* procedure. The SAS syntax *proc print* requests printed output.

The seventh statement in the program begins with the SAS keyword *var*. This keyword identifies the variables to be used in executing the *proc print* statement. Here, we have chosen *firstname* and *glucose* as the variables to be printed. Thus, the first name and glucose value will be printed for all data lines in the data set. Output from *proc print* and output that may be automatically printed by other SAS procedures is printed to the Output window described above. We can obtain a paper copy of the Output window by using the File>Print drop down menu.

The last statement in the program begins with the SAS keyword *run*. This is an important statement because it instructs SAS to run all procedures specified since the end of the data file or since the previous *run* statement. If we omit the *run* statement in the program shown in Insert 0.1, the *proc print* statement will not be executed.

Reading the ALSM data files: The ALSM text comes with a disk containing numerous data sets. We recommend that you transfer these data from the supplied disk to a permanent storage device. For instance, we created two directories named *ALRM* and *KUTNERDATA* on the C: drive and transferred all the ALSM data sets to these directories. All SAS illustrations in our book specify a path to one of these directories. As you write SAS code to perform statistical analyses of other data, you will need to modify the path specified within the illustrative SAS syntax to identify the storage device and directory for the data sets relevant to each application.

In text Chapter 1, the authors present the Toluca Company data set in Table 1.1. To read this data set, we start SAS and in the Editor window type the syntax as shown in Insert 0.2 – Method 1. (In Insert 0.2 and throughout this book, an * in an insert box represents a comment that explains some of the syntax.) The *data* statement tells SAS that we want to create a data set named Toluca. The *infile* statement identifies the path to the Toluca Company data set. Note that the directories for chapters 1 – 9 have 2 spaces between the word "chapter" and the corresponding chapter number. Thus, the *infile* statement must also contain 2 spaces as in "chapter 1." The input statement tells SAS the variable names to be assigned to the 2 variables in the data set. Variable names are determined by the user but must be consistent with naming conventions within SAS. In general, the variable name can consist of no more than 10 characters, cannot begin with a number, and cannot contain special characters. Execution of the syntax in Insert 0.1 – Method 1 will read the data for the Toluca Company data set into the variables *lotsize* and *workhrs*. *Lotsize* and *workhrs* will then be available for use with other SAS syntax. We execute the syntax in Insert 0.1 by selecting Run > Submit from the dropdown menu or by clicking the 犬 symbol.

We can enter data directly into the SAS Editor (syntax file) as shown in Insert 0.2 – Method 2. On text page 3, the authors present a data set containing the number of units sold (X) and the dollar sales amount (Y) for 3 time periods. As with Method 1, the *data* statement tells SAS that we want to create a data set named *example* and the *input* statement tells SAS the variable names to be assigned to the 3 variables in the imbedded data set. We name the three variables *period*, *units*, and *sales*, respectively, as shown in Insert 0.2. These names are arbitrary but follow conventions for variable names within SAS. The *datalines* statement indicates to SAS that the subsequent lines will contain data until a semicolon ";" is encountered. The syntax in Insert 0.2 – Method 2 will read the data for the example given on text page 3 into the variables *period*, *units*, and *sales*. *Period*, *units*, and *sales* will then be available for use with other SAS syntax.

The user must define by the *input* statement the type of variable to be read. That is, we can define a variable as a numeric, string (alphanumeric), or various other types of variables. For instance, each of the 3 variables defined on text page 3 is a numeric variable and can have only numeric values. If we were to enter the name of a city, such as "Memphis," we would have to define the variable as a string variable so that alpha-numeric characters could be entered to represent the city name. A string variable is defined by placing a $ character after the variable name, for example:

input city $

In Insert 0.2 – Method 2, we can define *units* as a string variable. But, once a variable is defined as a string, mathematical operations cannot be performed on the variable. So, we can take the square root of *units* if it is defined as a numeric variable but not if it is defined as a string variable.

INSERT 0.2	INSERT 0.2 continued
* Method 1; data Toluca; infile 'C:\alrm\chapter 1 data sets\ch01ta01.txt'; input lotsize workhrs;	* Method 2; data example; input period units sales; datalines; 1 75 150 2 25 50 3 130 260 ;

Creating a new variable: Suppose in the Toluca Company example above we wish to find the square of *lotsize* for use in polynomial regression. In Insert 0.3 we open the Toluca Company example as before and then compute a new variable, *lotsqr*, the square of *lotsize*. We can now use SAS *proc* statements to invoke predefined statistical routines. For instance, we can instruct SAS to use the predefined *means* routine to find the mean of *lotsize* and *lotsqr*. Since there will often be more than one data set created and available for use in a SAS session, we can optionally include on the *proc* statement a *date=dataset* statement (e.g., *data=toluca*) to identify the data set for use when executing the *proc* statement. Execution of Insert 0.3 will place the results as shown in SAS Output 0.1 in the Output window.

```
                              INSERT 0.3

data Toluca;
infile 'C:\alrm\chapter  1 data sets\ch01ta01.txt';
input lotsize workhrs;
lotsqr=lotsize**2;
proc means data=toluca;
 var lotsize lotsqr;
run;
```

SAS Output 0.1

Variable	N	Mean	Std Dev	Minimum	Maximum
lotsize	25	70.0000000	28.7228132	20.0000000	120.0000000
lotsqr	25	5692.00	4015.48	400.0000000	14400.00

In Insert 0.4, we read the Toluca Company data set as before and name the variables *lotsize* and *workhrs*. We then perform a regression analysis (*proc reg*) where the model statement specifies the dependent and independent variables to be used in the *model*, i.e.,

dependent variable = list of one or more independent variables.

In Insert 0.4, the dependent variable is *workhrs* and the single independent variable is *lotsize*. We can optionally request that residuals from the fitted model be saved by the *r* option on the *model* statement. We then tell SAS in which data set (*out=step2*) to store the results and to store the residuals (*r*) in a variable named *residual*. Now, the data set named *toluca* will contain *lotsize* and *workhrs*, and the data set named *step2* will contain *lotsize*, *workhrs*, and *residual*. Thus, to find the square of *residual*, we use *data step3* (the data file name *step3* is arbitrary) to issue a new data statement and then use *set step2* to identify *step2* as the data set to be used to find *ressqr=residual**2;*. Thus, we point SAS to the new data file (*step2*) to find the variable *residual* to be squared. We can then print (*proc print*) the values of *ressqr*.

```
                         INSERT 0.4

data Toluca;
  infile 'c:\alrm\chapter  1 data sets\ch01ta01.txt';
  input lotsize workhrs;
proc reg;
  model workhrs = lotsize / r;
  output out=step2 r=residual;
run;
data step3;
 set step2;
 ressqr=residual**2;
 run;
proc print;
 var ressqr;
 run;
```

SAS provides an extensive help system available from the Help dropdown menu. Additional help can be obtained at www.sas.com using SAS Notes® and other technical support options. SAS and all other SAS Institute Inc. product or service names are registered trademarks or trademarks of SAS Institute Inc. in the USA and other countries. We are grateful to SAS Technical Support for their assistance. SAS® software is licensed by:

SAS Institute Inc.
100 SAS Campus Drive
Cary, NC 27513-2414
USA
www.SAS.com

Chapter 1 SAS®

Linear Regression with One Predictor Variable

This chapter of the text introduces the simple linear regression model. The idea is to use statistical methods to find a model that allows us to predict the value of a dependent variable Y given the value of an independent variable X. We are given Y_i and X_i for a sample of n subjects and we want to find a "best fitting" model for predicting Y given X. The usual approach is to begin by assuming the model is of the form:

$$Y_i = \beta_0 + \beta_1 X_i + \varepsilon_i$$

for the ith subject, $i = 1, \ldots, n$. This is often referred to as a *simple linear regression model*. The first step is to find estimates of β_0 and β_1 so that the "fitted" model is best, as defined in the text, among all models of this form. The statistical analysis that involves estimating, constructing confidence intervals, and testing hypotheses about β_0 and β_1 is called *regression analysis*. The model is generalized in subsequent chapters to include more than one independent variable. The text introduces the basic concepts and gives easy to follow numerical examples that illustrate the ideas. Also, the text presents excerpts of a large data set in Table 1.1 followed by a description of the problem and details of a regression analysis. The text refers to this example as the Toluca Company example. A step-by-step set of SAS solutions is given below.

The Toluca Company Example

Data File: ch01ta01.txt

The Toluca Company manufactures refrigeration equipment and replacement parts (text page 19). The parts are manufactured in "runs" and groups of runs comprise lots of varying sizes. The data disk provided with the text contains data on 25 manufacturing runs under the file name ch01ta01.txt. For each run, this file contains data on lot size and work hours, defined as the number of labor hours required to produce the lot. The aim of the example is to investigate the relationship between work hours and lot size. We wish to fit a simple linear regression model that allows us to predict work hours from lot size. We let the variable names *workhrs* denote work hours and *lotsize* denote lot size, and take these to be the dependent variable Y and the independent variable X, respectively, in the simple linear regression model. See Chapter 0, "Working with SAS," for instructions on opening the Toluca Company data file. Note that the directories for Chapters 1-9 on the data disk provided with your text contain 2 spaces between the word "chapter" and the corresponding chapter number. Thus, the *infile* statement must also contain 2 spaces to identify the correct path. After opening and printing ch01ta01.txt, the first 5 lines of output should look like SAS Output 1.1.

SAS Output 1.1

Obs	lotsize	workhrs
1	80	399
2	30	121
3	50	221
4	90	376
5	70	361

Scatter plots: The text begins a regression analysis of the Toluca Company data with a scatter plot showing work hours plotted against lot size in Figure 1.10 (a & b), text page 20. We provide SAS syntax for constructing this scatter plot in Insert 1.1 and display the results in SAS Output 1.2 (a & b) below. To replicate the axes of text Figure 1.10 (a & b), we set the values of the horizontal axis (*haxis*) to range from 0 to 150 while incrementing by 50 units, and we set the values of the vertical axis (*vaxis*) to be range from 0 to 600 while incrementing by 100 units. Additionally, we could use the *proc gplot* procedure to generate the scatter plot with the regression line (text Figure1.10 b) by changing the *interpol=none* statement to *interpol=rl* (regression line) in Insert 1.1. The SAS *proc plot* procedure will also generate scatter plots although this procedure lacks some features available in *proc gplot*.

```
INSERT 1.1

*Produce Output 1.2a;
data Toluca;
infile 'C:\alrm\chapter  1 data sets\ch01ta01.txt';
input lotsize workhrs;
proc gplot;
  symbol1 value=dot interpol=none;
  plot workhrs*lotsize / haxis=0 to 150 by 50 vaxis=0 to 600 by 100;
run;

*Produce Output 1.2b;
data Toluca;
infile 'C:\alrm\chapter  1 data sets\ch01ta01.txt';
input lotsize workhrs;
proc reg;
  model workhrs = lotsize;
   plot workhrs*lotsize / haxis=0 to 150 by 50 vaxis=0 to 600 by 100;
run;
```

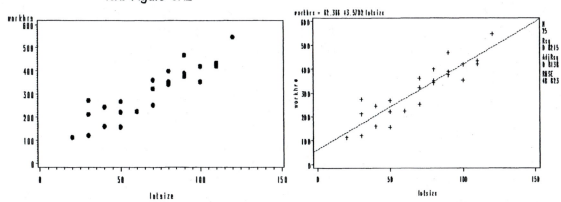

Estimation of β_0 and β_1: To find the least squares estimates b_0 and b_1 of β_0 and β_1, respectively, we follow the overview of the required computations that are outlined in Table 1.1, text page 19. In Insert 1.2, we show SAS syntax that performs these computations. We first find the means for *workhrs* ($\overline{X}=70$) and *lotsize* ($\overline{Y}=312.28$). Next, we find $X_i - \overline{X}$ (*xdev*), $Y_i - \overline{Y}$ (*ydev*), $(X_i - \overline{X})^2$ (*xdev2*), $(Y_i - \overline{Y})^2$ (*ydev2*), $(X_i - \overline{X})(Y_i - \overline{Y})$ (*xdev * ydev = cross*). The last step in Insert 1.2 is to find the sum of $(X_i - \overline{X})(Y_i - \overline{Y})$ ($\sum$ *cross*=70,690) and $(X_i - \overline{X})^2$ ($\sum$ *xdev2*=19,800). Using equation 1.10, text page 17, we calculate:

$$b_1 = \frac{\sum(X_i - \overline{X})(Y_i - \overline{Y})}{\sum(X_i - \overline{X})} = \frac{70,690}{19,800} = 3.5702$$

and

$$b_0 = \overline{Y} - b_1\overline{X} = 312.28 - 3.5702 * 70 = 62.365$$

INSERT 1.2

```
* Find mean of lotsize and workhrs;
data Toluca;
infile 'C:\alrm\chapter 1 data sets\ch01ta01.txt';
input lotsize workhrs;
proc means;
 var lotsize workhrs;
run;

* Calculate least squares estimates;
data Toluca;
infile 'C:\alrm\chapter 1 data sets\ch01ta01.txt';
input lotsize workhrs;
 xdev=(lotsize-70);
 ydev=workhrs-312.28;
 xdev2=(lotsize-70)**2;
 ydev2=(workhrs-312.28)**2;
 cross=xdev*ydev;
proc means sum;
 var cross xdev2;
run;
```

Estimated Regression Function: We used the SAS syntax shown in Insert 1.2 to demonstrate how SAS code can be written to provide intermediate results when we compute the parameter estimates b_0 and b_1. We now use the SAS Regression procedure *proc reg* to find b_0 and b_1. This procedure is shorter and easier to use, but it does not provide the results of all the intermediate computations shown on text page 19. In Insert 1.3, we request a regression analysis via the SAS statement *proc reg*. Next, we identify the dependent and independent variables via the *model* statement. Here, the statement: *model workhrs = lotsize* specifies the simple linear regression model with *workhrs* taken to be the Y variable (the dependent variable) and *lotsize* taken to be the X variable (the independent or predictor variable). Partial results are shown in SAS Output 1.3. The "Unstandardized Coefficients" shown under column heading "Parameter Estimate" give the results $b_0 = 62.36586$ and $b_1 = 3.57020$. Here, b_0 is given in the row labeled "Intercept" and b_1 is given in the row labeled "lotsize". These results are consistent with those shown on text page 20 and in the calculations of Insert 1.2 above. From the above regression analysis, we estimate the regression function to be: $\hat{Y} = 62.366 + 3.570(X)$.

INSERT 1.3

```
data Toluca;
infile 'C:\alrm\chapter  1 data sets\ch01ta01.txt';
input lotsize workhrs;
proc reg;
  model workhrs = lotsize;
run;
```

SAS Output 1.3

Analysis of Variance					
Source	DF	Sum of Squares	Mean Square	F Value	Pr > F
Model	1	252378	252378	105.88	<.0001
Error	23	54825	2383.71562		
Corrected Total	24	307203			

Parameter Estimates					
Variable	DF	Parameter Estimate	Standard Error	t Value	Pr > |t|
Intercept	1	62.36586	26.17743	2.38	0.0259
lotsize	1	3.57020	0.34697	10.29	<.0001

In Insert 1.4, we request the predicted value and residual for each lot size specified in the data, as in column 3 of text Table 1.2, in the *model* statement of *proc reg*. We put a slash after the predictor variable(s) listed in the model statement and then write *p* for predicted values and *r* for residuals. Thus, the statement: *model workhrs = lotsize / p r* instructs SAS to compute unstandardized predicted values and residuals for the specified regression model (Insert 1.4). Although not shown here, when we write *model workhrs = lotsize / p r*, SAS prints six columns of output: (1.) the dependent variable, (2.) the unstandardized predicted values, (3.) the standard errors of the predicted values, (4.) the residuals, (5.) the standard error of the residuals, and (6.) the Studentized residuals. Some of these results are not discussed until later in the text.

To get output results into the data file so we can perform calculations involving these results, we must use the *output* statement. The *output* statement instructs SAS to create a new data file that contains the original data and specified output. The *out = results* specification instructs SAS to store the new data file under the name we chose to call *results*. The code *p = yhat* specifies that the predicted values will be stored in the *results* data file as a new variable that we chose to call *yhat*. The code *r = residual* specifies that the residuals will be stored in the *results* data file as a new variable that we chose to call *residual*. That is, we store the predicted and residual values from the regression analysis and the original variables in a new data file that now comprises *lotsize, workhrs, run, yhat,* and *residual*. It is necessary to go through this procedure to get the calculated predicted values and residuals out of the output file and into a data file so we can perform additional calculations that involve these results.

At this point, we must specify a new *data step*. We do this by writing *data step2* where *step2* is the arbitrary name we have chosen for the new data set. We then write *set results* to identify *results* as the old data set to be used in the current instructions. Initially, the data set *step2* will be identical to data set *results*. Next, we compute the squared residual value using the statement *sqres=residual*residual*. The SAS system appends the data for *sqres* to the data set *step2*. Finally, we use *proc print* to print the first 5 lines of the data file. Because we do not specify in the *proc print* statement the data set to be printed, the most recent data set, *step2*, is printed. The printed results shown in SAS Output 1.4 are consistent with those shown in Table 1.2, text page 22. Note that the statement *run+1* that appears after the *input* statement was used to number the data lines in the data file. These numbers are stored in the original data file under the name we chose to call *run*. Once the data lines are numbered, the *where* statement can be used after the *print* statement to specify specific lines to be printed. Thus, the statement *where run le 5* used after the *print* statement instructs SAS to print the data lines whose *run* number is less than or equal to 5. The *var* statement that appears after the *print* statement identifies the variable names whose data values are to be printed.

INSERT 1.4	INSERT 1.4 continued

data Toluca;
infile 'C:\alrm\chapter 1 data sets\ch01ta01.txt';
input lotsize workhrs;
run+1;
proc reg;
  model workhrs = lotsize/ p r;
    output out=results p=yhat r=residual;
run;
	data step2;
	  set results;
	sqres=residual*residual;
	proc print;
	  where run le 5;
	  var lotsize workhrs yhat residual sqres;
	run;

SAS Output 1.4

Obs	lotsize	workhrs	yhat	residual	sqres
1	80	399	347.982	51.018	2602.83
2	30	121	169.472	-48.472	2349.53
3	50	221	240.876	-19.876	395.05
4	90	376	383.684	-7.684	59.04
5	70	361	312.280	48.720	2373.64

Chapter 2 SAS®

Inferences in Regression and Correlation Analysis

In this chapter, the authors introduce the fundamentals for making statistical inferences about the parameters of the regression model. The model of interest is:

$$Y_i = \beta_0 + \beta_1 X_i + \varepsilon_i$$

where:

β_0 and β_1 are unknown parameters

X_i are known constants for $i = 1, 2, \ldots, n$.

ε_i are unknown errors associated with the true model.

We assume the ε_i are independent $N(0, \sigma^2)$ for $i = 1, 2, \ldots, n$. The assumptions made here about the errors differ from those made in Chapter 1. The normality assumption is required by theoretical considerations used to develop confidence intervals and test statistics for making inferences involving the model parameters. Inferences were not considered in Chapter 1 and, therefore, normally distributed error terms were not required. The inferences of specific interest pertain to confidence intervals and tests of hypotheses for model parameters and functions of model parameters. The statistical analysis associated with estimation and inference involving regression models is called *regression analysis*.

Chapter 1 of the text presents formulas for the estimators b_0 and b_1 of the parameters β_0 and β_1, respectively. These estimators yield estimates that vary from sample to sample and, therefore, have a (sampling) distribution of their own. It is desirable then to make inferences about the true values of the parameters based on their sample estimates. Let β_j represent either β_0 or β_1 depending on whether $j = 0$ or 1 and let b_j denote the corresponding estimator. We can estimate the variance of b_j from a single sample of Y's and X's and the square root of this variance estimate is an estimate of the standard error of b_j. The text denotes the variance and standard error estimators by $s^2\{b_j\}$ and $s\{b_j\}$, respectively, and gives their computational formulas (see equation 2.9 page 43 and equation 2.23, text page 49).

Consider the null hypothesis:

$$H_0: \beta_j = 0$$

A statistic for testing this hypothesis against either a one or two-sided alternative is:

$$t = \frac{b_j}{s\{b_j\}}$$

Under the assumptions of the model this statistic is distributed as Student's t with $n - 2$ degrees of freedom.

Let $t(1 - \alpha/2; n - 2)$ denote the $(\alpha/2)100$ percentile of the t distribution with $n - 2$ degrees of freedom. The $1 - \alpha$ confidence limits for β_j are:

$$b_j \pm t(1 - \alpha/2; n - 2)\, s\{b_j\}$$

Chapter 2 of the text presents these formulas and others of inferential interest in the simple linear regression model.

Further Aspects of the Toluca Company Example

Data File: ch01ta01.txt

We return to the Toluca Company example first presented in Chapter 1 (text page 19). We let the variable names *workhrs* denote work hours and *lotsize* denote lot size, and take these to be the dependent variable Y and the independent variable X, respectively, in the simple linear regression model. See Chapter 0, "Working with SAS," for instructions on opening the Toluca Company data file. After opening and printing ch01ta01.txt, the first 5 lines of output should look like SAS Output 1.1.

SAS Output 1.1

Obs	lotsize	workhrs
1	80	399
2	30	121
3	50	221
4	90	376
5	70	361

We wish to perform a regression analysis using the model:

$$\text{workhrs} = \beta_0 + \beta_1(\text{lotsize}) + \varepsilon$$

Confidence Interval for β_1: On text page 46 the management team wants an estimate of β_1 with a 95% confidence interval. The $1 - \alpha$ confidence limits for β_1 are (equation 2.15, text page 45):

$$b_1 \pm t(1 - \alpha/2; n - 2)\, s\{b_1\}$$

We request confidence intervals for the regression coefficients using the *clb* option in the *model* statement given in Insert 2.1. From SAS Output 2.2 we see that the 95% confidence interval is $2.852 \le \beta_1 \le 4.288$, consistent with text page 46.

SAS Output 2.2

Analysis of Variance					
Source	DF	Sum of Squares	Mean Square	F Value	Pr > F
Model	1	252378	252378	105.88	<.0001
Error	23	54825	2383.71562		
Corrected Total	24	307203			

Root MSE	48.82331	**R-Square**	0.8215
Dependent Mean	312.28000	**Adj R-Sq**	0.8138
Coeff Var	15.63447		

Parameter Estimates							
Variable	DF	Parameter Estimate	Standard Error	t Value	Pr > |t|	95% Confidence Limits	
Intercept	1	62.36586	26.17743	2.38	0.0259	8.21371	116.51801
lotsize	1	3.57020	0.34697	10.29	<.0001	2.85244	4.28797

Tests of Hypothesis Concerning β_1: The t-test for H_0: $\beta_1 = 0$ is:

$$t^* = \frac{b_1}{s\{b_1\}}$$

with $n - 2$ degrees of freedom (equation 2.17, text page 47). We get the numerical value for this test statistic as part of the output from the SAS instructions given in Insert 2.1. In SAS Output

2.2 we see $(t^*) = 10.290$ for *lotsize* and the associated *p*-value = 0.000 (Pr>|t|). Since $p < 0.05$ we conclude $\beta_1 \neq 0$.

To test that $\beta_1 > 0$ (a one-sided test), we require that $|t^*| > t(1-\alpha; n-2)$. The standard output in SAS displays the *p*-value for a two-sided test. To get the *p*-value for a one-sided test, first determine whether the numerical value of the *t*-test is negative or positive and hence whether it tends to favor the specified one-sided alternative. A negative *t*-test favors H_a: $\beta_1 < 0$ whereas a positive *t*-test favors H_a: $\beta_1 > 0$. If the *t*-test favors the specified one-sided alternative, just divide the *p*-value displayed in the SAS output by 2. In the example, $(t^*) = 10.290$ is positive and this favors H_a: $\beta_1 > 0$ with *p*-value = 0.000/2 = 0.000. If the numerical value of the *t*-test does not favor the specified alternative, it is probably sufficient to quote $p > 0.50$ as the *p*-value. More precisely, the *p*-value for the one-sided *t*-test in this situation is 1 minus the *p*-value displayed in the SAS output divided by 2. In the present example, if we had specified H_a: $\beta_1 < 0$ and found $(t^*) = 10.290$, the *p*-value would be $1 - 0.000/2 = 1.000$. In this circumstance, we would not reject H_0.

Sometimes it is desirable to find the critical value $t(1-\alpha; n-2)$ corresponding to a *t*-test. To find $t(1-\alpha; n-2)$, use the SAS "*tinv*" *quantile* function (Insert 2.1 above) to request a new variable named *tvalue*. Let T denote a random variable that has a *t*-distribution with degrees of freedom = *df*. Suppose we want to find the value *t* such that $P(T > t) = \alpha$ for a value of α that we specify. Equivalently, suppose we want to find the value *t* such that $P(T \leq t) = 1-\alpha$. We can use the SAS *quantile function tinv*$(1-\alpha, df)$ for this purpose. When we specify $1-\alpha$ and *df*, this function returns the associated *t*-value. To find the critical value for testing H_a: $\beta_1 > 0$, controlling the level of significance at $\alpha = 0.05$, we must find *tvalue* = $t(1-\alpha; n-2)$ or *tvalue* = $t(0.95, 23)$. This critical value ($t = 1.71$) is obtained from the *quantile function* in Insert 2.1 and is printed to the output file by the *proc print* statement. Since the obtained *t*-value ($t = 10.29$) is greater than the critical value $t = 1.71$, we conclude $\beta_1 > 0$. If we want to obtain the critical value for a two-sided test where $\alpha = 0.05$, we find $t(1-\alpha/2; n-2)$ or $t(0.975, 23)$ using the above quantile function.

Confidence Interval for β_0: To obtain the 90% confidence interval for β_0 (text page 49), we specify *alpha* = 0.10 in the *model* statement and the 90% (rather than 95%) confidence intervals for the model parameters are printed. Notice that if we do not specify *alpha* in the *model* statement, SAS uses *alpha* = 0.05 by default. The complete model statement is

*model workhrs = lotsize / clb alpha = **0.10***;

Alternatively, we can find the 90% confidence interval through direct calculations as follows. We must find $t(1-\alpha/2; n-2)$. Note that SAS Output 2.2 presents the 95% confidence interval. Since we desire a 90% confidence interval, $\alpha = 0.10$ and $t(0.95, 23) = 1.71$. From SAS Output 2.2, we find the standard deviation of b_0 (Intercept) is $s\{b_0\} = 26.17$. From text equation 2.25 (equation 2.25, text page 49) the 90% confidence interval is:

$$b_0 \pm t(1-\alpha/2; n-2)\, s\{b_0\}$$

or

$$62.366 \pm 1.71 * 26.17$$

18

Simplifying this expression, we find the 90% confidence interval:

$$17.5 \le \beta_0 \le 107.2$$

Confidence Interval for $E\{Y_h\}$: Once specific sample data have been used to produce parameter estimates b_0 and b_1, we denote the fitted model as:

$$\hat{Y}_i = b_0 + b_1 X_i \qquad i = 1, 2, \dots, n$$

We call $\hat{Y}_i$ the *predicted value* of Y when the predictor variable is X_i. Let X_h denote a specific value of the independent variable in the simple linear regression model. As noted by the authors, "X_h may be a value which occurred in the sample, or it may be some other value of the predictor variable within the scope of the model." The corresponding predicted value is denoted $\hat{Y}_h$. We can select many random samples of data and different samples may produce different estimates b_0 and b_1 and hence different $\hat{Y}_h$. Hence, for any such X_h there is a distribution corresponding to the random variable $\hat{Y}_h$. This random variable has a mean and variance denoted $E\{\hat{Y}_h\} = E\{Y_h\}$ and $\sigma^2\{\hat{Y}_h\}$, respectively. Estimators of the mean and variance are $\hat{Y}_h$ and $s^2\{\hat{Y}_h\}$ (see equation 2.30, text page 53 for the formula for $s^2\{\hat{Y}_h\}$).

On text page 54, the authors use Toluca Company Example to find the 90% confidence interval for $E\{Y_h\}$ when lot size (X_h) = 65 units. The $1 - \alpha$ confidence limits are given in equation 2.33, text page 54:

$$\hat{Y}_h \pm t(1 - \alpha/2; n - 2) s\{\hat{Y}_h\}$$

To find $s^2\{\hat{Y}_h\}$ (equation 2.30, text page 53) we need the mean squared error (*MSE*), which is given in SAS Output 2.2 above (*MSE* = 2383.716). We use *proc means* (Insert 2.2 – Step 1) to find $\overline{X}$ = *lotsize mean* = 70. To find $(X_i - \overline{X})^2$ we first compute a new variable, *xdevsq* (Step 2). To find the sum of $\sum(X_i - \overline{X})^2$ =19,800 we use *proc means* (Step 2) with the *sum* option (SAS Output 2.3). We can now find:

$$s^2\{\hat{Y}_h\} = MSE\left[\frac{1}{n} + \frac{(X_h - \overline{X})^2}{\sum(X_i - \overline{X})^2}\right]$$

Thus,
$$s^2\{\hat{Y}_h\} = 2383.7\left[\frac{1}{25} + \frac{(65 - 70)^2}{19,800}\right] = 98.37$$

$$s\{\hat{Y}_h\} = \sqrt{s^2\{\hat{Y}_h\}} = 9.918$$

```
                          INSERT 2.2
* Step 1;
data Toluca Company;
  infile 'c:\alrm\chapter 1 data sets\ch01ta01.txt';
  input lotsize workhrs;
proc means;
 var lotsize ;
run;
* Step 2;
data Toluca Company;
  infile 'c:\alrm\chapter 1 data sets\ch01ta01.txt';
  input lotsize workhrs;
xdevsq=(lotsize-70)**2;
proc means sum;
 var xdevsq;
run;
* Step 3;
data Toluca Company;
yhat65=62.36586+(3.5702)*65;        * Predicted value given lot size = 65 units;
sdyhat=sqrt(2383.716*((1/25)+(((65-70)**2)/19800)));   * Sq root of Text eq 2.30;
ci65hi=yhat65+(1.714)*sdyhat;                   * Text eq 2.33;
ci65lo=yhat65-(1.714)*sdyhat;                   * Text eq 2.33;
proc print;
run;
```

To find the 90 percent confidence interval, we also need $t(1-\alpha/2; n-2)$. Using the *quantile function* introduced above where $t(1-\alpha/2; n-2) = t(0.95; 23)$, *tinv*(0.95, 23) returns $t(0.95, 23) = 1.71$. Using $X_h = 65$ units and the parameter estimates in SAS Output 2.2 above, we find

$$\hat{Y}_h = b_0 + b_1 X_h$$

or

$$\hat{Y}_h = 62.366 + 3.570(65) = 294.4$$

Substituting these numerical values into equation 2.33, text page 54, we obtain SAS Output 2.4 and

$$294.4 \ \pm \ 1.71\big(9.918\big)$$

or

$$277.44 \ \leq \ E\{Y_h\} \ \leq \ 311.36$$

SAS Output 2.3

Analysis Variable : xdevsq
Sum
19800.00

Obs	yhat65	sdyhat	ci65hi	ci65lo
1	294.429	9.91758	311.428	277.430

Confidence Band for Regression Line: To find the confidence band for the regression line as shown in equations 2.40 and 2.40a, text page 62, we use the Working-Hotelling $1-\alpha$ confidence band to establish boundary values for each *lotsize* value:

$$\hat{Y}_h \pm W\,s\{\hat{Y}_h\}$$

where:

$$W^2 = 2\,F(1-\alpha;\ 2, n-2)$$

We use text equations 2.28, 2.30, 2.40, and 2.40a to find the confidence band for the Toluca Company regression example. In Insert 2.3 we use the SAS *finv* quantile function of the form *finv(p,df1,df2)* to find F (*fvalue = finv(0.9, 2, 23) = 2.549*). We then find the upper (*bandhi*) and lower (*bandlo*) confidence bands and request the plot (*proc plot*) shown in SAS Output 2.7. This plot has an appearance similar to text Figure 2.6, text page 63.

```
                              INSERT 2.3

data Toluca Company;
  infile 'c:\alrm\chapter 1 data sets\ch01ta01.txt';
  input lotsize workhrs;
fvalue=finv(.9,2,23);
w2=sqrt(2*(fvalue));                           * Text eq 2.40a;
yhat=62.366+3.57*lotsize;                       * Text eq 228;
sdyhat=sqrt(2383.716*((1/25)+(((lotsize-70)**2)/19800)));   * Text eq 2.30;
bandhi=yhat+(w2*sdyhat);                        * Text eq 2.40;
bandlo=yhat-(w2*sdyhat);                        * Text eq 2.40;
proc plot;
 plot bandhi*lotsize bandlo*lotsize yhat*lotsize / overlay;
run;
```

SAS Output 2.7

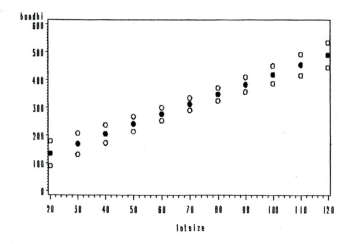

21

To replicate the plot on text page 63, we use *proc gplot* in Insert 2.4. We do not want to plot the predicted values of *Y* as in Insert 2.3, so we do not use *yhat*lotsize* in the *plot* statement in Insert 2.4. Additionally, we use *interpol=join* to connect the data points with straight lines. The data points will be connected in the order they occur in the input data set. Therefore, the data should be sorted by the horizontal axis variable prior to the *proc gplot* statement. We then specify that no symbol be used to plot the data points (*value=none*). Results of Insert 2.4 replicate text Figure 2.6 (SAS Output 2.8).

INSERT 2.4

```
data Toluca Company;
  infile 'c:\alrm\chapter  1 data sets\ch01ta01.txt';
  input lotsize workhrs;
fvalue=finv(.9,2,23);
w2=sqrt(2*(fvalue));                                            * Text eq 2.40a;
yhat=62.366+3.57*lotsize;                                       * Text eq 228;
sdyhat=sqrt(2383.716*((1/25)+(((lotsize-70)**2)/19800)));      * Text eq 2.30;
bandhi=yhat+(w2*sdyhat);                                        * Text eq 2.40;
bandlo=yhat-(w2*sdyhat);                                        * Text eq 2.40;
proc sort;
 by lotsize;
 run;
proc gplot;
   symbol1 value=none color=black interpol=join;
   symbol2 value=none color=black interpol=join;
   plot bandhi*lotsize bandlo*lotsize  / overlay;
run;
```

SAS Output 2.8

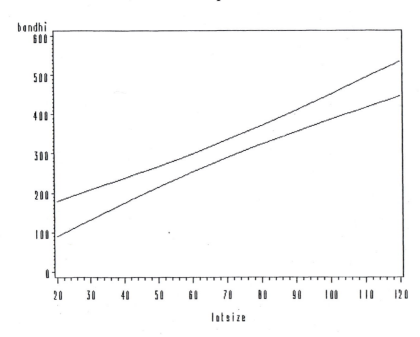

22

The coefficient of determination (R^2): From equation 2.72, text page 74, the coefficient of determination (R^2) is defined as Sum of Squares Regression / Sum of Squares Total; i.e.

$$R^2 = \frac{SSR}{SSTO} = 1 - \frac{SSE}{SSTO}$$

SAS prints the value of R^2 as part of the *proc reg* output (In SAS Output 2.2 above we see that *R-Square* = 0.8215). To compute R^2 directly, we refer to SAS Output 2.2 and find $SSR = 252{,}377.6$ and $SSTO = 307{,}203.0$. Thus $R^2 = 0.822$ and the correlation coefficient (r) = $+\sqrt{R^2}$ = 0.907. Note that here we have taken the positive square root of R^2 to find the correlation coefficient r because b_1 is positive indicating that the correlation coefficient is also positive.

Chapter 3 SAS®

Diagnostics and Remedial Measures

In Chapter 1 we learned that regression analysis involves using a sample of data values to find a linear model that will predict (the *dependent variables*) Y when the values of the (*independent variable*) X's are known. We also referred to the X's as *predictor variables*. We began with a sample of data where each sample unit provides an observation on Y (the dependent variable) and on one or more X's (the independent or predictor variables). Next, we formulated a model that we thought might specify the relationship between Y and the predictor variables. Once we decided on a model that we thought might be appropriate, we assumed the model was in fact an appropriate model for our purpose. We used the sample data to estimate parameters of the model and this estimation provided us with a fitted model. The adequacy of the estimates and of related statistical inferences depends on whether the specified model and the assumptions made in specifying the model are at least approximately true. In most applications, we do not know for certain in advance that the model we decide to use is appropriate for the specific analysis. In Chapter 3, the authors discuss methods for using the observed sample data to investigate the adequacy of a fitted regression model. A group of methods known as *regression diagnostics* are used for this purpose. When regression diagnostics identify inadequacies in the model, *remedial measures* can sometimes be used to correct or offset the inadequacies.

Many regression diagnostics are performed in terms of the residuals from the fitted model. Assuming the simple linear regression model is the specified model, the fitted model is denoted (equation 1.13, text page 21):

$$\hat{Y}_i = b_0 + b_1 X_i \qquad i = 1, \ldots, n$$

The estimates b_0 and b_1 are obtained from the sample data. Once they have been calculated and their numerical values obtained, we can substitute X_i into the fitted model and calculate the predicted value $\hat{Y}_i$ for the ith unit in the sample, $i = 1, 2, \ldots, n$. (See the example on text page 21). Ideally, the fitted model would predict the observed Y_i exactly for all $i = 1, 2, \ldots, n$ but this rarely happens in practice. Thus, there is usually a difference between the observed Y_i and its predicted value $\hat{Y}_i$. This difference is called the *residual*. The ith residual, denoted e_i, is defined as:

$$e_i = Y_i - \hat{Y}_i$$

In the discussion below, we use SAS to find the predicted values and the residuals for the sample data. We illustrate how to obtain graphs to perform graphical diagnostics discussed in the text. We then demonstrate how to produce regression diagnostics in terms of regression model residuals.

The Toluca Company Example Continued

Data File: ch01ta01.txt

We return to the Toluca Company example from Chapters 1 and 2 (text page 19, 46). We let the variable names *workhrs* denote work hours and *lotsize* denote lot size, and take these to be the dependent variable Y and the independent variable X, respectively, in the simple linear regression model. See Chapter 0, "Working with SAS," for instructions on opening the Toluca Company data file. After opening and printing ch01ta01.txt, the first 5 lines of the output should look like SAS Output 3.1.

SAS Output 3.1

Obs	lotsize	workhrs
1	80	399
2	30	121
3	50	221
4	90	376
5	70	361

Diagnostics for Predictor Variable: The authors begin by discussing graphical methods that can be used as diagnostic tools to see if there are any outlying X values in the sample. This is important because a few outlying X values could have too much influence on estimates of the model parameters and other aspects of the regression analysis. If the influence of a few outlying X values is dampened or eliminated altogether, we sometimes get a drastically different regression analysis.

We use SAS (Insert 3.1) to produce Figure 3.1 a-d shown on text page 101. A dot plot identical to text Figure 3.1a is not available in SAS but a bar chart (SAS Output 3.2) approximates that display of information. In the Toluca example there are 25 runs represented in the data file. Figure 3.1b, text page 101, shows a plot of *lotsize* against the run number. Run number is not available in the data file. However, the "*run+1;*" statement in Insert 3.1 creates a new variable named *run* which is a sequential number from 1 to 25 for each case. (Here, we assume that the original Toluca Company example is in order by run number.) We can now produce text Figure 3.1b as shown in SAS Output 3.2 below. The SAS procedure *proc univariate*, together with the related syntax shown in Insert 3.1, will produce a stem-and-leaf and box plots of *lotsize*. (SAS Output 3.2)

INSERT 3.1	INSERT 3.1 continued

data Toluca Company example;
  infile 'c:\alrm\chapter 1 data sets\ch01ta01.txt';
  input lotsize workhrs;
  run+1;
* text Figure 3.1a;
proc chart;
 vbar lotsize / levels=11;
	* text Figure 3.1b;
	goptions reset=all;
	symbol1 v=dot i=join c=black;
	proc gplot;
	  plot lotsize*run / vaxis = 0 to 150 by 50 ;
	run;
	* text Figure 3.1c & d;
	proc univariate plot;
	 var lotsize;
	run;

SAS Output 3.2 a – d

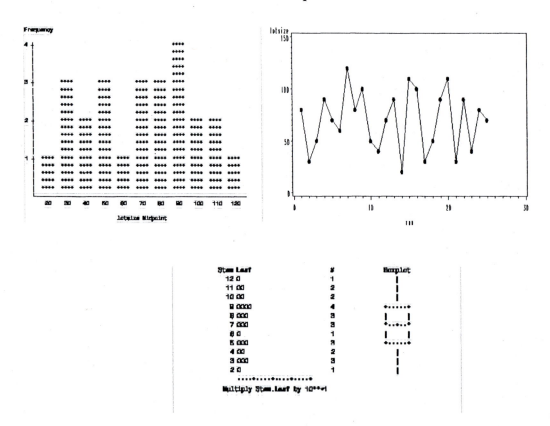

Diagnostics for Residuals: In Section 3.3, text page 103, the authors present informal diagnostic plots of *residuals*. Note that the authors make the distinction between *studentized* and *semistudentized* residuals. The authors point out that "both semistudentized residuals and studentized residuals can be very helpful in identifying outlying observations." SAS does not have an option to produce semistudentized residuals but it does produce studentized residuals. Studentized residuals are probably the more important of the two types of residuals. Therefore, we use studentized residuals in place of semistudentized residuals to present solutions to text chapter examples.

As before, we perform a regression analysis using the model:

$$workhrs = \beta_0 + \beta_1(lotsize) + \varepsilon$$

From Insert 3.2, we specify this regression model and request that unstandardized residuals be saved to a data set *step2* (*out = step2*) under a variable named *residual* (*r = residual*). To produce Figures 3.2 a, b, c, and d, text page 104, we use the syntax in Insert 3.2 (output not shown). The text presents numerous other diagnostic plots. For brevity, we do not present syntax for these other plots but relevant SAS statements are produced easily by a few modifications in the syntax shown in Inserts 3.1 and 3.2.

```
                              INSERT 3.2

data Toluca Company example;
  infile 'c:\alrm\chapter  1 data sets\ch01ta01.txt';
  input lotsize workhrs;
  run+1;
* Produce text Figure 3.2a;
proc reg;
  model workhrs = lotsize / r;
  output out=step2 r=residual;
  plot r.*lotsize;
run;
* Produce text Figure 3.2b;
proc plot data=step2;
 plot residual*run;
* Produce text Figure 3.2c & d;
proc univariate data=step2 plot;
 var residual;
run;
```

Correlation Test for Normality: On text page 111, the researchers for the Toluca Company calculate the coefficient of correlation between the ordered residuals and their expected value under normality. The expected value under normality of the kth smallest observation from a sample of size n is given by:

$$\sqrt{MSE}\left[z\left(\frac{k-0.375}{n+0.25}\right)\right]$$

The first step in obtaining the expected values of the ordered residuals under normality is to calculate $(k - 0.375)/(n + 0.25)$. (Insert 3.3) In the Toluca Company example, $n = 25$ and k is the rank of the ordered residuals. We rank the saved residuals (*residual*) using the *Proc Rank* procedure. The saved residuals are identified in the *proc rank* statement by the specification "*data = step2*". The "*out = step3*" option in the *proc rank* statement specifies the data file (*step3*) in which the ranks will be stored after the *proc ranks* statement has been executed. The *ranks ranke* statement creates another new variable, *ranke*, that is the variable name under which we chose to store the ranks of the variable *residual*, the unstandardized residual in the model with the predictor variable *lotsize* ($Y_i = \beta_0 + \beta_1 X_{i1} + \varepsilon_i$). In the next step of the program, we have written the statement "*data new*" followed by the statement "*set step3*". Thus, we have assigned the name "*new*" to this step and specified "*step3*" as the data file to be used. We use this approach so that we can carry out additional arithmetical operations involving the output (*ranke*) from the previous data step. Here, $(k - 0.375)/(n + 0.25)$ becomes $(ranke - 0.375)/(25 + 0.25)$. This quantity represents the cumulative probability ($0 \leq$ cumulative probability ≤ 1.0) of the standard normal distribution. We now obtain a standard score (z) associated with the cumulative probability calculated above. In SAS, the *Probit* function is *quantile* function that returns a quantile from the standard normal distribution. It takes the form *Probit(p)*, where $p =$ cumulative probability. For instance, if cumulative probability $= 0.50$ (*Probit*(0.50)) then $z = 0$ or if cumulative probability $= 0.8413$ (*Probit*(0.8413)) then $z = +1$. Thus, to obtain z in the Toluca Company example, we use

$$Probit ((ranke - 0.375)/(54 + 0.25))$$

Finally, we multiply this quantity by the square root of $MSE = 2383.716$ of the first order model (Chapter 2 – SAS Output 2.2). From the above, we compute the *expected value* as:

$$ev = sqrt(2383.716) * Probit ((ranke - 0.375)/(25 + 0.25)).$$

We can now obtain the coefficient of correlation between the residual and the expected value under normality (*ev*). The result of the correlation between *residual* and *ev* is 0.991 as reported on text page 115.

```
                          INSERT 3.3

  data Toluca Company example;
    infile 'c:\alrm\chapter  1 data sets\ch01ta01.txt';
    input lotsize workhrs;
  * Save residuals (/ r) in residual;
  proc reg;
    model workhrs = lotsize / r;
    output out=step2 r=residual;
  run;
  * Rank the residuals and place the rank in "ranke";
  proc rank data=step2 out=step3;
   var residual;
   ranks ranke;
  run;
  data new;
   set step3;
   ev = sqrt(2383.716) * Probit ((ranke - .375)/(25  + .25));
  proc corr;
   var ev residual;
   run;
```

Test for Constancy of Error Variance - Brown-Forsythe: The authors present two formal tests for constancy of error variance. We begin with the *Brown-Forsythe test* using the Toluca Company example, text page 117. For simplicity, we divided the process into steps:

- Step 1: (Insert 3.4) Divide the 25 data-lines into two subsets (*group*): those with *lotsize* between 20 and 70 (if *lotsize*<71 then *group*=1) and those with *lotsize* > 70(*else group*=2).
- Step 2: Use *proc means* to obtain the *median residual values* $\tilde{e}_1$ (group 1) = −19.87 and $\tilde{e}_2$ (group 2) = −2.68.
- Step 3: Find *absdevmd*, the absolute value (*abs*) of the residual minus the median residual value for the respective group, d_{i1} and d_{i2}.
- Step 4: Find the means of *absdevmd* for the two groups, $\bar{d}_1$ = 44.81 and $\bar{d}_2$ = 28.4.

28

- Step 5: Find *sqrdev,* the square of *absdevmd* minus the respective group mean of *absdevmd.*
- Step 6: Find the sum of *sqrdev* for the two groups, $\sum(d_{11} - \bar{d}_1)^2 = 12{,}567.86$ and $\sum(d_{12} - \bar{d}_2)^2 = 9{,}621.54.$

We now have the required values to calculate the *Brown-Forsythe statistic*:

$$s^2 = \frac{12{,}567.86 + 9{,}621.54}{25 - 2} = 964.75$$

$$s = \sqrt{964.75} = 31.06$$

$$t_{BF}^* = \frac{44.81 - 28.4}{31.06\sqrt{\frac{1}{13} + \frac{1}{12}}} = 1.319$$

INSERT 3.4	INSERT 3.4 continued

data Toluca Company example;
  infile 'c:\alrm\chapter 1 data sets\ch01ta01.txt';
  input lotsize workhrs;
* Step 1;
if lotsize<71 then group=1;
 else group=2;
proc reg;
  model workhrs = lotsize / r;
  output out=step2 r=residual;
run;
* Step 2;
proc sort data=step2;
 by group;
proc means data=step2 median;
 by group;
 var residual;
run;
	* Step 3;
	data step2;
	 set step2;
	if group=1 then absdevmd=abs(residual -(-19.88));
	if group=2 then absdevmd=abs(residual -(-2.68));
	* Step 4;
	proc means;
	 by group;
	  var absdevmd;
	 run;
	* Step 5;
	data new;
	 set step2;
	if group=1 then sqrdev=(absdevmd-44.81)**2;
	if group=2 then sqrdev=(absdevmd-29.45)**2;
	run;
	* Step 6;
	proc means sum;
	  by group;
	   var sqrdev;
	   run;

Test for Constancy of Error Variance - Breusch-Pagan Test: The second Test for *Constancy of Error Variance* considered by the authors is the *Breusch-Pagan Test* (text page 118). To compute the Breusch-Pagan test, we first save the residuals (*r=residual*) of the following model as shown in Insert 3.5:

$$workhrs = \beta_0 + \beta_1(lotsize) + \varepsilon$$

We now square *residual* and place the result in a variable named *ressqr* (e^2). The last step is to regress *ressqr* against *lotsize* in the usual manner. The last regression procedure in Insert 3.5 results in SAS Output 3.4 and contains $SSR^*=7,896,128$. SSE (54,825.459) is shown in SAS Output 3.5 and results from the first regression run in Insert 3.5. We now can find:

$$X^2_{BP} = \frac{SSR^*}{2} \div \left(\frac{SSE}{n} \right)^2$$

where SSR^* for regressing e^2 (*ressqr*) on X

and

SSE for regressing Y on X

$$X^2_{BP} = \frac{7,896,128}{2} \div \left(\frac{54,825}{25} \right)^2 = 0.821$$

INSERT 3.5

```
data Toluca Company example;
  infile 'c:\alrm\chapter  1 data sets\ch01ta01.txt';
  input lotsize workhrs;
proc reg;
  model workhrs = lotsize / r;
  output out=step2 r=residual;
data step2;
 set step2;
ressqr=residual**2;
proc reg;
  model ressqr = lotsize;
run;
```

SAS Output 3.4

Analysis of Variance					
Source	DF	Sum of Squares	Mean Square	F Value	Pr > F
Model	1	7896142	7896142	1.09	0.3070
Error	23	166395896	7234604		
Corrected Total	24	174292038			

30

Analysis of Variance					
Source	DF	Sum of Squares	Mean Square	F Value	Pr > F
Model	1	252378	252378	105.88	<.0001
Error	23	54825	2383.71562		
Corrected Total	24	307203			

Bank Example

Data File: ch03ta04.txt

F Test for Lack of Fit: On text pages 119-120, the authors discuss a formal test for determining if the regression function adequately fits the data. In an experiment involving 12 branch offices of a commercial bank, gifts were offered for customers who opened money market accounts. The value of the gift was proportional to the minimum deposit and there were 6 levels of minimum deposit used in the experiment. The researchers studied the relationship between the minimum deposit and value of the associated gift measured in terms of the size of minimum deposit (X) and the number of new accounts (Y) opened at each of the 12 branches. After opening and printing the Bank Example data (text Table 3.4), the first five lines of the output should look like SAS Output 3.6.

SAS Output 3.6

Obs	x	y
1	125	160
2	100	112
3	200	124
4	75	28
5	150	152

To compute the *Lack of Fit F** presented on text page 124, we switch to the *General Linear Model (GLM)* procedure. (Insert 3.6) We begin by fitting the full model to the data. This requires creating a new variable, *J*. As programmed in Insert 3.6, $j = 1$ if $X_1 = 75$, $j = 2$ if $X_2 = 100$ and so on. We now regress Y on X and J. Using the *class j* statement in *proc glm*, we specify that J is a classification variable. Thus, J identifies 6 discrete classifications based on the values of X. Insert 3.6 produces SAS Output 3.6 which shows that $SSE(F) = 1148.0$. From equation 3.16, text page 122, $SSE(F) = SSPE$. Therefore, $SSPE = 1148.0$. From equation 3.24, text page 124, we see that $SSLF = SSE(R) - SSPE$. If we were to regress Y on X, (reduced model) we would find that $SSE(R) = 14,741.6$ (not shown). Thus, $SSLF = 14,741.6 - 1148 = 13,593.6$. $SSLF = 13,593.6$ is given directly in SAS Output 3.6 under *Type III Sum of Squares* for J. Thus, regressing Y on X and J in *proc glm* gives us the quantities to find (text page 124):

$$F^* = \frac{SSLF}{c-2} \div \frac{SSPE}{n-c}$$

$$F^* = \frac{13{,}593.6}{4} \div \frac{1{,}148}{5} = 14.8$$

INSERT 3.6

```
* Full Model;
data Bank Example;
 infile 'c:\neter\ch03ta04.dat';
 input x y;
 if x=75 then j=1;
 if x=100 then j=2;
 if x=125 then j=3;
 if x=150 then j=4;
 if x=175 then j=5;
 if x=200 then j=6;
proc glm;
 class j;
 model y = x j;
run;
```

SAS Output 3.6

Source	DF	Sum of Squares	Mean Square	F Value	Pr > F
Model	5	18734.90909	3746.98182	16.32	0.0041
Error	5	1148.00000	229.60000		
Corrected Total	10	19882.90909			

R-Square	Coeff Var	Root MSE	y Mean
0.942262	12.94085	15.15256	117.0909

Source	DF	Type I SS	Mean Square	F Value	Pr > F
x	1	5141.33841	5141.33841	22.39	0.0052
j	4	13593.57068	3398.39267	14.80	0.0056

Source	DF	Type III SS	Mean Square	F Value	Pr > F
x	0	0.00000	.	.	.
j	4	13593.57068	3398.39267	14.80	0.0056

Box-Cox Transformations: SAS does not have a readily available option to generate *Box-Cox transformations* (text page 134). Insert 3.7 contains the necessary syntax in matrix language to produce Table 3.9 and Figure 3.17, text page 136. (SAS matrix language is covered in Chapter 5.) The text uses data on age (*X*) and plasma (*Y*) level of 25 children as presented in Table 3.8, text page 133, to illustrate the transformation procedure. The first 2 "*read all var*" statements set vectors **x** and **y** equal to *age* and *plasma*, respectively. This procedure uses a range of λ values starting at λ (*start*) = −2.3 and incrementing (*increment*) by a value of 0.1 for 34 iterations (*noiter*). A scatter plot of *SSE* as a function of λ is shown in SAS Output 3.7. The start, increment, and iteration values can be varied to accomplish different goals.

INSERT 3.7	INSERT 3.7 Continued

<pre>options ls=72 ps=30 nonumber nodate;
data plasma;
  infile 'c:\alrm\chapter 3 data sets\ch03ta08.txt';
  input age plasma;
run;
proc iml;
  use plasma;
  read all var {'plasma'} into y;
  read all var {'age'} into x;
  n = nrow(y);
  noiter = 34;
  start = -2.3;
  increment = 0.1;
  x = j(n,1,1)||x;
  hat =x*inv(x`*x)*x`;
  lambda = j(noiter,1);
  lambda[1,1] = start;
  do i = 2 to noiter;
    lambda[i,1]=lambda[i-1,1] + increment;
  end;</pre>
	<pre>sse = j(noiter,1,0);
	  do i = 1 to noiter;
	   lamb = lambda[i];
	        k2 = exp((1/n)*(j(1,n,1)*log(y)));
	        k1 = 1/(lamb*k2**(lamb-1));
	        if lamb > -1E-08 & lamb < 1E-08 then w =
	k2*log(y);
	        else w = k1*(y##lamb -j(n,1,1));
	        e = (i(n) - hat)*w;
	   sse[i] = e`*e;
	end;
	  print lambda [format = 5.1] sse [format = 10.4];
	  xy = lambda||sse;
	  call pgraf(xy,'*','Lambda','SSE','Plot for Box-Cox
	Transformation');
	quit;</pre>

SAS Output 3.7

Exploration of Shape of Regression Function – Lowess Method: The authors state that "the name *lowess* stands for locally weighted regression scatter plot smoothing." The lowess procedure divides the independent variables into groups or *local neighborhoods* and then fits a regression model to each local neighborhood of data. The procedure uses weighted least squares to fit regression models for each neighborhood with the weights being a function of the distance of the X's for a given subject in a neighborhood from the center of the neighborhood. The final fitted model is a blending of these fitted models in each neighborhood. A *smoothing parameter* must be specified in executing the lowess method. The smoothing parameter specifies the proportion of the total number of observations to be included in each neighborhood. Thus, if the total sample size is 50 and the smoothing parameter is 0.10, then 5 observations will be included in each local neighborhood used in executing the lowess method. We can adjust the smoothing parameter and examine a plot of the fitted loess curves together with the residual sum of squares to choose a reasonable fitting smooth curve.

In Insert 3.8, we present SAS syntax to produce Figure 3.19a, text page 140. Using the Toluca Company example, we use *proc loess* to specify that the lowess method be used to fit a smoothed curve to the data. The *model* option *smooth* = 0.5 specifies that the model be fit with smoothing parameter 0.5. The total sample size in the Toluca Company example is $n = 25$, so $(0.5)(25) \approx$ 12 observations will be included in local neighborhood in the analysis. (SAS Output 3.9) We print out the first 5 lines of the *results* data set (SAS Output 3.10) and produce a scatter plot of Y versus X with the fitted loess curve. (SAS Output 3.11)

INSERT 3.8

```
data toluca;
   infile 'c:\alrm\chapter  1 data sets\ch01ta01.txt';
   input x y;
proc loess;
   model y = x / smooth = 0.5 residual;
   ods output OutputStatistics = Results;
run;
proc print data=results (obs=5);
proc sort;
  by pred;
  run;
goptions reset=all;
proc gplot;
   symbol1 color=black value=none interpol=join;
   symbol2 color=black value=circle;
    title 'Scatter Plot and Lowess Curve';
   plot Pred*x DepVar*x / overlay haxis=0 to 150 by 50 vaxis=100 to 600 by 100 ;
run;
```

Output from *proc loess* Fit Summary	
Fit Method	kd Tree
Blending	Linear
Number of Observations	25
Number of Fitting Points	11
kd Tree Bucket Size	2
Degree of Local Polynomials	1
Smoothing Parameter	0.50000
Points in Local Neighborhood	12
Residual Sum of Squares	46341

SAS Output 3.10

Obs	SmoothingParameter	Obs	x	DepVar	Pred	Residual
1	0.5	1	80.00000	399.00000	360.04835	38.95165
2	0.5	2	30.00000	121.00000	180.61465	-59.61465
3	0.5	3	50.00000	221.00000	214.46246	6.53754
4	0.5	4	90.00000	376.00000	390.43038	-14.43038
5	0.5	5	70.00000	361.00000	304.84581	56.15419

SAS Output 3.11

Scatter Plot and Lowess Curve
SmoothingParameter=0.5

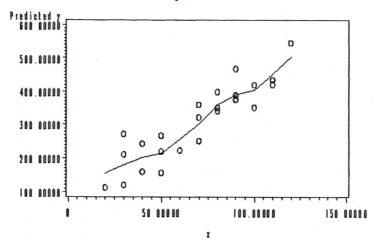

35

Chapter 4 SAS®

Simultaneous Inferences and Other Topics in Regression Analysis

The level of significance of a statistical test is the probability the test rejects the null hypothesis given that the null hypothesis is true. This probability is usually denoted α and is referred to as the probability of a Type I error. These concepts are in the context of a single application of the test. If the test is applied to multiple hypotheses we often want to make a simultaneous or joint statement about the probability of a Type I error given that all the hypotheses being tested are true. We call a set of tests under consideration a family of tests. If each test in a family of g tests is tested at level of significance α, the probability of making one or more Type I errors if all g hypotheses are true is α^* where:

$$\alpha^* \leq 1 - (1-\alpha)^g$$

This inequality is a form of the Bonferroni Equality. In this statement, equality holds if the tests are mutually independent. It is apparent that as g increases α^* approaches 1 and, unless we take corrective action, the probability is close to one that we falsely reject at least one hypothesis even if they are all true. The right side of the statement is approximately equal to $g\alpha$ if α is small; i.e.,

$$1 - (1-\alpha)^g \approx g\alpha$$

Therefore, if we perform each of g tests at the α/g level we get:

$$1 - \left(1 - \frac{\alpha}{g}\right)^g \approx \alpha$$

This approach to multiple testing is referred to as the Bonferroni method or procedure. Using the Bonferroni procedure, we perform each of g tests at the α/g level and are assured that the probability is $\leq \alpha$ of making one or more Type I errors if all g hypotheses are true. For example, if we perform 4 tests and use the $0.05/4 = 0.0125$ level of significance for each test, the probability we falsely reject one or more of the 4 corresponding hypotheses is less than or equal to 0.05.

If we are conducting a single two-sided test, we find critical values from the t-distribution by finding $t(1- \alpha/2; df)$ where df is the degrees of freedom of the test. Similarly, if we are conducting g two-sided multiple tests, we find critical values from the t-distribution by finding $t(1- \alpha/(2g); df)$ where df is the degrees of freedom of the test.

Analogous to multiple testing, we often want to set g confidence intervals with the knowledge that the confidence level is $\geq 100(1 - \alpha)$ percent that all g intervals bracket their respective objective. In the simple linear regression model, simultaneous (Bonferroni) confidence limits for estimating β_0 and β_1 are (equation 4.3, text page 156):

$$b_0 \pm Bs\{b_0\}$$

$$b_1 \pm Bs\{b_1\}$$

where $B = t(1 - \alpha/4; n - 2)$. Here $g = 2$ so that $\alpha/(2g) = \alpha/4$.

Section 4.2, text page 157, discusses simultaneous confidence intervals for the response means at different values of X. In addition to the Bonferroni procedure, the authors discuss the *Working-Hotelling* procedure. Section 4.3 discusses simultaneous prediction intervals for new observations. Section 4.4 presents the simple model for regression through the origin. Section 4.5 discusses the effects of measurement errors, while Section 4.6 presents inverse predictions.

More on The Toluca Company Example

Data File: ch01ta01.txt

We return to the Toluca Company example from Chapters 1, 2 and 3 (text page 19, 46, 156). See Chapter 0, "Working with SAS," for instructions on opening the Toluca Company data file. After opening and printing ch01ta01.dat, the first 5 lines of the output should look like SAS Output 4.1.

SAS Output 4.1

Obs	lotsize	workhrs
1	80	399
2	30	121
3	50	221
4	90	376
5	70	361

Bonferroni Joint Confidence Intervals for β_0 and β_1: On text page 156, the Toluca Company wants to estimate the 90 percent family confidence intervals for β_0 and β_1. To estimate the 90 percent confidence intervals for β_0 and β_1, the text reports $B = t(1 - 0.10/4; 23) = t(0.975; 23) = 2.069$. The *t*-value is actually based on $(1 - \alpha/(2g))$ where g is the number of joint intervals to be estimated. In the present example, we are estimating joint confidence intervals for β_0 and β_1 ($g=2$), so $B = t(1 - 0.10/(2*2); 23) = t(1 - 0.10/4; 23) = t(0.975; 23)$. In Insert 4.1, we use a *quantile function* to find $B = TINV(0.975, 23) = 2.068$. From SAS Output 1.3, we know b_0, $s\{b_0\}$, b_1, and $s\{b_1\}$. We then use equation 4.3, text page 156, and the Bonferroni procedure for developing joint confidence intervals for b_0 (*b0lo* and *b0hi*) and b_1 (*b1lo* and *b1hi*). The values for *b0lo*, *b0hi*, *b1lo*, and *b1hi* are written to each line in the Toluca Company date set. However, because the values are identical for each line, we need only to print the values for one observation. The (*obs=1*) option on the *proc print* statement causes only the first observation of the data set to be printed; it must be preceded by the *data=toluca* specification.

INSERT 4.1
```
data Toluca Company;
    infile 'c:\alrm\chapter  1 data sets\ch01ta01.txt';
    input lotsize workhrs;
b=tinv(.975,23);
b0lo=62.37-(b*26.18);
b0hi=62.37+(b*26.18);
b1lo=3.5702-(b*.3470);
b1hi=3.5702+(b*.3470);
run;
proc print data=toluca (obs=1);
    var b0lo b0hi b1lo b1hi;
run;
```

Simultaneous Estimation of Mean Responses: On text page 158, the Toluca Company wants to estimate the mean number of work hours required to produce lots of 30, 65, and 100 units where the family confidence coefficient is 0.90. In Chapter 2, we presented the steps to find the confidence interval for $E\{Y_h\}$ when lot size (X_h) = 65 units and the confidence band for the entire regression line. We repeat these steps here with fewer notations and more emphasis on SAS computational statements.

a. Working-Hotelling Procedure: We first find the 90 percent confidence interval for work hours when lot size (X_h) = 65 units. We use the Working-Hotelling $1-\alpha$ band (equations 2.40 and 2.40a, text page 61, and equation 2.30, text page 53) to establish boundary values for (X_h) = 65 units:

$$\hat{Y}_h \pm Ws\{\hat{Y}_h\}$$

where

$$W^2 = 2\,F(1-\alpha;\, 2,\, n-2)$$

and

$$s^2\{\hat{Y}_h\} = MSE\left[\frac{1}{n} + \frac{(X_h - \bar{X})^2}{\sum(X_i - \bar{X})^2}\right]$$

In Insert 4.2 – Method 1, we find the *F*-value (*fvalue*) associated with α = 0.90 and 2, 23 degrees of freedom. We then find $W = \sqrt{2 * fvalue}$. Next, we find $\hat{Y}_h$ (*yhat*) when X_h = 65 units using previously found parameter estimates (SAS Output 1.3), b_0 = 62.366 and b_1 = 3.570. We find $s\{\hat{Y}_h\}$ (*sdyhat*), the square root of text equation 2.30. Finally, we compute $\hat{Y}_h \pm$

$Ws\{\hat{Y}_h\}$ placing the lower boundary of the confidence interval in a variable named *bandlo* and the upper boundary of the confidence interval in a variable named *bandhi*. Execution of Insert 4.2 will print the 90 percent confidence interval for work hours when $X_h = 65$ units. After the syntax is working properly, as in Insert 4.2 – Method 1, we can rewrite the syntax in a more compact form if desired. Insert 4.2 Method 1 can be reduced to Method 2.

To find the confidence intervals for $X_h = 30$ and $X_h = 100$, simply change the computation of *yhat* and *sdyhat* in Insert 4.2 – Method 1 to reflect 30 or 100 units instead of 65 units. Using this method, old values for *bandlo* and *bandhi* will be overwritten each time you change the value of X_h. If this is undesirable, the syntax in Insert 4.3 will find the 90 percent confidence interval for each value of X_h. These intervals will be placed in unique variables, i.e., *bandlo30*, *bandhi30*, *bandlo65*, *bandhi65*, *bandlo00*, and *bandhi00*.

```
                              INSERT 4.2


* Method 1;
data Toluca;
 infile 'c:\alrm\chapter  1 data sets\ch01ta01.txt';
  input lotsize workhrs;

fvalue=finv(.9,2,23);
w=sqrt(2*fvalue);
yhat=62.366+(3.570*65);
sdyhat=sqrt(2383.716*((1/25)+((65-70)**2/19800)));
bandlo=yhat-(w*sdyhat);
bandhi=yhat+(w*sdyhat);
run;
proc print data=toluca (obs=1);
 var bandlo bandhi;
run;

* Method 2;
data Toluca;
  infile 'c:\alrm\chapter  1 data sets\ch01ta01.txt';
  input lotsize workhrs;
bandlo=(62.366+(3.570*65))-(sqrt(2*finv(.9,2,23))*sqrt(2383.716*((1/25)+((65-70)**2/19800))));
bandhi=(62.366+(3.570*65))+(sqrt(2*finv(.9,2,23))*sqrt(2383.716*((1/25)+((65-70)**2/19800))));
run;
proc print data=toluca (obs=1);
 var bandlo bandhi;
run;
```

```
                              INSERT 4.3
data Toluca Company;
  infile 'c:\alrm\chapter  1 data sets\ch01ta01.txt';
  input lotsize workhrs;
fvalue=finv(.9,2,23);
w=sqrt(2*fvalue);
yhat30=62.366+(3.570*30);
sdyhat30=sqrt(2383.716*((1/25)+((30-70)**2/19800)));
bandlo30=yhat30-(w*sdyhat30);
bandhi30=yhat30+(w*sdyhat30);
yhat65=62.366+(3.570*65);
sdyhat65=sqrt(2383.716*((1/25)+((65-70)**2/19800)));
bandlo65=yhat65-(w*sdyhat65);
bandhi65=yhat65+(w*sdyhat65);
yhat100=62.366+(3.570*100);
sdyhat00=sqrt(2383.716*((1/25)+((100-70)**2/19800)));
bandlo00=yhat100-(w*sdyhat00);
bandhi00=yhat100+(w*sdyhat00);
proc print data=toluca (obs=1);
 var bandlo30 bandhi30 bandlo65 bandhi65 bandlo00 bandhi00;
run;
```

b. Bonferroni Procedure: On text page 159, the authors use data from the Toluca Company example and the Bonferroni Procedure to estimate the mean number of work hours required to produce lots of 30, 65, and 100 units where the family confidence coefficient is 0.90. The Bonferroni confidence limits are:

$$\hat{Y}_h \pm Bs\{\hat{Y}_h\}$$

where:

$$B = t(1 - \alpha/2g; n–2)$$

and g is the number of joint confidence intervals to be estimated. In this example, there are three intervals in the family. Thus, $B = t(1 - 0.10/(2*3); 23) = t(1 - 0.10/6; 23) = t(1 - 0.01666; 23) = t(0.9833, 23)$. We can use the *TINV* function as before to find $B = TINV(0.98333, 23) = 2.263$. Computation of $s\{\hat{Y}_h\}$ is the same as for the Working-Hotelling procedure above including Insert 4.2. Thus, to use the Bonferroni Procedure to find the 90 percent confidence interval for work hours when $X_h = 65$ units, we use text equations 4.7 and 4.7a as in Insert 4.4 to find the upper (*bandhi*) and lower (*bandlo*) confidence limits. Confidence limits for $X_h = 30$ and $X_h = 100$ can be generalized from Inserts 4.2 and 4.3.

```
data Toluca Company;
  infile 'c:\alrm\chapter  1 data sets\ch01ta01.txt';
  input lotsize workhrs;
b=tinv(.98333,23);
yhat=62.366+(3.570*65);
sdyhat=sqrt(2383.716*((1/25)+((65-70)**2/19800)));
bandlo=yhat-(b*sdyhat);
bandhi=yhat+(b*sdyhat);
proc print data=toluca (obs=1);
 var bandlo bandhi;
run;
```

Prediction Intervals for New Observations: The Toluca Company now wants to predict the required work hours for lots of 80 and 100 units. The researchers first obtained S and B (text page 160) to determine which prediction interval was smaller. In Insert 4.5, we use the *TINV* and *FINV quantile* functions to find $S = 2.616$ (equation 4.8a, text page 160) and $B = 2.398$ (text equation 4.9a). Because the Bonferroni procedure produces the tighter limits, we use B to establish the 95% family coefficients.

We now calculate $\hat{Y}_h$ for 80 (*yhat80*) and 100 (*yhat100*) units. We then use equation 2.38a, text page 59, to find $s\{pred\}$ for 80 (*sdpre80*) and 100 (*sdpre00*) units. Finally, we use text equation 4.9, text page 160, to find the lower and upper 95% confidence limits for 80 (*bandlo80* and *bandhi80*, respectively) and 100 (*bandlo00* and *bandhi00*, respectively) units.

```
data Toluca Company;
  infile 'c:\alrm\chapter  1 data sets\ch01ta01.txt';
  input lotsize workhrs;
s=sqrt(2*finv(.95,2,23));
b=tinv(1-(.05/(2*2)),23);
yhat80=62.366+(3.570*80);
sdpre80=sqrt(2383.716*(1+(1/25)+((80-70)**2/19800)));
bandlo80=yhat80-(b*sdpre80);
bandhi80=yhat80+(b*sdpre80);
yhat100=62.366+(3.570*100);
sdpre00=sqrt(2383.716*(1+(1/25)+((100-70)**2/19800)));
bandlo00=yhat100-(b*sdpre00);
bandhi00=yhat100+(b*sdpre00);
proc print data=toluca (obs=1);
 var yhat80 bandlo80 bandhi80 yhat100 bandlo00 bandhi00;
run;
```

Inverse Predictions: The authors present an example of inverse prediction on text page 168. We do not have access to the source data file, however, and will use the Toluca Company for illustration. Suppose the auditing department of the Toluca Company's corporate home office requested that lot size $\hat{X}_{h(new)}$ be estimated with a 95% confidence interval when the work hours for a run is known to be $Y_{h(new)} = 300$. Although the accountants at the Toluca Company failed to appreciate the need for such a calculation, they complied with the request.

In Insert 4.6, we first find $\hat{X}_{h(new)} = Y_{h(new)} - 62.366 / 3.570 = 66.56$ using equation 4.31, text page 168, and parameter estimates from SAS Output 1.3. For equation 4.32, text page 169, we find t using $TINV(1-0.05/2, 23) = 2.07$ and place the result in *tvalue*. Using text equation 4.32a, we find $s^2\{predX\}$ (*sdprex*) = 13.95. Finally, we use text equation 4.32 to find:

$$\hat{X}_{h(new)} \pm t(1-\alpha/2;\ n-2)s\{predX\}$$

$$66.56 \pm 2.07*13.95$$

$$37.70 < \hat{X}_{h(new)} < 95.42$$

The auditors at the corporate home office conclude with 95% confidence that the number of hours required to produce the lot size of 300 units is between 37.70 and 95.42 hours. The auditors calculate the error to be 66.56/((95.42-37.70)/2) or approximately $\pm 43\%$.

INSERT 4.6

```
data Toluca Company;
  infile 'c:\alrm\chapter  1 data sets\ch01ta01.txt';
  input lotsize workhrs;
xhnew=(300-62.366)/3.570;
tvalue=tinv(1-.05/2,23);
sdprex=sqrt((2383.716/(3.570**2)*(1+(1/25)+((xhnew-70)**2/19800))));
prexlo=xhnew-(tvalue*sdprex);
prexhi=xhnew+(tvalue*sdprex);
proc print data=toluca (obs=1);
 var xhnew prexlo prexhi;
run;
```

The Charles Plumbing Supplies Example

Data File: ch04ta02.txt

Regression through the Origin: From text page 162, the Charles Plumbing Supplies Company studied the relationship between the number of work units performed (X) and the total variable labor costs (Y). After opening and printing ch04ta02.dat, the first 5 lines should appear as SAS Output 4.2. To perform regression through the origin, we use the *noint* option on the model statement to suppress the intercept term. Confidence limits are also requested (*clb*) on the model statement in Insert 4.7. This results in SAS Output 4.3 and is consistent with text pages 163-164.

SAS Output 4.2

Obs	x	y
1	20	114
2	196	921
3	115	560
4	50	245
5	122	575

INSERT 4.7

```
data Charles Plumbing;
  infile 'c:\alrm\chapter  4 data sets\ch04ta02.txt';
  input x y;
proc reg;
 model y = x / noint clb;
 run;
```

SAS Output 4.3

Analysis of Variance					
Source	DF	Sum of Squares	Mean Square	F Value	Pr > F
Model	1	4191980	4191980	18762.5	<.0001
Error	11	2457.65933	223.42358		
Uncorrected Total	12	4194438			

43

Parameter Estimates							
Variable	DF	Parameter Estimate	Standard Error	t Value	Pr > |t|	95% Confidence Limits	
x	1	4.68527	0.03421	136.98	<.0001	4.60999	4.76056

Parameter Estimates							
Variable	DF	Parameter Estimate	Standard Error	t Value	Pr > |t|	95% Confidence Limits	
x	1	4.68527	0.03421	136.98	<.0001	4.60999	4.76056

Matrix Approach to Simple
Linear Regression Analysis

The text begins Chapter 5 by presenting an overview of the algebra for vectors and matrices. In Chapter 5 of this manual, we introduce SAS/IML software through *proc iml*, a procedure that allows the user to write SAS statements for performing vector/matrix algebra. We follow examples in the text and show how to write SAS programs to perform operations such as matrix addition, subtraction and multiplication. Following the overview of matrix algebra, the text expresses the simple linear regression model as a matrix equation and then repeats the steps followed in Chapter 1 only now these steps are described using matrix algebra.

Again, we are given Y_i and X_i for a sample of n subjects and we want to find a "best fitting" model for predicting Y given X. In Chapter 1, the simple linear regression model for the ith subject, $i = 1, \ldots, n$ was written as :

$$Y_i = \beta_0 + \beta_1 X_i + \varepsilon_i$$

To summarize the key results of the matrix formulation, let the capital bold-faced letter **Y** represent the nx1 column vector containing the data for the dependent variable and the bold-faced letter **X** represent the nx2 matrix with the first column being a column vector of ones and the second column being the column vector of data for the independent variable; i.e.,

$$\mathbf{Y} = \begin{bmatrix} Y_1 \\ Y_2 \\ \vdots \\ Y_n \end{bmatrix} \quad \text{and} \quad \mathbf{X} = \begin{bmatrix} 1 & X_1 \\ 1 & X_2 \\ \vdots & \vdots \\ 1 & X_n \end{bmatrix}$$

Further, let:

$$\boldsymbol{\beta} = \begin{bmatrix} \beta_0 \\ \beta_1 \end{bmatrix} \quad \text{and} \quad \boldsymbol{\varepsilon} = \begin{bmatrix} \varepsilon_1 \\ \varepsilon_2 \\ \vdots \\ \varepsilon_n \end{bmatrix}$$

Using this notation, the simple linear regression model can be written:

$$\mathbf{Y} = \mathbf{X}\boldsymbol{\beta} + \boldsymbol{\varepsilon}$$

A few key results of the matrix formulation of the regression model are:

(1.) Matrix solution for the regression coefficients: $\mathbf{b} = \begin{bmatrix} b_0 \\ b_1 \end{bmatrix} = (\mathbf{X'X})^{-1} \mathbf{X'Y}$

(2.) Matrix solution for the predicted values: $\hat{\mathbf{Y}} = \mathbf{Xb} = \mathbf{X}(\mathbf{X'X})^{-1} \mathbf{X'Y} = \mathbf{HY}$

where $\mathbf{H} = \mathbf{X}(\mathbf{X'X})^{-1} \mathbf{X'}$ is called the *hat matrix*.

(3.) Matrix solution for the fitted model residuals: $\mathbf{e} = \mathbf{Y} - \hat{\mathbf{Y}} = \mathbf{Y} - \mathbf{Xb} = (\mathbf{I} - \mathbf{H})\mathbf{Y}$

From these equations, we begin to see that the computations required for regression analysis can be written as matrix expressions. As stated earlier, IML is a SAS procedure that performs matrix algebra. Most of our needs are met by SAS syntax that is more user friendly than that specific to IML, but occasionally we need to perform computations that are not directly available, and IML provides a convenient way to write programs according to our specifications. Moreover, it is instructional to write matrix language programs that perform regression analysis. We illustrate the use of IML by presenting SAS statements to compute (1.) – (3.) and other key matrix expressions for the regression analysis of data given in the Toluca Company example. We begin by introducing some basic mathematical operators used in the SAS/IML software.

Using *proc iml* for Matrix Operations: We initiate the IML procedure by writing *proc iml*. Next, we use IML syntax to write statements for performing one or more matrix operations. We end the procedure by writing *quit*. As in previous chapters, we terminate all SAS statements with a semi-colon. In the following, we illustrate some of the IML statements that are useful for programming a regression analysis.

A SAS program for finding the transpose of a matrix **A** and a vector **C** is given in Insert 5.1. In this program, the numerical values of the matrix **A** and the vector **C** are specified directly in the *iml* procedure. To accomplish this, we choose a name for the matrix and set that name equal to a quantity in braces. The SAS program does not differentiate between upper and lower case names and does not accept bold-face notation. Therefore, in SAS code we can write A = { } or a = { } to specify the matrix **A**. The matrix is specified by rows with row elements separated by one or more spaces and complete rows separated by a comma. It is not necessary to begin each row of a matrix on a new line of the program but it is helpful for proof-reading to do so and to line up the columns as we have done in specifying A and C in Insert 5.1. Thus, the three lines of code that immediately follow the *proc iml* statement specify the 3x2 matrix **A** and the next three lines specify the 3x1 vector **C**.

Insert 5.1 finds the transpose of **A** and **C**. The transpose operator is denoted by the back-quote character. Thus, the statement *AT = A`* exchanges the rows and columns of matrix **A** and stores the results in a matrix named **AT**. Similarly, the statement *CT = C`* exchanges the rows and columns of matrix **C** and stores the results in a matrix named **CT**. Alternatively, one can use AT=T(A) or CT=T(C) to find the transpose of **A** and **C**, respectively. The print statement in the next to last line of Insert 5.1 instructs SAS to print matrices **A**, **C**, **AT**, and **CT** (SAS Output 5.1). These results are given on text page 178.

```
                              INSERT 5.1

title 'Transpose of a matrix
 from text page 178";
proc iml;
 A = {2  5, 7 10,  3  4};
 C = { 4, 7, 10};
 AT = A`;
 CT = C`;
print A, AT, C, CT;
quit;
```

SAS Output 5.1

A	
2	5
7	10
3	4

AT		
2	7	3
5	10	4

C
4
7
10

CT		
4	7	10

Insert 5.2 shows SAS/IML syntax for text examples of matrix addition, subtraction, and multiplication, and finding the inverse of a matrix. The output is not presented for brevity. The symbol + denotes the addition operator and the symbol − denotes the subtraction operator. The asterisk symbol * denotes the multiplication operator. The IML function *inv(A)* finds the inverse of the matrix **A**. We have named the result *Ainv* but we could have chosen another convenient name. For example, we could have called the result *d* by writing *d = inv(A)*.

```
           INSERT 5.2                              INSERT 5.2 continued

title 'Addition and Subtraction of a matrix   title 'Multiplication of a matrix by a matrix
 from text page 180';                            from text page 182';
proc iml;                                      proc iml;
 A = {1 4, 2 5, 3 6};                           A = {2 5, 4 1};
 B = {1 2, 2 3, 3 4};                           B = {4 6, 5 8};
 C = A+B;                                        C = A*B;
 D = A-B;                                       print A B C;
print A, B, C, D;                              quit;
quit;
                                               title 'Inverse of a matrix from
title 'Multiplication of a matrix by a scalar   text page 189';
 (4) from text page 182';                      proc iml;
proc iml;                                        A = {2 4, 3 1};
 A = {2 7, 9 3};                               Ainv = inv(A);
 B = 4*A;                                       print A, Ainv;
print A, B;                                     quit;
quit;
```

Simple Linear Regression in Matrix Terms

The Toluca Company Example

Data File: 'ch01ta01.txt'

We use matrix methods to perform a simple linear regression analysis of the Toluca Company example (text page 19). The required steps are presented in text Chapter 5 and are not detailed here except in Insert 5.3. We begin the SAS program with the statement *data TolucaCo*. We assigned the arbitrary name *TolucaCo* to the data. Next, we identified the data file with the statement *infile* 'c:\alrm\chapter 1 data sets\ch01ta01.txt'. The statement *input lotsize workhrs* assigns names to the columns of data in the data file and stores the numerical data under these names. Excerpts from the **Y** vector (*workhrs*) and **X** matrix (a column of ones and a column of numerical values of *lotsize*) are given in equation 5.61 page 200 of the text. The *run* statement activates the *data* step and all the data are entered.

The *proc iml* statement initiates the IML procedure. The statement *read all var {'workhrs'} into y* stores the column of data named *workhrs* in the matrix (vector) *y*. Similarly, the next statement stores the column of data labeled *lotsize* in the matrix (vector) *x*. In this program we used lower case letters to denote matrices.

The statement $n = nrow(x)$ assigns the value of the number of rows in the matrix *x* to variable label *n*. The statement $p = ncol(x)$ assigns the value of the number of columns in the matrix *x* to variable label *p*.

The function $j(a,b,c)$ creates an *a*x*b* matrix whose elements all have the value *c*. Thus, $j(n,1,1)$ creates an *n*x1 matrix whose elements all have the value '1'.

The expression $c = a\|b$ concatenates the columns of the matrices *a* and *b* and stores the result in the matrix *c*. The result is a matrix whose first set of columns are the columns of *a* and whose next set of columns are the columns of *b*. This is called horizontal concatenation.

In Insert 5.3, the statement $x = j(n,1,1)\|x$ creates an *n*x1 matrix of ones, concatenates this created matrix with *x*, and stores the result in a new matrix named *x*. This results in a matrix *x* whose first column is a vector of ones and second column is a vector containing the data for *lotsize*. Here we have used *x* on both sides of the equal sign. This means that the "old" variable *x* is modified and the variable label *x* is used as the name for the "new" variable. The "old" variable is no longer associated with the name *x*.

The remaining statements are easy to follow. The statement $xpx = x`*x$ computes **X'X** and stores the result as a matrix named *xpx*; the statement $xpy = x`*y$ computes **X'Y** and stores the result as a matrix named *xpy*, and so on.

The print statement specifies printing **Y** (eq 5.61, text page 200), **X** (eq 5.61, text page 200), **Ŷ** (eq 5.71, text page 202), and **E** (**e**, eq 5.76, text page 203). Matrices **XPXINV** ($(\mathbf{X'X})^{-1}$, eq 5.64, text page 201), **B** (eq 5.60, text page 200), **YPY** ($\mathbf{Y'Y}$, text page 205), **CORRECT** (corrected

SSTO), **SSTO** (eq 5.83 and 5.89a, text page 204), **SSR** (**b'X'Y**, text page 205), **SSE** (**Y'Y−b'X'Y**, text page 205), **MSE**, **VARB** ($s^2\{b\}$, eq 5.94, text page 207), **XH**, **VARYHATH** ($s^2\{\hat{Y}\}$, eq 5.95 and 598, text page 208) are also presented. SAS Output 5.2 displays excerpts of output to illustrate the results.

INSERT 5.3	INSERT 5.3 continued
| ```
data TolucaCo;
  infile 'a:\ch01ta01.dat';
  input lotsize workhrs;
run;
proc iml;
  use ch01p0021;
  read all var {'workhrs'} into y;
  read all var {'lotsize'} into x;
  n = nrow(x);
  p = ncol(x);
  x = j(n,1,1)||x;
  xpx = x`*x;
  xpy = x`*y;
  xpxinv = inv(x`*x);
  b = inv(x`*x)*x`*y;
``` | ```
yhat = x*b;
 e = y - yhat;
 ypy = y`*y;
 correct = y`*j(n,n,1)*y/n;
 sstot = y`*y - y`*j(n,n,1)*y/n;
 ssr = b`*x`*y;
 sse = y`*y - b`*x`*y;
 mse = sse/(n-p);
 varb = mse*inv(x`*x);
 xh ={1, 65};
 varyhath = xh`*varb*xh;
print y x yhat e, xpx xpy, xpxinv,
 b, ypy correct sstot ssr sse mse, varb, xh,
varyhath;
quit;
``` |

SAS Output 5.2

Y	X		YHAT	E
399	1	80	347.98202	51.01798
121	1	30	169.47192	-48.47192
221	1	50	240.87596	-19.87596
376	1	90	383.68404	-7.68404
361	1	70	312.28	48.72

XPXINV		B	XH	VARB	
0.2874747	-0.003535	62.365859	1	685.25805	-8.427277
-0.003535	0.0000505	3.570202	65	-8.427277	0.1203897

VARYHATH	YPY	CORRECT	SSTOT	SSR	SSE	MSE
98.358367	2745173	2437970	307203.04	2690347.5	54825.459	2383.7156

Chapter 6 SAS®

Multiple Regression I

In many applications using regression analysis the model may involve more than one predictor variable. We call such a model the *multiple regression model* or the *general linear regression model*. We can write the general linear regression model as:

$$Y_i = \beta_0 + \beta_1 X_{i1} + \beta_2 X_{i2} + ... + \beta_{p-1} X_{i,p-1} + \varepsilon_i$$

where:

$\beta_0, \beta_1, ..., \beta_{p-1}$ are unknown model parameters with fixed values

$X_{i1}, ..., X_{i,p-1}$ are known constants

ε_i are independent $N(0, \sigma^2)$ random variables

$i = 1, ..., n$

In matrix notation, the general linear regression model is:

$$\mathbf{Y} = \mathbf{X}\boldsymbol{\beta} + \boldsymbol{\varepsilon}$$

where:

$\mathbf{Y}$ is the $n \times 1$ vector of response observations on the dependent variable
$\boldsymbol{\beta}$ is the $p \times 1$ vector of unknown model parameters
$\mathbf{X}$ is the $n \times p$ matrix of known constants
$\boldsymbol{\varepsilon}$ is a vector of independent $N(0, \sigma^2)$ random variables

Chapter 6 focuses on the special case where $p = 3$ and therefore only two predictor variables are in the general linear regression model. In the following, we give illustrative SAS syntax for performing a statistical analysis of the general linear regression model with $p = 3$.

Dwaine Studios, Inc. Example

Data File: ch06fi05.txt

Multiple Regression with Two Predictor Variables: Dwaine Studios, Inc. has locations in 21 medium size cities and is considering expansion into additional cities (text page 236). The company wants to predict sales (Y) in a community using the number of persons greater than 15 years in the community ($X1$) and per capita disposable income in the community ($X2$). See Chapter 0, "Working with SAS," for instructions on opening the Dwaine Studios data file and naming the variables $X1$, $X2$, and Y. After printing ch06fi05.txt, the first 5 lines of output should look like SAS Output 6.1.

SAS Output 6.1

Obs	x1	x2	y
1	68.5	16.7	174.4
2	45.2	16.8	164.4
3	91.3	18.2	244.2
4	47.8	16.3	154.6
5	46.9	17.3	181.6

The researchers began with the first order regression model. (Insert 6.1) Results are shown in SAS Output 6.2 and are consistent with Figure 6.5, text page 237. In Insert 6.1, we also present the matrix language syntax for estimation of the parameters. Notice that the **X** matrix on text page 237 contains a column of 1's and this column is not in the Dwaine Studios data file. Thus, in Insert 6.1 we first compute a variable, *X0* that is equal to 1 for each of the 21 cities in the data file. We then enter *proc iml* and set column vectors **CON**, **A**, **B**, and **Y** equal to *X0*, *X1*, *X2*, and *Y*, respectively. Next, we concatenate the **CON**, **A**, and **B** column vectors into the **X** matrix such that the **X** matrix is now as shown in equation 6.70, text page 237. (Although the method of constructing the **X** matrix in Insert 6.1 is different from the method presented in Chapter 5, both methods achieve the same outcome.) Next, we find **X'X** (*xtx*), **X'Y** (*xty*), $(\mathbf{X'X})^{-1}$ (*xtxinv*), and **b** $= (\mathbf{X'X})^{-1}\mathbf{X'Y}$. The "*print b*" statement will print the parameter estimates. Although we do not display the output from the "*print b*" statement, the estimates obtained through the matrix language program are equal to the estimates shown in SAS Output 6.2. We did not print **X'X**, **X'Y**, and $(\mathbf{X'X})^{-1}$, but we could do so and compare the numerical output to the text results shown on page 238-239 and the SAS regression analysis shown in SAS Output 6.2.

SAS Output 6.2

Analysis of Variance					
Source	DF	Sum of Squares	Mean Square	F Value	Pr > F
Model	2	24015	12008	99.10	<.0001
Error	18	2180.92741	121.16263		
Corrected Total	20	26196			

Root MSE	11.00739	**R-Square**	0.9167
Dependent Mean	181.90476	**Adj R-Sq**	0.9075
Coeff Var	6.05118		

Parameter Estimates					
Variable	DF	Parameter Estimate	Standard Error	t Value	Pr > |t|
Intercept	1	-68.85707	60.01695	-1.15	0.2663
x1	1	1.45456	0.21178	6.87	<.0001
x2	1	9.36550	4.06396	2.30	0.0333

INSERT 6.1

```
* Regresson analysis;
data dwaine;
  infile 'c:\alrm\chapter  6 data sets\ch06fi05.txt';
  input x1 x2 y;
proc reg;
 model y=x1 x2;
run;

* Matrix format;
data dwaine;
  infile 'c:\alrm\chapter  6 data sets\ch06fi05.txt';
  input x1 x2 y;
x0=1;
proc iml;
  use dwaine;
  read all var {'y'} into y;
  read all var {'x1'} into a;
  read all var {'x2'} into b;
  read all var {'x0'} into con;
x = (con||a||b);
xtx=x`*x;
xty=x`*y;
xtxinv=inv(x`*x);
b=inv(x`*x)*x`*y;
print b;
quit;
```

To produce the three-dimensional scatter plot shown in Figure 6.6(a)), text page 238, we use *proc g3d* from the SAS/Graph package (Insert 6.2). We first produce the three-dimensional scatter plot (SAS Output 6.3), and then rotate the plot by 45° in the second *proc g3d* (SAS Output 6.4). Optionally, we can rotate and tilt the plot in the same *proc g3d* statement, e.g., *scatter x2*x1=y / rotate=45 tilt=45;* .

INSERT 6.2

```
* Produce text Figure 6.6 3-D graphs;
data dwaine;
  infile 'c:\alrm\chapter  6 data sets\ch06fi05.txt';
  input x1 x2 y;
proc g3d data=dwaine;
  scatter x2*x1=y / shape='pyramid' caxis=black  noneedle;
title1 'Basic scatter plot';
run;
proc g3d data=dwaine;
  scatter x2*x1=y / shape='pyramid' caxis=black noneedle rotate=45;
title1 'Basic scatter plot';
run;

* Produce text Figures 6.8 and 6.9;
data dwaine;
  infile 'c:\alrm\chapter  6 data sets\ch06fi05.txt';
  input x1 x2 y;
proc reg;
 model y=x1 x2/ r p;
 output out=results r=residual p=yhat;
run;
data results;
 set results;
absresid=abs(residual);
x1x2=x1*x2;
proc plot;
* Produce text Figures 6.8 a-d;
 plot residual*yhat;
 plot residual*x1;
 plot residual*x2;
 plot residual*x1x2;
* Produce text Figures 6.9 a;
 plot absresid*yhat="*";
 run;
* Produce text Figures 6.9 b;
proc univariate normal plot;
 var residual;
run;
```

SAS Output 6.3

Basic scatter plot

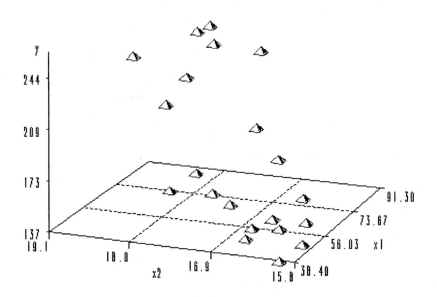

SAS Output 6.4

Basic scatter plot

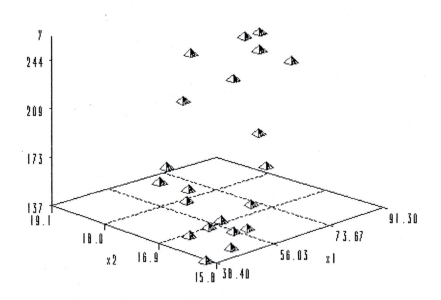

Analysis of Appropriateness of Model: Inspection of Figures 6.8 and 6.9, text pages 242-243, reveals that we need to produce the residuals and predicted values of *Y* based on the first order regression model. In Insert 6.2 above, we save the unstandardized residuals (*resesidual*) and predicted values (*yhat*) in the output file named *results* (*output out=results*). We also compute *absresid*, the absolute value of the residuals, and *x1x2*, the interaction term between *X1* and *X1*. *Proc plot* can now produce text Figures 6.8 a-d and 6.9a. *Proc univariate* is used to produce the normal probability plot shown in text Figure 6.9b.

On text page 243, the authors calculate the coefficient of correlation between the ordered residuals and their expected value under normality for the Dwaine Studios example. The expected value under normality of the kth smallest observation in a sample of size *n* is given by:

$$\sqrt{MSE}\left[z\left(\frac{k-0.375}{n+0.25}\right)\right]$$

The first step in obtaining the expected value of the ordered residuals under normality is to calculate $(k-0.375)/(n+0.25)$. (Insert 6.3) In the Dwaine Studios example, $n = 21$. Since *k* is the rank of the ordered residuals, we obtain the first order regression model and save the residuals (*residual*). We then use *proc rank* to create new variable (*ranke*) that is based on the value of *residual*. Thus, $(k-0.375)/(n+0.25)$ becomes $(ranke - 0.375)/(21 + 0.25)$. This quantity represents the cumulative probability ($0 \le$ cumulative probability ≤ 1.0) of the standard normal distribution. We now obtain a standard score (*z*) associated with the cumulative probability calculated above. In SAS, the *Probit* function is a *quantile function* and takes the form *Probit(p)*, where *p* = cumulative probability. For instance, if cumulative probability = 0.50 (*Probit*(0.50)) then $z = 0$. If cumulative probability = 0.8413 (*Probit*(0.8413)) then $z = +1$. Thus, to obtain *z* we use *Probit* $((ranke - 0.375)/(21 + 0.25))$. Finally, we multiply this quantity by the square root of *MSE* = 121.163 of the first order model (SAS Output 6.2). From the above, we compute the expected value (*ev*) as:

ev = *sqrt*(121.163) * *Probit* $((ranke - 0.375)/(21 + 0.25))$.

We can now obtain the coefficient of correlation between the residual and the expected value under normality (*ev*). The result of the correlation between *ev* and *residual* is 0.979 and is within rounding error of the correlation (0.980) reported on text page 243. The interpolated critical value from text Table B.6 for $n = 21$ and $\alpha = 0.05$ is 0.9525. The obtained correlation coefficient (0.980) is greater than the table value (0.9525), and we conclude that the distribution of the error terms appears to be reasonably close to a normal distribution.

On text page 244, the researchers tested the null hypothesis $H_0: \beta_1 = 0$ and $\beta_2 = 0$. The test result is found in the output of the first order regression model above (SAS Output 6.2). Because the *p*-value (<0.000) associated with $F = 99.103$ is less than the desired significance level ($\alpha = 0.05$), we conclude that sales are related to target population (*X1*) and disposable income (*X2*).

```
                              INSERT 6.3

data dwaine;
  infile 'c:\alrm\chapter  6 data sets\ch06fi05.txt';
  input x1 x2 y;
* Save residuals (/ r) in residual;
proc reg;
  model y=x1 x2/ r;
  output out=results r=residual;
run;
* Rank the residuals and place the rank in "rank";
proc rank data=results out=results;
  var residual;
  ranks ranke;
  run;
data results;
  set results;
  ev = sqrt(121.16263)*Probit((ranke - .375)/(21  + .25));
proc corr;
  var ev residual;
  run;
proc print;
  var ev;
  run;
```

We can use the ANOVA table in SAS Output 6.2 to find the *Coefficient of Multiple Determination* using equation 6.40, text page 226:

$$R^2 = \frac{SSR}{SSTO} = \frac{24,015.28}{26,196.21} = 0.917$$

$R^2 = 0.917$ is also given in the Model Summary table of SAS Output 6.2. Additionally, $R = 0.957$ and *Adjusted R Square* $= 0.907$ are presented in the Model Summary table.

Estimation of Regression Parameters: On text page 245, the researchers wish to jointly estimate β_1 and β_2 with a family confidence coefficient of 0.90. The confidence limits for β_k are given by equations 6.52 and 6.52a, text page 228:

$$b_k \pm Bs\{b_k\}$$

$$b_k \pm t(1-\alpha/2g; n-p)s\{b_k\}$$

where g = the number of intervals to be estimated and p = the number of parameters in the regression model. In the present discussion, we wish to estimate $g = 2$ intervals and there are 3 parameters in the regression model. We use the *quantile function TINV*(probability, df) where "probability" = $(1-0.90/2g)$ and df = $n - p$ or TINV(0.975, 18). Thus, in Insert 6.4, we find t and place its value in *tvalue*. We use the parameter estimates shown in SAS Output 6.2 (*b1* = 1.455 and *b2* = 9.366) and the standard deviation of each estimate (shown as "Standard Error" in SAS Output 6.2, $s\{b_1\}$ = 0.212 and $s\{b_2\}$ = 4.06) to find the lower (*b1lo* and *b2lo*) and upper (*b1hi* and *b2hi*) confidence limit for each estimated parameter. We print the limits using *proc print data=dwaine (obs=1);*.

```
                          INSERT 6.4

    data intervals;
    tvalue = tinv(.975,18);
    b1lo=1.45455-(tvalue*.211178);
    b1hi=1.45455+(tvalue*.211178);
    b2lo=9.3655-(tvalue*4.06395);
    b2hi=9.3655+(tvalue*4.06395);
    proc print;
     var b1lo b1hi b2lo b2hi;
    run;
```

Estimation of Mean Response: On text page 245 the authors wish to estimate the expected mean sales when the target population is 65.4 thousand persons and the per capita disposable income is 17.6 thousand dollars. They also estimate a 95 percent confidence interval for $E\{Y_h\}$. The $1-\alpha$ confidence limits for $E\{Y_h\}$ are given by text equations 6.59, text page 229:

where:

$$\hat{Y}_h \pm t(1-\alpha/2; n-p)s\{\hat{Y}_h\}$$

$$s^2\{\hat{Y}_h\} = MSE\left(\mathbf{X}_h'\left(\mathbf{X'X}\right)^{-1}\mathbf{X}_h\right)$$

In chapter 2 we found the confidence intervals for $E\{Y_h\}$ where there was one predictor variable in the model. However, as the number of predictor variables increases, the task of finding the variance of $\hat{Y}_h$ becomes increasingly laborious. Although equation 2.30, text page 53, can be generalized to the case of multiple regression ($p > 2$), the authors present the formulation of the variance of $\hat{Y}_h$ in matrix notation in text equation 6.58 shown above. We use this matrix formulation and *proc iml* to solve the current problem.

The matrix program shown in Insert 6.5 is an extension of the matrix program shown in Insert 6.1 above. We find *t* (*tvalue*) prior to entering the matrix program and after entering set the matrix **tvalue** to the variable *tvalue*. We then find $s^2\{\hat{Y}_h\}$ using the above notation. *MSE* = 121.163 is given in SAS Output 6.2 above. $\mathbf{X}_h'$ is defined in Insert 6.5 as shown on text page 246. We find $\hat{Y}_h$ (*yhath*) using text equation 6.55, text page 229. Finally, we compute and print the lower (*yhathlo*=185.29) and upper (*yhathlo*=196.91) confidence limits.

INSERT 6.5

```
data dwaine;
  infile 'c:\alrm\chapter  6 data sets\ch06fi05.txt';
  input x1 x2 y;
* Find t(1-alpha/2,n-p) from text equation 6.59;
tvalue=tinv(.975,18);
* Write a column of 1's into the Dwaine Studios data file;
x0=1;
proc iml;
  use dwaine;
  read all var {'y'} into y;
  read all var {'x1'} into a;
  read all var {'x2'} into b;
  read all var {'x0'} into con;
  read all var {'tvalue'} into tvalue;
x = (con||a||b);
xtx=x`*x;
xty=x`*y;
* Fine the b matrix using text equation 6.25;
b=inv(x`*x)*x`*y;
xtxinv=inv(x`*x);
* Define xh matrix per text page 246;
xh={1,65.4,17.6};
* Find standard deviation of yhat(new) per text equation 6.58;
sxh=sqrt(121.163*((xh`)*(xtxinv)*xh));
* Find yhat(new)using text equation 6.56;
yhath=xh`*b;
* Find confidence interval using text equation 6.59;
yhathlo=yhath-(tvalue*sxh);
yhathhi=yhath+(tvalue*sxh);
low = yhathlo[1,1];
high = yhathhi[1,1];
print low high;
quit;
```

Prediction Limits for New Observations: Dwaine Studios now wants to predict sales for two new cities (text page 247). Here, X_{h1} and X_{h2} equal 65.4 and 17.6, respectively, for City A and 53.1 and 17.7, respectively, for City B. To determine which prediction intervals (Scheffe versus Bonferroni) are preferable here, we find S and B using equations 6.65a and 6.66a, text page 231, where g = 2 and $1 - \alpha = 0.90$. In Insert 6.6, we compute S (s) and B (b) and print the two values. We find $S = 2.29$ and $B = 2.10$ so that the Bonferroni limits are tighter here and therefore more efficient.

INSERT 6.6

```
data dwaine;
  infile 'c:\alrm\chapter  6 data sets\ch06fi05.txt';
  input x1 x2 y;
s=sqrt(2*finv(.9,2,18));
b=tinv(1-(.1/(2*2)),18);
proc print data=dwaine (obs=1);
  var s b;
run;
```

To find the simultaneous Bonferroni prediction limits for city A, we use (equation 6.66, text page 231):

$$\hat{Y}_h \pm Bs\{pred\}$$

where (text equations 6.66a, 6.63a, and 6.58) :

$$B = t(1 - \alpha / 2g; n - p)$$

$$s^2\{pred\} = MSE + s^2\{\hat{Y}_h\}$$

$$s^2\{\hat{Y}_h\} = MSE\left(\mathbf{X}_h^{'}(\mathbf{X'X})^{-1}\mathbf{X}_h\right)$$

From Insert 6.7, we find the lower (*yhathlo*=167.71) and upper (*yhathhi*=214.49) 90% confidence limits for city A. We simply replace "*xh* = {1, 65.4, 17.6}." with "*xh* = {1, 53.1, 17.7}." in Insert 6.7and find the 90 percent confidence interval for city B: *yhathlo* = 149.08 and *yhathi* = 199.21.

INSERT 6.7

```
data dwaine;
  infile 'c:\alrm\chapter 6 data sets\ch06fi05.txt';
  input x1 x2 y;
* Find b(1-alpha/2g,n-p) from text equation 6.59;
b=tinv(1-(.1/(2*2)),18);
* Write a column of 1's into the Dwaine Studios data file;
x0=1;
proc iml;
  use dwaine;
  read all var {'y'} into y;
  read all var {'x1'} into a;
  read all var {'x2'} into b;
  read all var {'x0'} into con;
  read all var {'b'} into bon;
* Define the X matrix;
x = (con||a||b);
xtx=x`*x;
xpx=t(x)*x;
xty=x`*y;
* Fine the b matrix using text equation 6.25;
b=inv(t(x)*x)*t(x)*y;
xtxinv=inv(t(x)*x);
* Define xh matrix as on text page 247;
xh={1, 65.4, 17.6};
* Find standard deviation of new observation per text equation 6.58;
spre=sqrt(121.163+(121.163*(t(xh)*(xtxinv)*xh)));
* Find yhat(new);
yhath=t(xh)*b;
* Find confidence interval using text equation 6.66;
yhathlo=yhath-(bon*spre);
yhathhi=yhath+(bon*spre);
low = yhathlo[1,1];
high = yhathhi[1,1];
print low high;
quit;
```

Chapter 7 SAS®

Multiple Regression II

We use *sum of squared deviations* or *sum of squares* of various types as a quantitative measurement of variability that is attributable to different sources associated with parameters specified in the model. In previous chapters we defined the sum of squared deviations of the observations on the dependent variable Y_i from the overall sample mean $\overline{Y}$ as the (corrected) *total sum of squares*, denoted *SSTO*. We defined the sum of squared deviations of the fitted (predicted) values $\hat{Y}_i$ from $\overline{Y}$ as the *regression sum of squares* denoted *SSR*. We defined the sum of squared deviations of the observations Y_i from the fitted values $\hat{Y}_i$ as the *error sum of squares* denoted *SSE*. We found that:

$$SSTO = SSR + SSE$$

Suppose we fit a general linear model with $p - 1$ predictor variables and obtain *SST*, *SSR* and *SSE*. Now, suppose we add one or more predictor variables to the model and fit this "new" model. The observations Y_i will remain unchanged as will the mean $\overline{Y}$, but the $\hat{Y}_i$ with this new model may be different from the $\hat{Y}_i$ based on the first model. Thus, the numerical values of *SSR* and *SSE* will likely change. In fact, *SSR* will increase and, correspondingly, *SSE* will decrease by the same magnitude as the increase in *SSR*. We call this magnitude of change the *extra sum of squares* due to the predictor variable(s) that were added to the model. To avoid confusion we need additional notation to identify the variables that are in the model when *SSR* and *SSE* are computed.

It is easier to explain the extra sum of squares notation in terms of a specific example. Suppose predictor variables X_1, X_2 and X_3 are available for fitting a general linear regression model. If we fit a model with only X_1 in the model, we denote the sums of squares for regression and error as $SSR(X_1)$ and $SSE(X_1)$, respectively. If we fit a model that includes the predictor variables X_1 and X_2, we write $SSR(X_1, X_2)$ and $SSE(X_1, X_2)$ to denote the regression and error sums of squares, respectively. If we fit a model that includes X_1 and then add X_2 to the model and refit, the additional or extra regression sum of squares due to adding the additional predictor variable is denoted $SSR(X_2|X_1)$ and the reduction or extra error sum of squares is denoted $SSE(X_2|X_1)$. Similarly, if we fit a model that includes all three predictor variables, we write $SSR(X_1, X_2, X_3)$ and $SSE(X_1, X_2, X_3)$ to denote the regression and error sums of squares, respectively. If we fit a model that includes X_1 and then add X_2 and X_3 to the model and refit, the additional or extra regression sum of squares due to adding both additional predictor variables is denoted $SSR(X_2, X_3 |X_1)$ and the reduction or extra error sum of squares is denoted $SSE(X_2, X_3 |X_1)$. The extra sum of squares is also known as the *partial sum of squares*. It is obvious that we need to specify the predictor variables as being already in the model or as being added to the model when we discuss extra (partial) sums of squares.

In Chapter 7, the authors discuss methods used to make statistical inferences when adding and deleting predictor variables to the general linear regression model. The problem of deciding the merits of adding or deleting predictor variables in choosing an appropriate regression model is of particular interest. The extra sum of squares concept plays a fundamental role in the decision making process.

The Body Fat Example

Data File: ch07ta01.txt

Extra Sum of Squares: The text presents an excellent discussion of extra sum of squares. "Extra sum of squares measure the marginal reduction in error sum of squares when one or several predictor variables are added to the regression model, given that other predictor variables are already in the model." Many statistical packages use slightly different terminology to denote two major types of sum of squares: Type I and Type III. Type I sum of squares examines the sequential incremental improvement in the fit of the model as each independent variable is added to the model. Thus, the order of entry of variables into the model will affect the Type I sum of squares. Type I sum of squares is also called the hierarchical decomposition of sum of squares method. In contrast, Type III sum of squares for a particular predictor variable is the amount of increase in the regression sum of squares (decrease in error sum of squares) due to that predictor variable after all other terms in the model have been included. Thus, the Type III sums of squares for a given predictor is the reduction in error sum of squares achieved when that predictor variable is the last predictor variable added to the model. We will see how Type I and III sum of squares are used in the following examples.

On text page 256, researchers in the Body Fat example wished to develop a regression model to predict body fat from three predictor variables: triceps skin fold thickness, thigh circumference, and midarm circumference. They considered four regression models: (1.) body fat (Y) as a linear function of triceps skin fold thickness alone, (2.) body fat as a linear function of thigh circumference alone, (3.) body fat as a linear function of the two predictor variables triceps skin fold and thigh circumference, and (4.) body fat as a linear function of all three predictor variables.

See Chapter 0, "Working with SAS," for instructions on opening the Body Fat example (text Table 7.1) and renaming the variables $X1$, $X2$, $X3$, and Y. After opening ch07ta01.txt, the first 5 lines of output should look like SAS Output 7.1.

SAS Output 7.1

Obs	x1	x2	x3	y
1	19 5	43.1	29.1	11.9
2	24.7	49.8	28.2	22.8
3	30.7	51.9	37.0	18.7
4	29.8	54.3	31.1	20.1
5	19.1	42.2	30.9	12.9

In Insert 7.1, we regressed Y on $X1$ in the first analysis (SAS Output 7.2). Under the output labeled "*Analysis of Variance*", we see a column labeled "*Source*", under which we see "*Model*", "*Error*", and "*Corrected Total*". "*Source*" refers to source of variation. For our purposes here, "*Model*" means "*Regression Model*", or simply "*Regression.*" Under the column labeled "*DF*" we see the degrees of freedom associated with the sum of squares for each "*Source*": 1 degree(s) of freedom for regression, 18 for error, and 19 for the corrected total. Under the column labeled "*Sum of Squares*" we see that, $SSR(X1) = 352.270$, $SSE(X1) = 143.120$, and $SSTO = 495.390$. In the second analysis, we regressed Y on $X1$ and $X2$ (SAS Output 7.3). In this model, there are 2 degrees of freedom for regression and 17 for error. Also, $SSR(X1, X2) = 385.439$ and $SSE(X1, X2) = 109.951$. The difference

$$SSE(X2|X1) = SSE(X1) - SSE(X1, X2) = 143.120 - 109.951 = 33.169$$

is referred to as the *extra reduction in error sum of squares* achieved by adding $X2$ to a model that has $X1$ as the only predictor variable. Correspondingly,

$$SSR(X2|X1) = SSR(X1, X2) - SSR(X1) = 385.439 - 352.270 = 33.169$$

is the *extra increase in the regression sum of squares* achieved by adding $X2$ to a model that has $X1$ as the only predictor variable.

Note that $SSR(X2|X1)$ is not given in SAS Output 7.2 and 7.3. This is because, by default, SAS *proc reg* output displays only the regression and error sum of squares for a model specified in a SAS "*model*" statement and does not give the incremental change due to adding predictor variables to the model. To directly produce the extra sum of squares, we can use the *ss1* option in the model statement to request the Type I sum of squares. The syntax in Insert 7.2 requests Type I sum of squares based on a model with $X1$ and $X2$ as predictor variables (SAS Output 7.4). The Type I sum of squares $SSR(X2|X1) = 33.169$ here is the same as found earlier.

INSERT 7.1

```
data bodyfat;
    infile 'c:\alrm\chapter 7 data sets\ch07ta01.txt';
    input x1 x2 x3 y;
proc reg;
    model y=x1;
    model y=x1 x2;
run;
```

SAS Output 7.2

Y on *X1*

Analysis of Variance					
Source	DF	Sum of Squares	Mean Square	F Value	Pr > F
Model	1	352.26980	352.26980	44.30	<.0001
Error	18	143.11970	7.95109		
Corrected Total	19	495.38950			

SAS Output 7.3

Y on *X1* and *X2*

Analysis of Variance					
Source	DF	Sum of Squares	Mean Square	F Value	Pr > F
Model	2	385.43871	192.71935	29.80	<.0001
Error	17	109.95079	6.46769		
Corrected Total	19	495.38950			

INSERT 7.2

```
data bodyfat;
  infile 'c:\alrm\chapter  7 data sets\ch07ta01.txt';
  input x1 x2 x3 y;
proc reg;
 model y=x1 x2 / ss1;
run;
```

SAS Output 7.4

Parameter Estimates						
Variable	DF	Parameter Estimate	Standard Error	t Value	Pr > |t|	Type I SS
Intercept	1	-19.17425	8.36064	-2.29	0.0348	8156.76050
x1	1	0.22235	0.30344	0.73	0.4737	352.26980
x2	1	0.65942	0.29119	2.26	0.0369	33.16891

63

Test whether a single $\beta_k = 0$: On page 264, the researchers wished to test whether *X3* should be dropped from the model that contained *X1*, *X2*, and *X3*. That is, they wanted to test H_0: $\beta_3 = 0$. From Chapter 6, we know that we can use a *t*-test to test this hypothesis. The result, shown in SAS Output 7.5 (Parameter Estimates table), indicates $t = -1.37$ for *X3* with *p*-value for a two-sided test equal to 0.1896. Based on this finding, we do not reject H_0 and drop *X3* from the model. We get an equivalent *F*-test as follows. We regress *Y* on *X1*, *X2*, and *X3* (Insert 7.3). Results are shown in SAS Output 7.5. Under the column labeled "*Sum of Squares*" we see that, $SSR(X1, X2, X3) = 396.985$, $SSE(X1, X2, X3) = 98.405$, and $SSTO = 495.390$.

Recalling from SAS Output 7.3 above that $SSR(X1, X2) = 385.439$, we find:

$$SSR(X3|X1, X2) = SSR(X1, X2, X3) - SSR(X1, X2) = 396.985 - 385.439 = 11.546.$$

On adding *X3* to a model that already contains *X*1 and *X*2, we must estimate one additional parameter, so the partial sum of squares $SSR(X3|X1, X2)$ has one degree of freedom. Recalling from SAS Output 7.5 that $SSE(X1, X2, X3) = 98.405$ with 16 degrees of freedom, we find on substituting in equation 7.15, text page 264:

$$F^* = \frac{11.546}{1} \div \frac{98.405}{16} = 1.88.$$

Earlier, we found $t = -1.37$ for *X3*. We know that $t^2 \doteq F$, and this is easily verified in the present example because $(-1.37)^2 = 1.88$.

Alternatively, we can obtain both Type I and Type III sums of squares using *proc glm* with *X1*, *X2*, and *X3* as predictors. (Insert 7.3 & SAS Output 7.6). Using *proc glm*, we get by default both Type I and Type III sums of squares as part of the output. Note that the Type I and Type III sums of squares will always be the same for the last predictor variable that is added to the model. Thus, because *X3* was the last variable listed in specifying the predictor variables in the model statement, tests of the effect of *X3* based on Type I and Type III sums of squares are identical, SAS Output 7.6 Type I and III sum of squares = 11.454. However, when the statistical test is not based on the last variable in the model, test statistics based on Type I and Type III sum of squares test different hypotheses. Assume that we wish to determine if *X2* should be dropped from the above model. From the regression procedure using Type III sum of squares (Insert 7.3 - SAS Output 7.5), we see that $t = -1.11$ for *X2*. This is a test of the effect of *X2* controlling for all other variables in the model, i.e., *X1* and *X3*. From the *GLM* procedure Type I sum of squares (Insert 7.3 - SAS Output 7.6) we see that $F = 5.39$ for *X2*. This is a test of the effect of *X2* controlling for all variables that preceded it in the list of predictor variables specified in the model statement, i.e., controlling for *X1*. ($t^2 = F$, but $(-1.106)^2 \ne 5.393$). So, in the *X2* line of the analysis of variance, using Type III sum of squares, the *F*-test ($F = 1.22 = (-1.106)^2 = t^2$) is a test of the statistical significance of $SSR(X2|X1, X3)$, or, equivalently, $SSE(X2|X1, X3)$. On the other hand, the *F*-test ($F = 5.39$) in the *X2* line of the analysis of variance using Type I sum of squares tests the significance of $SSR(X2|X1)$. Note that SAS *GLM* prints both Type I and Type III sums of squares as part of the output by default.

Finally, we call attention to the t values for the first regression analysis from Insert 7.3 (SAS Output 7.5) in which we regress Y on $X1$, $X2$, and $X3$. In the second regression analysis of Insert 7.3, we use the same regression model as in the first regression analysis only now we specify that Type I sum of squares ($ss1$) be included in the output. Results of this maneuver are shown in SAS Output 7.7. Now we compare the t-values of SAS Output 7.5 to the t-values of SAS Output 7.7 where we requested Type I sum of squares and verify that the values are identical. Although the test for $X2$ (SAS Output 7.7) displays Type I sum of squares on the same line, the statistical test is not testing $SSR(X2|X1)$, but rather it is testing $SSR(X2|X1, X3)$, a Type III sum of squares or, equivalently, a Type I sum of squares for a model with $X2$ being the last predictor variable to enter the model. This illustrates a very important point: to properly interpret the output of a compute software program, we must know the type of sum of squares used in the analysis.

INSERT 7.3

```
data bodyfat;
  infile 'a:\ch07ta01.dat';
  input x1 x2 x3 y;

proc reg;
 model y=x1 x2 x3;
run;

proc reg;
 model y=x1 x2 x3 / ss1;
run;

proc glm;
 model y=x1 x2 x3;
run;
```

SAS Output 7.5

SAS Regression

Analysis of Variance					
Source	DF	Sum of Squares	Mean Square	F Value	Pr > F
Model	3	396.98461	132.32820	21.52	<.0001
Error	16	98.40489	6.15031		
Corrected Total	19	495.38950			

SAS Output 7.5 continued

Parameter Estimates					
Variable	**DF**	**Parameter Estimate**	**Standard Error**	**t Value**	**Pr > |t|**
Intercept	1	117.08469	99.78240	1.17	0.2578
x1	1	4.33409	3.01551	1.44	0.1699
x2	1	-2.85685	2.58202	-1.11	0.2849
x3	1	-2.18606	1.59550	-1.37	0.1896

SAS Output 7.6

SAS GLM

Source	**DF**	**Sum of Squares**	**Mean Square**	**F Value**	**Pr > F**
Model	3	396.9846118	132.3282039	21.52	<.0001
Error	16	98.4048882	6.1503055		
Corrected Total	19	495.3895000			

Source	**DF**	**Type I SS**	**Mean Square**	**F Value**	**Pr > F**
x1	1	352.2697968	352.2697968	57.28	<.0001
x2	1	33.1689128	33.1689128	5.39	0.0337
x3	1	11.5459022	11.5459022	1.88	0.1896

Source	**DF**	**Type III SS**	**Mean Square**	**F Value**	**Pr > F**
x1	1	12.70489278	12.70489278	2.07	0.1699
x2	1	7.52927788	7.52927788	1.22	0.2849
x3	1	11.54590217	11.54590217	1.88	0.1896

Parameter	**Estimate**	**Standard Error**	**t Value**	**Pr > |t|**
Intercept	117.0846948	99.78240295	1.17	0.2578
x1	4.3340920	3.01551136	1.44	0.1699
x2	-2.8568479	2.58201527	-1.11	0.2849
x3	-2.1860603	1.59549900	-1.37	0.1896

SAS Output 7.7

SAS Regression and display of Type I SS

Parameter Estimates						
Variable	**DF**	**Parameter Estimate**	**Standard Error**	**t Value**	**Pr > |t|**	**Type I SS**
Intercept	1	117.08469	99.78240	1.17	0.2578	8156.76050
x1	1	4.33409	3.01551	1.44	0.1699	352.26980
x2	1	-2.85685	2.58202	-1.11	0.2849	33.16891
x3	1	-2.18606	1.59550	-1.37	0.1896	11.54590

Test whether several $\beta_k = 0$: Continuing with the body fat example (text page 265), the researchers wished to determine if, in a single step, $X2$ and $X3$ should be dropped from the model that contained $X1$, $X2$, and $X3$. This is equivalent to testing the hypothesis H_0: $\beta_2 = \beta_3 = 0$. From SAS Output 7.6 above, we have the necessary information to find equation 7.18, text page 265:

$$F^* = \frac{SSR(X2 \mid X1) + SSR(X3 \mid X1, X2)}{2} \div MSE(X1, X2, X3)$$

$$F^* = \frac{33.169 + 11.546}{2} \div 6.15 = 3.63$$

In the above expression, we used the fact that

$$SSR(X2|X1) + SSR(X3|X1, X2) = SSR(X2, X3|X1)$$

Alternatively, there is an easier way to test H_0: $\beta_2 = \beta_3 = 0$. We use the *test* option that is available within *proc reg* (Insert 7.4). The *test* statement tests user-defined hypotheses about the parameters estimated in the preceding *model* statement. In Insert 7.4 we test the hypothesis that the coefficients for both $X2$ and $X3$ equal 0. We specify in the *test* statement a label (*x2x3*) for SAS to use in the output to identify the user-defined test. The test statistic $F = 3.64$ (SAS Output 7.8) represents the incremental effect of adding $X2$ and $X3$ to a model that contains $X1$, i.e., $SSR(X2, X3|X1)$.

```
                             INSERT 7.4
data bodyfat;
 infile 'c:\alrm\chapter  7 data sets\ch07ta01.txt';
  input x1 x2 x3 y;
proc reg;
 model y=x1 x2 x3;
 x2x3: test x2=x3=0;
run;
```

Test x2x3 Results for Dependent Variable y				
Source	DF	Mean Square	F Value	Pr > F
Numerator	2	22.35741	3.64	0.0500
Denominator	16	6.15031		

Coefficients of Partial Determination and Correlation: In the body fat example (text page 270) we obtain first the *Coefficients of Partial Correlation* for *X2* given *X1* is in the model, $r_{Y2|1}$ (Insert 7.5). This results in $r_{Y2|1} = 0.4814$ (output not shown). We now can find the *Coefficient of Partial Determination* by squaring the *Coefficient of Partial Correlation*, $0.4814^2 = 0.2317$.

INSERT 7.5

```
data bodyfat;
   infile 'c:\alrm\chapter 7 data sets\ch07ta01.txt';
   input x1 x2 x3 y;
proc corr;
var y x2;
   partial x1;
   run;
```

Dwaine Studios, Inc. Example

Data File: ch06fi05.txt

Standardized Multiple Regression Model: To produce the regression model with standardized coefficients, we specified the regression procedure with the model to regress *Y* on *X1* and *X2* using the Dwaine Studios, Inc. data (text page 276). We also requested descriptive statistics using the *simple* option in the *proc reg* statement. The *simple* option displays the sum, mean, variance, standard deviation, and uncorrected sum of squares for each variable used in *proc reg*. Partial output for this procedure is shown in SAS Output 7.9. Notice that we also used the *stb* option to request *standardized beta coefficients*. With the descriptive statistics, we can use equation 7.53, text page 276, to shift the *standardized regression coefficients* back to the *unstandardized regression coefficients*.

$$b_1 = \left(\frac{s_y}{s_1}\right) b_1^* = \frac{36.1913}{18.620}(.748) = 1.455$$

INSERT 7.6

```
data dwaine;
  infile 'c:\alrm\chapter  6 data sets\ch06fi05.txt';
  input x1 x2 y;
proc reg simple;
  model y=x1 x2 / stb;
  run;
```

SAS Output 7.9

		Descriptive Statistics			
Variable	**Sum**	**Mean**	**Uncorrected SS**	**Variance**	**Standard Deviation**
Intercept	21.00000	1.00000	21.00000	0	0
x1	1302.40000	62.01905	87708	346.71662	18.62033
x2	360.00000	17.14286	6190.26000	0.94157	0.97035
y	3820.00000	181.90476	721072	1309.81048	36.19130

			Parameter Estimates				
Variable	**DF**	**Parameter Estimate**	**Standard Error**	**t Value**	**Pr > |t|**	**Standardized Estimate**
Intercept	1	-68.85707	60.01695	-1.15	0.2663	0
x1	1	1.45456	0.21178	6.87	<.0001	0.74837
x2	1	9.36550	4.06396	2.30	0.0333	0.25110

Multicollinearity and Its Effects: When multiple predictor variables in a general linear regression model are correlated among themselves, we say there is *intercorrelation* or *multicollinearity* among these variables (text page 279). When there is multicollinearity among a set of predictor variables being considered for a general linear regression model, the extra regression (error) sum of squares for a given predictor or set of predictor variables will be different depending on which other predictor variables are in the model. On the other hand, if there is no multicollinearity among the predictor variables, the extra regression sum of squares will be the same no matter which other variables are included.

Work Crew Productivity Example

On text page 279, the authors present the results of an experiment on the effect of work crew size ($X1$) and level of pay ($X2$) on productivity (Y). The text presents results from a correlation matrix of the 3 variables and Table 7.7, the output of 3 separate regression models. We present the SAS syntax (Insert 7.7) for this example as a further illustration. The rationale closely follows that in the body fat example.

```
INSERT 7.7
data work;
  infile 'c:\alrm\chapter 7 data sets\ch07ta06.txt';
  input x1 x2 y;

proc corr;
  var x1 x2 y;
proc reg;
  model y=x1 x2;
  model y=x1;
  model y=x2;
  run;
```

More on the Body Fat Example

Data File: ch07ta01.txt

On text page 283, the authors revisit the Body Fat example (text page 256) to illustrate the effect of *multicollinearity*. In Insert 7.8, we explore the relation between the predictor variables by producing *scatter plots* and a *correlation matrix* (SAS Output 7.10) of *X1*, *X2*, and *X3*. The coefficient of correlation between *X1* and *X2* is $r_{12} = 0.9238$ and although *X3* is not strongly correlated with *X1* and *X2* individually, the multiple R^2 when *X3* is regressed on *X1* and *X2* is 0.990 (Insert 7.11). Thus, there is a strong correlation between *X3* and a linear function of *X1* and *X2*. To see the change in parameter estimates as variables are added to the model, we regressed *Y* on *X1* and *X2* (SAS Output 7.12) and *Y* on *X1*, *X2*, and *X3* (SAS Output 7.13). As noted in the text, the regression coefficient for *X2* changes in the two analyses from 0.659 to –2.857 due to the intercorrelations of the predictor variables. In Chapter 10, the authors explore formal methods that we can use to detect multicollinearity.

```
INSERT 7.8
data bodyfat;
  infile 'c:\alrm\chapter 7 data sets\ch07ta01.txt';
  input x1 x2 x3 y;

proc plot;
plot x1*x2;
plot x1*y;
plot x2*y;
run;

proc corr;
  var x1 x2 y;
  run;

proc reg;
  model x3=x2 x1;
  model y=x1 x2;
  model y=x1 x2 x3;
  run;
```

SAS Output 7.10

Pearson Correlation Coefficients, N = 20 Prob > |r| under H0: Rho=0			
	x1	**x2**	**y**
x1	1.00000	0.92384 <.0001	0.84327 <.0001
x2	0.92384 <.0001	1.00000	0.87809 <.0001
y	0.84327 <.0001	0.87809 <.0001	1.00000

SAS Output 7.11

X3 regressed on *X1* and *X2*

Root MSE	0.37699	R-Square	0.9904
Dependent Mean	27.62000	Adj R-Sq	0.9893
Coeff Var	1.36491		

SAS Output 7.12

Y regressed on *X1* and *X2*

Parameter Estimates					
Variable	DF	Parameter Estimate	Standard Error	t Value	Pr > |t|
Intercept	1	-19.17425	8.36064	-2.29	0.0348
x1	1	0.22235	0.30344	0.73	0.4737
x2	1	0.65942	0.29119	2.26	0.0369

SAS Output 7.13

Y regressed on *X1, X2,* and *X3*

Parameter Estimates					
Variable	DF	Parameter Estimate	Standard Error	t Value	Pr > |t|
Intercept	1	117.08469	99.78240	1.17	0.2578
x1	1	4.33409	3.01551	1.44	0.1699
x2	1	-2.85685	2.58202	-1.11	0.2849
x3	1	-2.18606	1.59550	-1.37	0.1896

Chapter 8 SAS®

Regression Models for Quantitative and Qualitative Predictors

In this chapter, the authors discuss some special types of general linear regression models. They discuss *polynomial regression models, interaction regression models, regression models with qualitative predictor variables,* and *more complex regression models.* Recall the simple linear regression model is of the form:

$$Y_i = \beta_0 + \beta_1 X_i + \varepsilon_i$$

This model is said to be a *first-order model* because the predictor variable appears in the model expressed to the first power; i.e., $X_i^1 = X_i$. Similarly, the model:

$$Y_i = \beta_0 + \beta_1 X_{i1} + \beta_2 X_{i2} + \varepsilon_i$$

is a first-order model because the two predictor variables X_{i1} and X_{i2} each appear in the model expressed to the first power.

The model:

$$Y_i = \beta_0 + \beta_1 x_i + \beta_2 x_i^2 + \varepsilon_i$$

where $x_i = X_i - \overline{X}$ is the *centered predictor variable*, is called a *polynomial regression model*. It is referred to as a *second-order model with one predictor* because the single predictor variable appears in the model expressed to the second power; i.e., x_i^2. Similarly, the polynomial regression model:

$$Y_i = \beta_0 + \beta_1 x_i + \beta_2 x_i^2 + \beta_3 x_i^3 + \varepsilon_i$$

where $x_i = X_i - \overline{X}$, is a *third-order model with one predictor variable*. The regression model:

$$Y_i = \beta_0 + \beta_1 x_{i1} + \beta_2 x_{i2} + \beta_{11} x_{i1}^2 + \beta_{22} x_{i2}^2 + \beta_{12} x_{i1} x_{i2} + \varepsilon_i$$

where $x_{i1} = X_{i1} - \overline{X}_1$ and $x_{i2} = X_{i2} - \overline{X}_2$, is a *second-order model with two predictor variables*. The cross-product term represents the *interaction effect* between x_1 and x_2. This nomenclature extends to models with any number of predictor variables.

The authors use indicator variables that take on values 0 and 1 in a regression model to identify classes or categories of a qualitative variable. They use several examples to illustrate how to fit and interpret a variety of higher-order models including models where some of the predictor variables are quantitative and others are qualitative.

The Power Cell Example

Data File: ch08ta01.txt

Using data from Table 8.1, text page 300, researchers studied the relationship between charge rate and temperature on the life of a power cell. There were three levels (0.6, 1.0, and 1.4 amperes) of charge rate ($X1$) and three levels (10, 20, and 30° C) of ambient temperature ($X2$). The dependent variable (Y) was defined as the number of discharge-charge cycles that a power cell underwent before failure. See Chapter 0, "Working with SAS," for instructions on opening the Power Cell data file and naming the variables Y, $X1$, and $X2$.

The researchers were uncertain of the expected response function, but decided to fit a second-order polynomial regression model. They first centered $X1$ and $X2$ around their respective means and scaled them using the absolute difference between adjacent levels of the variable. From Insert 8.1, we compute the coded values for $X1$ and $X2$ (x1code and x2code, respectively), the square of the coded values (x1code2 and x2code2, respectively), and the cross-product of $X1$ and $X2$ (x12inter). After executing the syntax in Insert 8.1, the printed output should look like SAS Output 8.1 and is consistent with Table 8.1, text page 300.

```
                          INSERT 8.1
data power;
  infile 'c:\alrm\chapter 8 data sets\ch08ta01.txt';
  input y x1 x2;
x1code=(x1-1)/.4;
x2code=(x2-20)/10;
x1code2=x1code**2;
x2code2=x2code**2;
x12inter=x1code*x2code;
run;
proc print;
run;
```

SAS Output 8.1

Obs	y	x1	x2	x1code	x2code	x1code2	x2code2	x12inter
1	150	0.6	10	-1	-1	1	1	1
2	86	1.0	10	0	-1	0	1	0
3	49	1.4	10	1	-1	1	1	-1
4	288	0.6	20	-1	0	1	0	0
5	157	1.0	20	0	0	0	0	0

Fitting the Model: We begin by obtaining the regression results of the second-order polynomial regression model and saving the unstandardized predicted values (*yhat*) and residuals (*residual*) in a file named *"results"* for future use (Insert 8.2). Partial results are shown in SAS Output 8.2. The Unstandardized Coefficients displayed under the column labeled "Parameter Estimate" in SAS Output 8.2 are the estimated regression coefficients shown in equation 8.16, text page 301.

```
                            INSERT 8.2
data power;
  infile 'c:\alrm\chapter  8 data sets\ch08ta01.txt';
  input  y x1 x2;
x1code=(x1-1)/.4;
x2code=(x2-20)/10;
x1code2=x1code**2;
x2code2=x2code**2;
x12inter=x1code*x2code;
run;
proc reg;
 model y=x1code x1code2 x2code x2code2 x12inter / r p;
 output out=results r=residual p=yhat;
run;
```

SAS Output 8.2

Analysis of Variance					
Source	DF	Sum of Squares	Mean Square	F Value	Pr > F
Model	5	55366	11073	10.57	0.0109
Error	5	5240.43860	1048.08772		
Corrected Total	10	60606			

Root MSE	32.37418	R-Square	0.9135
Dependent Mean	172.00000	Adj R-Sq	0.8271
Coeff Var	18.82220		

Parameter Estimates					
Variable	DF	Parameter Estimate	Standard Error	t Value	Pr > |t|
Intercept	1	162.84211	16.60761	9.81	0.0002
x1code	1	-55.83333	13.21670	-4.22	0.0083
x1code2	1	27.39474	20.34008	1.35	0.2359
x2code	1	75.50000	13.21670	5.71	0.0023
x2code2	1	-10.60526	20.34008	-0.52	0.6244
x12inter	1	11.50000	16.18709	0.71	0.5092

Residual Plots: In this section, we discuss SAS code for obtaining some simple graphical plots that are useful in assessing the adequacy of a fitted model. For brevity, we do not present the output plots. To produce the plots in Figure 8.5, text page 303, we continue with the SAS code shown in Insert 8.3 and request the residuals and predicted values of the current model using the *r* and *p* options in the *model* statement. The residual and predicted values are now available to be used within *proc reg* by specifying "*r.*" and "*p.*". That is, to produce text Figure 8.5 (a), we request a plot of *r.* (residual values) by *p.* (predicted values) using the code "*plot r.*p.*". To replicate the axes of text Figure 8.5 (a), we set the values of the horizontal axis (*haxis*) to range from 0 to 300 while incrementing by 100 units and we set the values of the vertical axis (*vaxis*) to range from 40 to 60 while incrementing by 20 units. Next we plot the residual values (*r.*) against *x1code* and *x2code*, and set the axes to correspond to those shown in Figure 8.5. Finally, we request a normal probability plot (*npp.*) for the residual values (*r.*).

```
                            INSERT 8.3

data power;
  infile 'c:\alrm\chapter  8 data sets\ch08ta01.txt';
  input  y x1 x2;
x1code=(x1-1)/.4;
x2code=(x2-20)/10;
x1code2=x1code**2;
x2code2=x2code**2;
x12inter=x1code*x2code;
run;
proc reg;
  model y=x1code x1code2 x2code x2code2 x12inter / r p;
  plot r.*p. / haxis=0 to 300 by 100 vaxis=-40 to 60 by 20;
  plot r.*x1code / haxis=-2 to 2 by 1 vaxis=-40 to 60 by 20;
  plot r.*x2code / haxis=-2 to 2 by 1 vaxis=-40 to 60 by 20;
  plot npp.*r.;
run;
```

Further Aspects of the Power Cell Example

Data File: ch08ta05.txt

Correlation Test for Normality: On text page 301, the researchers in the Power Cell example calculated the coefficient of correlation between the ordered residuals and their expected value under normality. The expected value under normality of the kth smallest observation from a sample of size n is given by:

$$\sqrt{MSE}\left[z\left(\frac{k - 0.375}{n + 0.25} \right) \right]$$

We find $MSE = 1048.088$ in SAS Output 8.2 above and here $n = 11$. In Chapter 3 we give a detailed description of the steps necessary to obtain z and k. In Insert 8.4, we regress Y on $X1$, $X2$, and $X1X2$ and save the residual values in a variable named *residual*. We then rank the residuals and place the rank in a variable named *rank*. We then compute *ev*, the expected value under normality and correlate this variable with *residual*. The resulting correlation is 0.984, as reported on the text page 301.

```
                              INSERT 8.4

data soap;
  infile 'c:\alrm\chapter 8 data sets\ch08ta05.txt';
  input  y x1 x2;
x1x2=x1*x2;
proc reg;
  model y=x1 x2 x1x2/ r;
  output out=results r=residual;
* Rank the residuals and place the rank in "rank";
proc rank data=results out=results;
  var residual;
  ranks rank;
run;
data new;
  set results;
  ev = sqrt(430.611) * Probit ((rank - .375)/(27  + .25));
proc corr;
  var ev residual;
  run;
```

Test of Fit: To perform a formal test of goodness of fit of the regression model, we use *proc glm* as detailed in Insert 8.5. We first compute a new variable (*J*) to represent each of the 9 combinations of *X1* and *X2*. We then regress *Y* on *J*, *x1code*, *x1code2*, *x2code*, *x2code2*, and *x12inter*. Additionally, in the *proc glm* statement we define *J* as a *class* variable. Thus, *J* identifies 9 discrete classifications based on the values of *X1* and *X2*. This produces the full model including $SSE(F) = 1404.6$ as shown in SAS Output 8.3 a. From equation 3.16, text page 122, $SSE(F) = SSPE$. Thus, $SSPE = 1404.6$. To produce the reduced model, we drop *J* from the previous model and refit the model in the second *proc glm* statement in Insert 8.5. This results in SAS Output 8.3 b. where $SSE(R) = 5240.4$. From equation 3.24, text page 123, $SSLF = SSE - SSPE$, or $SSLF = 5240.4 - 1404.6 = 3835.8$. In the present example, $n = 11$, $c = 9$ discrete classifications, and $p = 6$ parameters in the reduced model. We can now find:

$$F^* = \frac{SSLF}{c-p} \div \frac{SSPE}{n-c} = \frac{3835.8}{3} \div \frac{1404.6}{2} = 1.82$$

The *F*-value = 1.82 is identical to the Lack of Fit *F*-value reported on text page 302. The associated probability level of *F* is >0.05, and we conclude that the second-order polynomial regression is a reasonably good fitting model.

INSERT 8.5

```
data power;
  infile 'c:\alrm\chapter  8 data sets\ch08ta01.txt';
  input  y x1 x2;
x1code=(x1-1)/.4;
x2code=(x2-20)/10;
x1code2=x1code**2;
x2code2=x2code**2;
x12inter=x1code*x2code;
  if x2=10 & x1=0.6 then j=1;
  if x2=10 & x1=1.0 then j=2;
  if x2=10 & x1=1.4 then j=3;
  if x2=20 & x1=0.6 then j=4;
  if x2=20 & x1=1.0 then j=5;
  if x2=20 & x1=1.4 then j=6;
  if x2=30 & x1=0.6 then j=7;
  if x2=30 & x1=1.0 then j=8;
  if x2=30 & x1=1.4 then j=9;
proc glm;
  class j;
  model y=j x1code x1code2 x2code x2code2 x12inter;
run;
proc glm;
  model y=x1code x1code2 x2code x2code2 x12inter;
run;
```

SAS Output 8.3

a. Full Model

Source	DF	Sum of Squares	Mean Square	F Value	Pr > F
Model	8	59201.33333	7400.16667	10.54	0.0895
Error	2	1404.66667	702.33333		
Corrected Total	10	60606.00000			

b. Reduced Model

Source	DF	Sum of Squares	Mean Square	F Value	Pr > F
Model	5	55365.56140	11073.11228	10.57	0.0109
Error	5	5240.43860	1048.08772		
Corrected Total	10	60606.00000			

Coefficient of Multiple Determination: The coefficient of multiple correlation ($R = 0.956$), the coefficient of multiple determination ($R^2 = 0.914$) and the adjusted coefficient of multiple correlation ($Adj\ R^2 = 0.827$) are given in SAS Output 8.2 above.

Partial F-Test: The researchers now want to test whether a first-order model is appropriate. That is, they wish to decide if *x1code2*, *x2code2*, and *x12inter* can be dropped from the model; they test H_0: $\beta_{11} = \beta_{22} = \beta_{12} = 0$. In Insert 8.6, we use the *test* option available with the *proc reg* statement. That is, we request a test that *x1code2=x2code2=x12inter=0*. The "*b11b22b12:*" portion of the *test* statement is a label to identify the test on output. Partial results are shown in SAS Output 8.4. Consistent with text page 304, the *F*-value associated with this user defined test is 0.78 and the associated probability level ("Pr>F") is 0.5527. Thus, we fail to reject H_0: $\beta_{11} = \beta_{22} = \beta_{12} = 0$ and conclude that the first-order model is adequate.

INSERT 8.6

```
data power;
   infile 'c:\alrm\chapter 8 data sets\ch08ta01.txt';
   input  y x1 x2;
x1code=(x1-1)/.4;
x2code=(x2-20)/10;
x1code2=x1code**2;
x2code2=x2code**2;
x12inter=x1code*x2code;
proc reg;
  model y=x1code x2code x1code2 x2code2 x12inter;
   b11b22b12: test x1code2=x2code2=x12inter=0;
run;
```

SAS Output 8.4

Test b11b22b12 Results for Dependent Variable y				
Source	**DF**	**Mean Square**	**F Value**	**Pr > F**
Numerator	3	819.96491	0.78	0.5527
Denominator	5	1048.08772		

First-Order Model: Based on the above analysis, the researchers chose to fit the first-order model:

$$Y_i = \beta_0 + \beta_1 x_{i1} + \beta_2 x_{i2} + \varepsilon_i$$

From Insert 8.7 we use *"proc reg"* together with *"model y = x1code x2code"* to produce the first-order model with results as shown in SAS Output 8.5(a). The regression coefficients are identical to those reported in equation 8.18, text page 304, and to the estimates shown below in SAS Output 8.5; i.e. (standardized) $b_1 = -55.83333$ and $b_2 = 75.50000$ with standard errors $s\{b_1\} = s\{b_2\} = 12.66584$.

```
INSERT 8.7

data power;
  infile 'c:\alrm\chapter  8 data sets\ch08ta01.txt';
  input  y x1 x2;
x1code=(x1-1)/.4;
x2code=(x2-20)/10;
x1code2=x1code**2;
x2code2=x2code**2;
x12inter=x1code*x2code;
proc reg;
 model y=x1code x2code ;
 model y = x1 x2 /clb alpha = 0.10;
run;
```

SAS Output 8.5

(a)

Parameter Estimates					
Variable	DF	Parameter Estimate	Standard Error	t Value	Pr > |t|
Intercept	1	172.00000	9.35435	18.39	<.0001
x1code	1	-55.83333	12.66584	-4.41	0.0023
x2code	1	75.50000	12.66584	5.96	0.0003

(b)

Parameter Estimates							
Variable	DF	Parameter Estimate	Standard Error	t Value	Pr > |t|	95% Confidence Limits	
Intercept	1	160.58333	41.61545	3.86	0.0048	64.61793	256.54874
x1	1	-139.58333	31.66461	-4.41	0.0023	-212.60206	-66.56461
x2	1	7.55000	1.26658	5.96	0.0003	4.62925	10.47075

Fitted First-Order Model in Terms of *X1* and *X2*: In Insert 8.7, we add a second *model* statement to *proc reg* to obtain a fitted first order regression model in terms of the original (untransformed) predictor variables *X1* and *X2*. The resulting estimated coefficients are shown in SAS Output 8.5(b) and in equation 8.19, text page 304; i.e., (unstandardized) $b_1' = -139.58333$ and $b_2' = 7.55000$ with respective standard errors $s\{b_1'\} = 31.66461$ and $s\{b_2'\} = 1.26658$.

Estimation of Confidence Limits for Regression Coefficients: The researcher now wished to estimate the Bonferroni 90% confidence limits in terms of the original predictor variables. We apply the confidence limits formula for β_1 and β_2 given in equation 6.52, text page 228. In Insert 8.8, we first find $B = t(1 - \alpha/2g; n - p)$. In this case, $\alpha = 0.10$ with two confidence intervals being estimated ($g = 2$), $n = 11$, and there are 3 parameters in the model ($p = 3$). Thus, in Insert 8.8 we find B = *tinv*(1-(0.10/4), 8) = 2.306. We obtain the numerical values $s\{b_1'\} = 31.66461$ and $s\{b_2'\} = 1.26658$ directly from SAS Output 8.5(b). Alternatively, we can find $s\{b_1'\}$ (*sdb1*) and $s\{b_2'\}$ (*sdb2*) from $s\{b_1\}$ and $s\{b_2\}$ as shown on text page 305. Finally, we use equation 6.52, text page 258 to find the two Bonferroni simultaneous 90% confidence intervals:

$$-212.63 \le \beta_1 \le -66.55$$

and

$$4.63 \le \beta_2 \le 10.47.$$

These confidence limits are equal to those printed as part of the output [SAS Output 8.5(b)] for the second *model* statement of Insert 8.7. In this second *model* statement, we use the option *clb* with *alpha* = 0.05. The confidence intervals calculated through the *cbl* option are separate confidence intevals rather than simultaneous confidence intervals. However, we can adjust α through the *alpha* option to get simultaneous confidence intervals. We use *alpha* = 0.05 to get 90% confidence intervals because:

$$1 - \alpha/2g = 1 - 0.10/4 = 1 - 0.05/2$$

and, hence, the separate 95% confidence intervals are identical to the simultaneous 90% confidence intervals.

INSERT 8.8

```
data intervals;
x1code=(x1-1)/.4;
x2code=(x2-20)/10;
B=tinv(1-(.1/4),8);
sdb1=(1/.4)*12.67;
sdb2=(1/10)*12.67;
b1lo=-139.59-(b*sdb1);
b1hi=-139.59+(b*sdb1);
b2lo=7.55-(b*sdb2);
b2hi=7.55+(b*sdb2);
run;
proc print;
 var b1lo b1hi b2lo b2hi;
 run;
```

Insurance Innovation Example

Data File: ch08ta02.txt

An economist studied the relationship between the adoption of new insurance innovations and the type of insurance company and the size of the insurance firm (text page 313, 317). The response variable (time to adoption) is coded Y, and the predictor variables are coded $X1$ for size of the firm and $X2$ for type of firm where $X2 = 0$ for mutual companies and $X2 = 1$ for stock companies. See Chapter 0, "Working with SAS," for instructions on opening ch08ta02.txt and naming variables Y, $X1$, and $X2$. After opening and printing the Insurance Innovation example, the first 5 lines in the output should look like SAS Output 8.6.

SAS Output 8.6

Obs	y	x1	x2
1	17	151	0
2	26	92	0
3	21	175	0
4	30	31	0
5	22	104	0

In Insert 8.9, we produce SAS Output 8.7, which replicates Figure 8.12, text page 318. To draw separate regression lines for mutual and stock companies, we use the interpolate (*interplo*) option on *symbol* statements to specify that a regression line (*rl*) be drawn. The first character to be used to plot $X2$ values is the *circle* and the second value of $X2$ is plotted using the *dot* character. We also include an optional plot title and set the horizontal and vertical axes to replicate the axes shown in Figure 8.12, text page 318.

INSERT 8.9

```
data insurance;
  infile 'c:\alrm\chapter 8 data sets\ch08ta02.txt';
  input  y x1 x2;
goptions reset=all;
proc gplot;
  title1 'Text Figure 8.12';
  symbol1 value=circle color=black interpol=rl;
  symbol2 value=dot color=black interpol=rl;
  footnote h=1.5 j=c 'Mutual Firm [circle] vs Stock Firm [dot]';
  plot y*x1=x2 / haxis=0 to 350 by 50 vaxis=0 to 40 by 5 nolegend;
run;
```

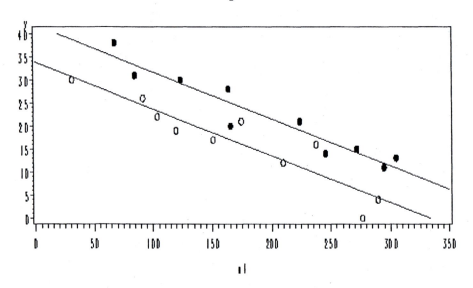

Text Figure 8.12

Mutual Firm [circle] vs Stock Firm [dot]

The economist was most interested in the effect of the type of insurance firm (*X2*) on the response variable. In Insert 8.10 we request the first-order model including confidence limits (*clb*) for the coefficients in the regression model. Consistent with text page 316, the 95% confidence interval for β_2 is displayed as $4.977 \le \beta_2 \le 11.134$. (SAS Output 8.8) This is not a simultaneous confidence interval like the intervals calculated in the previous example. Because the interval does not include zero, we conclude H_a: $\beta_2 \ne 0$, or that the type of insurance firm has a significant effect on the response variable. We can also reach this conclusion based on the probability level ($Pr>|t| = 0.000$) of the *t*-value ($t = 5.52$) associated with *X2*.

INSERT 8.10

```
data insurance;
  infile 'c:\alrm\chapter  8 data sets\ch08ta02.txt';
  input  y x1 x2;
proc reg;
  model y = x1 x2 / clb;
run;
```

SAS Output 8.8

						95% Confidence	
Variable	DF	Parameter Estimate	Standard Error	t Value	Pr > |t|	Limits	
Intercept	1	33.87407	1.81386	18.68	<.0001	30.04716	37.70098
x1	1	-0.10174	0.00889	-11.44	<.0001	-0.12050	-0.08298
x2	1	8.05547	1.45911	5.52	<.0001	4.97703	11.13391

Parameter Estimates (table title)

On text page 326, the economist wanted to test the hypothesis that there is no interaction between size (*X1*) and type (*X2*) of insurance company. Thus, the economist considered a regression model (equation 8.49, text page 324) that included the interaction term *X1X2*, the cross-product of *X1* and *X2*. In Insert 8.11, we compute *X1X2* and then fit the regression model with *X1*, *X2*, and *X1X2* as predictors. We test the hypothesis that there is no interaction in terms of β_3; i.e., we test H_0: $\beta_3 = 0$ against H_a: $\beta_3 \neq 0$. From SAS Output 8.9 and consistent with text page 326, we see the *t*-value associated with *X1X2* is $t = -0.02$, $p = 0.9821$. Thus, the economist concluded that the interaction is not statistically significant and, hence, the interaction term should be dropped from the model.

```
INSERT 8.11

data insurance;
  infile 'c:\alrm\chapter 8 data sets\ch08ta02.txt';
  input  y x1 x2;
  x1x2=x1*x2;
proc reg;
  model y = x1 x2 x1x2;
run;
```

SAS Output 8.9

Variable	DF	Parameter Estimate	Standard Error	t Value	Pr > |t|
Intercept	1	33.83837	2.44065	13.86	<.0001
x1	1	-0.10153	0.01305	-7.78	<.0001
x2	1	8.13125	3.65405	2.23	0.0408
x1x2	1	-0.00041714	0.01833	-0.02	0.9821

Parameter Estimates (table title)

Soap Production Lines Example

Data File: ch08ta05.txt

A company studied the relationship between production line speed ($X1$) and the amount of scrap (Y) generated on their 2 production lines ($X2$). The data are presented in Table 8.5, text page 330. After opening and printing ch08ta05.txt, the first 5 lines of output should look like SAS Output 8.10.

SAS Output 8.10

Obs	y	x1	x2
1	218	100	1
2	248	125	1
3	360	220	1
4	351	205	1
5	470	300	1

Based on Figure 8.16, text page 331, the researchers decided to fit a model with an interaction term:

$$Y_i = \beta_0 + \beta_1 X_{i1} + \beta_2 X_{i2} + \beta_3 X_{i1} X_{i2} + \varepsilon_i$$

Tentative Model: To produce the tentative model, we first compute a new variable, $X1X2$, the cross-product of $X1$ and $X2$. (Insert 8.12)   We then fit a model using Y as the dependent variable and $X1$, $X2$, and $X1X2$ as independent variables and save the unstandardized residuals (*residual*) and predicted values (*yhat*). This produces SAS Output 8.11, which is consistent with Table 8.6(a), text page 332. In Insert 8.13, we produce text Figure 8.16, text page 331, using *proc plot* to plot Y against $X1$ while displaying different symbols for the two values of $X2$.

```
INSERT 8.12

data soap;
  infile 'c:\alrm\chapter  8 data sets\ch08ta05.txt';
  input  y x1 x2;
x1x2=x1*x2;
proc reg;
 model y=x1 x2 x1x2/ r p;
 output out=results r=residual p=yhat;
run;
```

Analysis of Variance					
Source	DF	Sum of Squares	Mean Square	F Value	Pr > F
Model	3	169165	56388	130.95	<.0001
Error	23	9904.05692	430.61117		
Corrected Total	26	179069			

Parameter Estimates					
Variable	DF	Parameter Estimate	Standard Error	t Value	Pr > |t|
Intercept	1	7.57446	20.86970	0.36	0.7200
x1	1	1.32205	0.09262	14.27	<.0001
x2	1	90.39086	28.34573	3.19	0.0041
x1x2	1	-0.17666	0.12884	-1.37	0.1835

```
                                    INSERT 8.13
data soap;
  infile 'c:\alrm\chapter 8 data sets\ch08ta05.txt';
  input  y x1 x2;
proc plot;
 plot y * x1 = x2;
run;
```

Diagnostics: The researchers in the Soap Production Lines Example next calculated the coefficient of correlation between the ordered residuals and their expected values under normality. The expected value under normality of the kth smallest observation from a sample of n is given by:

$$\sqrt{MSE}\left[z\left(\frac{k-0.375}{n+0.25}\right)\right]$$

We find $MSE = 430.611$ in SAS Output 8.11 above and $n = 27$ in the Soap Production Lines Example. In Chapter 3 we give a detailed description of the steps necessary to obtain z and k. In Insert 8.14 we rank the residuals and place the rank in a variable named *rank*. We then compute the expected value under normality (*ev*) and correlate this variable with *residual*. The resulting correlation is 0.990, as reported on text page 331. From text Table B.6, the critical value for $\alpha = .05$ and $n = 28$ is 0.962. The calculated value is greater than the critical value found in the table, so we conclude there is sufficient evidence to support the assumption of normality of error terms.

```
                            INSERT 8.14

data soap;
  infile 'c:\alrm\chapter  8 data sets\ch08ta05.txt';
  input  y x1 x2;
x1x2=x1*x2;
proc reg;
 model y=x1 x2 x1x2/ r;
 output out=results r=residual;
* Rank the residuals and place the rank in "rank";
proc rank data=results out=results;
 var residual;
 ranks rank;
run;
data new;
 set results;
 ev = sqrt(430.611) * Probit ((rank - .375)/(27  + .25));
proc corr;
 var ev residual;
 run;
```

Continuing on text page 331, the authors formally test for constancy of error variance using the *Brown-Forsythe test* as described in Chapter 3. For simplicity, we again divide the process into steps:

- Step 1: (Insert 8.15) Divide the data file into two subsets. In the Soap Production Lines Example this has been done based on the value of $X2$ where $X2 = 1$ if production line = 1 and $X2 = 0$ if production line = 2. We also regress Y on $X1$, $X2$, and $X1X2$ and save the residual values (*residual*).
- Step 2: Use *proc means* with the *median* option to obtain the median residual values $\tilde{e}_1$ (Production line = 1, therefore, $X2 = 1$) = 5.4959 and $\tilde{e}_2$ (Production line = 2, therefore, $X2 = 0$) = −6.2203.
- Step 3: Find *absdevmd*, the absolute value (*abs*) of the residual minus the median residual value for the respective group, d_{i1} and d_{i2}.
- Step 4: Find the means of *absdevmd* for the two groups, $\bar{d}_1 = 16.132$ and $\bar{d}_2 = 12.648$.
- Step 5: Find *sqrdev,* the square of *absdevmd* minus the respective group mean of *absdevmd*.
- Step 6: Find the sum of *sqrdev* for the two production lines, $\sum \left(d_{11} - \bar{d}_1 \right)^2 = 2952.19$ and $\sum \left(d_{12} - \bar{d}_2 \right)^2 = 2045.82$.

We now have the values required to calculate the Brown-Forsythe statistic:

$$s^2 = \frac{2{,}952.20 + 2{,}04582}{27 - 2} = 199.921$$

$$s = \sqrt{199.921} = 14.139$$

$$t_{BF}^* = \frac{16.132 - 12.648}{14.139\sqrt{\dfrac{1}{15} + \dfrac{1}{12}}} = 0.636$$

Using $\alpha = 0.05$ and $df = 25$, the critical value of t can be obtained using a quantile function such as " $tvalue = tinv(0.975, 25)$ ", which will return 2.059. Since $t_{BF}^* = 0.636 < 2.059$, we conclude there is no significant lack of constancy of error variance.

INSERT 8.15	INSERT 8.15 continued
| ```
data soap;
  infile 'c:\alrm\chapter 8 data sets\ch08ta05.txt';
  input y x1 x2;
x1x2=x1*x2;
* Step 1;
proc reg;
  model y=x1 x2 x1x2/ r;
  output out=results r=residual;
* Step 2;
proc sort;
  by x2;
proc means median data=results;
  by x2;
  var residual;
* Step 3;
data results;
  set results;
if x2=0 then absdevmd=abs(residual-(-6.2203));
if x2=1 then absdevmd=abs(residual-(5.4959));
* Step 4;
proc means;
  var absdevmd;
  by x2;
``` | ```
* Step 5;
data results;
  set results;
if x2=0 then sqrdev=(absdevmd-12.6482)**2;
if x2=1 then sqrdev=(absdevmd-16.1321)**2;
* Step 6;
proc means data=results sum;
  by x2;
  var sqrdev;
run;

* Find tvalue;
data results;
  set results;
tvalue=tinv(0.975, 25);
proc print data=results (obs=1);
  var tvalue;
  run;
``` |

Inferences about Two Regression Lines: The researchers now wish to test the identity of the regression lines for the two soap production lines. The null and alternative hypotheses, respectively, are:

$$H_0 : \beta_2 = \beta_3 = 0$$

and

$$H_a : \text{not both } \beta_2 = 0 \text{ and } \beta_3 = 0$$

To test the null hypothesis using equation 7.27, text page 267, we need to produce text Table 8.6(b), text page 332, which lists Type I sum of squares. We request Type I sum of squares with the *ss1* option available on the *proc reg* statement (Insert 8.16). SAS Output 8.12 is the result of this *proc reg* procedure where we regressed Y on $X1$, $X2$, and $X1X2$. We can now use equation 8.56a, text page 333, to find $F^* = 22.65$. Alternatively, we can request a test in the *proc reg* procedure that the regression coefficients for $X2$ and $X1X2$ are both equal 0 (*x2x1x2: test x2=x1x2=0;*). The "*x2x1x2:*" portion of the statement is a label to identify the test in the output. From SAS Output 8.12, we see that the F-value for $H_0 : \beta_2 = \beta_3 = 0$ is $F = 22.647$. This is a test statistic for evaluating the effect of adding $X2$ and $X1X3$ to a model that already contains $X1$; this is, we test the hypothesis that the coefficients for $X2$ and $X1X2|X1$ are simultaneously zero. Since the computed F-value (22.65) is greater than the table F-value (5.67) when $\alpha = 0.01$, we conclude that the regression functions are not the same for the two production lines.

INSERT 8.16

```
data soap;
 infile 'c:\alrm\chapter 8 data sets\ch08ta05.txt';
 input y x1 x2;
x1x2=x1*x2;
proc reg;
 model y=x1 x2 x1x2 / ss1 clb;
x2x1x2: test x2=x1x2=0;
run;
```

SAS Output 8.12

Analysis of Variance					
Source	DF	Sum of Squares	Mean Square	F Value	Pr > F
Model	3	169165	56388	130.95	<.0001
Error	23	9904.05692	430.61117		
Corrected Total	26	179069			

Parameter Estimates						
Variable	DF	Parameter Estimate	Standard Error	t Value	Pr > |t|	Type I SS
Intercept	1	7.57446	20.86970	0.36	0.7200	2687271
x1	1	1.32205	0.09262	14.27	<.0001	149661
x2	1	90.39086	28.34573	3.19	0.0041	18694
x1x2	1	-0.17666	0.12884	-1.37	0.1835	809.62258

Test x2x1x2 Results for Dependent Variable y				
Source	DF	Mean Square	F Value	Pr > F
Numerator	2	9751.85064	22.65	<.0001
Denominator	23	430.61117		

The researcher also wanted to test whether the slopes of the regression lines for the two production lines were identical. The null and alternative hypotheses are:

$$H_0 : \beta_3 = 0$$

and

$$H_a : \beta_3 \neq 0$$

We can test the null hypothesis by equation 7.25, text page 267, or the partial F-test, text equation 7.24. Table 8.6(b), text page 332, and SAS Output 8.12 above provide the necessary information to find $F^* = 1.88$ (text equation 8.57a). Equivalently, we can use SAS Output 8.12 (Parameter Estimates Table) to obtain $t = -1.371$ for $X1X2$. Remember that $t^2 = F$ and $(-1.371)^2 = 1.88$. Thus, the t-statistic in SAS Output 8.12 using Type III sum of squares is a partial test of $X1X2|X1, X2$. Since the probability level 0.1835 is greater than the required $\alpha = 0.01$ we do not reject H_0: the slopes of the two regression functions are identical. Finally, to produce the 95% confidence limits for β_2, we use the *clb* option in Insert 8.16.

Chapter 9 SAS®

Building the Regression Model I: Model Selection and Validation

This chapter presents numerous strategies that are often used to build a regression model. These tactics include making use of theoretical relationships and knowledge gained from previous studies as well as information contained in a set of data available for analysis. We frequently have a large set of potential predictor variables and we wish to choose a subset of these variables to build a regression model that is efficient in its use of predictor variables. This process involves checking for outlying observations as well as investigating the contributions of potential predictor variables. The problem is complicated by the fact that there may be multicollinearity among the predictor variables. We may visually inspect relationships that are sometimes revealed in well-planned graphs. The authors discuss the criteria commonly used to select the predictor variables for inclusion or exclusion from the model. They then discuss three basic ways to validate a regression model once the selection process is in its final stages (see text page 369). These techniques are illustrated with well-chosen numerical examples.

Surgical Unit Example

Data File: ch09ta01.txt

A hospital studied the survival time (Y) of patients who had undergone a liver operation. The predictor or explanatory variables for the predictive regression model were blood clotting score ($X1$), prognostic index ($X2$), enzyme function score ($X3$), and liver function score ($X4$). The researchers also extracted from the preoperative evaluation the patients age ($X5$), sex ($X6$), and history of alcohol use, coded as two indicator variables, $X7$ (moderate use) and $X8$ (severe use). A representation of the Surgical Unit data set is shown in Table 9.1, text page 350. See Chapter 0, "Working with SAS," for instructions on opening the Surgical Unit data file and naming the variables $X1$, $X2$, $X3$, $X4$, $X5$, $X6$, $X7$, $X8$, Y, and *ylog*. After opening and printing ch09ta01.txt, the first 5 lines of printed output should look like SAS Output 9.1.

SAS Output 9.1

Obs	x1	x2	x3	x4	x5	x6	x7	x8	y	ylog
1	6.7	62	81	2.59	50	0	1	0	695	6.54
2	5.1	59	66	1.70	39	0	0	0	403	6.00
3	7.4	57	83	2.16	55	0	0	0	710	6.57
4	6.5	73	41	2.01	48	0	0	0	349	5.85
5	7.8	65	115	4.30	45	0	0	1	2343	7.76

The researchers selected a random sample of 108 patients. Because the researchers intended to validate the final model, the sample was split into a model-building set (first 54 patients) and a validation set (second 54 patients). To simplify the illustration, the authors used only the first four available predictors variables. We begin by regressing *Y* on *X1*, *X2*, *X3*, and *X4*, and saving the unstandardized residuals and predicted values. In Insert 9.1 we produce the regression analysis including plots shown in Figures 9.2 (a and b), text page 351 (SAS Output 9.2). In Insert 9.1, the *"plot r.*p.;"* statement instructs SAS to plot the residuals against the predicted values. The *"plot npp.*r.;"* statement requests a normal probability plot of the residuals (*r.*). Plot (a) of SAS Output 9.2 suggests both nonconstant error variances and curvature. That is, the variability of the residuals appears to increase as the magnitude of the predicted values increases. Plot (b) suggests the distribution of the residuals may not be a member of the family of normal distributions.

INSERT 9.1

```
data surgical;
  infile 'c:\alrm\chapter  9 data sets\ch09ta01.txt';
  input x1 x2 x3 x4 x5 x6 x7 x8 y ylog;
proc reg;
 model y = x1 x2 x3 x4;
  output out=results r=residual p=yhat;
  plot r.*p.;
  plot npp.*r. ;
run;
```

SAS Output 9.2

Plot (a)

Plot (b)

Because of the above findings, the investigator performed a logarithmic transformation of *Y*. We assigned the variable name *ylog* to the transformed data. Based on various diagnostics, the investigator then decided to use *ylog* as the response variable; to use *X1*, *X2*, *X3*, and *X4* as predictors; and to not include any interaction terms in the linear regression model. Using the first *proc reg* statement in Insert 9.2, we produce the regression analysis including plots shown in Figures 9.2 (c and d), text page 351 (SAS Output 9.2 – Plots c & d). Plot (c) of SAS Output 9.2 suggests both constant error variances and a first order model may be appropriate. Plot (d) suggests the distribution of the residuals more nearly normal compared to the residuals of the model for the untransformed *Y*.

The investigator also produced a correlation matrix and a scatter plot matrix to investigate pairwise correlations among the variables used in the model. We produce a correlation matrix for the variables in the *model* statement of the regression procedure by including the *corr* option in the regression statement; i.e., by writing *proc reg corr* as in the second *proc reg* statement in Insert 9.2 (Output not shown). An alternative way to produce a correlation matrix is to use the *proc corr* statement. We use the *proc corr* statement in Insert 9.2 to produce the correlation matrix shown SAS Output 9.3 and in Figure 9.3, text page 352. The *var* statement following the *proc corr* statement specifies the variables used in the correlation matrix. The *proc corr* statement produces the simple statistics (*n*, mean, standard deviation, sum, minimum, and maximum) as well as the correlation matrix. The correlation matrix output is shown in SAS Output 9.3. The correlation coefficients shown in the correlation matrix are Pearson's correlation coefficients. From the correlation matrix, we see that Pearson's correlation coefficient is 0.2462 for *ylog* and *X1*, 0.4699 for *ylog* and *X2*, and so on. There is redundancy in the correlation information shown above and below the main diagonal of the correlation matrix because the correlation between *ylog* and *X1* is the same as the correlation between *X1* and *ylog*, and so on. A *p*-value is given below each correlation coefficient. The *p*-value corresponds to a test of the null

92

hypothesis that the true correlation coefficient corresponding to the relevant sample estimate is zero; i.e., $\rho = 0$ for the indicated pair of variables. Thus, the correlation coefficient = 0.50242, with p-value = 0.0001, between *X1* and *X4* is indicative that the true correlation coefficient for *X1* and *X4* is significantly greater than 0.

We use the *proc plot* statement shown in Insert 9.2 to produce the scatter plots between pairs of variables specified in the *plot* statement. The SAS output for the scatter plots are not organized in the concise format shown in the text and are not shown here for brevity.

INSERT 9.2

```
data surgical;
  infile 'c:\alrm\chapter 9 data sets\ch09ta01.txt';
  input x1 x2 x3 x4 x5 x6 x7 x8 y ylog;

proc reg;
 model ylog = x1 x2 x3 x4;
  output out=results r=residual p=yhat;
   plot r.*p.;
   plot npp.*r. ;

proc reg corr;
  model ylog = x1 x2 x3 x4;

proc corr;
  var ylog x1 x2 x3 x4;

proc plot;
  plot ylog*(x1 x2 x3 x4)  x1*(x2 x3 x4)  x2*(x3 x4)  x3*x4;
run;
```

SAS Output 9.2 continued

Plot (c)

Plot (d)

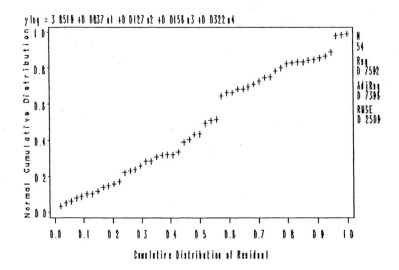

SAS Output 9.3

Correlation					
Variable	**x1**	**x2**	**x3**	**x4**	**ylog**
x1	1.0000	0.0901	-0.1496	0.5024	0.2462
x2	0.0901	1.0000	-0.0236	0.3690	0.4699
x3	-0.1496	-0.0236	1.0000	0.4164	0.6539
x4	0.5024	0.3690	0.4164	1.0000	0.6493
ylog	0.2462	0.4699	0.6539	0.6493	1.0000

Criteria for Model Selection

The next phase of the authors' model-building procedure calls for examining "whether all of the potential predictor variables are needed or whether a subset of them is adequate." We can choose from a rather long list of criteria for selecting or eliminating predicator variables.

In *proc reg*, the *selection=option* specifies the method used to select the regression model, where the option can be *forward* (or *f*), *backward* (or *b*), *stepwise*, *maxr*, *minr*, *rsquare*, *adjrsq*, *cp* or *none* (include all predictor variables). The default method is *none*.

All-Possible-Regressions. The *All-Possible-Regressions Procedure* compares the results obtained by fitting all possible subsets of potential predictor variables that could be used to build regression models. Based on various criteria, a small number of regression models are selected

94

for further evaluation. The number of candidate models, however, increases rapidly as the number of predictor variables increases. A study with only 3 predicator variables has $2^3 = 8$ possible first-order regression models, whereas one with 7 predictor variables has $2^7 = 128$. Thus, the all-possible-regressions procedure can be used when the number of potential predictor variables is relatively small, but becomes impractical for use when the number of predictor variables is very large.

In *proc reg*, the *selection=rsquare* option produces R^2, the proportion of variability attributable to the regression model, for all possible subsets of predictor variables that are specified in the *model* statement. For example, the SAS syntax given in Insert 9.3 produces SAS Output 9.4. The SAS output is arranged from largest to smallest values of R^2 for all one (predictor) variable models, then from largest to smallest values of R^2 for all two variable models, and so on. As noted in the text, the largest R^2 will always be realized for the model with all the predictor variables included. If we can, we want to choose a model with a smaller number of predictor variables but one with an R^2 reasonably close to the maximum.

SAS Output 9.4

Number in Model	R-Square	Variables in Model
1	0.4276	x3
1	0.4215	x4
1	0.2208	x2
1	0.0606	x1
2	0.6633	x2 x3
2	0.5995	x3 x4
2	0.5486	x1 x3
2	0.4830	x2 x4
2	0.4301	x1 x4
2	0.2627	x1 x2
3	0.7573	x1 x2 x3
3	0.7178	x2 x3 x4
3	0.6121	x1 x3 x4
3	0.4870	x1 x2 x4
4	0.7592	x1 x2 x3 x4

```
                              INSERT 9.3

data surgical;
  infile 'c:\alrm\chapter 9 data sets\ch09ta01.txt';
  input x1 x2 x3 x4 x5 x6 x7 x8 y ylog;
proc reg;
  model ylog = x1 x2 x3 x4 / selection = rsquare;
 run;
```

The SSE_p, R_p^2, $R_{a,p}^2$, C_p, AIC_p, SBC_p, and $PRESS_p$ values for all-possible-regression models are presented in Table 9.2, text page 353, for the Surgical Unit example when regressing *ylog* on *X1*, *X2*, *X3*, *X4*. In Insert 9.4, we request that the selection of possible models based on the adjusted R-square criterion (*selection=adjrsq*) and that R-square (*rsquare*), mean square error (*mse*), sum of squares error (*sse*), Mallows' C_p (*cp*), and Akaike's information criterion (*aic*) be printed for each model. A summary of the selection criteria shown in Table 9.2, text page 353, and those available as an option in the *model* statement using *proc reg* is displayed here in the table below Insert 9.4. The Schwarz Bayesian Criterion (SBC_p) shown in Table 9.2, text page 353, is not available in SAS.

Output for the first *proc reg* procedure in Insert 9.4 is presented in SAS Output 9.5. When we request residuals as an option in the *model* statement, SAS prints the $PRESS_p$ statistic after listing the residuals. The second *proc reg* statement of Insert 9.4 illustrates syntax that produces a listing of the residuals and the $PRESS_p$ statistic for an individual model (Output not shown).The *best*=option is used with the *rsquare*, *adjrsq*, and *cp* model selection options. If *selection=cp* or *selection=adjrsq* is specified, the *best*=option specifies the maximum number of subset models to be displayed. For *selection=rsquare*, the *best*=option sets the maximum number of subset models for each number of predictor variables. That is, if *best*=2 and there are 4 predictors variables in the *model* statement, the two best models based on *rsquare* will be displayed for all possible models with 1 predictor variable (only one model is available to be displayed), all possible models with 2 predictor variable, all possible models with 3 predictor variables, and all possible models with 4 predictor variables. If the *best*=option is omitted and there are less than 11 predictors variables, all possible subsets will be evaluated. If the *best*=option is omitted and the number of predictor variables is greater than 10, the maximum number of subsets will be equal to the number of predictor variables. The third *proc reg* statement and the corresponding *model* statement illustrates the use of the *best*=3 option (Output not shown).

```
                             INSERT  9.4
data surgical;
  infile 'c:\alrm\chapter 9 data sets\ch09ta01.txt';
  input x1 x2 x3 x4 x5 x6 x7 x8 y ylog;
proc reg;
  model ylog = x1 x2 x3 x4 / selection = adjrsq rsquare sse mse cp aic;

proc reg;
  model ylog = x1 x2 x3 x4 / r;

proc reg;
 model ylog = x1 x2 x3 x4 / selection =  adjrsq best=3;
 run;
```

Table 9.1

Text Table 9.2 Heading	SAS Output Heading (See SAS Output 9.5)	Comment
SSE_p	SSE	R_p^2 varies inversely with SSE_p
Not shown	MSE	
R_p^2	R-Square	
$R_{a,p}^2$	Adjusted R Square	
C_p	C(p)	
AIC_p	AIC	
SBC_p	Not available in SAS	
$PRESS_p$	Not computed for all possible regressions but is computed for one model at a time	Specify p or r as an option in the model statement and Press statistic is printed at the end of the list of predicted values and residuals.

SAS Output 9.5

Number in Model	Adjusted R-Square	R-Square	C(p)	AIC	MSE	SSE	Variables in Model
3	0.7427	0.7573	3.3905	-146.1609	0.06217	3.10854	x1 x2 x3
4	0.7396	0.7592	5.0000	-144.5895	0.06294	3.08396	x1 x2 x3 x4
3	0.7009	0.7178	11.4237	-138.0232	0.07228	3.61413	x2 x3 x4
2	0.6501	0.6633	20.5197	-130.4833	0.08456	4.31249	x2 x3
3	0.5889	0.6121	32.9320	-120.8442	0.09936	4.96782	x1 x3 x4
2	0.5838	0.5995	33.5041	-121.1126	0.10058	5.12970	x3 x4
2	0.5309	0.5486	43.8517	-114.6583	0.11335	5.78096	x1 x3
2	0.4627	0.4830	57.2149	-107.3236	0.12984	6.62201	x2 x4
3	0.4562	0.4870	58.3917	-105.7477	0.13140	6.57020	x1 x2 x4
1	0.4166	0.4276	66.4889	-103.8269	0.14099	7.33157	x3

Number in Model	Adjusted R-Square	R-Square	C(p)	AIC	MSE	SSE	Variables in Model
1	0.4104	0.4215	67.7148	-103.2615	0.14248	7.40873	x4
2	0.4078	0.4301	67.9721	-102.0669	0.14312	7.29905	x1 x4
2	0.2338	0.2627	102.0313	-88.1622	0.18515	9.44267	x1 x2
1	0.2059	0.2208	108.5558	-87.1781	0.19191	9.97918	x2
1	0.0425	0.0606	141.1639	-77.0788	0.23137	12.03147	x1

Automatic Search Procedures

SAS offers nine methods of variable selection: *forward* (or *f*), *backward* (or *b*), *stepwise*, *maxr*, *minr*, *rsquare*, *adjrsq*, *cp* or *none* (include all predictor variables). We illustrate below stepwise selection, forward selection, and backward selection.

Stepwise Selection: The *Stepwise* selection method first selects the best predictor variable (the predictor variable with the largest partial correlation with the response variable). In each step thereafter, a variable is either added or one of the variables already entered is dropped from the model. Additional variables are added to the model based on their incremental improvement to the reduction in error sum of squares. Variables are dropped from the model if their test for entry is not significant given the other variables in the model. The default and modifiable α limits for adding or dropping a variable are 0.50 and 0.15, respectively. The α limits for selecting variables for entry in the model (*sle*) and for selecting variables to stay in the model (*sls*) can be specified directly using the *sle* and *sls* options as shown in Insert 9.5. Consistent with text page 366, we have set *sle*=.1 and *sls*=.15.

The Stepwise method is used in Insert 9.5 to regress *ylog* on all eight *X* variables from the Surgical Unit Example with results shown in SAS Output 9.8. From SAS Output 9.8, we see that *X3* was entered at step 1 because *X3* had the highest partial *F*-value of all variables under consideration. At step 2, *X2* had the highest partial *F*-value of the variables not in the model and was added to the model at step 2. Of the variables not in the model after step 2, *X8* has the highest partial *F*-value and was added to the model at step 3. Again, of the variables not in the model after step 3, *X1* has the highest partial *F*-value and was added to the model at step 4. Beginning with step 2, the search algorithm compares the probability level of the partial correlation of the variables in the equation to the α level needed to remove a variable from the model. A variable is removed from the model if the *p*-value associated with the partial *F*-value is greater than the predetermined α level to remove. In the present example, none of the variables was removed from the model. Notice that the *p*-value associated with each predictor variable not in the model after step 4 (Stepwise Selection: Step 5 – SAS Output 9.8) is greater than the α level needed to add that variable to the model. Thus, the stepping process terminates with *X3*, *X2*, *X8*, and *X1* in the final model.

INSERT 9.5	INSERT 9.5 continued

data surgical;
  infile 'c:\alrm\chapter 9 data sets\ch09ta01.txt';
  input x1 x2 x3 x4 x5 x6 x7 x8 y ylog;
	proc reg;
	  model ylog = x1 x2 x3 x4 x5 x6 x7 x8/
	   selection = stepwise
	    sle=.1 sls=.15 details=all ;
	run;

SAS Output 9.8

Stepwise Selection: Step 1

Statistics for Entry DF = 1, 52				
Variable	**Tolerance**	**Model R-Square**	**F Value**	**Pr > F**
x1	1.000000	0.0606	3.35	0.0727
x2	1.000000	0.2208	14.74	0.0003
x3	1.000000	0.4276	38.84	<.0001
x4	1.000000	0.4215	37.89	<.0001
x5	1.000000	0.0210	1.12	0.2956
x6	1.000000	0.0538	2.96	0.0913
x7	1.000000	0.0160	0.85	0.3617
x8	1.000000	0.1390	8.39	0.0055

Stepwise Selection: Step 2

Statistics for Entry DF = 1, 51				
Variable	**Tolerance**	**Model R-Square**	**F Value**	**Pr > F**
x1	0.977610	0.5486	13.68	0.0005
x2	0.999443	0.6633	35.70	<.0001
x4	0.826591	0.5995	21.89	<.0001
x5	0.999834	0.4462	1.72	0.1960
x6	0.980475	0.4478	1.86	0.1781
x7	0.992766	0.4326	0.46	0.5025
x8	0.986198	0.5164	9.37	0.0035

Stepwise Selection: Step 3

	Statistics for Entry DF = 1, 50			
Variable	Tolerance	Model R-Square	F Value	Pr > F
x1	0.970108	0.7573	19.37	<.0001
x4	0.682979	0.7178	9.66	0.0031
x5	0.997531	0.6761	1.98	0.1651
x6	0.964220	0.6697	0.97	0.3283
x7	0.977269	0.6810	2.77	0.1023
x8	0.979642	0.7780	25.85	<.0001

Stepwise Selection: Step 4

	Statistics for Entry DF = 1, 49			
Variable	Tolerance	Model R-Square	F Value	Pr > F
x1	0.906955	0.8299	14.93	0.0003
x4	0.671275	0.8144	9.61	0.0032
x5	0.983952	0.7836	1.25	0.2687
x6	0.959734	0.7888	2.49	0.1211
x7	0.728783	0.7800	0.43	0.5158

Stepwise Selection: Step 5

	Statistics for Entry DF = 1, 48			
Variable	Tolerance	Model R-Square	F Value	Pr > F
x4	0.390402	0.8331	0.94	0.3380
x5	0.983823	0.8358	1.73	0.1944
x6	0.954457	0.8374	2.23	0.1418
x7	0.728750	0.8317	0.51	0.4782

Forward Elimination: The *Forward* method begins with no predictor variables in the model. In each step, the predictor variable with the largest partial *F*-value is entered in the model. This method continues to add variables with significant ($p < \alpha$ to add) partial *F*-values until none of the partial *F*-values is significant. To request the *forward* method in the present example, we simply replace *selection=stepwise* with *selection=forward* in the *model* statement in Insert 9.5. In the present example, the progression of predictor variable entry is the same as the *Stepwise* method shown in SAS Output 9.8. However, in contrast to the stepwise method, the *Forward* method makes no attempt to remove variables from the model. Since the *Stepwise* procedure above did not remove any predictor variables from the model and the *Forward* method makes no attempt to remove variables, the result of the *Stepwise* method (SAS Output 9.8) and *Forward* method (Output not shown) are the same in the present example, although this will not always be true.

Backward Elimination: The *Backward* method begins with all predictor variables in the model. Beginning with the one with the smallest partial *F*-value, the *backward* method then removes each predictor variable that does not have a significant ($p > \alpha$ to remove) partial *F*-value. To request the *backward* method in the present example, we simply replace *selection=stepwise* with *selection=backward* in the *model* statement in Insert 9.5. Consistent with text page 366, we have set *sle*=.1 and *sls*=.15. From SAS Output 9.9 we see that at step 1 all eight *X* variables are entered in the model. Because the probability level ("Pr>F") of *X4* is greater than the α needed to remove a variable and is greater than other probability levels of variables in the model, *X4* is removed from the model at step 2. *X7* and *X5* are then removed at steps 2 and 3, respectively, based on their significance levels. At Backward Elimination: Step 4 (SAS Output 9.9), the significance level for *X6* is 0.1418, which is less than the α to remove (*sls*=.15). Thus, *X6* is retained in the model. The final model contains *X1*, *X2*, *X3*, *X6*, and *X8*.

SAS Output 9.9

Backward Elimination: Step 1

Statistics for Removal DF = 1, 45				
Variable	Partial R-Square	Model R-Square	F Value	Pr > F
x1	0.0248	0.8213	7.26	0.0099
x2	0.1632	0.6829	47.73	<.0001
x3	0.2335	0.6126	68.29	<.0001
x4	0.0001	0.8460	0.03	0.8645
x5	0.0057	0.8404	1.68	0.2016
x6	0.0066	0.8396	1.92	0.1725
x7	0.0025	0.8436	0.74	0.3957
x8	0.0660	0.7801	19.31	<.0001

Backward Elimination: Step 2

	Statistics for Removal DF = 1, 46			
Variable	Partial R-Square	Model R-Square	F Value	Pr > F
x1	0.0489	0.7971	14.62	0.0004
x2	0.2087	0.6373	62.35	<.0001
x3	0.3981	0.4479	118.93	<.0001
x5	0.0068	0.8392	2.04	0.1597
x6	0.0076	0.8384	2.26	0.1392
x7	0.0026	0.8434	0.77	0.3835
x8	0.0659	0.7801	19.70	<.0001

Backward Elimination: Step 3

	Statistics for Removal DF = 1, 47			
Variable	Partial R-Square	Model R-Square	F Value	Pr > F
x1	0.0491	0.7944	14.72	0.0004
x2	0.2157	0.6277	64.75	<.0001
x3	0.3966	0.4468	119.07	<.0001
x5	0.0060	0.8374	1.80	0.1862
x6	0.0076	0.8358	2.29	0.1369
x8	0.0703	0.7731	21.10	<.0001

Backward Elimination: Step 4

	Statistics for Removal DF = 1, 48			
Variable	Partial R-Square	Model R-Square	F Value	Pr > F
x1	0.0487	0.7888	14.37	0.0004
x2	0.2207	0.6167	65.17	<.0001
x3	0.3966	0.4409	117.10	<.0001
x6	0.0076	0.8299	2.23	0.1418
x8	0.0761	0.7614	22.47	<.0001

Model Validation: The Surgical Unit Example Continued

Data File: ch09ta05.txt

Continuing with the Surgical Unit example, the researchers identified three candidate models using the model-selection criteria presented above: SSE_p, R_p^2, $R_{a,p}^2$, C_p, AIC_p, SBC_p, and $PRESS_p$. The researchers now wish to estimate the predictive capability of the three models using the *mean squared prediction error* ($MSPR$) described on text page 370. Model 1, given on text page 373, uses *ylog* as the response variable and *X1*, *X2*, *X3*, and *X8* as predictor variables.

In Insert 9.6, we first fit the regression model based on Model 1 using the Surgical Unit training data set presented in Table 9.1, text page 350. The estimated regression coefficients are given in SAS Output 9.10. We now open the Surgical Unit validation data set presented in Table 9.5, text page 374. After printing ch09ta05.txt, the first 5 lines of the data file should look like SAS Output 9.12.

```
                              INSERT 9.6
data surgical;
  infile 'c:\alrm\chapter 9 data sets\ch09ta01.txt';
  input x1 x2 x3 x4 x5 x6 x7 x8 y ylog;

proc reg;
  model ylog=x1 x2 x3 x8;
  run;
```

SAS Output 9.10

		Parameter Estimates			
Variable	**DF**	**Parameter Estimate**	**Standard Error**	**t Value**	**Pr > |t|**
Intercept	1	3.85242	0.19270	19.99	<.0001
x1	1	0.07332	0.01897	3.86	0.0003
x2	1	0.01419	0.00173	8.20	<.0001
x3	1	0.01545	0.00140	11.07	<.0001
x8	1	0.35297	0.07719	4.57	<.0001

SAS Output 9.11

Obs	x1	x2	x3	x4	x5	x6	x7	x8	y	ylog
1	7.1	23	78	1.93	45	0	1	0	302	5.710
2	4.9	66	91	3.05	34	1	0	0	767	6.642
3	6.4	90	35	1.06	39	1	0	1	487	6.188
4	5.7	35	70	2.13	68	1	0	0	242	5.489
5	6.1	42	69	2.25	70	0	0	1	705	6.558

From fitted results corresponding to Model 1 in equation 9.21, text page 373, we use the syntax in Insert 9.7 to compute $\hat{Y}_i$ ($m1$ is used to denote the predicted value for model 1), the predicted value of the ith observation in the validation data set using the regression coefficients (SAS Output 9.10) estimated from the training data set (Insert 9.6). We then find $devsq = \left(Y_i - \hat{Y}_i\right)^2$, where Y_i is the value of the response variable of the ith observation in the validation data. Finally, we use *proc means sum* to find the $\sum_{i=1}^{n^*}\left(Y_i - \hat{Y}_i\right)^2$ (SAS Output 9.13). We find by hand calculator $\sum_{i=1}^{n^*}\left(Y_i - \hat{Y}_i\right)^2 / n^* = 4.1773269 / 54 = 0.07735$.

We repeat the above process by estimating regression functions for Models 2 and 3 on text page 373 based on the Surgical Unit training data set and finding $\sum_{i=1}^{n^*}\left(Y_i - \hat{Y}_i\right)^2 / n^*$ when using the validation data set. This results in $MSPR = 0.0764$ and 0.0794, respectively. From the relative closeness of the three $MSPR$ values, the researchers concluded that the three candidate models performed equally in terms of predictive accuracy. Model 3 was discarded due to reversal of the sign of a regression coefficient from the training data set to the validation data set. Models 1 and 2 preformed equally well in the validation study. The final selection of Model 1 was based on Occam's razor; Model 1 required one less parameter than Model 2.

INSERT 9.7

```
data surgical;
 infile 'c:\alrm\chapter 9 data sets\ch09ta05.txt';
  input x1 x2 x3 x4 x5 x6 x7 x8 y ylog;
  m1=3.85241+(0.07332*x1)+(0.01418*x2)+(0.01545*x3)+(0.35296*x8);
devsq=(ylog-m1)**2;
 proc means sum;
  var devsq;
run;
```

SAS Output 9.13

Analysis Variable : devsq
Sum
4.1773269

Building the Regression
Model II: Diagnostics

This chapter is concerned with diagnostic techniques for identifying inadequacies of a fitted regression model. Graphical methods were used in previous chapters as an aid in deciding whether to use higher-order terms for a predictor variable in the model or whether to add predictor variables that have not been included in the model. Chapter 10 discusses graphs that can provide useful model-building information about a predictor variable, given that other predictor variables are already in the model. When we fit a regression model to a set of data, some observations may be outlying or extreme relative to most of the data. As shown in Figure 10.5, text page 391, an observation may contain a Y value, one or more X values, or both X and Y values that are outliers. Outlying observations may have too much influence on the estimates of the parameters of the model and, therefore, may require remedial steps. The authors discuss methods for detecting outliers and excessively influential observations. They also discuss remedial steps for dealing with these observations. In Section 10.5, text page 406, the authors continue their discussion of problems created when there is multicollinearity among the predictor variables of a regression model. They present informal methods of detecting multicollinearity problems on text page 407. They then define the variance inflation factor and show how it is used in more formal ways to check for serious multicollinearity among the predictor variables.

The Life Insurance Example

Data File: ch10ta01.txt

Table 10.1, text page 387, presents data from a study of the relationship between amount of insurance carried (Y) and annual income ($X1$) and a measure of risk aversion ($X2$). After opening the Life Insurance data file and naming the variables $X1$, $X2$, and Y, the first 5 lines of output should look like SAS Output 10.1.

SAS Output 10.1

Obs	x1	x2	y
1	45.010	6	91
2	57.204	4	162
3	26.852	5	11
4	66.290	7	240
5	40.964	5	73

We begin by regressing Y on $X1$ and $X2$ and generating the unstandardized residuals by using the *r* option on the *proc reg model* statement. (Insert 10.1) From within the *proc reg* procedure we add a title and then plot the residual values on the *y*-axis and $X2$ on the *x*-axis (*plot r.*x1;*) to produce text Figure 10.3 (a), text page 387, (SAS Output 10.2). To produce Figure 10.3 (b), we regress Y on $X2$ and save the unstandardized residual values in a variable named *res1* in data set *results*. We then regress $X1$ on $X2$ and save the unstandardized residuals in a variable named *res2* in the *results* data set. We use *proc gplot* to request a scatter plot with *res1* [$e(Y \mid X_2)$] on the y-axis and *res2* [$e(X_1 \mid X_2)$] on the x-axis. We also request that a dot (*value=dot*) be used to plot the data points, that a regression line (*interpol=rl*) be drawn through the data points, and that a vertical reference line be drawn from position 0 of the vertical axis (*vref=0*). We also define the values of the x and y axes. This produces SAS Output 10.3.

INSERT 10.1	**INSERT 10.1 continued**
```data life; infile 'c:\alrm\chapter 10 data sets\ch10ta01.txt'; input x1 x2 y; goptions reset=all; proc reg; model y=x1 x2 / r; title1 'Text Figure 10.3 a'; plot r.*x1; run; proc reg; model y=x2 / r; output out=results r=res1;```	```proc reg; model x1=x2 / r; output out=results r=res2; run; proc gplot; title1 'Text Figure 10.3 b'; symbol1 value=dot interpol=rl; plot res1*res2 / haxis=-25 to 50 by 25 vaxis=-150 to 300 by 50 vref=0; run;```

INSERT 10.1

```
data life;
   infile 'c:\alrm\chapter 10 data sets\ch10ta01.txt';
   input  x1 x2 y;
goptions reset=all;
proc reg;
 model y=x1 x2 / r;
 title1 'Text Figure 10.3 a';
 plot r.*x1;
 run;
proc reg;
 model y=x2 / r;
 output out=results r=res1;
proc reg;
 model x1=x2 / r;
 output out=results r=res2;
run;
proc gplot;
 title1 'Text Figure 10.3 b';
 symbol1 value=dot interpol=rl;
 plot res1*res2 / haxis=-25 to 50 by 25 vaxis=-150 to 300 by 50 vref=0;
 run;
```

SAS Output 10.2	SAS Output 10.3
Text Figure 10.3 a	Text Figure 10.3 b

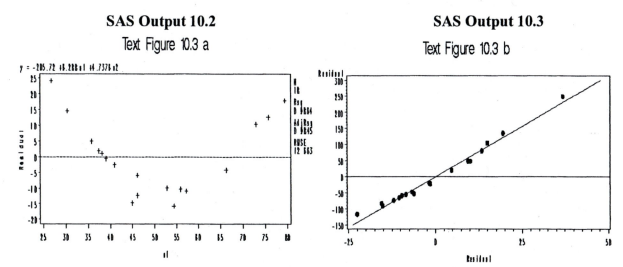

The Body Fat Example

Data File: ch07ta01.txt

We use the Body Fat example (Table 7.1, text page 257) to illustrate all regression diagnostics. See Chapter 0, "Working with SAS," for instructions on opening the Body Fat example and naming the variables *X1*, *X2*, *X3*, and *Y*. After opening ch07ta01.txt, the first 5 lines of output should look like SAS Output 10.4.

SAS Output 10.4

Obs	x1	x2	x3	y
1	19.5	43.1	29.1	11.9
2	24.7	49.8	28.2	22.8
3	30.7	51.9	37.0	18.7
4	29.8	54.3	31.1	20.1
5	19.1	42.2	30.9	12.9

Added-Variable Plots: We begin by regressing body fat (*Y*) on triceps skinfold thickness (*X1*) and thigh circumference (*X2*) (Insert 10.2). This results in the regression analysis shown in SAS Output 10.5. The fitted regression function is:

$$\hat{Y} = -19.174 + 0.222X_1 + 0.659X_2$$

INSERT 10.2

```
data bodyfat;
  infile 'c:\alrm\chapter 7 data sets\ch07ta01.txt';
  input x1 x2 x3 y;
proc reg;
 model y=x1 x2 ;
run;
```

107

SAS Output 10.5

Analysis of Variance					
Source	DF	Sum of Squares	Mean Square	F Value	Pr > F
Model	2	385.43871	192.71935	29.80	<.0001
Error	17	109.95079	6.46769		
Corrected Total	19	495.38950			

Parameter Estimates					
Variable	DF	Parameter Estimate	Standard Error	t Value	Pr > |t|
Intercept	1	-19.17425	8.36064	-2.29	0.0348
x1	1	0.22235	0.30344	0.73	0.4737
x2	1	0.65942	0.29119	2.26	0.0369

In Insert 10.3, we regress Y on $X1$ and $X2$ and use the r option on the *model* statement to request the residuals for this model. We save the residuals in a file named *results* using the statement *output out=results r=residual*. We specify the title of the plot and request that the residuals be plotted against $X1$ (*plot r.*x1*). We also request a second plot within the *proc reg* procedure. Because graphs are not created until a *run* statement is executed, we issue a *run* statement following the first plot statement. If we omitted the *run* statement that precedes the title for the second plot, the title for the second plot would overwrite the title for the first plot and be used for both plots. In the *plot r.*x2* statement, we request that the residual values be plotted against $X2$. The above maneuvers produce Figures 10.4 (a) and (c), text page 389 (SAS Output 10.6).

```
INSERT 10.3

data bodyfat;
  infile 'c:\alrm\chapter 7 data sets\ch07ta01.txt';
  input x1 x2 x3 y;
goptions reset=all;
proc reg;
 model y=x1 x2 / r ;
 output out=results r=residual;
 title 'Text Figure 10.4 a';
 plot r.*x1 ;
run;
 title 'Text Figure 10.4 c';
 plot r.*x2 ;
run;
```

SAS Output 10.6

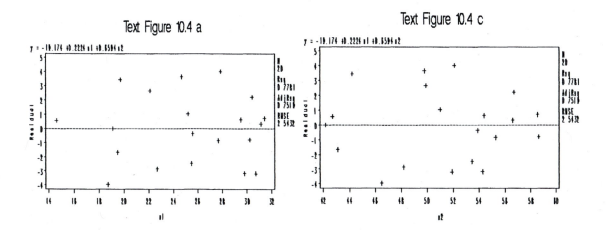

Text Figure 10.4 a

Text Figure 10.4 c

To produce Figures 10.4 b and d, text page 389 (SAS Output 10.7), we regress Y on $X1$, Y on $X2$, $X1$ on $X2$, and $X2$ on $X1$, and for each model save the residual values as *ryx1*, *ryx2*, *rx1x2*, and *rx2x1*, respectively (Insert 10.4). Since the intent of each regression analysis was only to generate residuals, we used the *noprint* option to suppress printing of standard output. We then use *proc gplot* to produce text Figures 10.4 b and d. Notice we requested that a *dot* be used to display data points on the graph and that a regression line be drawn through the data points (*symbol value=dot interpol=rl;*).

```
                          INSERT 10.4

proc reg;
 model y=x1 / r noprint;
 output out=results r=ryx1;
proc reg;
 model y=x2 / r noprint;
 output out=results r=ryx2;
proc reg;
 model x1=x2 / r noprint;
 output out=results r=rx1x2;
proc reg;
 model x2=x1 / r noprint;
 output out=results r=rx2x1;
 run;
proc gplot;
 title 'Text Figure 10.4 b';
 symbol value=dot interpol=rl;
 plot ryx2*rx1x2;
run;
proc gplot;
 title 'Text Figure 10.4 d';
 symbol value=dot interpol=rl;
 plot ryx1*rx2x1;
run;
```

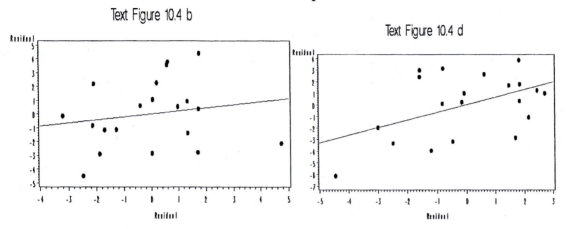

Text Figure 10.4 b

Text Figure 10.4 d

Illustration of Hat Matrix

Data File: ch10ta02.txt

On text page 393, the authors present a small data set to illustrate the relationship between the response variable and the predictor variables. After opening ch10ta02.txt and naming the variables *Y, X1*, and *X2*, the 4 lines of output should look like SAS Output 10.8. In Insert 10.5, we create a new variable named *X0* that is equal 1 for each line of data in the input file (there are 4 lines of data in this example). The data stored under the variable *X0* will be used to create a column of ones in the **X** matrix. We convert the data stored under the variable y to matrix (vector) form and call the resulting matrix y by issuing the statement *"read all var {'y'} into y"*. We create the matrix **X** whose columns are made up of the data stored under the variables *X0, X1*, and *X2*, respectively, by issuing the statement *"read all var {'x0' 'x1' 'x2'} into x"*. We then use the matrix syntax of *proc iml* and program various text equations to find the **B** (parameter estimates), **H** (hat matrix), **YHAT** (predicted values), and **VARCOVAR** (variance-covariance) matrices. Although the syntax only prints **VARCOVAR**, a *print* statement for any matrix can be added at any location in the matrix program.

SAS Output 10.8

Obs	y	x1	x2
1	301	14	25
2	327	19	32
3	246	12	22
4	187	11	15

INSERT 10.5	INSERT 10.5 continued

data hat;
  infile 'c:\alrm\chapter 10 data sets\ch10ta02.txt';
  input y x1 x2;
x0=1;
proc iml;
  use hat;
* Define Y matrix;
  read all var {'y'} into y;
* Create X matrix;
  read all var {'x0' 'x1' 'x2'} into x;
	* Find the B matrix using text equation 6.25;
	  b=inv(t(x)*x)*t(x)*y;
	* Find hat matrix (hat) by text equation 10.10;
	  hat=x*inv(t(x)*x)*t(x);
	* Find fitted values of y (yhat) by text equation 10.11;
	  yhat=hat*y;
	* Create a 4x4 idenity (I) matrix;
	  i=i(4);
	* Find variance-covariance matrix using text equation 10.13;
	  varcovar=574.9*(i-hat);
	  print varcovar;
	quit;

Formal Diagnostics: The remainder of the diagnostics on text pages 390-410 deals with *residuals, deleted residuals, leverage values, DFFITS, DFBETAS, Cook's distance measure,* and *variance inflation factors.* To produce these statistics we request the appropriate regression model as before. The options listed in SAS Output 10.9 are available on the *proc reg model* statement and will display the statistics shown under the Output heading. Using the options listed in SAS Output 10.10, you can save the selected statistics to a SAS data set.

SAS Output 10.9

SAS *proc reg **model*** statement option	Output
influence	Unstandardized residuals, studentized deleted residuals, leverage values, covariance ratio, DFFITS, DFBETAS
r	Unstandardized residual values
vif	Variance inflation factors

SAS Output 10.10

SAS *proc reg **output*** statement option	Description
Cookd=varname	Saves Cook's D influence statistics into *varname*
dffits=varname	Saves *dffits* value into *varname*
h=varname	Saves leverage values into *varname*
r=varname	Saves residual values into *varname*
rstudent=varname	Saves studentized deleted residual values into *varname*
student=varname	Saves studentized residual values into *varname*

111

Identifying Outlying *Y* Observations – Studentized Deleted Residuals: On text page 396 the researchers wished to examine whether there were outlying *Y* observations when using a regression model with the two predictor variables *X1* and *X2*. In Insert 10.6 – Step 1, we obtain a first order regression model with predictors *X1* and *X2* and request *influence* statistics. As noted in SAS Output 10.11, this results in the output of residuals (*residual*), studentized deleted residuals (*Rstudent*), leverage values (*Hat Diag H*), DFFITS, and DFBETAS for the current model. The first, third, and second columns of SAS Output 10.11 are consistent with the first, second and third columns, respectively, of Table 10.3, text page 397. Next, we save the studentized deleted residuals in a variable named *sdr*. (Insert 10.6 – Step 1)

The researchers now wish to determine if case 13 is an outlier based on the *studentized deleted residual* (text page 397). Using SAS it is just as easy to test for outliers for each of the 20 cases. Here, $\alpha = 0.10$, $n = 20$, and p = number of independent variables in the model (*X0*, *X1*, and *X2*) = 3 so that the appropriate Bonferroni critical value is $t(1-\alpha/2n;\ n-p-1) = t(1-0.10/2*20;\ 20-3-1) = t(0.9975, 16)$. In Insert 10.6 – Step 2, we use a *quantile* function to find *tvalue* = $t(0.9975; 16)$ = 3.2519. We then compare the absolute value of the *studentized deleted residual* (*abs(sdr)*) to *tvalue*. If the absolute value of the *studentized deleted residual* is greater than *tvalue*, we set *outlier* = 1, otherwise *outlier* = 0. Consistent with text page 398, all data lines with *outlier* = 1 should be considered outliers and, conversely, all data lines with *outlier* = 0 should be considered not to be outliers. If we were dealing with a large data file, more than 100 data lines, for example, we could search the entire data file by using the *where* option on the *proc print* statement to find all data lines with *outlier* = 1. We use *case+1* in the fourth line of Insert 10.6 to create a case number for each of the 20 cases. Thus we can print *case* for all cases *where outlier=1;* that is, if *outlier=1* we print the case number.

```
                            INSERT 10.6

* Step 1;
data bodyfat;
  infile 'c:\alrm\chapter  7 data sets\ch07ta01.txt';
  input x1 x2 x3 y;
  case+1;
proc reg;
 model y = x1 x2 / influence ;
 output out=results r=residual rstudent=sdr ;
 run;


* Step 2;
data results;
 set results;
tvalue=tinv(.9975,16);
if (abs(sd)) > tvalue then outlier=1;
if (abs(sdr)) <= tvalue then outlier=0;
proc print data=results;
 where outlier=1;
 var case;
 run;
```

			Hat Diag	Cov		DFBETAS		
Obs	Residual	RStudent	H	Ratio	DFFITS	Intercept	x1	x2
1	-1.6827	-0.7300	0.2010	1.3607	-0.3661	-0.3052	-0.1315	0.2320
2	3.6429	1.5343	0.0589	0.8443	0.3838	0.1726	0.1150	-0.1426
3	-3.1760	-1.6543	0.3719	1.1892	-1.2731	-0.8471	-1.1825	1.0669
4	-3.1585	-1.3485	0.1109	0.9768	-0.4763	-0.1016	-0.2935	0.1961
5	-0.000289	-0.000127	0.2480	1.5951	-0.0001	-0.0001	-0.0000	0.0001

Output Statistics

Identifying Outlying X Observations - Hat Matrix Leverage Values: To identify cases with potentially outlying X values, the researchers in the Body Fat example plotted triceps skinfold thickness ($X1$) against thigh circumference ($X2$) and identified each line by a case number (text page 399). SAS does not have a readily available way to include the case number on a scatter plot. In Insert 10.7 we produce that scatter plot of $X1$ and $X2$ using *proc gplot*. From SAS Output 10.12 we observe that two cases appear to be outlying with respect to the X values. A visual inspection indicates that the circled dot in the lower left corner of the plot is the only dot that has an $X1$ value less than 16. The other circled dot appears to have an $X1$ value greater than 30 and an $X2$ value less than 54. To find the case numbers corresponding to these dots, we use the *where* option on the *proc print* statement to print the case number for each selected case. Thus, a case number is printed if the condition "*where* (x1< 16) or (x1 > 30 *and* x2 < 54" is satisfied.

INSERT 10.7	**INSERT 10.7 continued**

data bodyfat;
 infile 'c:\alrm\chapter 7 data sets\ch07ta01.txt';
 input x1 x2 x3 y;
 case+1;
goptions reset=all;
proc gplot;
 symbol value=dot;
	plot x2*x1;
	 run;
	proc print ;
	 where (x1< 16) or (x1 > 30 and x2 < 54);
	 var case;
	 run;

SAS Output 10.12

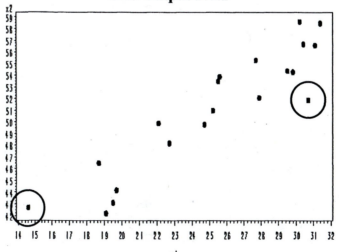

The ith diagonal element (h_{ii}) of the hat matrix is a measure of the distance between the point represented by the geometric coordinates of the X values for the ith case and the point represented by the coordinates of the means (the center of the distribution) of the X values for all n cases. The larger the value of h_{ii}, the farther the ith case is from the center of the distribution and the larger the effect of the X values for that case on the corresponding fitted value $(\hat{y}_i)$. Thus, h_{ii} is referred to as the *leverage* of the ith case. In Insert 10.8, we regress Y on $X1$ and $X2$ and request that leverage values be saved in a variable named *lev*. The values of *lev* are identical to the leverage values (h_{ii}) reported in column 2 of text Table 10.3.

The text defines a "large" leverage value as one that is more than twice the magnitude of the mean leverage value, defined as:

$$\bar{h} = \frac{p}{n}$$

where p is the number of independent variables (including the intercept term) and n is the number of cases. So, the leverage value (*lev*) is considered large in this example if *lev* > 2*(3/20). If so, we set *hilev* = 1, otherwise *hilev* = 0. We use the *where* option in the *proc print* procedure to list cases that the have *hilev*=1. After executing Insert 10.8, we see that case numbers 3 and 15 have high leverage values as indicated by *hilev* = 1 (output not shown).

```
                            INSERT 10.8

data bodyfat;
  infile 'c:\alrm\chapter  7 data sets\ch07ta01.txt';
  input x1 x2 x3 y;
  case+1;
proc reg;
 model y = x1 x2 / vif;
 output out=results h=lev;
 run;
data results;
 set results;
if lev > 2*(3/20)then hilev = 1;
if lev <= 2*(3/20) then hilev = 0;
proc print;
 where hilev=1;
 var case;
 run;
```

Identifying Influential Cases – DFFITS, Cook's Distance, and DFBETAS Measures: The researchers now wish to ascertain whether previously identified outlying cases were also influential cases. In Insert 10.9 we begin by specifying *proc reg* and with the *model* statement regressing Y against $X1$ and $X2$, and requesting *influence* statistics as an option in the *model* statement. We also save the *DFFITS* values in a variable named *dffits* and the *Cook's distance measure* in a variable named *cookd*. *DFBETAS* values can be printed as in SAS Output 10.11. The researcher can visually inspect *DFBETAS*, such as those shown in SAS Output 10.11 for the

Body Fat example, to determine if any values are indicative of influential cases. For large data sets, we use the syntax in Insert 10.9 to search for cases that may be influential.

```
                              INSERT 10.9

data bodyfat;
  infile 'c:\alrm\chapter  7 data sets\ch07ta01.txt';
  input x1 x2 x3 y;
    case+1;
proc reg;
  model y = x1 x2 / influence;
   output out=result1 cookd=cookd dffits=dffits;
     ods output outputstatistics=result2;
  run;
data result1;
  set result1;
  If (dffits > 2*sqrt(3/20))then dfflag=1;
  else dfflag=0;
  percent = 100*probf(cookd,3,17);
data result2;
  set result2;
  if (abs(dfb_x1) > 1) then b1flag=1;
   else b1flag=0;
  if (abs(dfb_x2) > 1) then b2flag=1;
   else b2flag=0;
data both;
  merge result1 result2;
  run;
proc print data=both;
  where dfflag=1 or percent > 20 or b1flag=1 or b2flag=1;
  var case dffits cookd percent dfb_x1 b1flag dfb_x2 b2flag;
  run;
```

A *DFFITS* value is judged to indicate an influential case if it exceeds 1 for a small to medium sample and $2\sqrt{p/n}$ for a large sample. In Insert 10.9, we create a new variable, *dfflag*, to indicate if the value of *DFFITS* exceeds $2\sqrt{p/n}$. We set *dfflag* = 1 if *DFFITS* (*dffits*) $> 2\sqrt{p/n}$, otherwise *dfflag* = 0. For *Cook's Distance measure* (D_i), the text authors suggest that D_i be compared to the *F*-distribution with $df1 = p$ and $df2 = n-p$ degrees of freedom. A case is not considered influential if the corresponding percentile value is less than 10 to 20 percent. However, a case is judged to have a major influence on the fitted regression function if the corresponding percentile value is near 50 percent or greater. In Insert 10.9 we use the probability function for the *F*-distribution (*probf*) with $df1 = 3$ (parameters) and $df2 = 17$ ($n-p$) degrees of freedom to find the proportion of the *F*-distribution that is less than D_i. We multiply this proportion by 100 to express the value as a percent. The result is saved as a new variable, *percent*. A case that has an absolute *DFBETAS* value greater than 1 for small to medium samples or an absolute *DFBETAS* greater than $2/\sqrt{n}$ for large samples may be considered to be an influential case. In Insert 10.9, we create two new variables, *b1flag* and *b2flag*. We then set *b1flag* = 1 if the absolute value (*abs*) of *dfb_x1* is greater than 0, otherwise *b1flag*=0. Similarly, b2flag = 1 if the absolute value (*abs*) of *dfb_x2* is greater than 0, otherwise *b2flag*=0.

To clarify the program structure of Insert 10.9, we first saved the Cook's *Distance measure* (*cookd*) and *DFFITS* (*dffits*) values in a data set named *result1* (*output out=result1 cookd=cookd dffits=dffits;*). *DFBETAS*, however, cannot be saved from this output statement. We must use the SAS Output Delivery System (ODS) to save these statistics. The "*ods output outputstatistics=result2;*" statement results in the *DFBETAS* statistics being saved in a data set named *result2*. *DFBETAS* for *X1* and *X2* are saved by default as *dbf_x1* and *dbf_x2*. We then point to the *result1* data set to test the *dffits* and *cookd* values. To test the *DFBETAS* values (*dbf_x1* and *dbf_x2*), we point to the *result2* data set. Since the *where* option in the *proc print* statement requires data from both *result1* and *result2* data sets, we merge the two data sets into one data set named *both*. The *data=both* option on the *proc print* statement points SAS to the *both* data set to test the conditions of the *where* statement.

We use the *where* option on the *proc print* statement to print all variables for cases that have *dfflag*=1 or have a *percent* value greater than 20 or *betaflag*=1. If we were to print all *dffit* and *percent* values, we would find that all values of *dfflag* = 0, indicating that no *DFFIT* value was greater than $2\sqrt{p/n}$. As reported on text page 404, we also would find that the percent value (*percent*) for case 3 is 30.6 percent and that the next largest percent value is for case 13 at 11 percent. Using *DFBETAS*, we find that *b1flag* = 1 and *b2flag* = 1 for case 3, indicating that *DFBETAS* for both *X1* and *X2* had an absolute value of greater than 1.

Influence on Inferences: Case 3 was identified as an outlying *X* observation and all three influence measures identified case 3 as influential. Thus, the researcher fitted regression functions with and without case 3. The researcher then calculated the percent difference between the predicted value of *Y* ($\hat{Y}_i$) based on the regression function with all 20 cases and the predicted value of *Y* ($\hat{Y}_{i(3)}$) based on the regression function when case 3 was omitted. From Insert 10.10, we begin this analysis by regressing *Y* on *X1* and *X2* and saving the *unstandardized predicted values* as *pred1*. We then use the *where* option in the *proc reg* procedure to select cases other than *case* 3 and again regress *Y* on *X1* and *X2*. (We used *case+1* to create the case number.) We do not save the *unstandardized predicted values* for this regression analysis because case 3 will not have a fitted value and we need the fitted values for all 20 cases; this analysis is only to find the parameter estimates for the model without case 3 in the data set. To find $\hat{Y}_{i(3)}$ for all 20 cases, we use the parameter estimates (shown on text page 406) from the regression function with case 3 omitted to compute *pred2*. We then find *pcinf*, the absolute value (*abs*) of (($\hat{Y}_{i(3)}$ - $\hat{Y}_i$)/ $\hat{Y}_i$)*100.

Finally, we use the *proc means* procedure to find the mean of *pcinf* = 3.1039. We can also generate a frequency distribution of *pcinf* using *proc freq* to see that the mean difference for 17 of the 20 cases is less than 5 percent. Based on this direct evidence, the researcher concluded that case 3 did not exert undue influence on the fitted regression function.

INSERT 10.10	INSERT 10.10 continued

data bodyfat;
  infile 'c:\alrm\chapter 7 data sets\ch07ta01.txt';
  input x1 x2 x3 y;
  case+1;
proc reg;
 model y = x1 x2 ;
 output out=results p=pred1;
 run;
proc reg;
 where case ne 3;
 model y = x1 x2 ;
 run;
	data results;
	 set results;
	pred2=-12.428+.5641*(x1)+.3635*(x2);
	pcinf=(abs((pred2-pred1)/pred1))*100;
	proc means;
	 var pcinf;
	 run;
	proc freq;
	 tables pcinf;
	 run;

Multicollinearity Diagnostics Variance Inflation Factor: The researchers now fitted a regression model with all three predictor variables. From text Chapter 7, we recall that triceps skinfold thickness and thigh circumference were highly correlated. We also found large changes in parameter estimates when a variable was added to the model and that one estimated coefficient was negative when a positive value was expected. Accordingly, the researchers were concerned that there may be *multicollinearity* among the predictor variables. They generated *Variance Inflation Factors* (VIF) as a formal test for the presence of *multicollinearity*. Insert 10.11 requests *collinearity diagnostics* (*vif*) and SAS Output 10.13 contains partial results. The *VIF*'s for *X1*, *X2*, and *X3* are identical to those reported on text page 409. SAS does not report the mean *VIF* value.

INSERT 10.11

```
data bodyfat;
  infile 'c:\alrm\chapter 7 data sets\ch07ta01.txt';
  input x1 x2 x3 y;
proc reg;
 model y = x1 x2 x3 / vif;
 run;
```

SAS Output 10.13

Parameter Estimates						
Variable	DF	Parameter Estimate	Standard Error	t Value	Pr > |t|	Variance Inflation
Intercept	1	117.08469	99.78240	1.17	0.2578	0
x1	1	4.33409	3.01551	1.44	0.1699	708.84291
x2	1	-2.85685	2.58202	-1.11	0.2849	564.34339
x3	1	-2.18606	1.59550	-1.37	0.1896	104.60601

Chapter 11 SAS®

Building the Regression Model III: Remedial Measures

When we detect inadequacies in a regression model that we are building, we take steps to improve the model so that it is more appropriate for the problem at hand. In earlier chapters, the authors used *remedial measures* such as transformations of Y "to linearize the regression relation, to make the error distributions more nearly normal, or to make the variances of the error terms more nearly equal." Further remedial measures are presented in Chapter 11 to improve model adequacy in the presence of unequal error variances, multicollinearity, and overly influential observations. The use of *weighted least squares* in regression analysis is discussed as an alternative to transformations in building models where the variances of the error terms are unequal. *Ridge regression* is presented as a method for dealing with serious multicollinearity among the predictor variables. *Robust regression* techniques are used to dampen the influence of outlying observations. Two methods of *nonparametric regression* are described: *lowess* and *regression trees*. The method of *bootstrapping* is presented to deal with the problem of estimating the precision of some of the complex estimators discussed in this chapter.

Unequal Error Variances Remedial Measures – Weighted Least Squares: Section 11.1 defines the *generalized multiple regression model*:

$$Y_i = \beta_0 + \beta_1 X_{i1} + \ldots + \beta_{p-1} X_{i,p-1} + \varepsilon_i$$

where

$\beta_0, \beta_1, \ldots, \beta_{p-1}$ are unknown parameters

$X_{i1}, X_{i2}, \ldots, X_{i,p-1}$ are known constants

ε_i are independent $N(0, \sigma_i^2)$

$i = 1, 2, \ldots, n$

The method of *weighted least squares* is frequently used to find estimators of the parameters in a generalized multiple regression model because the resulting estimators are *minimum variance unbiased estimators*. Let

$$w_i = \frac{1}{\sigma_i^2}$$

and

$$\mathbf{W} = \begin{bmatrix} w_1 & 0 & \cdots & 0 \\ 0 & w_2 & \cdots & 0 \\ \vdots & \vdots & \ddots & \vdots \\ 0 & 0 & \cdots & w_n \end{bmatrix}$$

Assume the σ_i^2 and hence the w_i are known. Then the weighted least squares (and maximum likelihood) estimators of the coefficients in the generalized multiple regression model are:

$$\mathbf{b_w} = (\mathbf{X'WX})^{-1} \mathbf{X'WY}$$

and the variance-covariance matrix of these estimators is:

$$\sigma^2\{\mathbf{b_w}\} = (\mathbf{X'WX})^{-1}$$

The σ_i^2 are unknown in most applications and the authors present methods for dealing with this circumstance.

The Blood Pressure Example

Data File: ch11ta01.txt

A researcher studied the relationship between diastolic blood pressure (*dbp*) and age (*age*). A sketch of the data is given in Table 11.1, text page 427. See Chapter 0, "Working with SAS," for instructions on opening the Blood Pressure example data file and naming the variables *age* and *dbp*. After opening ch11ta01.txt, the first 5 lines of output should look like SAS Output 11.1.

SAS Output 11.1

Obs	age	dbp
1	27	73
2	21	66
3	22	63
4	24	75
5	25	71

We begin the preliminary analysis of the residuals by fitting an *unweighted least squares* regression model ($Y_i = \beta_0 + \beta_1 X_{i1} + \varepsilon_i$) and saving the *unstandardized residuals (residual)*. (Insert 11.1) To produce the plots in Figure 11.1, text page 428, we use the SAS absolute value function to generate data values for a new variable, *absresid=abs(residual)*, which is the *absolute value of the unstandardized residual*. We produce Figure 11.1 using the *proc gplot* procedure and related syntax as given in Insert 11.1. The resulting plots are shown in SAS Output 11.2.

INSERT 11.1

```
data bp;
  infile 'c:\alrm\chapter 11 data sets\ch11ta01.txt';
  input age dbp;
proc reg;
 model dbp = age / r;
  output out=results r = residual;
data step2;
 set results;
  absresid=abs(residual);
goptions reset=all;
proc gplot;
  symbol color=black value=circle;
  plot dbp*age;
    run;
  plot residual*age;
    run;
  plot absresid*age;
run;
```

SAS Output 11.2

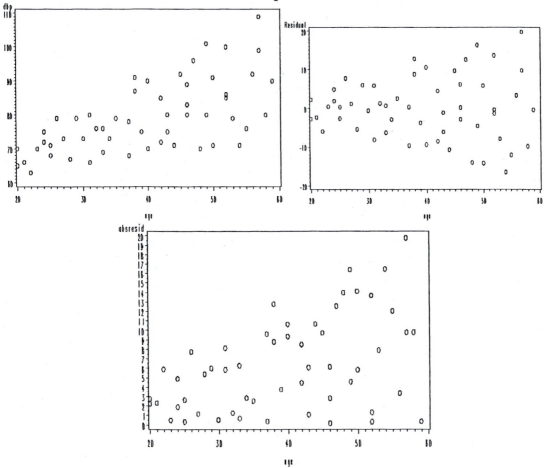

The plot of age against the *unstandardized residual* (*residual*) suggests that the error variance is not constant. From Figure 11.1c, text page 428, the researcher decided that a linear relation between the error standard deviation and *age* was reasonable. In *data step2* of Insert 11.2, we issue the statement *proc reg* with *model absresid = age / p* and obtain text equation 11.19, text page 428. The "*p*" following the slash requests the *fitted* (*unstandardized predicted*) *values*, denoted by $\hat{s}$ in the text. We use the statement *output out=results p = yhat* to specify that the predicted values are to be saved in an output file named *results* under the variable name *yhat*. In *data step3*, we specify *wt=1/(yhat**2)* to compute the weights following equation 11.16a, text page 425:

$$w_i = \frac{1}{(\hat{s}_i)^2} \text{ or } w_i = \frac{1}{(pre\_1)^2}.$$

The *proc print* statement results in a printout of the first five lines of the current data file (*step3*) as shown in SAS Output 11.3. This printout indicates that file *step2* is the same as the data presented in Table 11.1, text page 427.

INSERT 11.2	INSERT 11.2 continued
data bp;	
infile 'c:\alrm\chapter 11 data sets\ch11ta01.txt';	data step3;
input age dbp;	set results2;
line+1;	wt=1/(yhat**2);
proc reg;	proc print;
model dbp = age / r;	where line < 6;
output out=results1 r = residual;	proc reg;
data step2;	model dbp = age / clb;
set results1;	weight wt;
absresid=abs(residual);	run;
proc reg;	
model absresid = age / p;	
output out=results2 p = yhat;	
run;	

SAS Output 11.3

Obs	age	dbp	line	residual	absresid	yhat	wt
1	27	73	1	1.18224	1.18224	3.80117	0.06921
2	21	66	2	-2.33758	2.33758	2.61214	0.14656
3	22	63	3	-5.91761	5.91761	2.81031	0.12662
4	24	75	4	4.92233	4.92233	3.20666	0.09725
5	25	71	5	0.34230	0.34230	3.40483	0.08626

In *data step3* of Insert 11.2, we use weighted least squares to fit a regression model by regressing *dbp* on *age* using the statement *weight = wt* to specify *wt* as the weighting variable. We use the *clb* option in the model statement to get confidence limits for the model parameters. A partial output is shown in SAS Output 11.4 where we find:

$$\hat{Y} = 55.566 + 0.596\,X$$

and the 95% confidence interval is:

$$0.437 \le \beta_1 \le 0.755$$

consistent with text pages 428-429.

SAS Output 11.4

		Parameter Estimate	Standard Error	t Value	Pr > |t|	95% Confidence Limits	
Variable	DF						
Intercept	1	55.56577	2.52092	22.04	<.0001	50.50718	60.62436
age	1	0.59634	0.07924	7.53	<.0001	0.43734	0.75534

Multicollinearity Remedial Measures – Ridge Regression: One approach to estimating regression coefficients in the presence of multicollinearity among the predictor variables is to use a method known as *ridge regression*. The idea is to use estimators that have small bias but greater precision than their unbiased competitors. Let $\mathbf{r}_{XX}$ denote the correlation matrix of the X variables in the model of interest and let $\mathbf{r}_{XY}$ denote the vector of coefficients of simple correlation between Y and each X variable. The ridge standardized regression coefficients are:

$$\mathbf{b}^R = \left(\mathbf{r}_{XX} + c\mathbf{I}\right)^{-1}\mathbf{r}_{XY}$$

The constant c is the amount of bias in the estimators and $\mathbf{I}$ is the $(p-1)$ x $(p-1)$ *identity matrix*. When $c = 0$, $\mathbf{b}^R$ reduces to the standardized least squares estimators. When $c > 0$, the estimators are biased but more precise than ordinary least squares estimators. The strategy is to first obtain estimators based on $c = 0$. Then a small increment is added to c and another set of estimators is obtained. This process is continued for a large number of c values, usually values between 0 and 1. Then, we examine the *ridge trace* and *variance inflation factors* $(VIF)_k$ and try to choose the smallest value of c where the coefficients $\mathbf{b}^R$ first become stable and the $(VIF)_k$ are small. This requires judgement, but we take the value of $\mathbf{b}^R$ corresponding to the chosen c as the ridge estimate for the problem at hand. (See text page 434).

The Body Fat Example

Data File: ch07ta01.txt

On text page 434, a researcher studied the relationship between the amount of body fat (Y) and triceps skinfold thickness ($X1$), thigh circumference ($X2$), and midarm circumference ($X3$). See Chapter 0, "Working with SAS," for instructions on opening the Body Fat example data file and naming the variables. After opening the Body Fat example, the first 5 lines of output should look like SAS Output 11.5.

SAS Output 11.5

Obs	x1	x2	x3	y
1	19.5	43.1	29.1	11.9
2	24.7	49.8	28.2	22.8
3	30.7	51.9	37.0	18.7
4	29.8	54.3	31.1	20.1
5	19.1	42.2	30.9	12.9

In text Chapter 7, the researchers noted severe multicollinearity and decided that an appropriate alternative to ordinary least square regression was ridge regression. In Insert 11.3, we use *proc reg* and specify *outest = ridge* to request that variance inflation factors (*outvif*), standardized betas (*outstb*), and R^2 values be output to the *ridge* data set. The *ridge* = option requests a ridge regression analysis and specifies the values of the ridge constant k. (Here, k rather than c is used to represent the biasing constant.) Each value of k produces ridge regression estimates that are placed in the *outest = ridge* data set. The values of k are saved in the variable _RIDGE_. We write "*ridge = 0 to 1.0 by .002*" to specify the starting and ending constant value (biasing constant) and the value by which the constant will increment. We use the *plot* portion of the *proc reg* statement to produce SAS Output 11.6, which is consistent with Figure 11.3, text page 435. We use the two *proc print* statements to first print k and the standardized betas and then print k and the variance inflation factors. Partial results are shown in SAS Output 11.7 and are consistent with Tables 11.2 and 11.3, text page 434. Although we can print the variance inflation factors and standardized betas for each value of k, there is no readily available routine in SAS that will produce *r square* for a given biasing constant.

INSERT 11.3	**INSERT 11.3 continued**

data bodyfat;
  infile 'c:\alrm\chapter 7 data sets\ch07ta01.txt';
  input x1 x2 x3 y;
goptions reset=all;
proc reg outest = ridge outvif outstb rsquare ridge = 0 to 0.07 by .002;
  model y = x1 x2 x3 / influence vif;
  plot / ridgeplot;
  symbol1 value=dot color=black interpol=none;
  symbol2 value=circle color=black interpol=none;
 	
  symbol3 value=square color=black
	interpol=none;
	run;
	* print Table 11.2, text page 434;
	proc print data=ridge;
	  where _type_ = 'RIDGESTB';
	  var _ridge_ x1 x2 x3;
	run;
	* print Table 11.3, text page 434;
	proc print data=ridge;
	  where _type_ = 'RIDGEVIF'; var _ridge_ x1 x2 x3;
	
	run;

SAS Output 11.6

SAS Output 11.7

Obs	_RIDGE_	x1	x2	x3
4	0.000	4.26370	-2.92870	-1.56142
7	0.002	1.44066	-0.41129	-0.48127
10	0.004	1.00632	-0.02484	-0.31487
13	0.006	0.83002	0.13142	-0.24716
16	0.008	0.73433	0.21576	-0.21030

We can use the *ridge = value* statement to specify a single constant value (biasing constant) with which to produce estimated regression coefficients. Insert 11.4, for instance, we request a *ridge regression* using a *biasing constant* = 0.02. Partial (truncated) results are shown in SAS Output 11.8 and are consistent with the fitted regression model on text page 435.

INSERT 11.4

```
data bodyfat;
  infile 'c:\alrm\chapter  7 data sets\ch07ta01.txt';
  input x1 x2 x3 y;
proc reg outest = ridge outvif outstb ridge = .02;
  model y = x1 x2 x3;
 run;
proc print;
 where _type_ = 'RIDGESTB';
 var _ridge_ x1 x2 x3 ;
 run;
```

Obs	_RIDGE_	x1	x2	x3
4	0.02	0.54633	0.37740	-0.13687

Remedial Measures for Influential Cases - Iteratively Reweighted Least Squares (IRLS) Robust Regression. The text authors state "For robust regression, weighted least squares is used to reduce the influence of outlying cases by employing weights that vary inversely with the size of the residual. Outlying cases that have large residuals are thereby given smaller weights. The weights are revised as each iteration yields new residuals until the estimation process stabilizes." Two widely used weight functions, the *Huber* and *bisquare weight functions*, are described. These functions are used to dampen the effect of outlying observations.

Mathematics Proficiency Example

Data File: ch11ta04.txt

On text page 441, a researcher studied the relationship between the home environment and aggregate school performance (mathematics proficiency) for 37 states, the District of Columbia, Guam, and the Virgin Islands. The data are given by state and states are the study units in this example. The average mathematics proficiency score, denoted *Y*, is the dependent variable of interest. The predictor variables are parents (*X1*), home library (*X2*), reading (*X3*), watch TV (*X4*), and absences (*X5*). This example considers only the predictor variable *X2* (home library) which represents the percentage of eighth-grade students who had three or more types of reading materials at home. See Chapter 0, "Working with SAS," for instructions on opening the Mathematics Proficiency example data file and naming the variables. After opening the Mathematics Proficiency data file, the first 5 lines of output should look like SAS Output 11.9.

SAS Output 11.9

Obs	state	y	x1	x2	x3	x4	x5
1	Alabama	252	75	78	34	18	18
2	Arizona	259	75	73	41	12	26
3	Arkansas	256	77	77	28	20	23
4	Califom	256	78	68	42	11	28
5	Colorado	267	78	85	38	9	25

To produce the scatter plots (a) and (b) on text page 442 we first regress *Y* on *X2* and save the residuals (*residuals*). (Insert 11.5) We then use *proc gplot* to request a *scatter plot* of *Y* and *X2* (SAS Output 11.10) and *residual* and *X2* (SAS Output 11.11). From the plots, we notice that there are 3 states with outlying *Y* values (mathematics proficiency scores). Also, there are 6 states with low *X2* scores (resources) whose math proficiency scores are above the fitted regression line. We also issue *proc loess* to get the lowess regression fit as shown on Figure 11.5 (a), text page 442. (SAS Output not shown)

```
data math;
infile 'c:\alrm\chapter 11 data sets\ch11ta04.txt';
input state $  y x1 x2 x3 x4;
proc reg;
 model y = x2 / r;
  output out=results r = residual;
run;
goptions reset=all;
proc gplot;
 plot y*x2;
  symbol1 value=dot color=black interpol=rl;
 plot residual*x2;
  symbol1 value=dot color=black interpol=rl;
run;
proc loess data = math;
  model y = x2 / smooth = 0.5 to 0.8 by 0.1 residual;
  ods output OutputStatistics = Results;
run;
data step2;
  set results;
proc sort;
  by SmoothingParameter x2;
 run;
goptions reset=all;
proc gplot;
  by SmoothingParameter;
  symbol1 color=black value=none interpol=join ;
  symbol2 color=black value=circle;
   plot Pred*x2 DepVar*x2 / overlay ;
run;
```

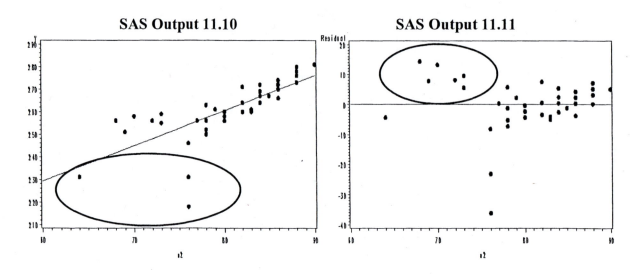

SAS Output 11.10   **SAS Output 11.11**

The researchers considered a second order model using *X2* (*homelib*) centered, and its square as the single predictor variable (equation 11.48, text page 443). To diminish the effect of outliers the researchers used *iteratively reweighted least squares* and the *Huber weight function*. We detail each step in the following and in Insert 11.7, although the output for each step is not shown. We begin in Insert 11.7 by centering *X2* (*x2cnt*) and finding the square of the centered variable (*x2cnt2*). Next, we issue *proc reg* and specify "*model y = x2cnt x2cnt2 / r*" to fit the second order model and compute the residuals. We then:

1) Save the unstandardized residuals in a data file named *step2* under the variable name *resid*.

2) Use *proc univariate* to find the median value (*median*$\{e_i\}$) of *resid* = 0.70629.

3) Compute (name arbitrary) *v1*, the absolute value of *resid* minus the median of the residuals ($|e_i - median\{e_i\}|$).

4) Find the median of [*median*$\{|e_i - median\{e_i\}|\}$] *v1* = 3.1488.

5) Use *proc univariate* to find the median absolute deviation estimator (*MAD*) = *median of v1 − constant* = 0.6745 (3.1488 / 0.6745) = 4.6683.

6) Compute the scaled residual, *u1* = *resid* ÷ *mad* = *resid* ÷ 4.6683.

7) Use the scaled residual in the computation of the Huber weight (*w*), where *w* = 1 if the absolute value of *u1* ≤ 1.345 and *w* = (1.345 / *absolute value of u1*) if the *absolute value of u1* > 1.345.

8) Regress *y* on *x2cnt* and *x2cnt2* using *w* as a weighting variable and save the unstandardized residuals. This produces the regression model: $\hat{Y} = 259.39 + 1.670\,x_2 + 0.064\,x_2^2$. The *proc print* statement in Step 8 of Insert 11.7 requests the current Huber weights (*w*) and residual values (*resid2*) as shown in SAS Output 11.12. These values are identical to columns 3 and 4 of Table 11.5, text page 444.

9) Return to Step 2 for the second iteration and use the residuals saved in Step 8 for the next iteration.

```
data math;
infile 'c:\alrm\chapter 11 data sets\ch11ta04.txt';
input state $  y x1 x2 x3 x4;
x2cnt=x2-80.4;
x2cnt2=x2cnt**2;
*  STEP 1;
proc reg;
 model y = x2cnt x2cnt2 / r;
 output out=step2 residual = resid;
run;
*  STEP 2;
proc univariate data = step2;
 var resid;
run;
*  STEP 3;
data new;
 set step2;
  v1 = abs(resid - 0.70629);
run;
```

```
*  STEP 4;
proc univariate;
 var v1;
run;
*  STEPS 5, 6 & 7;
data new;
 set step2;
  mad=3.1488 /.6745;
  u = resid / mad;
  if abs(u)<= 1.345 then wt=1;
  if abs(u) > 1.345 then wt=(1.345/abs(u));
run;
*  STEP 8;
proc reg;
 weight wt;
 model y = x2cnt x2cnt2 / r;
  output out=step3 residual = resid2;
run;
proc print data=step3;
 var wt resid2;
run;
```

SAS Output 11.12

Obs	wt	resid2
1	1.00000	-3.7542
2	0.59390	8.4297
3	1.00000	1.5411
4	0.60899	7.3822
5	1.00000	-1.4402

Nonparametric Regression: SAS/STAT uses proc loess for performing nonparametric regression using the lowess method. To our knowledge, SAS/STAT does not currently have a readily available method for performing regression trees.

Remedial Measures for Evaluating precision in Nonstandard Situations – Bootstrapping
To our knowledge, SAS/STAT has no readily available procedure for performing a bootstrap analysis in this application.

Autocorrelation in Time Series Data

In the context of the generalized multiple regression model, a time series is a set of data collected by observing a random variable and one or more independent variables at each time in a sequence of times. For example, company sales (the dependent variable) and industry sales (the independent variable) could be observed quarterly over a five-year interval. Or, net income (the dependent variable), gross revenues, and labor costs (the independent variables) for a company could be observed monthly over a three-year period. The error terms for regression models for times series data are often correlated and are, therefore, referred to as being *autocorrelated* or *serially correlated*. A generalized multiple regression model in which the error terms are autocorrelated is called an *autoregressive error model*. In this chapter, the authors of the text introduce the concept of *autocorrelation* and associated *autoregressive error models*. They discuss the *Durbin-Watson test for autocorrelation* as a means for detecting *autocorrelation* among the error terms of a model. They then discuss remedial measures for dealing with data where *autocorrelation* has been detected.

The Blaisdell Company Example

Data File: ch12ta02.txt

The Blaisdell Company (text page 488) used a trade association record of industry sales to predict their own sales. See Chapter 0, "Working with SAS," for instructions on opening the Blaisdell Company data file and naming the variables *company* and *industry*. After opening ch12ta02.txt, the first 5 lines of output should look like SAS Output 12.1.

SAS Output 12.1

Obs	company	industry
1	20.96	127.3
2	21.40	130.0
3	21.96	132.7
4	21.52	129.4
5	22.39	135.0

In Insert 12.1, we begin the analysis by producing a scatter plot of the company and industry sales data. (SAS Output 12.2) Since the scatter plot suggested that a linear regression model might be appropriate, the analyst working with Blaisdell Company fitted an ordinary least squares regression model and saved the unstandardized residuals (*residual*). To plot the residuals against time, we used the *time+1* statement in Insert 12.1 to create a sequential record number for each line in the Blaisdell Company data file. A plot of the residuals against *time* is shown in SAS Output 12.3.

INSERT 12.1	INSERT 12.1 Continued

* Produce Scatter Plot Output 12.2;
data Blaisdell;
  infile 'c:\alrm\chapter 12 data sets\ch12ta02.txt';
  input company industry;
time+1;
proc gplot;
 plot company*industry;
 run;
	proc reg;
	 model company = industry / r;
	  output out=results r=residual;
	run;
	data results;
	 set results;
	
	* Produce Scatter Plot Output 12.3;
	proc gplot;
	 symbol value=dot color=black interpol=none vref=0;
	 plot residual*time;
	 run;

SAS Output 12.2   SAS Output 12.3

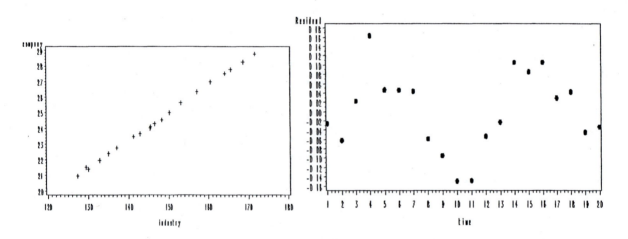

Durbin-Watson Test for Autocorrelation: Since SAS Output 12.3 indicates a positive autocorrelation in the error terms, the analyst produced the *Durbin-Watson Test for Autocorrelation*. To request the *Durbin-Watson* test, we use the first regression procedure in Insert 12.1 and modify the *model* statement to read, "*model company = industry / dw;*". Partial output is shown in SAS Output 12.4. The Durbin-Watson value = 0.735 as reported on text page 488. Using Table B.7, text page 675, we conclude that the error terms are positively autocorrelated.

SAS Output 12.4

Durbin-Watson D	0.735
Number of Observations	20
1st Order Autocorrelation	0.626

Cochrane-Orcutt Procedure: On text page 492, the analyst first used the *Cochrane-Orcutt procedure* to estimate the autocorrelation parameter ρ. Column 1 (e_t) of Table 12.3, text page 493, contains the residual values for the regression model fitted in Insert 12.1. Each line in text Table 12.3, column 2, is the residual value in column 1 for the preceding time period. In Insert 12.2, we use SAS' *Lag operation* that takes the form, *new=lag(old)* where *new* is the value of *old* for the previous case. That is, we use [*res_m1=lag(residual)*] to compute a new variable, *res_m1*, that is equal to the residual (*residual*) of the preceding time period (line) in the data file. This produces text Table 12.3, column 2, denoted by the symbol e_{t-1}. We also find *etm1et=residual*res_m1* which is the residual times the lagged residual. This produces text Table 12.3, column 3, denoted $e_{t-1}e_t$. We then square the lagged residual [*compute etm1et2=res_m1**2*] to produce text Table 12.3, column 4, denoted e_{t-1}^2. Finally, in SAS Output 12.5, we find the sum of *etm1et* = 0.0834478 and *etm1et2* = 0.1322127. We now obtain *r*, an estimate of ρ, by equation 12.22, text page 492:

$$r = 0.0834479 / 0.1333023 = 0.631166$$

INSERT 12.2	INSERT 12.2 continued

data Blaisdell;
  infile 'c:\alrm\chapter 12 data sets\ch12ta02.txt';
  input company industry;
time+1;
proc reg;
 model company = industry / r;
  output out=results r=residual;
run;
	*Produce Output 12.5;
	data results;
	 set results;
	res_m1=lag(residual);
	etm1et=residual*res_m1;
	etm1et2=res_m1**2;
	proc means sum;
	 var etm1et etm1et2;
	run;
	*Produce Output 12.6;
	data results;
	 set results;
	ypt=company-.631166*lag(company);
	xpt=industry-.631166*lag(industry);
	proc print;
	run;

SAS Output 12.5

Variable	Sum
etm1et	0.0834479
etm1et2	0.1322127

In Insert 12.2, we use equation 12.18, text page 491, to find Y_t' (*ypt*) and X_t' (*xpt*). This produces the 3rd and 4th columns of Table 12.4, text page 493. To complete the *Cochrane-Orcutt* procedure, we then regress *ytp* on *xpt* and request the Durbin-Watson statistic (syntax not show). Partial results are shown in SAS Output 12.6. The Durbin-Watson statistic = 1.65, consistent with text page 494. This leads to the conclusion that the autocorrelation of error terms is not significantly different from zero. From SAS Output 12.6 we note that $b_0' = -0.394$, $b_1' = 0.174$, $s\{b_0'\} = 0.16723$, and $s\{b_1'\} = 0.00296$. We use equation 12.20, text pages 491-492, to transform back to a fitted regression model in terms of the original variables and equation 12.21 to obtain estimated standard deviations of the back-transformed fitted model coefficients (syntax not shown).

SAS Output 12.6

Durbin-Watson D	1.650
Number of Observations	19
1st Order Autocorrelation	0.147

Parameter Estimates					
Variable	DF	Parameter Estimate	Standard Error	t Value	Pr > |t|
Intercept	1	-0.39411	0.16723	-2.36	0.0307
xpt	1	0.17376	0.00296	58.77	<.0001

Hildreth-Lu Procedure: The *Hildreth-Lu procedure* uses the value of ρ that minimizes the error sum of squares (*SSE*) for the transformed regression model. As noted in the text, we can repeatedly fit regression models while varying the value of ρ to find the value that minimizes *SSE*. An efficient method of producing Table 12.5, text page 495, is to use SAS' *IML* procedure to automatically perform the numerical search across a large range of ρ values as in Insert 12.3.

In Insert 12.3, use the *lag operation* to find Y_{t-1} (*ylag*) and X_{t-1} (*xlag*). Since there are 20 lines of data in the file with values for *company* and *industry*, the first line will have a missing value for the lagged variables *ylag* and *xlag*. If we read *ylag* and *xlag* into matrices and subsequently attempt to perform arithmetic using these variables, we will get an error due to the ***xlag*** and ***ylag*** vectors containing missing values. To circumvent the problem of missing values in the first row of these vectors, we read all variables into vectors that begin with a *t*, e.g., *txlag*. We then set a new vector equal to the 2nd through 20th row of the vector that begins with *t*, *xlag=txlag[2:20]* so that ***xlag*** now contains 19 rows that are equal to the last 19 rows of ***txlag*** 20x1 column vector.

To reproduce the *Hildreth-Lu* results shown in Table12.5, text page 495, we calculate *SSE* for a range of ρ values from 0.01 to 1.0 in increments of 0.01 (*do r=.01 to 1.0 by .01;*). We find X_t'

(*xstep1*) and concatenate *X0* (a column vectors of 1's) and *xstep1* to form matrix **xmat**. We find $Y_t^{'}$ (*ystep*) (also from equation 12.17, text page 491) and use this as our "*Y*" matrix. Finally, we use equations 5.60 and 5.85a, text pages 200 and 204, respectively, to find the *b* matrix and **SSE**. The numerical output from this insert (not shown) is consistent with the selected values of ρ and corresponding *SSE* values shown on Table 12.5, text page 495.

INSERT 12.3

```
data blaisdell;
 infile 'c:\alrm\chapter 12 data sets\ch12ta02.txt';
 input company industry;
x0=1;
ylag=lag(company);
xlag=lag(industry);
proc iml;
  use blaisdell;
  read all var {'x0'} into tx0;
  read all var {'xlag'} into txlag;
  read all var {'industry'} into tindustry;
  read all var {'ylag'} into tylag;
  read all var {'company'} into tcompany;
x0=tx0[2:20];
xlag=txlag[2:20];
industry=tindustry[2:20];
ylag=tylag[2:20];
company=tcompany[2:20];
do r=.01 to 1.0 by .01;
xstep1=industry-(r*xlag);
xmat=(x0||xstep1);
ystep1=company-(r*ylag);
* Find b matrix by text equation 5.56;
b=inv(t(xmat)*xmat)*t(xmat)*ystep1;
* Find sse by text equation 5.84a;
sse=t(ystep1)*ystep1-t(b)*t(xmat)*ystep1;
print r [format = 4.2] "   " sse [format = 6.5];
end;
quit;
```

First Difference Procedure: On text page 496, the analyst used the *First Difference procedure* where $\rho = 1.0$ for the transformed model (equation 12.17, text page 491), where $Y_t^{'} = Y_t - Y_{t-1}$ and $X_t^{'} = X_t - X_{t-1}$, and the regression model is based on "regression through the origin." In Insert 12.4, we compute $Y_t^{'}$ (*fdyp*) and $X_t^{'}$ (*fdxp*) using the *lag operation*. We then regress *fdyp* on *fdxp*, and specify that the fitted model has no intercept (*noint*). This results in SAS Output 12.7 and a fitted regression model $\hat{Y}^{'} = 0.168X^{'}$. To produce the Durbin-Watson statistic, we run the same regression model as above except we include the intercept term in the model. SAS Output 12.8 shows the Durbin-Watson statistic, which is consistent with text page 497.

INSERT 12.4

```
data Blaisdell;
  infile 'c:\alrm\chapter 12 data sets\ch12ta02.txt';
  input company industry;
fdyp=company-lag(company);
fdxp=industry-lag(industry);
proc reg;
 model fdyp = fdxp / noint;
 run;
proc reg;
 model fdyp = fdxp / dw;
 run;
```

SAS Output 12.7

		Parameter Estimates			
Variable	DF	Parameter Estimate	Standard Error	t Value	Pr > |t|
fdxp	1	0.16849	0.00510	33.06	<.0001

SAS Output 12.8

Durbin-Watson D	1.749
Number of Observations	19
1st Order Autocorrelation	0.116

We use equation 12.31, text pages 496-497, to transform the coefficients of the fitted model back to coefficients of a model fitted in terms of the original variables. If in the first regression procedure in Insert 12.1, we had modified the *proc reg* statement to read, "*proc reg simple;*" we would have obtained SAS Output 12.9. We use equation 12.31a and 12.31b, respectively, and SAS Output 12.7 and 12.9 to find:

$$b_0 = \overline{Y} - b_1' \overline{X}$$

$$b_0 = 24.5690 - 0.168(147.6250) = -0.30349$$

and

$$b_1 = b_1'$$

$$b_1 = 0.16849$$

134

Thus, the fitted model in terms of the original variables is:

$$\hat{Y} = -.30349 + 0.16849X$$

SAS Output 12.9

Descriptive Statistics					
Variable	Sum	Mean	Uncorrected SS	Variance	Standard Deviation
Intercept	20.00000	1.00000	20.00000	0	0
industry	2952.50000	147.62500	439411	186.73776	13.66520
company	491.38000	24.56900	12183	5.81001	2.41040

Forecasting with Autocorrelated Error Terms

Forecasting Based on Cochrane-Orcutt Estimates: On text page 500, the analyst forecasts the Blaisdell Company sales for the 21st quarter. The trade association's estimate for this quarter is $175.3 million. We use the *Cochrane-Orcutt* results presented in Insert 12.2 and SAS Output 12.6 where:

$$\hat{Y} = -0.3941 + 0.17376X'$$

We transform the model back to the original variables as shown on text page 497, which leads to:

$$\hat{Y} = -1.0685 + 0.17376X$$

In Insert 12.5, we find X_t' (*xpt*) and Y_t' (*ypt*) for subsequent use and set the estimate of ρ: (r) = 0.631166. We find (*e*) $e_{20} = Y_{20} - \hat{Y}_{20}$ where $Y_{20} = 28.78$ and $\hat{Y}_{20} = -1.0685 + 0.17376*171.7$. Using the above fitted regression model, the predicted value (*yhat*) $\hat{Y}_{21}$ when the independent variable is $X_{21} = 175.3$, is $-1.0685 + 0.17376*175.3 = 29.392$. We then compute F_{21} (*forcast*) = $\hat{Y}_{21} + re_{20} = 29.40$. We find X_{n+1}' where $X_{n+1} = 175.3$ (X_{21} above), $r = 0.631166$, and $X_{20} = 171.7$. Thus:

$$X_{n+1}' = 175.3 - 0.631166*171.7 = 66.629$$

Using the above numerical results, we find $s\{pred\}$ using equation 2.38, text page 59. Here, *MSE* = 0.0045097 (regress *ypt* on *xpt*), $(X_h - \bar{X})^2 = [(66.929 - 56.3186)**2]$, and $\sum(X_i - \bar{X})^2 = 515.8551$. Thus, text equation 2.38a:

$$s^2\{pred\} = MSE\left[1 + \frac{1}{n} + \frac{(X_h - \overline{X})^2}{\sum(X_i - \overline{X})^2}\right]$$

where $n = 19$, $X_h = X'_{n+1}$, $\overline{X}$ = mean of XPT, and $X_i = XPT_i$, becomes:

$$s\{pred\} = \sqrt{0.004509\left[1 + \frac{1}{19} + \frac{(66.929 - 56.3186)^2}{515.8551}\right]}$$

The value of $spred$ = 0.07570 is consistent with text page 500. Finally, we find $tvalue$ = $idf.t(.975,17)$ = 2.11 and then compute the lower ($cilo$) and upper ($cihi$) prediction intervals as F_{21} ($forcast$) = $29.40 \pm 2.11 * 0.0757$ or $29.24 \leq Y_{21(new)} \leq 29.56$.

INSERT 12.5

```
data Blaisdell;
  infile 'c:\alrm\chapter 12 data sets\ch12ta02.txt';
  input company industry;
ypt=company-.631166*lag(company);
xpt=industry-.631166*lag(industry);
r = 0.631166;
e = company-(-1.0685+(.17376*industry));
yhat = -1.0685+(.17376*175.3);
forecast = yhat+(r*e);
* Use text equation 2.38 to find s{pred} (spred);
* Find mean of xpt=56.3186 using proc means;
proc means;
 var xpt;
run;
data blaisdell;
 set blaisdell;
xptdif2=(xpt-56.3186)**2;
* Find sum of xptdif2 = 515.8551 using Analyze > Descriptives and Sum Option;
proc means sum;
 var xptdif2;
data blaisdell;
 set blaisdell;
spred=sqrt(0.0045097+ (0.0045097*((1/19)+(((66.929- 56.3186)**2)/515.8551))));
tvalue=tinv(.975,17);
cilo=29.4-(tvalue*spred);
cihi=29.4+(tvalue*spred);
proc print data=blaisdell (obs=1);
 var cilo cihi;
 run;
```

Forecasting Based on First Difference Estimates: On text page 501, the authors use the first differences fitted regression function to forecast sales for quarter 21. To find F_{21} we recall that the first part of the expression $[(-0.30349 + 0.16849*(175.3)]$ comes from equation 12.33, text page 497, and from $X_{21} = 175.3$ above. The latter part of the expression $\{1.0[28.78 + 0.30349 - 0.16849*171.70)]\}$ comes from text equation 12.33, the fact that $\rho = 1.0$ in the *First Difference* model, and $X_{20} = 171.70$. The forecasted value for the 21st quarter is $F_{21} = 29.39$ as shown on text page 501. We find the prediction intervals using equation 4.20, text page 162. We first find X_h^2 (*xh2*), which is the forecasted value (F_{21}) squared. We then find X_i^2 (*fdxp2*) and, subsequently, use *Descriptives* to find the sum of *fdxp2* = 185.42. We find X_{n+1}' (*xnp1*) = X_{21} - (r* X_{20}) where X_{20} = *industry*$_{20}$. The MSE = 0.00482 is from regressing *fdyp* on *fdxp* and specifying the fitted model with no intercept term. The statistic *tvalue* [*tinv*(.975,18)] is based on 18 *df*. First, 19 of the original 20 records were used in the analysis because we "lost" a record when we lagged to get *xpt* and *ypt*. (This was also true for the *Cochrane-Orcutt* procedure above where we used 17 *df* (*n*–2) to find *tvalue*.) We have 18 *df* (*n*–1) here because we estimated only 1 parameter (β_1) (this model has no intercept term.) We then find the 95% prediction intervals for $F_{21} = 29.39$ as shown on text page 501: $29.24 \leq Y_{21(new)} \leq 29.52$

INSERT 12.6

```
data Blaisdell;
  infile 'c:\alrm\chapter 12 data sets\ch12ta02.txt';
  input company industry;
fdyp=company-lag(company);
fdxp=industry-lag(industry);
xh2=29.39**2;
fdxp2=fdxp**2;
xnp1=175.3-(1.0*171.7);
xnp12=xnp1**2;
* find sum of fdxp2=185.42;
proc means sum;
 var fdxp2;
 run;
data blaisdell;
 set blaisdell;
spred=sqrt(.00482*(1+(12.96/185.42)));
tvalue=tinv(.975,18);
cilo=29.39-(tvalue*spred);
cihi=29.39+(tvalue*spred);
proc print data=blaisdell (obs=1);
 var cilo cihi;
run;
```

Forecasting Based on Hildreth-Lu Estimates: On text page 501, the authors find the 95 percent prediction interval based on the *Hildreth-Lu* procedure. Similar to the *Cochrane-Orcutt* procedure above, we first find Y_t' (*ytp*) and X_t' (*xpt*) using text equation 12.17, and set $r = 0.96$ as shown in Table 12.5, text page 495. (Insert 12.7) We transform the fitted regression model (equation 12.28, text page 496) back to a fitted model in terms of the original variables to obtain: $\hat{Y} = 1.7793 + .16045X$. We use this model to calculate e and $yhat$. Since X'_{n+1} is not given, we compute $xnp1 = X_{21} - (r * X_{20}) = X'_{n+1}$ (note that $X_{20} = industry_{20}$). We use equation 2.38, text page 59, to find $s^2\{pred\}$ ($spred$) where MSE is the mean square error from regressing ypt on xpt. The lower ($cilo$) and upper ($cihi$) prediction intervals are obtained by printing the 20th line in the current data set.

INSERT 12.7

```
data Blaisdell;
  infile 'c:\alrm\chapter 12 data sets\ch12ta02.txt';
  input company industry;
  line+1;
r = 0.96;
ypt=company-r*lag(company);
xpt=industry-r*lag(industry);
e = company-(1.7793+(.16045*industry));
yhat = 1.7793+(.16045*175.3);
forecast = yhat+(r*e);
xnp1=175.3-(.96*171.7);
* Use text equation 2.38 to find s{pred} (spred);
* Find mean of xpt=8.1912 using proc means;
proc means;
 var xpt;
 run;
data blaisdell;
 set blaisdell;
xptdif2=(xpt-8.1912)**2;
* Find sum of xptdif2 = 90.1088 using proc menas Sum Option;
proc means sum;
 var xptdif2;
 run;
data blaisdell;
 set blaisdell;
spred=sqrt(0.00422+ (0.00422*((1/19)+(((10.468- 8.1911)**2)/90.1088))));
tvalue=tinv(.975,17);
cilo=forecast-(tvalue*spred);
cihi=forecast+(tvalue*spred);
proc print;
 where line=20;
 var cilo cihi;
 run;
```

Chapter 13 SAS®

Non Linear Regression

The general linear regression model is:

$$Y_i = \beta_0 + \beta_1 X_{i1} + \beta_2 X_{i2} + \ldots + \beta_{p-1} X_{i,p-1} + \varepsilon_i$$

In this model, Y_i is a linear function of the $\beta's$ (the parameters). The general linear regression model can also be expressed as:

$$Y_i = f(\mathbf{X}_i, \boldsymbol{\beta}) + \varepsilon_i$$

where $\mathbf{X}_i$ is the vector of predictor variables for the ith subject, β is the vector of model parameters, and

$$f(\mathbf{X}_i, \boldsymbol{\beta}) = \beta_0 + \beta_1 X_{i1} + \beta_2 X_{i2} + \ldots + \beta_{p-1} X_{i,p-1}$$

The nonlinear regression model can be expressed as (text page 511):

$$Y_i = f(\mathbf{X}_i, \boldsymbol{\gamma}) + \varepsilon_i$$

In this representation of the nonlinear regression model, the authors use γ to denote the vector of parameters rather than β as a reminder that in this model $f(\mathbf{X}_i, \boldsymbol{\gamma})$ is a nonlinear function of the parameters.

Estimation of the parameters of a nonlinear regression model is usually based on the method of least squares or the method of maximum likelihood. However, it is usually not possible to find closed form "formulas" for the estimators of the parameters of nonlinear regression models. Instead, iterative search procedures are required. Thus, although the approach to finding estimators is the same as that used for linear regression models, the computations are much more tedious.

The problem reduces to one of finding values of the parameters that maximize (minimize) a nonlinear function of the parameters. Many search procedures have been developed for finding the maxima (minima) of nonlinear functions. SAS offers five methods for estimating regression parameters and statistics for models that are not linear in their parameters. The default method is Gauss-Newton. Other available options that may be specified (e.g., *proc nlin method=marquardt;*) are Marquardt, Newton, Gradient, and DUD.

Severely Injured Patients Example

Data File: ch13ta01.txt.

A hospital administrator wanted to predict long-term recovery among a group of severely injured patients (text page 514). The predictor variable used in the regression model was number of days of hospitalization and the response variable was a long-term recovery index measure. See Chapter 0, "Working with SAS," for instructions on opening the Severely Injured Patient data file and naming the variables *index* and *days*. After opening ch13ta01.txt, the first 5 lines of output should look like SAS Output 13.1.

SAS Output 13.1

Obs	index	days
1	54	2
2	50	5
3	45	7
4	37	10
5	35	14

The administrator began by producing a scatter plot (Insert 13.1 – SAS Output 13.2) of the data, which suggested an exponential relationship between number of days hospitalized and long-term recovery. A review of related literature also suggested an exponential relationship. Thus, the administrator explored the appropriateness of a two-parameter nonlinear exponential regression model (text page 514).

INSERT 13.1

```
data Injured;
   infile 'c:\alrm\chapter 13 data sets\ch13ta01.txt';
   input index days;
goptions reset=all;
proc gplot;
   symbol color=black value=circle;
    plot index*days;
run;
```

SAS Output 13.2

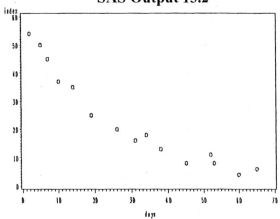

To fit this nonlinear regression model, we first find the initial starting values $g_0^{(0)}$ and $g_1^{(0)}$ (text page 521). We create a new variable, *logy*, the logarithmic transformation of *index*, and perform an ordinary least squares regression using *logy* as the response variable and *days* as the predictor variable using the syntax shown in Insert 13.2. From SAS Output 13.3, we find the parameter estimates for this model to be $b_0 = 4.0371$ and $b_1 = -0.03797$. Using a hand-held calculator, we find $g_0^{(0)} =$ exponential of $b_0 = \exp(4.0371) = 56.6646$ and $g_1^{(0)} = b_1 = -0.03797$ (text page 521). We now use SAS *proc nlin* as shown in Insert 13.3 to produce estimates of the parameters of the nonlinear model and related results. The final least square estimates, including the *MSE*, shown in SAS Output 14.4 are consistent with Table 13.3, text page 524. The 95% confidence intervals for β_0 and β_1 are also shown in SAS Output 13.4.

INSERT 13.2

```
data Injured;
 infile 'c:\alrm\chapter 13 data sets\ch13ta01.txt';
 input index days;
logy=log(index);
goptions reset=all;
proc reg;
 model logy = days;
run;
```

INSERT 13.3

```
data Injured;
 infile 'c:\alrm\chapter 13 data sets\ch13ta01.txt';
 input index days;
logy=log(index);
proc nlin;
 parms g0 = 56.6646 g1 = -0.03797;
 model index = g0*exp(g1*days);
run;
```

SAS Output 13.3

		Parameter Estimates			
Variable	**DF**	**Parameter Estimate**	**Standard Error**	**t Value**	**Pr > |t|**
Intercept	1	4.03716	0.08410	48.00	<.0001
days	1	-0.03797	0.00228	-16.62	<.0001

SAS Output 13.4

Iter	g0	g1	Sum of Squares
0	56.6646	-0.0380	56.0867
1	58.5578	-0.0395	49.4638
2	58.6055	-0.0396	49.4593
3	58.6065	-0.0396	49.4593

NOTE: Convergence criterion met.

Estimation Summary	
Method	Gauss-Newton
Iterations	3
R	9.015E-6
PPC(g1)	1.405E-6
RPC(g1)	0.000043
Object	7.896E-8
Objective	49.4593
Observations Read	15
Observations Used	15
Observations Missing	0

NOTE: An intercept was not specified for this model.

Source	DF	Sum of Squares	Mean Square	F Value	Approx Pr > F
Regression	2	12060.5	6030.3	1585.01	<.0001
Residual	13	49.4593	3.8046		
Uncorrected Total	15	12110.0			
Corrected Total	14	3943.3			

Parameter	Estimate	Approx Std Error	Approximate 95% Confidence Limits	
g0	58.6065	1.4722	55.4261	61.7869
g1	-0.0396	0.00171	-0.0433	-0.0359

Approximate Correlation Matrix		
	g0	g1
g0	1.0000000	-0.7071473
g1	-0.7071473	1.0000000

On text page 530, the authors generated bootstrap samples to check the appropriateness of large-sample inferences. To our knowledge, SAS/STAT has no readily available procedure for generating bootstrap samples in this application.

Learning Curve Example

Data File: ch13ta04.txt

An electronic products manufacturer produces a new product at two different locations: location A ($X1$=1) and location B ($X1$=0). (Text page 533) The response variable was relative efficiency, a measure related to production costs at each location. See Chapter 0, "Working with SAS," for instructions on opening the Learning Curve Example data file and naming the variables $X1$, $X2$, and Y. After opening ch13ta04.txt, the first 5 lines of output should look like SAS Output 13.5.

143

Obs	x1	x2	y
1	1	1	0.483
2	1	2	0.539
3	1	3	0.618
4	1	5	0.707
5	1	7	0.762

It was well known that production efficiency of a new product initially increases with time and then levels off. We use the syntax in Insert 13.4 to produce the scatter plot of relative efficiency (*Y*) and time (*X2*) with separate symbols to be used for Locations A and B (SAS Output 13.6). The engineers decided to fit an exponential model that used location (*X1*) and the relationship between relative efficiency (*Y*) and time (*X2*). The selected nonlinear model (equation 13.38, text page 534) was:

$$Y_i = \gamma_0 + \gamma_1 X_{i1} + \gamma_3 \exp(\gamma_2 X_{i2}) + \varepsilon_i$$

On text page 535, the authors detailed the rationale for determining the starting values for estimates of the parameters: $g_0^{(0)} = 1.025$, $g_1^{(0)} = -0.0459$, $g_2^{(0)} - 0.122$, and $g_3^{(0)} = -0.5$. Continuing in Insert 13.4, we specify *proc nonlin* and define the above non-linear regression model to be used in the nonlinear regression analysis. Results are shown in Output 13.8 and are consistent with Table 13.5, text page 535.

INSERT 13.4

```
data learning;
   infile 'c:\alrm\chapter 13 data sets\ch13ta04.txt';
   input x1 x2 y;
*Produce scatter plot shown in Figure 13.5, text page 534
proc gplot;
   symbol1 color=black value=circle interpol=join;
   symbol2 color=black value=dot i=join;
   plot y*x2=x1;
   run;
*Perform nonlinear regression analysis
proc nlin;
  parms g0 = 1.025 g1 = -0.0459 g2 = -.122 g3 = -0.5 ;
  model y = g0+g1*x1+g3*(exp(g2*x2));
  run;
```

SAS Output 13.6

SAS Output 13.8

Iter	g0	g1	g2	g3	Sum of Squares
0	1.0250	-0.0459	-0.1220	-0.5000	0.0160
1	1.0157	-0.0473	-0.1343	-0.5505	0.00330
2	1.0156	-0.0473	-0.1348	-0.5524	0.00329
3	1.0156	-0.0473	-0.1348	-0.5524	0.00329
4	1.0156	-0.0473	-0.1348	-0.5524	0.00329

NOTE: Convergence criterion met.

Estimation Summary	
Method	Gauss-Newton
Iterations	4
R	6.969E-6
PPC(g2)	1.149E-6
RPC(g2)	0.000017

Estimation Summary	
Object	1.08E-8
Objective	0.003293
Observations Read	30
Observations Used	30
Observations Missing	0

Source	DF	Sum of Squares	Mean Square	F Value	Approx Pr > F
Regression	4	22.8541	5.7135	2272.64	<.0001
Residual	26	0.00329	0.000127		
Uncorrected Total	30	22.8574			
Corrected Total	29	0.8667			

Parameter	Estimate	Approx Std Error	Approximate 95% Confidence Limits	
g0	1.0156	0.00367	1.0081	1.0231
g1	-0.0473	0.00411	-0.0557	-0.0388
g2	-0.1348	0.00436	-0.1438	-0.1258
g3	-0.5524	0.00816	-0.5692	-0.5357

Approximate Correlation Matrix				
	g0	g1	g2	g3
g0	1.0000000	-0.5595744	0.4112806	-0.1441959
g1	-0.5595744	1.0000000	-0.0000000	-0.0000000
g2	0.4112806	-0.0000000	1.0000000	0.5603318
g3	-0.1441959	-0.0000000	0.5603318	1.0000000

Neural Networks

On text page 537, the authors introduce Neural Network Modeling. To our knowledge, SAS/STAT has no readily available procedure for generating neural networks.

Chapter **14** SAS®

Logistic Regression,
Poisson Regression,
And Generalized
Linear Models

In this chapter, the authors consider nonlinear regression models for dependent variables that are categorical. In the simplest case, the dependent variable is binary and has two possible outcomes. Examples of binary outcome categories are success versus failure, disease absent versus disease present, and good performance versus bad performance. At the next level, the dependent variable is multinomial and has more than two possible outcomes. Examples of multinomial outcome categories are complete success, partial success, failure; no disease, minimum disease, moderate disease, severe disease; and performance on an increasing scale of 1 to 5. Lastly, the dependent variable may be a count of the number of events where large counts are rare and thought to be distributed as a Poisson random variable. Examples include counts of the number of accidents at a particular intersection, the number of people with a rare disease, and the number of sales.

One type of nonlinear regression model for categorical random variables is known as the logistic regression model. If the dependent variable is binary, we refer to the model as a logistic regression model whereas, if it is multinomial, we refer to the model as a polynomial or polytomous logistic regression model. If the dependent variable has a Poisson distribution, we refer to the nonlinear regression model as the Poisson regression model. This chapter of the text focuses on the statistical analysis of data based on the logistic model but also gives the essentials for the polytomous logistic regression model and the Poisson regression model.

Linear and nonlinear models considered in the text, including the three models mentioned above, belong to a family of models called *generalized linear models*. The salient feature of generalized linear models is that the initial model formulation is the same for each application with the exception of the specification of a link function. Thus, a unified approach to fitting regression models is provided. A concise description of generalized linear models is given on text pages 623-624.

Simple Logistic Regression

The Programming Task Example

Data File: ch14ta01.txt

An analyst studied the relationship between computer programming experience and success in completing a complex programming task within a specified time period (text page 565). That is, the response variable was coded $Y=1$ if the task was successfully completed and $Y=0$ if the task was not successfully completed. The predictor variable was the number of months of previous programming experience. See Chapter 0, "Working with SAS," for instructions on opening the Programming Task example data file (Table 14.1, text page 566) and naming the variables X, Y, and *FITTED*. After opening ch14ta01.txt, the first 5 lines of output should look like SAS Output 11.1.

SAS Output 11.1

Obs	x	y	fitted
1	14	0	0.31026
2	29	0	0.83526
3	6	0	0.11000
4	25	1	0.72660
5	18	1	0.46184

We begin the preliminary analysis by plotting Y against X values and overlaying a curve representing the fitted values plotted against X. (Insert 14.1 - SAS 14.2a) In a second graph, we plot the Y against X values and overlay a Lowess curve. (Insert 14.1 - SAS Output 14.2b) The plots suggest the underlying model is a sigmoidal S-shaped function. Accordingly, the analyst decided to use logistic regression to analyze the data.

Continuing in Insert 14.1, we issue the *proc logistic* statement with "*model y = x / cl*" to perform a logistic regression analysis using Y as the response variable and X as the single predictor variable. The *cl* option requests confidence intervals for the parameters of the model. We specify "*output out = estimates p = pie*" to save the predicted values (fitted values) to an output file named *estimates* under a variable named *pie*. Finally, we issue a *proc print data = estimates* to print the fitted estimates as shown in Table 14.1, column (3), text page 566. From the results shown in SAS Output 14.3, we see that the estimate of the model intercept is $b_0 = -3.0597$ and the estimate of the coefficient for X is $b_1 = 0.1615$. Further, the estimate of the odds ratio is 1.175. Thus, we estimate that the odds of successfully completing the task increase by 17.5% with each additional month of experience. These results are consistent with those given on text page 567. The printout of the fitted values (not shown) indicates that they are also consistent those reported in Table 14.1 of the text.

In some applications, the response variable is coded as 0 for non-event and 1 for event, and in other applications the coding is reversed. This coding is important because, by default, *proc logistic* models the probability of response levels of the lowest ordered value, i.e., response = 0, the non-event, relative to the highest ordered value, i.e., response = 1, the event. There are several ways to reverse this order of modeling. One is to code the response 0 for an event and 1 for a non-event but this is counterintuitive. Another option is to choose either the *ascending* or *descending* option on the *proc logistic* statement. The appropriate choice of the *ascending* or *descending* option depends on how the response variable (Y) is coded in the data file. We must be careful in using *proc logistic* to correctly use the ordering option and interpret the results accordingly.

In Insert 14.1, we specified the *descending* option for the logistic regression procedure and obtained 1.175 as an estimate of the odds ratio. If we executed the procedure without the *descending* option, the resulting odds ratio would be 0.851. Given what we now know about the *ascending* and *descending* options with *proc reg*, we know that 1/0.851 = 1.175 so we can use these options to estimate odds ratios according to our interest and the problem at hand. Since the event (task completed successfully) is coded internally as 0, the odds ratio obtained from *proc reg* estimates the odds that the task is completed successfully. Although it does not matter mathematically how the event or non-event is coded, it is less confusing to have the event we want to model (task completed successfully rather than unsuccessfully) in the numerator. Thus, in Insert 14.1, we include the *descending* option on the *proc logistic* statement to override the default.

```
                              INSERT 14.1
data program;
  infile 'c:\alrm\chapter 14 data sets\ch14ta01.txt';
  input x y fitted;
run;
*Produce plot of y vs x and fitted vs x shown in SAS Output 14.2 (a);
data graphs;
  set program;
proc sort;
  by fitted;
proc gplot;
   symbol1 color=black value=none interpol=join ;
   symbol2 color=black value=circle;
   title 'Scatter Plot fitted vs months';
   plot fitted*x y*x / overlay haxis=0 to 40 by 10 vaxis=0 to 1 by .5;
run;
*Produce Lowess Curve;
proc loess;
  model y = x / smooth = 0.4 to 0.8 by 0.1 residual;
  ods output OutputStatistics = Results;
run;
*Produce plot of y vs x and Lowess pred vs x shown in SAS Output 14.2 (b);
proc sort data = results;
 by smoothingparameter pred;
 run;
goptions reset=all;
proc gplot;
  by SmoothingParameter;
  symbol1 color=black value=none interpol=join ;
  symbol2 color=black value=circle;
   title 'Scatter Plot and Lowess Curve';
  plot Pred*x DepVar*x / overlay haxis=0 to 40 by 10 vaxis=0 to 1 by .5;
run;
*Run logistic regression analysis;
proc logistic  data = program descending;
 model y = x /  cl ;
 output out = estimates p = pie;
proc print data = estimates;
run;
```

(a)   (b)

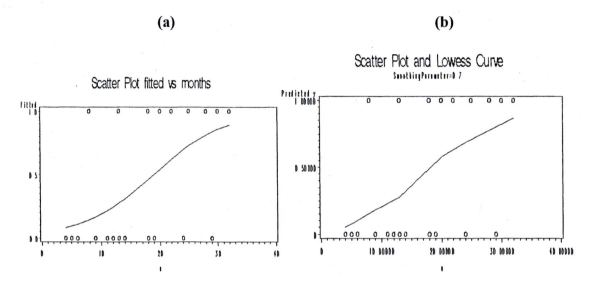

SAS Output 14.3

Analysis of Maximum Likelihood Estimates					
Parameter	DF	Estimate	Standard Error	Chi-Square	Pr > ChiSq
Intercept	1	-3.0597	1.2594	5.9029	0.0151
x	1	0.1615	0.0650	6.1760	0.0129

Odds Ratio Estimates		
Effect	Point Estimate	95% Wald Confidence Limits
x	1.175	1.035 1.335

Wald Confidence Interval for Parameters			
Parameter	Estimate	95% Confidence Limits	
Intercept	-3.0597	-5.5280	-0.5914
x	0.1615	0.0341	0.2888

The Coupon Effectiveness Example
Data File: ch14ta02.txt

Marketing researchers mailed packets containing promotional material and related coupons to 1000 selected homes. Two hundred homes each received one of 5 different coupons that offered price reductions of 5, 10, 15, 20, or 25 dollars. Thus, the predictor variable was the amount of price reduction and the response variable (Y) was coded to indicate whether or not the home redeemed the coupon within a six-month period. See Chapter 0, "Working with SAS," for instructions on opening the Coupon Effectiveness example data file (Table 14.2, text page 569) and naming the variables X, n, Y, and *pro*. After opening ch14ta02.txt, the 5 lines of output should look like SAS Output 14.4.

SAS Output 14.4

Obs	x	n	y	pro
1	5	200	30	0.150
2	10	200	55	0.275
3	15	200	70	0.350
4	20	200	100	0.500
5	30	200	137	0.685

In Insert 14.2, we input the data in the form of Table 14.2, text page 569 (SAS Output 14.4). Next, we issue the *proc logistic* statement and specify *model y/n = x*. Here, Y is the number of coupons redeemed and n is the number of households that received a coupon with price reduction X. Thus, *y/n* is the proportion of coupons redeemed at each price reduction x. Execution of the logistic procedure with this model produces SAS Output 14.5 with $b_0 = -2.0443$, $b_1 = 0.0968$, and odds ratio = 1.102 as shown on text page 570.

Following the model statement in Insert 14.2, we specify "*output out = estimates p = pie.*" This requests estimates of the predicted values to be stored in a file named *estimates* under the variable name *pie*. We then specify "*proc print data=estimates*" to print (SAS Output 14.5) the model based estimates in Column (5) of Table 14.2, text page 569.

INSERT 14.2

```
data Program;
  infile 'c:\alrm\chapter 14 data sets\ch14ta02.txt';
  input x n y pro;
proc logistic;
  model y/n = x;
output out = estimates p = pie;
run;
proc print data = estimates;
run;
```

SAS Output 14.5

Analysis of Maximum Likelihood Estimates					
Parameter	DF	Estimate	Standard Error	Chi-Square	Pr > ChiSq
Intercept	1	-2.0443	0.1610	161.2794	<.0001
x	1	0.0968	0.00855	128.2924	<.0001

Odds Ratio Estimates			
Effect	Point Estimate	95% Wald Confidence Limits	
x	1.102	1.083	1.120

SAS Output 14.5 continued – Model Based Estimates

Obs	x	n	y	pro	pie
1	5	200	30	0.150	0.17362
2	10	200	55	0.275	0.25426
3	15	200	70	0.350	0.35621
4	20	200	100	0.500	0.47311
5	30	200	137	0.685	0.70280

Multiple Logistic Regression

The Disease Outbreak Example – Model Building

Data File: ch14ta03.txt and appenc10.txt

Note: Data for the Disease Outbreak example are available in two files: ch14ta03.txt and appenc10.txt. There are differences in the files that we will identify. For all analyses involving the Disease Outbreak example, we must pay close attention to the data file we use, i.e., ch14ta03.txt versus appenc10.txt. We will be unable to match the chapter results if we use the wrong file.

Using ch14ta03.txt, a researcher studied the relationship between disease outbreak ($Y=1$ if disease was present and $Y=0$ if disease was not present) and the individual's age ($X1$), socioeconomic status (represented by indicator variables $X2$ and $X3$), and the sector in which the individual lived ($X4$ coded 0 or 1). See Chapter 0, "Working with SAS," for instructions on opening the Disease Outbreak example data file (Table 14.3, text page 574) and naming the variables *case, X1, X2, X3, X4, and Y*. After opening ch14ta03.txt, the first 5 lines of output should look like SAS Output 14.6a.

SAS Output 14.6 (a)

Obs	case	x1	x2	x3	x4	y
1	1	33	0	0	0	0
2	2	35	0	0	0	0
3	3	6	0	0	0	0
4	4	60	0	0	0	0
5	5	18	0	1	0	1

Similar to the steps for requesting the logistic regression analysis in the previous example (Insert 14.1), for the Disease Outbreak example we enter *Y* as the dependent variable and *X1, X2, X3*, and *X4* as covariates. Partial results are shown in SAS Output 14.7(a). The regression function is consistent with equation 14.46, text page 574. The odds ratio (listed under *Point Estimate*) for *X1*=1.03, indicating that, because age is coded in units of years, the risk of disease increases by 1.03 or approximately 3% for each additional year of age. The odds ratio for *X4*=4.83, indicating that individuals living in sector 2 are 4.829 times more likely to have contracted the disease compared to individuals living in sector 1.

As noted above, data file ch14ta03.txt comprises the first 98 cases of a sample of 196 cases used in the Disease Outbreak example. The entire 196 cases are available in the data file appenc10.txt. After opening appenc10.txt and naming the variables *case, age, status, sector, y,* and *other*, the first 10 lines of output should look like SAS Output 14.6(b). In this file, socioeconomic status is represented by one variable (*status*) where *status* = 1 if status is "upper," *status* = 2 if status is "middle," and *status* = 3 if status is "lower." The sector is coded *sector* = 1 if the individual lives in sector 1 and *sector* = 2 if the individual lives in sector 2.

SAS Output 14.6 (b)

Obs	case	age	status	sector	y	other
1	1	33	1	1	0	1
2	2	35	1	1	0	1
3	3	6	1	1	0	0
4	4	60	1	1	0	1
5	5	18	3	1	1	0
6	6	26	3	1	0	0
7	7	6	3	1	0	0
8	8	31	2	1	1	1
9	9	26	2	1	1	0
10	10	37	2	1	0	0

In ch14ta03.txt, two indicator variables (*X2, X3*) were used to represent the 3 levels of socioeconomic status. We illustrate the use *status* as a *class* variable to represent socioeconomic status. However, SAS uses the larger of the coded values as the reference category, and our desired reference category (upper) is coded 1. Accordingly, we compute a new variable named *newstat* where we simply reverse the coding of *status* so that upper socioeconomic status (*newstat=3*) will now be the reference category. Using this coding scheme we can enter *age*, *newstat*, and *sector*, as predictor variables and specify *newstat* as a *class* variable in the *proc logistic* procedure (Insert 14.3).

For each variable specified as a *class* variable, SAS will automatically code a set of indicator variables. Thus, we replaced *X2* and *X3* in the analysis that produced the partial output shown in SAS Output 14.7(a) with *newstat*. We also replaced *X1* with *age*, although these two variables are equal, and replaced *X4* with *sector*. This results in SAS Output 14.7(b). So, SAS Output 14.7(a) is a result of using *X1, X2, X3*, and *X4* as predictors from the ch14ta03.txt data set. On the other hand, the partial output shown in SAS Output 14.7(b) is a result of using *age, newstat*, and *sector* as predictors from the appenc10.txt data set (and using *where case* < 99). Although the variables used in the two models were coded differently, they contain the same "information." Thus, the two analyses produce identical the odd ratios. The coding scheme used to produce SAS Output 14.7(b) also yields an overall test statistic that is indicative of lack of significance for the *newstat* variable, $p = 0.547$.

SAS Output 14.7

(a)

	Odds Ratio Estimates		
Effect	Point Estimate	95% Wald Confidence Limits	
x1	1.030	1.003	1.058
x2	1.505	0.465	4.868
x3	0.737	0.226	2.408
x4	4.829	1.807	12.907

(b)

	Odds Ratio Estimates		
Effect	Point Estimate	95% Wald Confidence Limits	
age	1.030	1.003	1.058
newstat 1 vs 3	0.737	0.226	2.408
newstat 2 vs 3	1.505	0.465	4.868
sector	4.829	1.807	12.907

154

Polynomial Logistic Regression

The Initial Public Offerings Example

Data File: appenc11.txt

A researcher studies the relationship between whether or not a company was financed by venture capital (*VC*) and the face value (*facval*) of the company (text page 575). See Chapter 0, "Working with SAS," for instructions on opening the IPO example data file and naming the variables *case, VC, FACEVAL, SHARES,* and *X3*. After opening appenc11.txt, the first 5 lines of output should look like SAS Output 14.8.

SAS Output 14.8

Obs	case	vc	faceval	shares	x3
1	1	0	1200000	3000000	0
2	2	0	1454000	1454000	1
3	3	0	1500000	300000	0
4	4	0	1530000	510000	0
5	5	0	2000000	800000	0

In Insert 14.4, we find *LNFACE*, the natural logarithm of *FACEVAL*. We use *proc loess* and *proc gplot* to generate a scatter plot of *VC* and *LNFACE* and overlay a Lowess curve [SAS Output 14.9(a)]. We then regress *VC* against *LNVACE* and save the fitted values (*linpie*) to a file named *linear*. In the next *proc plot* statement we use *linpie* and other values as shown to generate the first order logistic curve [SAS Output 14.9 (b)]. SAS Output 14.9 (a) and (b) display the Lowess curve and the first order logistic curve, respectively, as shown on Figure 14.9 (a), text page 575. The mound shaped relationship of SAS Output 14.9 (a) was not adequately depicted by the first order regression fit of SAS Output 14.9 (b). This indicated that a first-order logistic regression would not be appropriate; the authors decided to explore a second-order model using *LNFACE* (centered) and *LNFACE* (centered) squared as predictors. Continuing in Insert 14.4, we center *LNFACE* (*xcnt*), find its square (*xcnt2*), and regress *VC* on *xcnt* and *xcnt2*. Partial results of this model are shown in SAS Output 14.10 and are consistent with Table 14.5, text page 576. Finally, we use *proc gplot* to generate a scatter plot of the estimated probabilities (*pie*) against *xcnt* with an overlay of *VC* against *xcnt* [SAS Output 14.9 (c)]. This second order logistic curve is consistent with Figure 14.9 (b), text page 575.

INSERT 14.4	INSERT 14.4 continued

data ipo;
  infile 'c:\alrm\appendix c data sets\appenc11.txt';
  input case vc faceval shares x3;
Inface = LOG(faceval);
*Run lowess analysis;
proc loess;
  model vc = Inface / smooth = 0.5 residual;
  ods output OutputStatistics = Results;
run;
*Produce scatter plot and lowess curve;
data graph1;
  set results;
proc sort;
  by Inface;
  run;
goptions reset=all;
proc gplot;
  by SmoothingParameter;
  symbol1 color=black value=none interpol=join;
  symbol2 color=black value=circle;
   title 'Scatter Plot and Lowess Curve';
  plot Pred*Inface DepVar*Inface / overlay ;
run;
*Run 1st order logistic regression analysis;
proc logistic data = ipo descending;
  model vc = Inface;
  output out = linear p = linpie;
run;
*Produce scatterplot and fitted 1st order logistic;
data graph2;
  set linear;
proc sort;
  by Inface;
	proc gplot;
	  symbol1 color=black value=none interpol=join ;
	  symbol2 color=black value=circle;
	   title 'Scatter Plot and 1st Order Logit Curve';
	  plot linpie*Inface vc*Inface / overlay;
	run;
	
	* Find mean of Inface=16.7088 ;
	proc means;
	  var Inface;
	run;
	*Run 2nd order logistic regression analysis;
	data step2;
	  set linear;
	xcnt = 16.7088 - Inface ;
	xcnt2 = xcnt ** 2 ;
	proc logistic descending;
	  model vc = xcnt xcnt2/ cl;
	  output out = estimates p = pie;
	run;
	*Produce scatter plot and fitted 2nd order logistic;
	data graph;
	  set estimates;
	proc sort;
	  by xcnt;
	  proc gplot;
	  symbol1 color=black value=none interpol=join ;
	  symbol2 color=black value=circle;
	   title 'Scatter Plot and 2nd Order Logit Curve';
	  plot pie*xcnt vc*xcnt / overlay ;
	run;

SAS Output 14.9

(a)   (b)

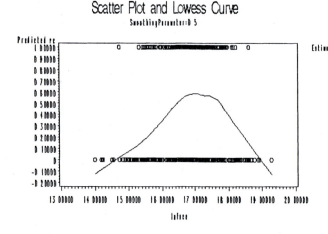

(c)

Scatter Plot and 2nd Order Logit Curve

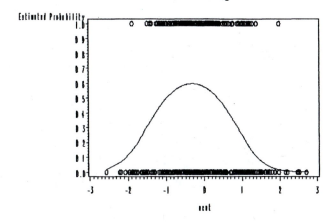

SAS Output 14.10

Analysis of Maximum Likelihood Estimates					
Parameter	DF	Estimate	Standard Error	Chi-Square	Pr > ChiSq
Intercept	1	0.3004	0.1240	5.8741	0.0154
xcnt	1	-0.5517	0.1385	15.8718	<.0001
xcnt2	1	-0.8615	0.1404	37.6504	<.0001

Inferences about Regression Parameters: **The Programming Task Example**

On text page 578, the authors wish to test $H_0 : \beta_1 \leq 0$ versus $H_a : \beta_1 > 0$. The test for β_1 in SAS Output 14.3 is a two-sided test. For a one-sided test, we simply divide the probability level (0.0129 listed under *Pr > ChiSq* and across from *x*) by 2. This yields the one-sided probability level of 0.0065 as noted on text page 579. The text authors report $z^* = 2.485$ and the square of z is equal to the Wald statistic, which is distributed approximately as chi-square distribution with 1 degree of freedom. Thus, the Wald statistic is $X^2 = 2.485^2 = 6.176$ as shown in SAS Output 14.3.

The confidence interval for β_1 shown in SAS Output 14.3 is consistent with text page 579. This is a result of the *cl* option on the *proc logistic* statement in Insert 14.1. We know from SAS Output 14.3 that $b_1 = 0.161$ and $s\{b_1\} = 0.065$. For a 95% confidence interval, we require $z = 1.96$. We compute the 95% confidence interval directly from these results as follows:

$$0.161 \pm 1.96(0.065)$$

or

$$0.034 \leq \beta_1 \leq 0.288.$$

The Disease Outbreak Example

Data File: ch14ta03.txt

On text page 581, the researchers now wish to determine if $X1$ can be dropped from the model in the Disease Outbreak Example. We use *proc logistic* (syntax not shown) to regress Y on $X2$, $X3$, and $X4$ and refer to this as the reduced model (reduced because $X1$ is no longer in the model). In SAS Output 14.11, we see that –2 Log Likelihood statistic = 106.204. We now regress Y on $X1$, $X2$, $X3$, and $X4$ and refer to this as the full model. From SAS Output 14.11, the –2 Log Likelihood statistic = 101.054. Using equation 14.60, text page 581, we find $G^2 = 106.204 - 101.054 = 5.15$. For $\alpha = 0.05$ we require $X^2(.95;1) = 3.84$. Since our computed G^2 value (5.15) is greater than the critical value (3.84) we conclude H_a, that $X1$ should not be dropped from the model.

SAS Output 14.11

Reduced Model

Model Fit Statistics		
Criterion	Intercept Only	Intercept and Covariates
AIC	124.318	114.204
SC	126.903	124.544
-2 Log L	122.318	106.204

Full Model

Model Fit Statistics		
Criterion	Intercept Only	Intercept and Covariates
AIC	124.318	111.054
SC	126.903	123.979
-2 Log L	122.318	101.054

Automatic Model Selection Methods: The Disease Outbreak Example

Data File: appenc10.txt

Best Subsets Procedure. SAS' *proc logistic* offers a best subset procedure. We specify on the *proc logistic* statement that n models with the highest score chi-square statistics for each model

158

size. The *best* option is used exclusively with *selection=score*. For example, we can specify that the 2 models with the highest score chi-square statistics be displayed for models with one, two, three, and four predictor variables, e.g., "*model y = x1 x2 x3 x4 / selection=score best=2;*". Additionally, the $-2\log_e L(\mathbf{b})$, AIC_p and SBC_p statistics are available for each *proc logistic* analysis but are not displayed as part of the best subset procedure.

Stepwise Model Selection. SAS' *proc logistic* offers stepwise selection, forward selection, and backward selection. The methods generally follow the description of selection procedures described for multiple linear regression in Chapter 9.

From the appenc10.txt data file, we create four new variables to match the coding scheme of ch14ta03.txt and we select the first 98 cases (Insert 14.5). That is, socioeconomic status will be represented by two indicator variables: $X2 = 1$ if class is middle, otherwise $X2 = 0$, and $X3=1$ if class is lower, otherwise $X3 = 0$. Thus, upper socioeconomic status is the reference class. Also, $X4 = 0$ if the individual lives in sector 1 and $X4=1$ if the individual lives in sector 2. Finally, to use the same variable names as the text, we set $X1=age$.

We present the syntax to perform forward stepwise selection in Insert 14.5. Partial results are shown in SAS Output 14.12. At Step 0, before any variables are entered into the model, $X4$ has the lowest probability level of the 4 variables under consideration and, thus, is entered into the model at Step 1. Of the variables not in the model after Step 1, $X1$ has the lowest probability level of the three candidate variables and is entered into the model at Step 2. Of the variables not in the model after Step 2, $X2$ and $X3$ both have probability levels greater than the probability level required for entering a variable into the model and the stepping process stops.

Although we arrive at the same conclusion as the text, the *constant* values in SAS Output 14.12 (Analysis of Maximum Likelihood Estimates) do not match those displayed in Table 14.11, text page 585. In the model specified in Insert 14.5, we used $X1$, $X2$, $X3$, and $X4$ as predictor variables. The text example used *age*, *status*, and *sector* as predictors. Both sets of predictors contain the same "information" but socioeconomic status and city sector are parameterized differently in the two models. Thus, although we arrive at the same conclusion regarding the regression coefficients, the intercepts differ due to the different parameterization.

INSERT 14.5

```
data disease;
  infile 'c:\alrm\appendix c data sets\appenc10.txt';
  input case age status sector y other;
x1=age;
if status eq 2 then x2=1; else x2=0;
if status eq 3 then x3=1; else x3=0;
if sector eq 2 then x4=1; else x4=0;
proc logistic descending;
  where case < 99;
  model y =  x1 x2 x3 x4 / selection=forward detail;
run;
```

SAS Output 14.12 Step 0 – Intercept only

Analysis of Effects Not in the Model			
Effect	DF	Score Chi-Square	Pr > ChiSq
x2	1	1.4797	0.2238
x3	1	3.9087	0.0480
x4	1	14.7805	0.0001
x1	1	7.5802	0.0059

After Step 1

Analysis of Effects Not in the Model			
Effect	DF	Score Chi-Square	Pr > ChiSq
x2	1	0.6638	0.4152
x3	1	1.1549	0.2825
x1	1	5.2385	0.0221

After Step 2

Analysis of Effects Not in the Model			
Effect	DF	Score Chi-Square	Pr > ChiSq
x2	1	0.9681	0.3252
x3	1	0.7332	0.3919

Summary of Variables in Final Model

Analysis of Maximum Likelihood Estimates					
Parameter	DF	Estimate	Standard Error	Chi-Square	Pr > ChiSq
Intercept	1	-2.3350	0.5111	20.8713	<.0001
x4	1	1.6734	0.4873	11.7906	0.0006
x1	1	0.0293	0.0132	4.9455	0.0262

Tests for Goodness of Fit

Pearson Chi-Square Goodness of Fit Test. Using the Coupon Effectiveness example (ch14ta02.txt), the authors present 3 goodness of fit measures (text page 586) including the *Pearson Chi-Square Goodness of Fit*. In Insert 14.6, we open the Coupon Effectiveness data file. To request the *Pearson Chi-Square Goodness of Fit* test, we use the *aggregate* and *scale* options on the *model* statement, i.e.," *model y/n = x / aggregate=(x) scale=pearson;*". This produces SAS Output 14.13. The Pearson Chi-Square test statistic = 2.1486, consistent with the value (X^2=2.15) reported on text page 588.

Deviance Goodness of Fit Test. SAS will compute the *Deviance Goodness of Fit* statistic as described above. Notice from SAS Output 14.13 that the Deviance test statistic = 2.1668, consistent with the value [$DEV(X_0,X_1)$=2.16] reported on text page 586. This statistic can also be obtained as described in the text. As noted on text page 588, the *deviance goodness of fit test* for logistic regression is analogous to the *F lack of fit test* discussed in previous chapters. We present the steps without the specific syntax. Find –2 log likelihood (1191.973) for the reduced model by regressing Y on X using the Coupon Effectiveness example described above. To find –2 log likelihood for the saturated model, we first compute j=1 if X=5, j=2 if X=10, … , j=5 if X=30. Now use *proc logistic* to regress Y on X and j, and specify j as a *class* variable. This results in –2 log likelihood for the saturated model = 1189.806. The difference in the 2 values is 2.167, consistent with text page 589 where $DEV(X_0,X_1)$ = 2.16.

Hosmer-Lemeshow Goodness of Fit Test. On text page 590, the authors calculated the Hosmer-Lemeshow goodness of fit test for the Disease Outbreak example. They based the calculation on 5 classes. SAS, however, uses approximately 10 classes based on the percentiles of the estimated probabilities. To generate the Hosmer-Lemeshow goodness of fit statistic, we use the *lackfit* option on the *proc logistic* model statement, e.g., *model y = x1 x2 x3 x4 / lackfit;*. Partial results are found in SAS Output 14.14. Note that $X^2 = 9.180$ ($p = 0.327$) and the text reports $X^2 =1.98$ ($p = 0.58$). Although the difference in magnitudes of the test statistics is large, the p-values lead to the same conclusion. The discrepancy is due to the test statistics being based on different contingency tables, i.e., 2x5 versus 2x10. The use of 20 cells (2x10) decreases the expected frequencies per cell relative to the use of 10 cells (2x5). However, Hosmer and Lemeshow take a liberal approach to expected values and argue that their method is an accurate assessment of goodness of fit.

INSERT 14.6

```
data Program;
  infile 'c:\alrm\chapter 14 data sets\ch14ta02.txt';
  input x n y pro;
proc logistic;
  model y/n = x / aggregate=(x) scale=pearson;
run;
```

161

Deviance and Pearson Goodness-of-Fit Statistics				
Criterion	DF	Value	Value/DF	Pr > ChiSq
Deviance	3	2.1668	0.7223	0.5385
Pearson	3	2.1486	0.7162	0.5421

SAS Output 14.14

Hosmer and Lemeshow Goodness-of-Fit Test		
Chi-Square	DF	Pr > ChiSq
9.1871	8	0.3268

Logistic Regression Diagnostics and Detection of Influential Observations

Logistic Regression Residuals and Influence on Pearson Chi-Square and the Deviance Statistics. On text page 591, the authors demonstrate the calculation of various residuals and other statistics for the Disease Outbreak example. We illustrate the steps needed to produce the statistics presented in Tables 14.9 and 14.11 (text pages 593 and 599, respectively). In Insert 14.7, we use the first 98 cases of the Disease Outbreak data file as given in appenc10.txt and compute $X1$, $X2$, $X3$, and $X4$ as before. In *proc logistic*, the diagonal elements of the hat matrix (leverage values) are available only through the *ods* output system. Thus, we specify *influence* on the *model* statement. This creates an *ods* output table named *influence*. In the *ods output* statement we put the contents of the *influence* table into a file named *results2*. By default, the diagonal elements of the hat matrix are stored in a variable named *hatdiag*. In the *output* statement immediately following the *model* statement we set *yhat = p* (estimated probability, $\hat{\pi}_i$), *chires = reschi* (Pearson residual, r_{Pi}), *devres = resdev* (deviance residual, dev_i), *difchsq = difchisq* (delta chi-square, ΔX_i^2), and *difdev = difdev* (delta deviance, Δdev_i). (Here, *p*, *reschi*, *resdev*, *difchisq,* and *difdev* are SAS key words for the respective variables.) We then *merge results1* and *results2* into one file named *both* so that the data for all variables will be assessable in one data file. We then use equation 14.81 (text page 592) to find *rsp* (studentized Pearson residual, r_{SPi}) and equation 14.87 (text page 600) to find *cookd* (Cook's Distance, D_i). Printed output (first 5 lines) is shown in SAS Output 14.15. These values are consistent with Tables 14.9 and 14.11 (text pages 593 and 599, respectively). These values can be used to generate various plots as displayed in the text. For example, we can generate Figure 14.15 (d), text page 600, by using *proc gplot* to *plot difdev*yhat;.*

INSERT 14.7

```
data disease;
  infile 'c:\alrm\appendix c data sets\appenc10.txt';
  input case age status sector y other;
x1=age;
if status eq 2 then x2=1; else x2=0;
if status eq 3 then x3=1; else x3=0;
if sector eq 2 then x4=1; else x4=0;
proc logistic descending;
 where case < 99;
 model y = x1 x2 x3 x4 / influence ;
 output out = results1 p = yhat reschi=chires resdev=devres
   difchisq=difchisq difdev=difdev;
 ods output influence=results2 ;
 run;
data both;
 merge results1 results2;
 rsp=chires/(sqrt(1-hatdiag));
 cookd=((chires**2)*hatdiag)/(5*(1-hatdiag)**2);
proc print;
 var yhat chires rsp hatdiag devres difchisq difdev cookd;
run;
```

SAS Output 14.15

Obs	yhat	chires	rsp	HatDiag	devres	difchisq	difdev	cookd
1	0.20898	-0.51399	-0.52425	0.0387	-0.68473	0.2748	0.4795	0.002215
2	0.21898	-0.52951	-0.54054	0.0404	-0.70308	0.2922	0.5061	0.002461
3	0.10581	-0.34400	-0.34985	0.0332	-0.47295	0.1224	0.2277	0.000841
4	0.37100	-0.76800	-0.80486	0.0895	-0.96293	0.6478	0.9852	0.012737
5	0.11082	2.83262	2.86899	0.0252	2.09755	8.2311	4.6070	0.042535

Inferences about Mean Response

On text page 603, the authors wish to calculate the 95% confidence interval for a new observation. Completion of this task requires that we find $s^2\{b\}$ for use in equation 14.92, text page 602. To generate this variance-covariance matrix, we use the *covb* option on the *proc logistic* model statement, e.g., *model y = x1 x2 x3 x4 / covb;*. We could now use SAS *iml* matrix language to find $X_h' s^2\{b\} X_h$, where X_h is given on text page 603.

Prediction of a New Observation: The Disease Outbreak Example

Data File: appenc10.txt

We use the first 96 cases of appenc10.txt for this analysis. The authors wish to obtain the best cutoff point for predicting whether the outcome of a new observation will be "1" or "0". If 0.5 is used as the cutoff point, for example, the prediction rule would be: if $\hat{\pi}_h \geq 0.5$, predict the outcome will be "1"; otherwise predict it will be "0". Table 14.12, text page 605, displays the classification table based on text equation 14.95. That is, because 0.316 is the proportion of the diseased individuals in the sample, we use 0.316 as the starting cutoff point.

163

In Insert 14.8, we save the predicted probability in a variable named *yhat* (*p=yhat*) and then set *newgp*=1 if *yhat* is greater than or equal to 0.316, otherwise *newgp*=0. We then select the first 98 cases from the Disease Outbreak data file and form a 2x2 table of *Y* values (diseased versus non-diseased) by *newgp* values (predicted diseased versus predicted non-diseased). This produces SAS Output 14.16. We could produce text Table 14.12 (b) by changing the value in the *if* statement from 0.316 to 0.325 in Insert 14.8.

INSERT 14.8

```
data disease;
  infile 'c:\alrm\appendix c data sets\appenc10.txt';
  input case age status sector y other;
x1=age;
if status eq 2 then x2=1; else x2=0;
if status eq 3 then x3=1; else x3=0;
if sector eq 2 then x4=1; else x4=0;
proc logistic descending;
 where case < 99;
 model y = x1 x2 x3 x4 / outroc=roc ;
 output out = results p = yhat;
 run;
data results;
 set results;
 if yhat ge .316 then newgp=1; else newgp=0;
proc freq;
 where case < 99;
 table y*newgp / nopercent norow nocol;
 run;
proc gplot data=roc;
  symbol1 color=black value=none interpol=join ;
 plot _SENSIT_ * _1MSPEC_;
run;
```

SAS Output 14.16

Table of y by newgp			
y	**newgp**		
Frequency	**0**	**1**	**Total**
0	49	18	67
1	8	23	31
Total	57	41	98

There were 8+23=31 (false negatives + true positives) diseased individuals and 49+18=67 (true negatives + false positives) non-diseased individuals. The fitted regression function correctly predicted 23 of the 31 diseased individuals. Thus, the sensitivity is calculated as true positives /

(false negatives + true positives) = 23 / 8 + 23 = 0.7419 as reported on text page 606. The logistic regression function's specificity is defined as true negatives / (false positives + true negatives) = 48 / (18 + 48) = 0.727. This is not consistent with text page 607 where the specificity is reported as 47 / 67 = 0.7014. The difference comes from numerator used to calculate specificity. Table 14.12 (a), text page 605, uses 47 and we determined the number of true negatives to be 49. We assumed that the regression model was to be based on using *age, status,* and *sector* as predictors. If we use *age* and *sector* as suggested by the stepwise regression above, the classification table will match Table 14.12, text page 605.

To approximate Figure 14.17, text page 606, we use the *outroc* option on the *model* statement. This saves the data necessary to produce the ROC curve in a data file named *roc* (*outroc=roc*). We can view the contents of the *roc* data file by specifying *proc contents data=roc; run;*. Two of the variables stored in the *roc* data set are *_sensit_* (sensitivity) and *_1mspec_* (1-specificity). In the *proc gplot* we plot *_sensit_* against *_1mspec_* to form the ROC curve (SAS Output 14.17) presented in Figure 14.17, text page 606.

SAS Output 14.17

Validation of Prediction Error Rate:

The Disease Outbreak Example – Validation Data Set

Data File: appenc10.txt

On text page 607, the researchers now wish to use the regression function based on the Model-Building data set to classify observations in the Validation data set. After opening appenc10.txt and naming the variables *case, age, status, sector, y,* and *other,* the first 10 lines of output should look like SAS Output 14.18.

SAS Output 14.18

Obs	case	age	status	sector	y	other
1	1	33	1	1	0	1
2	2	35	1	1	0	1
3	3	6	1	1	0	0
4	4	60	1	1	0	1
5	5	18	3	1	1	0
6	6	26	3	1	0	0
7	7	6	3	1	0	0
8	8	31	2	1	1	1
9	9	26	2	1	1	0
10	10	37	2	1	0	0

In Inert 14.9 we first compute *X1, X2, X3*, and *X4* as before. We compute the estimated probabilities (*yhat*) for each case using the regression function (equation 14.46, text page 574) based on the model-building data set. We then use prediction rule 14.96 (text page 606) to establish group membership (*newgp*) where *newgp* = 1 if *yhat* ≥ 0.325 and *newgp* = 0 if *yhat* < 0.325. We also select on cases 99 to 196. Finally, we use the *proc freq* procedure to form a 2x2 table of *Y* values (diseased versus non-diseased) by *newgp* values (predicted diseased versus predicted non-diseased). Results are shown in SAS Output 14.19 and are consistent with text page 608. The off-diagonal percentages indicate that 12 (46.2%) of the 26 diseased individuals were incorrectly classified (prediction error) as non-diseased. Twenty-eight (38.9%) of the 72 non-diseased individuals were incorrectly classified as diseased.

INSERT 14.9

```
data disease;
  infile 'c:\alrm\appendix c data sets\appenc10.txt';
  input case age status sector y other;
x1=age;
if status eq 2 then x2=1; else x2=0;
if status eq 3 then x3=1; else x3=0;
if sector eq 2 then x4=1; else x4=0;
yhat=(1+exp(2.3129-(.02975*x1)-(.4088*x2)+(.30525*x3)-(1.5747*x4)))**-1;
if yhat ge .325 then newgp=1; else newgp=0;
proc freq;
 where case > 98;
 table y * newgp / nocol nopct;
run;
```

SAS Output 14.19

Table of y by newgp			
y	**newgp**		
Frequency **Row Pct**	**0**	**1**	**Total**
0	44 61.11	28 38.89	72
1	12 46.15	14 53.85	26
Total	56	42	98

Polyotomous Logistic Regression for Nominal and Ordinal Response:

Pregnancy Duration Example

Data File: ch14ta13.txt

On text page 609, a researcher studied the relationship between gestation period and several predictor variables. Gestation period was classified as less than 36 weeks ($Y=1$), 36 to 37 weeks ($Y=2$), and greater than 37 weeks ($Y=3$). After opening ch14ta13.txt and naming the variables *case, Y, RC1, RC2, RC3, X1, X2, X3, X4,* and *X5*, the first 5 lines of output should look like SAS Output 14.20. In Insert 14.10, we specify *proc logistic* with *X1, X2, X3, X4,* and *X5* as predictor variables; *X2, X3, X4,* and *X5* as *class* variables; and *Y* as the dependent variable. Since there are 3 levels of *Y*, SAS will assume that the variable is ordinal and perform Ordinal Logistic Regression. Results are shown in SAS Output 14.21 and are consistent with Figure 14.19, text page 618.

SAS Output 14.20

Obs	case	y	rc1	rc2	rc3	x1	x2	x3	x4	x5
1	1	1	1	0	0	150	0	0	0	1
2	2	1	1	0	0	124	1	0	0	0
3	3	1	1	0	0	128	0	0	0	1
4	4	1	1	0	0	128	1	0	0	1
5	5	1	1	0	0	133	0	0	1	1

INSERT 14.10

```
data Pregnancy;
  infile 'c:\alrm\chapter 14 data sets\ch14ta13.txt';
  input case y rc1 rc2 rc3 x1 x2 x3 x4 x5;
  x2=1-x2;
  x3=1-x3;
  x4=1-x4;
  x5=1-x5;
proc logistic ;
  class  x2 x3 x4 x5;
  model y = x1 x2 x3 x4 x5;
  run;
```

SAS Output 14.21

Testing Global Null Hypothesis: BETA=0			
Test	Chi-Square	DF	Pr > ChiSq
Likelihood Ratio	47.1740	5	<.0001
Score	36.1844	5	<.0001
Wald	32.3954	5	<.0001

Type III Analysis of Effects			
Effect	DF	Wald Chi-Square	Pr > ChiSq
x1	1	17.4958	<.0001
x2	1	11.3137	0.0008
x3	1	6.0426	0.0140
x4	1	12.4767	0.0004
x5	1	12.3683	0.0004

Analysis of Maximum Likelihood Estimates						
Parameter		DF	Estimate	Standard Error	Chi-Square	Pr > ChiSq
Intercept		1	6.2303	1.5826	15.4982	<.0001
Intercept2		1	8.3251	1.6838	24.4446	<.0001
x1		1	-0.0489	0.0117	17.4958	<.0001
x2	0	1	0.9880	0.2937	11.3137	0.0008
x3	0	1	0.6817	0.2773	6.0426	0.0140
x4	0	1	0.8349	0.2364	12.4767	0.0004
x5	0	1	0.7958	0.2263	12.3683	0.0004

Odds Ratio Estimates			
Effect	Point Estimate	95% Wald Confidence Limits	
x1	0.952	0.931	0.974
x2 0 vs 1	7.214	2.281	22.815
x3 0 vs 1	3.910	1.318	11.595
x4 0 vs 1	5.311	2.103	13.415
x5 0 vs 1	4.911	2.023	11.924

The steps to perform polyotomous logistic regression for an ordinal response completely generalize to the case where there is a nominal response. Use Insert 14.10 and add the *link=glogit* option, i.e., "*model y = x1 x2 x3 x4 x5 / link=glogit;*". The resulting syntax will produce the appropriate analysis for a multinomial response (output not shown). Note that this *link* option is available in Release 8.2 or higher. For users of earlier releases, SAS does not offer a direct solution if the response variable is polyotomous nominal and any of the predictor variables is continuous. If all predictor variables are nominal, *proc catmod* may be used.

Poisson Regression: Miller Lumber Company Example

Data File: ch14ta14.txt

The Miller Lumber Company conducted an in-store customer survey. The researcher counted the number of customers who visited the store from each nearby census tract. The researcher also collected and subsequently retained five (quantitative) predictor variables for use in the Poisson Regression. See Chapter 0, "Working with SAS," for instructions on opening the Miller Lumber Company data file and naming the Y, $X1$, $X2$, $X3$, $X4$, and $X5$. The first 5 lines of output should look like SAS Output 14.22. Table 14.14, text page 622, appears to indicate that the variables are arranged in the data file in the order $X1$, $X2$, $X3$, $X4$, $X5$, and Y. By printing the data set, we sometimes find that the order of the variables listed in the SAS *input* statement is not consistent with the order in data file.

SAS Output 14.22

Obs	y	x1	x2	x3	x4	x5
1	9	606	41393	3	3.04	6.32
2	6	641	23635	18	1.95	8.89
3	28	505	55475	27	6.54	2.05
4	11	866	64646	31	1.67	5.81
5	4	599	31972	7	0.72	8.11

Poisson regression is available in the *proc genmod* procedure (Insert 14.11). *Proc genmod* fits a generalized linear model to the data. There are a number of link functions and probability distributions that can be specified by the user. We complete the Miller Lumber analysis by specifying the Poisson distribution on the *model* statement. Results are shown in SAS Output 14.23 below and are consistent with Table 14.15, text page 622.

```
                        INSERT 14.11
data Miller;
  infile 'c:\alrm\chapter 14 data sets\ch14ta14.txt';
  input y x1 x2 x3 x4 x5;
proc genmod;
  model y = x1 x2 x3 x4 x5 /
  dist = poisson ;
run;
```

SAS Output 14.23

Analysis Of Parameter Estimates							
Parameter	DF	Estimate	Standard Error	Wald 95% Confidence Limits		Chi-Square	Pr > ChiSq
Intercept	1	2.9424	0.2072	2.5362	3.3486	201.57	<.0001
x1	1	0.0006	0.0001	0.0003	0.0009	18.17	<.0001
x2	1	-0.0000	0.0000	-0.0000	-0.0000	30.63	<.0001
x3	1	-0.0037	0.0018	-0.0072	-0.0002	4.37	0.0365
x4	1	0.1684	0.0258	0.1179	0.2189	42.70	<.0001
x5	1	-0.1288	0.0162	-0.1605	-0.0970	63.17	<.0001
Scale	0	1.0000	0.0000	1.0000	1.0000		

Chapter 15 SAS®

Analysis of Data in Designed Experimental and Observational Studies

In the previous chapters, the authors of the text focused on linear and nonlinear statistical models to investigate the relationship between an observed response vector **Y** and one or more independent variables or predictors arranged in a "design" matrix **X**. These models were called *regression models*. The analysis of regression models typically emphasizes the individual contribution of each independent variable (one of the X's) toward predicting the value of the dependent variable Y. Independent variables are added to or deleted from the regression model, according to their importance, in order to choose an appropriate model for predicting Y given the values of the X's. The analysis of variance in terms of these regression models is an important step in the investigation of a suitable model for a specific problem.

In Chapter 15, the authors give an overview of important types of designed studies and issues involved in the use of various designs. Here, emphasis is on investigating differences among the response means for subjects that are categorized in different groups where the groups of interest are determined by the study design. Again, the analysis of variance is an important approach to investigating these differences. Linear models are formulated for this purpose and these models are referred to as *analysis of variance models*.

The mathematical equation is the same for the regression model and the analysis of variance model, and both can be expressed as

$$Y = X\beta + \varepsilon$$

A model of this form is referred to as the *general linear model*. In both the regression model and the analysis of variance model, **Y** is an observed response vector. In the regression model, the first column of **X** is a vector of ones (which is omitted if an intercept term is to be omitted) followed by one or more column vectors, each containing the data for a single independent variable; and **β** is a vector of parameters (intercept and one or more coefficients, one parameter for each column vector of **X**). Typically, the **X** matrix is of full rank implying that there are no linear dependencies among its columns. In the analysis of variance model, the columns of **X** are "indicator" variables that identify the group to which a given response is linked (typically each column of **X** is a variable whose values are 0's, 1's, and −1's). For each specific problem, there are many ways to specify these indicator variables. The following example illustrates the analysis of variance model for data collected in a completely randomized design.

171

15.1 Single Factor Studies: Fixed Effects

Lipid Study Example

Researchers studied the effect of 4 experimental drug treatments on subsequent changes in lipid concentrations. Twenty patients with a diagnosis of hyperlipidemia participated in the study. Each of four experimental drugs was randomly assigned to five patients. Let y_{ij} denote the change in lipid concentration of the jth patient, $j = 1, 2, \ldots, 5$, treated with the ith experimental drug, $i = 1, 2, \ldots, 4$. The data were arranged for analysis as follows:

Drug A		Drug B		Drug C		Drug D	
Subject	Response	Subject	Response	Subject	Response	Subject	Response
1	$Y_{11}=12$	6	$Y_{21}=7$	11	$Y_{31}=6$	16	$Y_{41}=4$
2	$Y_{12}=9$	7	$Y_{22}=7$	12	$Y_{32}=8$	17	$Y_{42}=3$
3	$Y_{13}=10$	8	$Y_{23}=5$	13	$Y_{33}=2$	18	$Y_{43}=2$
4	$Y_{14}=11$	9	$Y_{24}=6$	14	$Y_{34}=3$	19	$Y_{44}=3$
5	$Y_{15}=8$	10	$Y_{25}=9$	15	$Y_{35}=6$	20	$Y_{45}=4$

We refer to the single classification variable *drug* (treatment) as the *factor* in this study and we refer to the four types of drugs as *levels* of the factor. For the SAS analysis, we arbitrarily coded the response variable as *y* and the 4 levels of treatment (Drug A, Drug B, Drug C, and Drug D) *drug*=1, *drug*=2, *drug*=3, or *drug*=4, respectively. The 20 observations of *y* and *drug* values are given in SAS Output 15.1.

SAS Output 15.1

y	drug	y	drug	y	drug	y	drug
12	1	7	2	6	3	4	4
9	1	7	2	8	3	3	4
10	1	5	2	2	3	2	4
11	1	6	2	3	3	3	4
8	1	9	2	6	3	4	4

We can write the specific form of the general linear model for these data in many different ways, all of which will produce the same numerical values of the relevant test statistics. The different forms of the model are determined by the way we define the indicator variables in the design matrix **X**. We provide here 3 specific models as illustrative examples. In each of these illustrative models, the design matrix **X** has four columns, each defined by values of an indicator variable. We denote the indicator variables as X_0, X_1, X_2, and X_3, respectively.

To analyze the data using SAS, we can enter the values of the **X** matrix for a given analysis of variance model along with the values for the **Y** vector in the same manner we entered data for the regression models analyzed in previous chapters. Alternatively, we can use SAS syntax to generate the values of the matrix **X**. We use this latter approach in the examples that follow. Once we have entered the data and have generated or entered the values of the matrix **X**, we can use *proc reg* to request an (regression) analysis of variance. We can also use *proc glm*.

Alternatively, we can enter, as part of the data, the group to which each observation in the **Y** vector belongs and specify that this group membership variable is a *class* variable (categorical variable). *Proc glm* will then automatically generate code for parameterizing an effects model, as defined below.

In SAS Output 15.1, we see that *drug* has been coded using allocated codes (see text page 321). That is, we have used one variable (*drug*) to code the 4 categories (levels) of the experimental drug. We arbitrarily coded Drug A=1, Drug B=2, Drug C=3, and Drug D=4. As we will see, allocated codes can be very convenient; however, allocated codes can also be misused. The current coding 1, 2, 3, and 4 seems to imply an equal distance between each level of *drug*, an implication that is not tenable. We could have arbitrarily coded Drug A=3, Drug B=1, Drug C=4, and Drug D=2, or, for that matter, we could have coded Drug A=a, Drug B=b, Drug C=c, and Drug D=d (note that we cannot use *proc reg* if we use alphanumeric coding for the values of indicator variables). Thus, the value of the allocated code is only an arbitrary label to represent a category of *drug*. Given that *drug* is an allocated numeric code, application of SAS *proc reg* where *y* is specified to be the dependent variable and *drug* the independent variable will produce erroneous results because the *proc reg* will handle *drug* as a continuous variable as opposed to a categorical variable.

Indicator variables, however, do not necessarily imply order or magnitude of spacing between categories. We will use indicator variables to represent the $c=4$ types (categories) of experimental drugs, and illustrate two effects models (remember there are many choices for effects models) and the cell means model with each specific model parameterization depending on our choice of indicator variables. We also demonstrate the use of allocated codes where the *General Linear Model* procedure (*proc glm*) automatically assigns values to indicator variables for an analysis of variance effects model.

Effects Model 1

One model can be expressed by defining the indicator variables to have values as follows:

$$X_0 = 1 \text{ (always)} \quad X_1 = \begin{cases} 1 & \text{if } drug = 1 \\ -1 & \text{if } drug = 4 \\ 0 & \text{otherwise} \end{cases} \quad X_2 = \begin{cases} 1 & \text{if } drug = 2 \\ -1 & \text{if } drug = 4 \\ 0 & \text{otherwise} \end{cases} \quad X_3 = \begin{cases} 1 & \text{if } drug = 3 \\ -1 & \text{if } drug = 4 \\ 0 & \text{otherwise} \end{cases}$$

The model can then be expressed in the general linear model (matrix form) $\mathbf{Y} = \mathbf{X}\boldsymbol{\beta} + \boldsymbol{\varepsilon}$ with specific matrices

$$
\begin{bmatrix}
Y_{11} \\
Y_{12} \\
Y_{13} \\
Y_{14} \\
Y_{15} \\
Y_{21} \\
Y_{22} \\
Y_{23} \\
Y_{24} \\
Y_{25} \\
Y_{31} \\
Y_{32} \\
Y_{33} \\
Y_{34} \\
Y_{35} \\
Y_{41} \\
Y_{42} \\
Y_{43} \\
Y_{44} \\
Y_{45}
\end{bmatrix}
=
\begin{bmatrix}
1 & 1 & 0 & 0 \\
1 & 1 & 0 & 0 \\
1 & 1 & 0 & 0 \\
1 & 1 & 0 & 0 \\
1 & 1 & 0 & 0 \\
1 & 0 & 1 & 0 \\
1 & 0 & 1 & 0 \\
1 & 0 & 1 & 0 \\
1 & 0 & 1 & 0 \\
1 & 0 & 1 & 0 \\
1 & 0 & 0 & 1 \\
1 & 0 & 0 & 1 \\
1 & 0 & 0 & 1 \\
1 & 0 & 0 & 1 \\
1 & 0 & 0 & 1 \\
1 & -1 & -1 & -1 \\
1 & -1 & -1 & -1 \\
1 & -1 & -1 & -1 \\
1 & -1 & -1 & -1 \\
1 & -1 & -1 & -1
\end{bmatrix}
\begin{bmatrix}
\mu \\
\tau_1 \\
\tau_2 \\
\tau_3
\end{bmatrix}
+
\begin{bmatrix}
\varepsilon_{11} \\
\varepsilon_{12} \\
\varepsilon_{13} \\
\varepsilon_{14} \\
\varepsilon_{15} \\
\varepsilon_{21} \\
\varepsilon_{22} \\
\varepsilon_{23} \\
\varepsilon_{24} \\
\varepsilon_{25} \\
\varepsilon_{31} \\
\varepsilon_{32} \\
\varepsilon_{33} \\
\varepsilon_{34} \\
\varepsilon_{35} \\
\varepsilon_{41} \\
\varepsilon_{42} \\
\varepsilon_{43} \\
\varepsilon_{44} \\
\varepsilon_{45}
\end{bmatrix}
$$

Thus, because Y_{11} denotes the response for a subject who received Drug A (*drug*=1), the "X variables" for observation Y_{11} are $X_0 = 1$, $X_1 = 1$, $X_2 = 0$, and $X_3 = 0$. These values appear in the first row (line) of the matrix $\mathbf{X}$ shown above. In fact, Y_{12}, Y_{13}, Y_{14}, and Y_{15}, respectively, denote responses for subjects who received Drug A and their X variables are identical to those for Y_{11}. Similarly, Y_{21}, Y_{22}, Y_{23}, Y_{24}, and Y_{25}, respectively, are responses for subjects who received Drug B (*drug* = 2), and the "X variables" for each of these Y's are $X_0 = 1$, $X_1 = 0$, $X_2 = 1$, and $X_3 = 0$. These values appear in rows (lines) 2 through 5 of the matrix $\mathbf{X}$ shown above. Similar coding is displayed in subsequent rows of the matrix $\mathbf{X}$. We see that our choice of the matrix $\mathbf{X}$ is key to our specification of the model.

The analysis of variance model specified above is called an *effects model*. For purposes of discussion here, we shall refer to this model as *Effects Model 1*. In this effects model, we assume the expected values of a random observation from subjects in the four drug groups (cells) are μ_1, μ_2, μ_3, and μ_4, respectively, and the overall expected value is μ. We further assume there is an "effect" for each of the four cells (perhaps the effect is zero) denoted τ_1, τ_2, τ_3, and τ_4, respectively, the effect is the difference between the cell mean and the overall mean, and the sum of the effects is zero so that $\tau_4 = -\tau_1 - \tau_2 - \tau_3$. In this context, the effects for the four cells are as follows:

$$\tau_1 = \mu_1 - \mu$$
$$\tau_2 = \mu_2 - \mu$$
$$\tau_3 = \mu_3 - \mu$$

$$\tau_4 = -\tau_1 - \tau_2 - \tau_3$$
$$= -(\mu_1 - \mu) - (\mu_2 - \mu) - (\mu_3 - \mu)$$
$$= 3\mu - (\mu_1 + \mu_2 + \mu_3)$$
$$= 3\left(\frac{\mu_1 + \mu_2 + \mu_3 + \mu_4}{4}\right) - 4\left(\frac{\mu_1 + \mu_2 + \mu_3}{4}\right)$$
$$= 3\left(\frac{\mu_4}{4}\right) + \left(\frac{\mu_4}{4}\right) - \left(\frac{\mu_1 + \mu_2 + \mu_3}{4}\right) + \left(\frac{\mu_4}{4}\right)$$
$$= \mu_4 - \mu$$

Thus, once τ_1, τ_2, and τ_3 are known, τ_4 is also known. In fact, once any three of the four effects parameters are known, the fourth is also known. We therefore say there are three *degrees of freedom* for estimating the effects parameters.

Effects Model 2

Another model can be expressed by defining the indicator variables to have values as follows:

$$X_0 = 1 \text{ (always)} \quad X_1 = \begin{cases} 1 & \text{if } drug = 1 \\ 0 & \text{otherwise} \end{cases} \quad X_2 = \begin{cases} 1 & \text{if } drug = 2 \\ 0 & \text{otherwise} \end{cases} \quad X_3 = \begin{cases} 1 & \text{if } drug = 3 \\ 0 & \text{otherwise} \end{cases}$$

As for the previous model, the model associated with these indicator variables is a special case of the general linear model (matrix form) $\mathbf{Y} = \mathbf{X\beta} + \mathbf{\varepsilon}$ but here the specific matrices are

$$
\begin{bmatrix} y_{11} \\ y_{12} \\ y_{13} \\ y_{14} \\ y_{15} \\ y_{21} \\ y_{22} \\ y_{23} \\ y_{24} \\ y_{25} \\ y_{31} \\ y_{32} \\ y_{33} \\ y_{34} \\ y_{35} \\ y_{41} \\ y_{42} \\ y_{43} \\ y_{44} \\ y_{45} \end{bmatrix}
=
\begin{bmatrix}
1 & 1 & 0 & 0 \\
1 & 1 & 0 & 0 \\
1 & 1 & 0 & 0 \\
1 & 1 & 0 & 0 \\
1 & 1 & 0 & 0 \\
1 & 0 & 1 & 0 \\
1 & 0 & 1 & 0 \\
1 & 0 & 1 & 0 \\
1 & 0 & 1 & 0 \\
1 & 0 & 1 & 0 \\
1 & 0 & 0 & 1 \\
1 & 0 & 0 & 1 \\
1 & 0 & 0 & 1 \\
1 & 0 & 0 & 1 \\
1 & 0 & 0 & 1 \\
1 & 0 & 0 & 0 \\
1 & 0 & 0 & 0 \\
1 & 0 & 0 & 0 \\
1 & 0 & 0 & 0 \\
1 & 0 & 0 & 0
\end{bmatrix}
\begin{bmatrix} \mu \\ \tau_1 \\ \tau_2 \\ \tau_3 \end{bmatrix}
+
\begin{bmatrix} \varepsilon_{11} \\ \varepsilon_{12} \\ \varepsilon_{13} \\ \varepsilon_{14} \\ \varepsilon_{15} \\ \varepsilon_{21} \\ \varepsilon_{22} \\ \varepsilon_{23} \\ \varepsilon_{24} \\ \varepsilon_{25} \\ \varepsilon_{31} \\ \varepsilon_{32} \\ \varepsilon_{33} \\ \varepsilon_{34} \\ \varepsilon_{35} \\ \varepsilon_{41} \\ \varepsilon_{42} \\ \varepsilon_{43} \\ \varepsilon_{44} \\ \varepsilon_{45} \end{bmatrix}
$$

For our discussion here, we shall refer to this model as *Effects Model 2*. In this effects model, we again assume the expected value of a random observation from subjects in the four drug groups (cells) are $\mu_1, \mu_2, \mu_3,$ and μ_4, respectively, and the overall expected value is μ. We further assume there is an "effect" for each of the first three cells (perhaps the effect is zero) denoted $\tau_1, \tau_2,$ and τ_3, respectively, and τ_4, the effect for cell 4, is always equal to 0. The effects for the four cells are as follows:

$$\tau_1 = \mu_1 - \mu_4$$
$$\tau_2 = \mu_2 - \mu_4$$
$$\tau_3 = \mu_3 - \mu_4$$
$$\tau_4 = \mu_4 - \mu_4 = 0$$

Thus, the expected value of a random observation from cell 4 is μ and cell 4 is referred to as the *reference cell*.

Hypothesis to be Tested in Effects Models 1 and 2

Both of the above effects models have four columns in the design matrix and four degrees of freedom for the model. Both have a first column that specifies an overall mean for the response variable (one degree of freedom) and both have three columns that correspond to "effects for the first three cells" of the design (three degrees of freedom, one for each column or effect). In both models we are interested in testing the (global) hypothesis

$$H_0 : \mu_1 = \mu_2 = \mu_3 = \mu_4$$

or, equivalently,

$$H_0 : \tau_1 = \tau_2 = \tau_3 = 0$$

The test statistic for evaluating this hypothesis is a function of the regression sum of squares attributable to adding the indicator variables X_1, X_2, and X_3 to a model that contains only the variable X_0 (i.e., a model that contains no terms other than a term for the overall mean or the reference cell). We denote this added sum of squares as $SS(X_1, X_2, X_3 | X_0)$.

Using SAS *proc reg* to Analyze Effects Models 1 and 2

In this section, we provide SAS programs to produce analyses for *Effects Models 1 and 2*. Unless otherwise specified, SAS automatically creates X_0, a column of ones, so that a parameter corresponding to the overall mean (*Effects Model 1*) or a reference cell (*Effects Model 2*) is included in the model. To represent the $c=4$ experimental drugs, we use SAS programming syntax to create for each model $c-1=3$ indicator variables (*X1, X2, X3*) that signify the drug effect associated with each response.

We entered the data shown in SAS Output 15.1 into a SAS syntax program and named the variables *y* and *drug*. The syntax to parameterize the *Effects Models 1 and 2*, respectively, is shown in Insert 15.1. Note that both models, by default, contain intercept terms so that we do not have to specify explicit code to generate X_0. Regression analyses based on both parameterizations result in identical *Model Summary* and *ANOVA* tables (SAS Output 15.2). The numerical value of the test statistic for both models is $F = 14.75$ with degrees of freedom = 3 and *p*-value (*Pr>F*) < 0.0001.

Note that the parameter estimates for the two parameterizations are different (SAS Output 15.3). For reference, the cell means for the sample data are given by the descriptive statistics shown in SAS Output 15.4. Note that the intercept for *Effects Model 1* is the overall sample mean 6.25 whereas the intercept for *Effects Model 2* is the sample mean for *drug* = 4. For *Effects Model 1*, the parameter estimates for the indicator variables *X1, X2*, and *X3* are equal to the respective difference between the mean of the response variable for each drug category and the overall sample mean. For example, the parameter estimate for *X1* is the difference between the mean response for subjects in the *drug* = 1 group and mean response for all subjects in the four drug categories; i.e., $10.0 - 6.25 = 3.75$.

For the parameter estimates based on *Effects Model 2*, we see that the parameter estimate for *X1*, the indicator variable for *drug*=1, is equal to the mean response for *drug* = 1 minus the mean response for *drug* = 4; i.e., 10.0 –3.2 = 6.8.

INSERT 15.1	INSERT 15.1 continued
Title 'Effects Model 1';	Title 'Effects Model 2';
data income;	data income;
input y drug @@;	input y drug @@;
if drug = 1 then x1=1;	if drug = 1 then x1=1;
if drug = 4 then x1=-1;	if drug ne 1 then x1=0;
if drug ne 1 and drug ne 4 then x1=0;	if drug = 2 then x2=1;
if drug = 2 then x2=1;	if drug ne 2 then x2=0;
if drug = 4 then x2=-1;	if drug = 3 then x3=1;
if drug ne 2 and drug ne 4 then x2=0;	if drug ne 3 then x3=0;
if drug = 3 then x3=1;	datalines;
if drug = 4 then x3=-1;	12 1 9 1 10 1 11 1
if drug ne 3 and drug ne 4 then x3=0;	8 1 7 2 7 2 5 2
datalines;	6 2 9 2 6 3 8 3
12 1 9 1 10 1 11 1	2 3 3 3 6 3 4 4
8 1 7 2 7 2 5 2	3 4 2 4 3 4 4 4
6 2 9 2 6 3 8 3	;
2 3 3 3 6 3 4 4	proc reg;
3 4 2 4 3 4 4 4	model y = x1 x2 x3 ;
;	run;
proc reg;	
model y = x1 x2 x3 ;	
run;	

SAS Output 15.2

Analysis of Variance					
Source	DF	Sum of Squares	Mean Square	F Value	Pr > F
Model	3	126.15000	42.05000	14.75	<.0001
Error	16	45.60000	2.85000		
Corrected Total	19	171.75000			

Root MSE	1.68819	R-Square	0.7345
Dependent Mean	6.25000	Adj R-Sq	0.6847
Coeff Var	27.01111		

178

SAS Output 15.3

Parameter Estimates – Effects Model 1

Parameter Estimates					
Variable	**DF**	**Parameter Estimate**	**Standard Error**	**t Value**	**Pr > |t|**
Intercept	1	6.25000	0.37749	16.56	<.0001
x1	1	3.75000	0.65383	5.74	<.0001
x2	1	0.55000	0.65383	0.84	0.4126
x3	1	-1.25000	0.65383	-1.91	0.0740

Parameter Estimates – Effects Model 2

Parameter Estimates					
Variable	**DF**	**Parameter Estimate**	**Standard Error**	**t Value**	**Pr > |t|**
Intercept	1	3.20000	0.75498	4.24	0.0006
x1	1	6.80000	1.06771	6.37	<.0001
x2	1	3.60000	1.06771	3.37	0.0039
x3	1	1.80000	1.06771	1.69	0.1112

SAS Output 15.4

Level of drug	N	y	
		Mean	**Std Dev**
1	5	10.0000000	1.58113883
2	5	6.8000000	1.48323970
3	5	5.0000000	2.44948974
4	5	3.2000000	0.83666003

Cell Means Model

Another analysis of variance model of interest is the *Cell Means Model* or, simply, the *Means Model*, which can be expressed by defining the indicator variables to have values as follows:

$$X_1 = \begin{cases} 1 & \text{if } drug = 1 \\ 0 & \text{otherwise} \end{cases} \qquad X_2 = \begin{cases} 1 & \text{if } drug = 2 \\ 0 & \text{otherwise} \end{cases}$$

$$X_3 = \begin{cases} 1 & \text{if } drug = 3 \\ 0 & \text{otherwise} \end{cases} \qquad X_4 = \begin{cases} 1 & \text{if } drug = 4 \\ 0 & \text{otherwise} \end{cases}$$

Here we have not defined X_0 because in this model we do not wish to have an intercept term. The parameters of this model are simply the means of the 4 drug groups (cells of the design). The model associated with these indicator variables is another special case of the general linear model (matrix form) $\mathbf{Y} = \mathbf{X\beta} + \boldsymbol{\varepsilon}$. The $\mathbf{X}$ matrix has 4 columns, each comprised of values of one of the 4 indicator variables.

As in the previous models, we wish to test the hypothesis

$$H_0 : \mu_1 = \mu_2 = \mu_3 = \mu_4$$

but here we "decompose" the hypothesis into three simultaneous hypotheses of the form

$$H_0 : \begin{cases} \mu_1 - \mu_2 = 0 \\ \mu_2 - \mu_3 = 0 \\ \mu_3 - \mu_4 = 0 \end{cases}$$

This is but one of many ways of specifying the components of the decomposition. Each component of the simultaneous hypotheses is a *contrast* (a linear function of the four means) that is equal to 0. We can write the simultaneous hypothesis in vector-matrix form as follows. First, we write the means in vector form:

$$\boldsymbol{\mu} = \begin{bmatrix} \mu_1 \\ \mu_2 \\ \mu_3 \\ \mu_4 \end{bmatrix}$$

and define a vector of zeros as

$$\mathbf{0} = \begin{bmatrix} 0 \\ 0 \\ 0 \\ 0 \end{bmatrix}$$

Next, we define a contrast matrix $\mathbf{L}$ as a matrix whose elements are non-negative constants such that the elements in each row of the matrix sum to 0.

The hypothesis can then be written in terms of the *general linear hypothesis* as

$$H_0 : \mathbf{L\mu} = \mathbf{0}$$

or

$$H_0 : \begin{bmatrix} 1 & -1 & 0 & 0 \\ 0 & 1 & -1 & 0 \\ 0 & 0 & 1 & -1 \end{bmatrix} \begin{bmatrix} \mu_1 \\ \mu_2 \\ \mu_3 \\ \mu_4 \end{bmatrix} = \begin{bmatrix} 0 \\ 0 \\ 0 \end{bmatrix}$$

or

$$H_0 : \begin{bmatrix} \mu_1 - \mu_2 \\ \mu_2 - \mu_3 \\ \mu_3 - \mu_4 \end{bmatrix} = \begin{bmatrix} 0 \\ 0 \\ 0 \end{bmatrix}$$

The specific matrices for the *Cell Means Model* are

$$\begin{bmatrix} y_{11} \\ y_{12} \\ y_{13} \\ y_{14} \\ y_{15} \\ y_{21} \\ y_{22} \\ y_{23} \\ y_{24} \\ y_{25} \\ y_{31} \\ y_{32} \\ y_{33} \\ y_{34} \\ y_{35} \\ y_{41} \\ y_{42} \\ y_{43} \\ y_{44} \\ y_{45} \end{bmatrix} = \begin{bmatrix} 1 & 0 & 0 & 0 \\ 1 & 0 & 0 & 0 \\ 1 & 0 & 0 & 0 \\ 1 & 0 & 0 & 0 \\ 1 & 0 & 0 & 0 \\ 0 & 1 & 0 & 0 \\ 0 & 1 & 0 & 0 \\ 0 & 1 & 0 & 0 \\ 0 & 1 & 0 & 0 \\ 0 & 1 & 0 & 0 \\ 0 & 0 & 1 & 0 \\ 0 & 0 & 1 & 0 \\ 0 & 0 & 1 & 0 \\ 0 & 0 & 1 & 0 \\ 0 & 0 & 1 & 0 \\ 0 & 0 & 0 & 1 \\ 0 & 0 & 0 & 1 \\ 0 & 0 & 0 & 1 \\ 0 & 0 & 0 & 1 \\ 0 & 0 & 0 & 1 \end{bmatrix} \begin{bmatrix} \mu_1 \\ \mu_2 \\ \mu_3 \\ \mu_4 \end{bmatrix} + \begin{bmatrix} \varepsilon_{11} \\ \varepsilon_{12} \\ \varepsilon_{13} \\ \varepsilon_{14} \\ \varepsilon_{15} \\ \varepsilon_{21} \\ \varepsilon_{22} \\ \varepsilon_{23} \\ \varepsilon_{24} \\ \varepsilon_{25} \\ \varepsilon_{31} \\ \varepsilon_{32} \\ \varepsilon_{33} \\ \varepsilon_{34} \\ \varepsilon_{35} \\ \varepsilon_{41} \\ \varepsilon_{42} \\ \varepsilon_{43} \\ \varepsilon_{44} \\ \varepsilon_{45} \end{bmatrix}$$

Using SAS *proc reg* to Analyze the Cell Means Model

A direct test of the global hypothesis $H_0 : \mu_1 = \mu_2 = \mu_3 = \mu_4$ in terms of the *Cell Means Model* is readily available in SAS *proc reg*. In Insert 15.2, we illustrate the SAS syntax used to generate the indicator variables for the *Cell Means Model*. We specify code for *proc reg* where *y* is the dependent variable and *X1, X2, X3,* and *X4* are independent variables. We further specify that the model will not contain an intercept (*noint*). Next, we specify a *test* statement to test the general linear hypothesis: $H_0 : \mu_1 = \mu_2 = \mu_3 = \mu_4$. In the *test* statement, the code *x1-x2* specifies the hypothesis $\mu_1 - \mu_2 = 0$, *x2-x3* specifies $\mu_2 - \mu_3 = 0$, and *x3-x4* specifies $\mu_3 - \mu_4 = 0$. The fact that the three specified hypotheses are separated by commas and listed in a single *test* statement indicates three hypotheses are to be tested simultaneously yielding a single *F* value with 3 degrees of freedom. The *F* value (not shown) produced by this *test* statement is identical to $F=14.75$ for the *Effects Model 1* and *Effects Model 2* shown in (SAS Output 15.2).

Using SAS *proc glm* to analyze Effects Model

As an alternative to using *proc reg* to test the hypothesis $H_0 : \mu_1 = \mu_2 = \mu_3 = \mu_4$, we now illustrate the use of SAS's *General Linear Model* procedure (Insert 15.2 - *proc glm*). In Insert 15.2, we specify *proc glm* where *y* is the dependent variable and *drug* is a class variable. That is, we use the *class* statement to specify that the variable *drug* (allocated code) is a categorical variable; this specification is not directly available in *proc reg*. Execution of Insert 15.2 (*proc glm*) results in SAS Output 15.5. Note that the $R^2=0.7345$ from the *proc reg* output (SAS Output 15.2) and that, from the *proc glm* output (SAS Output 15.5), $R^2 = 0.734$. Additionally, the test statistics for the *proc reg* ANOVA table are identical to those found in the *proc glm* summary table. The parameter estimates produced by the procedure *proc glm* (SAS Output 15.5) are identical to the parameter estimates for the regression analysis based on *Effects Model 2*. Based on the specification that *drug* is a categorical variable (listed in the *class* statement), SAS' *proc glm* internally parameterized the model as an *Effects Model 2*. Thus, *proc glm* eliminates the SAS program steps of explicitly defining indicator variables for a specific model parameterization by internally providing a "regression formulation" of an analysis of variance effects model. In many subsequent text chapters, the authors present both an analysis of variance and regression approach to chapter problems. Since *proc glm* is based on a regression formulation that makes the proper adjustments for unbalanced designs, we will present most of the illustrative examples using only *proc glm*.

Other Model Parameterizations

We see that there are many ways to specify analysis of variance models for a given set of data. Typically, each specification requires different assumptions about the parameters and therefore imposes different restrictions on these parameters. Estimates of the parameters are not unique because they may be different for different parameterizations of the model even though the data remain the same for the different specifications. In the output (SAS Output 15.5) of SAS *proc glm*, the letter 'B' is printed in the column next to the parameter estimates to indicate that they are not unique and numerical estimates may be different for different parameterizations of the model. However, provided they are formulated properly, the test statistics for the relevant hypotheses are unique in that they (the respective test statistics) have the same numerical value for each parameterization. Moreover, we can show that, for each parameterization, the set of estimates yields the same predicted value of *y* for any given subject's set of X's.

INSERT 15.2	INSERT 15.2 continued

Title 'Cell means model w/o intercept';
data lipid;
  input y drug @@;
if drug = 1 then x1=1;
if drug ne 1 then x1=0;
if drug = 2 then x2=1;
if drug ne 2 then x2=0;
if drug = 3 then x3=1;
if drug ne 3 then x3=0;
if drug = 4 then x4=1;
if drug ne 4 then x4=0;
datalines;
12 1 9 1 10 1 11 1
8 1 7 2 7 2   5 2
6 2 9 2 6 3   8 3
2 3 3 3 6 3   4 4
3 4 2 4 3 4   4 4
;
proc reg;
 model y = x1 x2 x3 x4 / noint;
 test x1-x2, x2-x3, x3-x4;
 run;
	Title 'GLM model';
	data income;
	  input y drug @@;
	datalines;
	12 1 9 1 10 1 11 1
	8 1 7 2 7 2 5 2
	6 2 9 2 6 3 8 3
	2 3 3 3 6 3 4 4
	3 4 2 4 3 4 4 4
	;
	proc glm;
	 class drug;
	 model y = drug ;
	 run;

SAS Output 15.5

proc glm output

Source	DF	Sum of Squares	Mean Square	F Value	Pr > F
Model	3	126.1500000	42.0500000	14.75	<.0001
Error	16	45.6000000	2.8500000		
Corrected Total	19	171.7500000			

R-Square	Coeff Var	Root MSE	y Mean
0.734498	27.01111	1.688194	6.250000

183

Parameter	Estimate		Standard Error	t Value	Pr > |t|
Intercept	3.200000000	B	0.75498344	4.24	0.0006
drug 1	6.800000000	B	1.06770783	6.37	<.0001
drug 2	3.600000000	B	1.06770783	3.37	0.0039
drug 3	1.800000000	B	1.06770783	1.69	0.1112
drug 4	0.000000000	B	.	.	.

15.2 Multifactor Studies: Fixed Effects

Growth Hormone Example

Data File: ch23ta01.txt

On text page 954 the authors present the two-factor Growth Hormone Example that has six cells with unequal sample sizes. A researcher studied the effect of a child's gender (Factor A) and bone development (Factor B) on the rate of hormone-induced growth (Y). We let Y_{ijk}, denote the growth, where $i = 1, 2, 3$ represents the levels of Factor A, $j = 1, 2$ represents the levels of Factor B and $k = 1, 2, \ldots, n_{ij}$ represents the kth subject in the ij^{th} "cell" of the design. The data from text Table 23.1 are:

Data for Growth Hormone Example

Gender (Factor A)	Bone Development (Factor B)		
	Severe (B₁)	Moderate (B₂)	Mild (B3)
Male (A₁)	$Y_{111}=1.4$ $Y_{112}=2.4$ $Y_{113}=2.2$	$Y_{121}=2.1$ $Y_{122}=1.7$	$Y_{131}=0.7$ $Y_{132}=1.1$
Female (A₂)	$Y_{211}=2.4$	$Y_{221}=2.5$ $Y_{222}=1.8$ $Y_{223}=2.0$	$Y_{231}=0.5$ $Y_{232}=0.9$ $Y_{233}=1.3$

Eighteen children, 3 per cell or combination of levels of Factor A and B, began the study. However, four of the children were unable to complete the study. Thus, data for these four children were not available and the resulting treatment sample sizes were unequal. See Chapter 0, "Working with SAS," for instructions on opening the Growth Hormone Example and naming the variables y, *gender*, *bonedev*, and *rep*. After opening and printing ch23ta01.txt, the first 5 lines of output should look like SAS Output 15.6.

SAS Output 15.6

Obs	y	gender	bonedev	rep
1	1.4	1	1	1
2	2.4	1	1	2
3	2.2	1	1	3
4	2.1	1	2	1
5	1.7	1	2	2

As in the single factor data discussed above, many analysis of variance models can be specified for this data structure. We shall discuss here only the *Effects Model 1* and the *Cell Means Model.*

Effects Model 1

To formulate an *effects model* (we called this model *Effects Model 1* in the previous section) for this unbalanced design, the authors use the following indicator variables as shown on text page 955:

$$X_1 = \begin{cases} 1 & \text{if gender} = 1 \\ -1 & \text{if gender} = 2 \end{cases} \qquad X_2 = \begin{cases} 1 & \text{if } bonedev = 1 \\ -1 & \text{if } bonedev = 3 \\ 0 & \text{otherwise} \end{cases} \qquad X_3 = \begin{cases} 1 & \text{if } bonedev = 2 \\ -1 & \text{if } bonedev = 3 \\ 0 & \text{otherwise} \end{cases}$$

and

$$X_4 = X_1 * X_2$$

$$X_5 = X_1 * X_3$$

Here, *X1*, *X2*, and *X3* are indicator variables analogous to those defined in the previous example, and *X4* (the product of *X1* and *X2*) and *X5* (the product of *X1* and *X3*) are indicator variables that define effects for interaction between gender and bone development.

In this effects model, we assume the expected values of a random observation from subjects in the six factor combinations (cells) are $\mu_{11}, \mu_{12}, \mu_{21}, \mu_{22}, \mu_{31}$, and μ_{32}, respectively, and the overall expected value is μ. We further assume there is a "main effect" for each level of Factor A, a "main effect" for each level of Factor B, and an effect of interaction at each level of Factor A with each level of Factor B. As shown in Table 23.2, text page 956, the matrix form of this effects model is

$$
\begin{bmatrix}
Y_{111} \\
Y_{112} \\
Y_{113} \\
Y_{121} \\
Y_{122} \\
Y_{131} \\
Y_{132} \\
Y_{211} \\
Y_{221} \\
Y_{222} \\
Y_{223} \\
Y_{231} \\
Y_{232} \\
Y_{233}
\end{bmatrix}
=
\begin{bmatrix}
1 & 1 & 1 & 0 & 1 & 0 \\
1 & 1 & 1 & 0 & 1 & 0 \\
1 & 1 & 1 & 0 & 1 & 0 \\
1 & 1 & 0 & 1 & 0 & 1 \\
1 & 1 & 0 & 1 & 0 & 1 \\
1 & 1 & -1 & -1 & -1 & -1 \\
1 & 1 & -1 & -1 & -1 & -1 \\
1 & -1 & 1 & 0 & -1 & 0 \\
1 & -1 & 0 & 1 & 0 & -1 \\
1 & -1 & 0 & 1 & 0 & -1 \\
1 & -1 & 0 & 1 & 0 & -1 \\
1 & -1 & -1 & -1 & 1 & 1 \\
1 & -1 & -1 & -1 & 1 & 1 \\
1 & -1 & -1 & -1 & 1 & 1
\end{bmatrix}
\begin{bmatrix}
\mu \\
\alpha_1 \\
\beta_1 \\
\beta_2 \\
(\alpha\beta)_{11} \\
(\alpha\beta)_{12}
\end{bmatrix}
+
\begin{bmatrix}
\varepsilon_{111} \\
\varepsilon_{112} \\
\varepsilon_{113} \\
\varepsilon_{121} \\
\varepsilon_{122} \\
\varepsilon_{131} \\
\varepsilon_{132} \\
\varepsilon_{211} \\
\varepsilon_{221} \\
\varepsilon_{222} \\
\varepsilon_{223} \\
\varepsilon_{231} \\
\varepsilon_{232} \\
\varepsilon_{233}
\end{bmatrix}
$$

where μ denotes the overall mean, α_1 denotes the main effect of level A$_1$ of Factor A, $\alpha_2 = -\alpha_1$ denotes the main effect of level A$_2$ of Factor A, β_1 denotes the main effect of level B$_1$ of Factor B, β_2 denotes the main effect of level B$_2$ of Factor B, $\beta_3 = -\beta_1 - \beta_2$ denotes the main effect of level B$_3$ of Factor B, $(\alpha\beta)_{ij}$ is the effect of interaction at level A$_i$ of Factor A and level B$_j$ of Factor B, $(\alpha\beta)_{21} = -(\alpha\beta)_{11}$, and $(\alpha\beta)_{13} = -(\alpha\beta)_{11} - (\alpha\beta)_{12}$.

Cell Means Model

The following indicator variables are used for the cell means model for the growth hormone example:

$$X_1 = \begin{cases} 1 \text{ if gender} = 1 \text{ and bonedev} = 1 \\ 0 \text{ otherwise} \end{cases}$$

$$X_2 = \begin{cases} 1 \text{ if gender} = 1 \text{ and bonedev} = 2 \\ 0 \text{ otherwise} \end{cases}$$

$$X_3 = \begin{cases} 1 \text{ if gender} = 1 \text{ and bonedev} = 3 \\ 0 \text{ otherwise} \end{cases}$$

$$X_4 = \begin{cases} 1 \text{ if gender} = 2 \text{ and bonedev} = 1 \\ 0 \text{ otherwise} \end{cases}$$

$$X_5 = \begin{cases} 1 \text{ if gender} = 2 \text{ and bonedev} = 2 \\ 0 \text{ otherwise} \end{cases}$$

$$X_6 = \begin{cases} 1 \text{ if gender} = 2 \text{ and bonedev} = 3 \\ 0 \text{ otherwise} \end{cases}$$

The cell means model can be represented as

$$\begin{bmatrix} Y_{111} \\ Y_{112} \\ Y_{113} \\ Y_{121} \\ Y_{122} \\ Y_{131} \\ Y_{132} \\ Y_{211} \\ Y_{221} \\ Y_{222} \\ Y_{223} \\ Y_{231} \\ Y_{232} \\ Y_{233} \end{bmatrix} = \begin{bmatrix} 1 & 0 & 0 & 0 & 0 & 0 \\ 1 & 0 & 0 & 0 & 0 & 0 \\ 1 & 0 & 0 & 0 & 0 & 0 \\ 0 & 1 & 0 & 0 & 0 & 0 \\ 0 & 1 & 0 & 0 & 0 & 0 \\ 0 & 0 & 1 & 0 & 0 & 0 \\ 0 & 0 & 1 & 0 & 0 & 0 \\ 0 & 0 & 0 & 1 & 0 & 0 \\ 0 & 0 & 0 & 0 & 1 & 0 \\ 0 & 0 & 0 & 0 & 1 & 0 \\ 0 & 0 & 0 & 0 & 1 & 0 \\ 0 & 0 & 0 & 0 & 0 & 1 \\ 0 & 0 & 0 & 0 & 0 & 1 \\ 0 & 0 & 0 & 0 & 0 & 1 \end{bmatrix} \begin{bmatrix} \mu_{11} \\ \mu_{12} \\ \mu_{13} \\ \mu_{21} \\ \mu_{22} \\ \mu_{23} \end{bmatrix} + \begin{bmatrix} \varepsilon_{111} \\ \varepsilon_{112} \\ \varepsilon_{113} \\ \varepsilon_{121} \\ \varepsilon_{122} \\ \varepsilon_{131} \\ \varepsilon_{132} \\ \varepsilon_{211} \\ \varepsilon_{221} \\ \varepsilon_{222} \\ \varepsilon_{223} \\ \varepsilon_{231} \\ \varepsilon_{232} \\ \varepsilon_{233} \end{bmatrix}$$

where μ_{11} represents the mean for the cell in row 1, column 1; μ_{12} represents the mean for the cell in row 1, column 2; and so on.

Hypotheses to be Tested in Two-Factor Model With Interaction

There are three primary hypotheses of interest and they can be expressed in terms of the parameters of the cell means model or the effects model:

1. The means for the 2 levels of Factor A are equal; i.e.,

$$(cell~means)~H_0 : \mu_{11} + \mu_{12} + \mu_{13} = \mu_{21} + \mu_{22} + \mu_{23}$$

or, equivalently, the 2 main effects for Factor A are equal to zero; i.e.,

$$(effects)~H_0 : \alpha_1 = \alpha_2 = 0$$

2. The means for the 3 levels of Factor B are equal; i.e.,

$$(\text{cell means}) \, H_0 : \mu_{11} + \mu_{21} = \mu_{12} + \mu_{22} = \mu_{13} + \mu_{23}$$

or, equivalently, the 3 main effects for Factor B are equal to zero; i.e.,

$$(\text{effects}) \, H_0 : \beta_1 = \beta_2 = \beta_3 = 0$$

3. The difference between the means for the two levels of Factor A is the same for all levels of Factor B; i.e.,

$$(\text{cell means}) \, H_0 : \mu_{11} - \mu_{21} = \mu_{12} - \mu_{22} = \mu_{13} - \mu_{23}$$

or, equivalently, the interaction effects are all equal to zero; i.e.,

$$(\text{effects}) \, H_0 : (\alpha\beta)_{11} = (\alpha\beta)_{21} = \ldots = (\alpha\beta)_{23} = 0$$

Sums of Squares Types I, II, III, and IV

The analysis of variance typically is performed in terms of an effects model such as the one above. In that context, the sum of squared deviations from the overall mean is referred to as the corrected total sum of squares. This "corrected total sum of squares," SSCT is partitioned into a sum of squares due to Factor A (SSA), a sum of squares due to Factor B (SSB), a sum of squares due to interactions between Factor A and Factor B (SSAB), and a residual or "error" sum of squares (SSE). If the number of observations is the same in all cells of the design (equal cell sizes), we can show that

$$\text{SSCT} = \text{SSA} + \text{SSB} + \text{SSAB} + \text{SSE} \quad \text{(provided cell sizes are equal)}$$

However, it is not true in general that this equality is true if the cell sizes are not all equal; i.e.,

$$\text{SSCT} \neq \text{SSA} + \text{SSB} + \text{SSAB} + \text{SSE} \quad \text{(if cell sizes are unequal)}$$

There are different ways to compute SSA, SSB, and SSAB. For the model with terms for Factors A, B, and AB interactions as potential parameters, 4 types of sum of squares are defined as follows:

SS(A) = Type I SSA where Factor A is the only factor in the model (Factor B and AB interactions are not in the model -- they are ignored). Here we are using SS(A) for brevity to denote SS(indicator variables for the levels of A). Similar notation is used in the following discussion.

SS(B) = Type I SSB where Factor B is the only factor in the model (Factor A and AB interactions are not in the model -- they are ignored).

SS(AB) = Type I SSAB where AB interaction terms are the only effects in the model (Factors A and B are not in the model -- they are ignored).

SS(A|B) = Type II SSA, the additional increase in the model sum of squares (reduction in the error sum of squares) achieved by adding Factor A to the model that already has Factor B in the model (AB interactions are not in the model – they are ignored). We say this is the sum of squares for A "adjusted for B."

SS(B|A) = Type II SSB, the additional increase in the model sum of squares (reduction in the error sum of squares) achieved by adding Factor B to the model that already has Factor A in the model (AB interactions are not in the model – they are ignored). We say this is the sum of squares for B "adjusted for A."

SS(AB|A, B) = Type II SSAB, the additional increase in the model sum of squares (reduction in the error sum of squares) achieved by adding all AB interactions to the model that already has Factors A and B in the model We say this is the sum of squares for AB "adjusted for A and B."

SS(A|B, AB) = Type III SSA (= Type IV SSA in this data structure), the additional increase in the model sum of squares (reduction in the error sum of squares) achieved by adding Factor A to the model that already has Factor B and all AB interactions in the model.

SS(B|A, AB) = Type III SSB (= Type IV SSB in this data structure), the additional increase in the model sum of squares (reduction in the error sum of squares) achieved by adding Factor B to the model that already has Factor A and all AB interactions in the model.

SS(AB|A, B) = Type III SSAB (= Type IV SSAB in this data structure), the additional increase in the model sum of squares (reduction in the error sum of squares) achieved by adding all AB interactions to the model that already has Factors A and B in the model.

For the structure considered here, if the cell sizes are all equal, the 4 types of sums of squares are also all equal. If the cell sizes are unequal but proportionate, Type I = Type II and Type III = Type IV for SSA and SSB, and the 4 types are equal for SSAB. Our purpose in analyzing analysis of variance models will be satisfied by using Type III sums of squares for most of the data structures considered in the text. Exceptions, such as data structures where some cells have no observations available for analysis, will be discussed in later chapters.

SAS Syntax for Analyzing Two Factor Effects Model 1

The authors fitted a Full Model and 3 Reduced Models, as shown in Table 23.3, text page 957. Equation 2.70, text page 73, was used to find the test statistics for the main effects for Factors A and B and the interaction effect. A summary of the study effects is shown in ANOVA Table 23.4, text page 959.

Using the regression approach (text page 953) to perform this two-factor analysis of variance, we parameterize the model as shown on text page 955. (Insert 15.3) We then use these indicator variables in *proc reg* (text equations 23.11, 23.15, 23.17, and 23.18) to fit the full and reduced models shown in Table 23.3, text page 957. We use the strategy of fitting a model that includes all model parameters (full model) and then fitting a model that has deleted terms corresponding to effects to be tested (reduced model). Next we calculate test statistics using (text equation 2.70):

$$F^* = \frac{SSE(R) - SSE(F)}{df_R - df_F} \div \frac{SSE(F)}{df_F}$$

To test the hypothesis that all interaction effects are equal to zero, we fit the Full Model, which contains indicator variables representing the main effects and all possible interaction effects, and find SSE (Residual Sum of Squares) = 1.300 and $df_F = 8$ (SAS Output 15.7). We then fit the Reduced Model that contains only indicator variables representing the main effects, and find SSE = 1.375 and $df_F = 10$ (SAS Output 15.8). Thus, to test $H_0 : (\alpha\beta)_{11} = (\alpha\beta)_{12} = 0$ (text equation 23.14a), we calculate

$$F^* = \frac{1.375 - 1.300}{10 - 8} \div \frac{1.300}{8} = 0.23$$

as shown on text page 958. Since this calculated F^* is less than the critical value for $\alpha = 0.05$, we conclude that interaction effects are not statistically significant.

To test the Factor A (*gender*) main effects, we use the output of the Full Model (SAS Output 15.7) and the output of the reduced model (SAS Output 15.9) that contains *x2*, *x3*, *x4*, and *x5* (all effects except *x1*). We then calculate

$$F^* = \frac{1.420 - 1.300}{9 - 8} \div \frac{1.300}{8} = 0.74$$

Similarly, we find F^* for the Factor B (bone development) main effects using SAS Output 15.7 and 15.10. Table 23.4, text page 959, is a consolidated ANOVA table that contains a summary of the analysis of variance obtained using the regression approach.

We carried out the same analysis (Insert 15.3) using SAS' *proc glm* as an alternative to *proc reg*. In specifying *proc glm*, we indicate that *y* (growth) is the dependent variable and *gender* and *bonedev* are *class* variables. Here, *gender* and *bonedev* are variables defined in the input data and in this case are variables whose values are allocated codes. We specify *gender* and *bonedev* to be *class* variables. Thus, SAS will automatically generate indicator variables for an analysis of variance model. To obtain a full factorial model that includes main effects for *gender* and *bonedev* and all possible interactions in SAS's *proc glm*, we specify *model y = gender | bonedev* which is equivalent to *model y = gender bonedev gender*bonedev*, where *gender*bonedev* denotes interaction between gender and bone development categories. Also, in SAS *proc glm*, the *Type I* and *III sums of squares* are printed by default. Partial results shown in SAS Output 15.11 are identical to those shown in text Table 23.4 and to the statistics calculated above using *proc reg*. Thus, we will use *proc glm* in subsequent chapters when the authors refer to the regression approach to analysis of variance.

INSERT 15.3	INSERT 15.3 continued
`data growth;` `  infile 'c:\kutnerdata\chapter 23 data sets\ch23ta01.txt';` `  input y gender bonedev rep;` `if gender = 1 then x1=1;` `if gender = 2 then x1=-1;` `if bonedev = 1 then x2=1;` `if bonedev = 3 then x2=-1;` `if bonedev ne 1 and bonedev ne 3 then x2=0;` `if bonedev = 2 then x3=1;` `if bonedev = 3 then x3=-1;` `if bonedev ne 2 and bonedev ne 3 then x3=0;` `x4=x1*x2;` `x5=x1*x3;` `Title "Full Model - equation 23.11";` `proc reg;` ` model y = x1 x2 x3 x4 x5;` `run;`	`Title "Reduced Model - equation 23.15";` `proc reg;` ` model y = x1 x2 x3;` `run;` `Title "Reduced Model - equation 23.17";` `proc reg;` ` model y = x2 x3 x4 x5;` `run;` `Title "Reduced Model - equation 23.18";` `proc reg;` ` model y = x1 x4 x5;` `run;` `Title "GLM Model";` `proc glm;` ` class gender bonedev;` ` model y = gender	bonedev;` `run;`

SAS Output 15.7
Full Model – Equation 23.11

Analysis of Variance					
Source	DF	Sum of Squares	Mean Square	F Value	Pr > F
Model	5	4.47429	0.89486	5.51	0.0172
Error	8	1.30000	0.16250		
Corrected Total	13	5.77429			

SAS Output 15.8
Reduced Model – Equation 23.15

Analysis of Variance					
Source	DF	Sum of Squares	Mean Square	F Value	Pr > F
Model	3	4.39886	1.46629	10.66	0.0019
Error	10	1.37543	0.13754		
Corrected Total	13	5.77429			

SAS Output 15.9

Reduced Model – Equation 23.17

Analysis of Variance					
Source	DF	Sum of Squares	Mean Square	F Value	Pr > F
Model	4	4.35429	1.08857	6.90	0.0080
Error	9	1.42000	0.15778		
Corrected Total	13	5.77429			

SAS Output 15.10

Reduced Model – Equation 23.18

Analysis of Variance					
Source	DF	Sum of Squares	Mean Square	F Value	Pr > F
Model	3	0.28457	0.09486	0.17	0.9124
Error	10	5.48971	0.54897		
Corrected Total	13	5.77429			

SAS Output 15.11

GLM Model

Source	DF	Type III SS	Mean Square	F Value	Pr > F
gender	1	0.12000000	0.12000000	0.74	0.4152
bonedev	2	4.18971429	2.09485714	12.89	0.0031
gender*bonedev	2	0.07542857	0.03771429	0.23	0.7980

Analysis of Single-Factor Studies

The analysis of variance (ANOVA) for a dependent (response) variable of interest is the partitioning of the total sum of squares for the dependent variable into component sums of squares associated with identifiable sources of variation. Once the partitioning is complete, we can use the component sums of squares to test whether variation attributed to some sources is significantly greater than variability attributed to other sources. In this chapter, we are concerned with linear statistical models that are convenient for performing an ANOVA and testing hypotheses about group means for the dependent variable. In this context, we are interested in testing whether variability among group means is significantly greater than the variability among observations within the groups.

Kenton Food Company Example

Data File: ch16ta01.txt

The Kenton Food Company (text page 685) studied the relationship between sales (Y) and the type of package design for a new breakfast cereal. Here, store was the experimental unit. Each of 20 stores was assigned to one package design such that there were 5 stores assigned to each design. One store was unable to fulfill the study requirement and was dropped from the study. See Chapter 0, "Working with SAS," for instructions on opening the Kenton Food Company Example and naming the variables *y*, *package*, and *store*. After opening and printing ch16ta01.txt, the first 5 lines of output should look like SAS Output 16.1.

SAS Output 16.1

Obs	y	package	store
1	11	1	1
2	17	1	2
3	16	1	3
4	14	1	4
5	15	1	5

We begin the analysis (Insert 16.1) by reproducing the scatter plot in Figure 16.3, text page 686, (SAS Output 16.2). We then request the *General Linear Model (proc glm)* procedure where Y is the response variable and *package* is the single independent (*class*) variable. Although Type I, II, III, or IV sum of squares (See Chapter 15 of this manual) can be requested in *proc glm*, Type I and III sum of squares are the default and either type serves our purpose here. We also request means for the 4 levels of *package*. Execution of *proc glm* in Insert 16.1 results in SAS Output 16.3, which is consistent with the decomposition of *SSTO* (text page 692), breakdown of degrees of freedom (text page 693), and the mean sales per store (text page 688). See the table following SAS Insert 16.1 for correspondence between the abbreviations used in the text versus terminologies used in SAS. On text page 699 the authors wish to test that the means (sales) are the same for the four package designs. Consistent with the text, from SAS Output 16.3 we find the *F*-value for Model is 18.59 and its associated *p*-value is 0.000. Because *package* is the only factor in the study, the *Model F*-value and the *F*-value for *package* are equal. Based on the *p*-value of 0.000, we conclude that there are significant differences among the sales means for the four package designs.

INSERT 16.1	INSERT 16.1 continued

data Kenton;
infile 'c:\kutnerdata\chapter 16 data sets\ch16ta01.txt';
  input y package store;
 	
*** Produce text Figure 16.3;
proc gplot;
 symbol value=circle;
 title 'Text Figure 16.3';
 plot y*package/haxis=0 to 5;
 run;
	proc glm;
	  class package;
	  model y = package;
	   means package;
	run;

Text abbreviation	SAS terminology
SSTR	Sum of Squares –Model
SSE	Sum of Squares - Error
SSTO	Sum of Squares – Corrected Total
MSTR	Mean Square –Model
MSE	Mean Square – Error

SAS Output 16.2

Text Figure 16.3

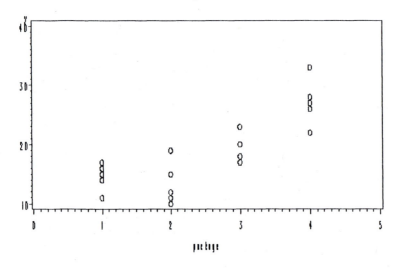

194

SAS Output 16.3

Source	DF	Sum of Squares	Mean Square	F Value	Pr > F
Model	3	588.2210526	196.0736842	18.59	<.0001
Error	15	158.2000000	10.5466667		
Corrected Total	18	746.4210526			

Source	DF	Type III SS	Mean Square	F Value	Pr > F
package	3	588.2210526	196.0736842	18.59	<.0001

Level of package	N	y Mean	Std Dev
1	5	14.6000000	2.30217289
2	5	13.4000000	3.64691651
3	4	19.5000000	2.64575131
4	5	27.2000000	3.96232255

Regression Approach to Single-Factor Analysis of Variance

On text page 704 the authors illustrate the regression approach to a single-factor analysis of variance. In Chapter 15 of this manual we presented the general linear model and discussed the construction of indicator variables for use in the regression approach to analysis of variance. We indicated that *proc glm* will generate indicator variables for the regression approach automatically and give the same test statistics as those obtained by our defining indicator variables directly and using SAS' *proc reg*. Here, we give one further example of defining indicator variables and using SAS' *proc reg* in a single factor design. In all subsequent chapters, however, the reader is referred to Chapter 15 of this manual when the text refers to the Regression Approach to ANOVA.

In Insert 16.2, we define indicator variables *X1, X2*, and *X3* as shown on text page 707 (referred to in Chapter 15 as *Effects Model 1*). We then perform a regression analysis using *Y* as the response variable and *X1, X2,* and *X3* as independent variables. Results are shown in SAS Output 16.4 and are consistent with the results reported on text page 707, Table 16.4 (c), and the *proc glm* output presented in SAS Output 16.3 where *package* was the single factor in the model. The variable (factor) *package* has values that were specified by allocated coding (see Chapter 15) but *proc glm* automatically codes indicator variables to be used in a regression analysis of variance model. We could also define our own choice of indicator variables and specify these as independent variables in the *model* statement for *proc glm*. This would also result in a Correct Model *F* value of 18.59.

INSERT 16.2	INSERT 16.2 continued

* Regression Approach to Single-Factor Analysis of Variance.
data Kenton;
infile 'c:\kutnerdata\chapter 16 data sets\ch16ta01.txt';
  input y package store;
x1=0;
if package=1 then x1=1;
if package=4 then x1=-1;
x2=0;
	if package=2 then x2=1;
	if package=4 then x2=-1;
	x3=0;
	if package=3 then x3=1;
	if package=4 then x3=-1;
	proc reg;
	  model y=x1 x2 x3;
	  run;

SAS Output 16.4

Source	DF	Sum of Squares	Mean Square	F Value	Pr > F
Model	3	588.2210526	196.0736842	18.59	<.0001
Error	15	158.2000000	10.5466667		
Corrected Total	18	746.4210526			

Source	DF	Type III SS	Mean Square	F Value	Pr > F
package	3	588.2210526	196.0736842	18.59	<.0001

Randomization Tests

SAS does not have a readily available test for conducting the randomization test presented on text page 712.

Chapter 17 SAS®

Analysis of Factor Level Effects in Single Factor Studies

In Chapter 16, the authors discussed the analysis of variance for the single-factor ANOVA model. The focus was on an F-test aimed at testing the null hypothesis that the factor level means are all equal; i.e., an F-test aimed at testing

$$H_0 : \mu_1 = \mu_2 = \cdots = \mu_r$$

where r is the number of factor level means. If this hypothesis is rejected, we usually pursue further analyses to investigate the nature of differences among the means. This often involves testing hypotheses and constructing confidence intervals on subsets of the factor level means. When we investigate these sub-hypotheses and confidence intervals, we usually want to use procedures for making simultaneous inferences to preserve the overall significance level at the stated level α for testing hypotheses and the overall confidence level at the stated $100(1-\alpha)\%$ level for constructing multiple interval estimates. In this chapter, the authors present various procedures that are widely used to make simultaneous inferences pertaining to subsets of the factor level means.

Rust Inhibitor Example

Data File: ch17ta02.txt

Researchers tested the effectiveness of four brands of rust inhibitor. Forty experimental units were assigned randomly to the four brands with 10 units assigned to each brand. The response variable was coded so that higher values indicated more rust inhibitor effectiveness. See Chapter 0, "Working with SAS," for instructions on opening the Rust Inhibitor Example and naming the variables y, *brand*, and *unit*. After opening and printing ch17ta02.txt, the first 5 lines of output should look like SAS Output 17.1.

The researcher first wished to determine if there were any significant differences among the response (effectiveness) means for the four rust inhibitors. Here we use *proc glm* where Y is the dependent variable and *brand* is the single *class* variable. Again, *proc glm* automatically creates indicator variables suitable for an effects model analysis of variance. Partial results are presented in SAS Output 17.2 and are consistent with Table 17.2 (b), text page 735. The researchers concluded that there were statistically significant differences among the rust inhibitor means, $F(3, 36) = 866.118, p < 0.000$.

SAS Output 17.1

Obs	y	brand	unit
1	43.9	1	1
2	39.0	1	2
3	46.7	1	3
4	43.8	1	4
5	44.2	1	5

SAS Output 17.2

Source	DF	Sum of Squares	Mean Square	F Value	Pr > F
Model	3	15953.46600	5317.82200	866.12	<.0001
Error	36	221.03400	6.13983		
Corrected Total	39	16174.50000			

Source	DF	Type III SS	Mean Square	F Value	Pr > F
brand	3	15953.46600	5317.82200	866.12	<.0001

Kenton Food Company Example

Data File: ch16ta01.txt

The Kenton Food Company (text page 865-686) studied the relationship between sales (Y) and the type of package design for a new breakfast cereal. Here, store was the experimental unit. Each of 20 stores was assigned to one package design such that there were 5 stores assigned to each design. One store was unable to fulfill the study requirement and was dropped from the study. See Chapter 0, "Working with SAS," for instructions on opening the Kenton Food Company Example and naming the variables y, *package*, and *store*. After opening and printing ch16ta01.txt, the first 5 lines of output should look like SAS Output 17.3.

SAS Output 17.3

Obs	y	package	store
1	11	1	1
2	17	1	2
3	16	1	3
4	14	1	4
5	15	1	5

The Line Plot shown in Figure 17.1, text page 736, is not available in SAS. Text Figure 17.2 (a) can be obtained using *proc chart*, and the Main Effect Plot [Figure 17.2 (b), text page 736] with box and whiskers added can be obtained (output not shown) using *proc boxplot* as also shown in Insert 17.1.

```
INSERT 17.1

data Kenton;
infile 'c:\kutnerdata\chapter 16 data sets\ch16ta01.txt';
  input y package store;
*** Produce text Figure 17.2 a;
proc chart;
 vbar package / midpoints=1 to 4 ;
run;
*** Produce text Figure 17.2 b with box and whiskers;
proc boxplot;
 plot y * package / boxconnect vaxis=0 to 40 by 10;
 run;
```

Review of SAS Methods for Multiple Comparisons and Estimating and Testing Hypotheses About Contrasts

Before continuing the Kenton Food Company example, we review some of the methods available in SAS for Contrasts and Post Hoc comparisons. We will see that there are many ways to request multiple comparisons in SAS. Each method, however, is typically used in different situations or to test different hypotheses. Using *proc glm*, sub-hypotheses can be specified using *means*, *lsmeans*, or *contrast* statements.

The *means* statement takes the form:

   means effects </ options>;

Only effects specified as *class* variables can be used in the *means* statement. For each specified effect, SAS computes the arithmetic means and standard deviations of all continuous variables in the model. For example, suppose A and B are two factors where A has two levels and B has 3 levels. The SAS statements:

   proc glm;
     class a b;
     model y = a b a*b;
     means a b a*b;
   run;

will result in a printing of the means and standard deviations for the two levels of A, the three levels of B, and the six combinations (cells) of levels of A and B.

As an option in the means statement, we may also request pairwise comparisons for main effects but not for interaction effects. Procedures available for performing tests for pairwise comparisons include: *Bonferroni, Duncan, Dunnett, Gabriel, LSD, Scheffe, Sidak, SNK, Tukey, Waller*, and others. We may also specify the overall alpha level (e.g., *alpha=0.01*) for the set of comparisons (the default is *alpha* = 0.05). In the *means* statement, all comparisons are based on unadjusted means. Thus, for unbalanced designs or for designs with a covariate in the model, the *means* statement may not be appropriate.

For illustration, assume that we have a *class* variable named *drug* that has 4 levels (*d1, d2, d3*, and *d4*). We can request the six pairwise comparisons of the means (*d1* vs *d2, d1* vs *d3*, etc.) using the *Bonferroni* method for testing these comparisons with an overall alpha level of 0.1 by specifying:

> *means drug / bon alpha=.1;*

Thus, each of the six comparisons is made at the $\alpha/6 = 0.1/6 = 0.0167$ level of significance with the assurance that the overall probability (that at least one of the six null hypotheses will be rejected if all six are all true) is no greater than $\alpha = 0.1$.

SAS provides many additional options for use in the *means* statement, four of which are useful in the present discussion. The *cldiff* option, when used with the *bon, gabriel, scheffe, sidak, smm, gt2, t, lsd,* and/or *tukey* options, requests confidence intervals for all pairwise differences between means where the intervals are adjusted (using the specified method of adjustment) for simultaneous coverage at the $100x(1-\alpha)\%$ level. The *clm* option, when used with the *bon, gabriel, scheffe, sidak, smm, t,* and/or *lsd* options, requests simultaneous confidence intervals for the mean of each level of all the effects variables specified in the *means* statement. The option *e = effect* specifies the denominator mean square that is to be used in the multiple comparison tests (the default is the residual mean square). The effect specified in this option must be a term in the *model* statement; otherwise the default is invoked. The option *etype = n*, where *n* = 1, 2, 3, or 4 indicates the type of sum of squares to be used in computing the denominator mean square for the effect specified in the *e = effect* option.

The *lsmeans* statement takes the form:

> *lsmeans effects </ options>;*

Only effects specified as *class* variables can be used in the *lsmeans* statement. The SAS *lsmeans* statement produces least squares means (*lsmeans*), sometimes referred to as adjusted means. For unbalanced designs or models that contain covariates, the *lsmeans* statement may be more appropriate than the *means* statement. Additionally, we may request multiple comparisons for main effects and for interaction means. Procedures available for multiple comparisons include: *Bonferroni, Dunnett, Scheffe, Sidak, Tukey,* and others. We may also specify the overall alpha level (e.g., *alpha=0.01*) for the set of comparisons. All comparisons are based on adjusted means. The *adjust=method, clm, cl,* and *pdiff* options are used with the *lsmeans* statement. *Adjust=method* specifies the method of adjustment (e.g., *adjust = bon*), *clm* specifies confidence limits for the adjusted mean of each level of the all effects variables specified in the *lsmeans* statement, *cl* specifies confidence limits for the differences between adjusted means for all possible pairs of levels for each effect variable specified in the *lsmeans* statement, and the *pdiff* option requests that *p*-values for pairwise tests of no differences between the adjusted means. For illustration, assume that we have an unbalanced design with *class* variables named *A* and *B* that have 2 and 3 levels, respectively, as above. We can request 6 pairwise comparisons of the adjusted means together with simultaneous confidence intervals using the *Bonferroni* method with an overall alpha level of 0.1 by the statement:

lsmeans a*b / adjust=bon cl pdiff alpha=.1;

Whereas options in the *means* and *lsmeans* statements can be used to perform pairwise tests of the hypotheses that the two means in each pair are equal, we do not have the option in these statements to test hypotheses involving other functions of the means. We can use the *contrast* statement to test hypotheses that certain linear functions of the means are equal to zero. As stated in Chapter 15 of this manual, contrasts (L) are linear functions of a set of means where in this function the coefficients of the means sum to zero. For theoretical reasons used in the development of the F-statistic for testing general linear hypotheses about the mean, we require that these hypotheses be contrasts according to the formal definition. We can specify contrasts within *proc glm* using the *contrast* statement, which takes the form:

contrast 'label' effect values < ... effect values > < / options >;

The values are the (constants) coefficients that define the linear function (L) as indicated in Chapter 15 and further illustrated in the next section. Unlike the *means* and *lsmeans* statements, the *contrast* statement offers no protection against Type I error for multiple contrasts. The *contrast* statement provides a test of the hypothesis that the specified contrast is equal to zero but it does not provide an estimate of the contrast. We can use the *estimate* statement to obtain such an estimate. This statement has the form:

estimate 'label' effect values < ... effect values > < / options >;

In the next section, we provide examples to illustrate use of the *contrast* and *estimate* statements, respectively, to test more general hypotheses than the pairwise comparisons tested by the *means* and *lsmeans* statements and to estimate linear functions of the model parameters.

Kenton Food Company Example Continued

Estimation and Testing of Factor Level Means

Inferences for a Single Factor Level Mean

On text page 738 the sales manager wishes to estimate the sales mean for package design 1 with a 95% confidence interval. To produce this confidence interval, we specify *proc glm* and the *lsmeans* statement in Insert 17.2. This statement produces the adjusted means, 95% (by default) confidence limits (*cl*), and probability levels and confidence limits for differences between factor level means as shown in SAS Output 17.4. These results are consistent with the 95% confidence interval reported on text page 738.

```
                              INSERT 17.2

data Kenton;
infile 'c:\kutnerdata\chapter 16 data sets\ch16ta01.txt';
  input y package store;
proc glm;
  class package;
  model y = package;
  lsmeans package / pdiff cl ;
  estimate 'Package design 3 vs 4' package 0 0 1 -1;
  estimate '3-color (package 1&2) vs 5-color (package 3&4)' package .5 .5 -.5 -.5;
run;
```

SAS Output 17.4

package	y LSMEAN	95% Confidence Limits	
1	14.600000	11.504380	17.695620
2	13.400000	10.304380	16.495620
3	19.500000	16.038991	22.961009
4	27.200000	24.104380	30.295620

Inferences for Differences between Two Factor Level Means

On text page 740, the sales manager wishes to estimate the difference between the sales means for package designs 3 and 4 using a 95% confidence interval. The *lsmeans* statement of Insert 17.2 also produces this analysis as shown in SAS Output 17.5. These results are consistent with the 95% confidence interval reported on text page 740. The authors also present test statistic (17.18) $t^* = -3.53$. In Insert 17.2, we use an *estimate* statement to estimate the specified linear function of the means. Results of the *estimate* statements are found in SAS Output 17.6.

SAS Output 17.5

		Difference Between Means	95% Confidence Limits for LSMean(i)- LSMean(j)	
i	j			
1	2	1.200000	-3.177868	5.577868
1	3	-4.900000	-9.543430	-0.256570
1	4	-12.600000	-16.977868	-8.222132
2	3	-6.100000	-10.743430	-1.456570
2	4	-13.800000	-18.177868	-9.422132
3	4	-7.700000	-12.343430	-3.056570

Least Squares Means for Effect package

SAS Output 17.6

Parameter	Estimate	Standard Error	t Value	Pr > |t|
Package design 3 vs 4	-7.70000000	2.17853162	-3.53	0.0030
3-color (package 1&2) vs 5-color (package 3&4)	-9.35000000	1.49705266	-6.25	<.0001

Inferences for Contrasts of Factor Level Means

Illustrations of Contrasts: We extend the use of the *contrast* statement introduced in Chapter 15 of this manual to specify various custom hypotheses for the contrasts presented on text page 741. As noted in text Chapter 15, linear contrasts (L) are linear functions of factor level means where the contrast coefficients c_i sum to zero. A linear combination of m sample means takes the form:

$$L = c_1 \mu_1 + c_2 \mu_2 + \cdots + c_m \mu_m$$

In SAS, the *contrast* statement is useful for specifying custom hypotheses that otherwise may be not readily available. Upon execution of a *contrast* statement, SAS presents test results for the specified custom hypothesis. We present some specific examples that use the *contrast* statement to request test statistics in terms of the following four contrasts (text page 741).

Each of these contrasts is a function of four means: μ_1, μ_2, μ_3, and μ_4. These are the "population" sales means for the four levels of *package* in the text Kenton Food Example.

Contrast #1: $L = \mu_1 - \mu_2$

Contrast #2: $L = \dfrac{\mu_1 + \mu_2}{2} - \dfrac{\mu_3 + \mu_4}{2}$

Contrast #3: $L = \dfrac{\mu_1 + \mu_3}{2} - \dfrac{\mu_2 + \mu_4}{2}$

Contrast #4: $L = \mu_1 - \dfrac{\mu_1 + \mu_2 + \mu_3 + \mu_4}{4}$

Contrast #1: The researchers wish to test the hypothesis that the sales means for the two 3-color designs are equal, i.e., the mean for *package*=1 is equal to the mean for *package*=2. Thus, they wish to test the "null" hypothesis

$$H_0 : \mu_1 - \mu_2 = 0$$

If we let $c_1 = 1$, $c_2 = -1$, $c_3 = 0$, and $c_4 = 0$, we see that the left side of the equation for the hypothesis is a contrast L that can be written as

$$L = (1)\mu_1 + (-1)\mu_2 + (0)\mu_3 + (0)\mu_4$$

The corresponding SAS *contrast* statement to test the hypothesis is

> *contrast* 'Package 1 vs Package 2=0' *package* 1 –1 0 0;

We estimate the contrast by executing the statement

> *estimate* 'Package 1 - Package 2' *package* 1 –1 0 0;

Contrast #4: The researchers wish to test the hypothesis that the sales mean for package design 1 is equal to the overall mean. The overall mean is

$$\mu = \dfrac{\mu_1 + \mu_2 + \mu_3 + \mu_4}{4}$$

The hypothesis can be expressed as

$$H_0 : \mu_1 = \mu$$

or as

$$H_0 : \mu_1 - \mu = 0$$

or, substituting for μ, as

$$H_0 : \mu_1 - \frac{\mu_1 + \mu_2 + \mu_3 + \mu_4}{4} = 0$$

or, multiplying by 4 and combining terms, as

$$H_0 : \ 3\mu_1 - \mu_2 - \mu_3 - \mu_4 = 0$$

Again, we see that the left side of the hypothesis is a contrast. The corresponding SAS *contrast* statement to test the hypothesis is

> *contrast* 'Package 1 vs All designs' *package*   3 –1 –1 –1;

We return to the hypothesis expressed as

$$H_0 : \mu_1 - \mu = 0$$

and recall that in the effects model, we define

$$\tau_1 = \mu_1 - \mu$$

as the "effect" of package design 1. Thus, we can also express the hypothesis as

$$H_0 : \tau_1 = 0$$

Suppose we wish to estimate the treatment effect (a contrast) for package design 1; i.e., suppose we wish to estimate

$$\tau_1 = \frac{3\mu_1 - \mu_2 - \mu_3 - \mu_4}{4}$$

We accomplish this goal by executing the statement

> *estimate* 'Package 1 vs All designs' *package* .75 -.25 -.25 -.25;

Note that we prefer to avoid using decimal fractions for the coefficients in *contrast* and *estimate* statements because for contrasts like 2/3 –1/3 –1/3, use of 0.6667 –0.3333 –0.3333 does not work: i.e., the sum of the coefficients must be exactly zero in order for the contrast to be estimable (use of 0.6666 –0.3333 –0.3333 does work because the contrast coefficients sum exactly to zero). However, we can use the *divisor* option in the *estimate* statement to estimate functions that require decimal fractions. For example, we could execute the following as an alternative to the previous *estimate* statement:

estimate 'Package 1 vs All designs' *package* 3 -1 -1 –1 / divisor = 4;

Syntax shown in the *contrast* statements of Insert 17.3 will produce test statistics for the 4 contrasts listed above and presented on text page 741. Contrasts of interest in analyzing interactions will be discussed in Chapter 19 of this manual.

INSERT 17.3

```
data Kenton;
infile 'c:\kutnerdata\chapter 16 data sets\ch16ta01.txt';
  input y package store;
proc glm;
  class package;
  model y = package;
  contrast 'Contrast #1' package 1 –1 0 0;
  estimate 'Package 1 - Package 2' package  1  –1  0  0;
  contrast 'Contrast #2' package 1 1 –1 –1;
  contrast 'Contrast #3' package 1 –1 1 –1;
  contrast 'Contrast #4' package 3 –1 –1 –1 ;
  estimate 'Package 1 vs All designs' package .75 -.25 -.25 -.25;
run;
```

On text page 743, the sales manager wishes to compare the mean sales of 3-color designs (*package* 1 and *package* 2) to the mean sales of 5-color designs (*package*=3 and *package*=4) with a 95% confidence interval. In Insert 17.2, we use an *estimate* statement (second *estimate* statement) for this analysis. Results of the *estimate* statement are given in SAS Output 17.6. The *t* value and $s\{\hat{L}\}$ (Standard Error) are consistent with text page 743. Note that neither the *estimate* nor the *contrast* statement produces confidence intervals and that neither *means* nor *lsmeans* can be used to produce confidence intervals for these "custom" functions. The statistics provided in SAS Output 17.6 can be used to calculate the desired confidence intervals via a hand calculator.

Simultaneous Inference Procedures

***Tukey* Multiple Comparison Procedure**: SAS offers many options for conducting post hoc analyses that can be accessed from the *proc glm means* or *lsmeans* statement. For example, on text page 748 the authors estimated all pairwise comparisons in the Rust Inhibitor example using the *Tukey* procedure. We request *proc glm* with *Y* as the dependent variable and *brand* as the single independent variable (*class* variable), and specify *Tukey* in the *lsmeans* statement. Partial results are shown in SAS Output 17.7. The 95% confidence limits are consistent with those reported in Table 17.3, text page 749. Additionally, the difference in the response means between brands A (1) and D (4) are not statistically significant, $p=0.0933$. The adjusted mean for Brand B is significantly greater than all other brands. Brand C is significantly greater than brands A and D but significantly less than Brand B. SAS makes the proper adjustment in the *Tukey* procedure when there are unequal sample sizes as reported on text page 749-751.

INSERT 17.4

```
data rust;
infile 'c:\kutnerdata\chapter 17 data sets\ch17ta02.txt';
  input y brand unit;
proc glm;
 class brand;
 model y = brand;
  lsmeans brand / adjust=tukey alpha=.05 cl pdiff;
run;
```

SAS Output 17.7

brand	y LSMEAN	LSMEAN Number
1	43.1400000	1
2	89.4400000	2
3	67.9500000	3
4	40.4700000	4

Least Squares Means for effect brand
Pr > |t| for H0: LSMean(i)=LSMean(j)

Dependent Variable: y

i/j	1	2	3	4
1		<.0001	<.0001	0.0933
2	<.0001		<.0001	<.0001
3	<.0001	<.0001		<.0001
4	0.0933	<.0001	<.0001	

Least Squares Means for Effect brand				
I	j	Difference Between Means	Simultaneous 95% Confidence Limits for LSMean(i)-LSMean(j)	
1	2	-46.300000	-49.284465	-43.315535
1	3	-24.810000	-27.794465	-21.825535
1	4	2.670000	-0.314465	5.654465
2	3	21.490000	18.505535	24.474465
2	4	48.970000	45.985535	51.954465
3	4	27.480000	24.495535	30.464465

On text page 750, the authors illustrate simultaneous inference procedures for unbalanced designs. Using the Keeton Food Company example shown above, the researcher wished to compare the performance of the four package designs using the *Tukey* procedure and a family confidence coefficient equal to 90 percent. Since the numbers of observations for the different package designs are unequal, the estimated standard deviations must be calculated for each pairwise comparison. However, SAS will make the necessary adjustments as shown on text page 751 (text equation 17.30, page 747). The confidence intervals shown on text page 751 are obtained by modifying the Kenton Food Company example syntax as shown in Insert 17.2. The *lsmeans* statement is changed to: *"lsmeans package / adjust=tukey alpha=.1 pdiff cl;"*.

Scheffe **Multiple Comparison Procedure**: The researcher in the Kenton Food Company example used the *Scheffe* procedure and a family confidence coefficient of 90 percent to estimate the four contrasts shown on text page 754. L_1 and L_2 represent linear combinations of factor level means that are not available via the *lsmeans* statement. We can execute *contrast* or *estimate* statements as for Contrast #1 and Contrast #3 in Insert 17.3 above but neither will produce confidence intervals, adjusted by the *Scheffe* method or otherwise. To obtain the *Scheffe* adjusted confidence interval as shown on text page 754, we use the *finv* function to find $S=2.7330$ (Insert 17.5) and SAS Output 17.6 to find $\hat{L}_1 = -9.35$ and $s\{\hat{L}_1\}=1.497$. We then use equation 17.43, text page 753, to find the desired interval. L_3 and L_4 are simple pairwise comparisons and their confidence limits can be obtained by specifying the *Scheffe* procedure as shown in the *lsmeans* statement of Insert 17.5.

INSERT 17.5	INSERT 17.5 continued

data Kenton;
infile 'c:\kutnerdata\chapter 16 data sets\ch16ta01.txt';
  input y package store;
s=sqrt(3*finv(.9,3,15));
B=tinv(1-(.025/(2*2)),15);
proc print data=kenton (obs=1);
  var s b;
run;
	proc glm;
	  class package;
	  model y = package;
	  lsmeans package / adjust=scheffe alpha=.1 cl pdiff;
	  run;

Bonferroni **Multiple Comparison Procedure**: The researcher in the Kenton Food Company example used the *Bonferroni* procedure and a family confidence coefficient of 97.5 percent to estimate the two contrasts shown on text page 756. As in the *Scheffe* example, L_1 and L_2 represent linear combinations of factor level means that are not pairwise differences, and therefore are not available via the *lsmeans* statement. To obtain the *Bonferroni* adjusted confidence interval for L_1 as shown on text page 757, we use the *tinv* function to find $B=2.8366$ (Insert 17.5) and SAS Output 17.6 to find $\hat{L}_1 = -9.35$ and $s\{\hat{L}_1\}=1.497$. We can then use equation 17.46, text page 756, to find the desired interval.

Analysis of Means

The Analysis of Means testing procedure presented on text page 758 is not readily available in SAS.

ANOVA Diagnostics and Remedial Measures

In this chapter, the authors discuss diagnostics and remedial measures to improve the appropriateness of the analysis of variance model. Their discussion begins with analysis of residuals for ANOVA models, procedures that closely parallel the use of residual analysis for regression models. In section 18.3, the authors discuss tests for constancy of error variance. Next, the authors discuss models that employ weighted least squares and transformations as remedial measures for models that have deficiencies identified in the diagnostic process. In section 18.6, the authors describe the effects of departures from the model. The authors conclude the chapter with a discussion of the nonparametric rank F test.

Residual Analysis

Rust Inhibitor Example

Data File: ch17ta02.txt

From text page 734, researchers tested the effectiveness of four brands of rust inhibitor. Forty experimental units were assigned randomly to the four brands with 10 units assigned to each brand. The response variable was coded so that higher values indicated more rust inhibitor effectiveness. See Chapter 0, "Working with SAS," for instructions on opening the Rust Inhibitor Example and naming the variables *y*, *brand*, and *unit*. After opening and printing ch17ta02.txt, the first 5 lines of output should look like SAS Output 17.1.

To produce the residual plots shown in Figure 18.1, text page 777, we use *proc glm* and save the residuals (*r=residual*) and predicted values (*p=predicted*) based on a model where *Y* is the dependent variable and *brand* is the single independent variable (*class* variable). (Insert 18.1) We then use *proc gplot* to plot the residuals on the Y-axis and predicted values on the X-axis. Results are shown in SAS Output 18.1 and are consistent with text Figure 18.1, a *residual plot against fitted values*. We use the procedure *proc capability* and specify the *qqplot* option to produce a normal probability plot, also shown text Figure 18.1. To produce the aligned dot plot shown in text Figure 18.1, we again use the *proc gplot* procedure (output not shown) and enter *brand* on the Y-axis and *residual* on the X-axis.

INSERT 18.1	INSERT 18.1 continued

data rust;
infile 'c:\kutnerdata\chapter 17 data
sets\ch17ta02.txt';
  input y brand unit;
proc glm;
 class brand;
 model y = brand;
 output out=results r=residual p=predicted;
run;
	*** Produce Figure 18.1, residual by predicted;
	proc gplot data=results;
	 plot residual*predicted / haxis = 30 to 100 by 10;
	 run;
	*** Produce Figure 18.1, normal probability;
	goptions reset=all;
	proc capability ;
	 symbol1 value=dot;
	  var residual;
	  qqplot ;
	run;

SAS Output 18.1

SAS Output 18.2

210

Tests for Constancy of Error Variance

ABT Electronic Example

Data File: ch18ta02.txt

Engineers at the ABT Electronics Corporation evaluated five types of flux used to solder joints. Forty circuit boards were randomly selected and each of the five types of flux was randomly assigned to 8 of the circuit boards. A mechanical device then measured the force required to break the soldered joint. This force, referred to as pull strength by the engineers, was the response variable. See Chapter 0, "Working with SAS," for instructions on opening the ABT Electronic Example (text page 783) and naming the variables *y*, *flux*, and *board*. After opening and printing ch18ta02.txt, the first 5 lines of output should look like SAS Output 18.3.

SAS Output 18.3

Obs	y	flux	board
1	14.87	1	1
2	16.81	1	2
3	15.83	1	3
4	15.47	1	4
5	13.60	1	5

On text page 783, the researchers plotted the response variable against the flux types in Figure 18.6, text page 784. To reproduce Figure 18.6 (SAS Output 18.4), we use *proc gplot* and enter *Y* on the X-axis and *flux* on the Y-axis. (Insert 18.2.) Consistent with the text, flux type 3 has a greater magnitude of variation than the other flux types.

INSERT 18.2	INSERT 18.2 continued

data abt;
infile 'c:\kutnerdata\chapter 18 data sets\ch18ta02.txt';
  input y flux board;
*** Produce Figure 18.4;
goptions reset=all;
proc gplot;
 plot flux*y / haxis=0 to 30 by 10 vaxis=0 to 5;
 run;
*** Correlation Test for Normality;
proc glm;
 class flux;
 model y = flux;
  output out=step2 r=residual;
run;
	proc capability ;
	 where flux=1;
	  var residual;
	  probplot;
	run;
	proc rank data=step2 out=step3;
	 where flux=1;
	 var residual;
	 ranks ranke;
	run;
	data new;
	 set step3;
	ev=sqrt(2.109)* Probit ((ranke-.375)/(8+.25));
	proc corr;
	 var ev residual;
	  run;

The researchers wished to perform the *Hartley Test*. Since the *Hartley Test* requires approximate normality, the researcher first plotted normal probability plots of residuals for each treatment. In Insert 18.2, we first use *proc glm* to save the residuals for the ABT Electronic Example. To produce normal probability plots for each treatment, we use *proc capability* and the *where* option as shown in Insert 18.2 to select only one flux type at a time when producing the normal probability plot. (Output not shown)

The researchers then performed a formal test of normality of error terms that was discussed in text Chapter 3. Computational details for the *Correlation Test for Normality*, the correlation between the ordered residuals and their expected value under normality, were presented in Chapter 3 of this manual. In Insert 18.2, we obtain the mean squared error (*MSE*=2.109) for the model where *Y* is the dependent variable and *flux* in the independent variable (*class* variable), and we save the residuals (*r=residual*). We then select (*where flux=1*) only *flux* type 1, rank the residuals, and place the rank in a variable named *ranke*. We then use equation 3.6, text page 111, to find the expected value (*ev*) of the error terms. Finally, we correlate *ev* with *residual*. The resulting correlation is 0.982 and is consistent with text page 783. Since our obtained correlation is greater than the critical value in text Table B.6, we conclude that the error terms among *flux* type 1 are normally distributed. To perform the same operation for *flux* type 2, change both *where* statements in Insert 18.2 to *where flux=2*.

SAS Output 18.4

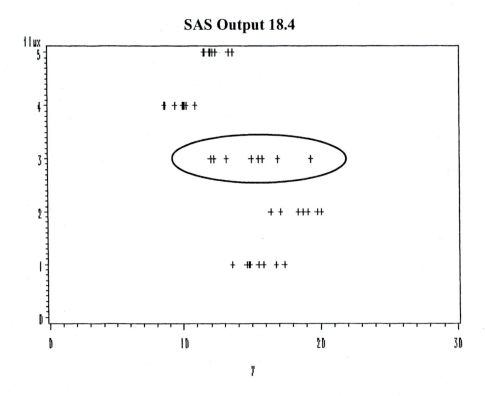

To formally test for constancy of error variance, we conduct a *Hartley Test* as described on text page 782. This test is based on the ratio of the largest factor level variance to the smallest factor level variance. In Insert 18.3, we request the variance of each factor level in the ABT Electronics Example. Results are not shown. We now find $H = 6.183 / 0.592 = 10.44$. Since $H = 10.44 >$ the critical value we conclude that the variances of the five factor levels are not all equal.

INSERT 18.3	INSERT 18.3 continued
| ```
data abt;
infile 'c:\kutnerdata\chapter 18 data sets\ch18ta02.txt';
  input y flux board;
proc sort;
 by flux;
run;
``` | ```
proc means var;
 by flux;
 var y;
 run;
``` |

On text page 784, the researchers in the ABT Electronics Example performed a *Brown-Forsythe* test for constancy of error variance. This test is based on the absolute deviation of each Y value from its respective factor level median. In this application, we specify SAS statements to perform summary calculations and retain the values for subsequent calculations. In Insert 18.4, we use the *proc means* and *output* statements to find and retain the median of Y for each value of *flux*. We specify that the median of the Y values be placed in a file name *temp*. We use the *merge* function to specify that the *abt* and *temp* data sets be merged into a data set named *combine*. We then compute the absolute value of the deviation (*absdev*) of each Y value from its respective factor level median. Finally, we perform an ANOVA using *proc glm* where *absdev* is the dependent variable and *flux* is the single independent variable. Results are shown in SAS Output 18.5 where $F_{BF}^* = 2.936$, $p = 0.034$, consistent with text page 785. Optionally, we can use the *proc glm means* option, *hovtest=bf*, to request the Brown Forsythe test as shown in Insert 18.4.

INSERT 18.4	INSERT 18.4 continued
| ```
data abt;
infile 'c:\kutnerdata\chapter 18 data sets\ch18ta02.txt';
  input y flux board;
proc sort;
 by flux;
******** Find median of Y for each level of flux;
proc means noprint;
 by flux;
 var y;
 output out=temp (drop=_type_ _freq_)
median=flux_y;
run;
data combine;
 merge abt temp;
 by flux;
run;
``` | ```
proc sort;
 by flux;
data combine;
 set combine;
absdev=abs(y-flux_y);
proc glm;
 class flux;
  model absdev = flux;
run;

**  SAS hovtest option for Brown Forsythe;
proc glm;
 class flux;
 model y = flux;
 means flux / hovtest=bf;
 run;
``` |

SAS Output 18.5

Source	DF	Sum of Squares	Mean Square	F Value	Pr > F
Model	4	9.34771500	2.33692875	2.94	0.0341
Error	35	27.86062500	0.79601786		
Corrected Total	39	37.20834000			

Weighted Least Squares

ABT Electronics Example

Continuing with the ABT Electronics Example on text page 787, because there is evidence that the error variances are not constant across *flux* levels, we use weighted least squares regression as a remedial measure. In Insert 18.5, we use the *proc means output* statement to find the variance of *Y* for each level of *flux*. We use the *merge* function to combine the *abt* and *temp* files into a file named *combine*. We use the coding presented on text page 787 to create *X1* though *X5*, use equation 18.14 (text page 786) to compute the weight (w_{ij}), and set *X=1*. We then use *proc reg* where *Y* is the dependent variable; *X1, X2, X3, X4,* and *X5* are independent variables; *wt* is the weight variable; and we do not include an intercept in the model (*noint*). This produces Figure 18.7 (a), text page 788. (Output not shown.) We then produce Figure 18.7 (b), with *proc reg* where *Y* is the dependent variable, *X* is the independent variable, *wt* is the weight variable, and there is no intercept in the model. We can now use equation 18.15, text page 787, to find $F_W^* = 81.05$, as shown on text page 789.

INSERT 18.5	INSERT 18.5 continued
| ```
data abt;
infile 'c:\kutnerdata\chapter 18 data sets\ch18ta02.txt';
  input y flux board;
proc sort;
 by flux;
*** Find median of Y for each level of flux;
proc means noprint;
 by flux;
 var y;
 output out=temp (drop=_type_ _freq_) var=flux_y;
run;
data combine;
 merge abt temp;
 by flux;
run;
proc sort;
 by flux;
``` | ```
data combine;
 set combine;
if flux=1 then x1=1;else x1=0;
if flux=2 then x2=1;else x2=0;
if flux=3 then x3=1;else x3=0;
if flux=4 then x4=1;else x4=0;
if flux=5 then x5=1;else x5=0;
wt=1/flux_y;
x=1;
*** Produce Figure 18.7 a;
proc reg;
 model y = x1 x2 x3 x4 x5 / noint;
  weight  wt;
run;
*** Produce Figure 18.7 b;
proc reg;
 model y = x / noint;
  weight  wt;
run;
``` |

Box-Cox Procedure

Servo-Data, Inc. Example

Data File: ch18ta05.txt

The Servo-Data, Inc., wished to study the relationship between location of mainframe computer installations and the amount of time between computer failures, the response variable. See Chapter 0, "Working with SAS," for instructions on opening the Servo-Data Example and naming the variables *y*, *location*, and *interval*. After opening and printing Table 18.5, text page 791, the first 5 lines of output should look like SAS Output 18.6.

SAS Output 18.6

Obs	y	location	interval
1	4.41	1	1
2	100.65	1	2
3	14.45	1	3
4	47.13	1	4
5	85.21	1	5

Here we use the Box-Cox procedure to identify a power transformation of the type Y^λ that may be helpful in correcting for non-constancy of error variance and lack of normality. We presented syntax for the Box-Cox transformation in Chapter 3 of this manual. The independent variable was continuous in the example of Chapter 3. In the present example, independent variables represent three levels of a single factor. Here, we have modified the syntax from Chapter 3 to accommodate the use of indicator variables to represent levels of a factor in the ANOVA model rather than directly using one or more continuous variables in the regression model. (Insert 18.6)

This procedure uses a range of λ values starting at λ (*start*) = -1 and incrementing (*incremen*) by a value of 0.1 for 21 iterations (*noiter*). The syntax will list the values of λ and *SSE* (consistent with Table 18.6, text page 792) and plot *SSE* as a function of λ (not shown). The start, increment, and iterations values can be varied to specify choices suitable for different data sets.

```
options ls=72 ps=30 nonumber nodate;
data servo;
  infile 'c:\kutnerdata\chapter 18 data sets\ch18ta05.txt';
  input y location interval;
proc iml;
  use servo var{y location};
  read all;
  n = nrow(y);
  x1 = J(n,1,1);
  x2 = J(n,1,1);
    do i = 1 to n;
            if location[i] = 2 then x1[i] =  0;
            if location[i] = 3 then x1[i] = -1;
            if location[i] = 1 then x2[i] =  0;
            if location[i] = 3 then x2[i] = -1;
          end;
  noiter = 21;
  start = -1;
  increment = .1;
  x = J(n,1,1)||x1||x2;
  hat =x*inv(x`*x)*x`;
  lambda = j(noiter,1);
  lambda[1,1] = start;
  do i = 2 to noiter;
    lambda[i,1]=lambda[i-1,1] + increment;
  end;
  sse = j(noiter,1,0);
  do i = 1 to noiter;
    lamb = lambda[i];
          k2 = exp((1/n)*(j(1,n,1)*log(y)));
          k1 = 1/(lamb*k2**(lamb-1));
          if lamb > -1E-08 & lamb < 1E-08 then w = k2*log(y);
          else w = k1*(y##lamb -j(n,1,1));
          e = (i(n) - hat)*w;
    sse[i] = e`*e;
end;
  print lambda [format = 5.1] sse [format = 10.4];
  xy = lambda||sse;
  call pgraf(xy,'*','Lambda','SSE','Plot for Box-Cox Transformation');
quit;
```

Nonparametric Rank *F* Test

Servo-Data, Inc. Example

Data File: ch18ta05.txt

On text page 796, the authors present the nonparametric rank *F* test as an alternative to performing transformations of *Y* in the presence of non-normality or non-constancy of error variances. Servo-Data, Inc. wished to compare the length of time between computer failures (*Y*) during 5 failure intervals (*interval*) at three different locations (*location*). See Chapter 0, "Working with SAS," for instructions on opening the Servo-Data Example and naming the variables *y*, *location*, and *interval*. After opening and printing Table 18.5, text page 791, the first 5 lines of output should look like SAS Output 18.6.

Initial examination of the data indicates the presence of non-normality or non-constancy of error variances. On text page 796, the researchers performed the nonparametric rank F test and presented the *Kruskal-Wallis* test. In Insert 18.7, we rank the dependent variable (Y) and place the ranks into a variable named *ranky*. Results (output not shown) of the *GLM* procedure using *ranky* as the dependent variable are $F_R^* = 2.898$, $p = 0.094$, consistent with text page 796. Results of the *Kruskal-Wallis* test are $X_{KW}^2 = 4.560$, $p = 0.102$.

Multiple Pairwise Testing Procedure: On text page 797, the authors now wish to perform multiple pairwise testing following a significant rank F test. We use the steps in the last *proc glm* statement in Insert 18.7 to obtain the three confidence intervals.

INSERT 18.7	INSERT 18.7 continued

data abt;
  infile 'c:\kutnerdata\chapter 18 data sets\ch18ta05.txt';
  input y location interval ;
proc rank;
 var y;
 ranks ranky;
run;
*** Produce GLM with rank of y as dependent;
proc glm;
 class location;
  model ranky=location;
run;
*** Produce Kruskal-Wallis with y as dependent;
proc sort;
 by location;
run;
proc npar1way wilcoxon;
 var y;
 class location;
run;
	data abt;
	  infile 'c:\kutnerdata\chapter 18 data sets\ch18ta05.txt';
	  input y location interval ;
	proc glm;
	 class location;
	 model ranky=location;
	 means location / cldiff bon alpha = 0.1;
	run;

Chapter 19 SAS®

Two-Factor Studies with Equal Sample Size

In this chapter, the authors discuss two-factor studies with equal sample size. The typical model for these studies includes terms for estimating and testing hypotheses relevant to investigating the main effects of the two factors and possible interaction between the two factors. If the interactions are not statistically significant, we can focus the analysis directly on main effects. On the other hand, if they are significant, we must investigate differences among the means for the levels of each factor separately at each level of the other factor.

Castle Bakery Company Example

Data File: ch19ta07.txt

On text page 833, researchers studied the effect of shelf display height (bottom, middle, top) and width (regular, wide) on the number of cases (Y) of Italian bread sold during the study period. See Chapter 0, "Working with SAS," for instructions on opening the Castle Bakery Example and naming the variables y, $height$, $width$, and rep. After opening and printing ch19ta07.txt, the first 5 lines of output should look like SAS Output 19.1.

SAS Output 19.1

Obs	Y	height	width	rep
1	47	1	1	1
2	43	1	1	2
3	46	1	2	1
4	40	1	2	2
5	62	2	1	1

The researcher first plotted the estimated treatment means, Figure 19.8, text page 836. In Insert 19.1 we use *proc glm* to save the least square (adjusted) means and *proc gplot* to reproduce this figure as shown in SAS Output 19.2. Inspection of the graph suggests that the middle display height may be associated with more sales than the bottom and top display heights. Additionally, there appears to be little difference in sales means between the wide and regular display widths. The researchers now wished to formally test the effects of display height and width. We have already used *proc glm* (Insert 19.1) where we specified Y as the dependent variable and *height|width* as the independent variables (*class* variables). The vertical line between *height* and *width* indicates that the model will contain main effects for *height* and *width* and the *height*width* interaction effects. We also specified that least square means be printed and saved. Results are shown in SAS Outputs 19.3 and 19.4, and are consistent with Table 19.9 and Figure 19.9, text page 842. On text page 845, the researchers test for interaction effects between *height* and *width*. From SAS Output 19.3, we see that for the *height*width* interaction term, $F(2, 6)=1.16$, $p=0.3747$. Thus, we conclude that the interaction between display height and display width is not statistically significant. Since we failed to find significant interaction between the two factors, we test hypotheses about the main effects of *height* and *width*. For display *height*, we find $F(2, 6)=74.71$, $p<0.000$ and conclude that the means for the three levels of *height* are not all equal. For display width we find $F(2, 6)=1.16$, $p=0.3226$ and conclude that the means for the two levels of *width* are not significantly different. These findings are consistent with the analysis of main effects reported on text page 845-846.

INSERT 19.1	INSERT 19.1 continued

*** Figure 19.8;
data Bakery ;
infile 'c:\kutnerdata\chapter 19 data sets\ch19ta07.txt';
  input Y height width rep;
proc glm;
 class height width;
 model y = height|width;
  lsmeans height|width / out=lsmeans;
  run;
proc sort data=lsmeans;
by height width;
run;
	goptions reset=all;
	symbol1 v=circle i=join c=blue;
	symbol2 v=square i=join c=red;
	proc gplot data=lsmeans;
	 where ((height>0 and height<4)and (width>0 and width<3));
	 title 'Figure 19.8';
	 plot lsmean*height=width / haxis=0 to 4 by 1 vaxis=30 to 70 by 10;
	run;

SAS Output 19.2

Figure 19.8

SAS Output 19.3

Source	DF	Type III SS	Mean Square	F Value	Pr > F
height	2	1544.000000	772.000000	74.71	<.0001
width	1	12.000000	12.000000	1.16	0.3226
height*width	2	24.000000	12.000000	1.16	0.3747

219

SAS Output 19.4

height	width	Y LSMEAN
1	1	45.0000000
1	2	43.0000000
2	1	65.0000000
2	2	69.0000000
3	1	40.0000000
3	2	44.0000000

On text page 843, the authors plot the residuals against the predicted values [Figure 19.10 (a), text page 843] and present a normality plot of the residuals [Figure 19.10 (b)]. The syntax to reproduce Figures 19.10 (a) & (b) and 19.12 (a) & (b) is presented in Insert 19.2 (output not shown). The syntax to find the coefficient of correlation between the ordered residuals and their expected value under normality was presented in Chapter 18 of this manual and is not repeated here.

INSERT 19.2	INSERT 19.2 continued
| ```
data Bakery ;
infile 'c:\kutnerdata\chapter 19 data sets\ch19ta07.txt';
  input Y height width rep;
* plot figure 19.10;
proc glm;
 class height width;
 model y = height|width;
 means height|width;
 output out=results r=residual p=yhat;
run;


*** Produce Figure 19.10a;
goptions reset=all;
proc gplot data=results;
 title 'Figure 19.10a';
 plot residual*yhat / haxis=35 to 75 by 10;
run;
``` | ```
*** Produce Figure 19.10b;
goptions reset=all;
proc capability data=results;
 symbol1 value=dot;
 title 'Figure 19.10b';
  var residual;
  qqplot;
run;


*** Produce Figure 19.12a;
goptions reset=all;
proc chart data=results;
 title 'Figure 19.12a';
  vbar height / discrete type=mean sumvar=y;
run;
*** Produce Figure 19.12b;
goptions reset=all;
proc chart data=results;
 title 'Figure 19.12b';
  vbar width / discrete type=mean sumvar=y;
run;
``` |

Analyses of Factor Effects when Factors do not Interact

Estimates Based on Treatment Means

Pairwise Comparisons of Factor Level Means: Since SAS Output 19.2 and the formal analysis shown in SAS Output 19.3 failed to detect significant interaction effects, the authors plotted bar graphs of the *height* and *width* factor level means. In Insert 19.2 we produce Figure 19.12 (a) and (b), text page 853 (output not shown).

On text page 853, the authors test all pairwise comparisons among the shelf height means using the *Tukey* procdure and a family significance level of $\alpha = 0.05$. Additionally, they wish to estimate the differences in sales means between the middle shelf height and the other two heights. In Insert 19.3, we use *proc glm* to specify a full factorial model ($y = height|weight$) and request all pairwise comparisons among adjusted factor level (*height*) means by the *Tukey* method. Results are shown in SAS Output 19.5 and 19.6. We see that the middle height (*height*=2) had a significantly higher sales mean $\left(\overline{Y}_{2..} = 67\right)$ than the bottom $\left(\overline{Y}_{1.} = 44, p = 0.0001\right)$ and top $\left(\overline{Y}_{3.} = 42, p = 0.0001\right)$ heights. The difference between the bottom and top shelf height means was not statistically significant, *p*=0.6714. This is also seen in SAS Output 19.5 along with the 95% confidence intervals for the differences between the middle shelf height and the bottom and top shelf heights. Both SAS Output 19.5 and 19.6 are consistent with text page 854-855.

INSERT 19.3	INSERT 19.3 continued

data Bakery ;
infile 'c:\kutnerdata\chapter 19 data sets\ch19ta07.txt';
  input Y height width rep;
proc glm;
 class height width;
 model y = height|width;
 lsmeans height / adjust=tukey cl pdiff;
run;
	data Bakery ;
	infile 'c:\kutnerdata\chapter 19 data sets\ch19ta07.txt';
	  input Y height width rep;
	proc glm;
	 class height width;
	 model y = height|width;
	 lsmeans height|width / cl pdiff;
	  run;

SAS Output 19.5

		Difference Between Means	Simultaneous 95% Confidence Limits for LSMean(i)-LSMean(j)	
i	j			
1	2	-23.000000	-29.973998	-16.026002
1	3	2.000000	-4.973998	8.973998
2	3	25.000000	18.026002	31.973998

Least Squares Means for Effect height

221

SAS Output 19.6

height	Y LSMEAN	LSMEAN Number
1	44.0000000	1
2	67.0000000	2
3	42.0000000	3

Least Squares Means for effect height
Pr > |t| for H0: LSMean(i)=LSMean(j)

Dependent Variable: Y

i/j	1	2	3
1		0.0001	0.6714
2	0.0001		<.0001
3	0.6714	<.0001	

On text page 855, the authors wish to estimate the sales means for the middle and top shelf heights for the regular display width only. The estimate will be made using the *Bonferroni* procedure to construct a 90% family confidence interval ($\alpha = 0.1$). In Insert 19.3, the second *proc glm* specifies estimated (adjusted) means for the *height*width* interaction.

SAS will print (output not shown) the estimated marginal means for each of the six cells and also the 95% (by default) confidence intervals. However, these confidence intervals are not adjusted using a *Bonferroni* approach. That is, each interval essentially assumes that there is g=1 group for which the confidence interval is being constructed. Thus, requesting *proc glm* together with *lsmeans* and confidence intervals with $\alpha = 0.1$ will not match the intervals on text page 855, which are based on g=2. Since SAS does not allow us to specify g=2 in the calculation of the interval, we can still produce the intervals shown on text page 855 by specifying $\alpha = 0.1 / 2 = 0.05$, which is the default alpha level. Results are shown in SAS Output 19.7 and are consistent with text page 855.

SAS Output 19.7

height	width	Y LSMEAN	95% Confidence Limits	
1	1	45.000000	39.438095	50.561905
1	2	43.000000	37.438095	48.561905
2	1	65.000000	59.438095	70.561905
2	2	69.000000	63.438095	74.561905
3	1	40.000000	34.438095	45.561905
3	2	44.000000	38.438095	49.561905

Analysis of Factor Effect when Interactions are Important

On text page 856, a researcher at a junior college studied the effect of teaching method (Abstract versus Standard) and student's quantitative ability (Excellent vs Good vs Moderate) on the acquisition of mathematical knowledge. The data file for this example is not available, so we will present the syntax only for analyzing the Mathematics Learning Example. We let Y represent the response variable and *method* and *ability* represent the two independent variables. In Insert 19.4, we plot the estimated (adjusted) means to produce Figures 19.13 (a) and (b), text page 859.

On text page 859, the authors analyzed the response in terms of the logarithmic and square root transformations. To investigate the square root transformation, we compute a new variable named *ysqrt* (Insert 19.4), which is the square root of Y, the response variable [ysqrt=sqrt(y).] and specify *proc glm* with *ysqrt* as the response variable. To investigate the logarithmic transformation, we create another variable arbitrarily named *ylog10* [*ylog10* = *log(y)*], which is the log base 10 of Y and specify *proc glm* with *ylog10* as the response variable.

The researcher next wished to investigate the nature of the interaction effects shown in Figure 19.13, text page 859. Specifically, the researcher wished to estimate the difference between the learning means for the two teaching methods separately within each of the three levels of quantitative ability. We use a *Bonferroni* multiple comparison procedure with a 95% confidence coefficient for this. In Insert 19.5 we specify *proc glm* with the *model* statement y = *method|ability* (a full factorial model). We request least squares means for the six combinations of *method*ability* and specify the *slice* option. This *slice* option specifies that we want to test the effects of method (abstract versus standard) within of the three levels of *ability*. These effects are sometimes referred to as *simple effects*.

Execution of this syntax results in an "*ability*method effect sliced by ability for y*" table (not shown) that compares the abstract method of instruction to the standard method of instruction separately within each of the three levels of *ability*. Finally, the family of confidence intervals given on text page 860 is for difference between means for *method* of instruction within each of the 3 levels of *ability*, not for difference between *ability* levels for each level of *method*. To produce the *Bonferroni* adjusted confidence intervals for differences in *method* of instruction for each of the 3 levels of *ability*, we specify $\alpha = 0.05/3 = 0.016666$ in Insert 19.5. This produces simultaneous 95 percent confidence intervals for the family of three differences in *method* of instruction means.

INSERT 19.4

```
data math ;
infile ' math data file' not available;
  input Y method ability;
*** Figure 19.13;
proc glm;
 class method ability;
 model y = method|ability;
  lsmeans method|ability / out=lsmeans;
  run;
proc sort data=lsmeans;
by method ability;
run;
goptions reset=all;
symbol1 v=circle i=join c=blue;
symbol2 v=square i=join c=red;
proc gplot data=lsmeans;
 where ((ability>0 and ability<4)and (method>0 and method<3));
 title 'Figure 19.13a';
 plot lsmean*ability=method / vaxis=70 to 100 by 10;
run;
goptions reset=all;
symbol1 v=circle i=join c=blue;
symbol2 v=square i=join c=red;
symbol3 v=dot i=join c=green;
proc gplot data=lsmeans;
 where ((ability>0 and ability<4)and (method>0 and method<3));
 title 'Figure 19.13b';
 plot lsmean*method=ability / vaxis=70 to 100 by 10 haxis=1 to 2 by 1;
run;

* Sq root and log transformations;
data math;
 set math;
ysqrt = sqrt (y);
ylog10 = log(y);
proc glm;
 class method ability;
 model y = method|ability;
  run;
 proc glm;
 class method ability;
 model y = method|ability;
  run;
```

```
                                    INSERT 19.5

proc glm;
 class ability method;
  model y = method|ability ;
   lsmeans method*ability / slice=ability cl alpha = 0.016666 pdiff;
run;
```

Testing Custom Hypotheses and Estimating Custom Functions (text page 860).

In this section, we further illustrate use of the *contrast* and *estimate* statements (introduced in Chapter 15 and also discussed in Chapter 17 of this manual) to test custom hypotheses about the means and estimate custom functions of the means. We choose applications from the hypothetical Mathematics Learning Example. In that example, there are six "population" means associated with the combinations of levels of *method* and *ability* and we denote these cell means as follows:

	ability=1	*ability=2*	*ability=3*
method=1	μ_{11}	μ_{12}	μ_{13}
method=2	μ_{21}	μ_{22}	μ_{23}

The marginal means for the two levels of *method* are:

$$\mu_{1+} = \mu_{11} + \mu_{12} + \mu_{13}$$

$$\mu_{2+} = \mu_{21} + \mu_{22} + \mu_{23}$$

(We use '+' in the subscript to denote summation over the values of the subscript whereas the text uses '.').

The marginal means for the three levels of *ability* are:

$$\mu_{+1} = \mu_{11} + \mu_{21}$$

$$\mu_{+2} = \mu_{12} + \mu_{22}$$

$$\mu_{+3} = \mu_{13} + \mu_{23}$$

Example 1. Marginal Means for *method*. In SAS, we can use the *contrast* and *estimate* statements to request analyses in terms of the cell means or the marginal means. Suppose we are interested in comparing the mean for *method*=1 to the mean for *method*=2. We can express the null hypothesis for this comparison as

$$H_{0:} : \mu_{1+} - \mu_{2+} = 0$$

If we let $c_1 = 1$, $c_2 = -1$ then the left side of the null hypothesis can be written as a contrast L where

$$L = (1)\mu_{1+} + (-1)\mu_{2+}$$

The corresponding SAS *contrast* statement to test the hypothesis H_0 is

contrast 'Method 1 - Method 2=0' *method* 1 –1;

This *contrast* statement is not needed because the test is already given by the F-test for *method* in the analysis of variance table that is printed out on execution of *proc glm*. We may wish to estimate the difference $\mu_{1+} - \mu_{2+}$, however, and this can be accomplished by executing the statement

estimate 'Method 1 - Method 2' *method* 1 –1;

Example 2. Marginal Means for *ability*. Suppose we are interested in comparing students with excellent quantitative ability (*ability*=1) to students with moderate quantitative ability (*ability*=3). We can express the null hypothesis for this comparison as

$$H_0 : \mu_{+1} - \mu_{+3} = 0$$

If we let $c_1 = 1$, $c_2 = 0$, $c_3 = -1$ then the left side of the null hypothesis can be written as a contrast L where

$$L = (1)(\mu_{+1}) + (0)(\mu_{+2}) + (-1)(\mu_{+3}) = \mu_{+1} - \mu_{+3}$$

The corresponding *contrast* statement to test the hypothesis is

contrast 'Ability 1 - Ability 3=0' *ability* 1 0 –1;

If we wish to estimate the contrast we execute the statement

estimate 'Ability 1 - Ability 3' *ability* 1 0 –1;

We can also express the null hypothesis for this example as

$$H_0 : (\mu_{11} + \mu_{21}) - (\mu_{13} + \mu_{23}) = 0$$

or, equivalently, as

$$H_0 : \mu_{11} - \mu_{13} + \mu_{21} - \mu_{23} = 0$$

These are all variations of the same hypothesis expressed above in terms of marginal means and the same *contrast* and *estimate* statements are applicable. When we faced with the analysis of a hypothesis that is expressed in terms of the cell means, we must recognize situations in which we can rewrite the expression in terms of the marginal means for analysis using the *contrast* statement.

Example 3. Marginal Means for *ability*. If we wish to compare the mean of students with excellent *ability* level (*ability*=1) to the average of the means of the students at *ability* levels 2 and 3, then the null hypothesis is

$$H_0 : \mu_{+1} - \left(\frac{\mu_{+2} + \mu_{+3}}{2} \right) = 0$$

or, equivalently,

$$H_0 : 2\mu_{+1} - \mu_{+2} - \mu_{+3} = 0$$

The left side of the null hypothesis can be written as a contrast L where

$$L = (2)(\mu_{+1}) + (-1)(\mu_{+2}) + (-1)(\mu_{+3})$$

The corresponding *contrast* statement is

> *contrast* '2*Ability 1 –(Ability 2 + 3)' *ability* 2 –1 –1;

We can obtain an estimate the difference between the mean of students with excellent *ability* level (*ability*=1) and the average of the means of the students at *ability* levels 2 and 3 by executing the statement

> *estimate* 'Ability 1 –0.5(Ability 2 + 3)' *ability* 1 –0.5 –0.5;

or

> *estimate* 'Ability 1 –0.5(Ability 2 + 3)' *ability* 2 –1 –1 / divisor=2;

Example 4. Interaction Functions of Cell Means. In this section, we illustrate use of the *contrast* and *estimate* statements statement to analyze simple effects for interactions. To illustrate, on text page 860 the authors wish to test the difference in learning between the standard and abstract methods for students with moderate quantitative ability (*ability*=3) versus students with good quantitative ability (*ability*=2). This is a simple effect of interaction between *method* and two levels of *ability*. We first consider the null hypothesis of no interaction between method and ability. This hypothesis can be written as

$$H_0 : \begin{cases} (\mu_{11} - \mu_{12}) - (\mu_{21} - \mu_{22}) = 0 \\ (\mu_{12} - \mu_{13}) - (\mu_{22} - \mu_{23}) = 0 \end{cases}$$

On execution of *proc glm*, we obtain a printout of the analysis of variance that includes the result of the *F*-test for this hypothesis. The hypothesis has two parts and we can test these separately. For example, the sub-hypothesis for the second line of the hypothesis is

$$H_0 : (\mu_{12} - \mu_{13}) - (\mu_{22} - \mu_{23}) = 0$$

or, equivalently,

$$H_0 : (\mu_{23} - \mu_{13}) - (\mu_{22} - \mu_{12}) = 0$$

The left side of this latter form is the contrast estimated on text page 860; i.e.,

$$L = (\mu_{23} - \mu_{13}) - (\mu_{22} - \mu_{12})$$

which can be rewritten as:

$$L = (0)\mu_{11} + (1)\mu_{12} + (-1)\mu_{13} + (0)\mu_{21} + (-1)\mu_{22} + (1)\mu_{23}$$

The corresponding *contrast* statement is

>   *contrast* '(M2A3-M1A3)-(M2A2-M1A2=0)' *method*ability* 0 1 –1 0 –1 1;

We can obtain an estimate of the contrast by executing the statement

>   *estimate* '(M2A3-M1A3)-(M2A2-M1A2)' *method*ability* 0 1 –1 0 –1 1;

In summary, the SAS code for the above four examples are shown in Insert 19.6.

```
                              INSERT 19.6

proc glm;
 class method ability  ;
  model y = method | ability ;
  contrast 'Method 1 - Method 2=0' method 1 –1;
  estimate 'Method 1 - Method 2' method 1 –1;
  contrast 'Ability 1 - Ability 3=0' ability 1 0 –1;
  estimate 'Ability 1 - Ability 3' ability 1 0 –1;
  contrast '2*Ability 1 –( Ability 2 + 3)=0' ability 2 –1 –1;
  estimate 'Ability 1 –0.5( Ability 2 + 3)' ability 1 –0.5 –0.5;
  contrast '(M2A3-M1A3)-(M2A2-M1A2)=0' method*ability   0  1 –1  0 –1  1;
  estimate '(M2A3-M1A3)-(M2A2-M1A2)' method*ability   0  1 –1  0 –1  1;
  run;
```

Chapter 20 SAS®

Two-Factor Studies – One Case per Cell

In Chapter 19, the authors discuss two-factor studies in which there are an equal number (n > 1) of subjects at each combination of levels of the two factors. They refer to each combination of levels of the two factors as a "cell." In Chapter 20, they consider two factor studies in which there is one subject per cell for every cell. When there is only one subject per cell, we cannot estimate the error variance σ^2 and, therefore, we must use *Tukey's test for additivity* to test for interaction between the two factors.

Insurance Premium Example

Data File: ch20ta02.txt

An insurance analyst studied insurance premiums of six cities of different sizes and from two different regions of the state. There was only one observation per cell for each of the six combinations of the two factors, city size (3 levels) and region (2 levels). See Chapter 0, "Working with SAS," for instructions on opening the Insurance Premium Example and naming the variables *y*, *city*, and *region*. After opening and printing ch20ta02.txt, the first 5 lines of output should look like SAS Output 20.1.

SAS Output 20.1

Obs	y	city	region
1	140	1	1
2	100	1	2
3	210	2	1
4	180	2	2
5	220	3	1

In Insert 20.1, we begin the analysis by producing text Figure 20.1, text page 883. (Output not shown.) As noted by the authors, the lines are only moderately lacking in parallelism and there could be a slight interaction between region and city size. Accordingly, the analyst calculated the *Tukey* test for interaction, referred to as the *Tukey Test for Additivity* on text page 886. This test is not readily available in SAS but may be obtained by the syntax shown in Insert 20.2. We use three sets of *proc means* and *output* statements to find $\overline{Y}$ values for each level of *city* ($\overline{Y}_{i.}$) and region ($\overline{Y}_{.j}$) and the overall mean $\overline{Y}$. We use *merge* statements to combine the resulting three sets of output (means) in a data file named *combine*. We then specify SAS syntax to find *SSA*, *SSB*, *SSAB**, and *SSRem** by equations on text pages 886-887 and finally find F^* by text equation 20.11. Results are shown in SAS Output 20.2 and are consistent with calculations presented on text page 888. Since $F^* = 6.75$ is less than the specified $F(.90; 1, 1)=39.9$, the authors concluded that there was no significant interaction between *city* and *region* and proceeded with the no-interaction model (equation 20.1, text page 881).

INSERT 20.1	INSERT 20.1 continued
| ```
data insurance;
 infile 'c:\kutnerdata\chapter 20 data sets\ch20ta02.txt';
 input y city region;
goptions reset=all;
symbol1 v=circle i=join c=blue;
symbol2 v=square i=join c=red;
symbol3 v=dot i=join c=green;
``` | ```
proc gplot data=insurance;
 title 'Figure 20.1';
 plot y*region=city / haxis=0 to 3 ;
run;
``` |

INSERT 20.2	INSERT 20.2
| ```
data insurance;
 infile 'c:\kutnerdata\chapter 20 data sets\ch20ta02.txt';
 input y city region;
constant=1;
proc sort;
 by city;
************* Find mean Y for each level of city;
proc means noprint;
 by city;
 var y;
 output out=city (drop=_type_ _freq_) mean=city_y;
run;
data combine;
 merge insurance city;
 by city;
run;
proc sort;
 by region;
************** Find mean Y for each level of region;
proc means noprint;
 by region;
 var y;
 output out=region (drop=_type_ _freq_) mean=reg_y;
run;
data combine;
 merge combine region;
 by region;
run;
``` | ```
*************** Find mean Y for all cases;
proc means noprint;
 by constant;
 var y;
 output out=all (drop=_type_ _freq_) mean=all_y;
run;
data combine;
 merge combine all;
 by constant;
run;
data combine;
 set combine;
t=(y-all_y)**2;
a=(city_y-all_y)**2;
b=(reg_y-all_y)**2;
c=(city_y-all_y)*(reg_y-all_y)*y;
proc means noprint;
 by constant;
 var t a b c;
 output out=sum (drop=_type_ _freq_)
  sum = t_sum a_sum b_sum c_sum ;
run;
** t_sum=ssto a_sum=ssa b_sum=ssb;
** c_sum=Sum(Ybar[i.]-Ybar[..])(Ybar[ij]-Ybar[..])Y[ij];
data sum;
 set sum;
dfa=2;
dfb=3;
ssab=(c_sum**2)/((a_sum/dfa)*(b_sum/dfb));
ssrem=t_sum-a_sum-b_sum-ssab;
********* F by text equation 21.11;
F=(ssab/1)/(ssrem/(dfa*dfb-dfa-dfb));
proc print;
 title 'Tukey Test for Additivity';
 var a_sum b_sum t_sum ssab ssrem f ;
run;
``` |

Obs	a_sum	b_sum	t_sum	ssab	ssrem	F
1	9300	1350	10750	87.0968	12.9032	6.75

In Insert 20.3, we produce the no-interaction model using the *proc glm*. Results shown in SAS Output 20.3 are consistent with Table 20.2 (b), text page 882 and text pages 883-884, and indicate that there are significant main-effects for *city* [$F(2, 2)=93.0$, $p=0.011$] and for *region* [$F(1, 2)=27.0$, $p=0.035$].

INSERT 20.3

```
data insurance;
 infile 'c:\kutnerdata\chapter 20 data sets\ch20ta02.txt';
 input y city region;
proc glm;
 class city region;
 model y = city region;
 run;
```

SAS Output 20.3

Source	DF	Type III SS	Mean Square	F Value	Pr > F
city	2	9300.000000	4650.000000	93.00	0.0106
region	1	1350.000000	1350.000000	27.00	0.0351

On text page 884, the authors estimate the treatment means by text equation 20.5. In Insert 20.4, we again use the *proc means* and *output* statements to find means for each level of *city* ($\overline{Y}_{i.}$) and *region* ($\overline{Y}_{.j}$) and the overall mean $\overline{Y}$. We then use text equation 20.5 to find *muhat* ($\hat{\mu}_{ij}$). Execution of Insert 20.4 will result in the SAS Output 20.4.

SAS Output 20.4

Obs	y	city	region	muhat
1	140	1	1	135
2	210	2	1	210
3	220	3	1	225
4	100	1	2	105
5	180	2	2	180
6	200	3	2	195

INSERT 20.4	INSERT 20.4
| ```
data insurance;
 infile 'c:\kutnerdata\chapter 20 data
sets\ch20ta02.txt';
 input y city region;
constant=1;
proc sort;
 by city;
**************** Find mean Y for each level of
city;
proc means noprint;
 by city;
 var y;
 output out=city (drop=_type_ _freq_)
mean=city_y;
run;
data combine;
 merge insurance city;
 by city;
run;
proc sort;
 by region;
*************** Find mean Y for each level of
region;
proc means noprint;
 by region;
 var y;
 output out=region (drop=_type_ _freq_)
mean=reg_y;
run;
``` | ```
data combine;
 merge combine region;
 by region;
run;
***************** Find mean Y for all cases;
proc means noprint;
 by constant;
 var y;
 output out=all (drop=_type_ _freq_) mean=all_y;
run;
data combine;
 merge combine all;
 by constant;
run;
data combine;
 set combine;
muhat=city_y+reg_y-all_y;
proc print;
 title 'Estimation of Treatment Means';
 var y city region muhat;
run;
``` |

Finally, on text page 885, the authors parameterize an effects model and we can use the estimates obtained on fitting this model to find the confidence intervals for the treatment means. As discussed in Chapter 15 of this manual, *proc glm* internally defines indicator variables for an effects model. Thus, *proc glm* is used in Insert 20.5 where we save the predicted (*p=predicted*) values and the lower (*lclm=cllo*) and upper (*uclm=clhi*) limits of the confidence interval for the predicted values. Execution if Insert 20.5 results in SAS Output 20.5. Notice that *muhat* calculated in Insert 20.4 (SAS Output 20.4) is equal to the predicted value (*predicted*) saved by the syntax in Insert 20.5 (SAS Output 20.5).

	INSERT 20.5	INSERT 20.5 continued

	data insurance;
	  infile 'c:\kutnerdata\chapter 20 data sets\ch20ta02.txt';
	  input y city region;
	proc glm;
	  class city region;
	  model y = city region;
	  output out=results lclm=cllo uclm=clhi p=predicted;
	run;
		proc print;
		  title 'Est of Tx Means & Confidence Intervals';
		  var y city region predicted cllo clhi;
		run;

SAS Output 20.5

Obs	y	city	region	predicted	cllo	clhi
1	140	1	1	135	110.159	159.841
2	100	1	2	105	80.159	129.841
3	210	2	1	210	185.159	234.841
4	180	2	2	180	155.159	204.841
5	220	3	1	225	200.159	249.841
6	200	3	2	195	170.159	219.841

Chapter 21 SAS®

Randomized Complete Block Designs

The authors present randomized block designs in Chapter 21. They state that "A randomized block design is a restricted randomization design in which the experimental units are first sorted into homogeneous groups, called *blocks*, and the treatments are then assigned at random within the blocks." With effective blocking, we can obtain a more precise estimate of error variance and, hence, more efficient tests of hypotheses about the treatment factor which is usually our primary goal. The simplest randomized block designs have one treatment factor (with multiple levels) in addition to the blocking factor and are thus called two factor studies.

When each level of treatment is included exactly once in each block, we call the design a *randomized complete block design*. The randomized complete block design is a two-factor study with one subject per cell. We usually assume there is no block by treatment interaction in the analysis of data collected using a randomized complete block design. If we include n > 1 subjects per cell in a randomized block design, we call the design a *generalized randomized block design*. We can test for block by treatment interaction in generalized randomized block designs.

Risk Premium Example
Data File: ch21ta01.txt

On text page 895, investigators studied the relationship between three methods of quantifying risk premium and subsequent confidence in the method. Fifteen executives were studied with age of executive used as a blocking variable. Five blocks (age groups) were used; block 1 comprised the three oldest executives, block 2 comprised the next three oldest executives, and so on. The three methods were randomly assigned to the three executives separately within each block. Thus, the design is a *randomized complete block design*. See Chapter 0, "Working with SAS," for instructions on opening the Risk Premium Example and naming the variables *Y*, *block*, and *method*. After opening and printing ch21ta01.txt, the first 5 lines of output should look like SAS Output 21.1.

SAS Output 21.1

Obs	y	block	method
1	1	1	1
2	5	1	2
3	8	1	3
4	2	2	1
5	8	2	2

234

How to Randomize

The 15 executives were grouped into five blocks according to age. Within each block, we assigned a "tag" number (1,2,3) to each executive so that none of the executives within a block have the same tag number. This step of the randomization process was done manually but could be automated, a step that would be especially convenient for large samples.

On text page 895, the authors indicate that random permutations are used to assign "treatments" to experimental units (executives) within each block. That is, there are six permutations of the three treatment methods. The six permutations are "CWU", "CUW", "WCU", "WUC", "UCW", and "UWC". In Insert 21.1, we first generate a data file with six lines, each with a random number between 0 and 1000 from a uniform distribution. We assign one of the six permutations to each of the six lines, assign a rank to the line based on the value of the random number, and sort the file based on the rank variable (*rrandom*). Each execution of Insert 21.1 will yield different results. Output from one execution is shown in SAS Output 21.2. The fifth permutation (UCW) has been assigned to block 1, the forth permutation (WUC) has been assigned to block 2, and so on. Starting with block 1, the youngest (or oldest) group of three executives, we assign method U to the executive (tag) numbered 1, method C to the executive numbered 2, and method W to the executive numbered 3. We proceed to block 2, the next youngest (oldest) age group, and assign executive numbered 1 to method W, executive numbered 2 to method U, and method C to the executive numbered 3. We continue in this fashion until the treatment assignment is complete for all age groups. Thus, we will have used random permutations to assign treatments to experimental units within each block. Note that the third permutation (WCU) was assigned to block 6 and will not be used because the first five permutations will determine the 15 required assignments for the subjects in the 5 blocks of the study. If the number of executives were 33, for instance, we would assign the 18 youngest (oldest) executives based on the first execution of program and then assign the final 15 executives based on a second execution of the program.

INSERT 21.1	INSERT 21.1 continued

/* Generate random numbers using the RANUNI function with a seed of zero. Using zero as the argument in ranuni causes the computer clock to be used as the seed. This results in a different series of random numbers each time the program is executed, unless the program is executed at exactly the same time of day. */
 	
* Create 6 lines each with a random;
* number between 0 and 1000;
data random;
 do perm=1 to 6;
 rannum=1000*(ranuni(0));
 output;
 end;
* Assign permutations to the six lines;
data random;
 set random;
format order a;
	if perm=1 then order="CWU";
	if perm=2 then order="CUW";
	if perm=3 then order="WCU";
	if perm=4 then order="WUC";
	if perm=5 then order="UCW";
	if perm=6 then order="UWC";
	* Find rank based on the value of the random number;
	proc rank;
	 var rannum;
	 ranks rrandom;
	run;
	proc sort;
	 by rrandom;
	run;
	proc print noobs;
	run;

SAS Output 21.2

perm	rannum	order	rrandom
5	19.093	UCW	1
4	279.485	WUC	2
6	310.521	UWC	3
2	327.213	CUW	4
1	556.304	CWU	5
3	680.599	WCU	6

In Insert 21.2, we use *proc glm* to produce the ANOVA table shown in Table 21.3, text page 899. We enter *block* and *method* as *class* variables and then specify a model that contains main effects only. For subsequent use, we request pairwise comparisons using the *Tukey* procedure. (Output not shown.) The syntax to calculate the *Tukey Test for Additivity* (text page 903) was presented in Chapter 20 of this manual and is generalizable to the current problem. We also present syntax to produce the graphs as shown in Figure 21.5 (a) and (b).

Analysis of Treatment Effects: On text page 905, the researcher used the *Tukey* procedure to obtain all pairwise comparisons with a 95% family confidence coefficient. This syntax is presented in Insert 21.2. Partial results are shown in SAS Output 21.3 and are consistent with the results presented on text page 905. For completeness, in Insert 21.3 we show the syntax for using each of the procedures given on text page 904, equations 21.9 a – d.

INSERT 21.2	INSERT 21.2

<pre>data risk;
 infile 'c:\kutnerdata\chapter 21 data
sets\ch21ta01.txt';
 input y block method;
proc glm;
 class block method;
 model y = block method;
 lsmeans method / adjust=tukey cl pdiff;
 output out=results r=residual p=predicted;
run;</pre>
	<pre>goptions reset=all;
	proc gplot data=results;
	 Title 'Text Figure 21.5(a)';
	 symbol value=dot;
	 plot residual*predicted / haxis = 0 to 20 by 5;
	 symbol1 v=dot c=black;
	 run;
	goptions reset=all;
	proc capability ;
	 Title 'Text Figure 21.5(b)';
	 symbol value=dot;
	  var residual;
	  qqplot ;
	run;</pre>

		Difference Between Means	Simultaneous 95% Confidence Limits for LSMean(i)-LSMean(j)	
i	**j**			
1	**2**	-4.200000	-7.321443	-1.078557
1	**3**	-9.000000	-12.121443	-5.878557
2	**3**	-4.800000	-7.921443	-1.678557

Least Squares Means for Effect method

```
                          INSERT 21.3
compute n=5.
compute r=3.
compute alpha=.05.
compute g=3.
exe.
* Single comparison - equation 27.9a.
compute t=IDF.T((1-(alpha/2)), (n-1)*(r-1)).
exe.
* Tukey comparison -  equation 27.9b.
compute T = (1/sqrt(2))*IDF.SRANGE((1-alpha),r,((n-1)*(r-1))) .
exe.
* Scheffe procedure - equation 27.9c.
compute S2=(r-1)*IDF.F((1-alpha),(r-1),(n-1)*(r-1)).
exe.
* Bonferroni procedure - equation 27.9d.
compute B=IDF.T((1-(alpha/2*g)), (n-1)*(r-1)).
exe.
```

Generalized Randomized Block Design: In the previous *randomized complete block design*, we assumed there was no *block* by *method* interaction and executed a model that included only main effects. However, use of the additive (main effects only) model will decrease the power of the test for treatment effects if the block effect is fixed and there is interaction between the block and treatment effects. The *generalized randomized block design* allows for investigation of the block by treatment interaction even when the block effects are fixed as in the example presented in Table 21.4, text page 907. For this analysis, we use *proc glm* and enter the variables *distraction* and *gender* as *class* variables and specify "*model y = distraction|gender*" to indicate a full factorial model. Results of this analysis will be consistent with Figure 21.6, text page 908.

Note that text Figure 21.6 displays Type I sum of squares (Sums of square Types I, II, III, and IV are discussed in Chapter 15 of this manual). Type I and Type III sums of squares yield identical results when the design is *balanced* (cells have equal sample sizes) as in the present example. However, Type III sum of squares should be used when the design is unbalanced (cells do not all have the same sample sizes).

Chapter 22 SAS®

Analysis of Covariance

We learned in previous chapters that we may reduce the error variance by using randomized block designs. The impact is narrower confidence intervals and greater sensitivity in tests of hypotheses relevant to the factor(s) of primary interest. In this chapter, the authors present the *analysis of covariance* as an additional method for reducing error variance. A covariance model includes the features of an ANOVA model and also includes one or more quantitative variables as "covariates." The idea is to account for the variability in the response variable that can be attributed to a linear regression type of relationship with the covariate(s). Once this variability has been quantified, we can "remove" it from the estimate of error variance; otherwise, it is pooled with the estimate of error variance.

We must exercise caution when we perform an analysis of covariance because the analysis is based on the rather strong assumption of *parallelism* or *constancy of slopes*. To see how the assumption works, consider a single factor study with a single covariate. The authors illustrate the models for analysis of covariance in text equations 22.1 – 22.7. The expected response for a specific subject depends not only on the treatment (level of the factor) the subject receives but also the value of the covariate for that subject. The analysis of covariance model specifies separate regression lines all with the same slope (coefficient for the covariate) for the treatments. The difference between the means of any two treatments is the same for all values of the covariate because the regression lines are parallel (they have the same slopes). If the analysis of covariance model is specified as

$$Y_{ij} = \mu_Y + \tau_i + \gamma\left(X_{ij} - \mu_X\right) + \varepsilon_{ij}$$

then $\tau_i - \tau_j$ measures the difference between the response mean with treatment i and the response mean with treatment j for any value of the covariate X. Thus, we can use unbiased estimators of $\tau_i - \tau_j$ to investigate differences between response means for the ith and j^{th} treatments. We can show that the residual mean square is the appropriate estimate of error variance.

Because the assumption of parallelism is so important in the analysis of covariance, it usually is desirable to conduct a formal test of this assumption. An example is given in the text, and SAS syntax for that example is given in the following section.

Single Factor Covariance Analysis

Cracker Promotion Example

Data File: ch22ta01.txt

On text page 926, a company studied the effect of three sales promotions on the number of cases of crackers sold. The number of cases sold in the study period is coded Y, the sales promotion/treatment is arbitrarily coded t, and number of cases sold in the period preceding the study period is coded x. Thus, Y is the response variable, t is a factor, and x is a covariate or concomitant variable. See Chapter 0, "Working with SAS," for instructions on opening the Cracker Promotion Example and naming the variables Y, x, t, and *store*. After opening and printing ch22ta01.txt, the first 5 lines of output should look like SAS Output 22.1.

SAS Output 22.1

Obs	y	x	t	store
1	38	21	1	1
2	39	26	1	2
3	36	22	1	3
4	45	28	1	4
5	33	19	1	5

To develop the full regression model on text page 926 (equation 22.13), we create indicator variables ($i1$, $i2$) for the treatment variable (t) as shown on text page 926. Additionally, we create a new variable, *x_center*, which is the covariate (x) centered by subtracting the overall mean $\overline{X} = 25$ from the original value of the covariate x. Finally, to subsequently test for parallel slopes, we create two new variables, *i1x* and *i2x* where *i1x=i1*x_center* and *i2x=i2*x_center*. (Insert 22.1)

The authors begin the analysis by generating a symbolic scatter plot of Y and X, various residual plots, and the *Correlation Test for Normality* (text pages 927-928). The computational details of the *Correlation Test for Normality* are presented in Chapters 3 and 18 of this manual. The syntax for the various text plots and the *Correlation Test for Normality* is given without comment in Insert 22.1.

The Full Model can now be obtained using *proc reg* to regress Y on *x_center*, *i1*, and *i2*. (Insert 22.1) SAS Output 22.1 and 22.2 are partial output of the above full model solution and are consistent with Table 22.3, text page 928.

INSERT 22.1	INSERT 22.1 continued

```
data cracker;
infile 'c:\kutnerdata\chapter 22 data sets\ch22ta01.txt';
input  y x t store;
if t =  1 then i1 = 1 ;
if t =  3 then i1 = -1;
if t =  2 then i1 = 0;
if t =  2 then i2 = 1;
if t =  3 then i2 = -1;
if t =  1 then i2 = 0;
x_center=x-25;
i1x=i1*x_center;
i2x=i2*x_center;

* Produce Figure 22.5;
goptions reset=all;
proc gplot;
 symbol1 c=black value=circle;
 symbol2 c=black value=dot;
 symbol3 c=black value=square;
 title 'Figure 22.5';
 plot y*x=t / haxis=15 to 35 by 5;
run;

* Save residuals;
proc reg;
 model y = i1 i2 x_center;
 output out=step2 r=residual;
run;

* Produce Figure 22.6(a);
goptions reset=all;
proc gplot;
 symbol1 c=black value=dot;
 title 'Figure 22.6(a)';
 plot t*residual / vaxis=0 to 4 by 1;
 run;
```

```
* Produce Figure 22.6(b);
goptions reset=all;
proc capability;
 title 'Figure 22.6(b)';
 qqplot residual;
 symbol1 c=black value=dot;
 run;

* Correlation Test for Normality;
proc rank data=step2 out=step3;
  var residual;
  ranks r_res;
data new;
 set step3;
 percent=(r_res-.375)/(15+.25);
 ev=sqrt(3.506)*probit((r_res-.375)/(15+.25));
proc corr;
 var ev residual;
 run;

***** Full Model;
proc reg;
  model y = x_center i1 i2;
run;
***** Reduced Model;
proc reg;
  model y=x_center;
run;
```

SAS Output 22.1

Analysis of Variance					
Source	DF	Sum of Squares	Mean Square	F Value	Pr > F
Model	3	607.82869	202.60956	57.78	<.0001
Error	11	38.57131	3.50648		
Corrected Total	14	646.40000			

SAS Output 22.2

Parameter Estimates					
Variable	DF	Parameter Estimate	Standard Error	t Value	Pr > |t|
Intercept	1	33.80000	0.48349	69.91	<.0001
x_center	1	0.89856	0.10258	8.76	<.0001
i1	1	6.01741	0.70826	8.50	<.0001
i2	1	0.94202	0.69868	1.35	0.2047

Test for Treatment Effects

To test treatment effects, we use the reduced model shown in equation 22.15, text page 929. Again, we use *proc reg* with *x_center* as the only independent variable. (Insert 22.1) This yields SAS Output 22.3, which is consistent with Table 22.4, text page 929. We can now calculate the partial F^* value from SAS Output 22.1 and 22.3, as shown on text page 929:

$$F^* = \frac{SSE(R) - SSE(F)}{(n_T - 2) - [n_T - (r+1)]} \div \frac{SSE(F)}{n_T - (r+1)}$$

$$F^* = \frac{455.722 - 38.571}{13 - 11} \div \frac{38.571}{11} = 59.5$$

SAS Output 22.3

Analysis of Variance					
Source	DF	Sum of Squares	Mean Square	F Value	Pr > F
Model	1	190.67778	190.67778	5.44	0.0364
Error	13	455.72222	35.05556		
Corrected Total	14	646.40000			

Alternatively, we can use *proc glm* to test for treatment effects. (Insert 22.2) We enter *t* as a *class* variable and *x_center* as a covariate. Insert 22.2 results in SAS Output 22.4; the calculated *F* value for *t* is 59.48 consistent with the F^* value calculated above. This indicates that, controlling for the number of cases sold in the preceding period, there are significant differences in the number of cases of crackers sold among the treatment groups.

INSERT 22.2	INSERT 22.2 continued

data cracker;
infile 'c:\kutnerdata\chapter 22 data sets\ch22ta01.txt';
input y x t store;
if t = 1 then i1 = 1 ;
if t = 3 then i1 = -1;
if t = 2 then i1 = 0;
if t = 2 then i2 = 1;
if t = 3 then i2 = -1;
if t = 1 then i2 = 0;
	x_center=x-25;
	i1x=i1*x_center;
	i2x=i2*x_center;
	proc glm;
	 class t;
	 model y=t x_center;
	 run;

SAS Output 22.4

Source	DF	Type III SS	Mean Square	F Value	Pr > F
t	2	417.1509137	208.5754568	59.48	<.0001
x_center	1	269.0286915	269.0286915	76.72	<.0001

Using the SAS *proc reg*, yet another solution is to enter *x_center, i1,* and *i2* as independent variables and use the *test* statement as in Insert 22.3 to test the effect of *i1* and *i2*. This results in $F=59.48$. (SAS Output 22.5) This F value is identical to and the interpretation is the same as for the F^* (text page 929) and F obtained using *proc glm* (SAS Output 22.4).

INSERT 22.3	INSERT 22.3 continued

data cracker;
infile 'c:\kutnerdata\chapter 22 data sets\ch22ta01.txt';
input y x t store;
if t = 1 then i1 = 1 ;
if t = 3 then i1 = -1;
if t = 2 then i1 = 0;
if t = 2 then i2 = 1;
if t = 3 then i2 = -1;
if t = 1 then i2 = 0;
	proc reg;
	 model y = x_center i1 i2;
	 i1i2: test i1=0, i2=0;
	 run;

SAS Output 22.5

Test i1i2 Results for Dependent Variable y				
Source	DF	Mean Square	F Value	Pr > F
Numerator	2	208.57546	59.48	<.0001
Denominator	11	3.50648		

Estimation of Treatment Effects

To obtain the estimated treatment effects and adjusted estimated treatment effects shown on text page 930 - 932, we use *proc glm*. (Insert 22.4) This procedure results in SAS Output 22.6. Note that the comparison of $\tau_1 - \tau_2 = 5.075$ presented on text page 930, for instance, is found below in SAS Output 22.6 along with the *Scheffe* adjusted 95 percent confidence interval. SAS Output 22.6 also displays the adjusted estimated treatment means reported on text page 932. We see there was a significant difference ($p = 0.0058$) in the estimated means of Treatment 1 versus Treatment 2. Also, the adjusted means of Treatment 1 and Treatment 2 were 39.817 and 34.742, respectively. Thus, Treatment 1 resulted in significantly more cracker sales on average than Treatment 2. Differences between means for Treatment 1 versus Treatment 3 and Treatment 2 versus Treatment 3 were also statistically significant.

INSERT 22.4	INSERT 22.4 continued

data cracker;
infile 'c:\kutnerdata\chapter 22 data sets\ch22ta01.txt';
input y x t store;
if t = 1 then i1 = 1 ;
if t = 3 then i1 = -1;
if t = 2 then i1 = 0;
if t = 2 then i2 = 1;
if t = 3 then i2 = -1;
if t = 1 then i2 = 0;
x_center=x-25;
i1x=i1*x_center;
i2x=i2*x_center;
	proc glm;
	 class t;
	 model y=t x_center;
	 lsmeans t / pdiff cl adjust=scheffe;
	run;

SAS Output 22.6

Least Squares Means for Effect t				
		Difference Between Means	Simultaneous 95% Confidence Limits for LSMean(i)-LSMean(j)	
i	j			
1	2	5.075390	1.607052	8.543728
1	3	12.976831	9.574367	16.379294
2	3	7.901441	4.546608	11.256273

SAS Output 22.6 continued

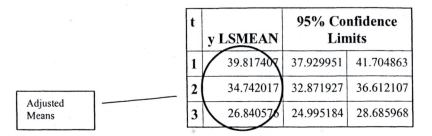

t	y LSMEAN	95% Confidence Limits	
1	39.817407	37.929951	41.704863
2	34.742017	32.871927	36.612107
3	26.840576	24.995184	28.685968

Adjusted Means

Least Squares Means for effect t **Pr > |t| for H0: LSMean(i)=LSMean(j)** **Dependent Variable: y**			
i/j	**1**	**2**	**3**
1		0.0058	<.0001
2	0.0058		0.0001
3	<.0001	0.0001	

Test for Parallel Slopes

The usual ANOVA assumptions apply to Analysis of Covariance, and SAS solutions for testing these assumptions were presented in Chapter 18 of this manual. An additional assumption of Covariance is that the slopes of regression lines for the different treatments are equal (text page 932). This is referred to in the text as Constancy of Slopes. To obtain the general linear model (equation 22.23, text page 932), we regress Y on x_center, $i1$, $i2$, $i1x$, and $i2x$. (Insert 22.5)

In SAS Output 22.7 below, we produced text Table 22.5 including the $SSE=31.521$ and in SAS Output 22.1 above we have $SSE(R)=38.571$, quantities needed to calculate the $F^*=1.01$ as shown on text page 933.

INSERT 22.5	**INSERT 22.5 continued**

data cracker;
 infile 'c:\kutnerdata\chapter 22 data
 sets\ch22ta01.txt';
 input y x t store;
 if t = 1 then i1 = 1 ;
 if t = 3 then i1 = -1;
 if t = 2 then i1 = 0;
	if t = 2 then i2 = 1;
	 if t = 3 then i2 = -1;
	 if t = 1 then i2 = 0;
	 x_center=x-25;
	 i1x=i1*x_center;
	 i2x=i2*x_center;
	 proc reg;
	  model y = x_center i1 i2 i1x i2x;
	 run;

SAS Output 22.7

Analysis of Variance					
Source	DF	Sum of Squares	Mean Square	F Value	Pr > F
Model	5	614.87916	122.97583	35.11	<.0001
Error	9	31.52084	3.50232		
Corrected Total	14	646.40000			

Alternatively, SAS *proc glm* can be used to test for interaction between the covariate and the factor. (Insert 22.6) We create a model that includes a term for interaction between t (factor) and x (covariate). From SAS Output 22.8, we see that the $t*x$ interaction term has an obtained F value of 1.01. This is the same value ($F^*=1.01$) reported on text page 933. Both *proc reg and proc glm* yield an $F=1.01$, $p=0.403$, a result that suggests the assumption of equal treatment slopes is tenable in this example.

INSERT 22.6	INSERT 22.6 continued

data cracker;
infile 'c:\kutnerdata\chapter 22 data sets\ch22ta01.txt';
input y x t store;
if t = 1 then i1 = 1 ;
if t = 3 then i1 = -1;
if t = 2 then i1 = 0;
	if t = 2 then i2 = 1;
	if t = 3 then i2 = -1;
	if t = 1 then i2 = 0;
	x_center=x-25;
	i1x=i1*x_center;
	i2x=i2*x_center;
	proc glm;
	 class t;
	  model y =t|x;
	run;

SAS Output 22.8

Source	DF	Type III SS	Mean Square	F Value	Pr > F
t	2	1.2632832	0.6316416	0.18	0.8379
x	1	243.1412380	243.1412380	69.42	<.0001
x*t	2	7.0504731	3.5252366	1.01	0.4032

Covariance for Two-Factor Studies and Randomized Complete Block Designs

The authors present a two-factor covariance example. The syntax presented for the previous one-factor covariance study generalizes completely to two-factor studies. Additional syntax for this example will not be presented.

Chapter 23 SAS®

Two-Factor Studies Unequal Sample Sizes

As stated in Chapter 16 of this manual, the analysis of variance (ANOVA) for a dependent (response) variable of interest is the partitioning of the total sum of squares for the dependent variable into component sums of squares associated with identifiable sources of variation. Once the partitioning is complete, we can use the component sums of squares to test whether variability attributed to some sources is significantly greater than variability attributed to other sources. In two-factor studies, if the sample sizes are equal in all cells (the number of subjects is the same for all combinations of levels of the two factors), the components of the ANOVA decomposition are said to be orthogonal and the sum of the component sums of squares is equal to the corrected total sum of squares. On the other hand, if the sample sizes are unequal, the components are *not* orthogonal and the sum of the component sums of squares is *not* equal to the corrected total sum of squares. The regression approach to ANOVA for two-factor studies with unequal sample sizes is to compute sequential sums of squares for each component (Factor 1, Factor 2, and Factor 1 by Factor 2 interaction) as if all the model effects for each component in turn are the last to be added to the regression model. This procedure produces respective component sum of squares for Factor 1, Factor 2, and Factor 1 by Factor 2 interaction that are adjusted in a sense for all the other component effects having been entered in the model. The sums of squares relative to this procedure are referred to as the Type III sums of squares. The four types of sums of squares that are available in SAS *proc glm* are discussed in Chapter 15. In SAS, *proc glm* uses an underlying regression approach; analysis of variance tables based on both Type I and Type III sums of squares are printed as the default. Thus, we can use *proc reg* and write SAS code to define independent variables directly to produce the ANOVA, but it is easier to use *proc glm* because this procedure requires less code (See Chapter 15 for additional discussion).

Growth Hormone Example

Data File: ch23ta01.txt

A researcher studied the effect of a child's bone development and gender on the rate of hormone-induced growth (*Y*). Eighteen children, 3 per factor combination, began the investigation. However, four of the children were unable to complete the study. Thus, data for these four children were not available and the resulting sample sizes for the cells (factor combinations) were unequal. See Chapter 0, "Working with SAS," for instructions on opening the Growth Hormone Example (Table 23.1, text page 954) and naming the variables *Y*, *gender*, *bonedev*, and *rep*. After opening and printing ch23ta01.txt, the first 5 lines of output should look like SAS Output 23.1.

Obs	y	gender	bonedev	rep
1	1.4	1	1	1
2	2.4	1	1	2
3	2.2	1	1	3
4	2.1	1	2	1
5	1.7	1	2	2

We begin the analysis of the Growth Hormone Example by reproducing Figure 23.1, text page 955. (Insert 23.1 - Output not shown) Results indicate that a child's bone development may be related to hormone-induced growth rate and that there may be interaction between gender and bone development. On text page 953, the authors analyze the regression model to investigate these effects. The regression model was used because of the unequal sample sizes. However, as we discussed in Chapter 15, *proc glm* uses a regression approach and prints results based on Type III sums of squares. Thus, *proc glm* provides the analysis of interest when the within cell sample sizes are unequal. We present all solutions in this chapter using *proc glm*.

INSERT 23.1	INSERT 23.1 continued
```data growth; infile 'c:\kutnerdata\chapter 23 data sets\ch23ta01.txt'; input y gender bonedev rep; *** Produce Figure 23.1; proc glm; class gender bonedev; model y = gender|bonedev; lsmeans gender|bonedev / out=lsmeans; run; proc sort data=lsmeans; by gender bonedev; run;```	```goptions reset=all; symbol1 v=circle i=join c=blue; symbol2 v=square i=join c=red; proc gplot data=lsmeans; where ((bonedev>0 and bonedev<4)and (gender>0 and gender<3)); title 'Figure 23.1'; plot lsmean*bonedev=gender / haxis=0 to 4 by 1 vaxis=0 to 3 by 1; run; * Produce Table 23.4 & pairwise comparisons; proc glm data=growth; class gender bonedev; model y = gender|bonedev; lsmeans bonedev / adjust=tukey alpha=.1 cl pdiff; run;```

To produce ANOVA Table 23.4, text page 959, we use *proc glm* and specify *Y* as the dependent variable; *gender* and *bonedev* as *class* variables; and the full factorial model *y = gender | bonedev*. (Insert 23.1) Results are shown in SAS Output 23.2 and are consistent with text Table 23.4. Neither the *gender* by *bonedev* interaction nor the *gender* main effect was statistically significant. However, there were significant differences among the means for the three levels of *bondev* ($p=0.003$). The authors now investigate the nature of the differences among the levels of *bonedev* by performing pairwise comparisons using the *Tukey* procedure and a 90% family confidence coefficient. These comparisons are requested in the last *proc glm* statement of Insert 23.1 and results in SAS Output 23.3, which is consistent with text page 963.

Source	DF	Type III SS	Mean Square	F Value	Pr > F
gender	1	0.12000000	0.12000000	0.74	0.4152
bonedev	2	4.18971429	2.09485714	12.89	0.0031
gender*bonedev	2	0.07542857	0.03771429	0.23	0.7980

SAS Output 23.3

		Difference Between Least Squares Means for Levels of Bonedev		
i	j	Difference Between Means	Simultaneous 90% Confidence Limits for LSMean(i)-LSMean(j)	
1	2	0.200000	-0.507807	0.907807
1	3	1.300000	0.592193	2.007807
2	3	1.100000	0.479212	1.720788

Single Degree Of Freedom Test

On text page 964, the authors wish to determine whether children with mildly depressed bone development experience, on average, a significant increase in growth rate during the study period. Thus, we want to test if the growth rate mean is ≤ 0 for children with level 3 bone development regardless of the child's gender. This hypothesis can be stated as

$$H_0 : \mu_{+3} \leq 0$$

We specify *proc glm* and the *estimate* statements as shown in Insert 23.2. Finally, since we are comparing one group to zero (as opposed to comparing two groups to each other) we must include a coefficient for the intercept term. Execution of this syntax results in SAS Output 23.4, which is consistent with text page 964, where $t^* = 4.89$. The *p*-value in SAS Output 23.4 is Pr > |t| = 0.0012 corresponding to a two-sided test. We divide this *p*-value by 2 to get the *p*-value for the one-sided test; i.e., Pr(t > + 4.89) = 0.0006.

INSERT 23.2

```
data growth;
infile 'c:\kutnerdata\chapter 23 data sets\ch23ta01.txt';
input y gender bonedev rep;
proc glm;
class gender bonedev;
model y = gender|bonedev;
estimate 'bonedev level 3 mean' bonedev 0 0 1 intercept 1;
run;
```

SAS Output 23.4

Parameter	Estimate	Standard Error	t Value	Pr > |t|
bonedev level 3 mean	0.90000000	0.18399502	4.89	0.0012

Empty Cells in Two-Factor Studies

Data File: ch23ta06.txt

Missing Observations in Randomized Complete Block Designs: On text page 968 the authors present a data set that contains 3 treatments and 3 blocks where the observation for block 1, treatment 1 is missing. See Chapter 0, "Working with SAS," for instructions on opening the Table 23.6, text page 954, and naming the variables *Y*, *block*, and *tx*. After opening and printing ch23ta06.txt, the first 5 lines of output should look like SAS Output 23.5.

SAS Output 23.5

Obs	y	block	tx
1	10	1	2
2	9	1	3
3	11	2	1
4	10	2	2
5	7	2	3

In Insert 23.3, we specify *proc glm* where *block* and *tx* are *class* variables, and the *model* statement indicates that *y* is the response variable. We specify a model that includes main effects but does not include interaction effects. We further use the *lsmeans* statement to request adjusted means, confidence intervals for the means and pairwise differences between the means, and *p*-values for the test statistics for the pairwise tests of equal means for the levels of *tx*. The *adjust = method* option was not specified in the *lsmeans* statement so the confidence intervals and *p*-values are not intended to provide simultaneous inferences. Results (not shown) are consistent with all statistics presented on text page 970.

INSERT 23.3

```
data ta23_6;
  infile 'c:\kutnerdata\chapter 23 data sets\ch23ta06.txt';
  input y block tx;
proc glm;
 class block tx;
 model y = block tx;
 lsmeans tx / cl pdiff;
run;
```

ANOVA Inferences When Treatment Means Are of Unequal Importance

Tests for Factor Main Effects by Use of Equivalent Regression Models

In the Growth Hormone example (text page 972), the authors indicate that females receive growth hormone treatment twice as often as males and that the 2:1 ratio is consistent across each level of bone development. The authors present a regression formulation to test the effect of bone development while adjusting the analysis for the unequal importance of treatment means. Again, we use *proc glm* to test the null hypothesis, which can be stated by equation 23.37a, text page 972 as:

$$H_0 : \begin{cases} \dfrac{2\mu_{11} + \mu_{21}}{3} - \dfrac{2\mu_{12} + \mu_{22}}{3} = 0 \\[3mm] \dfrac{2\mu_{11} + \mu_{21}}{3} - \dfrac{2\mu_{13} + \mu_{23}}{3} = 0 \end{cases}$$

If we multiply through by 3, the first half of the above can be rewritten as:

$$2\mu_{11} + 1\mu_{21} - 2\mu_{12} - 1\mu_{22} = 0$$

Rearranged, the left side of this equation can be written as:

$$2\mu_{11} - 2\mu_{12} + 0\mu_{13}$$
$$1\mu_{21} - 1\mu_{22} + 0\mu_{23}$$

Thus, the contrast coefficients for *gender*bonedev* are 2 –2 0 1 –1 0, or rearranged:

$$\begin{matrix} 2 & -2 & 0 \\ 1 & -1 & 0 \end{matrix}$$

To find the coefficients for *gender*, we sum each of the two rows to find:

$$0 \; 0$$

To find the coefficients for *bonedev*, we sum each of the three columns to find:

$$3 \; -3 \; 0$$

Since both coefficients for *gender* are zeros, we can omit the *gender* specification from the *contrast* statement. We specify *proc glm* with the *class*, *model*, and *contrast* statements shown in Insert 23.4.and write syntax for the first half of H_0 as shown in lines 2 and 3 of the *contrast* statement; i.e.

bonedev 3 -3 0
gender*bonedev 2 -2 0 1 -1 0,

We then repeat the above algorithm to find the contrast coefficients for the second half of H_0, which are *bonedev* 3 0 –3 and *gender*bonedev* 2 0 –2 1 0 –1. We complete the syntax for H_0 in lines 4 and 5 of the contrast statement; i.e.

bonedev 3 0 -3
gender*bonedev 2 0 -2 1 0 –1;

Since the both halves of H_0 are specified in one contrast statement (separated by a comma), the resulting test statistic will be based on a simultaneous test of both halves. Execution of this syntax results in the SAS Output 23.6, which is consistent with text page 974.

INSERT 23.4

```
data growth;
  infile 'c:\kutnerdata\chapter 23 data sets\ch23ta01.txt';
  input y gender bonedev rep;
proc glm;
  class gender bonedev;
  model y = gender|bonedev;
  contrast 'page 972-974 example'
              bonedev 3 -3 0
              gender*bonedev 2 -2 0 1 -1 0,
              bonedev 3 0 -3
              gender*bonedev 2 0 -2 1 0 -1;
run;
```

SAS Output 23.6

Contrast	DF	Contrast SS	Mean Square	F Value	Pr > F
page 972-974 example	2	3.45428571	1.72714286	10.63	0.0056

Tests for Factor Effects when Weights are Proportional to Sample Sizes

In the Growth Hormone study, assume that the treatment sample sizes are proportional to the treatment means. We wish to study the relationship between *gender* and the weighted means for the response "change in rate of growth." This is stated on text page 979 as:

$$H_0: \frac{3}{7}\mu_{11} + \frac{2}{7}\mu_{12} + \frac{2}{7}\mu_{13} = \frac{1}{7}\mu_{21} + \frac{3}{7}\mu_{22} + \frac{3}{7}\mu_{23}$$

251

and can be rewritten as:

$$H_0: \ 3\mu_{11} + 2\mu_{12} + 2\mu_{13} - \mu_{21} - 3\mu_{22} - 3\mu_{23} = 0$$

Rearranging the left side of the equation of the hypothesis, we have:

$$3\mu_{11} + 2\mu_{12} + 2\mu_{13}$$

$$-1\mu_{21} - 3\mu_{22} - 3\mu_{23}$$

Thus, the *gender*bonedev* interaction coefficients are:

$$\begin{array}{rrr} 3 & 2 & 2 \\ -1 & -3 & -3 \end{array}$$

To find the coefficients for *gender*, we sum each of the two rows to find:

$$7 \quad -7$$

To find the coefficients for *bonedev*, we sum each of the three columns to find:

$$2 \quad -1 \quad -1$$

Again, we specify *proc glm* with the *class*, *model*, and *contrast* statements shown in Insert 23.5. Execution of this syntax (output not shown) results in the F^* value shown on text page 979.

INSERT 23.5

```
data growth;
  infile 'c:\kutnerdata\chapter 23 data sets\ch23ta01.txt';
  input y gender bonedev rep;
proc glm;
  class gender bonedev;
  model y = gender|bonedev;
  contrast 'text page 914 contrast'
            gender 7 -7
            bonedev 2 -1 -1
            gender*bonedev 3 2 2 -1 -3 -3;
run;
```

Chapter 24 SAS®

Multifactor Studies

In this chapter, the authors discuss studies with three or more factors. This presentation is a generalization of the discussion for two factor studies. The primary difference between studies with two factors and those with three or more factors is that the additional factors create more main effects and more possibilities for interactions, and ordinarily we must consider these additional effects in the analysis. Consider, for example, a four-factor study with factors denoted by A, B, C, and D. There are four main effects (A, B, C, D), six two factor interactions (AB, AC, AD, BC, BD, CD), four three factor interactions (ABC, ABD, ACD, BCD), and one four factor interaction (ABCD). Unless we have prior knowledge that some of these effects are not present, we typically include all of them in the model and in significance tests associated with the analysis of variance. The analysis can be cumbersome but is relatively straightforward.

Stress Test Example

Data File: ch24ta04.txt

A researcher studied the relationship between exercise tolerance (Y) and gender, body fat, and smoking history. See Chapter 0, "Working with SAS," for instructions on opening the Stress Test Example (Table 24.4 (a), text page 1004) and naming the variables Y, *gender*, *fat*, *smoke*, and *rep*. After opening and printing ch24ta04.txt, the first 5 lines of output should look like SAS Output 24.1.

SAS Output 24.1

Obs	y	gender	fat	smoke	rep
1	24.1	1	1	1	1
2	29.2	1	1	1	2
3	24.6	1	1	1	3
4	20.0	2	1	1	1
5	21.9	2	1	1	2

To produce the estimated treatment and factor level means presented in Table 24.4 (b), text page 1004, we use the *lsmeans* option from within *proc glm* to save the least square means as shown in Insert 24.1. The plots shown in Figure 24.5 (a) and (b), text page 1007, can be generated by *proc gplot*. Partial results are shown in SAS Output 24.2.

INSERT 24.1	INSERT 24.1 continued

data stress;
  infile 'c:\kutnerdata\chapter 24 data sets\ch24ta04.txt';
  input y gender fat smoke rep;
 	
*** Produce Table 24.4 b & Figure 24.7;
proc glm ;
  class gender fat smoke;
  model y = gender|fat|smoke;
  output out=results r=residual;
  lsmeans gender|fat|smoke / out=lsmeans;
run;
 	
*** Produce Figure 24.5 a and b;
proc sort data=lsmeans;
  by descending lsmean;
run;
goptions reset=all;
symbol1 v=circle i=join c=blue;
symbol2 v=dot i=join c=red;
	proc gplot data=lsmeans;
	  title 'Figure 24.5 Male';
	  where gender=1 and (smoke=1 or smoke=2);
	plot lsmean*fat=smoke / haxis=0 to 3 by 1 vaxis=0
	to 30 by 10;
	run;
	proc gplot data=lsmeans;
	  title 'Figure 24.5 Female';
	  where gender=2 and (smoke=1 or smoke=2);
	plot lsmean*fat=smoke / haxis=0 to 3 by 1 vaxis=0
	to 30 by 10;
	run;
	
	*** Produce Figure 24.6;
	proc capability data=results;
	  title 'Figure 24.6';
	symbol1 v=dot c=black;
	  var residual;
	  qqplot residual;
	run;

SAS Output 24.2

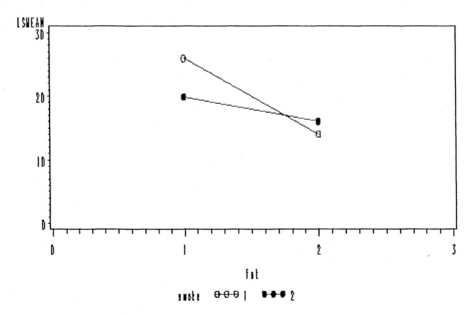

Residual Analysis: To produce the normal probability plot of residuals and the correlation between the ordered residuals and their expected value under normality, as reported on text page 1006, in Insert 24.1 we specify *proc glm* where *Y* is the dependent variable and full factorial model containing *gender*, *fat*, and *smoke* as *class* variables. We also specify that residuals from the specified model be saved. The normal probability plot of residuals (Figure 24.6, text page

254

1007) can be reproduced using *proc capability* as shown in Insert 24.1. The correlation coefficient between the ordered residuals and their expected value under normality can be calculated as discussed in Chapter 18 of this manual.

For the Stress Test Example (text page 1011), there are 3 main effects for factors (*gender, fat, smoking*), 3 two-factor interactions (*gender* by *fat, gender* by *smoking, fat* by *smoking*), and 1 three-factor interaction (*gender* by *fat* by *smoking*) for a total of 7 potential tests. The researchers tested for these 7 factor effects and used the *Kimball* inequality (equation 24.25, text page 1010) to control the family level of significance at 0.10. This resulted in a $\alpha_i = 0.015$ being used to determine statistical significance of each of the 7 tests while maintaining the family level of significance at a level that does not exceed 0.10. The *proc glm* statement from Insert 24.1 results in SAS Output 24.3. To test for the three-factor interaction, we note that $F(1, 16)=0.20$, $p=0.66$. For $\alpha_i = 0.015$ we require $F^* > 7.42$ or $p < 0.015$. Thus, the authors concluded that the three-factor interaction is not statistically significant. To test the two-factor interactions, we inspect the F values as discussed on text page 1012, or we can use the probability level (*Pr>F*) for each two-factor interaction to determine significance. From SAS Output 24.3 we find that the probability levels of the *gender*fat* (*p*=0.244) and *gender*smoke* (*p*=0.292) interactions are both greater than the Kimball inequality $\alpha_i = 0.015$. Thus, we conclude that the *gender*fat* and *gender*smoke* interactions are not statistically significant. The probability level of the *fat*smoke* interaction (*p*=0.013) is less than the required alpha level (0.015), so we conclude that there is significant *fat*smoke* interaction. Main effects for *fat* and *smoke* were not tested because each interacted with another factor. The researchers did test the main effect for *gender*, $F(1, 16)=18.915$, $p = 0.0005$, and concluded that *gender* is statistically significant.

SAS Output 24.3

Source	DF	Type III SS	Mean Square	F Value	Pr > F
gender	1	176.5837500	176.5837500	18.92	0.0005
fat	1	242.5704167	242.5704167	25.98	0.0001
gender*fat	1	13.6504167	13.6504167	1.46	0.2441
smoke	1	70.3837500	70.3837500	7.54	0.0144
gender*smoke	1	11.0704167	11.0704167	1.19	0.2923
fat*smoke	1	72.4537500	72.4537500	7.76	0.0132
gender*fat*smoke	1	1.8704167	1.8704167	0.20	0.6604

On text page 1018, the researchers wish to test separately for persons with low and high body fat, the difference in exercise tolerance for light smokers and heavy smokers. These effects are sometimes called the *simple effects* of smoking. The researchers also wish to test the main effect for *gender* in the same analysis. Thus, there are three planned comparisons, and the researchers wish to use the *Bonferroni* method to construct 3 confidence intervals with a 95% family confidence coefficient.

We specify *proc glm* as indicated in Insert 24.2. The *slice* option on the *lsmeans* statement indicates that we wish to test the effect of *fat* within each level of *smoke*; that is, we compare light and heavy smokers (*smoke*) at each level of *fat*. To produce the *Bonferroni* adjusted 95% confidence intervals, we set the alpha level on each *lsmeans* statement to $\alpha = 0.05/3 = 0.01666$. That is, specifying *adjust=* will not simultaneously adjust for each of the three comparisons because the comparisons are specified on separate *lsmeans* statements. Execution of Insert 24.2 results in SAS Output 24.4. This output indicates a 98.334% $[100(1-0.01666)\%]$ confidence interval for each comparison. The family confidence interval is $100[1-(3)(0.01666)]\% = 95\%$. Thus, the confidence intervals are consistent with those reported on text page 1018.

On text page 1019, the authors note that regression analysis can be used to analyze multifactor studies with unequal cell sizes. As we discussed in Chapter 15 of this manual, *proc glm* uses a regression based approach and thus we can use *proc glm* to analyze multifactor studies with unequal cell sizes. However, we must be careful that the analysis of variance and associated contrasts are based on Type III sums of squares.

INSERT 24.2

```
data stress;
 infile 'c:\kutnerdata\chapter 24 data sets\ch24ta04.txt';
  input y gender fat smoke rep;
proc sort;
 by fat smoke ;
 run;
proc glm;
 class gender fat smoke;
  model y = gender|fat|smoke;
  lsmeans fat*smoke / slice=smoke cl pdiff alpha=0.01666;
  lsmeans gender / cl pdiff alpha=0.01666;
run;
```

SAS Output 24.4

Least Squares Means for Effect fat*smoke				
i	j	Difference Between Means	98.334% Confidence Limits for LSMean(i)-LSMean(j)	
1	2	6.900000	2.184343	11.615657
1	3	9.833333	5.117676	14.548991
1	4	9.783333	5.067676	14.498991
2	3	2.933333	-1.782324	7.648991
2	4	2.883333	-1.832324	7.598991
3	4	-0.050000	-4.765657	4.665657

Least Squares Means for Effect gender				
i	j	Difference Between Means	98.334% Confidence Limits for LSMean(i)-LSMean(j)	
1	2	5.425000	2.090527	8.759473

Random and Mixed-Effects Models

In previous discussion of ANOVA models, the authors restricted attention to methods for models in which all factors were fixed effects factors. The ANOVA model in which the factor levels for all factors are considered fixed is called model I, or the *fixed effects model*. In model I studies, the factor levels included in the study are the only ones of interest relative to the inferences made in the conclusions. In some studies, the factor levels are a sample from "a larger population of potential factor levels," and the researcher wishes that relevant conclusions pertain to that larger population. The effects for such factors are called random effects and the ANOVA model with all random effects (the levels of every factor included in the model is a sample from some larger population) is referred to as model II or the *random effects model*. The ANOVA model that includes some fixed effects factors and some random effects, is called model III, or a *mixed effects model* or simply a *mixed model*.

Example of Single-Factor Study Model II: Factor Effects Random

Apex Enterprises Example

Data File: ch25ta01.txt

Apex Enterprises studied personnel officer evaluation ratings of potential employees. Five of the company's personnel officers were randomly selected, and four job applicants were randomly assigned to each of the five officers. Thus, each officer rated four job applicants. See Chapter 0, "Working with SAS," for instructions on opening the Apex Enterprises Example and naming the variables *Y*, *officer*, and *candidate*. After opening and printing ch25ta01.txt, the first 5 lines of output should look like SAS Output 25.1.

SAS Output 25.1

Obs	y	officer	candidate
1	76	1	1
2	65	1	2
3	85	1	3
4	74	1	4
5	59	2	1

We begin the Apex Enterprises analysis by generating ANOVA Table 25.2 (text page 1037) using SAS *proc glm*. (Insert 25.1) Because the five officers are perceived as a random sample from a very large "population" of officers, we refer to the factor *officer* as a random factor. The twenty candidates also are viewed as a random sample from a very large "population" of candidates, so we use ANOVA model II (all factors are random). The ratings of candidates by each officer are assumed to follow a normal distribution with mean μ_i and variance σ^2 (the variance for each officer is the same), i = 1, 2, ... , ∞ . The variability among the μ_i is denoted σ^2_μ .

Test of hypothesis $\sigma^2_\mu = 0$

To carry out the test of the null hypothesis that $\sigma^2_\mu = 0$, we specify that *officer* is a random factor in *proc glm*. (Insert 25.1) Partial results are shown in SAS Output 25.1. Consistent with text page 1037, we conclude that the means for officers in the population (of officers) are not all equal, or $\sigma^2_\mu > 0$, $F(4,15)=5.39$, $p=0.0068$.

Estimation of μ

To construct confidence intervals for functions of σ^2 and σ^2_μ and carry out additional analyses illustrated in the Apex Enterprises Example, we use SAS *proc mixed* in Insert 25.1. Note that the *method* option can be used to specify the estimation method [*ml* = maximum likelihood, *reml* = residual (restricted) maximum likelihood, *miqvue0* = minimum variance quadratic unbiased estimates] for the covariance parameters. The default *method = reml*. In Insert 25.1, we specify *method = reml* to illustrate where to place the option specification.

From text page 1039, we estimate the mean rating (μ) of all personnel officers with a 90% confidence interval. This is accomplished by the "model y = / cl alpha=.1;" statement. That is, we specify that SAS estimate the overall mean of Y (μ) and construct 90% confidence limits. From SAS Output 25.2, *Solution for Fixed Effects* table, the estimate is $\hat{\mu}_\bullet$ =71.45. The confidence limits ($61.9768 \le \mu \le 80.9232$) are consistent with text page 1039.

INSERT 25.1	INSERT 25.1 continued

data apex;
infile 'c:\kutnerdata\chapter 25 data sets\ch25ta01.txt';
  input y officer candidate;
proc print data=apex (obs=5);
run;
proc glm;
  class officer;
  model y = officer;
  random officer;
run;
	proc mixed method = reml asycov cl covtest
	alpha=.1;
	  class officer;
	  model y = / cl alpha=.1;
	  random officer;
	run;

SAS Output 25.1
Proc GLM

Source	DF	Sum of Squares	Mean Square	F Value	Pr > F
Model	4	1579.700000	394.925000	5.39	0.0068
Error	15	1099.250000	73.283333		
Corrected Total	19	2678.950000			

Source	DF	Type III SS	Mean Square	F Value	Pr > F
officer	4	1579.700000	394.925000	5.39	0.0068

SAS Output 25.2
Proc Mixed

Covariance Parameter Estimates							
Cov Parm	Estimate	Standard Error	Z Value	Pr Z	Alpha	Lower	Upper
officer	80.4104	70.1333	1.15	0.1258	0.1	29.5215	865.42
Residual	73.2833	26.7593	2.74	0.0031	0.1	43.9774	151.39

Asymptotic Covariance Matrix of Estimates			
Row	Cov Parm	CovP1	CovP2
1	officer	4918.68	-179.01
2	Residual	-179.01	716.06

Solution for Fixed Effects								
Effect	Estimate	Standard Error	DF	t Value	Pr > |t|	Alpha	Lower	Upper
Intercept	71.4500	4.4437	4	16.08	<.0001	0.1	61.9768	80.9232

260

Estimation of $\left(\sigma_\mu^2 + \sigma^2\right)$ **and** $\sigma_\mu^2 / \left(\sigma_\mu^2 + \sigma^2\right)$

From text page 1042, we estimate $\left(\sigma_\mu^2 + \sigma^2\right)$ and $\sigma_\mu^2 / \left(\sigma_\mu^2 + \sigma^2\right)$ with 90% confidence intervals. From text equation 25.23 we find that an estimate of σ^2 is $\hat{\sigma}_\mu^2 = s_\mu^2 = 80.4$, which was generated by *proc mixed* in Insert 25.1 and is given in SAS Output 25.2. An estimate of σ^2 is given by $MSE = 73.28$ (equation 25.6, text page 1035) and is shown in SAS Output 25.1. In Insert 25.2 we use equation 25.18, text page 1040, to calculate confidence intervals for $\left(\sigma_\mu^2 + \sigma^2\right)$ and $\sigma_\mu^2 / \left(\sigma_\mu^2 + \sigma^2\right)$ as shown on text page 1040-1041. The lower and upper limits of $\left(\sigma_\mu^2 + \sigma^2\right)$ are stored in variables named *l* and *u*. The corresponding limits for $\sigma_\mu^2 / \left(\sigma_\mu^2 + \sigma^2\right)$ are stored in *lstar* and *ustar*.

INSERT 25.2	INSERT 25.2 continued

data apex;
infile 'c:\kutnerdata\chapter 25 data sets\ch25ta01.txt';
  input y officer candidate;
* Use text equation 25.18;
n=4;
r=5;
mstr=394.925;
mse=73.28333;
alpha=0.05;
	fl=finv(1-alpha,r-1,r*(n-1));
	fu=finv(alpha,r-1,r*(n-1));
	l=1/n*((mstr/mse)*(1/fl)-1);
	u=1/n*((mstr/mse)*(1/fu)-1);
	lstar=l/(1+l);
	ustar=u/(1+u);
	proc print data=apex (obs=1);
	  var l u lstar ustar;
	run;

Estimation of σ^2

On text page 1042, the authors estimate σ^2 with a 90% confidence interval. In Insert 25.1, *proc mixed*, we requested that the asymptotic covariance matrix of the covariance parameters be displayed and that 90% confidence limits be computed to estimate the parameters (*asycov cl covtest alpha=.1;*). The c*ovtest* option produces asymptotic standard errors and Wald Z-tests for the covariance parameter estimates. The Wald Z value in the *Covariance Parameter Estimates* table is the estimate of the parameter divided by its standard error. From the SAS Output 25.2, *Covarinace Parameter Estimate* table, we see that a 90% confidence interval is calculated to be $43.9774 \le \sigma^2 \le 151.39$, which is consistent with text page 1042.

Point and Interval estimation of σ_μ^2

The authors next estimate σ_μ^2. As noted above, $\hat{\sigma}_\mu^2 = s_\mu^2 = 80.4$ as shown in SAS Output 25.2, *Covariance Parameter Estimates* table, in the row labeled *officer* and column labeled *estimate*. Next, the authors wish to estimate σ_μ^2 using a 90% confidence interval. They note that exact interval estimates are not possible, but that several approximations are available. SAS uses a *Satterthwaite* approximation for parameters that have a default lower boundary constraint of zero. A Wald Z-score and normal quantiles are used to construct the limits for parameters without the constraint of zero. Note, however, that this interval ($29.5215 \le \sigma_\mu^2 \le 865.42$, SAS Output 25.2) is not consistent with the interval ($30.9 \le \sigma_\mu^2 \le 685.2$) presented on text page 1044. The approximate interval estimate of σ_μ^2 given on text page 1044 can be computed on a hand calculator and is not detailed here.

On text page 1045 the authors present an improved procedure for computing approximate confidence intervals for σ_μ^2 based on a modified large sample (*MLS*) procedure. In Insert 25.3, we use the computational formulas presented in Table 25.3, text page 1045, to estimate a confidence interval for σ_μ^2 based on the *MLS* procedure. The lower and upper limits for σ_μ^2 are given by *cl90l* and *cl90u*, respectively. The lower and upper limits for σ_μ are given by *sqrt90l* and *sqrt90u*, respectively.

If candidate rating means for personnel officers are equal for all personnel officers in the population, we expect the variance component for *officer* to be small. We therefore wish to test the null hypothesis that this variance component is equal to 0. From the Wald Z-score and corresponding one-tailed probability (Pr Z=0.1258) in SAS Output 25.2, we would conclude that the variance component for *officer* is not significantly greater than 0. However, the Wald Z can be unreliable when used with small samples, and contrary to this conclusion, results of *proc glm* presented above suggest that the rating means are not equal for all officers in the population, or that $\sigma_\mu^2 > 0$. Additionally, the *intraclass correlation* defined by equation 25.3, page 1034, is $\sigma_\mu^2 / (\sigma_\mu^2 + \sigma^2)$=80.4/80.4+73.28=0.5229. Thus, about 52% of the total variability among individual candidate ratings can be attributed to variability among rating means for officers. If the variance component for *officer* is 0, the variability among candidate ratings is due solely to differences among candidates and none is due to differences among means for officers in the population. Using equations 25.18, text page 1040, we find that the confidence limits of the 90% (and 95%, not shown) confidence interval for $\sigma_\mu^2 / (\sigma_\mu^2 + \sigma^2)$ do not include 0. This finding leads us to reject the hypothesis that the proportion $\sigma_\mu^2 / (\sigma_\mu^2 + \sigma^2)$ (of the total variance of candidate ratings accounted for by variance among means for officers) is 0. As alternative tests of the hypothesis that σ_μ^2=0, we used the *Satterthwaite* procedure (text page1043), the *MLS* procedure (text page 1045), and the SAS approximation shown in SAS Output 25.2. None of the three sets of 90% confidence limits included 0. Thus, we are led to reject the hypothesis that the variance component for *officer* is 0 by any of the three procedures. (Note that 95% intervals are narrower than their 90% counterparts so that the corresponding three sets of 95% confidence necessarily do not include 0).

In summary, the Wald Z test, which can be unreliable when used with small samples, fails to reject the hypothesis $\sigma_\mu^2 = 0$. However, the *glm* procedure, the *intraclass correlation coefficient* confidence interval, and the three methods of interval estimation of σ_μ^2 all led to the conclusion that there are significant differences among candidate rating means for officers.

```
data apex;
infile 'c:\neter\ch24ta01.dat';
  input y officer candidate;
n=4;
c1=1/n;
c2=-1/n;
* ms1=mstr;
ms1=394.925;
*ms2=mse;
ms2=73.28333;
lhat=(ms1-ms2)/n;
f1=finv(.95,4,9999);
f2=finv(.95,15,9999);
f3=finv(.95,9999,4);
f4=finv(.95,9999,15);
f5=finv(.95,4,15);
f6=finv(.95,15,4);
g1=1-(1/f1);
g2=1-(1/f2);
g3=((f5-1)**2-(g1*f5)**2-(f4-1)**2)/f5;
g4=f6*(((f6-1)/f6)**2-(((f3-1)/f6)**2)-g2**2);
hl=(((g1*c1*ms1)**2)+(((f4-1)*c2*ms2)**2)-g3*c1*c2*ms1*ms2)**.5;
hu=(((f3-1)*c1*ms1)**2+((g2*c2*ms2)**2)-(g4*c1*c2*ms1*ms2))**.5;
cl90l=lhat-hl;
cl90u=lhat+hu;
sqrt90l=sqrt(cl90l);
sqrt90u=sqrt(cl90u);
run;
proc print data=apex (obs=1);
 var f1 f2 f3 f4 f5 f6 g1 g2 g3 g4 hl hu cl90l cl90u sqrt90l sqrt90u;
run;
```

ANOVA Models II and III with Unequal Sample Sizes

Sheffield Food Company Example

Data File: ch25ta12.txt

The Sheffield Food Company studied the reliability of two methods of determining the milk fat content of yogurt. Each method was to be used at 4 laboratories to determine the milk fat content of 12 samples of yogurt that had a known fat content. "Method of measurement" was considered to be a fixed factor with 2 levels: a propriety method of the Sheffield Food Company and a governmental method. "Laboratory" was considered to be a random factor with 4 levels; i.e. 4 laboratories. Due to technical problems, each laboratory was unable to establish a fat content for some samples by use of the governmental method. Thus, an ANOVA *mixed model* (model III) for unequal sample sizes is appropriate. See Chapter 0, "Working with SAS," for instructions on opening the Sheffield Food Company Example and naming the variables *fat, measure,* and *lab*. After opening and printing ch25ta12.txt, the first 5 lines of output should look like SAS Output 25.3.

SAS Output 25.3

Obs	fat	measure	lab
1	5.19	1	1
2	5.09	1	1
3	4.09	1	2
4	3.99	1	2
5	3.75	1	2

On text page 1075, the researchers obtained the maximum likelihood estimates of the parameters and standard deviations of the maximum likelihood estimators. In Insert 25.4 we first recode *measure* into a variable we arbitrarily named *xmeas* so that the variable for method of measurement will have values 1 = Sheffield method or -1 = government method instead of 1 = Sheffield method or 2 = government method. We request a mixed model analysis where the method of estimation is maximum likelihood (*ml*) and the asymptotic covariance matrix is printed. Partial results are shown in SAS Output 25.4. The estimated parameters and estimated standard deviations of the estimators for the parameters are found in the *Solution for Fixed Effects* table ($\hat{\mu}_{..} = 3.6941$ and $\hat{\alpha}_1 = 0.6329$, and corresponding standard deviations are listed under *Estimate* and *Standard Error*, and *Covariance Parameter Estimates* ($\hat{\sigma}^2 = 0.023$ is listed as *Residual Estimate*, $\hat{\sigma}^2_\beta = 0.097$ is listed as *lab Estimate*). The estimated variances of the estimators of the parameters σ^2 and σ^2_β are found in the *Asymptotic Covariance Matrix of Estimates* table. For instance, from text Table 25.14, the estimated standard deviation of $\hat{\sigma}^2_\beta$ is $s\{\hat{\sigma}^2_\beta\} = 0.071$. From the *Asymptotic Covariance Matrix of Estimates* table below, we see that the estimate of the variance of $\hat{\sigma}^2_\beta$ is $s^2\{\hat{\sigma}^2_\beta\} = 0.005068$ and the standard deviation is $s\{\hat{\sigma}^2_\beta\} = \sqrt{0.005068} = 0.0711898$. Likewise, the estimate of the variance of $\hat{\sigma}^2$ is $s^2\{\hat{\sigma}^2\} = 0.000035$ and the standard deviation is $s\{\hat{\sigma}^2\} = \sqrt{0.000035} = 0.006$.

An estimate of variance component for interaction and an estimate of the standard deviation of the corresponding estimator cannot be found directly in SAS Output 25.4. In equation 25.42, text page 1049, the variance of the error term is not expressed as $\sigma^2_{\alpha\beta}$ but rather as $(a-1)\sigma^2_{\alpha\beta}/a$. In the present example, $a = 2$ and the above expression can be rearranged as $\frac{1}{2}\alpha^2_{\alpha\beta} = \frac{\sigma^2_{\alpha\beta}}{2}$. From text Table 25.14 we find that $\hat{\sigma}^2_{\alpha\beta} = 0.086$. The SAS estimate for the interaction component is 0.04285 as shown below in the *Covariance Parameter Estimates* table, in the row labeled *xmeas*lab* under the column labeled *estimate*. If we multiply the SAS result by 2, we obtain the estimate (2)(0.04285) = 0.0857 in agreement with the estimate reported in text Table 25.14. An estimate of the standard deviation of the estimator $\hat{\sigma}^2_{\alpha\beta}$ is found using the variance of the estimate of the variance of the *xmeas*lab* parameter shown below in the *Asymptotic Covariance Matrix of Estimates* as $s^2\{\hat{\sigma}^2_{\alpha\beta}\} = 0.001052$. If we multiply this estimate by $(2)^2 = 4$, we get the estimate $(4)(0.001052) = 0.004208$, in rough agreement with the value 0.0041 given in text Table 25.14. Thus, the estimate of the standard deviation of $\sigma^2_{\alpha\beta}$ is $\sqrt{0.004208} = 0.0649$ as shown in text Table 25.14.

INSERT 25.4

```
data one;
infile 'c:\kutnerdata\chapter 25 data sets\ch25ta12.txt';
  input fat measure lab;
  if measure = 1 then xmeas =  1;
  if measure = 2 then xmeas = -1;
proc mixed method = ml asycov;
  class lab;
  model fat = xmeas / cl;
  random lab xmeas*lab;
run;
```

SAS Output 25.4

Covariance Parameter Estimates	
Cov Parm	**Estimate**
lab	0.09729
xmeas*lab	0.04285
Residual	0.02325

Asymptotic Covariance Matrix of Estimates				
Row	**Cov Parm**	**CovP1**	**CovP2**	**CovP3**
1	lab	0.005068	0.000081	-0.00001
2	xmeas*lab	0.000081	0.001052	-7.34E-6
3	Residual	-0.00001	-7.34E-6	0.000035

Solution for Fixed Effects								
Effect	**Estimate**	**Standard Error**	**DF**	**t Value**	**Pr > |t|**	**Alpha**	**Lower**	**Upper**
Intercept	3.6941	0.1581	3	23.36	0.0002	0.05	3.1910	4.1973
xmeas	0.6329	0.1067	3	5.93	0.0096	0.05	0.2933	0.9725

Type 3 Tests of Fixed Effects				
Effect	Num DF	Den DF	F Value	Pr > F
xmeas	1	3	35.17	0.0096

The bootstrap method described on text page 1076 is not readily available in SAS.

Chapter 26 SAS®

Nested Designs, Subsampling and Partially Nested Designs

In previous chapters when two or more factors were involved in an experiment, the factors were *crossed* in the sense that every level of each factor occurred with all levels of every other factor. This was the situation in randomized complete block designs and in full factorial experiments where we investigated interactions among factors. In Chapter 26, the authors discuss *nested factors*. We say factor B is nested within factor A if each level of factor A contains different levels of factor B. We may encounter many variations in nested and crossed factors. For example, we could have factor A crossed with factor B and factor C nested within all the combinations of levels of A and B. Further, we could have factor C nested within factor B where factor B is itself nested within factor A. Closely related to the concept of nested factors is the notion of *subsampling*. Subsampling occurs when more than one observation is made on the response variable of interest for each (primary) study unit. The authors give an example in which batches of flour mix (primary study unit) are randomly assigned to treatment. Three loaves of bread (subsamples) from each batch of flour mix are then observed for each treatment. The authors refer to situations in which some factors are crossed and others are nested as *partially nested*, *partially hierarchical*, or *cross-nested designs*. Variations in the use of crossed and/or nested factors and subsampling lead to different considerations in the statistical analysis of relevant data.

Training School Example

Data File: ch26ta01.txt

A manufacturing company operates a training school in each of three districts. Each school has two instructors. Because each school has its own set of two instructors, we say that instructors are nested within schools. The company wished to investigate the effect of training school and instructors on student learning. Classes were formed at each training school and randomly assigned to one of the two instructors within the school. See Chapter 0, "Working with SAS," for instructions on opening the Training School Example and naming the variables *Y*, *school*, *instruct*, and *session*. After opening and printing ch26ta01.txt, the first 5 lines of output should look like SAS Output 26.1.

SAS Output 26.1

Obs	y	school	instruct	session
1	25	1	1	1
2	29	1	1	2
3	14	1	2	1
4	11	1	2	2
5	11	2	1	1

On text page 1095, the authors viewed both *school* and *instruct* as fixed factors. In Insert 26.1, we specify *proc glm* where *Y* is the dependent variable and *school* and *instruct* are *class* variables with instructor (*instruct*) nested within school (*school*). We indicate the nesting in the *model* statement by writing

model y = school instruct(school);

Execution of the first *proc glm* statement in Insert 26.1 results in SAS Output 26.2. This output is consistent with Table 26.4, text page 1097. To test for factor effects in this nested two-factor study, we refer to SAS Output 26.2. From these results, we find $F(2, 6)=11.18$, $p=0.0095$, and conclude that there are significant differences among learning score means for *school*. The result of the test of equal learning score means for instructors within schools is $F(3, 6)=27.02$, $p=0.0007$, so we conclude differences between instructors are significant in at least one school.

INSERT 26.1	INSERT 26.1 continued

data training;
infile 'c:\kutnerdata\chapter 26 data
                sets\ch26ta01.txt';
 input y school instruct session;
proc glm;
class school instruct;
 model y = school instruct(school);
 lsmeans school / cl ;
 lsmeans school / cl pdiff adjust=tukey alpha=.1;
run;
	data training;
	infile 'c:\kutnerdata\chapter 26 data
	                sets\ch26ta01.txt';
	 input y school instruct session;
	proc glm;
	class school instruct;
	 model y = school|instruct;
	 lsmeans school*instruct / slice=school cl pdiff
	                adjust=bon alpha=.5;
	run;

SAS Output 26.2

Source	DF	Sum of Squares	Mean Square	F Value	Pr > F
Model	5	724.0000000	144.8000000	20.69	0.0010
Error	6	42.0000000	7.0000000		
Corrected Total	11	766.0000000			

Source	DF	Type III SS	Mean Square	F Value	Pr > F
school	2	156.5000000	78.2500000	11.18	0.0095
instruct(school)	3	567.5000000	189.1666667	27.02	0.0007

Estimation of Factor Level Means μ_i

On text page 1101, the authors wish to estimate the response mean for the Atlanta school with a 95% confidence interval. We use the first *lsmeans* statement (under the first *proc glm*) in Insert 26.1 to find the estimated marginal means and confidence intervals (95% by default) for each level of *school*. Results (not shown) are consistent with text page 1101.

On text page 1101, the authors performed pairwise comparisons of the learning score means for the three schools using the *Tukey* test and a 90% confidence interval. This analysis is specified in the second *lsmeans* statement (under the first *proc glm*) in Insert 26.1. Results (not shown) are consistent with text page 1101.

Estimation of Treatment Means μ_{ij}

On text page 1102, the authors compare the learning score means of the two instructors within each of the three schools using the *Bonferroni* procedure and a 90% confidence interval. In the second *proc glm* of Insert 26.1, we specify *model y = school|instruct*. We use the *lsmeans* statement and *slice* option to specify *Bonferroni* adjusted comparisons of instructor (*instruct*) within each level of school (*school*). This specification will result in 15 comparisons. However, we are interested in only three comparisons and the effective alpha level would be 0.1/3=0.0333. To find the equivalent *Bonferroni* adjusted alpha level for 3 of the 15 comparisons, we solve for alpha (alpha/15=0.0333) to find alpha=0.5. That is, to construct the 90% confidence intervals for the three comparisons shown on text page 1102, given that SAS is going to produce 15 comparisons, we specify alpha=0.5 in the second *proc glm* statement in Insert 26.1. Results (not shown) are consistent with text page 1102.

On text page 1103, the authors estimate the overall mean with a 95% confidence interval. The calculations are performed easily on a hand calculator and are not detailed here.

Unbalanced Nested Two-Factor Designs

On text page 1104 the authors present an unbalanced nested two-factor design and use the regression approach for analyzing the data. As we discussed in Chapter 15 of this manual, *proc glm* is a regression-based approach and can be used with unbalanced data as shown in Table 26.6 (a), text page 1105, without recoding the data as shown in Table 26.6 (b). Thus, execution of the syntax described in Insert 26.1, using the data from text Table 26.6 (a), will result in the analysis of variance table shown in Table 26.7, text page 1106.

Subsampling in Single-Factor Study with Completely Randomized Design

Bread Crustiness Example

Data File: ch26ta09.txt

On text page 1109, researchers studied the relationship between oven temperature (three levels) and a measure of bread crustiness (the response). There were two experimental units (batches of flour mix) randomly assigned to each treatment, and three subsamples were selected from each batch. See Chapter 0, "Working with SAS," for instructions on opening the Bread Crustiness Example and naming the variables *Y*, *temp*, *batch*, and *obser*. After opening and printing ch26ta09.txt, the first 5 lines of output should look like SAS Output 26.3.

SAS Output 26.3

Obs	y	temp	batch	obser
1	4	1	1	1
2	7	1	1	2
3	5	1	1	3
4	12	1	2	1
5	8	1	2	2

In Insert 26.2 we designate *batch* and *temp* as *class* variables, and specify *model y = temp batch(temp)*. This syntax produces SAS Output 26.3. Notice that the *SS*, *df*, and *MS* terms are consistent with Table 26.10, text page 1110. [*Error Sum of Squares*, SAS Output 26.3 = *Observation units (OE) Sum of Squares*, text Table 26.10] However, the test statistic (*F*=45.09) for the hypothesis that all *temp* effects are equal to zero is not consistent with *F**=7.21 as reported on text page 1109. This is because SAS uses the error mean square (2.611) as the denominator for the test statistic by default instead of the batch within temperature mean square [*Mean Square* for *batch(temp)* =16.33 in SAS Output 26.3] as shown in equation 26.38a, text page 1108. To specify syntax for a test that uses the correct mean square in its denominator, we use the *test* subcommand from within *proc glm* to test a (numerator) mean square for a specified factor against a specified denominator mean square. That is, we add the *test* subcommand to request a test for temperature effects (*h=temp*) using the mean square for batches within temperature setting as the denominator mean square [*e=batch(temp)*] in the *F*-test. This results in SAS Output 26.4, which is consistent with the *F**=7.21 reported on text page 1109. We use the error mean square (2.611) as the denominator for the test statistic for evaluating *batch* differences. The value of the resulting test statistic is shown in SAS Output 26.3 as *F*=6.26 for the effect of *batch(temp)*, which is consistent with text page 1110.

270

```
data bread;
infile 'c:\kutnerdata\chapter 26 data sets\ch26ta09.txt';
  input y temp batch obser;
proc glm;
 class temp batch;
 model y = temp batch(temp);
 test h=temp e=batch(temp);
run;
```

SAS Output 26.3

Source	DF	Sum of Squares	Mean Square	F Value	Pr > F
Model	5	284.4444444	56.8888889	21.79	<.0001
Error	12	31.3333333	2.6111111		
Corrected Total	17	315.7777778			

Source	DF	Type III SS	Mean Square	F Value	Pr > F
temp	2	235.4444444	117.7222222	45.09	<.0001
batch(temp)	3	49.0000000	16.3333333	6.26	0.0084

SAS Output 26.4

Custom Hypothesis Tests

Tests of Hypotheses Using the Type III MS for batch(temp) as an Error Term					
Source	DF	Type III SS	Mean Square	F Value	Pr > F
temp	2	235.4444444	117.7222222	7.21	0.0715

On text page 1111, the authors wish to find the 95% confidence interval for bread baked at the low temperature and to estimate the difference in means for the measure of crustiness for breads baked at low versus high temperatures. The calculations are performed easily on a hand calculator and are not detailed here.

On text page 1112 the authors wish to estimate σ^2, the variance component for variability among response means for batches within temperatures, with a 95% confidence interval. [See Chapter 25 (Random and Fixed Effects Models) of this manual for example syntax.]

Three-Factor Partially Nested Designs

Group Decision Making Example

Data File: ch26ta12.txt

On text page 1115 the authors present a partially nested design with three factors: A, B, and C. A and B are crossed, C is nested within A, and B and C are crossed. See Chapter 0, "Working with SAS," for instructions on opening the Group Decision Making Example and naming the variables Y, a, b, c, and k. After opening and printing ch26ta12.txt, the first 5 lines of output should look like SAS Output 26.5.

SAS Output 26.5

Obs	y	a	b	c	k
1	16	1	1	1	1
2	20	1	1	1	2
3	14	1	1	2	1
4	19	1	1	2	2
5	7	2	1	1	1

In Insert 26.3, we use the rationale described under *Development of Model*, text page 1114, and specify the *model* statement according to the model shown in Equation 6.48 text page 1115. To test for the effect of nationality as shown on text page 1117, we add the *test* statement to indicate that we wish to test the effect of a while using the mean square for c nested within a [$c(a)$] as the denominator. The result of this custom test is $F^*=1681.00$, $p=0.0006$, consistent with text page 1118. Continuing in Insert 26.3, we use equation 26.50 and 26.50a (text page 1118) to estimate the difference between response means for the U.S. and foreign teams. The resulting lower (*lhatlo*) and upper (*lhathi*) confidence limits (not shown) will be printed.

INSERT 26.3	INSERT 26.3 continued

data group;
infile 'c:\kutnerdata\chapter 26 data
              sets\ch26ta12.txt';
 input y a b c k;
proc glm;
 class a b c;
 model y = a b c(a) a*b b*c(a) ;
 test h=a e=c(a);
run;
	data group;
	infile 'c:\kutnerdata\chapter 26 data
	              sets\ch26ta12.txt';
	 input y a b c k;
	lhat=20.25-10.00;
	t=tinv(1-(.05/2),(2-1)*2);
	lhatlo=lhat-t*sqrt((2*.25)/8);
	lhathi=lhat+t*sqrt((2*.25)/8);
	proc print data=group (obs=1);
	 var lhatlo lhathi;
	run;

Chapter 27 SAS®

Repeated Measures and Related Designs

In this chapter, the authors take up studies in which the response variable is observed repeatedly, perhaps under different experimental conditions. In a weight loss study, for example, subjects may be weighed weekly during a 6 week study period to assess possible changes in weight across time. In this context, "subject" is considered to be a block and the individual subjects are considered to be a random sample from a large population of subjects. Thus, "subject" may be viewed as a random factor (blocks random). SAS and other software packages provide many options for analyzing repeated measures data. For example, if the subjects compose a single group of subjects of interest, we can analyze the data following the steps used for analyzing a randomized complete block design where subjects are regarded as blocks. (See text Figure 27.1) If there are multiple groups, we can use the analysis of variance for split plot designs. These methods are univariate approaches to the analysis of multivariate data because repeated measures data are inherently multivariate data. Of course, multivariate analysis of variance can also be performed. There are advantages to using univariate approaches if they are appropriate but the univariate methods require the covariance matrix (for the inherently multivariate data structure) to have the property of sphericity relative to the hypothesis being tested. Mauchley's test for sphericity is useful for checking whether the property is plausible. On the other hand, the sphericity assumption for the covariance matrix is not required for multivariate analysis. SAS' *proc glm – repeated* statement is useful for analyzing repeated measures data, and we provide an overview of the statement in this chapter.

Single-Factor Experiments with Repeated Measures on All Treatments

Wine-Judging Example

Data File: ch27ta02.txt

In the Wine-Judging example, six judges rated the overall excellence of four wine types. See Chapter 0, "Working with SAS," for instructions on opening the Wine-Judging Example and naming the variables *Y, judge,* and *wine*. After opening and printing ch27ta02.txt, the first 5 lines of output should look like SAS Output 27.1.

SAS Output 27.1

Obs	y	judge	wine
1	20	1	1
2	24	1	2
3	28	1	3
4	28	1	4
5	15	2	1

The researchers considered the six judges to be a random sample from a large population of potential judges; thus, they considered the effects associated with *judge* to be random. They considered effects associated with *wine* to be fixed because the four wines were the only wines of interest. From Figure 27.2, text page 1133, the researchers concluded that there did not appear to be significant interaction between *judge* and *wine*; thus, an additive model was adopted. A single-factor repeated measures analysis was performed to test for differences in the response variable (*Y*) among the 4 levels of *wine*. In Insert 27.1 we specify that *wine* and *judge* are *class* variables and that *judge* is a random factor. By lack of the same specification, *wine* is a fixed factor. We use the *lsmeans* statement to obtain the *Tukey* procedure and the 95% family confidence intervals for the four levels of *wine*. Results are shown in SAS Output 27.2 and are consistent with the ANOVA Table presented on text page 1133 (Figure 27.3) and the pairwise comparisons shown on text page 1137.

INSERT 27.1	INSERT 27.1 continued

data wine;
infile 'c:\kutnerdata\chapter 27 data
           sets\ch27ta02.txt';
  input y judge wine;
proc print data=wine (obs=5);
run;
	proc glm;
	  class judge wine;
	   model y=judge wine;
	    random judge;
	    lsmeans wine / adjust=tukey cl pdiff;
	run;

SAS Output 27.2

Source	DF	Sum of Squares	Mean Square	F Value	Pr > F
Model	8	357.3333333	44.6666667	41.88	<.0001
Error	15	16.0000000	1.0666667		
Corrected Total	23	373.3333333			

Source	DF	Type III SS	Mean Square	F Value	Pr > F
judge	5	173.3333333	34.6666667	32.50	<.0001
wine	3	184.0000000	61.3333333	57.50	<.0001

SAS Output 27.2 continued

		Difference Between Means	Simultaneous 95% Confidence Limits for LSMean(i)-LSMean(j)	
i	**j**			
1	2	-2.000000	-3.718582	-0.281418
1	3	-6.666667	-8.385248	-4.948085
1	4	-6.000000	-7.718582	-4.281418
2	3	-4.666667	-6.385248	-2.948085
2	4	-4.000000	-5.718582	-2.281418
3	4	0.666667	-1.051915	2.385248

Title above table: **Least Squares Means for Effect wine**

Review of Syntax for SAS Repeated Statement

In SAS, the *repeated* statement can be used with *proc glm* to provide many useful features for the analysis of repeated measures. The general setup for the SAS statements in a repeated measures analysis is as follows:

> *proc glm* <options>;
>   *class* variables;
>   *model* dependent variables = independent variables < / option*s* >;
>   *repeated* factor name < levels < (level values) >> < transformation > / option;
>   run;

In the *model* statement above, the repeated measures must be listed as dependent variables; hence, the model will be a multivariate model. This may require rearranging the data in the input data file or using SAS programming code to create a data set that contains the rearranged data.

In the Wine-Judging Example, we rearrange the data as follows so that each line of data contains the judge number and scores for the four wines assigned by one judge:

SAS Output 27.3

Obs	judge	y1	y2	y3	y4
1	1	20	24	28	28
2	2	15	18	23	24
3	3	18	19	24	23
4	4	26	26	30	30
5	5	22	24	28	26

Given this latter file structure, we illustrate how to input the data with the data embedded directly in the program as shown in Insert 27.2. We then execute *proc glm* with the model given as

$$model\ y1\text{-}y4 = \ ;$$

Here, there is only one group of subjects (judges) in the experiment. There are four responses (the dependent variables) for each subject and there are no independent variables. Thus, in the model statement, nothing appears after the "=" symbol. Next, we execute three repeated statements, the first being

$$repeated\ wine\ 4\ (1\ 2\ 3\ 4)\ contrast\ (1)\ /\ nom\ summary\ printe;$$

Here, we arbitrarily assigned the factor name *wine* to label the factor for the repeated measures. We use the "4" after *wine* to indicate there are four levels of the factor *wine*. The expression (1 2 3 4) labels the four levels of wine. The expression *contrast* (1) requests tests of all pairwise contrasts that involve *wine* level 1 (1 vs 2, 1 vs 3, and 1 vs 4). After the slash, the option *nom* specifies that no multivariate test results are to be printed. The option *summary* produces analysis of variance tables for each contrast. The option *printe* displays the *Mauchly* test for the hypothesis of Sphericity of the covariance matrix The *repeated* statement displays the *Greenhouse-Geisser* epsilon and the *Huynh-Feldt* epsilon for use if Mauchley's test suggests the assumption of Sphericity is not tenable.

The second and third *contrast* statements insure that all pairwise comparisons are generated. This method is used for making pairwise comparisons from within the *proc glm – repeated* statement but is not equivalent to the pairwise comparisons made using *proc glm* in Insert 27.1 or to those reported on text page 1137. The *repeated - contrast* procedure uses separate error terms for each comparison, and each contrast is equivalent to a paired t-test. This method is also valid but more conservative than the method in Insert 27.1 and the method reported by the text.

Partial results of Insert 27.2 are shown in SAS Output 27.4. From the table labeled *Sphericity Tests*, we conclude that the assumption of Sphericity is tenable, *Mauchly's Criterion* $X^2 = 3.89, p = 0.5652$. Thus, we base the test for equality of taste score means for wines on the unadjusted F test, and disregard the Greenhouse-Geisser and Huynh-Feldt adjustments. Note that the methods shown in Insert 27.1 and 27.2 both yield an $F=57.5$ for testing the hypothesis that the rating means for the four wine types are equal, consistent with text page 1133.

```
data wine;
  input judge y1 y2 y3 y4;
datalines;
1      20      24      28      28
2      15      18      23      24
3      18      19      24      23
4      26      26      30      30
5      22      24      28      26
6      19      21      27      25
;
proc glm ;
  model y1-y4= ;
        repeated wine 4 (1 2 3 4) contrast (1) / nom summary printe;
        repeated wine 4 (1 2 3 4) contrast (2) / nom summary;
        repeated wine 4 (1 2 3 4) contrast (3) / nom summary;
run;
```

SAS Output 27.4

GLM – Repeated Measures

Sphericity Tests				
Variables	DF	Mauchly's Criterion	Chi-Square	Pr > ChiSq
Transformed Variates	5	0.0618258	10.360564	0.0656
Orthogonal Components	5	0.3515625	3.8910912	0.5652

Source	DF	Type III SS	Mean Square	F Value	Pr > F	Adj Pr > F G - G	Adj Pr > F H - F
score	3	184.0000000	61.3333333	57.50	<.0001	<.0001	<.0001
Error(score)	15	16.0000000	1.0666667				

Greenhouse-Geisser Epsilon	0.6038
Huynh-Feldt Epsilon	0.9270

At times it is advantageous to use an analysis as shown in Insert 27.1 or a repeated measures analysis as shown in Insert 27.2, but the data file is not structured as needed for the desired procedure. For instance, assume that we wish to use the *proc glm - repeated* option but 1,000 data records have been entered in the format shown in SAS Output 27.1. This format is not compatible with the *proc glm - repeated* option. The syntax shown in Insert 27.3 - Method 1 will convert the data file as shown in SAS Output 27.1 to the structure as shown in SAS Output 27.3, which is compatible with the *proc glm - repeated* option. The syntax shown in Insert 27.4 -

Methods 2 and 3 will each convert the data file as shown in SAS Output 27.3 to the structure as shown in SAS Output 27.1, which is compatible with Insert 27.1.

INSERT 27.3	INSERT 27.3 continued

data wine;
infile 'c:\kutnerdata\chapter 27 data sets\ch27ta02.txt';
  input y judge wine;
 	
* **METHOD 1** - One measurement per line to multiple; * *
* measurements per line;
* Restructure Output 26.1 to Output 26.3;
proc sort;
 by judge wine ;
data new;
	retain judge score1-score4;
	 set wine;
	array score(4) score1 - score4;
	 by judge;
	score(wine)=y;
	if last.judge then output;
	keep judge score1 - score4;
	proc print data=new noobs;
	run;

INSERT 27.4	INSERT 27.4 continued

* METHOD 2 - Multiple measurements per line to;
* one measurement per line;
data wine;
  input judge score1 score2 score3 score4;
   datalines;
1   20   24   28   28
2   15   18   23   24
3   18   19   24   23
4   26   26   30   30
5   22   24   28   26
6   19   21   27   25
;
data new;
retain y judge wine;
 set wine;
array score (4);
 do wine=1 to 4;
y=score(wine);
keep y judge wine;
output ;
end;
proc print data=new noobs;
run;
	* METHOD 3 - Multiple measurements per line to;
	* one measurement per line;
	data wine (keep = y judge wine);
	retain y judge wine;
	  input judge score1 score2 score3 score4;
	y=score1; wine=1; output;
	y=score2; wine=2; output;
	y=score3; wine=3; output;
	y=score4; wine=4; output;
	datalines;
	1 20 24 28 28
	2 15 18 23 24
	3 18 19 24 23
	4 26 26 30 30
	5 22 24 28 26
	6 19 21 27 25
	;
	proc print data=wine noobs;
	 run;

Ranked Data

In Table 27.4, text page 1138, the authors present the results of six subjects' ranking of coffee sweeteners. The data are arranged in ch27ta04.txt in the following order: *Y*, *subject*, and *sweetener*. Additionally, the ratings have already been ranked within each subject so that *Y* represents a rank variable. Here we simply specify a main-effects only model in *proc glm* where the rank (*Y*) is the dependent variable and *subject* and *sweetener* are *class* variables (program not shown). This will result in $F_R^* = 7.50$ for sweetener as reported on text page 1138. The pairwise comparisons reported on text page 1139 can be calculated on a hand calculator except for text equation 27.9a. To find $B = z(1 - \alpha / 2g) = 2.326$ execute the following statement: "B=probit(10.2/(2*10));".

Two-Factor Experiments with Repeated Measures on One Factor: Analysis of Factor Effects without Interaction

Athletic Shoe Sales Example

Data File: ch27ta07.txt

Market researchers selected 10 test markets (*market*) to study the effect of two advertising campaigns (*campaign*). The outcome measure was athletic shoe sales (*Y*) and data were collected for three 2-week periods (*period*). See Chapter 0, "Working with SAS," for instructions on opening the Athletic Shoe Sales Example and naming the variables *Y*, *market*, *campaign*, and *period*. After opening and printing ch27ta07.txt, the first 5 lines of output should look like SAS Output 27.5.

SAS Output 27.5

Obs	y	market	campaign	period
1	958	1	1	1
2	1005	2	1	1
3	351	3	1	1
4	549	4	1	1
5	730	5	1	1

The researchers first visually inspected the relationship between *campaign* and *period*. Based on Figure 27.6, text page 1146, and other diagnostics, they concluded that a repeated measures model was appropriate. *Campaign* and *period* were considered fixed factors. Levels of *market* were considered a random sample from a large population of potential markets and, thus, *market* was considered to be a random factor. Additionally, *market* was nested within *campaign* because 5 test markets were assigned to the first advertising campaign and 5 different test markets were assigned to the second campaign. In Insert 27.5, we specify the appropriate model and request a *Tukey* procedure with a 99% confidence interval as shown on text page 1148. Execution of Insert 27.5 results in SAS Output 27.6. With one exception, this output is consistent with Figure 27.7, text page 1147, and the confidence intervals shown on text page 1148. However, the test statistic (F=469.7) for the effect of *campaign* is not consistent with F^*=0.73 reported on text page 1147. This is due to the mean square error (MSE=357.96) being used as the denominator for the test statistic instead of $MSS(A)$= [MS for *market(campaign)*]=16.33 as shown in equation 27.14b, text page 1143. To specify this custom hypothesis, we use the *test* subcommand from within *proc glm* to test an hypothesis term against a specified error term. That is, we add the *test* subcommand to request a test for treatment (*campaign*) using MS for *market(campaign)* as the error term. Results of this custom hypothesis are shown in SAS Output 27.6 where F=0.73.

```
                           INSERT 27.5

data shoe;
infile 'c:\kutnerdata\chapter 27 data sets\ch27ta07.txt';
  input y market campaign period ;
proc glm;
   class campaign period market;
   model y = campaign period market(campaign) campaign*period;
   random market;
   test h=campaign e=market(campaign);
   lsmeans period / adjust=tukey cl pdiff alpha=.01;
 run;
```

SAS Output 27.6

Source	DF	Sum of Squares	Mean Square	F Value	Pr > F
Model	13	2069296.000	159176.615	444.67	<.0001
Error	16	5727.467	357.967		
Corrected Total	29	2075023.467			

Source	DF	Type III SS	Mean Square	F Value	Pr > F
campaign	1	168150.533	168150.533	469.74	<.0001
period	2	67073.067	33536.533	93.69	<.0001
market(campaign)	8	1833680.933	229210.117	640.31	<.0001
campaign*period	2	391.467	195.733	0.55	0.5892

Tests of Hypotheses Using the Type III MS for market(campaign) as an Error Term					
Source	DF	Type III SS	Mean Square	F Value	Pr > F
campaign	1	168150.5333	168150.5333	0.73	0.4166

Least Squares Means for Effect period			
i	j	Difference Between Means	Simultaneous 99% Confidence Limits for LSMean(i)-LSMean(j)
1	2	-80.400000	-109.031863	-51.768137
1	3	32.000000	3.368137	60.631863
2	3	112.400000	83.768137	141.031863

As noted above, there are advantages to using univariate approaches (Insert 27.5) but the univariate methods require the covariance matrix to have the property of sphericity relative to the hypothesis being tested. Mauchley's test for sphericity is useful for testing this assumption but is not available from the syntax in Insert 27.5. To obtain Mauchley's test for sphericity, we use the *proc glm – repeated* statement. The *repeated* statement, however, requires that the data file be structured as multiple (repeated) measurements per line, which is not the structure shown in SAS Output 27.5 (text Table 27.7). In Insert 27.6, we read the data file shown in Table 27.5 and use the logic of syntax in Insert 27.3 to convert the file to multiple measurements per line. After executing Insert 27.6, the first five lines of printed output will look like SAS Output 27.7. We then specify *proc glm* where *sales1*, *sales2*, and *sales3* are dependent variables and *campaign* is a *class* variable. We also specify *period* as the label of the three levels of shoe sales. Partial output of this *proc glm* is shown in SAS Output 27.8. Notice that the *F* values for *campaign*, *period*, and *campaign*period* in SAS Output 27.8 are consistent with SAS Output 27.6 above and text Figure 27.7. However, from the table labeled *Sphericity Tests* in SAS Output 27.8, we find that the assumption of sphericity is rejected, $X^2 = 7.97, p = 0.0186$. Given that the sphericity assumption is not supported, we can adjust the univariate tests using the methods of Greenhouse and Geisser or Huynh and Feldt. For example, the adjusted *Greenhouse-Geisser* and *Huynh-Feldt* probability level for the *period*campaign* interaction are listed under *G-G* and *H-F*, respectively, as *p*=0.5075 and *p*=0.5387.

The *Greenhouse-Geisser* adjustment is conservative, especially for small samples; the *Huynh-Feldt* adjustment is more liberal than the *Greenhouse-Geisser* adjustment. When we do not reject the assumption of sphericity and the *p*-value of the test is large, say $p > 0.15$, we would quote the *p*-value for the unadjusted F test (in this case for testing *campaign*period* and *campaign*); if the sphericity p-value is modestly large, say $0.15 \leq p < 0.05$, we would quote the *p*-values based on the *Huynh-Feldt* adjustment; if the sphericity *p*-value is small, say $0.05 \leq p < 0.01$, we would quote the *p*-values based on the *Greenhouse-Geisser* adjustment; and if the sphericity *p*-value is very small, say $p \leq 0.01$, we would use multivariate tests. The multivariate tests are not discussed in the text and are usually presented in a separate course on multivariate analysis. We point out here that the multivariate tests make no assumptions regarding the within-subject covariance matrix and hence they are valid for all covariance structures. But the univariate tests are more powerful provided the covariance matrix for the repeated measures has the property of sphericity or "near spherecity." *Wilks' Lambda*, *Pillai's Trace*, *Hotelling-Lawley Trace*, and *Roy's Greatest Root* are also displayed in SAS Output 27.8 below. The *F* values for these four multivariate tests are identical in many situations including the present example but that is not always the case. None of the four is uniformly superior to the others and SAS prints all four test results so the analyst can choose differently for different situations.

SAS Output 27.7

Obs	campaign	market	sales1	sales2	sales3
1	1	1	958	1047	933
2	1	2	1005	1122	986
3	1	3	351	436	339
4	1	4	549	632	512
5	1	5	730	784	707

```
data shoe;
infile 'c:\kutnerdata\chapter 27 data sets\ch27ta07.txt';
  input y market campaign period ;
* METHOD 1 - One measurement per line to multiple measurements per line;
proc sort;
 by campaign market period;
data new;
retain campaign market sales1-sales3;
 set shoe;
array sales(3) sales1 - sales3;
 by campaign market;
sales (period)=y;
if last.market then output;
keep campaign market sales1 - sales3;
proc print data=new (obs=5);
run;
proc glm data=new;
 class campaign;
   model sales1 - sales3 = campaign / nouni ;
     repeated period 3 / printe;
run;
```

SAS Output 27.8

Sphericity Tests				
Variables	DF	Mauchly's Criterion	Chi-Square	Pr > ChiSq
Transformed Variates	2	0.2073483	11.013488	0.0041
Orthogonal Components	2	0.3201301	7.9731943	0.0186

Manova Test Criteria and Exact F Statistics for the Hypothesis of no period Effect
H = Type III SSCP Matrix for time
E = Error SSCP Matrix

S=1   M=0   N=2.5

Statistic	Value	F Value	Num DF	Den DF	Pr > F
Wilks' Lambda	0.06892566	47.28	2	7	<.0001
Pillai's Trace	0.93107434	47.28	2	7	<.0001
Hotelling-Lawley Trace	13.50838421	47.28	2	7	<.0001
Roy's Greatest Root	13.50838421	47.28	2	7	<.0001

SAS Output 27.8 continued

Manova Test Criteria and Exact F Statistics for the Hypothesis of no period*campaign Effect
H = Type III SSCP Matrix for time*campaign
E = Error SSCP Matrix

S=1   M=0   N=2.5

Statistic	Value	F Value	Num DF	Den DF	Pr > F
Wilks' Lambda	0.57604042	2.58	2	7	0.1451
Pillai's Trace	0.42395958	2.58	2	7	0.1451
Hotelling-Lawley Trace	0.73598930	2.58	2	7	0.1451
Roy's Greatest Root	0.73598930	2.58	2	7	0.1451

Source	DF	Type III SS	Mean Square	F Value	Pr > F
campaign	1	168150.533	168150.533	0.73	0.4166
Error	8	1833680.933	229210.117		

Source	DF	Type III SS	Mean Square	F Value	Pr > F	Adj Pr > F G - G	Adj Pr > F H - F
period	2	67073.06667	33536.53333	93.69	<.0001	<.0001	<.0001
period*campaign	2	391.46667	195.73333	0.55	0.5892	0.5075	0.5387
Error(period)	16	5727.46667	357.96667				

Greenhouse-Geisser Epsilon	0.5953
Huynh-Feldt Epsilon	0.7274

Two-Factor Experiments with Repeated Measures on Both Factors

Blood Flow Example
Data File: ch27ta12.txt

On text page 1158, a researcher studied the effects of drug A (levels = A_1 and A_2) and drug B (levels = B_1 and B_2) on blood flow in 12 human subjects. Each subject received each of the four treatments (A_1B_1, A_1B_2, A_2B_1, A_2B_2) in a random order over several days. The half-life of each drug was such that there was no carryover effect. The 12 subjects were considered to be a random sample from a large population of potential subjects; thus *subject* was considered a random factor and drug *A* and drug *B* were fixed factors. See Chapter 0, "Working with SAS," for instructions on opening the Blood Flow Example and naming the variables *Y*, *subject*, *a*, and *b.* After opening and printing ch27ta12.txt, the first 5 lines of output should look like SAS Output 27.9.

SAS Output 27.9

Obs	y	subject	a	b
1	2	1	1	1
2	-1	2	1	1
3	0	3	1	1
4	3	4	1	1
5	1	5	1	1

To produce the test statistics given in Figure 27.11, text page 1159, we specify *proc glm* where *Y* is the dependent variable, *A* and *B* are fixed factors, *subject* is a random factor, and use *model* to specify the effects shown in Figure 27.11. (Insert 27.7) This will result in SAS Output 27.10 and is consistent with Figure 27.11 with the exception of the *F* values for *A* and *B*. The discrepancy is due to mean square error (*MSE*) being used as the denominator for the *F* statistics instead of *MSAS* and *MSBS* as shown in equations 27.24b and 27.25b, respectively, on text page 1155. To specify these custom hypotheses, we use the *test* subcommand from within *proc glm* to test hypothesis terms against specified error terms. That is, we add the *test* subcommand to request a test for treatments (*A*) and (*B*) using *MSAS* and *MSBS*, respectively, as the error terms. Results of these custom hypotheses are shown in SAS Output 27.10.

INSERT 27.7	INSERT 27.7 continued
| ```
data blood;
infile 'c:\kutnerdata\chapter 27 data sets\ch27ta12.txt';
  input y subject a b;
proc print data=blood (obs=5);
run;
proc glm;
class subject a b;
 model y = subject a b a*b subject*a subject*b;
  random subject;
   test h=a e=a*subject  ;
   test h=b e=b*subject ;
   lsmeans a*b / pdiff cl adjust=bon alpha=.06;
run;
``` | ```
*** proc glm – repeated statement ***;

data blood;
 input subject a1b1 a1b2 a2b1 a2b2;
datalines;
1    2    10    9    25
2   -1     8    6    21
3    0    11    8    24
4    3    15   11    31
5    1     5    6    20
6    2    12    9    27
7   -2    10    8    22
8    4    16   12    30
9   -2     7    7    24
10  -2    10   10    28
11   2     8   10    25
12  -1     8    6    23
;
proc glm data=blood;
        model a1b1 a1b2 a2b1 a2b2 = / nouni;
        repeated trt 4 (1 2 3 4) / printe;
run;
proc glm data=blood;
        model a1b1 a1b2 a2b1 a2b2 = / nouni;
        repeated a 2 (1 2), b 2 (1 2);
run;
``` |

SAS Output 27.10

Source	DF	Sum of Squares	Mean Square	F Value	Pr > F
Model	36	4085.500000	113.486111	99.87	<.0001
Error	11	12.500000	1.136364		
Corrected Total	47	4098.000000			

Source	DF	Type III SS	Mean Square	F Value	Pr > F
subject	11	258.500000	23.500000	20.68	<.0001
a	1	1587.000000	1587.000000	1396.56	<.0001
b	1	2028.000000	2028.000000	1784.64	<.0001
a*b	1	147.000000	147.000000	129.36	<.0001
subject*a	11	22.500000	2.045455	1.80	0.1720
subject*b	11	42.500000	3.863636	3.40	0.0269

Tests of Hypotheses Using the Type III MS for subject*a as an Error Term					
Source	DF	Type III SS	Mean Square	F Value	Pr > F
a	1	1587.000000	1587.000000	775.87	<.0001

Tests of Hypotheses Using the Type III MS for subject*b as an Error Term					
Source	DF	Type III SS	Mean Square	F Value	Pr > F
b	1	2028.000000	2028.000000	524.89	<.0001

Note that for the $A*B$ interaction, $F=129.360$, $p<0.0001$. Given the significant interaction effect and the results of text Figure 27.12, on page 1160, the authors proceeded to make 5 pairwise comparisons to study the nature of the interaction. Note that the text specifies a *Bonferroni* procedure with a 95 percent family confidence coefficient. Using the *lsmeans* statement in Insert 27.7, we request all (6) possible *Bonferroni* adjusted pairwise comparisons for the $A*B$ interaction. However, the *lsmeans* statement will produce 6 comparisons, and we are interested in only 5 of the 6. To construct the 95% confidence intervals shown on text page 1161, we specify an alpha=(0.05/5)*6=0.06 in Insert 27.6 to obtain SAS Output 27.9.

SAS Output 27.11

		Difference Between Means	Simultaneous 94% Confidence Limits for LSMean(i)-LSMean(j)	
i	j			
1	2	-9.500000	-10.851629	-8.148371
1	3	-8.000000	-9.351629	-6.648371
1	4	-24.500000	-25.851629	-23.148371
2	3	1.500000	0.148371	2.851629
2	4	-15.000000	-16.351629	-13.648371
3	4	-16.500000	-17.851629	-15.148371

In the second column of Insert 27.7, we entered the data as shown in Table 27.12, text page 1158. This structure is suitable for SAS *repeated* statement. As part of the first *proc glm* statement we specify

repeated trt 4 (1 2 3 4) / *printe*;

This assigns the factor name *trt* to the 4 repeated measures and the valucs 1, 2, 3, and 4 to the four levels of *trt*. The *printe* option specifies the residual error matrix for the model is to be printed together with the result for Mauchley's test for overall sphericity. In the second *proc glm* statement we specify

repeated a 2 (1 2), *b* 2 (1 2);

This assigns the factor name *a* to the 4 repeated measures (dependent variables defined on the *model* statement) and the values 1 and 2 to the two levels of *a*. It also assigns the factor name *b* to the 4 repeated measures and the values 1 and 2 to the two levels of *b*. Because *a* is listed first, the first two repeated measures (*a1b1* and *a1b2*) will be assigned level 1 of *a* and the second two (*a2b1* and *a2b2*) will be assigned level 2 of *a*. Similarly, because *b* is listed second, the first repeated measure (*a1b1*) will be assigned level 1 of *b*, the second repeated measure (*a1b2*) will be assigned level 2 of *b*, the third repeated measure (*a2b1*) will be assigned level 1 of *b*, and the fourth repeated measure (*a2b2*) will be assigned level 2 of *b*. The resulting values of the test statistics will be identical to those shown in SAS Output 27.10.

Split-Plot Designs

On text page 1162 the authors describe Split-Plot Designs. For the layout shown in text Figure 27.13 (text page 1163), assume that the response variable is bushels of vegetables produced per split-plot treatment as shown in the following reproduction of text Figure 27.13. To analyze this data set, we use the variable names *a*, *b*, and *field* to represent the factors irrigation method, fertilizer type, and field, respectively, and the variable name *Y* to represent the response variable as shown in Insert 27.8. We then use *proc glm* and specify *Y* as the dependent variable, *a* and *b* as *class* variables, and *field* as a random factor. We use the *model* statement to specify main effects for *a*, *b*, and *field* and a two-way interaction between *a* and *b*. We also specify that *field* in nested within *a* [*field(a)*] as noted on text page 1163 and shown in Insert 27.8. Execution of Insert 27.8 (output not shown) indicates that neither the two-way interaction nor the main effect for fertilizer type is statistically significant. However, we do find a significant main effect for irrigation method $[F(1, 2) = 225.00. p = 0.004]$. We show the syntax for a repeated measures approach to the Split-Plot Example in the second *proc glm* statement shown in Insert 27.8. The sample sizes within irrigation methods are too small in this example to support Mauchly's test of sphericity but we nevertheless specify the *printe* option for illustration. Although we do not show the output, the computed values of the test statistics are the same for the two programs shown in Insert 27.8.

Fields

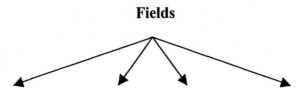

	Field 1	Field 2	Field 3	Field 4
Split Plot	A_2B_2 Fertilizer 2 Y = 6 bushels	A_1B_1 Fertilizer 1 Y = 6 bushels	A_1B_2 Fertilizer 2 Y = 4 bushels	A_2B_1 Fertilizer 1 Y = 7 bushels
Split Plot	A_2B_1 Fertilizer 1 Y = 9 bushels	A_1B_2 Fertilizer 2 Y = 2 bushels	A_1B_1 Fertilizer 1 Y = 3 bushels	A_2B_2 Fertilizer 2 Y = 8 bushels

Irrigation method (A) A_2 A_1 A_1 A_2

Whole-Plot Treatments

INSERT 27.8	INSERT 27.8 continued

<pre>data splitplot;
  input a b field y;
  label a = 'Irrigation method'
    b = 'Fertilizer type';
datalines;
2   2   1   6
2   1   1   9
1   1   2   6
1   2   2   2
1   2   3   4
1   1   3   3
2   1   4   7
2   2   4   8
;
proc glm;
  class a b field;
  model y = a b field(a) a*b;
  random field(a);
  test h=a e=field(a);
run;</pre>
	<pre>data splitplot;
	  input a field yb1 yb2;
	  label a = 'Irrigation method';
	datalines;
	2 1 9 6
	1 2 6 2
	1 3 3 4
	2 4 7 8
	;
	proc glm;
	  class a ;
	    model yb1 yb2 = a / nouni ;
	    repeated fertilizer 2 (1 2) / printe;
	run;</pre>

INSERT 27.8

```
data splitplot;
  input a b field y;
  label a = 'Irrigation method'
      b = 'Fertilizer type';
datalines;
2       2       1       6
2       1       1       9
1       1       2       6
1       2       2       2
1       2       3       4
1       1       3       3
2       1       4       7
2       2       4       8
;
proc glm;
 class a b field;
 model y = a b field(a) a*b;
 random field(a);
 test h=a e=field(a);
 run;


data splitplot;
  input a field yb1 yb2;
  label a = 'Irrigation method';
datalines;
2 1 9 6
1 2 6 2
1 3 3 4
2 4 7 8
;
proc glm;
 class a ;
   model yb1 yb2 = a / nouni ;
   repeated fertilizer 2 (1 2) / printe;
 run;
```

Chapter 28 SAS®

Latin Square, Balanced Incomplete Block, and Related Designs

In some randomized block designs it may be impossible to use all treatments in every block. Suppose, for example, we wished to investigate the effects of 4 treatments using a randomized block design but there are only 3 experimental units available per block. We can use a *balanced incomplete block design* in which every pair of treatments is used the same number of times in the experiment. We can represent the experimental layout as follows:

Block	Treatment			
1	A	_	C	D
2	_	B	C	D
3	A	B	C	_
4	A	B	_	D

Note that the design is balanced because every pair of treatments (AB, AC, AD, BC, BD, and CD) is used twice in the experiment. We would randomly assign the treatments separately within each block as usual. The number of blocks required for balancing depends upon the number of treatments that can be used in each block (i.e., upon the number of experimental units available per block).

In some experiments, we wish to block on more than one factor. For example, we might wish to block on gender (Male, Female) and socio-economic status (Low, Medium, High). We could create 6 blocks (Male-Low, Male-Medium, Male-High, Female-Low, Female-Medium, Female-High). If there are 4 treatments we can represent the experimental layout as follows:

Block	Treatment			
1	A	B	C	D
2	A	B	C	D
3	A	B	C	D
4	A	B	C	D
5	A	B	C	D
6	A	B	C	D

Again, we would randomly assign the treatments separately within each block as usual. In this layout, every treatment is used exactly once in every block so the design is a randomized complete block design. Moreover, every treatment is used in every block and the 6 blocks use every combination of the levels of the two blocking factors. We say that we have made full use of the blocking factors.

The number of experimental units required to make full use of multiple blocking factors in a randomized complete block design is sometimes too large and we may want to use a randomized incomplete block design. A design in which each treatment appears once and only once in each row (blocking factor 1) and once and only once in each column (blocking variable 2) is called a *Latin Square design*. Latin squares designs are a special type of incomplete block designs that may be useful when we have two blocking factors. However, use of a Latin square design is possible only when the number of levels of both blocking factors equals the number of levels of the treatment factor. An example of a 4x4 Latin square follows:

Block Factor 1	Block Factor 2			
	1	2	3	4
1	A	B	C	D
2	D	A	B	C
3	C	D	A	B
4	B	C	D	A

In this chapter the authors discuss balanced incomplete block designs including the Latin square design and other variations. The steps required for using SAS to analyze data collected in these designs are the same as those used for previously discussed designs.

Balanced Incomplete Block Designs

Food Product Taste-Testing Example

Data File: ch28ta02.txt

Researchers wished to test consumer preference of five breakfast cereals. However, previous research has demonstrated that consumers are not able to discriminate among more than 3 cereals. Thus, the 10 consumers each rated three of the five cereals on a 10-point scale. This experiment represents a balanced incomplete block design with five treatments (cereals) and block size of three. See Chapter 0, "Working with SAS," for instructions on opening the Food Product Taste-Testing Example and naming the variables i, j, y, $z1$, $z2$, $z3$, $z3$, $z4$, $z5$, $z6$, $z7$, $z8$, $z8$, $z9$, $x1$, $x2$, $x3$, $x4$. After opening and printing ch28ta02.txt, the first 5 lines of output should look like SAS Output 28.1.

SAS Output 28.1

Obs	i	j	y	z1	z2	z3	z4	z5	z6	z7	z8	z9	x1	x2	x3	x4
1	1	1	6	1	0	0	0	0	0	0	0	0	1	0	0	0
2	1	2	6	1	0	0	0	0	0	0	0	0	0	1	0	0
3	1	3	8	1	0	0	0	0	0	0	0	0	0	0	1	0
4	2	1	3	0	1	0	0	0	0	0	0	0	1	0	0	0
5	2	2	7	0	1	0	0	0	0	0	0	0	0	1	0	0

In Table 28.2 (SAS Output 28.1), i and j are allocated codes that represent block and treatment, respectively. The "z" and "x" variables are indicator variables (see text page 1178) representing block and treatment. The authors begin the analysis of this balanced incomplete block design by presenting a regression approach. As we discussed in Chapter 15 of this manual, we use the alternative regression based *proc glm* and allocated codes.

In Insert 28.1, we specify *proc glm* where y is the dependent variable and i and j are class variables; we also specify that the model is a main effects only model. Results shown in SAS Output 28.2 are consistent with the F statistics shown on text page 1179. On text page 1180-1181 the authors present the least squares estimates of the five treatment means and 10 pairwise comparisons of treatment means based on the *Tukey* procedure. The comparisons are based on least squares means and we specify this analysis using the *lsmeans* statement. Results (output not shown) are consistent with text page 1181.

```
                          INSERT 28.1

data taste;
infile 'c:\kutnerdata\chapter 28 data sets\ch28ta02.txt';
  input i j y z1 z2 z3 z4 z5 z6 z7 z8 z9 x1 x2 x3 x4 ;
proc glm;
 class j i;
 model y = j i;
 lsmeans j / cl pdiff adjust=tukey;
 run;
```

SAS Output 28.2

Source	DF	Type III SS	Mean Square	F Value	Pr > F
j	4	50.44444444	12.61111111	15.66	<.0001
i	9	40.27777778	4.47530864	5.56	0.0015

Latin Square Designs

Background Music Example
Data File: ch28ta04.txt

Investigators studied the relationship between various types of background music and productivity of bank tellers. Day of week and week of study were blocking variables. See Chapter 0, "Working with SAS," for instructions on opening the Background Music Example (Table 28.4, text page 1187) and naming the variables *Y, week, day,* and *trt*. After opening and printing ch28ta04.txt, the first 5 lines of output should look like SAS Output 28.3.

SAS Output 28.3

Obs	y	week	day	trt
1	18	1	1	4
2	13	2	1	3
3	7	3	1	1
4	17	4	1	5
5	21	5	1	2

We begin by producing all indices needed to perform the diagnostic and inferential analyses described on text page 1191. The researchers analyzed residuals by various plots, and performed the *Bonferroni* outlier test and *Tukey's* test of additivity. The *Bonferroni* outlier test and the *Tukey* test for additivity were discussed in Chapters 10 and 20, respectively, of this manual.

For the Latin Square design, as illustrated in Table 28.4, text page 1187, we use *week*, *day*, and *trt* as *class* variables, and assume that there are no interactions involving these three variables. While specifying this model in Insert 28.2, we request that pairwise comparisons be made between the different types of background music (*trt*) and 90% confidence intervals. I'm not sure what you mean here.] Partial results of Insert 28.2 are shown in SAS Output 28.4. Notice that the $F=10.58$ associated with *trt* is consistent with the value reported for treatment effects reported on text page 1192. The confidence intervals (not shown) from the *Tukey* specification indicate three homogenous subgroups (SAS Output 28.4) consistent with text page 1192

```
                              INSERT 28.2

data music;
  infile 'c:\kutnerdata\chapter 28 data sets\ch28ta04.txt';
input y week day trt;
proc print data=music (obs=5);
run;
proc glm;
 class week day trt;
  model y = week day trt ;
   lsmeans trt / adjust=tukey pdiff cl alpha=.1;
    output out=results r=residual h=lev1 rstudent=stud;
run;
```

SAS Output 28.4

Source	DF	Type III SS	Mean Square	F Value	Pr > F
week	4	82.0000000	20.5000000	1.31	0.3226
day	4	477.2000000	119.3000000	7.60	0.0027
trt	4	664.4000000	166.1000000	10.58	0.0007

	Least Squares Means for effect trt Pr > |t| for H0: LSMean(i)=LSMean(j) Dependent Variable: y				
i/j	1	2	3	4	5
1		0.0004	0.0433	0.0025	0.0110
2	0.0004		0.0967	0.7947	0.3242
3	0.0433	0.0967		0.4821	0.9262
4	0.0025	0.7947	0.4821		0.8996
5	0.0110	0.3242	0.9262	0.8996	

Additional Replications with Latin Square Designs

Retraining Program Experiment

Data File: ch28ta08.txt

Researchers studied the relationship between three different reward methods and achievement. Age and IQ were used as blocking factors and there were 2 replications per cell as shown in Table 28.8, text page 1197. See Chapter 0, "Working with SAS," for instructions on opening the Retraining Program Experiment Example and naming the variables *Y*, *iq*, *age*, and *trt*. After opening and printing ch28ta08.txt, the first 5 lines of output should look like SAS Output 28.5.

SAS Output 28.5

Obs	y	iq	age	trt
1	19	1	1	2
2	16	1	1	2
3	24	2	1	3
4	22	2	1	3
5	10	3	1	1

To compute the *Lack of Fit F** presented on text page 1196, we use the approach described in Chapter 3 of this manual. We begin by fitting the full model to the data. This requires creation of a new variable, *lof*. In Insert 28.3, we define *iq*, *age*, and *trt* as character variables (alphanumeric) that are each 1 position in length (*length* and *input* statements). We then create *lof*, which is the concatenation of *iq*, *age*, and *trt*. The first and second observations in SAS Output 28.5 will have a *lof* value of "112", the third and fourth observations will have a *lof* value of "213", and so on. Thus, *lof* identifies 9 discrete classifications based on the values of *iq*, *age*, and *trt*.

We now regress y on iq, age, trt, and lof (all as *class* variables) in the first *proc glm* statement. (Remember that iq, age, trt, and lof are allocated variables and can not be used in *proc reg*.) Insert 28.3 produces SAS Output 28.6 which shows that $SSE(F) = 36.0$. From equation 3.16, text page 122, $SSE(F) = SSPE$. Therefore, $SSPE = 36.0$. From equation 3.24, text page 124, we see that $SSLF = SSE(R) - SSPE$. In the second *proc glm* statement regress y on iq, age, and trt (reduced model), to find that $SSE(R) = 52.333$ (SAS Output 28.7). Thus, $SSLF = 52.333 - 36.0 = 16.333$. $SSLF = 16.333$ is given directly in SAS Output 28.6 under *Type III Sum of Squares* for lof. Thus, regressing y on iq, age, trt, and lof in *proc glm* gives us the quantities to find the usual lack of fit test statistic, equation 3.25: $F^*=MSLF/MSPE=2.04$. The second *proc glm* in Insert 28.3 also produces the remainder of Table 28.8 (b), text page 1197.

INSERT 28.3

```
data training;
  infile 'c:\kutnerdata\chapter 28 data sets\ch28ta08.txt';
  length iq age trt $ 1;
  input y  iq $ age $ trt $ ;
lof=iq || age || trt;
proc glm;
 title 'Produce full model & SSPE';
 class iq age trt lof;
  model y =  iq  age  trt lof;
  run;
proc glm;
 title 'Produce Table 28.8 b, reduced model, & SSE';
 class iq age trt;
 model y = iq age trt ;
 run;
```

SAS Output 28.6

Full Model

Source	DF	Sum of Squares	Mean Square	F Value	Pr > F
Model	8	562.0000000	70.2500000	17.56	0.0001
Error	9	36.0000000	4.0000000		
Corrected Total	17	598.0000000			

Source	DF	Type III SS	Mean Square	F Value	Pr > F
iq	0	0.00000000	.	.	.
age	0	0.00000000	.	.	.
trt	0	0.00000000	.	.	.
lof	2	16.33333333	8.16666667	2.04	0.1857

294

Reduced Model

Source	DF	Sum of Squares	Mean Square	F Value	Pr > F
Model	6	545.6666667	90.9444444	19.12	<.0001
Error	11	52.3333333	4.7575758		
Corrected Total	17	598.0000000			

Source	DF	Type III SS	Mean Square	F Value	Pr > F
iq	2	364.3333333	182.1666667	38.29	<.0001
age	2	34.3333333	17.1666667	3.61	0.0624
trt	2	147.0000000	73.5000000	15.45	0.0006

Replications in Repeated Measures Studies

Apple Sales Example

Data File: ch28ta11.txt

Researchers used a Latin Square crossover design to study the effect of 3 different displays on apple sales. There were six stores in the study; two were randomly assigned to each of the treatment order patterns. See Chapter 0, "Working with SAS," for instructions on opening the Apple Sales Example and naming the variables *Y*, *pattern*, *order*, *display*, and *stores*. After opening and printing ch28ta11.txt, the first 5 lines of output should look like SAS Output 28.8.

SAS Output 28.8

Obs	y	pattern	order	display	stores
1	9	1	1	2	1
2	4	1	1	2	2
3	12	2	1	1	1
4	13	2	1	1	2
5	7	3	1	3	1

For this analysis, we specify *proc glm* where *Y* is the dependent variable; *pattern*, *order*, *display*, and *stores* are *class* variables; and specify a model that contains main effects only for the 4 *class* variables. Our *model* statement indicates that *stores* are nested within *pattern* [*model y = pattern order display stores(pattern)* ;]. Results are not shown but are consistent with Table 28.11 (b) and the treatment (*display*) $F^*=37.18$ reported on text page 1200.

Chapter 29 SAS®

Exploratory Experiments: Two-Level Factorial and Fractional Factorial Designs

In this chapter, the authors discuss strategies for using exploratory experiments aimed at investigating a large number of factors that may be related to the response outcome. By including a large number of factors in the early stages of inquiry, we may be able to identify the most important factors and focus on these in future experiments. When we investigate multiple factors, the size of a full factorial experiment may become prohibitively large. However, we may be able to carefully select a subset of all the possible combinations of levels of the factors and run the experiment using only this *fraction* of the full factorial study. Using a *fractional factorial* combination of factor levels, we can study a large number of factors in a single experiment with a relatively small number of experimental subjects. To see how we might use a fractional factorial study, consider an experiment with three factors denoted A, B, and C, each with two levels denoted A_1, A_2, B_1, B_2, and C_1, C_2, respectively. In the full factorial, there are $2^3 =$ eight possible combinations of levels of the factors:

$$A_1B_1C_1$$
$$A_2B_1C_1$$
$$A_1B_2C_1$$
$$A_2B_2C_1$$
$$A_1B_1C_2$$
$$A_2B_1C_2$$
$$A_1B_2C_2$$
$$A_2B_2C_2$$

Thus, we say there are 8 factor combinations or 8 treatments, and a minimum of 8 experimental subjects are required if we are to run a full factorial experiment (subjects are randomly assigned to the 8 treatments with one subject per treatment). An analysis of variance *effects model* for the 2^3 full factorial study is given in equation 29.2 of the text. We can arrange the X variables for the model as follows:

Treatment	X_1	X_2	X_3
1	−1	−1	−1
2	1	−1	−1
3	−1	1	−1
4	1	1	−1
5	−1	−1	1
6	1	−1	1
7	−1	1	1
8	1	1	1

A one-half fraction of the treatment combinations is:

$$A_2B_1C_1$$
$$A_1B_2C_1$$
$$A_1B_1C_2$$
$$A_2B_2C_2$$

An analysis of variance effects model for this fractional factorial study is

$$Y_i = \beta_0 X_{i0} + \beta_1 X_{i1} + \beta_2 X_{i2} + \beta_3 X_{i3} + \varepsilon_i$$

where:

ε_i are independent $N(0, \sigma^2)$

$X_0 \equiv 0$

$$X_1 = \begin{cases} -1 & \text{if observation is from level } A_1 \text{ of factor A} \\ 1 & \text{if observation is from level } A_2 \text{ of factor A} \end{cases}$$

$$X_2 = \begin{cases} -1 & \text{if observation is from level } B_1 \text{ of factor B} \\ 1 & \text{if observation is from level } B_2 \text{ of factor B} \end{cases}$$

$$X_3 = \begin{cases} -1 & \text{if observation is from level } C_1 \text{ of factor C} \\ 1 & \text{if observation is from level } C_2 \text{ of factor C} \end{cases}$$

but only the indicated combinations of levels of A, B, and C are used. We can arrange the X variables for the model as follows:

Treatment	X_1	X_2	X_3
1	1	−1	−1
2	−1	1	−1
3	−1	−1	1
4	1	1	1

In this example, we can estimate 7 effects using the full factorial study: the 3 main effects of A, B, and C; the 3 two-factor interaction effects AB, AC, BC; and the three factor interaction ABC. In the fractional factorial, we can estimate only the 3 main effects. Nevertheless, fractional factorial studies can be very useful especially in exploratory investigations.

Stress Test Example

Data File: ch24ta04.txt

In the Stress Test Example researchers studied the effects of gender, body fat, and smoking history on exercise tolerance. See Chapter 0, "Working with SAS," for instructions on opening the Stress Test Example (Table 24.4 (a), text page 1004) and naming the variables *Y, gender, fat, smoke,* and *rep*. After opening and printing ch24ta04.txt, the first 5 lines of output should look like SAS Output 24.1.

The authors present further aspects of the analysis on text page 1215 in terms of the effects model defined by the design matrix $\mathbf{X}$ shown in Table 29.1, text page 1213. We obtain the results shown in Figure 29.1, text page 1215, by executing the syntax given below in Insert 29.1. We use a series of *if* statements to recode the variables *gender*, *fat*, and *smoking* and subsequently produce the design matrix shown in Table 29.1. We specify *proc print* to list the first 5 lines of data, including the newly recoded variables, as shown in SAS Output 29.1. We next specify the *proc glm* statement to produce the results in Figure 29.1, of text page 1215. Because we wish to use the recoded values of *gender*, *fat*, and *smoking* in the model, we omit the *class* statement so that *proc glm* will handle all independent variables listed in the *model* statement as non-classification variables. Otherwise, the variables listed in the *class* statement will be handled as classification variables and *proc glm* will define internally indicator variables for an effects model that is different from the model used in the text. Finally, we specify the model and use the *solution* option to obtain the parameter estimates, standard error estimates of parameter estimators, and *t*-values together with *p*-values for the hypothesis that each parameter in turn is equal to zero. The results shown in below SAS Output 29.2 are consistent with those presented in Figure 29.1, text page 1215. We obtain the pooled sum of squares for the three main effects from SAS Output 29.2 by adding the individual sums for *gender*, *fat*, and *smoking* and get Sum of Squares (main effects) = 176.5837500 + 242.5704167 + 70.3837500 = 489.5379167. Similarly, we get Sum of Squares (2-way interactions) = 13.6504167 + 11.0704167 + 72.4537500 = 97.1745834. These results are consistent with text page 1215.

INSERT 29.1	INSERT 29.1 continued

data stress;
infile 'c:\kutnerdata\chapter 24 data sets\ch24ta04.txt';
  input y gender fat smoking subj;
  if gender = 1 then gender = -1;
  if gender = 2 then gender = 1;
  if fat = 1 then fat = -1;
	if fat = 2 then fat = 1;
	  if smoking = 1 then smoking = -1;
	  if smoking = 2 then smoking = 1;
	proc print data=stress (obs=5);
	proc glm;
	  model y = gender|fat|smoking /solution;
	run;

SAS Output 29.1

Obs	y	gender	fat	smoking	subj
1	24.1	-1	-1	-1	1
2	29.2	-1	-1	-1	2
3	24.6	-1	-1	-1	3
4	20.0	1	-1	-1	1
5	21.9	1	-1	-1	2

Source	DF	Type III SS	Mean Square	F Value	Pr > F
gender	1	176.5837500	176.5837500	18.92	0.0005
fat	1	242.5704167	242.5704167	25.98	0.0001
gender*fat	1	13.6504167	13.6504167	1.46	0.2441
smoking	1	70.3837500	70.3837500	7.54	0.0144
gender*smoking	1	11.0704167	11.0704167	1.19	0.2923
fat*smoking	1	72.4537500	72.4537500	7.76	0.0132
gender*fat*smoking	1	1.8704167	1.8704167	0.20	0.6604

Parameter	Estimate	Standard Error	t Value	Pr > |t|
Intercept	16.27083333	0.62367916	26.09	<.0001
gender	-2.71250000	0.62367916	-4.35	0.0005
fat	-3.17916667	0.62367916	-5.10	0.0001
gender*fat	0.75416667	0.62367916	1.21	0.2441
smoking	-1.71250000	0.62367916	-2.75	0.0144
gender*smoking	-0.67916667	0.62367916	-1.09	0.2923
fat*smoking	1.73750000	0.62367916	2.79	0.0132
gender*fat*smoking	-0.27916667	0.62367916	-0.45	0.6604

Pecos Foods Corporation Example

Data File: ch29ta02.txt

The Pecos Food Corporation conducted a study to investigate the effects of process temperature ($x1$), an antimicrobial agent ($x2$), moisture level ($x3$), and acidity ($x4$) on the microbial growth in a fruit bar (y). The four factors were studied at high and low levels as defined on text page 1216. The response (y) is the natural logarithm of the microbial count. See Chapter 0, "Working with SAS," for instructions on opening the Pecos Foods Corporation Example (Table 29.2, text page 1217) and naming the variables y, $x0$, $x1$, $x2$, $x3$, $x4$, $x12$, $x13$, $x14$, $x23$, $x24$, $x34$, $x123$, $x124$, $x134$, $x234$, and $x1234$. After opening and printing ch29ta02.txt, the first 5 lines of output should look like SAS Output 29.3.

SAS Output 29.3

Obs	y	x0	x1	x2	x3	x4	x12	x13	x14	x23	x24	x34	x123	x124	x134	x234	x1234
1	5.55	1	-1	-1	-1	-1	1	1	1	1	1	1	-1	-1	-1	-1	1
2	4.47	1	1	-1	-1	-1	-1	-1	-1	1	1	1	1	1	1	-1	-1
3	5.19	1	-1	1	-1	-1	-1	1	1	-1	-1	1	1	1	-1	1	-1
4	5.32	1	1	1	-1	-1	1	-1	-1	-1	-1	1	-1	-1	1	1	1
5	10.54	1	-1	-1	1	-1	1	-1	1	-1	1	-1	1	-1	1	1	-1

In Insert 29.2 (Full Model Analysis), we first obtain the results shown in Figure 29.2, text page 1217 by regressing y on $x1$ through $x1234$ as shown in SAS Output 29.3. Partial results shown in SAS Output 29.4 are consistent with text Figure 29.2. The researchers decided that all three-factor and four-factor interactions were unimportant and dropped these terms from the previous model. In Insert 29.2 (Reduced Model Analysis) we produce Figure 29.3, text page 1219. A truncated parameter estimate table is shown in SAS Output 29.5. We can now find the percent contribution to the sum of squares for each factor using equation 29.16 and results from SAS Output 29.4 and 29.5. From text page 1220 we find the percent contribution of $x3$:

$$\frac{n_T b_3^2}{SSTO}(100) = \frac{16(1.403)^2}{91.628}(100) = 3\%$$

INSERT 29.2	INSERT 29.2 continued
| ```
data pecos;
  infile 'c:\kutnerdata\chapter 29 data
sets\ch29ta02.txt';
  input y x0 x1 x2 x3 x4 x12 x13 x14 x23 x24 x34
                x123 x124 x134 x234 x1234;
/* If only Y x1 x2 x3 x4 were available, the
  following syntax would create x12 through x1234.
  x12 = x1*x2;
  x13 = x1*x3;
  x14 = x1*x4;
  x23 = x2*x3;
  x24 = x2*x4;
  x34 = x3*x4;
  x123 = x1*x2*x3;
``` | ```
x124 = x1*x2*X4;
x134 = X1*X3*X4;
x234 = X2*X3*X4;
x1234 = X1*X2*X3*X4; */;
proc print data=pecos (obs=5);
*** Full Model Analysis;
proc glm;
  model y = x1 x2 x3 x4 x12 x13 x14 x23
            x24 x34 x123 x124 x134 x234
            x1234 / solution;
run;
*** Reduced Model Analysis;
proc glm;
  model y = x1 x2 x3 x4 x12 x13 x14 x23
                x24 x34 / solution;
run;
``` |

300

SAS Output 29.4

Source	DF	Sum of Squares	Mean Square	F Value	Pr > F
Model	15	91.62849375	6.10856625	.	.
Error	0	0.00000000		.	
Corrected Total	15	91.62849375			

(Truncated Table)

Parameter	Estimate	Standard Error	t Value	Pr > |t|
Intercept	6.740625000	.	.	.
x1	-0.124375000	.	.	.
x2	-1.250625000	.	.	.
x3	1.403125000	.	.	.

SAS Output 29.5

(Truncated Table)

Parameter	Estimate	Standard Error	t Value	Pr > |t|
Intercept	6.740625000	0.16733317	40.28	<.0001
x1	-0.124375000	0.16733317	-0.74	0.4907
x2	-1.250625000	0.16733317	-7.47	0.0007
x3	1.403125000	0.16733317	8.39	0.0004

Lack of Fit. On text page 1223, the authors posit a scenario in which four replicate observations are made at the center point of the 2^4 factorial combinations of treatment levels used in the Pecos Food Corporation Example. We use the SAS code given in Insert 29.3 to obtain a test for lack of fit of the full model. The hypothetical data for the center point are appended to the original data set to provide a total of 20 lines of data, which are embedded in the syntax. The results are shown in SAS Output SAS Output 29.6; we can now find $F=22.2$ by equation 6.68b or refer to the *lof* test statistic in SAS Output 29.6.

INSERT 29.3	INSERT 29.3

data pecostwo;
  input id y x1 x2 x3 x4 ;
  if id le 16 then lof = id;
  if id gt 16 then lof = 17;
  x12 = x1*x2;
  x13 = x1*x3;
  x14 = x1*x4;
  x23 = x2*x3;
  x24 = x2*x4;
  x34 = x3*x4;
  x123 = x1*x2*x3;
  x124 = x1*x2*X4;
  X134 = X1*X3*X4;
  X234 = X2*X3*X4;
  X1234 = X1*X2*X3*X4;
datalines;
01 5.55 -1 -1 -1 -1
02 4.47 1 -1 -1 -1
03 5.19 -1 1 -1 -1
04 5.32 1 1 -1 -1
05 10.54 -1 -1 1 -1
	06 11.56 1 -1 1 -1
	07 5.08 -1 1 1 -1
	08 5.45 1 1 1 -1
	09 5.12 -1 -1 -1 1
	10 5.63 1 -1 -1 1
	11 6.18 -1 1 -1 1
	12 5.24 1 1 -1 1
	13 10.73 -1 -1 1 1
	14 10.33 1 -1 1 1
	15 6.53 -1 1 1 1
	16 4.93 1 1 1 1
	17 7.23 0 0 0 0
	18 7.89 0 0 0 0
	19 7.80 0 0 0 0
	20 7.39 0 0 0 0
	;
	proc glm;
	  class lof;
	  model y = x1 x2 x3 x4 x12 x13 x14 x23
	             x24 x34 x123 x124 x134
	             x234 x1234 lof;
	run;

SAS Output 29.6

Source	DF	Sum of Squares	Mean Square	F Value	Pr > F
Model	16	93.86964500	5.86685281	58.07	0.0032
Error	3	0.30307500	0.10102500		
Corrected Total	19	94.17272000			

(Partial Table)

Source	DF	Type I SS	Mean Square	F Value	Pr > F
x1	1	0.24750625	0.24750625	2.45	0.2155
X1234	1	0.27825625	0.27825625	2.75	0.1956
lof	1	2.24115125	2.24115125	22.18	0.0181

The Iowa Aluminum Corporation Example

Data File: ch29ta07.txt

The Iowa Aluminum Corporation manufactures sheet aluminum from recycled aluminum beverage containers (text page 1233). Six factors that might affect the quality of the product were considered:

1. coolant temperature ($x1$)
2. percentage of oil in the coolant ($x2$)
3. volume 1 of coolant ($x3$)
4. volume 2 of coolant ($x4$)
5. volume 3 of coolant ($x5$)
6. strip speed ($x6$)

Low and high levels for each of these six factors were used in an experiment with the goal to improve the quality of the aluminum. The response variable was a surface impurity score. Only 20 experimental units were available for the study so $2^6 = 64$ factorial combinations of treatments (a full factorial) could not be investigated. Instead, the company conducted a study using a one-quarter fractional factorial plan with an additional four observations made at the center point. The design matrix and the observed data are shown in Table 29.7. See Chapter 0, "Working with SAS," for instructions on opening the Stress Test Example (Table 29.7, text page 1236) and naming the variables $x1$, $x2$, $x3$, $x4$, $x5$, $x6$, and y. After opening and printing ch29ta07.txt, the first 5 lines of output should look like SAS Output 29.7.

SAS Output 29.7

Obs	x1	x2	x3	x4	x5	x6	y
1	-1	-1	-1	-1	-1	-1	4
2	1	-1	-1	-1	1	-1	6
3	-1	1	-1	-1	1	1	7
4	1	1	-1	-1	-1	1	2
5	-1	-1	1	-1	1	1	3

In Insert 29.4, the first *proc glm* statement produces (output not shown) the initial factorial model as shown in Figure 29.9, text page 1237. From Figure 29.9, the researchers identified active effects for $x2$, $x5$, $x6$, and the interaction between $x1$ and $x3$. We fitted a regression model based on these four effects and produced the *lack of fit* test for the model. In Insert 29.4; we derived a *lof* variable based on the nine possible combinations of $x2$, $x5$, $x6$, and $x1x3$; and specified *lof* as a *class* variable. Partial results of this analysis are shown in SAS Output 29.8 and are consistent with the *lack of fit* $F^*=0.04$ reported on text page 1235 and Figure 29.10, text page 1238.

```
data aluminum;
  infile 'c:\kutnerdata\chapter 29 data sets\ch29ta07.txt';
  input x1 x2 x3 x4 x5 x6 y;
  label x1 = 'cooltemp'
      x2 = 'oilpct'
      x3 = 'coolvol1'
      x4 = 'coolvol2'
      x5 = 'coolvol3'
      x6 = 'stripspd';
proc print data=aluminum (obs=5);
run;
* Produce initial model;
proc glm;
  model y = x1-x6 x1*x2 x1*x3 x1*x4 x1*x5 x1*x6 x2*x4 x2*x6
        x1*x2*x4 x1*x2*x6 / solution;
run;
* Produce model with active effects and lof;
data alumtwo;
  set aluminum;
  x13 = x1*x3;
  if x2 = -1 and x5 = -1 and x6 = -1 and x13 =  1 then lof = 1;
  if x2 = -1 and x5 = -1 and x6 =  1 and x13 =  1 then lof = 2;
  if x2 = -1 and x5 =  1 and x6 = -1 and x13 = -1 then lof = 3;
  if x2 = -1 and x5 =  1 and x6 =  1 and x13 = -1 then lof = 4;
  if x2 =  0 and x5 =  0 and x6 =  0 and x13 =  0 then lof = 5;
  if x2 =  1 and x5 = -1 and x6 = -1 and x13 = -1 then lof = 6;
  if x2 =  1 and x5 = -1 and x6 =  1 and x13 = -1 then lof = 7;
  if x2 =  1 and x5 =  1 and x6 = -1 and x13 =  1 then lof = 8;
  if x2 =  1 and x5 =  1 and x6 =  1 and x13 =  1 then lof = 9;
proc sort;
  by x2 x5 x6 x13;
proc print;
 var y x2 x5 x6 x13;
proc glm;
  class lof;
  model y = x2 x5 x6 x13 lof/ solution;
run;
```

SAS Output 29.8

Source	DF	Type III SS	Mean Square	F Value	Pr > F
x2	0	0.00000000	.	.	.
x5	0	0.00000000	.	.	.
x6	0	0.00000000	.	.	.
x13	0	0.00000000	.	.	.
lof	4	0.20000000	0.05000000	0.04	0.9958

The Caramel Example

Data File: ch29ta10.txt

On text page 1248, researchers wished to study the relationship between three recipe ingredients and the plasticity of caramel. Plasticity measured on a scale of 1 to 100, where 100 indicated complete plasticity; the target value was 70. The three ingredients investigated were brown sugar ($x1$), sweetened condensed milk ($x2$), and light corn syrup ($x3$). An experiment was run using a full factorial 2^3 with four replicates for each treatment combination. Text Table 29.10 contains the coded values for the three ingredients ($x1 - x3$) and the interaction between the three ingredients ($x12 - x123$), the replicates ($y1 - y4$), the sample variances ($s2$), the logarithms of the sample variances ($logs2$), and estimated weights (w). See Chapter 0, "Working with SAS," for instructions on opening the Caramel Example (Table 29.10, text page 1248) and naming the variables $x1$, $x2$, $x3$, $x12$, $x13$, $x23$, $x123$, $y1$, $y2$, $y3$, $y4$, $s2$, $logs2$, and w. After opening and printing ch29ta10.txt, the first 5 lines of output should look like SAS Output 29.9.

SAS Output 29.9

Obs	x1	x2	x3	x12	x13	x23	x123	y1	y2	y3	y4	s2	logs2	w
1	-1	-1	-1	1	1	1	-1	42	65	70	73	197.67	5.287	0.0102
2	1	-1	-1	-1	-1	1	1	50	52	55	63	32.67	3.486	0.0322
3	-1	1	-1	-1	1	-1	1	61	70	78	79	70.00	4.248	0.0102
4	1	1	-1	1	-1	-1	-1	48	51	55	60	27.00	3.296	0.0322
5	-1	-1	1	1	-1	-1	1	65	74	74	77	27.00	3.296	0.0322

The analyst fitted the dispersion model shown in text equation 29.40 as a first step in the analysis. That is, the researchers regressed *logs2* on the coded values of the three ingredients and all possible interaction combinations. In the first *proc glm* of Insert 29.5 we specify the *model* statement as *model logs2 = x1 | x2 | x3* to indicate main effects and all possible interactions of the three main effects. Results are not shown but the parameter estimates are consistent with Figure 29.13(a), text page 1249. We also use the *ods output* function to save the parameter estimates for subsequent use in the normal probability plot as shown in Figure 29.13(b) and SAS Output 29.10(a). From this analysis the researchers identified one nonzero dispersion effect and decided to use weighted least squares regression (estimated variance function based on equation 29.44) for estimation of parameters in the location effects model. (See Chapters 11 of this manual and the text for additional computational details of weighted least squares regression.) To perform this analysis, we restructure the data file as shown in SAS Output 29.9. The restructured file will contain 4 records for each record in SAS Output 29.9. Each of the 4 new records will contain one of the *y* values ($y1 - y4$) from the original file. Using the new file (*carameltwo*), we specify the *model* statement as *model y= x1 | x2 | x3* to indicate main effects and all possible interactions of the three main effects, and specify *w* as the weight variable. Resulting parameter estimates (not shown) are consistent with Figure 29.14(a). SAS Output 29.10(b) is consistent with the Figure 29.14(b).

INSERT 29.5	INSERT 29.5 continued

data caramel;
  infile 'c:\kutnerdata\chapter 29 data
                     sets\ch29ta10.txt';
  input x1 x2 x3 x12 x13 x23 x123
       y1 y2 y3 y4 s2 logs2 w;
  label x1 = 'brownsug'
      x2 = 'condmilk'
      x2 = 'cornsyrp';
* Produce Figure 29.13(a) & save parameter
                       estimates;
proc glm;
  model logs2 = x1 | x2 | x3 / solution;
  ods output ParameterEstimates = Results;
run;
* Produce Figure 29.13(b);
 goptions reset=all;
proc capability data=results;
  where parameter ne 'Intercept ';
  symbol1 value=dot;
  var estimate;
  qqplot ;
run;
	* Produce Figure 29.14(a);
	data carameltwo;
	  set caramel;
	  y = y1; output;
	  y = y2; output;
	  y = y3; output;
	  y = y4; output;
	proc print data=carameltwo;
	run;
	proc glm;
	  model y = x1 | x2 | x3 / solution;
	  weight w;
	  ods output ParameterEstimates = Results2;
	run;
	 goptions reset=all;
	proc capability data=results2;
	  where parameter ne 'Intercept ';
	  symbol1 value=dot;
	  var estimate;
	  qqplot ;
	run;

SAS Output 29.10

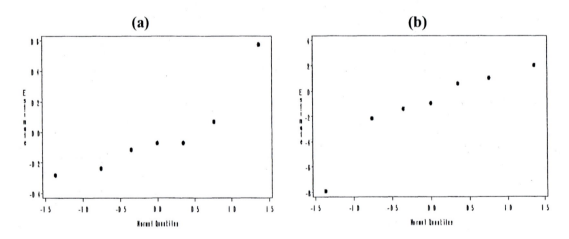

(a)   (b)

Clutch Slave Cylinder Example

Data File: ch29ta12.txt

An automotive company conducted research to identify a clutch slave cylinder design that minimized fluid leakage. The response variable was fluid leakage; the five control factors were body inner diameter ($X1$), body outer diameter ($X2$), seal inner diameter ($X3$), seal outer diameter ($X4$), and seal design ($X5$); and the two noise factors were temperature and load. See Chapter 0, "Working with SAS," for instructions on opening the Clutch Slave Cylinder Example (Table 29.12, text page 1252) and naming the variables $x1$, $x2$, $x3$, $x4$, $x5$, $y1$, $y2$, $y3$, $y4$, *logs2*, and w. After opening and printing ch29ta12.txt, the first 5 lines of output should look like SAS Output 29.11.

Obs	x1	x2	x3	x4	x5	y1	y2	y3	y4	logs2	w
1	-1	-1	-1	-1	-1	0.8	0.4	0	0.0	-1.920	1.245
2	1	-1	-1	1	-1	3.2	0.0	0	0.0	0.940	0.195
3	-1	1	-1	1	-1	0.0	0.0	0	2.4	0.365	1.245
4	1	1	-1	-1	-1	5.8	0.0	0	2.8	2.036	0.195
5	-1	-1	1	1	-1	0.0	3.0	0	2.4	0.912	1.245

In Insert 29.6, we estimate the dispersion model by regressing *logs2* on the first dispersion effect from each of the 16 pairs shown in equation 29.46, text page 1253. We also save the parameter estimates for use in a normal probability plot. Results are consistent with Figure 29.15(a) (not shown) and (b) (SAS Output 29.12). From the plot, the researchers found active dispersion effects for *x5* and *x15*. In the second *proc glm*, we eliminate the inactive effects and estimate the subset dispersion model. Partial results in SAS Output 29.13 are consistent with equation 29.48, test page 1254.

SAS Output 29.12

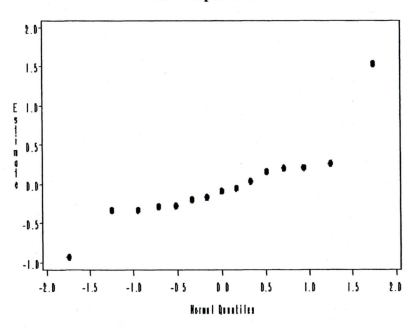

The researchers elected to fit a weighted least squares regression model to estimate the location model. In Insert 29.6 we restructure the original data file (ch29ta12.txt, shown in SAS Output 29.11). The restructured file will contain 4 records for each record in SAS Output 29.11. Each of the 4 new records will contain one of the *y* values (*y1 – y4*) from the original file. Using the new file (*clutchtwo*), we specify the *model* statement as *model y = x1 x2 x3 x4 x5 x12 x13 x14 x15 x25 x35 x45 x125 x135 x145 / solution;*, and specify *w* as the weight variable. Resulting parameter estimates and normal probability plot (not shown) are consistent with Figure 29.16(a)

& (b). Both Figure 29.16 (a) and (b) indicate that *x15* (β_{15}) is the only active location effect. Thus, in the last *proc glm* of Insert 29.9 we specify *model y = x5 / solution* to produce equation 29.49, text page 1254.

<table>
<tr><td>

INSERT 29.6

```
data clutch;
  infile 'c:\kutnerdata\chapter 29 data
                  sets\ch29ta12.txt';
  input x1 x2 x3 x4 x5 y1 y2 y3 y4 logs2 w;
  x12 = x1*x2;
  x13 = x1*x3;
  x14 = x1*x4;
  x15 = x1*x5;
  x25 = x2*x5;
  x35 = x3*x5;
  x45 = x4*x5;
  x125 = x1*x2*x5;
  x135 = x1*x3*x5;
  x145 = x1*x4*x5;
  label x1 = 'bodyinner'
      x2 = 'bodyouter'
      x3 = 'sealinner'
      x4 = 'sealouter'
      x5 = 'sealdesig';
* Produce Fig 29.15(a) &
      save parameter estimates;
proc glm;
  model logs2 = x1 x2 x3 x4 x5 x12
            x13 x14 x15 x25 x35 x45
            x125 x135 x145 / solution;
  ods output ParameterEstimates = Results;
run;
* Produce Figure 29.15(b);
 goptions reset=all;
proc capability data=results;
  where parameter ne 'Intercept ';
  symbol1 value=dot;
  var estimate;
  qqplot ;
run;
```

</td><td>

INSERT 29.6 continued

```
* Produce equation 29.48;
proc glm data=clutch;
  model logs2 = x5 x15 / solution;
run;
data clutchtwo;
  set clutch;
  y = y1; output;
  y = y2; output;
  y = y3; output;
  y = y4; output;
proc glm;
  model y = x1 x2 x3 x4 x5 x12 x13 x14
            x15 x25 x35 x45
            x125 x135 x145 / solution;
  weight w;
  ods output ParameterEstimates = Results2;
run;
* Produce Figure 29.16(b);
 goptions reset=all;
proc capability data=results2;
  where parameter ne 'Intercept ';
  symbol1 value=dot;
  var estimate;
  qqplot ;
run;
* Produce equation 29.49;
proc glm data=clutch;
  model y = x5 / solution;
run;
```

</td></tr>
</table>

SAS Output 29.13

Parameter	Estimate	Standard Error	t Value	Pr > |t|
Intercept	2.240875000	0.22087135	10.15	<.0001
x5	1.534000000	0.22087135	6.95	<.0001
x15	-0.925875000	0.22087135	-4.19	0.0011

Chapter 30 SAS®

Response Surface Methodology

The goal of *response surface* techniques is to determine the levels of the factors under investigation that produce an optimum response. The methods involve choosing wisely the levels of factors to include in an experiment, fitting linear regression models, and then estimating the combination of factor levels that produces the optimum response. Sometimes the optimum response is not found in the range of the levels chosen for initial experimentation but the results from that experiment point toward a range for additional experimentation. In the regression model, the dependent variable is the response y and the independent variables are a function of the levels of the factors. The independent variables typically are linear and quadratic terms representing levels of the factors. Thus, the regression model is usually a first or second-order model and the predicted values lie on the surface of the curve described by the fitted model. In this chapter, the authors discuss the design and analysis of experiments using response surface methods in studies where the goal is to find the combination of levels of quantitative factors that produce the best quantitative response.

Analysis of Response Surface Experiments

Dorle Exterior Trim Example

Data File: ch30fill.txt

The Dorle Exterior Trim manufacturing company found blemishes on the surface of automobile bumpers during the initial production of a new model. A response surface experiment was conducted to study the relationship between three key process variables and the suspected cause of the blemishes, and to identify the optimum operating levels of the three process variables. See Chapter 0, "Working with SAS," for instructions on opening the Dorle Exterior Trim Example and naming the variables Y, $x1$, $x2$, and $x3$. After opening and printing ch30fill.txt, the first 5 lines of output should look like SAS Output 30.1.

SAS Output 30.1

Obs	y	x1	x2	x3
1	63	-1	-1	1
2	12	1	-1	1
3	64	-1	1	1
4	26	1	1	1
5	59	-1	-1	-1

The researcher considered a three-factor second-order response function as given by the general expression shown in equation 30.1, text page 1267. The three factors were chemical temperature ($x1$), mold temperature ($x2$), and curing time ($x3$). We use *proc rsreg* in Insert 30.1 to specify this model. Notice that we specify a *model* statement that includes only the three original factors $x1$, $x2$, and $x3$, i.e., the additional factors needed for the second-order model are constructed internally by *proc rsreg*. Execution of Insert 30.1 results in (output not shown) p values greater than or equal to 0.6 for each term involving curing time ($x3$, $x3*x1$, $x3*x2$, $x3*x1$, and $x3*x3$).

INSERT 30.1

```
* Orginal 3 factor model;
data dorle;
infile 'c:\kutnerdata\chapter 30 data sets\ch30fi11.txt';
  input y x1 x2 x3;
proc rsreg;
   model y = x1 x2 x3 ;
run;
```

Based on the results from fitting a three-factor model above, the researchers dropped curing time ($x3$) and adopted a two-factor second-order response surface model with chemical temperature ($x1$) and mold temperature ($x2$) as explanatory variables. In Insert 30.2, after reading the data file, we create a variable named *id* for each record in the *dorle* data file and reverse the coding of $x1$ into a variable named *x1rev* for subsequent use as noted on text page 1389. We specify a model where $x1$ and $x2$ are explanatory variables and, for subsequent plotting, request that the predicted values based on this model be saved in an output file named *dorleout*. Partial results of this *proc rsreg* are shown in SAS Output 30.2 and are consistent with Figure 30.11, text page 1289.

The predicted values for the two-factor model are saved in a data file named *dorleout*; however, they are saved under the name *y*, *_TYPE_=PREDICT*. Since we wish to later merge the *dorle* and *dorleout* files, in the next *data* statement we rename *y* to *yhat* and add a variable named *id* to the *dorleout* file. In the *merge* statement we merge *dorle* and *dorleout* data files by matching on the *id* variable. This results in the original variables from the *dorle* data file and the predicted values (renamed to *yhat*) of the *dorleout* data file being merged into a file named *all*. We can now use *proc g3grid* to produce a grid (*dorleplot*) to be used on the next *proc g3d* statement; the grid (axis –1 to 1 by 0.125) will be 16x16. Results of the *proc g3d* the statement are shown in SAS Output 30.3 and are consistent with Figure 30.12 (a), text page 1290. Because the data set *dorle* contains a relatively small number of points, the lines will appear as connected lines. Using the output from *proc g3grid* as the input data set on the *proc gcontour* statement will result in smoothed lines. This output is shown in SAS Output 30.4 and is consistent with text Figure 30.12 (b).

INSERT 30.2		**INSERT 30.2 continued**	

```
data dorle;
infile 'c:\kutnerdata\chapter 30 data sets\ch30fi11.txt';
   input y x1 x2 x3;
id+1;
x1rev=0;
if x1=1 then x1rev=-1;
if x1=-1 then x1rev=1;
label x1rev='Chem Temp'
     x2='Mold Temp';
proc rsreg data=dorle out=dorleout;
    model y = x1 x2 / predict;
run;
data dorleout (rename=(y=yhat));
 set dorleout;
 id+1;
data all;
 merge dorle dorleout;
 by id;
 run;
goptions reset=all;
proc g3grid data=all out=dorleplot;
  grid x2*x1rev=yhat / axis1=-1 to 1 by 0.125
                 axis2=-1 to 1 by 0.125;
run;
```

```
proc g3d data=dorleplot;
  title "g3d";
  plot x2*x1rev=yhat /
            tilt=66
            rotate=40
            xticknum=5
            yticknum=5
            zmax=80
            zmin=0
            zticknum=5
            grid;
run;
quit;
goptions reset=all;
axis2 length=22;
proc gcontour data=dorleplot;
  plot x2*x1rev=yhat /
    levels = 10 20 30 40 50
            autolabel=(check=none)
            vaxis=axis2
            nolegend;
run;
quit;
```

SAS Output 30.2

Regression	DF	Type I Sum of Squares	R-Square	F Value	Pr > F
Linear	2	5075.300000	0.6894	87.31	<.0001
Quadratic	2	1854.363485	0.2519	31.90	<.0001
Crossproduct	1	112.500000	0.0153	3.87	0.0749
Total Model	5	7042.163485	0.9566	48.46	<.0001

Parameter	DF	Estimate	Standard Error	t Value	Pr > |t|	Parameter Estimate from Coded Data
Intercept	1	16.301887	2.221627	7.34	<.0001	16.301887
x1	1	-22.300000	1.704856	-13.08	<.0001	-22.300000
x2	1	3.200000	1.704856	1.88	0.0873	3.200000
x1*x1	1	12.443396	3.097911	4.02	0.0020	12.443396
x2*x1	1	3.750000	1.906087	1.97	0.0749	3.750000
x2*x2	1	11.943396	3.097911	3.86	0.0027	11.943396

Factor	DF	Sum of Squares	Mean Square	F Value	Pr > F	Label
x1	3	5554.338275	1851.446092	63.70	<.0001	
x2	3	646.909704	215.636568	7.42	0.0054	Mold Temp

Factor	Critical Value		Label
	Coded	Uncoded	
x1	0.938443	0.938443	
x2	-0.281292	-0.281292	Mold Temp
Predicted value at stationary point: 5.388176			

SAS Output 30.3

g3d

SAS Output 30.4

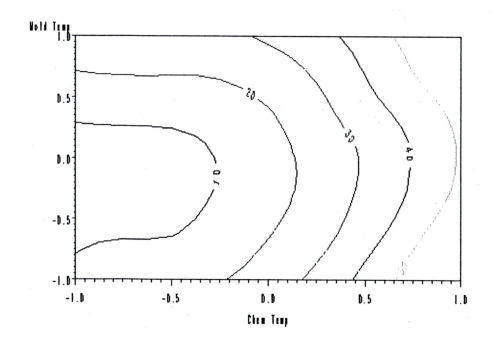

SPSS® Solutions

Chapter 0 SPSS®

Working with SPSS®

The purpose of this chapter is to introduce the requisite methods for entering, creating, and opening the data files provided with *Applied Linear Statistical Models, 5th Edition* by Kutner, Nachtsheim, Neter, and Li (2004). Although we will work with many SPSS programs as we progress through *Applied Linear Statistical Models,* the present chapter is not intended to be a comprehensive review of the SPSS capabilities.

SPSS is a modular, integrated, product line for the analytical process. The SPSS products are available using a simple point-and-click graphical interface and can be used for:

- Planning
- Data collection
- Data access and management
- Report writing
- Statistical analysis
- File handling

SPSS is available for most mainframe and personal computers running under the Windows® or Macintosh® operating systems. The modules required to perform the analyses in the forthcoming chapters are SPSS Base®, SPSS Advanced Models®, and SPSS Regression Models®.

Starting SPSS: Most compute systems have an SPSS icon on the desktop. Double click the icon to start SPSS and, if needed, close the window that may be superimposed over SPSS Output 0.1. The SPSS *Data Editor* screen will appear as shown in SPSS Output 0.1.

SPSS Output 0.1

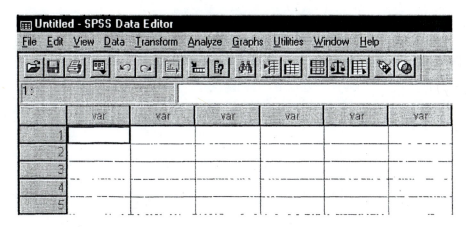

SPSS *Data Editor*: SPSS' *Data Editor* is versatile spreadsheet-like system that can be used for entering, editing, defining, and displaying data. It is from this window that most of the procedures used in this book will be performed.

Entering data in the *Data Editor*: On text page 3, the authors present a data set containing the number of units sold (X) and the dollar sales amount (Y) for 3 time periods. To enter this data, we first name the variables to be entered. Click ($\checkmark$) the Variable View tab in the lower left hand corner of the *Data Editor*. Name the three variables *period*, *units*, and *sales*, respectively, as shown in SPSS Output 0.2. These names are arbitrary but follow conventions for variable names within SPSS. In general, the name must be no more than 8 characters, cannot contain a special character, and must begin with one of the alphabetic letters a through z. So, instead of using *units* as the name for the variable "Number of Units Sold," we could have used *unit*, *unitsold*, *sold*, *x*, or any other name that was within the naming convention for a variable. From the screen shown in SPSS Output 0.2, we can also define the type of variable, the width of the display for each variable as well as define missing values, variable labels, and value labels. For instance, each of the 3 variables defined on text page 3 contains only numeric values and, thus, should be defined as *numeric* variables under the *Type* column. If we were to enter the name of a city, such as "New York," we would have to define the variable as a *String* variable in the *Type* column so that non-numeric characters could be entered to represent the city name. But, once a variable is defined as a *String*, mathematical operations cannot be performed on the variable. So, we can take the square root of *units* if it is defined as a *Numeric* variable but not if it is defined as a *String* variable. A variable label for *units* such as "Number of Units Sold" can also be defined. The variable label will be included in addition to or in place of the variable name in program output. We may also define *Value Labels* for any variable. For instance, we could assign *Value Labels* for *period* where 1="January thru April," 2="May thru August," and 3="Sept thru Dec." Finally, the column labeled *Decimals* in SPSS Output 0.2 indicates the number of decimal places displayed in the *Data Editor*. It does not affect the number of decimals that can be entered and stored in SPSS. A column Width=8 and Decimal=2 is the default settings in SPSS and throughout this book we will use these default values.

After naming the variables *period*, *units*, and *sales* in the *Data Editor*, $\checkmark$ the Data View tab in the lower left hand corner of the *Data Editor* and enter the 3 columns of data shown on text page 3. The *Data Editor* will now appear as SPSS Output 0.3.

SPSS Output 0.2

		Name	Type	Width	Decimals	Label	Values	Missing	Columns
1		period	Numeric	8	2		None	None	8
2		units	Numeric	8	2		None	None	8
3		sales	Numeric	8	2		None	None	8
4									
5									

SPSS Output 0.3

Untitled - SPSS Data Editor

File Edit View Data Transform Analyze Graphs Utilities Window Help

3 : sales | 260

	period	units	sales	var	var
1	1.00	75.00	150		
2	2.00	25.00	50		
3	3.00	130.00	260		
4					
5					

Reading Data files into the *Data Editor*: A SPSS data file that has been saved by SPSS will have a "*sav*" extension. To read a SPSS data file, simply ✔ Open from the *Data Editor* and point SPSS to the appropriate file. However, the data files provided with *Applied Linear Statistical Models* are "*txt*" files and must be read using SPSS's Text Import Wizard. To open the Toluca Company example from text Chapter 1 (Table 1.1, text page 19), ✔ Open ✔ Data and point SPSS to ch01ta01.txt in the appropriate directory. (We recommend that you transfer your data files from the disk provided with your text to a directory on a permanent disk drive, e.g., C:\alrm*.) SPSS will recognize that the requested file is not a SPSS file and open the Import Wizard. (SPSS Output 0.4) For most files, we simply need to ✔ Next 5 times and then ✔ Finish. The *Data Editor* will now look like SPSS Output 0.5. Note that the default variable names are *v1* and *v2*. We can rename the variables *lotsize* and *workhrs* as described above and add value labels, variable labels, etc. as appropriate. We can now save 💾 the data file, by default, as a SPSS .sav file type.

SPSS Output 0.4

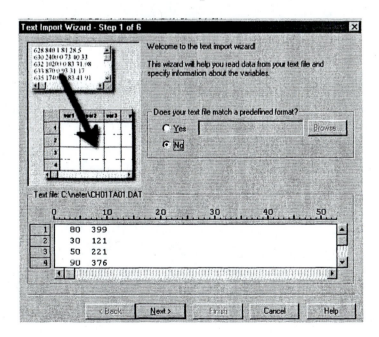

SPSS Output 0.5

	v1	v2	var	var	var
1	80.00	399 00			
2	30 00	121 00			
3	50 00	221 00			
4	90 00	376 00			
5	70 00	361 00			

Note that the default file type to be opened when using the ☞ icon is determined by the current Window type in SPSS. That is, while in the *Data Editor*, pressing the ☞ icon will only display files that are SPSS Data Files (*.sav* extension). While in the *Syntax Editor*, pressing the ☞ icon will only display files that are syntax files (*.sps* extension). Thus, if we are in an SPSS Output file (*.spo* extension), for example, and want to open a syntax file, we must ✔ File, ✔ Open, ✔ Syntax to view files in the current directory that are syntax files (*.sps* extension).

Creating a new variable: Suppose in the Toluca Company example above we wish to find the square of *lotsize* for use in polynomial regression. From the *Data Editor* ✔ Transform ✔ Compute. This will open a Compute Variable dialogue box. (SPSS Output 0.6) Insert 0.1 details the steps to create a new variable, *lotsqr*, the square of *lotsize*. In Insert 0.1 and throughout this book, an * in an insert box represents a comment statement or instructions needed to complete the current task. Following the steps in Insert 0.1 up to but not including ✔ OK will result in a Compute Variable dialogue box identical to SPSS Output 0.6. When we ✔ OK, *lotsqr* will be computed and placed in the *Data Editor* with *lotsize* and *workhrs*. Use of Insert 0.1 presupposes that the Toluca Company data file is open in the *Data Editor* and the variables are named *lotsize* and *workhrs*.

SPSS Output 0.6

```
                              INSERT 0.1

   ✔ Transform
   ✔ Compute
   * Type "lotsqr" in the Target Variable" box.
   ✔ lotsize
   ✔ ▶
   ✔ **
   ✔ 2
   ✔ OK
```

There may be times when we need to begin writing SPSS code for a data analysis before the complete data set is available. For instance, in the Toluca Company example, the analyst may have only a portion of a data set available but because of time constraints needs to begin writing the code for the final data analysis. Suppose that the analyst knows from past experience with the Toluca Company that a polynomial regression will be required. The analyst can develop and save the computational steps necessary for finding *lotsqr* prior to having the complete data set. Repeat the steps in Insert 0.1 up to but not including ✔ OK. Instead of ✔ OK, ✔ Paste. SPSS will paste the syntax into a SPSS *Syntax Editor*. If we now ✔ Run, and ✔ All in the SPSS *Syntax Editor*, *lotsqr* will be computed and placed in the *Data Editor* with *lotsize* and *workhrs*.

However, since the complete data set is not available, we simply click save 🖫 in the *Syntax Editor* (SPSS Output 0.7) to save the syntax file for later use.

SPSS Output 0.7

We can also create a syntax file by ✔ File, ✔ New, ✔ Syntax from the *Data Editor*. Once in the *Syntax Editor*, we can type the desired syntax so that the *Syntax Editor* looks like SPSS Output 0.7. For many applications the use of the point-and-click Compute Variable dialogue box is convenient and practical. For other applications, it is easier to open the *Syntax Editor* and type the appropriate syntax. For example, in SPSS Chapter 3 we find the expected value under normality,

$$ev = \text{sqrt}(2383.716) * \text{probit} ((rres\_1 - .375)/(25 + .25)).$$

Although this calculation can be done in a Compute Variable dialogue box, it is simpler and less prone to error to type a *Compute* statement in the *Syntax Editor* for this computation.

319

Many SPSS procedures allow the user to save various statistics. For example, we can specify that unstandardized residuals for a regression model be saved to the *Data Editor*. By default, the residuals will be saved in a variable named *res_1*. If we save the residuals for a second model, they will be saved as *res_2* if *res_1* has not been deleted from the *Data Editor*. In this book, we may instruct you to save residuals for use in subsequent calculations. For each set of instructions we assume that all previous residuals have been deleted from the *Data Editor* and the current residuals will be saved as *res_1*. If they will be saved as *res_3*, for example, you should use *res_3* in the calculation instead of *res_1*.

Default settings in SPSS: In the SPSS *Data Editor*, the user has available a number of options for customizing the software. These options can be edited by ✔ Edit, ✔ Options. (SPSS Output 0.8) If the system is set to Display Names, SPSS will display the Variable Name in a dialogue box. If the system is set to Display Labels, SPSS will display the Variable Label followed by the Variable Name in parentheses in a dialogue box. For example, if we save the unstandardized residuals from a regression procedure, they are saved under the Variable Name *res_1* with the Variable Label "Unstandardized Residuals." Selecting Display Names will result in SPSS Output 0.9 and selecting Display Labels will result in SPSS Output 0.10. We will use the Display Names option under Variable List throughout this text. The other option that may cause a difference in appearance of data files is the number of decimals displayed. We use Decimal Places=2 throughout this book unless otherwise specified. This option is found under the Data tab in the Options dialogue box.

SPSS Output 0.8

SPSS Output 0.9

SPSS Output 0.10

SPSS provides an extensive help system available from the Help dropdown menu. Additional help can be obtained at www.spss.com/tech using AnserNet and other technical support options. We are grateful to SPSS Technical Support for their assistance. SPSS® software is licensed by:

SPSS Inc. Headquarters
233 S. Wacker Drive
11th floor
Chicago, Illinois 60606
www.SPSS.com

Chapter **1** SPSS®

Linear Regression with One Predictor Variable

This chapter of the text introduces the simple linear regression model. The idea is to use statistical methods to find a model that allows us to predict the value of a dependent variable Y given the value of an independent variable X. We are given Y_i and X_i for a sample of n subjects and we want to find a "best fitting" model for predicting Y given X. The usual approach is to begin by assuming the model is of the form:

$$Y_i = \beta_0 + \beta_1 X_i + \varepsilon_i$$

for the ith subject, i = 1, ... , n. This is often referred to as a *simple linear regression model*. The first step is to find estimates of β_0 and β_1 so that the "fitted" model is best, as defined in the text, among all models of this form. The statistical analysis that involves estimating, constructing confidence intervals, and testing hypotheses about β_0 and β_1 is called *regression analysis*. The model is generalized in subsequent chapters to include more than one independent variable. The text introduces the basic concepts and gives easy to follow numerical examples that illustrate the ideas. Also, the text presents excerpts of a large data set in Table 1.1 followed by a description of the problem and details of a regression analysis. The text refers to this example as the Toluca Company example. A step-by-step set of SPSS solutions is given below.

The Toluca Company Example

Data File: ch01ta01.txt

The Toluca Company manufactures refrigeration equipment and replacement parts (text page 19). The parts are manufactured in "runs" and groups of runs comprise lots of varying sizes. The data disk provided with the text contains data on 25 manufacturing runs under the file name ch01ta01.txt. For each run, this file contains data on lot size and work hours, defined as the number of labor hours required to produce the lot. The aim of the example is to investigate the relationship between work hours and lot size. We wish to fit a simple linear regression model that allows us to predict work hours from lot size. We let the variable names *workhrs* denote work hours and *lotsize* denote lot size, and take these to be the dependent variable Y and the independent variable X, respectively, in the simple linear regression model. See Chapter 0, "Working with SPSS," for instructions on opening the Toluca Company data file and renaming the variables *lotsize* and *workhrs*. After opening ch01ta01.txt, the first 5 lines in the SPSS *Data Editor* should look like SPSS Output 1.1.

SPSS Output 1.1

Scatter plots: The text begins a regression analysis of the Toluca Company data with a scatter plot showing work hours plotted against lot size in Figure 1.10 (a & b), text page 20. We provide SPSS syntax for constructing this scatter plot in Insert 1.1 and display the results in SPSS Output 1.2 (a & b) below.

INSERT 1.1

* Produce Scatter Plot.
✔ Graphs
✔ Scatter
✔ Simple
✔ Define
✔ *lotsize*
✔ ▶(to the X axis)
✔ *workhrs*
✔ ▶(to the Y axis)
✔ OK

* **Release 11.5 and lower**: To draw the regression line as shown in text Figure 1.10(b),
* double click on the graph in the SPSS Viewer. This brings up a SPSS Chart Editor window.
✔ Chart
✔ Options
✔ Total (under Fit Line)
✔ OK
* Close the Chart Editor.

* **Release 12.0 and higher**: To draw the regression line as shown in text Figure 1.10(b), .
* double click on the graph in the SPSS Viewer. This brings up a SPSS Chart Editor.
* window. Double click on any data point on the graph.
✔ Chart
✔ Add Chart Element
✔ Fit Line at Total
✔ Linear
✔ OK
* Close the Chart Editor.

(a)   **SPSS Output 1.2**   **(b)**

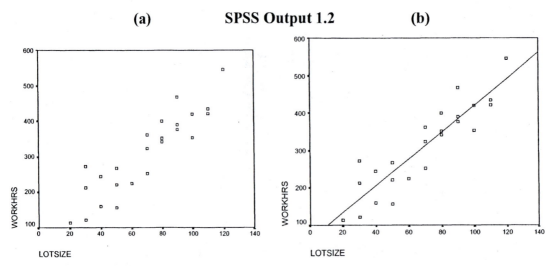

Estimation of β_0 and β_1: To find the least squares estimates b_0 and b_1 of β_0 and β_1, respectively, we follow the overview of the required computations that are outlined in Table 1.1, text page 19. In Insert 1.2, we show the SPSS syntax that performs these computations. We first find the means for *workhrs* ($\overline{X} = 70$) and *lotsize* ($\overline{Y} = 312.28$). Next we find $X_i - \overline{X}$ (*xdev*), $Y_i - \overline{Y}$ (*ydev*), $(X_i - \overline{X})^2$ (*xdev2*), $(Y_i - \overline{Y})^2$ (*ydev2*), $(X_i - \overline{X})(Y_i - \overline{Y})$ (*xdev * ydev = cross*). The last step in Insert 1.2 is to find the sum of $(X_i - \overline{X})(Y_i - \overline{Y})$ ($\sum$ *cross*=70,690) and $(X_i - \overline{X})^2$ ($\sum$ *xdev2*=19,800). Using equation 1.10, text page 17, we calculate:

$$b_1 = \frac{\sum (X_i - \overline{X})(Y_i - \overline{Y})}{\sum (X_i - \overline{X})} = \frac{70{,}690}{19{,}800} = 3.5702$$

and

$$b_0 = \overline{Y} - b_1 \overline{X} = 312.28 - 3.5702 * 70 = 62.365$$

INSERT 1.2	INSERT 1.2 continued
* Find mean of *lotsize* and *workhrs*. ✔ Analyze ✔ Descriptive Statistics ✔ Descriptives ✔ *lotsize* ✔ ▶ ✔ *workhrs* ✔ ▶ ✔ OK * Calculate least squares estimates. ✔ File ✔ New ✔ Syntax * Type the following syntax. compute xdev=(lotsize-70). compute ydev=workhrs-312.28. compute xdev2=(lotsize-70)**2.	compute ydev2=(workhrs-312.28)**2. compute cross=xdev*ydev. execute. ✔ Run ✔ All * Find sum of *cross* and *xdev2*. ✔ Analyze ✔ Descriptive Statistics ✔ Descriptives ✔ *cross* ✔ ▶ ✔ *xdev2* ✔ ▶ ✔ Options ✔ Sum ✔ Continue ✔ OK

Estimated Regression Function: We used the SPSS syntax shown in Insert 1.2 to demonstrate how SPSS code can be written to provide intermediate results when we compute the parameter estimates b_0 and b_1. We now use SPSS' *Regression* procedure to find b_0 and b_1. This procedure is shorter and easier to use but it does not provide the results of the intermediate computations shown on text page 19. In Insert 1.3, we request a regression analysis where *workhrs* is regressed on *lotsize*. Partial results are shown in SPSS Output 1.3. Notice that the "Unstandardized Coefficients" shown under column heading B give the results $b_0 = 62.366$ and $b_1 = 3.570$. Here b_0 is given in the row labeled (Constant) and b_1 is given in the row labeled LOTSIZE. These results are consistent with those shown on text page 20 and in the calculations of Insert 1.2 above. We can easily obtain more precision in the SPSS output for parameter estimates. For example, after executing Insert 1.3, the output file will appear as SPSS Output 1.3. Double click on the Coefficients table and then double click on the "62.366." The output will display the estimate $b_0 = 62.3658585$.

INSERT 1.3

- ✔ Analyze
- ✔ Regression
- ✔ Linear
- ✔ *workhrs*
- ✔ ▶ (to the Dependent box)
- ✔ *lotsize*
- ✔ ▶ (to the Independent box)
- ✔ OK

SPSS Output 1.3

ANOVA[b]

Model		Sum of Squares	df	Mean Square	F	Sig.
1	Regression	252377.6	1	252377.581	105.876	.000[a]
	Residual	54825.459	23	2383.716		
	Total	307203.0	24			

a. Predictors: (Constant), LOTSIZE

b. Dependent Variable: WORKHRS

Coefficients[a]

Model		Unstandardized Coefficients		Standardized Coefficients	t	Sig.
		B	Std. Error	Beta		
1	(Constant)	62.366	26.177		2.382	.026
	LOTSIZE	3.570	.347	.906	10.290	.000

a. Dependent Variable: WORKHRS

From the above regression analysis, we estimate the regression function to be: $\hat{Y}= 62.377 +$ 3.570(X). To estimate the mean response (the mean number of work hours required) or predicted value for each lot size specified in the data as in column 3 of Table 1.2, text page 22, we instruct SPSS to save the unstandardized predicted values for the regression analysis (Insert 1.4). Similarly, to obtain the residuals as in column 4 of text Table 1.2, we instruct SPSS to save the unstandardized residuals. SPSS saves the unstandardized predicted values and the unstandarized residuals in the active *Data Editor* as *pre_1* and *res_1*, respectively. (SPSS Output 1.4). The partial results shown in SPSS Output 1.4 are consistent with those shown in text Table 1.2 with the exception of the Squared Residual. To produce the squared residual, simply open a Syntax File or use a dialogue box as shown in Insert 1.5. We compute the square of the individual residuals as *res_1*res_1* and store the result as a new variable that we have arbitrarily called *sqres*. *Sqres* will be saved in the active *Data Editor*.

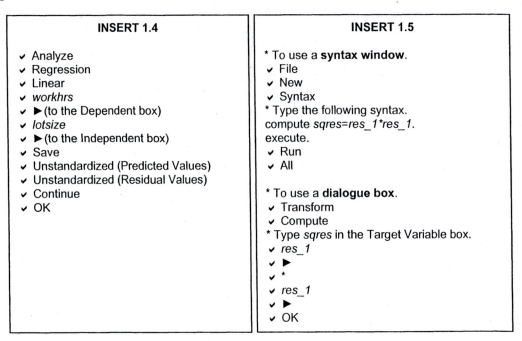

INSERT 1.4	INSERT 1.5
✔ Analyze	* To use a **syntax window**.
✔ Regression	✔ File
✔ Linear	✔ New
✔ *workhrs*	✔ Syntax
✔ ▶ (to the Dependent box)	* Type the following syntax.
✔ *lotsize*	compute *sqres=res_1*res_1*.
✔ ▶ (to the Independent box)	execute.
✔ Save	✔ Run
✔ Unstandardized (Predicted Values)	✔ All
✔ Unstandardized (Residual Values)	
✔ Continue	* To use a **dialogue box**.
✔ OK	✔ Transform
	✔ Compute
	* Type *sqres* in the Target Variable box.
	✔ *res_1*
	✔ ▶
	✔ *
	✔ *res_1*
	✔ ▶
	✔ OK

SPSS Output 1.4

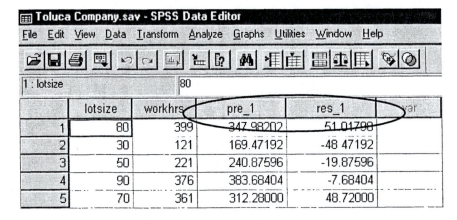

Chapter 2 SPSS®

Inferences in Regression and Correlation Analysis

In this chapter, the authors introduce the fundamentals for making statistical inferences about the parameters of the regression model. The model of interest is:

$$Y_i = \beta_0 + \beta_1 X_i + \varepsilon_i$$

where:

β_0 and β_1 are unknown parameters
X_i are known constants for $i = 1, 2, \ldots, n$.
ε_i are unknown errors associated with the true model.

We assume the ε_i are independent $N(0, \sigma^2)$ for $i = 1, 2, \ldots, n$. Note that the assumptions made here about the errors differ from those made in Chapter 1. The normality assumption is required by theoretical considerations used to develop confidence intervals and test statistics for making inferences involving the model parameters. Inferences were not considered in Chapter 1 and, therefore, normally distributed error terms were not required. The inferences of specific interest pertain to confidence intervals and tests of hypotheses for model parameters and functions of model parameters. The statistical analysis associated with estimation and inference involving regression models is called *regression analysis*.

Chapter 1 of the text presents formulas for the estimators b_0 and b_1 of the parameters β_0 and β_1, respectively. These estimators yield estimates that vary from sample to sample and, therefore, have a (sampling) distribution of their own. It is desirable then to make inferences about the true values of the parameters based on their sample estimates. Let β_j represent either β_0 or β_1 depending on whether $j = 0$ or 1 and let b_j denote the corresponding estimator. We can estimate the variance of b_j from a single sample of Y's and X's and the square root of this variance estimate is an estimate of the standard error of b_j. The text denotes the variance and standard error estimators by $s^2\{b_j\}$ and $s\{b_j\}$, respectively, and gives their computational formulas (see equation 2.9 page 43 and equation 2.23 page 49 of the text).

Consider the null hypothesis:

$$H_0: \beta_j = 0$$

A statistic for testing this hypothesis against either a one or two-sided alternative is:

$$t = \frac{b_j}{s\{b_j\}}$$

Under the assumptions of the model this statistic is distributed as Student's t with $n - 2$ degrees of freedom.

Let $t(1 - \alpha/2; n - 2)$ denote the $(\alpha/2)100$ percentile of the t distribution with $n - 2$ degrees of freedom. The $1 - \alpha$ confidence limits for β_j are:

$$b_j \pm t(1 - \alpha/2; n - 2)\, s\{b_j\}$$

Chapter 2 of the text presents these formulas and others of inferential interest in the simple linear regression model.

Further Aspects of the Toluca Company Example

Data File: **ch01ta01.txt**

We return to the Toluca Company example first presented in Chapter 1 (text page 19). We let the variable names *workhrs* denote work hours and *lotsize* denote lot size, and take these to be the dependent variable Y and the independent variable X, respectively, in the simple linear regression model. See Chapter 0, "Working with SPSS," for instructions on opening the Toluca Company data file and renaming the variables *lotsize* and *workhrs*. After opening ch01ta01.txt, the first 5 lines in the SPSS *Data Editor* should look like SPSS Output 2.1.

SPSS Output 2.1

	lotsize	workhrs	var	var	var
1	80	399			
2	30	121			
3	50	221			
4	90	376			
5	70	361			

Toluca Company.sav - SPSS Data Editor
File Edit View Data Transform Analyze Graphs Utilities Window Help
1 : lotsize   80

We wish to perform a regression analysis using the model:

$$\text{workhrs} = \beta_0 + \beta_1(\text{lotsize}) + \varepsilon$$

Confidence Interval for β_1: On text page 46 the management team wants an estimate of β_1 with a 95% confidence interval. The $1 - \alpha$ confidence limits for β_1 are (equation 2.15, text page 45):

$$b_1 \pm t(1 - \alpha/2; n-2)\, s\{b_1\}$$

We request confidence intervals for the regression coefficients using SPSS by the instructions given in Insert 2.1. From SPSS Output 2.2 we see that the 95% confidence interval is $2.852 \le \beta_1 \le 4.288$, consistent with text page 46.

Tests of Hypothesis Concerning β_1: The t-test for H_0: $\beta_1 = 0$ is:

$$t^* = \frac{b_1}{s\{b_1\}}$$

with $n - 2$ degrees of freedom (equation 2.17, text page 47). We get the numerical value for this test statistic as part of the output from the SPSS instructions given in Insert 2.1. In SPSS Output 2.2 we see $(t^*) = 10.290$ for *lotsize* and the associated p-value $= 0.000$ (Sig.). Since $p<0.05$ we conclude $\beta_1 \ne 0$.

To test that $\beta_1 > 0$ (a one-sided test), we require that $|t^*| > t(1-\alpha; n-2)$. The standard output in SPSS displays the p-value for a two-sided test. To get the p-value for a one-sided test, first determine whether the numerical value of the t-test is negative or positive and hence whether it tends to favor the specified one-sided alternative. A negative t-test favors H_a: $\beta_1 < 0$ whereas a positive t-test favors H_a: $\beta_1 > 0$. If the t-test favors the specified one-sided alternative, just divide the p-value displayed in the SPSS output by 2. In the example, $(t^*) = 10.290$ is positive and this favors H_a: $\beta_1 > 0$ with p-value $= 0.000/2 = 0.000$. If the numerical value of the t-test does not favor the specified alternative, it is probably sufficient to quote $p > 0.50$ as the p-value. More precisely, the p-value for the one-sided t-test in this situation is 1 minus the p-value displayed in the SPSS output divided by 2. In the present example, if we had specified H_a: $\beta_1 < 0$ and found $(t^*) = 10.290$, the p-value would be $1 - 0.000/2 = 1.000$. In this circumstance, we would not reject H_0.

INSERT 2.1

- ✔ Analyze
- ✔ Regression
- ✔ Linear
- ✔ *workhrs*
- ✔ ▶ (to the Dependent box)
- ✔ *lotsize*
- ✔ ▶ (to the Independent box)
- ✔ Statistics
- ✔ Confidence Intervals (under Regression coefficients)
- ✔ Continue
- ✔ OK

SPSS Output 2.2

Model Summary[b]

Model	R	R Square	Adjusted R Square	Std. Error of the Estimate
1	.906[a]	.822	.814	48.823

a. Predictors: (Constant), LOTSIZE

b. Dependent Variable: WORKHRS

ANOVA[b]

Model		Sum of Squares	df	Mean Square	F	Sig.
1	Regression	252377.6	1	252377.581	105.876	.000[a]
	Residual	54825.459	23	2383.716		
	Total	307203.0	24			

a. Predictors: (Constant), LOTSIZE

b. Dependent Variable: WORKHRS

Coefficients[a]

Model		Unstandardized Coefficients B	Unstandardized Coefficients Std. Error	Standardized Coefficients Beta	t	Sig.	95% Confidence Interval for B Lower Bound	95% Confidence Interval for B Upper Bound
1	(Constant)	62.366	26.177		2.382	.026	8.214	116.518
	LOTSIZE	3.570	.347	.906	10.290	.000	2.852	4.288

a. Dependent Variable: WORKHRS

Sometimes it is desirable to find the critical value $t(1-\alpha; n-2)$ corresponding to a t-test. To find $t(1-\alpha; n-2)$ in SPSS, use a Compute Variable ($\checkmark$ Transform $\checkmark$ Compute) dialogue box (SPSS Output 2.3) to request a new variable named *tvalue*. Let T denote a random variable that has a t-distribution with degrees of freedom = df. Suppose we want to find the value t such that $P(T > t)$ = α for a value of α that we specify. Equivalently, suppose we want to find the value t such that $P(T \le t) = 1-\alpha$.. We can use the SPSS *inverse distribution function IDF.T*$(1-\alpha, df)$ for this purpose. When we specify $1-\alpha$ and df, this function returns the associated t-value. To find the critical value for testing H_a: $\beta_1 > 0$ controlling the level of significance at $\alpha = 0.05$, we must find $t(1-\alpha; n-2)$ or $t(0.95, 23)$. This critical value ($t = 1.71$) is obtained from the Compute Variable dialogue box (SPSS Output 2.3) and is written into each of the 25 data-lines in the Toluca *Data Editor*. Since the obtained t-value ($t = 10.29$) is greater than the critical value $t = 1.71$, we conclude $\beta_1 > 0$. If we want to obtain the critical value for a two-sided test where $\alpha = 0.05$, we find $t(1-\alpha/2; n-2)$ or $t(0.975, 23)$ using the above *inverse distribution function*.

SPSS Output 2.3

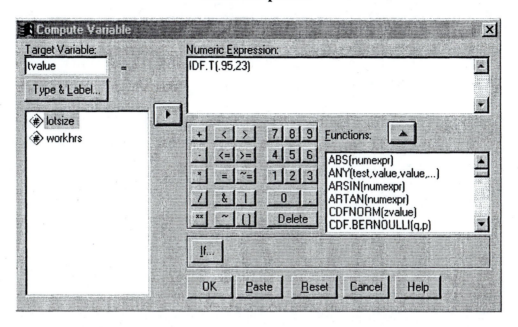

Confidence Interval for β_0: To obtain the 90% confidence interval for β_0 (text page 49), we must find $t(1-\alpha/2; n-2)$. (Note that Output 2.2 presents the 95% confidence interval.) Since we desire a 90% confidence interval, $\alpha = 0.10$ and $t(0.95, 23) = 1.71$. From Output 2.2, we find the standard deviation of b_0 (Constant) is $s\{b_0\} = 26.17$. From equation 2.25, text page 49, the 90% confidence interval is:

$$b_0 \pm t(1-\alpha/2; n-2) s\{b_0\}$$

or

$$62.366 \pm 1.71 * 26.17$$

Simplifying this expression, we find the 90% confidence interval:

$$17.5 \leq \beta_0 \leq 107.2$$

Confidence Interval for $E\{Y_h\}$: Once specific sample data have been used to produce parameter estimates b_0 and b_1, we denote the fitted model as:

$$\hat{Y}_i = b_0 + b_1 X_i \qquad i = 1, 2, \ldots, n$$

We call $\hat{Y}_i$ the *predicted value* of Y when the predictor variable is X_i. Let X_h denote a specific value of the independent variable in the simple linear regression model. As noted by the authors, "X_h may be a value which occurred in the sample, or it may be some other value of the predictor variable within the scope of the model." The corresponding predicted value is denoted $\hat{Y}_h$. We can select many random samples of data and different samples may produce different estimates

331

b_0 and b_1 and hence different $\hat{Y}_h$. Hence, for any such X_h there is a distribution corresponding to the random variable $\hat{Y}_h$. This random variable has a mean and variance denoted $E\{\hat{Y}_h\} = E\{Y_h\}$ and $\sigma^2\{\hat{Y}_h\}$, respectively. Estimators of the mean and variance are $\hat{Y}_h$ and $s^2\{\hat{Y}_h\}$ (see equation 2.30, text page 53 for the formula for $s^2\{\hat{Y}_h\}$).

On text page 54, the authors use Toluca Company Example to find the 90% confidence interval for $E\{Y_h\}$ when lot size (X_h) = 65 units. The $1 - \alpha$ confidence limits are given in equation 2.33, text page 54:

$$\hat{Y}_h \pm t(1 - \alpha/2; n - 2)\, s\{\hat{Y}_h\}$$

To find $s^2\{\hat{Y}_h\}$ (equation 2.30, text page 53) we need the mean squared error (*MSE*), which is given in SPSS Output 2.2 above (*MSE* = 2383.716). To find $\overline{X}$, we use ✔ Analyze ✔ Descriptive Statistics ✔ Descriptives to find the mean for *lotsize* = 70. To find $(X_i - \overline{X})^2$ we use a Compute Variable dialogue box (✔ Transform ✔ Compute) and enter the syntax as shown in SPSS Output 2.4. This results in a new variable named *xdev2* being placed in your active *Data Editor*. To find the sum of this variable ($\sum(X_i - \overline{X})^2$) we use ✔ Analyze ✔ Descriptive Statistics ✔ Descriptives ✔ Options ✔ Sum and move *xdev2* to the Variables box. This produces SPSS Output 2.5, which contains the sum of *xdev2* = 19,800. We can now find:

$$s^2\{\hat{Y}_h\} = MSE\left[\frac{1}{n} + \frac{(X_h - \overline{X})^2}{\sum(X_i - \overline{X})^2}\right]$$

Thus,

$$s^2\{\hat{Y}_h\} = 2383.7\left[\frac{1}{25} + \frac{(65 - 70)^2}{19,800}\right] = 98.37$$

$$s\{\hat{Y}_h\} = \sqrt{s^2\{\hat{Y}_h\}} = 9.918$$

To find the 90 percent confidence interval, we also need $t(1-\alpha/2;\ n-2)$. Using the *inverse distribution function* introduced above (SPSS Output 2.3) where $t(1-\alpha/2;\ n-2) = t(0.95;\ 23)$, *IDF.T*(0.95, 23) returns $t(0.95, 23) = 1.71$. Using $X_h = 65$ units and the parameter estimates in Output 2.2 above, we find:

$$\hat{Y}_h = b_0 + b_1 X_h$$

or

$$\hat{Y}_h = 62.366 + 3.570(65) = 294.4$$

Substituting these numerical values into equation 2.33, text page 54, we obtain:

$$294.4 \pm 1.71(9.918)$$

or

$$277.44 \le E\{Y_h\} \le 311.36$$

SPSS Output 2.4

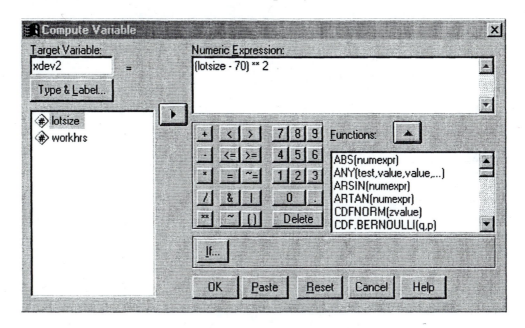

SPSS Output 2.5

Descriptive Statistics

	N	Minimum	Maximum	Sum	Mean	Std. Deviation
XDEVSQ	25	.00	2500.00	19800.00	792.0000	764.26435
Valid N (listwise)	25					

Confidence Band for Regression Line: To find the confidence band for the regression line as shown in equations 2.40 and 2.40a, text page 62, we use the Working-Hotelling $1-\alpha$ confidence band to establish boundary values for each *lotsize* value:

$$\hat{Y}_h \pm W\, s\{\hat{Y}_h\}$$

where:

$$W^2 = 2\,F(1-\alpha;\ 2, n-2)$$

In Insert 2.2, we use the SPSS *inverse distribution function IDF.F*$(1-\alpha, df_1, df_2)$ to find the critical *F*-value for the *F*-distribution with $1-\alpha = 0.90$ and $df_1 = 2$ and $df_2 = 23$ degrees of freedom and place the result in a new variable named *fvalue*. This results in SPSS writing the *F*-value associated with *IDF.F*$(0.9, 2, 23) = 2.55$ into every line in the *Data Editor*.

We now use text equations 2.28, 2.30, 2.40, and 2.40a to find the confidence band for the Toluca Company regression example. Insert 2.2 contains the necessary syntax to compute the upper (*bandhi*) and lower (*bandlo*) confidence bands. Notice that we have presented the syntax to be used in a *Syntax Editor*. Dialogue boxes could have been used in place of the *Syntax Editor*. We can now use ✔ Graphs ✔ Scatter ✔ Overlay ✔ Define to request (SPSS Output 2.6) the plot as shown in SPSS Output 2.7. This plot is equivalent to Figure 2.6, text page 63.

INSERT 2.2

```
✔ File
✔ New
✔ Syntax
* Type the following syntax.
compute fvalue=idf.f(.9,2,23).
compute w=sqrt((fvalue)*2).
compute yhat=62.366+3.57*lotsize.
compute sdyhat=sqrt(2383.716*((1/25)+(((lotsize-70)**2)/19800))).
compute bandhi=yhat+(w*sdyhat).
compute bandlo=yhat-(w*sdyhat).
execute.
✔ Run
✔ All
```

SPSS Output 2.6

SPSS Output 2.7

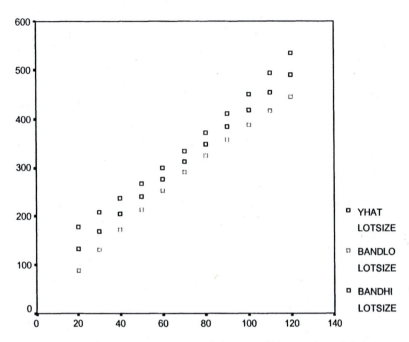

Now that we have a grasp of the computation of the confidence band for a regression line, we use SPSS' charting capabilities in Insert 2.3 to produce SPSS Output 2.8, which is equivalent to Output 2.7 above and to text Figure 2.6. For both SPSS Output 2.7 and 2.8, the range of values for the x-axis and y-axis is not identical to text Figure 2.6. The SPSS *Chart Editor* can additionally be used to modify a chart to conform to the values shown in text Figure 2.6.

INSERT 2.3

* Produce Scatter Plot.
✔ Graphs
✔ Scatter
✔ Simple
✔ Define
✔ *lotsize*
✔ ► (to the X axis)
✔ *workhrs*
✔ ► (to the Y axis)
✔ OK
* To draw the confidence bandsas shown in text Figure 2.6,.
* double click on the graph in the SPSS Viewer. This brings.
* up a SPSS Chart Editor window.
✔ Chart
✔ Options
✔ Total (under Fit Line)
✔ Fit Options
✔ Mean (under Regression Prediction Lines)
* Type "90" in Confidence Interval box.
✔ Continue
✔ OK
* Close the Chart Editor.

SPSS Output 2.8

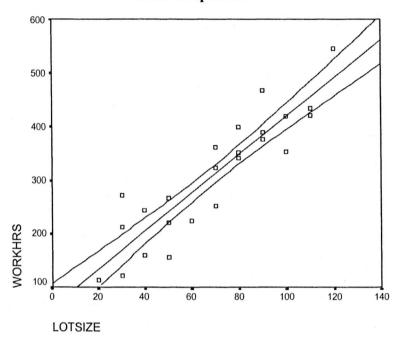

LOTSIZE

The coefficient of determination (R^2): From equation 2.72, text page 74, the coefficient of determination (R^2) is defined as Sum of Squares Regression / Sum of Squares Total; i.e.

$$R^2 = \frac{SSR}{SSTO} = 1 - \frac{SSE}{SSTO}$$

From SPSS Output 2.2 given above, we find $SSR = 252{,}377.6$ and $SSTO = 307{,}203.0$. Thus R^2 = 0.822 and the correlation coefficient (r) = $+\sqrt{R^2}$ = 0.907.

Chapter **3** SPSS®

Diagnostics and Remedial Measures

In Chapter 1 we learned that regression analysis involves using a sample of data values to find a linear model that will predict (the *dependent variable*) Y when the values of the (*independent variable*) X's are known. We also referred to the X's as *predictor variables*. We began with a sample of data where each sample unit provides an observation on Y (the dependent variable) and on one or more X's (the independent or predictor variables). Next, we formulated a model that we thought might specify the relationship between Y and the predictor variables. Once we decided on a model that we thought might be appropriate, we assumed the model was in fact an appropriate model for our purpose. We used the sample data to estimate parameters of the model and this estimation provided us with a fitted model. The adequacy of the estimates and of related statistical inferences depends on whether the specified model and the assumptions made in specifying the model are at least approximately true. In most applications, we do not know for certain in advance that the model we decide to use is appropriate for the specific analysis.

In Chapter 3, the authors discuss methods for using the observed sample data to investigate the adequacy of a fitted regression model. A group of methods known as *regression diagnostics* are used for this purpose. When regression diagnostics identify inadequacies in the model, *remedial measures* can sometimes be used to correct or offset the inadequacies.

Many regression diagnostics are performed in terms of the residuals from the fitted model. Assuming the simple linear regression model is the specified model, the fitted model is denoted (equation 1.13, text page 21):

$$\hat{Y}_i = b_0 + b_1 X_i \qquad i = 1, \ldots, n$$

The estimates b_0 and b_1 are obtained from the sample data. Once they have been calculated and their numerical values obtained, we can substitute X_i into the fitted model and calculate the predicted value $\hat{Y}_i$ for the ith unit in the sample, $i = 1, 2, \ldots, n$. (See the example on text page 21). Ideally, the fitted model would predict the observed Y_i exactly for all $i = 1, 2, \ldots, n$ but this rarely happens in practice. Thus, there is usually a difference between the observed Y_i and its predicted value $\hat{Y}_i$. This difference is called the *residual*. The ith residual, denoted e_i, is defined as:

$$e_i = Y_i - \hat{Y}_i$$

In the discussion below, we use SPSS to find the predicted values and the residuals for the sample data. We illustrate how to obtain graphs to perform graphical diagnostics discussed in the text. We then demonstrate how to produce regression diagnostics in terms of regression model residuals.

337

The Toluca Company Example Continued

Data File: ch01ta01.txt

We return to the Toluca Company example from Chapters 1 and 2 (text page 19, 46). See Chapter 0, "Working with SPSS," for instructions on opening the Toluca Company data file and renaming the variables *lotsize* and *workhrs*. After opening ch01ta01.txt, the first 5 lines in your SPSS *Data Editor* should look like SPSS Output 3.1.

SPSS Output 3.1

	lotsize	workhrs	var	var	var
1	80	399			
2	30	121			
3	50	221			
4	90	376			
5	70	361			

Diagnostics for Predictor Variable: The authors begin by discussing graphical methods that can be used as diagnostic tools to see if there are any outlying X values in the sample. This is important because a few outlying X values could have too much influence on estimates of the model parameters and other aspects of the regression analysis. If the influence of a few outlying X values is dampened or eliminated altogether, we sometimes get a drastically different regression analysis.

We use SPSS (Insert 3.1) to produce Figure 3.1 a-d shown on text page 101. A dot plot identical to text Figure 3.1a is not available in SPSS but a bar chart (SPSS Output 3.2) approximates that display of information. In the Toluca example, there are 25 runs represented in the data file. Text Figure 3.1b is a plot of *lotsize* against the run number but the data file does not contain the run number. SPSS has a system variable named *$casenum* that is simply a sequential count of the data file records. That is, *$casenum* equals 1 for the first record, 2 for the second record, etc. However, *$casenum* is a "dynamic" variable in that it can change values as the data file is restructured by various procedures such as sorting the file. Thus, we need to convert *$casenum* to a variable in the active Toluca *Data Editor* for use in subsequent analyses. This is accomplished by the *compute run=$casenum* command in Insert 3.1. The active *Data Editor* will now contain a variable named *run*, whose values are a sequential numbering of the data-lines from 1 to 25. (Here, we assume the original Toluca Company data-lines are in order by run number.) We can now produce text Figure 3.1b as shown in SPSS Output 3.2. Next, we use SPSS' Explore to produce a stem-and-leaf and box plots of *lotsize*. (SPSS Output 3.2)

INSERT 3.1	**INSERT 3.1 continued**
* text Figure 3.1a. ✔ Graph ✔ Bar ✔ Simple ✔ Define ✔ *lotsize* ✔ ►(to the Category axis) ✔ OK * text Figure 3.1b. ✔ File ✔ New ✔ Syntax * Type the following syntax. compute run=$casenum. execute. ✔ Run ✔ All	✔ Graph ✔ Line ✔ Simple ✔ Define ✔ *lotsize* ✔ ►(to the Variable) ✔ *run* ✔ ►(to the Category axis) ✔ OK * text Figure 3.1c and d. ✔ Analyze ✔ Descriptive Statistics ✔ Explore ✔ *lotsize* ✔ ►(to the Dependent List) ✔ OK

SPSS Output 3.2 a - d

```
LOTSIZE Stem-and-Leaf Plot

 Frequency    Stem &  Leaf

      .00       0 .
     4.00       0 .  2333
     5.00       0 .  44555
     4.00       0 .  6777
     7.00       0 .  8889999
     4.00       1 .  0011
     1.00       1 .  2

 Stem width:   100
 Each leaf:        1 case(s)
```

Diagnostics for Residuals: In text Section 3.3, the authors present informal diagnostic plots of *residuals*. Note that the authors make the distinction between *studentized* and *semistudentized* residuals. The authors point out that "both semistudentized residuals and studentized residuals can be very helpful in identifying outlying observations." SPSS does not have an option to produce semistudentized residuals but it does produce studentized residuals. Studentized residuals are probably the more important of the two types of residuals. Therefore, we use studentized residuals in place of semistudentized residuals to present solutions to text chapter examples.

As before, we perform a regression analysis using the model:

$$workhrs = \beta_0 + \beta_1(lotsize) + \varepsilon$$

In Insert 3.2, we specify this regression model and request that unstandardized residuals be saved to the active *Data Editor*. By default the residuals are saved as *res_1*. To produce text Figures 3.2 a, b, and c, simply use the syntax in Insert 3.1 above, replacing *lotsize* with *res_1*. To produce text Figure 3.2d, request a normality plot from the Explore dialogue box. (Insert 3.2) Notice that the standard SPSS output has the observed residual values on the *x*-axis, opposite of text Figure 3.2d. Using SPSS *Chart Editor*, we can switch the axis positions so the plot appears as text Figure 3.2d as shown in SPSS Output 3.3. The text presents numerous other diagnostic plots. For brevity, we do not present these plots but you should be able to produce them easily by generalizing the syntax shown in Inserts 3.1 and 3.2.

INSERT 3.2	**INSERT 3.2 continued**
✔ Analyze	* text Figure 3.1d.
✔ Regression	✔ Analyze
✔ Linear	✔ Descriptive Statistics
✔ *workhrs*	✔ Explore
✔ ▶ (to the Dependent box)	✔ *res_1*
✔ *lotsize*	✔ ▶ (to the Dependent List)
✔ ▶ (to the Independent box)	✔ Plots
✔ Save	✔ Normality plots with tests
✔ Unstandardized (Residual Values)	✔ Continue
✔ Continue	✔ OK
✔ OK	* Double click the chart you wish to edit.
	✔ Series
	✔ Displayed
	* Use the Simple Scatterplot Displayed Data dialogue.
	* to reverse the plot axises.
	✔ OK
	* Close the Chart Editor.

SPSS Output 3.3

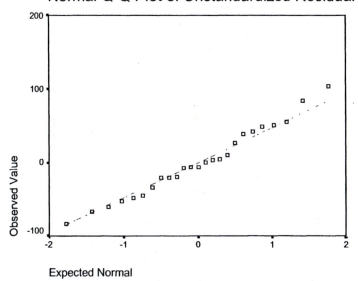

Normal Q-Q Plot of Unstandardized Residual

Correlation Test for Normality: On text page 111, the authors calculate the coefficient of correlation between the ordered residuals and their expected value under normality for the Toluca Company Example. The expected value under normality of the kth smallest observation from a sample of size n is given by:

$$\sqrt{MSE}\left[z\left(\frac{k-0.375}{n+0.25}\right)\right]$$

The first step in obtaining the expected value of the ordered residuals under normality is to calculate $(k - 0.375)/(n + 0.25)$. The syntax for this is shown in Insert 3.3. In the Toluca Company example, $n = 25$ and k is the rank of the ordered residuals. We rank the saved residuals (*res_1*) using the Rank Case function. SPSS creates another new variable, *rres_1*, that is the rank based on the value of *res_1*, the unstandardized residual based on a model with *lotsize* as the predictor variable. Thus, $(k - 0.375)/(n + 0.25)$ becomes $(rres\_1 - 0.375)/(25 + 0.25)$. This quantity represents the cumulative probability ($0 \leq$ cumulative probability ≤ 1.0) of the standard normal distribution. We now obtain a standard score (z) associated with the cumulative probability calculated above. In SPSS, the Probit function is an *inverse distribution function*. It takes the form *Probit*(p), where p = cumulative probability. For instance, if cumulative probability = 0.50 [*Probit*(0.50)] then $z = 0$. If cumulative probability = 0.8413 (*Probit*(0.8413)) then $z = +1$. Thus, to obtain z we use *Probit* $((rres\_1 - 0.375)/(25 + 0.25))$. Finally, we multiply this quantity by the square root of the mean squared error, $MSE = 2383.716$ of the first order model (Chapter 2 – SPSS Output 2.2). From the above, we compute the expected value as:

$$ev = sqrt(2383.716) * Probit ((rres\_1 - 0.375)/(25 + 0.25)).$$

341

We can now obtain the coefficient of correlation between the residual (*res_1*) and the expected value under normality (*ev*). The result of the correlation between *ev* and *res_1* is 0.992 and is within rounding error of the correlation (0.991) reported on text page 115.

INSERT 3.3

- ✔ Analyze
- ✔ Regression
- ✔ Linear
- ✔ *workhrs*
- ✔ ▶ (to the Dependent box)
- ✔ *lotsize*
- ✔ ▶ (to the Independent box)
- ✔ Save
- ✔ Unstandardized (Residual Values)
- ✔ Continue
- ✔ OK
- ✔ Transform
- ✔ Rank Cases
- ✔ *res_1*
- ✔ ▶ (to the Variables box)
- ✔ *OK*

- ✔ Transform
- ✔ Compute
- * Type "ev" in Target Variable box
- * Scroll down the list of functions
- ✔ SQRT(numexpr)
- ✔ ▲
- Type "2383.716"
- ✔ to the right of the closing) in the numeric expression
- ✔ *
- Scroll through the list of functions
- ✔ PROBIT(prob)
- ✔ ▲
- * Type "("
- ✔ *rres_1*
- ✔ ▶
- Type "-.375)/(25+.25)"
- ✔ OK

- ✔ Analyze
- ✔ Correlate
- ✔ Bivariate
- ✔ *ev*
- ✔ ▶
- ✔ *res_1*
- ✔ ▶
- ✔ OK

Note that the Transform>Compute (bracketed) portion of Insert 3.3 is cumbersome and prone to error. As we discussed in Chapter 0, "Working with SPSS," it is sometimes easier to work in a *Syntax Editor* window than to use a dialogue box (point-and-click). In doing so, we can type the formula for *ev* in a *Syntax Editor* in lieu of using a dialogue box. This is shown in Insert 3.4. Thus, the steps setoff with a single bracket in Insert 3.3 can be replaced by the steps in Insert 3.4. Both approaches accomplish the same outcome but the latter is much simpler.

INSERT 3.4

- ✔ File
- ✔ New
- ✔ Syntax

compute *ev* = sqrt(2383.716) * Probit((*rres_1* - .375)/(25 + .25)).
execute.

- ✔ Run
- ✔ All

Test for Constancy of Error Variance - Brown-Forsythe: The authors present two formal tests for constancy of error variance. We begin with the *Brown-Forsythe* test using the Toluca Company example (text page 117). For simplicity, we have divided the process into steps:

- Step 1: (Insert 3.5) Divide the 25 data-lines into two subsets (*group*): those with *lotsize* between 20 and 70 (*lotsize*<=70) and those with *lotsize* > 70. Insert 3.5 contains syntax for using the Recode procedure and for using the If – Then procedure. Both procedures yield the same result.
- Step 2: Use *Explore* to obtain the median residual values $\tilde{e}_1$ (group 1) = −19.87 and $\tilde{e}_2$ (group 2) = −2.68.
- Step 3: Find *absdevmd*, the absolute value (*abs*) of the residual minus the median residual value for the respective group, d_{i1} and d_{i2}.
- Step 4: Find the means of *absdevmd* for the two groups, $\bar{d}_1 = 44.81$ and $\bar{d}_2 = 28.4$.
- Step 5: Find *sqrdev*, the square of *absdevmd* minus the respective group mean of *absdevmd*.
- Step 6: Find the sum of *sqrdev* for the two groups, $\sum(d_{i1} - \bar{d}_1)^2 = 12{,}567.86$ and $\sum(d_{i2} - \bar{d}_2)^2 = 9{,}621.54$.

We now have the required values to calculate the *Brown-Forsythe* statistic:

$$s^2 = \frac{12{,}567.86 + 9{,}621.54}{25 - 2} = 964.75$$

$$s = \sqrt{964.75} = 31.06$$

$$t_{BF}^* = \frac{44.81 - 28.4}{31.06\sqrt{\dfrac{1}{13} + \dfrac{1}{12}}} = 1.319$$

INSERT 3.5	**INSERT 3.5 continued**

* Step 1.
✔ File
✔ New
✔ Syntax
recode lotsize (0 thru 70=1) (else=2) into group .
execute .
* OR.
if (lotsize le 70)group=1.
if (lotsize gt 70)group=2.
execute.
✔ Run
✔ All
 	
* Step 2.
✔ Analyze
✔ Descriptive Statistics
✔ Explore
✔ *res_1*
✔ ▶(to the Dependent List)
✔ *group*
✔ ▶(to the Factor List)
✔ OK
 	
*Step 3.
✔ File
✔ New
✔ Syntax
* Type the following syntax.
if (group=1) absdevmd=abs(res_1-(-19.88)).
if (group=2) absdevmd=abs(res_1-(-2.68)).
execute.
✔ Run
✔ All
	* Step 4.
	✔ Analyze
	✔ Descriptive Statistics
	✔ Explore
	✔ *absdevmd*
	✔ ▶(to the Dependent List)
	✔ *group*
	✔ ▶(to the Factor List)
	✔ OK
	
	* Step 5.
	✔ File
	✔ New
	✔ Syntax
	* Type the following syntax.
	if (group=1) sqrdev=(absdevmd-44.81)**2.
	if (group=2) sqrdev=(absdevmd-29.45)**2.
	execute.
	✔ Run
	✔ All
	
	* Step 6.
	✔ Analyze
	✔ Compare Means
	✔ Means
	✔ *sqrdev*
	✔ ▶(to the Dependent List)
	✔ *group*
	✔ ▶(to the Independent List)
	✔ Options
	✔ Sum
	✔ ▶(to the Cell Statistics)
	✔ Continue
	✔ OK

Test for Constancy of Error Variance - Breusch-Pagan Test: The second Test for *Constancy of Error Variance* considered by the authors is the *Breusch-Pagan Test* (text page 118). To compute the *Breusch-Pagan* test we first save the residual values of the following model as shown in Insert 3.6:

$$workhrs = \beta_0 + \beta_1(lotsize) + \varepsilon$$

The residual values are saved in the active *Data Editor* as *res_1*. If we have *res_1* saved from a previous run, we do not need to resave the residuals. We now square *res_1* and place the result in a variable named *ressqr* (e^2). The last step is to regress *ressqr* against *lotsize* in the usual manner. The last regression procedure in Insert 3.6 results in SPSS Output 3.4 and contains SSR*=7,896,128. SSE (54,825.459) is shown in SPSS Output 3.5 and results from the first regression run in Insert 3.6. We now can find:

$$X_{BP}^2 = \frac{SSR^*}{2} \div \left(\frac{SSE}{n}\right)^2$$

where SSR^* from regressing e^2 (*ressqr*) on X and SSE from regressing Y on X:

$$X_{BP}^2 = \frac{7,896,128}{2} \div \left(\frac{54,825}{25}\right)^2 = 0.821$$

INSERT 3.6

- ✔ Analyze
- ✔ Regression
- ✔ Linear
- ✔ *workhrs*
- ✔ ▶ (to the Dependent box)
- ✔ *lotsize*
- ✔ ▶ (to the Independent box)
- ✔ Save
- ✔ Unstandardized (Residual Values)
- ✔ Continue
- ✔ OK

- ✔ File
- ✔ New
- ✔ Syntax
* Type the following syntax.
compute *ressqr=res_1**2*.
execute.
- ✔ Run
- ✔ All

- ✔ Analyze
- ✔ Regression
- ✔ Linear
- ✔ *ressqr*
- ✔ ▶ (to the Dependent List)
- ✔ *lotsize*
- ✔ ▶ (to the Independent List)
- ✔ OK

ANOVA[b]

Model		Sum of Squares	df	Mean Square	F	Sig.
1	Regression	7896142	1	7896141.961	1.091	.307[a]
	Residual	1.66E+08	23	7234604.179		
	Total	1.74E+08	24			

a. Predictors: (Constant), LOTSIZE

b. Dependent Variable: RESSQR

SPSS Output 3.5

ANOVA[b]

Model		Sum of Squares	df	Mean Square	F	Sig.
1	Regression	252377.6	1	252377.581	105.876	.000[a]
	Residual	54825.459	23	2383.716		
	Total	307203.0	24			

a. Predictors: (Constant), LOTSIZE

b. Dependent Variable: WORKHRS

The Bank Example

Data File: ch03ta04.txt

F **Test for Lack of Fit**: On text page 119, the authors present a formal test for determining if the regression function adequately fits the data. In an experiment involving 12 branch offices of a commercial bank, gifts were offered for customers who opened money market accounts. The gift was proportional to the minimum deposit and there were 6 levels of minimum deposit used in the experiment. The researchers studied the relationship between the minimum deposit and associated gift (*mindep*) and the number of new accounts (*newaccts*) opened at each of the 12 branches. After opening the Bank Example data (Table 3.4, text page 120), the first five lines of the *Data Editor* should look like SPSS Output 3.6.

To generate the Lack of Fit F* presented on text page 124, we switch to SPSS' *General Linear Model* (*GLM*) procedure. We demonstrate two ways of obtaining the lack of fit test in SPSS. The first is a longer method and is presented to parallel the solution presented in the text. We begin by fitting the full model to the data. This requires that we create a new variable, *J*. As noted in Insert 3.7, $j = 1$ if $X_1 = 75$, $j = 2$ if $X_2 = 100$ and so on. We now regress *Y* (*newaccts*) on *X* (*mindep*) and *J*. This is accomplished by the syntax shown in Insert 3.7 – Method 1. Note that we enter *J* as a fixed factor. Thus, *J* identifies 6 discrete classifications based on the values of *X*.

SPSS Output 3.6

```
lof table 3.4.sav - SPSS Data Editor
File  Edit  View  Data  Transform  Analyze  Graphs  Utilities  W
```

11 : newaccts		136		
	mindep	newaccts	var	var
1	125 00	160 00		
2	100 00	112 00		
3	200 00	124 00		
4	75 00	28 00		
5	150 00	152 00		

Insert 3.7 - Method 1 produces SPSS Output 3.7a. Notice that $SSE = 1148.0$ and from text equation 3.16, $SSE(F) = SSPE$; therefore, $SSPE = 1148.0$. From text equation 3.24, we see that $SSLF = SSE(R) - SSPE$. If we were to regress *newaccts* on *mindep*, (reduced model) we would find that $SSE(R) = 14{,}741.6$. This is accomplished by the syntax shown in Insert 3.7 – Method 2, and the results are shown in SPSS Output 3.7b. Thus, $SSLF = 14{,}741.6 - 1148 = 13{,}593.6$. Notice, however, that this quantity is given in SPSS Output 3.7a under *Type III Sum of Squares* for J. Thus, regressing Y on X and J in SPSS' General Linear Model procedure gives us the quantities to find:

$$F^* = \frac{SSLF}{c-2} \div \frac{SSPE}{n-c}$$

or

$$F^* = \frac{13{,}593.6}{4} \div \frac{1{,}148}{5} = 14.8$$

(see text page 124). Now that we understand the computation of the lack of fit test, we note that SPSS has an easy way to request the lack of fit test. We simply use the *Lack of Fit* option within SPSS' *GLM* to perform the same test. Insert 3.7 - Method 2 contains the necessary steps to produce SPSS Output 3.7b and we do so without creating J. Again, notice the lack of fit $F = 14.8$, consistent with text page 124.

SPSS Output 3.7a

Tests of Between-Subjects Effects

Dependent Variable: NEWACCTS

Source	Type III Sum of Squares	df	Mean Square	F	Sig.
Corrected Model	18734.909[a]	5	3746.982	16.320	.004
Intercept	2729.288	1	2729.288	11.887	.018
MINDEP	.000	0	.	.	.
J	13593.571	4	3398.393	14.801	.006
Error	1148.000	5	229.600		
Total	170696.000	11			
Corrected Total	19882.909	10			

a. R Squared = .942 (Adjusted R Squared = .885)

347

INSERT 3.7	INSERT 3.7 continued

* Full Model.
✔ File
✔ New
✔ Syntax
* Type the following.
if (mindep = 75)j=1.
if (mindep = 100)j=2.
if (mindep = 125)j=3.
if (mindep = 150)j=4.
if (mindep = 175)j=5.
if (mindep = 200)j=6.
execute.
✔ Run
✔ All

* Method 1.
✔ Analyze
✔ General Linear Model
✔ Univariate
✔ *newaccts*
✔ ► (to the Dependent box)

✔ *j*
✔ ► (to the Fixed factors)
✔ *mindep*
✔ ► (to the Covariate box)
✔ OK

* Method 2.
✔ Analyze
✔ General Linear Model
✔ Univariate
✔ *newaccts*
✔ ► (to the Dependent box)
✔ *mindep*
✔ ► (to the Covariate box)
✔ Options
✔ Lack of Fit
✔ Continue
✔ OK

SPSS Output 3.7b

Tests of Between-Subjects Effects

Dependent Variable: NEWACCTS

Source	Type III Sum of Squares	df	Mean Square	F	Sig.
Corrected Model	5141.338[a]	1	5141.338	3.139	.110
Intercept	2714.916	1	2714.916	1.658	.230
MINDEP	5141.338	1	5141.338	3.139	.110
Error	14741.571	9	1637.952		
Total	170696.000	11			
Corrected Total	19882.909	10			

a. R Squared = .259 (Adjusted R Squared = .176)

Lack of Fit Tests

Dependent Variable: NEWACCTS

Source	Sum of Squares	df	Mean Square	F	Sig.
Lack of Fit	13593.571	4	3398.393	14.801	.006
Pure Error	1148.000	5	229.600		

Box-Cox Transformations: SPSS does not have a readily available option to generate *Box-Cox transformations* (text page 134). Insert 3.8 contains the necessary syntax in matrix language to produce Table 3.9 and Figure 3.17, text page 136. (SPSS matrix language will be covered in

Chapter 5.) The syntax requires the data file presented in Table 3.8, text page 133, to be open in the active *Data Editor* and the variables to be named *age*, *plasma*, and *logy*. Note that the syntax in Insert 3.8 will overwrite the active *Data Editor*; save the contents of the *Data Editor* as needed. The first two "get statements" set vectors **x** and **y** equal to *age* and *plasma*, respectively. This procedure uses a range of λ values starting at λ (*start*) = -2.3 and incrementing (*incremen*) by a value of 0.1 for 34 iterations (*noiter*). A plot of SSE as a function of λ is shown in SPSS Output 3.8. The start, increment, and iterations values can be varied to specify choices suitable for different data sets.

INSERT 3.8

```
✔ File
✔ New
✔ Syntax
matrix.
get x / variables = age.
get y / variables = plasma.

compute start = -2.3.
compute noiter = 34.
compute incremen = 0.1.

compute n=nrow(y).
compute x = {make(n,1,1),x}.
compute hat = x*inv(t(x)*x)*t(x).
compute lambda = {make(noiter,1,1)}.
compute lambda(1,1)=start.
loop i = 2 to noiter.
  compute lambda(i,1)=lambda(i-1,1) + incremen.
end loop.
  compute sse={make(noiter,1,0)}.
loop i = 1 to noiter.
  compute lamb = lambda(i).
  compute k2 = exp((1/n)&*({make(1,n,1)}*ln(y))).
  compute k1 = 1/(lamb*k2**(lamb-1)).
  do if (lamb > -.00000001 and lamb < .00000001).
  compute w=k2*ln(y).
  else.
  compute w = k1*( y&**lamb-{make(n,1,1)}).
  end if.
  compute e=(ident(n) - hat)*w.
  compute sse(i)=t(e)*e.
end loop.
compute newm={lambda,sse}.
  print newm.
  save newm / outfile=*.
end matrix.
graph
 /scatterplot(bivar)=col1 with col2
 /missing=listwise
 /title= 'Plot of Box-Cox text Figure 3.17'.
 execute.
✔ Run
✔ All
```

SPSS Output 3.8

Plot of Box-Cox Text Figure 3 17

Exploration of Shape of Regression Function – Lowess Method: The authors state that "the name *lowess* stands for locally weighted regression scatter plot smoothing." The lowess procedure divides the independent variables into groups or *local neighborhoods* and then fits a regression model to each local neighborhood of data. The procedure uses weighted least squares to fit regression models for each neighborhood with the weights being a function of the distance of the *X*'s for a given subject in a neighborhood from the center of the neighborhood. The final fitted model is a blending of these fitted models in each neighborhood. The proportion of the total number of observations to be included in each neighborhood (*percent of points to fit*) can be specified; the default value is 50%. SPSS also allows us to specify the *number of iterations*; the default value is 3. We can adjust the size of successive neighborhoods and iterations and examine a plot of the fitted loess curves to choose a reasonable fitting smooth curve.

In Insert 3.9, we present SPSS syntax to produce Figure 3.19a, text page 140. Using the Toluca Company example, we produce a scatter plot of *lotsize* and *workhrs*. In the *Chart Editor* we then request the lowess smoothed curve as shown in SPSS Output 3.9. SPSS does not produce the lowess curve and confidence bands on the same scatter plot.

```
                              INSERT 3.9

   ✔ Graphs
   ✔ Scatter
   ✔ Simple
   ✔ Define
   ✔ lotsize
   ✔ ▶ (to the X axis)
   ✔ workhrs
   ✔ ▶ (to the Y axis)
   ✔ OK
   * To draw the regression line as shown in text Figure 1.10(b),.
   * double click on the graph in the SPSS Viewer.  This brings up a.
   * SPSS Chart Editor window. For Release 12.0 and higher see.
   * Insert 1.1.
   ✔ Chart
   ✔ Options
   ✔ Total (under Fit Line)
   ✔ Fit Options
   ✔ Lowess
   ✔ Continue
   ✔ OK
   * Close the Chart Editor.
```

SPSS Output 3.9

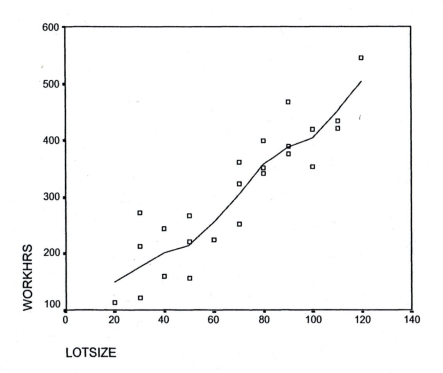

Simultaneous Inferences and Other Topics in Regression Analysis

The level of significance of a statistical test is the probability the test rejects the null hypothesis given that the null hypothesis is true. This probability is usually denoted α and is referred to as the probability of a Type I error. These concepts are in the context of a single application of the test. If the test is applied to multiple hypotheses we often want to make a simultaneous or joint statement about the probability of a Type I error given that all the hypotheses being tested are true. We call a set of tests under consideration a family of tests. If each test in a family of g tests is tested at level of significance α, the probability of making one or more Type I errors if all g hypotheses are true is α^* where:

$$\alpha^* \leq 1 - (1-\alpha)^g$$

This inequality is a form of the Bonferroni Equality. In this statement, equality holds if the tests are mutually independent. It is apparent that as g increases α^* approaches 1 and, unless we take corrective action, the probability is close to one that we falsely reject at least one hypothesis even if they are all true. The right side of the statement is approximately equal to $g\alpha$ if α is small; i.e.,

$$1 - (1-\alpha)^g \approx g\alpha$$

Therefore, if we perform each of g tests at the α/g level we get:

$$1 - \left(1 - \frac{\alpha}{g}\right)^g \approx \alpha$$

This approach to multiple testing is referred to as the Bonferroni method or procedure. Using the Bonferroni procedure, we perform each of g tests at the α/g level and are assured that the probability is $\leq \alpha$ of making one or more Type I errors if all g hypotheses are true. For example, if we perform 4 tests and use the $0.05/4 = 0.0125$ level of significance for each test, the probability we falsely reject one or more of the 4 corresponding hypotheses is less than or equal to 0.05.

If we are conducting a single two-sided test, we find critical values from the t-distribution by finding $t(1- \alpha / 2; df)$ where df is the degrees of freedom of the test. Similarly, if we are conducting g two-sided multiple tests, we find critical values from the t-distribution by finding $t(1- \alpha / (2g); df)$ where df is the degrees of freedom of the test.

Analogous to multiple testing, we often want to set g confidence intervals with the knowledge that the confidence level is $\geq 100(1 - \alpha)$ percent that all g intervals bracket their respective objective. In the simple linear regression model, simultaneous (Bonferroni) confidence limits for estimating β_0 and β_1 are (equation 4.3, text page 156):

$$b_0 \pm Bs\{b_0\}$$

$$b_1 \pm Bs\{b_1\}$$

where $B = t(1 - \alpha/4; n - 2)$. Here $g = 2$ so that $\alpha/(2g) = \alpha/4$.

Section 4.2, text page 157, discusses simultaneous confidence intervals for the mean responses at different values of X. In addition to the Bonferroni procedure, the authors discuss the *Working-Hotelling* procedure. Section 4.3 discusses simultaneous prediction intervals for new observations. Section 4.4 presents the simple model for regression through the origin while Section 4.5 discusses the effects of measurement errors while Section 4.6 presents inverse predictions.

More on The Toluca Company Example

Data File: ch01ta01.txt

We return to the Toluca Company example from Chapters 1, 2 and 3 (text page 19, 46, 156). See Chapter 0, "Working with SPSS," for instructions on opening the Toluca Company data file and renaming the variables *lotsize* and *workhrs*. After opening ch01ta01.dat, the first 5 lines in your SPSS *Data Editor* should look like SPSS Output 4.1.

SPSS Output 4.1

	lotsize	workhrs	var	var	var
1	80	399			
2	30	121			
3	50	221			
4	90	376			
5	70	361			

Bonferroni Joint Confidence Intervals for β_0 and β_1: On text page 156, the Toluca Company wants to estimate the 90 percent family confidence intervals for β_0 and β_1. To estimate the 90 percent confidence intervals for β_0 and β_1, the text reports $B = t(1 - 0.10/4; 23) = t(0.975; 23) =$

2.069. The *t*-value is actually based on $(1 - \alpha/(2g))$ where g is the number of joint intervals to be estimated. In the present example, we are estimating joint confidence intervals for β_0 and β_1 ($g=2$), so $B = t(1- 0.10/(2*2); 23) = t(1 - 0.10/4; 23) = t(0.975; 23)$. Thus, we use SPSS' *inverse distribution function* to find $B = IDF.T(0.975, 23) = 2.068$. From SPSS Output 1.3, we know b_0, $s\{b_0\}$, b_1, and $s\{b_1\}$. In Insert 4.1 we use equation 4.3, text page 156, and the Bonferroni procedure for developing joint confidence intervals for b_0 (*b0lo* and *b0hi*) and b_1 (*b1lo* and *b1hi*).

INSERT 4.1

```
✔ File
✔ New
✔ Syntax
* Type the following syntax.
compute b=idf.t(.975,23).
compute b0lo=62.37-(b*26.18).
compute b0hi=62.37+(b*26.18).
compute b1lo=3.5702-(b*.3470).
compute b1hi=3.5702+(b*.3470).
execute.
✔ Run
✔ All
```

Simultaneous Estimation of Mean Responses: On text page 158, the Toluca Company wants to estimate the mean number of work hours required to produce lots of 30, 65, and 100 units where the family confidence coefficient is 0.90. In Chapter 2 we presented the steps to find the confidence interval for $E\{Y_h\}$ when lot size (X_h) = 65 units and the confidence band for the entire regression line. We repeat these steps here with fewer notations and more emphasis on SPSS computational statements.

a. Working-Hotelling Procedure: We first find the 90 percent confidence interval for work hours when lot size (X_h) = 65 units. We use the Working-Hotelling $1-\alpha$ band (text equations 2.40, 2.40a, 2.30) to establish boundary values for (X_h) = 65 units:

$$\hat{Y}_h \pm Ws\{\hat{Y}_h\}$$

where

$$W^2 = 2 F(1- \alpha; 2, n-2)$$

and

$$s^2\{\hat{Y}_h\} = MSE\left[\frac{1}{n} + \frac{(X_h - \bar{X})^2}{\sum(X_i - \bar{X})^2}\right]$$

In Insert 4.2 – Method 1, we first find the *F*-value (*fvalue*) associated with $\alpha = 0.90$ and 2, 23 degrees of freedom. We then find $W = \sqrt{2 * fvalue}$. Next, we find $\hat{Y}_h$ (*yhat*) when $X_h = 65$ units using previously found parameter estimates (SPSS Output 1.3), $b_0 = 62.366$ and $b_1 = 3.570$. We

354

find $s\{\hat{Y}_h\}$ (*sdyhat*), the square root of text equation 2.30. Finally, we compute $\hat{Y}_h \pm Ws\{\hat{Y}_h\}$ placing the lower boundary of the confidence interval in a variable named *bandlo* and the upper boundary of the confidence interval in a variable named *bandhi*. Execution of Insert 4.2 will place in the *Data Editor* the 90 percent confidence interval for *workhrs* when $X_h = 65$ units. After the syntax is working properly, as in Insert 4.2 – Method 1, we can rewrite the syntax in a more compact form if desired. Insert 4.2 Method 1 can be reduced to Method 2.

To find the confidence intervals for $X_h = 30$ and $X_h = 100$, simply change the computation of *yhat* and *sdyhat* in Insert 4.2 – Method 1 to reflect 30 or 100 units instead of 65 (bolded) units. Using this method, old values for *bandlo* and *bandhi* will be overwritten each time you change the value of X_h. If this is undesirable, the syntax in Insert 4.3 will find the 90 percent confidence interval for each value of X_h. These intervals will be placed in unique variables, i.e., *bandlo30*, *bandhi30*, *bandlo65*, *bandhi65*, *bandlo00*, and *bandhi00*.

INSERT 4.2

```
* Method 1.
✔ File
✔ New
✔ Syntax
* Type the following syntax.
compute fvalue=idf.f(.9,2,23).
compute w=sqrt(2*fvalue).
compute yhat=62.366+(3.570*65).
compute sdyhat=sqrt(2383.716*((1/25)+((65-70)**2/19800))).
compute bandlo=yhat-(w*sdyhat).
compute bandhi=yhat+(w*sdyhat).
execute.
✔ Run
✔ All
```

INSERT 4.2 continued

```
* Method 2.
✔ File
✔ New
✔ Syntax
* Type the following syntax.
compute fvalue=idf.f(.9,2,23).
compute w=sqrt(2*fvalue).
compute bandlo=(62.366+(3.570*65))-(sqrt(2*idf.f(.9,2,23))*sqrt(2383.716*((1/25)+((65-70)**2/19800)))).
compute bandhi=(62.366+(3.570*65))+(sqrt(2*idf.f(.9,2,23))*sqrt(2383.716*((1/25)+((65-70)**2/19800)))).
execute.
✔ Run
✔ All
```

```
                        INSERT 4.3
  ✔ File
  ✔ New
  ✔ Syntax
* Type the following syntax.
compute fvalue=idf.f(.9,2,23).
compute w=sqrt(2*fvalue).
compute yhat30=62.366+(3.570*30).
compute sdyhat30=sqrt(2383.716*((1/25)+((30-70)**2/19800))).
compute bandlo30=yhat30-(w*sdyhat30).
compute bandhi30=yhat30+(w*sdyhat30).
compute yhat65=62.366+(3.570*65).
compute sdyhat65=sqrt(2383.716*((1/25)+((65-70)**2/19800))).
compute bandlo65=yhat65-(w*sdyhat65).
compute bandhi65=yhat65+(w*sdyhat65).
compute yhat100=62.366+(3.570*100).
compute sdyhat00=sqrt(2383.716*((1/25)+((100-70)**2/19800))).
compute bandlo00=yhat100-(w*sdyhat00).
compute bandhi00=yhat100+(w*sdyhat00).
execute.
  ✔ Run
  ✔ All
```

b. Bonferroni Procedure: On text page 159, the authors use data from the Toluca Company example and the Bonferroni Procedure to estimate the mean number of work hours required to produce lots of 30, 65, and 100 units where the family confidence coefficient is 0.90. The Bonferroni confidence limits are:

$$\hat{Y}_h \pm Bs\{\hat{Y}_h\}$$

where:

$$B = t(1 - \alpha/2g; n-2)$$

and g is the number of joint confidence intervals to be estimated. In this example, there are three intervals in the family. Thus, $B = t(1 - 0.10/(2*3); 23) = t(1 - 0.10/6; 23) = t(1 - 0.01666; 23) = t(0.9833, 23)$. We can use the *IDF.T* function as before to find $B = idf.t(0.98333, 23) = 2.263$. Computation of $s\{\hat{Y}_h\}$ is the same as for the Working-Hotelling procedure above including Insert 4.2. Thus, to use the Bonferroni Procedure to find the 90 percent confidence interval for work hours when $X_h = 65$ units, we use text equations 4.7 and 4.7a as in Insert 4.4 to find the upper (*bandhi*) and lower (*bandlo*) confidence limits. Confidence limits for $X_h = 30$ and $X_h = 100$ can be generalized from Inserts 4.2 and 4.3.

```
                          INSERT 4.4

  ✔ File
  ✔ New
  ✔ Syntax
* Type the following syntax.
compute b=idf.t(.98333,23).
compute yhat=62.366+(3.570*65).
compute sdyhat=sqrt(2383.716*((1/25)+((65-70)**2/19800))).
compute bandlo=yhat-(b*sdyhat).
compute bandhi=yhat+(b*sdyhat).
execute.
  ✔ Run
  ✔ All
```

Prediction Intervals for New Observations: The Toluca Company now wants to predict the required work hours for lots of 80 and 100 units. The researchers first obtained S and B (text page160) to determine which prediction interval was smaller. Insert 4.5 uses the *IDF.T* and *IDF.F inverse distribution functions* to find $S = 2.616$ (equation 4.8a, text page 160) and $B = 2.398$ (equation 4.9a, text page 160). Because the Bonferroni procedure produces the tighter limits, we use B to establish the 95% family coefficients.

We now calculate $\hat{Y}_h$ for 80 (*yhat80*) and 100 (*yhat100*) units. We then use equation 2.38a, text page 59, to find $s\{pred\}$ for 80 (*sdpre80*) and 100 (*sdpre00*) units. Finally, we use equation 4.9, text page 160, to find the lower and upper 95% confidence limits for 80 (*bandlo80* and *bandhi80*, respectively) and 100 (*bandlo00* and *bandhi00*, respectively) units.

```
                          INSERT 4.5

  ✔ File
  ✔ New
  ✔ Syntax
compute s=sqrt(2*idf.f(.95,2,23)).
compute b=idf.t(1-(.05/(2*2)),23).
compute yhat80=62.366+(3.570*80).
compute sdpre80=sqrt(2383.716*(1+(1/25)+((80-70)**2/19800))).
compute bandlo80=yhat80-(b*sdpre80).
compute bandhi80=yhat80+(b*sdpre80).
compute yhat100=62.366+(3.570*100).
compute sdpre00=sqrt(2383.716*(1+(1/25)+((100-70)**2/19800))).
compute bandlo00=yhat100-(b*sdpre00).
compute bandhi00=yhat100+(b*sdpre00).
execute.
  ✔ Run
  ✔ All
```

Inverse Predictions: The authors present an example of inverse prediction on text page 168. We do not have access to the source data file, however, and will use the Toluca Company for illustration. Suppose the auditing department of the Toluca Company's corporate home office requested that lot size $\hat{X}_{h(new)}$ be estimated with a 95% confidence interval when the work hours for a run is known to be $Y_{h(new)} = 300$. Although the accountants at the Toluca Company failed to appreciate the need for such a calculation, they complied with the request.

In Insert 4.6 we first find $\hat{X}_{h(new)} = Y_{h(new)} - 62.366 / 3.570 = 66.56$ using equation 4.31, text page 168, and parameter estimates from SPSS Output 1.3. For equation 4.32, text page 169, we find t using $IDF.T(1-0.05/2, 23) = 2.07$ and place the result in *tvalue*. Using equation 4.32a, text page 169, we find $s^2\{predX\}$ (*sdprex*) = 13.95. Finally, we use text equation 4.32 to find:

$$\hat{X}_{h(new)} \pm t(1-\alpha/2;\ n-2)s\{predX\}$$

$$66.56 \pm 2.07*13.95$$

$$37.70 < \hat{X}_{h(new)} < 95.42$$

The auditors at corporate the home office conclude with 95% confidence that the number of hours required to produce the lot size of 300 units is between 37.70 and 95.42 hours. The auditors calculate the error to be 66.56/((95.42-37.70)/2) or approximately $\pm 43\%$.

INSERT 4.6

✔ File
✔ New
✔ Syntax
* Inverse prediction.
compute xhnew=(300-62.366)/3.570.
compute tvalue=IDF.T(1-.05/2,23).
compute sdprex=sqrt((2383.716/(3.570**2)*(1+(1/25)+((**xhnew**-70)**2/19800)))).
compute prexlo=xhnew-(tvalue*sdprex).
compute prexhi=xhnew+(tvalue*sdprex).
execute.
✔ Run
✔ All

The Charles Plumbing Supplies Example

Data File: ch04ta02.txt

Regression through the Origin: From text page 162, the Charles Plumbing Supplies Company studied the relationship between the total labor costs (Y) and the number of work units performed (X). The authors use data from this example to illustrate fitting a regression model that has no intercept term and thus the fitted line passes through the origin. The explicit regression model used for this purpose is given in equation 4.10, page 161 of the text. After opening ch04ta02.txt and renaming the variables X and Y, the first 5 lines in the *Data Editor* should appear as SPSS Output 4.2. To perform regression through the origin, simply uncheck the Include Constant in Equation option (Insert 4.6). This results in SPSS Output 4.3 and is consistent with text pages 163-164.

SPSS Output 4.2

Untitled - SPSS Data Editor

File Edit View Data Transform Analyze Graphs Utilities Window Help

1 : x   20

	x	y	var	var	var
1	20.00	114.00			
2	196.00	921.00			
3	115.00	560.00			
4	50.00	245.00			
5	122.00	575.00			

INSERT 4.6

- ✔ Analyze
- ✔ Regression
- ✔ Linear
- ✔ *y*
- ✔ ► (to the Dependent box)
- ✔ *x*
- ✔ ► (to the Independent box)
- ✔ Options
- ✔ Include Constant in Equation * Uncheck the box.
- ✔ Continue
- ✔ Statistics
- ✔ Confidence Intervals (under Regression coefficients)
- ✔ Continue
- ✔ OK

SPSS Output 4.3

ANOVA[c,d]

Model		Sum of Squares	df	Mean Square	F	Sig.
1	Regression	4191980	1	4191980.341	18762.480	.000[a]
	Residual	2457.659	11	223.424		
	Total	4194438[b]	12			

a. Predictors: V1

b. This total sum of squares is not corrected for the constant because the constant is zero for regression through the origin.

c. Dependent Variable: V2

d. Linear Regression through the Origin

Coefficients[a,b]

		Unstandardized Coefficients		Standardized Coefficients			95% Confidence Interval for B	
		B	Std. Error	Beta	t	Sig.	Lower Bound	Upper Bound
1		4.685	.034	1.000	136.976	.000	4.610	4.761

a. Dependent Variable: V2

b. Linear Regression through the Origin

Chapter 5 SPSS®

Matrix Approach to Simple Linear Regression Analysis

The text begins Chapter 5 by presenting an overview of the algebra for vectors and matrices. In Chapter 5 of this manual, we introduce *MATRIX - END MATRIX* commands, which are only available through the *Syntax Editor*. These commands allow the user to write SPSS statements for performing vector/matrix algebra. We follow examples in the text and show how to write SPSS programs to perform operations such as matrix addition, subtraction and multiplication. Following the overview of matrix algebra, the text expresses the simple linear regression model as a matrix equation and then repeats the steps followed in Chapter 1, only now these steps are described using matrix algebra.

Again, we are given Y_i and X_i for a sample of n subjects and we want to find a "best fitting" model for predicting Y given X. In Chapter 1, the simple linear regression model for the ith subject, $i = 1, \ldots , n$ was written as:

$$Y_i = \beta_0 + \beta_1 X_i + \varepsilon_i$$

To summarize the key results of the matrix formulation, let the capital bold-faced letter **Y** represent the nx1 column vector containing the data for the dependent variable and the bold-faced letter **X** represent the nx2 matrix with the first column being a column vector of ones and the second column being the column vector of data for the independent variable; i.e.,

$$\mathbf{Y} = \begin{bmatrix} Y_1 \\ Y_2 \\ \vdots \\ Y_n \end{bmatrix} \quad \text{and} \quad \mathbf{X} = \begin{bmatrix} 1 & X_1 \\ 1 & X_2 \\ \vdots & \vdots \\ 1 & X_n \end{bmatrix}$$

Further, let

$$\boldsymbol{\beta} = \begin{bmatrix} \beta_0 \\ \beta_1 \end{bmatrix} \quad \text{and} \quad \boldsymbol{\varepsilon} = \begin{bmatrix} \varepsilon_1 \\ \varepsilon_2 \\ \vdots \\ \varepsilon_n \end{bmatrix}$$

Using this notation, the simple linear regression model can be written:

$$\mathbf{Y} = \mathbf{X}\boldsymbol{\beta} + \boldsymbol{\varepsilon}$$

A few key results of the matrix formulation of the regression model are:

(1.) Matrix solution for the regression coefficients: $\quad \mathbf{b} = \begin{bmatrix} b_0 \\ b_1 \end{bmatrix} = (\mathbf{X'X})^{-1}\mathbf{X'Y}$

(2.) Matrix solution for the predicted values: $\quad \hat{\mathbf{Y}} = \mathbf{Xb} = \mathbf{X}(\mathbf{X'X})^{-1}\mathbf{X'Y} = \mathbf{HY}$

where $\mathbf{H} = \mathbf{X}(\mathbf{X'X})^{-1}\mathbf{X'}$ is called the *hat matrix*.

(3.) Matrix solution for the fitted model residuals: $\quad \mathbf{e} = \mathbf{Y} - \hat{\mathbf{Y}} = \mathbf{Y} - \mathbf{Xb} = (\mathbf{I} - \mathbf{H})\mathbf{Y}$

From these equations, we begin to see that the computations required for regression analysis can be written as matrix expressions. As stated earlier, *MATRIX* is an SPSS procedure that performs matrix algebra. Most of our needs are met by other SPSS syntax that is more user friendly than that specific to *MATRIX*, but occasionally we need to perform computations that are not directly available, and *MATRIX* provides a convenient way to write programs according to our specifications. Moreover, it is instructional to write matrix language programs that perform regression analysis. We illustrate the use of *MATRIX* by presenting SPSS statements to compute (1.) – (3.) above and other key matrix expressions for the regression analysis of data given in the Toluca Company example. We begin by introducing some basic mathematical operators used in the SPSS *MATRIX* software.

Using *MATRIX* – *END MATRIX* for Matrix Operations: We initiate the *MATRIX* procedure with the keyword *MATRIX*. Next, we use *MATRIX* syntax to write statements for performing one or more matrix operations. We end the procedure with *END MATRIX*. In the following, we illustrate some of the *MATRIX* statements that are useful for programming a regression analysis.

An SPSS program for finding the transpose of a matrix **A** and a vector **C** is given in Insert 5.1. In this program, the numerical values of the matrix **A** and the vector **C** are specified directly in the *MATRIX* procedure. When this is done, the name you assign to the matrix is set equal to a quantity in braces. The SPSS program does not differentiate between upper and lower case names. Therefore, in SPSS code we can write "A = { }" or "a = { }" to specify the matrix **A**. The matrix is specified by rows with row elements separated by commas and complete rows separated by semicolons. Thus, the three lines of code that immediately follow the *MATRIX* statement specify the 3x2 matrix **A** and the next three lines specify the 3x1 vector **C**.

Insert 5.1 then finds the transpose of **A** and **C**. The transpose operator takes the form of *TRANSPOS*(M) or *T*(M). Thus, the statement "*COMPUTE AT = TRANSPOS(A)*." and "*COMPUTE AT=T(A)*." exchanges the rows and columns of matrix **A** and stores the results in a matrix named **AT**. Similarly, the statement "*COMPUTE CT = T(C)*." exchanges the rows and columns of matrix **C** and stores the results in a matrix named **CT**. The print statements in the next lines of Insert 5.1 instruct SPSS to print matrices **A**, **AT**, **C**, and **CT** (Output 5.1). These results are given on text page 178 and 179.

```
                    INSERT 5.1

title "Transpose of a matrix from text page 178".
matrix.
compute A = {2,5;7,10;3, 4}.
compute C = {4; 7;10}.
compute AT = T(A).
compute CT = T(C).
print A.
print AT.
print C.
print CT.
end matirx.
```

SPSS Output 5.1

```
Run MATRIX procedure:

A
     2     5
     7    10
     3     4

AT
     2     7     3
     5    10     4

C
     4
     7
    10

CT
     4     7    10

------ END MATRIX -----
```

Insert 5.2 shows *MATRIX* syntax for text examples of matrix addition, subtraction, and multiplication, and finding the inverse of a matrix. The output is not presented for brevity. The symbol "+" denotes the addition operator and the symbol "–" denotes the subtraction operator. The asterisk symbol "*" denotes the multiplication operator. The *MATRIX* function *inv(A)* finds the inverse of the matrix **A**. We have named the result *Ainv* but we could have chosen another convenient name. For example, we could have called the result *d* by writing *d* = *inv(A)*.

INSERT 5.2


```
title 'Addition and Substraction of a matrix from text page 180'.
matrix.
compute a={1,4;2,5;3,6}.
compute b={1,2;2,3;3,4}.
compute apb = a + b.
compute amb = a - b.
print a.
print b.
print apb.
print amb.
end matirx.

title 'Multiplication of a matrix by a scalar (4) from text page 182'.
matrix.
compute A = {2, 7; 9, 3}.
compute B = 4*A.
print A.
print B.
end matrix.

title 'Multiplication of a matrix by a matrix from text page 182'.
matrix.
compute A = {2, 5; 4, 1}.
compute B = {4, 6; 5, 8}.
compute C = A*B.
print A.
print B.
print C.
end matrix.

title 'Inverse of a matrix from text page 189'.
matrix.
compute a={2,4;3,1}.
compute ainv = inv(a).
print a.
print ainv.
end matirx.
```

The Toluca Company Example

Data File: ch01ta01.txt

We use matrix methods to perform a simple linear regression analysis of the Toluca Company example (text page 19). The required steps are presented in text Chapter 5 and are not detailed here except in Insert 5.3. For the *MARTIX* program in Insert 5.3 to function, the Toluca Company example data file must be the active file in your *Data Editor*. See Chapter 0, "Working with SPSS," for instructions on opening the Toluca Company data file and renaming the variables *lotsize* and *workhrs*. After opening ch01ta01.txt, the first 5 lines in your SPSS *Data Editor* should look like SPSS Output 1.1.

The *MATRIX* statement initiates the *MATRIX* procedure. The statement "*GET X / VARIABLES = LOTSIZE.*" stores the column of data named *lotsize* in matrix (vector) **X**. Similarly, the next statement stores the column of data labeled *workhrs* in matrix (vector) **Y**.

The statement $n = nrow(x)$ assigns the value of the number of rows in matrix **X** to variable label *n*. The statement $p = ncol(x)$ assigns the value of the number of columns in matrix **X** to variable label *p*.

The function *MAKE(a,b,c)* creates an *axb* matrix whose elements all have the value *c*. Thus, *MAKE(n,1,1)* creates an *n*x1 matrix whose elements all have the value '1'. The "*COMPUTE X = {MAKE(N,1,1), X}*" statement creates the *n*x1 matrix and concatenates it with the column vector **X** defined above as the column of *lotsize* values. Thus, **X** is now equal to **X** defined in equation 5.61 of text page 200.

The remaining statements are easy to follow. The statement $xpx = transpos(x)*x$ computes **X'X** and stores the result as a matrix named *xpx*; the statement $xpy = transpos(x)*y$ computes **X'Y** and stores the result as a matrix named *xpy*, and so on.

The print statement requests the printing of **Y** (eq 5.61, text page 200), **X** (eq 5.61, text page 200), $\hat{\mathbf{Y}}$ (eq 5.71, text page 202), and **E** (**e**, eq 5.76, text page 203) **XPXINV** ($(\mathbf{X'X})^{-1}$, eq 5.64, text page 201), **B** (eq 5.60, text 200), **YPY** ($\mathbf{Y'Y}$, (eq 5.13, text page 185), **CORRECT** (corrected SSTO), **SSTO** (eq 5.83, text page 204 and 5.89a, text page 206), **SSR** (b'X'Y, text page 205), **SSE** (Y'Y-b'X'Y, text page 205), **MSE**, **VARB** ($s^2\{b\}$, eq 5.94, text page 207), **XH**, **VARYHATH** ($s^2\{\hat{Y}\}$, eq 5.98, text page 208). Output 5.2 displays the first 5 lines of **X** and **Y** matrices for illustration.

```
                              INSERT 5.3

matrix.
get x / variables = lotsize.
get y /variables = workhrs.
compute n=nrow(x).
compute x={make(n,1,1),x}.
compute p=ncol(x).
compute xpx=transpos(x)*x.
compute xpy=transpos(x)*y.
compute xinv=inv(t(x)*x).
compute b=inv(t(x)*x)*t(x)*y.
compute yhat=x*b.
compute e=y-yhat.
compute ypy=t(y)*y.
compute correct=(t(y)*(make(n,n,1))*y/n).
compute sstot=t(y)*y-t(y)*(make(n,n,1))*y/n.
compute ssr=t(b)*t(x)*y.
compute sse=t(y)*y-t(b)*t(x)*y.
compute mse=sse/(n-p).
compute varb=mse*inv(t(x)*x).
compute xh={1;65}.
compute varyhath=t(xh)*varb*xh.
print y / title "Y = Work Hours" .
print x / title "X = Lot Size" .
print yhat / title "Predicted Values".
print xinv / title "X Inverse".
print e / title "Residual Values".
print xpy / title "(XPY), Y = Work Hours" .
print xpx / title "(XPX), X = Lot Size" .
print xinv / title "X'X inverse".
print b / title "Parameter estimates".
print correct / title "Corrected sum of squares".
print sstot / title "Total sum of squares".
print ssr / title "Sum of squares regression".
print sse / title "Sum of squares error".
print mse / title "Mean square error".
print varb / title "Variance of b".
end matrix.
execute.
```

SPSS Output 5.2

Y Matrix	X Matrix	
399	1	80
121	1	30
221	1	50
376	1	90
361	1	70

Chapter **6** SPSS®

Multiple Regression I

In many applications using regression analysis, the model may involve more than one predictor variable. We call such a model the *multiple regression model* or the *general linear regression model*. We can write the general linear regression model as:

$$Y_i = \beta_0 + \beta_1 X_{i1} + \beta_2 X_{i2} + ... + \beta_{p-1} X_{i,p-1} + \varepsilon_i$$

where:

$\beta_0, \beta_1, ..., \beta_{p-1}$ are unknown model parameters with fixed values

$X_{i1}, ..., X_{i,p-1}$ are known constants

ε_i are independent $N(0, \sigma^2)$ random variables

$i = 1, ..., n$

In matrix notation, the general linear regression model is

$$\mathbf{Y} = \mathbf{X}\boldsymbol{\beta} + \boldsymbol{\varepsilon}$$

where:

$\mathbf{Y}$ is the nx1 vector of response observations on the dependent variable

β is the px1 vector of unknown model parameters

$\mathbf{X}$ is the nxp matrix of known constants

ε is a vector of independent $N(0, \sigma^2)$ random variables

Chapter 6 focuses on the special case where $p = 3$ and therefore only two predictor variables are in the general linear regression model. In the following, we give illustrative SPSS syntax for performing a statistical analysis of the general linear regression model with $p = 3$.

Dwaine Studios, Inc. Example

Data File: ch06fi05.txt

Multiple Regression with Two Predictor Variables: Dwaine Studios, Inc. has locations in 21 medium size cities and is considering expansion into additional cities (text page 236). The company wants to predict sales (*Y*) in a community using the number of persons greater than 15 years in the community (*X1*) and per capita disposable income in the community (*X2*). See Chapter 0, "Working with SPSS," for instructions on opening the Dwaine Studios data file and renaming the variables *X1*, *X2*, and *Y*. After opening ch06fi05.txt, the first 5 lines in your SPSS *Data Editor* should look like SPSS Output 6.1.

| dwaine studio example.sav - SPSS Data Editor |

File Edit View Data Transform Analyze Graphs Utilities Window Help

5 : y   181.6

	x1	x2	y	var	var
1	68.50	16.70	174.40		
2	45.20	16.80	164.40		
3	91.30	18.20	244.20		
4	47.80	16.30	154.60		
5	46.90	17.30	181.60		

The researchers began with the first order regression model. (Insert 6.1) Results are shown in SPSS Output 6.2 and are consistent with Figure 6.5, text page 237. In Insert 6.1 we also present the matrix language syntax for estimating the parameters. Notice that the **X** matrix on text page 237 contains a column of 1's and that this column is not in the Dwaine Studios data file. Thus, in Insert 6.1 we first compute a variable, *X0* that is equal to 1 for each of the 20 cities in the data file. We then enter the SPSS *MATRIX* language (notice the line that specifies *matrix* in Insert 6.1) and set column vectors **CON**, **A**, **B**, and **Y** equal to *X0*, *X1*, *X2*, and *Y*, respectively. Next, we concatenate the **CON**, **A**, and **B** column vectors into the **X** matrix such that the **X** matrix is now as shown in equation 6.70, text page 237. (Although the method of constructing the **X** matrix in Insert 6.1 is different from the method presented in Chapter 5, both methods achieve the same outcome.) Next, we find $\mathbf{X'X}$ (*xtx*) , $\mathbf{X'Y}$ (*xty*), $(\mathbf{X'X})^{-1}$ (*xtxinv*), and $\mathbf{b} = (\mathbf{X'X})^{-1} \mathbf{X'Y}$. The "*print b.*" statement will print the parameter estimates. Although we do not display the output from the "*print b.*" statement, the estimates obtained through the matrix language program are equal to the estimates shown in SPSS Output 6.2. We did not print $\mathbf{X'X}$, $\mathbf{X'Y}$, and $(\mathbf{X'X})^{-1}$, but we could do so and compare the numerical output to the text results shown on text pages 238-239 and the SPSS regression analysis shown in SPSS Output 6.2.

INSERT 6.1	INSERT 6.1 continued	INSERT 6.1 continued
* Regresson analysis. ✔ Analyze ✔ Regression ✔ Linear ✔ *y* ✔ ► (to the Dependent box) ✔ *x1* ✔ ► (to the Independent box) ✔ *x2* ✔ ► (to the Independent box) ✔ OK	* Matrix format. ✔ File ✔ Open ✔ Syntax * Type the following syntax. compute x0=1. execute. matrix. get con / variables =x0. get a / variables = x1. get b / variables = x2. get y /variables=y.	compute x = {con, a, b} . compute xtx=t(x)*x. comute xty=t(x)*y. compute xtxinv=inv(t(x)*x). compute b=inv(t(x)*x)*t(x)*y. print b. end matrix. execute. ✔ Run ✔ All

SPSS Output 6.2

Model Summary

Model	R	R Square	Adjusted R Square	Std. Error of the Estimate
1	.957[a]	.917	.907	11.00739

a. Predictors: (Constant), X2, X1

ANOVA[b]

Model		Sum of Squares	df	Mean Square	F	Sig.
1	Regression	24015.282	2	12007.641	99.103	.000[a]
	Residual	2180.927	18	121.163		
	Total	26196.210	20			

a. Predictors: (Constant), X2, X1

b. Dependent Variable: Y

Coefficients[a]

Model		Unstandardized Coefficients		Standardized Coefficients		
		B	Std. Error	Beta	t	Sig.
1	(Constant)	-68.857	60.017		-1.147	.266
	X1	1.455	.212	.748	6.868	.000
	X2	9.366	4.064	.251	2.305	.033

a. Dependent Variable: Y

To produce the three-dimensional scatter plot shown on text page 238 (text Figure 6.6(a)), we ✔ Graph ✔ Scatter ✔ 3-D ✔ Define and set our dialogue as shown SPSS Output 6.3. (Note that we have entered Variable Labels in the Dwaine Studio data file.) The result is shown in SPSS Output 6.4. Clicking on the three-dimensional scatter plot will open the *Chart Editor*. You can now rotate the plot by ✔ Format ✔ 3-D rotation to rotate the chart to the desired position.

SPSS Output 6.3

369

SPSS Output 6.4

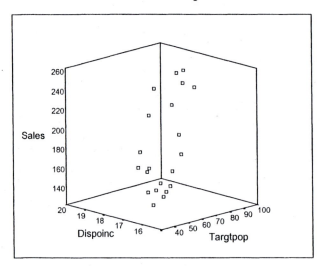

Analysis of Appropriateness of Model: Inspection of Figures 6.8 and 6.9, text pages 242-243, reveals that we need to produce the residuals and predicted values of *Y* based on the first order regression model. Insert 6.2 saves the unstandardized residuals (*res_1*) and predicted values (*pre_1*) in the *Data Editor*. We now use a Syntax File to produce *absresid*, the absolute value of the residuals, and *x1x2*, the interaction term between *X1* and *X1*. Text Figures 6.8 a-d can now be produced by using ✔ Graph ✔ Scatter ✔ Matrix ✔ Define (not shown in Insert 6.9) and setting the dialogue box as shown in SPSS Output 6.5 (including moving *absresid* into the Matrix Variables box – not visible.) This results in SPSS Output 6.6; note that the first four plots in the first row are equivalent to text Figures 6.8 a-d and that the plot in row 1, column 2 is equivalent to text Figure 6.9a. The last section of Insert 6.2 will produce text Figure 6.9b although the axes will be reversed compared to the text. Reversing the axes will result in SPSS Output 6.7.

INSERT 6.2	INSERT 6.2 continued
✔ Analyze ✔ Regression ✔ Linear ✔ *y* ✔ ▶ (to the Dependent box) ✔ *x1* ✔ ▶ (to the Independent box) ✔ *x2* ✔ ▶ (to the Independent box) ✔ Save ✔ Unstandardized (Under residuals) ✔ Unstandardized (Under predicted values) ✔ Continue ✔ OK ✔ File ✔ Open ✔ Syntax * Type the following syntax.	compute absresid=abs(res_1). compute x1x2=x1*x2. execute. ✔ Run ✔ All * Produce text Figure 6.9b. ✔ Analyze ✔ Descriptive Statistics ✔ Explore ✔ *res_1* ✔ ▶ (to the Dependent List) ✔ Plots ✔ Normal probability plot with tests ✔ Continue ✔ OK * Double click on the chart to open the Chart Editor. ✔ Series ✔ Displayed * Reverse axis's and close Chart Editor.

SPSS Output 6.5

SPSS Output 6.6

SPSS Output 6.7

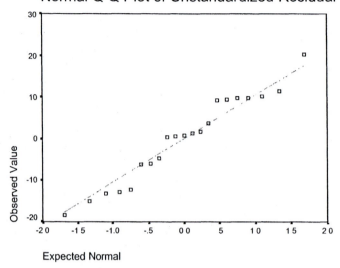

Normal Q-Q Plot of Unstandardized Residual

SPSS Output 6.6 and 6.7 do not indicate any serious problems with the response function including non-constancy of error terms. SPSS Output 6.6 (*x1x2*res_1*) indicates that there is no striking interaction effect in the regression model. The authors report that the normal probability plot of the residuals is moderately linear (SPSS Output 6.7).

On text page 243, the authors calculate the coefficient of correlation between the ordered residuals and their expected value under normality for the Dwaine Studios example. The expected value under normality of the kth smallest observation in a sample of size n is given by:

$$\sqrt{MSE}\left[z\left(\frac{k - 0.375}{n + 0.25}\right)\right]$$

The first step in obtaining the expected value of the ordered residuals under normality is to calculate $(k - 0.375)/(n + 0.25)$. (Insert 6.3) In the Dwaine Studios example, $n = 21$. Since k is the rank of the ordered residuals, we rank the saved residuals (*res_1*, saved in Insert 6.2 above) using the Rank Case function. SPSS creates another new variable, *rres_1*, that is the rank of the value of *res_1*, the unstandardized residual based on a model with *x1* and *x2* as the predictor variables. Thus, $(k - 0.375)/(n + 0.25)$ becomes $(rres\_1 - 0.375)/(21 + 0.25)$. This quantity represents the cumulative probability ($0 \leq$ cumulative probability ≤ 1.0) of the standard normal distribution. We now must obtain a standard score (z) associated with the cumulative probability calculated above. In SPSS, the *Probit* function is an *inverse density function* and takes the form *Probit*(*p*), where *p* = cumulative probability. For instance, if the cumulative probability = 0.50 (*Probit*(0.50)) then $z = 0$. If the cumulative probability = 0.8413 (*Probit*(0.8413)) then $z = +1$. Thus, to obtain z we use *Probit* ((*rres_1* $- 0.375)/(21 + 0.25)$). Finally, we multiply this quantity by the square root of *MSE* = 121.163 of the first order model (SPSS Output 6.2). From the above, we compute the expected value as:

$$ev = sqrt(121.163) * Probit((rres\_1 - 0.375)/(21 + 0.25)).$$

INSERT 6.3

- ✔ Transform
- ✔ Rank Cases
- ✔ *res_1*
- ✔ ▶ (to the Variables box)
- ✔ OK

- ✔ File
- ✔ New
- ✔ Syntax

compute *ev* = sqrt(121.163) * Probit ((*rres_1* - 0.375)/(21 + 0.25)).
execute.

- ✔ Run
- ✔ All

- ✔ Analyze
- ✔ Correlate
- ✔ Bivariate
- ✔ *ev*
- ✔ ▶
- ✔ *res_1*
- ✔ ▶
- ✔ OK

We can now obtain the coefficient of correlation between the residual and the expected value under normality (*ev*). The result of the correlation between *ev* and *res_1* is 0.980 and is consistent with the correlation reported on text page 243. The interpolated critical value from Table B.6, text page 673, for $n = 21$ and $\alpha = 0.05$ is 0.9525. The obtained correlation coefficient (0.980) is greater than the table value (0.9525) and we conclude that the distribution of the error terms appears to be reasonably close to a normal distribution.

On text page 244, the researchers tested the null hypothesis $Ho: \beta_1 = 0$ and $\beta_2 = 0$. The test result is found in the output of the first order regression model above (SPSS Output 6.2). Because the *p*-value (<0.000) associated with F = 99.103 is less than the desired significance level ($\alpha = 0.05$), we conclude that sales are related to target population (*X1*) and disposable income (*X2*).

We can use the ANOVA table in SPSS Output 6.2 to find the *Coefficient of Multiple Determination* using text equation 6.40:

$$R^2 = \frac{SSR}{SSTO} = \frac{24,015.28}{26,196.21} = 0.917$$

$R^2 = 0.917$ is also given in the Model Summary table of SPSS Output 6.2. Additionally, $R = 0.957$ and *Adjusted R Square* = 0.907 are presented in the Model Summary table.

Estimation of Regression Parameters: On text page 245, the researchers wish to jointly estimate β_1 and β_2 with a family confidence coefficient of 0.90. The confidence limits for β_k are given by equations 6.52 and 6.52a, text page 228:

$$b_k \pm Bs\{b_k\}$$

$$b_k \pm t(1 - \alpha/2g; n - p)s\{b_k\}$$

where g = the number of intervals to be estimated and p = the number of parameters in the regression model. In the present discussion, we wish to estimate $g = 2$ intervals and there are 3 parameters in the regression model. We use the *inverse distribution function* (*IDF.T*(probability, *df*) where "probability" = $(1 - 0.90/2g)$ and $df = n - p$ or *IDF.T*(0.975, 18). Thus, in Insert 6.4 we find t and place its value in *tvalue*, which is written on each line in the *Data Editor*. We use the parameter estimates shown in SPSS Output 6.2 ($b1 = 1.455$ and $b2 = 9.366$). We use the standard deviation of each estimate (shown as "*Std. Error*" in SPSS Output 6.2, $s\{b_1\} = 0.212$ and $s\{b_2\} = 4.06$) to find the lower (*b1lo* and *b2lo*) and upper (*b1hi* and *b2hi*) confidence limit for each estimated parameter. These limits are written into the *Data Editor*.

INSERT 6.4

✔ File
✔ New
✔ Syntax
```
compute tvalue = IDF.T(.975,18) .
compute b1lo=1.45455-(tvalue*.211178).
compute b1hi=1.45455+(tvalue*.211178).
compute b2lo=9.3655-(tvalue*4.06395).
compute b2hi=9.3655+(tvalue*4.06395).
execute.
```
✔ Run
✔ All

Estimation of Mean Response: On text page 245 the authors wish to estimate the expected mean sales when the target population is 65.4 thousand persons and the per capita disposable income is 17.6 thousand dollars. They also estimate a 95 percent confidence interval for $E\{Y_h\}$. The $1 - \alpha$ confidence limits for $E\{Y_h\}$ are given by equations 6.59 and 6.58:

$$\hat{Y}_h \pm t(1 - \alpha/2; n - p)s\{\hat{Y}_h\}$$

where:

$$s^2\{\hat{Y}_h\} = MSE\left(X'_h (X'X)^{-1} X_h\right)$$

In chapter 2 we found the confidence intervals for $E\{Y_h\}$ where there was one predictor variable in the model. However, as the number of predictor variables increases, the task of finding the variance of $\hat{Y}_h$ becomes increasingly laborious. Although text equation 2.30 can be generalized to the case of multiple regression ($p > 2$), the authors present the formulation of the variance of $\hat{Y}_h$ in matrix terms in equation 6.58 (text page 229) presented above. We use this equation and SPSS' *Matirix* program to solve the current problem.

The matrix program shown in Insert 6.5 is a continuation of the matrix program shown in Insert 6.1 above. We find t prior to entering the matrix program and after entering set the matrix **tvalue** to the variable *tvalue*. We then find $s^2\{\hat{Y}_h\}$ using the above notation. $MSE = 121.163$ is given in SPSS Output 6.2 above. $\mathbf{X}_h'$ is defined in Insert 6.5 as shown on text page 246. We find $\hat{Y}_h$ (*yhath*) using equation 6.55, text page 229. The lower (*yhathlo*=185.29) and upper (*yhathlo*=196.91) confidence limits are then computed and printed.

INSERT 6.5

```
* Find t(1-alpha/2,n-p) from text equation 6.59.
compute tvalue = IDF.T(.975,18) .
* Write a column of 1's into the Dwaine Studios data file.
compute x0=1.
execute.
matrix.
get con / variables =x0.
get a / variables = x1.
get b / variables = x2.
* Define the Y matrix.
get y /variables=y.
get tvalue /variables=tvalue.
* Define the X matrix.
compute x = {con, a, b} .
compute xtx=t(x)*x.
comute xty=t(x)*y.
* Fine the b matrix using text equation 6.25.
compute b=inv(t(x)*x)*t(x)*y.
compute xtxinv=inv(t(x)*x).
* Define xh matrix as on text page 246.
compute xh={1;65.4;17.6}.
* Find standard deviation of yhat(new) per text equation 6.58.
compute sxh=sqrt(121.163*(t(xh)*(xtxinv)*xh)).
* Find yhat(new) using text equation 6.56..
compute yhath=t(xh)*b.
* Find confidence interval using text equation 6.59.
compute yhathlo=yhath-(tvalue*sxh).
compute yhathhi=yhath+(tvalue*sxh).
print yhathlo(1,1).
print yhathhl(1,1).
end matrix.
execute.
```

Prediction Limits for New Observations: Dwaine Studios now wants to predict sales for two new cities (text page 247). Here, X_{h1} and X_{h2} equal 65.4 and 17.6, respectively, for City A and 53.1 and 17.7, respectively, for City B. To determine which prediction intervals are preferable here, we find S and B using text equations 6.65a and 6.66a (text page 231) where $g = 2$ and $1 - \alpha = 0.90$. Insert 6.6 computes S (s) and B (b) and writes the two variables into the *Data Editor*. Note that $S = 2.29$ and $B = 2.10$ so that the Bonferroni limits are tighter here and therefore more efficient.

INSERT 6.6

- ✔ File
- ✔ New
- ✔ Syntax
```
compute s=sqrt(2*idf.f(.9,2,18)).
compute b=idf.t(1-(.1/(2*2)),18).
execute.
```
- ✔ Run
- ✔ All

To find the simultaneous Bonferroni prediction limits for city A, we use (text equation 6.66):

$$\hat{Y}_h \pm Bs\{pred\}$$

where (text equations 6.66a, 6.63a, and 6.58):

$$B = t(1 - \alpha/2g; n - p)$$

$$s^2\{pred\} = MSE + s^2\{\hat{Y}_h\}$$

$$s^2\{\hat{Y}_h\} = MSE\left(\mathbf{X'_h}\left(\mathbf{X'X}\right)^{-1}\mathbf{X_h}\right)$$

From Insert 6.7, we find the lower (*yhathlo*=167.71) and upper (*yhathhi*=214.49) 90% confidence limits for city A. To find the intervals for city B, simply replace "*xh* = {1, 65.4, 17.6}." with "*xh* = {1, 53.1, 17.7}." in Insert 6.7. Insert 6.7 so modified will find the 90 percent confidence interval for city B: *yhathlo* = 149.08 and *yhathi* = 199.21 consistent with text page 246.

INSERT 6.7

```
* Find b(1-alpha/2g,n-p) from text equation 6.59.
compute b = IDF.T(1-(.1/(2*2)),18) .
* Write a column of 1's into the Dwaine Studios data file.
compute x0=1.
execute.
matrix.
get con / variables =x0.
get a / variables = x1.
get b / variables = x2.
* Define the Y matrix.
get y /variables=y.
get bon /variables=b.
* Define the X matrix.
compute x = {con, a, b} .
compute xtx=t(x)*x.
compute xty=t(x)*y.
* Fine the b matrix using text equation 6.25.
compute b=inv(t(x)*x)*t(x)*y.
compute xtxinv=inv(t(x)*x).
* Define xh matrix as on text page 246.
compute xh={1;65.4;17.6}.
* Find standard deviation of yhat(new) per text equation 6.63a.
compute spre=sqrt(121.163+(121.163*(t(xh)*(xtxinv)*xh))).
print xh.
* Find yhat(new) using text equation 6.56.
compute yhath=t(xh)*b.
* Find confidence interval using text equation 6.66.
compute yhathlo=yhath-(bon*spre).
compute yhathhi=yhath+(bon*spre).
print yhathlo(1,1).
print yhathhl(1,1).
end matrix.
execute.
```

Chapter 7 SPSS®

Multiple Regression II

We use *sum of squared deviations* or *sum of squares* of various types as a quantitative measurement of variability that is attributable to different sources associated with parameters specified in the model. In previous chapters we defined the sum of squared deviations of the observations on the dependent variable Y_i from the overall sample mean $\overline{Y}$ as the (corrected) *total sum of squares*, denoted *SSTO*. We defined the sum of squared deviations of the fitted (predicted) values $\hat{Y}_i$ from $\overline{Y}$ as the *regression sum of squares* denoted *SSR*. We defined the sum of squared deviations of the observations Y_i from the fitted values $\hat{Y}_i$ as the *error sum of squares* denoted *SSE*. We found that:

$$SSTO = SSR + SSE$$

Suppose we fit a general linear model with $p - 1$ predictor variables and obtain *SST*, *SSR* and *SSE*. Now, suppose we add one or more predictor variables to the model and fit this "new" model. The observations Y_i will remain unchanged as will the mean $\overline{Y}$, but the $\hat{Y}_i$ with this new model may be different from the $\hat{Y}_i$ based on the first model. Thus, the numerical values of *SSR* and *SSE* will likely change. In fact, *SSR* will increase and, correspondingly, *SSE* will decrease by the same magnitude as the increase in *SSR*. We call this magnitude of change the *extra sum of squares* due to the predictor variable(s) that were added to the model. To avoid confusion we need additional notation to identify the variables that are in the model when *SSR* and *SSE* are computed.

It is easier to explain the extra sum of squares notation in terms of a specific example. Suppose predictor variables X_1, X_2 and X_3 are available for fitting a general linear regression model. If we fit a model with only X_1 in the model, we denote the sums of squares for regression and error as $SSR(X_1)$ and $SSE(X_1)$, respectively. If we fit a model that includes the predictor variables X_1 and X_2, we write $SSR(X_1, X_2)$ and $SSE(X_1, X_2)$ to denote the regression and error sums of squares, respectively. If we fit a model that includes X_1 and then add X_2 to the model and refit, the additional or extra regression sum of squares due to adding the additional predictor variable is denoted $SSR(X_2|X_1)$ and the reduction or extra error sum of squares is denoted $SSE(X_2|X_1)$. Similarly, if we fit a model that includes all three predictor variables, we write $SSR(X_1, X_2, X_3)$ and $SSE(X_1, X_2, X_3)$ to denote the regression and error sums of squares, respectively. If we fit a model that includes X_1 and then add X_2 and X_3 to the model and refit, the additional or extra regression sum of squares due to adding both additional predictor variables is denoted $SSR(X_2, X_3|X_1)$ and the reduction or extra error sum of squares is denoted $SSE(X_2, X_3|X_1)$. The extra sum of squares is also known as the *partial sum of squares*. It is obvious that we need to specify the predictor variables as being already in the model or as being added to the model when we discuss extra (partial) sums of squares.

In Chapter 7, the authors discuss methods used to make statistical inferences when adding and deleting predictor variables to the general linear regression model. The problem of deciding the merits of adding or deleting predictor variables in choosing an appropriate regression model is of particular interest. The extra sum of squares concept plays a fundamental role in the decision making process.

The Body Fat Example

Data File: ch07ta01.txt

Extra Sum of Squares: The text presents an excellent discussion of extra sum of squares. "Extra sum of squares measure the marginal reduction in error sum of squares when one or several predictor variables are added to the regression model, given that other predictor variables are already in the model." Many statistical packages use slightly different terminology to denote two major types of sum of squares: Type I and Type III. Type I sum of squares examines the sequential incremental improvement in the fit of the model as each independent variable is added to the model. Thus, the order of entry of variables into the model will affect the Type I sum of squares. Type I sum of squares is also called the hierarchical decomposition of sum of squares method. In contrast, Type III sum of squares for a particular predictor variable is the amount of increase in the regression sum of squares (decrease in error sum of squares) due to that predictor variable after all other terms in the model have been included. Thus, the Type III sums of squares for a given predictor is the reduction in error sum of squares achieved when that predictor variable is the last predictor variable added to the model. We will see how Type I and III sum of squares are used in the following examples.

On text page 256, researchers in the Body Fat example wished to develop a regression model to predict body fat from three predictor variables: triceps skin fold thickness, thigh circumference, and midarm circumference. They considered four regression models: (1.) body fat (Y) as a linear function of triceps skin fold thickness alone, (2.) body fat as a linear function of thigh circumference alone, (3.) body fat as a linear function of the two predictor variables triceps skin fold and thigh circumference, and (4.) body fat as a linear function of all three predictor variables.

See Chapter 0, "Working with SPSS," for instructions on opening the Body Fat example (text Table 7.1) and renaming the variables $X1$, $X2$, $X3$, and Y. After opening ch07ta01.txt, the first 5 lines in your SPSS *Data Editor* should look like SPSS Output 7.1.

SPSS Output 7.1

	x1	x2	x3	y	var
1	19.50	43 10	29.10	11 90	
2	24 70	49 80	28 20	22 80	
3	30 70	51 90	37 00	18 70	
4	29 80	54 30	31 10	20 10	
5	19 10	42 20	30 90	12 90	

In Insert 7.1, we regressed Y on $X1$ in the first analysis (SPSS Output 7.2). In the second analysis, we regressed Y on $X1$ and $X2$ (SPSS Output 7.3). In the third regression analysis of Insert 7.1, we use the Block feature (SPSS Output 7.4) available in SPSS. That is, we entered $X1$ at block 1 and $X2$ at block 2 (SPSS Output 7.5). Thus, Model 1 of SPSS Output 7.5 represents a regression model where Y has been regressed on $X1$ and Model 2 represents a regression model where Y has been regressed on $X1$ and $X2$. Note that $SSE(X1) = 143.120$ and $SSE(X1, X2) = 109.951$ in SPSS Output 7.5 and $SSE(X1) = 143.120$ and $SSE(X1, X2) = 109.951$ in SPSS Output 7.2 and 7.3 for the two separate analyses. This is consistent with Table 7.2, text page 257. The difference $SSE(X2|X1) = SSE(X1) - SSE(X1, X2) = 143.120 - 109.951 = 33.169$ is referred to as the *extra reduction in error sum of squares* achieved by adding $X2$ to a model that has $X1$ as the only predictor variable. Correspondingly, $SSR(X2|X1) = SSR(X1, X2) - SSR(X1) = 385.439 - 352.270 = 33.169$ is the *extra increase in the regression sum squares* achieved by adding $X2$ to a model that has $X1$ as the only predictor variable. Note that $SSE(X2|X1) = SSR(X2|X1) = 33.169$ is not given in SPSS Output 7.2, 7.3, or 7.5. This is because SPSS Regression output displays only the *total regression* and *error sum of squares* for a given model and not the incremental change due to adding predictor variables to the model. To directly produce the extra sum of squares, we need Type I sum of squares that is available in the SPSS *General Linear Model* (*GLM*) procedure. The syntax in Insert 7.2 requests Type I sum of squares based on a model with $X1$ and $X2$ as predictor variables (SPSS Output 7.6). The Type I sum of squares $SSR(X2|X1) = 33.169$ here is the same as found earlier.

INSERT 7.1	INSERT 7.1 continued
✔ Analyze ✔ Regression ✔ Linear ✔ *y* ✔ ► (to the Dependent box) ✔ *x1* ✔ ► (to the Independent box) ✔ OK ✔ Analyze ✔ Regression ✔ Linear ✔ *y* ✔ ► (to the Dependent box) ✔ *x1* ✔ ► (to the Independent box) ✔ *x2* ✔ ► (to the Independent box) ✔ OK	✔ Analyze ✔ Regression ✔ Linear ✔ *y* ✔ ► (to the Dependent box) ✔ *x1* ✔ ► (to the Independent box) ✔ Next ✔ *x2* ✔ ► (to the Independent box) ✔ OK

SPSS Output 7.2
Y on *X1*

ANOVA[b]

Model		Sum of Squares	df	Mean Square	F	Sig.
1	Regression	352.270	1	352.270	44.305	.000[a]
	Residual	143.120	18	7.951		
	Total	495.389	19			

a. Predictors: (Constant), X1

b. Dependent Variable: Y

SPSS Output 7.3
Y on *X1* and *X2*

ANOVA[b]

Model		Sum of Squares	df	Mean Square	F	Sig.
1	Regression	385.439	2	192.719	29.797	.000[a]
	Residual	109.951	17	6.468		
	Total	495.389	19			

a. Predictors: (Constant), X2, X1

b. Dependent Variable: Y

SPSS Output 7.4

SPSS Output 7.5

Y on *X1* and *X2* using Block feature

ANOVA[c]

Model		Sum of Squares	df	Mean Square	F	Sig.
1	Regression	352.270	1	352.270	44.305	.000[a]
	Residual	143.120	18	7.951		
	Total	495.389	19			
2	Regression	385.439	2	192.719	29.797	.000[b]
	Residual	109.951	17	6.468		
	Total	495.389	19			

a. Predictors: (Constant), X1

b. Predictors: (Constant), X1, X2

c. Dependent Variable: Y

INSERT 7.2

- ✔ Analyze
- ✔ General Linear Model
- ✔ Univariate
- ✔ Y
- ✔ ► (to the Dependent box)
- ✔ x1
- ✔ ► (to the Covariate box)
- ✔ x2
- ✔ ► (to the Covariate box)
- ✔ Model
- ✔ Sum of Squares ▼
- * Select Type I.
- ✔ Continue
- ✔ OK

SPSS Output 7.6

Tests of Between-Subjects Effects

Dependent Variable: Y

Source	Type I Sum of Squares	df	Mean Square	F	Sig.
Corrected Model	385.439[a]	2	192.719	29.797	.000
Intercept	8156.761	1	8156.761	1261.154	.000
X1	352.270	1	352.270	54.466	.000
X2	33.169	1	33.169	5.128	.037
Error	109.951	17	6.468		
Total	8652.150	20			
Corrected Total	495.389	19			

a. R Squared = .778 (Adjusted R Squared = .752)

Test whether a single $\beta_k = 0$: On text page 264, the researchers wished to test whether $X3$ should be dropped from a model that contained $X1$, $X2$, and $X3$. That is, they wanted to test H_0: $\beta_3 = 0$. From Chapter 6, we know that we can use the t^* to test this hypothesis. But, to continue with the general linear test approach, we use the block feature and regress Y on $X1$ at block 1, $X2$ at block 2, and $X3$ at block 3 (Insert 7.3). Results are shown in SPSS Output 7.7. We first find $SSR(X3|X1, X2) = SSR(X1, X2, X3) - SSR(X1, X2)$ or $396.985 - 385.439 = 11.546$ and $SSE(X1, X2, X3) = 98.405$. Thus, from equation 7.15, text page 264, $F^* = \dfrac{11.546}{1} \div \dfrac{98.405}{16} = 1.88$. This is consistent with the regression procedure SPSS Output 7.7 which shows $t = -1.37$ for $X3$ at Model 3. That is, we know that $t^2 = F$ and $(-1.37)^2 = 1.88$. Based on this finding, we do not reject H_0 and drop $X3$ from the model. Requesting Type I sum of squares in GLM with $X1$, $X2$, and $X3$ as predictors results in SPSS Output 7.8 (syntax not shown). The F-value associated with $X3$ is 1.877. Regression analysis yields Type III sum of squares and GLM yields Type I sum of squares (if requested) but we arrive at the same conclusion regarding H_0: $\beta_3 = 0$. Remember the test of H_0: $\beta_3 = 0$ is a conditional test, given that $X1$ and $X2$ are already in the model. The test for $X3$ (Regression Output 7.7 – Coefficients - Model 3) is a test of the significance of adding $X3$ to a model that already includes all other predictors being considered, i.e., $X1$ and $X2$. The test for $X3$ using GLM and requesting Type I sum of squares (GLM Output 7.8) has the same interpretation. Thus, because $X3$ was the last variable entered into the model, inferential tests of the effect of $X3$ based on Type I and Type III sum of squares test the same hypothesis. However, when the statistical test is not based on the last variable in the model, Type I and Type III sum of squares test different hypotheses. Assume that we wish to determine if $X2$ can be dropped from the above model. From the regression procedure using Type III sum of squares (SPSS Output 7.7 – Model 3) we see that $t = -1.106$ for $X2$. This is the effect of $X2$ controlling for all other variables in the model, i.e., $X1$ and $X3$. From the GLM procedure (SPSS Output 7.8) we see that $F = 5.393$ for $X2$. This is the effect of $X2$ controlling for all variables that preceded it in the model, i.e., $X1$. ($t^2 = F$, but $(-1.106)^2 \ne 5.393$). So, using Type III sum of squares we get a test of the statistical significance of $SSR(X2|X1, X3)$, or, equivalently, $SSE(X2|X1, X3)$. On the other hand, using the GLM procedure, the test associated with the Type I sum of squares tests the significance of $SSR(X2|X1)$. The default sum of squares in SPSS GLM is Type III. This also illustrates a very important point: to properly interpret the output of a computer software program, we must know the type of sum of squares used in the analysis.

INSERT 7.3

- ✔ Analyze
- ✔ Regression
- ✔ Linear
- ✔ y
- ✔ ► (to the Dependent box)
- ✔ x1
- ✔ ► (to the Independent box)
- ✔ Next
- ✔ x2
- ✔ ► (to the Independent box)
- ✔ Next
- ✔ x3
- ✔ ► (to the Independent box)
- ✔ OK

SPSS Output 7.7

SPSS Regression

ANOVA[d]

Model		Sum of Squares	df	Mean Square	F	Sig.
1	Regression	352.270	1	352.270	44.305	.000[a]
	Residual	143.120	18	7.951		
	Total	495.389	19			
2	Regression	385.439	2	192.719	29.797	.000[b]
	Residual	109.951	17	6.468		
	Total	495.389	19			
3	Regression	396.985	3	132.328	21.516	.000[c]
	Residual	98.405	16	6.150		
	Total	495.389	19			

a. Predictors: (Constant), X1

b. Predictors: (Constant), X1, X2

c. Predictors: (Constant), X1, X2, X3

d. Dependent Variable: Y

Coefficients[a]

Model		Unstandardized Coefficients		Standardized Coefficients		
		B	Std. Error	Beta	t	Sig.
1	(Constant)	-1.496	3.319		-.451	.658
	X1	.857	.129	.843	6.656	.000
2	(Constant)	-19.174	8.361		-2.293	.035
	X1	.222	.303	.219	.733	.474
	X2	.659	.291	.676	2.265	.037
3	(Constant)	117.085	99.782		1.173	.258
	X1	4.334	3.016	4.264	1.437	.170
	X2	-2.857	2.582	-2.929	-1.106	.285
	X3	-2.186	1.595	-1.561	-1.370	.190

a. Dependent Variable: Y

SPSS Output 7.8

SPSS GLM

Tests of Between-Subjects Effects

Dependent Variable: Y

Source	Type I Sum of Squares	df	Mean Square	F	Sig.
Corrected Model	396.985[a]	3	132.328	21.516	.000
Intercept	8156.761	1	8156.761	1326.237	.000
X1	352.270	1	352.270	57.277	.000
X2	33.169	1	33.169	5.393	.034
X3	11.546	1	11.546	1.877	.190
Error	98.405	16	6.150		
Total	8652.150	20			
Corrected Total	495.389	19			

a. R Squared = .801 (Adjusted R Squared = .764)

Test whether several $\beta_k = 0$: Continuing with the body fat example (text page 265), the researchers wished to determine if $X2$ and $X3$ could be dropped from the model that contained $X1$, $X2$, and $X3$. This is equivalent to testing the hypothesis Ho: $\beta_2 = \beta_3 = 0$. From SPSS Output 7.8 above, we have the necessary information to find equation 7.18, text page 265:

$$F^* = \frac{SSR(X2 \mid X1) + SSR(X3 \mid X1, X2)}{2} \div MSE(X1, X2, X3)$$

$$F^* = \frac{33.169 + 11.546}{2} \div 6.15 = 3.63$$

However, there is an easier way to test H_0: $\beta_2 = \beta_3 = 0$. We use SPSS regression procedure and enter $X1$ at block 1 and $X2$, $X3$ at block 2, and request a R^2 Change statistic (Insert 7.4). In SPSS Output 7.9, Model 1 contains $X1$ and Model 2 contains $X1$, $X2$, and $X3$. The R^2 Change $F = 3.635$ represents the incremental effect of adding $X2$ and $X3$ to a model that contains $X1$, i.e., $SSR(X2, X3 \mid X1)$.

INSERT 7.4	INSERT 7.4 continued
✔ Analyze	✔ *x2*
✔ Regression	✔ ▶ (to the Independent box)
✔ Linear	✔ *x3*
✔ *y*	✔ ▶ (to the Independent box)
✔ ▶ (to the Dependent box)	✔ Statistics
✔ *x1*	✔ R square Change
✔ ▶ (to the Independent box)	✔ Continue
✔ Next	✔ OK

SPSS Output 7.9

Model Summary

Model	R	R Square	Adjusted R Square	Std. Error of the Estimate	Change Statistics				
					R Square Change	F Change	df1	df2	Sig. F Change
1	.843[a]	.711	.695	2.81977	.711	44.305	1	18	.000
2	.895[b]	.801	.764	2.47998	.090	3.635	2	16	.050

a. Predictors: (Constant), X1

b. Predictors: (Constant), X1, X3, X2

Coefficients of Partial Determination and Correlation: In the body fat example (text page 270) we obtain first the *Coefficient of Partial Correlation* for *X2* given *X1* is in the model, $r_{Y2|1}$. (Insert 7.5) This results in $r_{Y2|1} = 0.482$ (output not shown). We now can find the *Coefficient of Partial Determination* by squaring the *Coefficient of Partial Correlation*, $0.482^2 = 0.232$.

INSERT 7.5

✔ Analyze
✔ Correlate
✔ Partial
✔ *y*
✔ ► (to Variable box)
✔ *x2*
✔ ► (to Variable box)
✔ *x1*
✔ ► (to Controlling for: box)
✔ OK

Standardized Multiple Regression Model: To produce the standardized regression model, we use the regression procedure to regress *Y* on *X1* and *X2* using the Dwaine Studio data (ch06fi05.txt) and request Descriptives under the Statistics option (syntax not shown). Partial output for this procedure is shown in SPSS Output 7.10. Notice that standardized beta coefficients are standard output using SPSS regression procedure. With the descriptive statistics, we can use equation 7.53, text page 276, to shift the standardized regression coefficients back to the unstandardized regression coefficients.

$$b_1 = \left(\frac{s_y}{s_1}\right) b_1^* = \frac{36.1913}{18.620}(.748) = 1.455$$

SPSS Output 7.10

Descriptive Statistics

	Mean	Std. Deviation	N
Y	181.9048	36.19130	21
X1	62.0190	18.62033	21
X2	17.1429	.97035	21

Coefficients[a]

Model		Unstandardized Coefficients		Standardized Coefficients	t	Sig.
		B	Std. Error	Beta		
1	(Constant)	-68.857	60.017		-1.147	.266
	X1	1.455	.212	.748	6.868	.000
	X2	9.366	4.064	.251	2.305	.033

a. Dependent Variable: Y

Multicollinearity and Its Effects: When multiple predictor variables in a general linear regression model are correlated among themselves, we say there is *intercorrelation* or *multicollinearity* among these variables (text page 279). When there is multicollinearity among a set of predictor variables being considered for a general linear regression model, the extra regression (error) sum of squares for a given predictor or set of predictor variables will be different depending on which other of these predictor variables are in the model. On the other hand, if there is no multicollinearity among the predictor variables, the extra regression sum of squares will be the same no matter which other variables are included.

Work Crew Productivity Example: On text page 279, the authors present the results of an experiment on the effect of work crew size (*X1*) and level of pay (*X2*) on productivity (*Y*). The text presents results from a correlation matrix of the 3 variables and Table 7.7, the output of 3 separate regression models. We present the SPSS syntax for this example as a further illustration. The rationale closely follows that in the body fat example.

Note that we have presented the entire solution in syntax form, as opposed to using the graphical point-and-click interface. Additionally, we present a compact method of requesting the 3 regression models. That is, in one regression procedure, we regress *Y* on *X1* and *X2* (*enter=x1 x2*); this generates the regression model presented in Table 7.7 (a), text page 280. We then remove *X2* (*remove=x2*) from the model. This generates a model with *X1* only [text Table 7.7 (b)]. Finally, we remove *X1* (*remove=x1*) and enter *X2* (*enter=x2*) to generate a model with *X2* as the only predictor variable.

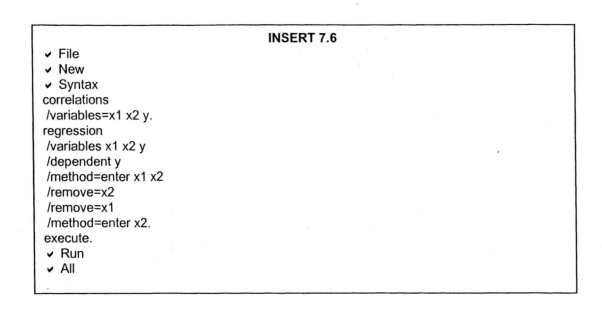

```
INSERT 7.6
✔ File
✔ New
✔ Syntax
correlations
 /variables=x1 x2 y.
regression
 /variables x1 x2 y
 /dependent y
 /method=enter x1 x2
 /remove=x2
 /remove=x1
 /method=enter x2.
execute.
✔ Run
✔ All
```

More on the Body Fat Example: On text page 283, the authors revisit the Body Fat example (text page 256) to illustrate the effect of *multicollinearity*. In Insert 7.7, we explore the relation between the predictor variables by producing a *scatter matrix* (SPSS Output 7.11) and *correlation matrix* (SPSS Output 7.12) of *X1*, *X2*, and *X3*. Note that $r_{12} = 0.924$ and although *X3* is not strongly correlated with *X1* and *X2* individually, the multiple R^2 when *X3* is regressed on *X1* and *X2* is 0.990. Thus, there is a strong correlation between *X3* and a linear function of *X1* and *X2* (Output 7.13). To see the change in parameter estimates as variables are added to the model, we regressed *Y* on *X2* and *Y* on *X1*, *X2*, and *X3* (SPSS Output 7.14). As noted in the text, the regression coefficient for *X2* changes in the two analyses from 0.659 to -2.857 due to the intercorrelations of the predictor variables. In Chapter 10, the authors explore formal methods to detect multicollinearity.

INSERT 7.7	INSERT 7.7 continued
✔ Graph ✔ Scatter ✔ Matrix ✔ Define ✔ *x1* ✔ ► (to the Matrix variables box) ✔ *x2* ✔ ► (to the Matrix variables box) ✔ *x3* ✔ ► (to the Matrix variables box) ✔ OK	✔ Analyze ✔ Correlate ✔ Bivariate ✔ *x1* ✔ ► (to the Variables box) ✔ *x2* ✔ ► (to the Variables box) ✔ *x3* ✔ ► (to the Variables box) ✔ OK

SPSS Output 7.11

SPSS Output 7.12

Correlations

		X1	X2	X3
X1	Pearson Correlation	1	.924**	.458*
	Sig. (2-tailed)	.	.000	.042
	N	20	20	20
X2	Pearson Correlation	.924**	1	.085
	Sig. (2-tailed)	.000	.	.723
	N	20	20	20
X3	Pearson Correlation	.458*	.085	1
	Sig. (2-tailed)	.042	.723	.
	N	20	20	20

**. Correlation is significant at the 0.01 level (2-tailed).

*. Correlation is significant at the 0.05 level (2-tailed).

SPSS Output 7.13

X3 regressed on X1 and X2

Model Summary

Model	R	R Square	Adjusted R Square	Std. Error of the Estimate
1	.995ᵃ	.990	.989	.37699

a. Predictors: (Constant), X2, X1

SPSS Output 7.14

Y regressed on *X1* and *X2*

Coefficients^a

Model		Unstandardized Coefficients		Standardized Coefficients	t	Sig.
		B	Std. Error	Beta		
1	(Constant)	-19.174	8.361		-2.293	.035
	X1	.222	.303	.219	.733	.474
	X2	.659	.291	.676	2.265	.037

a. Dependent Variable: Y

Y regressed on *X1, X2,* and *X3*

Coefficients^a

Model		Unstandardized Coefficients		Standardized Coefficients	t	Sig.
		B	Std. Error	Beta		
1	(Constant)	117.085	99.782		1.173	.258
	X1	4.334	3.016	4.264	1.437	.170
	X2	-2.857	2.582	-2.929	-1.106	.285
	X3	-2.186	1.595	-1.561	-1.370	.190

a. Dependent Variable: Y

Chapter 8 SPSS®

Regression Models for Quantitative and Qualitative Predictors

In this chapter, the authors discuss some special types of general linear regression models. They discuss *polynomial regression models, interaction regression models, regression models with qualitative predictor variables,* and *more complex regression models.* Recall the simple linear regression model is of the form:

$$Y_i = \beta_0 + \beta_1 X_i + \varepsilon_i$$

This model is said to be a *first-order model* because the predictor variable appears in the model expressed to the first power; i.e., $X_i^1 = X_i$. Similarly, the model:

$$Y_i = \beta_0 + \beta_1 X_{i1} + \beta_2 X_{i2} + \varepsilon_i$$

is a first-order model because the two predictor variables X_{i1} and X_{i2} each appear in the model expressed to the first power.

The model:

$$Y_i = \beta_0 + \beta_1 x_i + \beta_2 x_i^2 + \varepsilon_i$$

where $x_i = X_i - \overline{X}$ is the *centered predictor variable*, is called a *polynomial regression model*. It is referred to as a *second-order model with one predictor* because the single predictor variable appears in the model expressed to the second power; i.e., x_i^2. Similarly, the polynomial regression model:

$$Y_i = \beta_0 + \beta_1 x_i + \beta_2 x_i^2 + \beta_3 x_i^3 + \varepsilon_i$$

where $x_i = X_i - \overline{X}$, is a *third-order model with one predictor variable*. The regression model:

$$Y_i = \beta_0 + \beta_1 x_{i1} + \beta_2 x_{i2} + \beta_{11} x_{i1}^2 + \beta_{22} x_{i2}^2 + \beta_{12} x_{i1} x_{i2} + \varepsilon_i$$

where $x_{i1} = X_{i1} - \overline{X}_1$ and $x_{i2} = X_{i2} - \overline{X}_2$, is a *second-order model with two predictor variables*. The cross-product term represents the interaction effect between x_1 and x_2. This nomenclature extends to models with any number of predictor variables.

The authors use indicator variables that take on values 0 and 1 in a regression model to identify classes or categories of a qualitative variable. They use several examples to illustrate how to fit and interpret a variety of higher-order models including models where some of the predictor variables are quantitative and others are qualitative.

The Power Cell Example

Data File: ch08ta01.txt

Using data from Table 8.1, text page 300, researchers studied the relationship between charge rate and temperature on the life of a power cell. There were three levels (0.6, 1.0, and 1.4 amperes) of charge rate ($X1$) and three levels (10, 20, and 30° C) of ambient temperature ($X2$). The dependent variable (Y) was defined as the number of discharge-charge cycles that a power cell underwent before failure. See Chapter 0, "Working with SPSS," for instructions on opening the Power Cell example and renaming the variables Y, $X1$, and $X2$.

The researchers were uncertain of the expected response function, but decided to fit a second-order polynomial regression model. They first centered $X1$ and $X2$ around their respective means and scaled them using the absolute difference between adjacent levels of the variable. From Insert 8.1, we have computed the coded values for $X1$ and $X2$ ($x1code$ and $x2code$, respectively), the square of the coded values ($x1code2$ and $x2code2$, respectively), and the cross-product of $X1code$ and $X2code$ ($x12inter$). After executing the syntax in Insert 8.1, the active *Data Editor* should look like Output 8.1 and is consistent with Table 8.1, text page 300.

INSERT 8.1

- File
- New
- Syntax

* Type the following syntax.
```
compute x1code=(x1-1)/.4.
compute x2code=(x2-20)/10.
compute x1code2=x1code**2.
compute x2code2=x2code**2.
compute x12inter=x1code*x2code.
execute.
```
- Run
- All

SPSS Output 8.1

power cell example.sav - SPSS Data Editor

File Edit View Data Transform Analyze Graphs Utilities Window Help

19:

	y	x1	x2	x1code	x2code	x1code2	x2code2	x12inter
1	150.00	.60	10.00	-1.00	-1.00	1.00	1.00	1.00
2	86.00	1.00	10.00	.00	-1.00	.00	1.00	.00
3	49.00	1.40	10.00	1.00	-1.00	1.00	1.00	-1.00
4	288.00	.60	20.00	-1.00	.00	1.00	.00	.00
5	157.00	1.00	20.00	.00	.00	.00	.00	.00

Fitting the Model: We begin by obtaining the regression results of the second-order polynomial regression model and saving the unstandardized predicted values and residuals for future use (Insert 8.2). Partial results are shown in Output 8.2. The Unstandardized Coefficients in Output 8.2 are the estimated regression coefficients used in equation 8.16, text page 301.

```
┌─────────────────────────────────────────────────────────────┐
│                         INSERT 8.2                          │
│                                                             │
│   ✔ Analyze                                                 │
│   ✔ Regression                                              │
│   ✔ Linear                                                  │
│   ✔ y                                                       │
│   ✔ ▶ (to the Dependent box)                                │
│   ✔ x1code                                                  │
│   ✔ ▶ (to the Independent box)                              │
│   ✔ x2code                                                  │
│   ✔ ▶ (to the Independent box)                              │
│   ✔ x1code2                                                 │
│   ✔ ▶ (to the Independent box)                              │
│   ✔ x2code2                                                 │
│   ✔ ▶ (to the Independent box)                              │
│   ✔ x12inter                                                │
│   ✔ ▶ (to the Independent box)                              │
│   ✔ Save                                                    │
│   ✔ Unstandardized (Residual Values)                        │
│   ✔ Unstandardized (Predicted Values)                       │
│   ✔ Continue                                                │
│   ✔ OK                                                      │
└─────────────────────────────────────────────────────────────┘
```

SPSS Output 8.2

Model Summary

Model	R	R Square	Adjusted R Square	Std. Error of the Estimate
1	.956[a]	.914	.827	32.37418

a. Predictors: (Constant), X12INTER, X2CODE2, X2CODE, X1CODE, X1CODE2

ANOVA[b]

Model		Sum of Squares	df	Mean Square	F	Sig.
1	Regression	55365.561	5	11073.112	10.565	.011[a]
	Residual	5240.439	5	1048.088		
	Total	60606.000	10			

a. Predictors: (Constant), X12INTER, X2CODE2, X2CODE, X1CODE, X1CODE2

b. Dependent Variable: Y

393

Coefficients[a]

Model		Unstandardized Coefficients		Standardized Coefficients		
		B	Std. Error	Beta	t	Sig.
1	(Constant)	162.842	16.608		9.805	.000
	X1CODE	-55.833	13.217	-.556	-4.224	.008
	X2CODE	75.500	13.217	.751	5.712	.002
	X1CODE2	27.395	20.340	.184	1.347	.236
	X2CODE2	-10.605	20.340	-.071	-.521	.624
	X12INTER	11.500	16.187	.093	.710	.509

a. Dependent Variable: Y

Residual Plots: In this section we produce Figure 8.5, text page 303. The easiest way to produce the various plots of residuals and other values is with the *scatterplot matrix* procedure. That is, we request a *scatterplot matrix* of the unstandardized residuals (*res_1*) saved in Insert 8.2 above with the predicted value of Y ($\hat{Y}$), *x1code*, and *x2code* (Insert 8.3).

INSERT 8.3

✔ Graph
✔ Scatter
✔ Matrix
✔ Define
✔ *res_1*
✔ ► (to the Matrix variables box)
✔ *x1code*
✔ ► (to the Matrix variables box)
✔ *x2code*
✔ ► (to the Matrix variables box)
✔ *pre_1*
✔ ► (to the Matrix variables box)
✔ OK

Power Cell Example

Data File: ch08ta05.txt

Correlation Test for Normality: On text page 301, the researchers in the Power Cell example calculate the coefficient of correlation between the ordered residuals and their expected value under normality. The expected value under normality of the kth smallest observation from a sample of size n is given by:

$$\sqrt{MSE}\left[z\left(\frac{k-0.375}{n+0.25}\right)\right]$$

We find *MSE* = 1048.088 in Output 8.2 above and in this case $n = 11$. In Chapter 3 we give a detailed description of the steps necessary to obtain z and k. Insert 8.5 assumes that the residuals have been saved (*res_1*) from Insert 8.2 above. In Insert 8.4, we rank the residuals and place the rank in a variable named (by default) *rres_1*. We then compute *ev*, the expected value under normality and correlate this variable with *res_1*. The resulting correlation is 0.975, within rounding error of the value (0.974) reported on the text page 301.

INSERT 8.4

✔ File
✔ New
✔ Syntax
* Type the following syntax.
Rank
  variables=res_1.
Compute *ev* = sqrt(1048.088) * probit((*rres_1* - .375)/(11 + .25)).
Correlations
  /variables=ev res_1.
execute.
✔ Run
✔ All

Test of Fit: To perform a formal test of goodness of fit of the regression model, we use the *GLM* procedure as detailed in Insert 8.5. Output 8.3 contains the partial results of Insert 8.5. The *F*-value = 1.82 is identical to the Lack of Fit *F*-value reported on text page 302. Since the associated probability level of *F* is >0.05, we conclude that the second-order polynomial regression model is a good fit.

INSERT 8.5

✔ Analyze
✔ General Linear Model
✔ Univariate
✔ *y*
✔ ▶ (to the Dependent box)
✔ *x1code*
✔ ▶ (to the Covariate box)
✔ *x2code*
✔ ▶ (to the Covariate box)
✔ *x1code2*
✔ ▶ (to the Covariate box)
✔ *x2code2*
✔ ▶ (to the Covariate box)
✔ *x12code*
✔ ▶ (to the Covariate box)
✔ Options
✔ Lack of Fit
✔ Continue
✔ OK

Output 8.3

Lack of Fit Tests

Dependent Variable: Y

Source	Sum of Squares	df	Mean Square	F	Sig.
Lack of Fit	3835.772	3	1278.591	1.820	.374
Pure Error	1404.667	2	702.333		

Coefficient of Multiple Determination: The coefficient of multiple correlation ($R = 0.956$), the coefficient of multiple determination ($R^2 = 0.914$) and the adjusted coefficient of multiple correlation ($Adj\ R^2 = 0.827$) are given in Output 8.2 above.

Partial F Test: The researchers now want to test whether a first-order model is appropriate. That is, they wish to decide if $x1code2$, $x2code2$, and $x12inter$ can be dropped from the model; they test H_0: $\beta_{11} = \beta_{22} = \beta_{12} = 0$. Instead of using the extra sum of squares approach to test this null hypothesis, we use the block option within SPSS *Regression* (Insert 8.6). We enter $x1code$ and $x2code$ at block 1 and the higher-order variables at block 2, and request the R^2 Change statistic. Partial results are shown in Output 8.4. Consistent with text page 304, the F-value associated with the change in R^2 when the higher-order variables are added to a model that contain only the first-order variables is 0.782 and the associated probability level ("Sig. F Change") is 0.553. Thus, we fail to reject H_0: $\beta_{11} = \beta_{22} = \beta_{12} = 0$ and conclude that the first-order model is adequate.

INSERT 8.6

- ✔ Analyze
- ✔ Regression
- ✔ Linear
- ✔ y
- ✔ ▶ (to the Dependent box)
- ✔ x1code
- ✔ ▶ (to the Independent box)
- ✔ x2code
- ✔ ▶ (to the Independent box)
- ✔ Next
- ✔ x1code2
- ✔ ▶ (to the Independent box)
- ✔ x2code2
- ✔ ▶ (to the Independent box)
- ✔ x12code
- ✔ ▶ (to the Independent box)
- ✔ Statistics
- ✔ R squared change
- ✔ Continue
- ✔ OK

Output 8.4

Model Summary

Model	R	R Square	Adjusted R Square	Std. Error of the Estimate	R Square Change	F Change	df1	df2	Sig. F Change
						Change Statistics			
1	.934[a]	.873	.841	31.02486	.873	27.482	2	8	.000
2	.956[b]	.914	.827	32.37418	.041	.782	3	5	.553

a. Predictors: (Constant), X2CODE, X1CODE

b. Predictors: (Constant), X2CODE, X1CODE, X12INTER, X2CODE2, X1CODE2

First-Order Model: Based on the above analysis, the researchers chose to fit the first-order model:

$$Y_i = \beta_0 + \beta_1 x_{i1} + \beta_2 x_{i2} + \varepsilon_i$$

From Insert 8.7 we produce the first-order model; results are shown in Output 8.5. The regression coefficients are identical to those reported on text page 304, and b_1 and b_2 are identical to the same estimates shown in Output 8.2 above.

INSERT 8.7

- ✔ Analyze
- ✔ Regression
- ✔ Linear
- ✔ *y*
- ✔ ▶(to the Dependent box)
- ✔ *x1code*
- ✔ ▶(to the Independent box)
- ✔ *x2code*
- ✔ ▶(to the Independent box)
- ✔ OK

SPSS Output 8.5

Coefficients[a]

Model		Unstandardized Coefficients		Standardized Coefficients	t	Sig.
		B	Std. Error	Beta		
1	(Constant)	172.000	9.354		18.387	.000
	X1CODE	-55.833	12.666	-.556	-4.408	.002
	X2CODE	75.500	12.666	.751	5.961	.000

a. Dependent Variable: Y

Fitted First-Order Model in Terms of X: The first-order regression model above can be transformed back to the original variables by use of text equation 8.15. We can also obtain a fitted first order regression model by regressing Y on the original (untransformed) predictor variables $X1$ and $X2$. (Insert 8.8) The resulting estimated coefficients (not shown) are consistent with equation 8.19, text page 304; i.e., (unstandardized) $b_1' = -139.58$ and $b_2' = 7.55$ with standard errors $s\{b_1'\} = 31.66$ and $s\{b_2'\} = 1.26$.

INSERT 8.8

- ✔ Analyze
- ✔ Regression
- ✔ Linear
- ✔ y
- ✔ ▶(to the Dependent box)
- ✔ x1
- ✔ ▶(to the Independent box)
- ✔ x2
- ✔ ▶(to the Independent box)
- ✔ OK

Estimation of Regression Coefficients: The researcher now wished to estimate the Bonferroni 90% confidence limits in terms of the original predictor variables. We apply the confidence limits formula for β_1 and β_2 given in equation 6.52, text page 228. In Insert 8.9, we first find $B = t(1 - \alpha/2g; n - p)$. In this case, $\alpha = 0.10$ with two confidence intervals being estimated ($g = 2$), $n = 11$, and there are 3 parameters in the model ($p = 3$). Thus, in Insert 8.9 we find $B = idf.t(1 - (0.10/4), 8) = 2.306$. We obtain the numerical values $s\{b_1'\}$ (*sdb1*) and $s\{b_2'\}$ (*sdb2*) as shown on text page 305. Finally, we use equation 6.52, text page 228, to find the two Bonferroni simultaneous 90% confidence intervals: $-212.63 \le \beta_1 \le -66.55$ and $4.63 \le \beta_2 \le 10.47$. The confidence limits are written into the *Data Editor*.

INSERT 8.9

- ✔ File
- ✔ New
- ✔ Syntax

* Type the following syntax.

```
compute B=idf.t(1-(.1/4),8).
compute sdb1=(1/.4)*12.67.
compute sdb2=(1/10)*12.67.
compute b1lo=-139.59-(b*sdb1).
compute b1hi=-139.59+(b*sdb1).
compute b2lo=7.55-(b*sdb2).
compute b2hi=7.55+(b*sdb2).
execute.
```

- ✔ Run
- ✔ All

Insurance Innovation Example

Data File: ch08ta02.txt

An economist studied the relationship between the adoption of new insurance innovations and the type of insurance company and the size of the insurance firm (text page 313, 316). The response variable (time to adoption) is coded Y, and the predictor variables are coded $X1$ for size of the firm and $X2$ for type of firm where $X2 = 0$ for mutual companies and $X2 = 1$ for stock companies. See Chapter 0, "Working with SPSS," for instructions on opening ch08ta02.txt and renaming variables Y, $X1$, and $X2$. After opening the Insurance Innovation example, the first 5 lines in the SPSS *Data Editor* should look like Output 8.6.

SPSS Output 8.6

	y	x1	x2	var
1	17.0	151.00	0	
2	26.0	92.00	0	
3	21.0	175.00	0	
4	30.0	31.00	0	
5	22.0	104.00	0	

In Insert 8.10, we first produce Output 8.7, which is consistent with Figure 8.12, text page 318. The economist was most interested in the type of insurance firm ($X2$) on the response variable. In Insert 8.11 we request the first-order model including confidence limits for the coefficients in the regression model. Consistent with text page 316, the 95% confidence interval for β_2 is displayed as $4.977 \leq \beta_2 \leq 11.134$ (SPSS Output 8.8). Note that this is not a simultaneous confidence interval like the intervals calculated in the previous example. Because the interval does not include zero, we conclude H_a: $\beta_2 \neq 0$ or that the type of insurance firm has a significant effect on the response variable. This conclusion can also be reached based on the probability level (*Sig.* = 0.000) of the *t*-value ($t = 5.521$) associated with $X2$.

INSERT 8.10	INSERT 8.10 continued
✔ Graph	
✔ Scatter	✔ OK
✔ Simple	* Open Chart Editor by double clicking on the graph
✔ Define	in the Viewer window.
✔ *y*	✔ Chart
✔ ▶ (to the Y axis box)	✔ Options
✔ *x1*	✔ Subgroups
✔ ▶ (to the X axis box)	✔ OK
✔ *x2*	* Close Chart Editor.
✔ ▶ (to the Set Markers by: box)	

SPSS Output 8.7

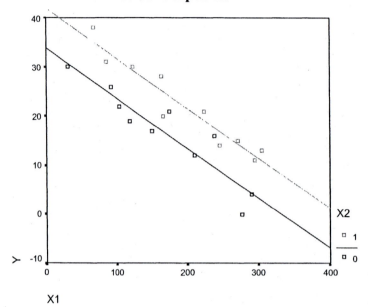

X1

INSERT 8.11

- ✔ Analyze
- ✔ Regression
- ✔ Linear
- ✔ *y*
- ✔ ► (to the Dependent box)
- ✔ *x1*
- ✔ ► (to the Independent box)
- ✔ *x2*
- ✔ ► (to the Independent box)
- ✔ Statistics
- ✔ Confidence Intervals
- ✔ Continue
- ✔ OK

SPSS Output 8.8

Coefficients[a]

Model		Unstandardized Coefficients		Standardized Coefficients	t	Sig.	95% Confidence Interval for B	
		B	Std. Error	Beta			Lower Bound	Upper Bound
1	(Constant)	33.874	1.814		18.675	.000	30.047	37.701
	X1	-.102	.009	-.911	-11.443	.000	-.121	-.083
	X2	8.055	1.459	.439	5.521	.000	4.977	11.134

a. Dependent Variable: Y

400

On text page 326, the economist wanted to test the hypothesis that there is no interaction between size ($X1$) and type ($X2$) of insurance company. Thus, he fitted a regression model (equation 8.49, text page 324) that included the interaction term $X1X2$, the cross-product of $X1$ and $X2$. In Insert 8.12, we compute $X1X2$ and then fit the regression model with $X1$, $X2$, and $X1X2$ as predictors. We test the hypothesis that there is no interaction in terms of β_3; i.e., we test H_0: $\beta_3 = 0$ against H_a: $\beta_3 \neq 0$. From Output 8.9 and consistent with text page 326, we see the t-value associated with $X1X2$ is -0.023, $p = 0.982$. Thus, the economist concluded that the interaction is not statistically significant and, hence, the interaction term should be dropped from the model.

INSERT 8.12

✔ File
✔ New
✔ Syntax
* Type the following syntax.
compute x1x2=x1*x2.
execute.
✔ Run
✔ All

✔ Analyze
✔ Regression
✔ Linear
✔ y
✔ ▶(to the Dependent box)
✔ x1
✔ ▶(to the Independent box)
✔ x2
✔ ▶(to the Independent box)
✔ x1x2
✔ ▶(to the Independent box)
✔ OK

SPSS Output 8.9

Coefficients[a]

Model		Unstandardized Coefficients		Standardized Coefficients	t	Sig.
		B	Std. Error	Beta		
1	(Constant)	33.838	2.441		13.864	.000
	X1	-.102	.013	-.909	-7.779	.000
	X2	8.131	3.654	.443	2.225	.041
	X1X2	.000	.018	-.005	-.023	.982

a. Dependent Variable: Y

Soap Production Lines Example

Data File: ch08ta05.txt

A company studied the relationship between production line speed (*X1*) and the amount of scrap (*Y*) generated on their 2 production lines (*X2*). The data are presented in Table 8.5, text page 330. After opening ch08ta05.txt and renaming the variables, the first 5 lines in the SPSS *Data Editor* should look like Output 8.10.

SPSS Output 8.10

```
┌────────────────────────────────────────────────┐
│ ▦ Untitled - SPSS Data Editor                   │
├────────────────────────────────────────────────┤
│ File  Edit  View  Data  Transform  Analyze  Graphs  Utilities  W │
├────────────────────────────────────────────────┤
│  [toolbar icons]                                 │
├────────────────────────────────────────────────┤
│ 1 : y                          │218              │
└────────────────────────────────────────────────┘
```

	y	x1	x2	var
1	218.00	100.00	1	
2	248.00	125.00	1	
3	360.00	220.00	1	
4	351.00	205.00	1	
5	470.00	300.00	1	

Based on text Figure 8.16, the researchers decided to fit a model with an interaction term:

$$Y_i = \beta_0 + \beta_1 X_{i1} + \beta_2 X_{i2} + \beta_3 X_{i1} X_{i2} + \varepsilon_i$$

To produce the Tentative Model (text page 330), we first compute a new variable, *X1X2*, the cross-product of *X1* and *X2*. (Insert 8.13)   We then fit a model using *Y* as the dependent variable and *X1*, *X2*, and *X1X2* as independent variables and save the unstandardized residuals (*res_1*) and predicted values (*pre_1*). This produces Output 8.11, which is consistent with Table 8.6(a), text page 332.

INSERT 8.13	INSERT 8.13 continued
✔ File	✔ ▶(to the Dependent box)
✔ New	✔ x1
✔ Syntax	✔ ▶(to the Independent box)
* Type the following syntax.	✔ x2
compute x1x2=x1*x2.	✔ ▶(to the Independent box)
execute.	✔ x1x2
✔ Run	✔ ▶(to the Independent box)
✔ All	✔ Save
✔ Analyze	✔ Unstandardized (Residual Values)
✔ Regression	✔ Unstandardized (Predicted Values)
✔ Linear	✔ Continue
✔ y	✔ OK

SPSS Output 8.11

ANOVA[b]

Model		Sum of Squares	df	Mean Square	F	Sig.
1	Regression	169164.7	3	56388.228	130.949	.000[a]
	Residual	9904.057	23	430.611		
	Total	179068.7	26			

a. Predictors: (Constant), X1X2, X1, X2

b. Dependent Variable: Y

Coefficients[a]

Model		Unstandardized Coefficients		Standardized Coefficients	t	Sig.
		B	Std. Error	Beta		
1	(Constant)	7.574	20.870		.363	.720
	X1	1.322	.093	1.010	14.273	.000
	X2	90.391	28.346	.552	3.189	.004
	X1X2	-.177	.129	-.242	-1.371	.184

a. Dependent Variable: Y

Diagnostics: Separate production line plots of the line speed ($X1$) against Y are requested in Insert 8.14. (Output not shown.) The researchers in the Soap Production Lines Example next calculated the coefficient of correlation between the ordered residuals and their expected values under normality. The expected value under normality of the kth smallest observation from a sample of size n is given by:

$$\sqrt{MSE}\left[z\left(\frac{k-.375}{n+.25} \right) \right]$$

We find $MSE = 430.611$ in Output 8.11 above and $n = 27$ in the Soap Production Lines Example. In Chapter 3 we give a detailed description of the steps necessary to obtain z and k. Insert 8.15 assumes that the residuals have been saved (res_1) from Insert 8.13 above. In Insert 8.15 we rank the residuals and place the rank in a variable named (by default) rres_1. We then compute the expected value under normality, ev, and correlate this variable with res_1. The resulting correlation is 0.990, as reported on text page 331. From Table B.6, text page 673, the critical value for $\alpha = .05$ and $n = 28$ is 0.962. The calculated value is greater than the critical value found in the table, so we conclude there is sufficient evidence to support the assumption of normality of error terms.

Continuing on text page 331, the authors formally test for constancy of error variance using the Brown-Forsythe test as described in Chapter 3. For simplicity, we again divide the process into steps:

- Step 1: (Insert 8.16) Divide the data file into two subsets. In the Soap Production Lines Example this has been done based on the value of $X2$ where $X2 = 1$ if production line = 1 and $X2 = 0$ if production line = 2. Also, execute Insert 8.13 to save the unstandardized residual values for the second order regression model where $X1$, $X2$, and $X1X2$ are predictor variables.

- Step 2: Use Explore to obtain the median residual values $\tilde{e}_1$ (Production line = 1, therefore, $X2 = 1$) = 5.4959 and $\tilde{e}_2$ (Production line = 2, therefore, $X2 = 0$) = -6.2203.

- Step 3: Find *absdevmd*, the absolute value (*abs*) of the residual minus the median residual value for the respective group, d_{i1} and d_{i2}.

- Step 4: Find the means of *absdevmd* for the two groups, $\bar{d}_1 = 16.132$ and $\bar{d}_2 = 12.648$.

- Step 5: Find *sqrdev*, the square of *absdevmd* minus the respective group mean of *absdevmd*.

- Step 6: Find the sum of *sqrdev* for the two production lines, $\sum(d_{i1} - \bar{d}_1)^2 = 2952.19$ and $\sum(d_{i2} - \bar{d}_2)^2 = 2045.82$.

We now have the values required to calculate the Brown-Forsythe statistic:

$$s^2 = \frac{2{,}952.20 + 2{,}04582}{27 - 2} = 199.921$$

$$s = \sqrt{199.921} = 14.139$$

$$t^*_{BF} = \frac{16.132 - 12.648}{14.139\sqrt{\dfrac{1}{15} + \dfrac{1}{12}}} = .636$$

Using $\alpha = 0.05$ and $df = 25$, the critical value of t can be obtained by the *inverse distribution function*, "compute IDF.T(0.975, 25) = IDF.T(0.975, 25)", which will return 2.060. Since $t^*_{BF} = 0.636 < 2.060$, we conclude that there is constancy of error variance. Further, we can find the two-sided p-value of $t^*_{BF} = 0.636$ using the *cumulative distribution function*. For example, in the *Syntax Editor* we can use "compute *tprob*=(1−CDF.T(*tvalue*, 25))*2 where *tvalue* = IDF.T(0.975, 25). The *CDF.T* function will return 0.5305, the two-side p-value where $t = 0.636$ and $df = 25$ as reported on text page 333.

INSERT 8.16

* Step 1.
* Use *X*2 for Step 1.

* Step 2.
- ✔ Analyze
- ✔ Descriptive Statistics
- ✔ Explore
- ✔ *res_1*
- ✔ ► (to the Dependent List)
- ✔ *x2*
- ✔ ► (to the Factor List)
- ✔ OK

*Step 3.
- ✔ File
- ✔ New
- ✔ Syntax
* Type the following syntax.
if (x2=0) absdevmd=abs(res_1-(-6.2203)).
if (x2=1) absdevmd=abs(res_1-(5.4959)).
execute.
- ✔ Run
- ✔ All

* Step 4.
- ✔ Analyze
- ✔ Descriptive Statistics
- ✔ Explore
- ✔ *absdevmd*
- ✔ ► (to the Dependent List)
- ✔ *x2*
- ✔ ► (to the Factor List)
- ✔ OK

* Step 5.
- ✔ File
- ✔ New
- ✔ Syntax
* Type the following syntax.
if (x2=0) *sqrdev*=(absdevmd-12.648)**2.
if (x2=1) *sqrdev*=(absdevmd-16.132)**2.
execute.
- ✔ Run
- ✔ All

* Step 6.
- ✔ Analyze
- ✔ Compare Means
- ✔ Means
- ✔ *sqrdev*
- ✔ ► (to the Dependent List)
- ✔ *group*
- ✔ ► (to the Independent List)
- ✔ Options
- ✔ Sum
- ✔ ► (to the Cell Statistics)
- ✔ Continue
- ✔ OK

Inferences about Two Regression Lines: The researchers now wish to test the identity of the regression lines for the two soap production lines. The null and alternative hypotheses, respectively, are:

$$H_0 : \beta_2 = \beta_3 = 0$$

and

$$H_a : not\ both\ \beta_2 = 0\ and\ \beta_3 = 0$$

To test the null hypothesis using equation 7.27, text page 267, we need to produce text Table 8.6(b), which lists Type I sum of squares. Type I sum of squares is only available in SPSS through the General Linear Model (*GLM*). Output 8.12 is the result using *GLM* to regress *Y* on *X1*, *X2*, and *X1X2* and requesting Type I sum of squares in the Model window. (Syntax not shown.) We can now use equation 8.56a, text page 333, to solve for $F^* = 22.65$ shown on text page 333. Alternatively, we can use the block option in the Regression procedure to test the current hypothesis. In Insert 8.17 we enter *X1* at block 1 and *X2*, *X1X2* at block 2, and request *R Squared Change* statistics. From Output 8.13, we see that the *F*-value for Model 2 is 22.647. This is the effect of adding *X2* and *X1X3* to a model that already contains *X1*; this is, we test the effect of *X2*, *X1X2|X1*. Since the computed *F*-value (22.647) is greater than the table *F*-value (5.67) when $\alpha = 0.01$, we conclude that the regression functions are not the same for the two production lines.

SPSS Output 8.12

Tests of Between-Subjects Effects

Dependent Variable: Y

Source	Type I Sum of Squares	df	Mean Square	F	Sig.
Corrected Model	169164.684[a]	3	56388.228	130.949	.000
Intercept	2687271.3	1	2687271.259	6240.598	.000
X1	149660.983	1	149660.983	347.555	.000
X2	18694.079	1	18694.079	43.413	.000
X1X2	809.623	1	809.623	1.880	.184
Error	9904.057	23	430.611		
Total	2866340.0	27			
Corrected Total	179068.741	26			

a. R Squared = .945 (Adjusted R Squared = .937)

INSERT 8.17	**INSERT 8.17 continued**
✔ Analyze	✔ x2
✔ Regression	✔ ▶(to the Independent box)
✔ Linear	✔ x1x2
✔ y	✔ ▶(to the Independent box)
✔ ▶(to the Dependent box)	✔ Statistics
✔ x1	✔ R squared change
✔ ▶(to the Independent box)	✔ Continue
✔ Next	✔ OK

SPSS Output 8.13

Model Summary

Model	R	R Square	Adjusted R Square	Std. Error of the Estimate	Change Statistics				
					R Square Change	F Change	df1	df2	Sig. F Change
1	.914[a]	.836	.829	34.29738	.836	127.229	1	25	.000
2	.972[b]	.945	.937	20.75117	.109	22.647	2	23	.000

a. Predictors: (Constant), X1

b. Predictors: (Constant), X1, X2, X1X2

Coefficients[a]

Model		Unstandardized Coefficients		Standardized Coefficients	t	Sig.
		B	Std. Error	Beta		
1	(Constant)	64.036	23.249		2.754	.011
	X1	1.196	.106	.914	11.280	.000
2	(Constant)	7.574	20.870		.363	.720
	X1	1.322	.093	1.010	14.273	.000
	X2	90.391	28.346	.552	3.189	.004
	X1X2	-.177	.129	-.242	-1.371	.184

a. Dependent Variable: Y

The researcher also wanted to test whether the slopes of the regression lines for the two production lines were identical. The null and alternative hypotheses are:

$$H_0 : \beta_3 = 0$$

and

$$H_a : \beta_3 \neq 0$$

We can test the null hypothesis by text equation 7.25 or the partial F-test, text equation 7.24. Text Table 8.6(b) and Output 8.12 above provide the necessary to information to find (text equation 8.57a) $F^* = 1.88$. Equivalently, we can use Output 8.13 (Coefficients Table) to obtain $t = -1.371$ for $X1X2$. Remember that $t^2 = F$ and $-1.371^2 = 1.88$. Thus, the t-statistic in Output 8.13 using Type III sum of squares is a partial test of $X1X2|X1, X2$. Since the probability level 0.184 is greater than the required $\alpha = 0.01$ we conclude H_0, that the slopes of the regression functions are not significantly different.

You may notice in Output 8.12 that $F = 1.88$ for $X1X2$ and that this output is based on Type I sum of squares. Remember that the order of entry into the model does not effect Type III sum of squares but does effect Type I sum of squares. Since $X1X2$ is entered into the model after $X1$ and $X2$ for Output 8.12 (Type I sum of squares), it is testing the effect of $X1X2|X1, X2$. Output 8.13 is based on Type III sum of squares so the order of entry does not matter. The two tests are identical here only because *X1X2* was the last variable entered into the model in Output 8.12. If, however, we used Output 8.12 to test the effect of *X2*, we would be testing the effect of *X2|X1*. If we use Output 8.13 to test the effect of *X2*, we would be testing the effect of *X2|X1, X1X2*. Notice that the effect of *X2* is Output 8.12 and Output 8.13 are not identical, that is $F = 41.413 \neq t^2 = 3.189^2$). Also note that we requested Type I sum of squares to produce Output 8.12; the default sum of squares in SPSS *General Linear Model* is Type III. Finally, to produce the 95% confidence limits for β_2, use Insert 8.17 and also ✔ Confidence Limits while in the Statistics window.

Chapter 9 SPSS®

Building the Regression Model I: Model Selection and Validation

This chapter presents numerous strategies that are often used to build a regression model. These tactics include making use of theoretical relationships and knowledge gained from previous studies as well as information contained in a set of data available for analysis. We frequently have a large set of potential predictor variables and we wish to choose a subset of these variables to build a regression model that is efficient in its use of predictor variables. This process involves checking for outlying observations as well as investigating the contributions of potential predictor variables. The problem is complicated by the fact that there may be multicollinearity among the predictor variables. We may visually inspect relationships that are sometimes revealed in well-planned graphs. The authors discuss the criteria commonly used to select the predictor variables for inclusion or exclusion from the model. They then discuss three basic ways to validate a regression model once the selection process is in its final stages (see text page 369). These techniques are illustrated with well-chosen numerical examples.

Surgical Unit Example

Data File: ch09ta01.txt

A hospital studied the survival time (Y) of patients who had undergone a liver operation. The predictor or explanatory variables for the predictive regression model were blood clotting score ($X1$), prognostic index ($X2$), enzyme function score ($X3$), and liver function score ($X4$). The researchers also extracted from the preoperative evaluation the patients age ($X5$), sex ($X6$), and history of alcohol use, coded as two indicator variables, $X7$ (moderate use) and $X8$ (severe use). A representation of the Surgical Unit data set is shown in Table 9.1, text page 350. See Chapter 0, "Working with SPSS," for instructions on opening the Surgical Unit data file and renaming the variables $X1, X2, X3, X4, X5, X6, X7, X8$, Y, and $ylog$. After opening ch09ta01.txt, the first 5 lines in the SPSS *Data Editor* should look like SPSS Output 9.1.

SPSS Output 9.1

	x1	x2	x3	x4	x5	x6	x7	x8	y	ylog
1	6.70	62 0	81 00	2 59	50 0	0	1	0	695	6 54
2	5 10	59 0	66 00	1 70	39 0	0	0	0	403	6 00
3	7 40	57 0	83 00	2 16	55 0	0	0	0	710	6 57
4	6.50	73 0	41 00	2 01	48 0	0	0	0	349	5 85
5	7 80	65 0	115 0	4 30	45 0	0	0	1	2343	7 76

The researchers selected a random sample of 108 patients. Because the researchers intended to validate the final model, the sample was split into a model-building set (first 54 cases) and a validation set (second 54 cases). To simplify the illustration, the researchers used only the first four available predictors variables. We begin by regressing Y on $X1$, $X2$, $X3$, and $X4$, and saving the unstandardized residuals and predicted values. (Syntax not shown.) In Insert 9.1 we produce Figures 9.2(a and b), text page 351, as shown in SPSS Output 9.2 (a and b). SPSS Output 9.2(a) suggests both nonconstant error variances and curvature. That is, the variability of the residual values increases as the magnitude of the predicted values increases. Additionally, when we add a Lowess curve (discussed in Chapter 4) to SPSS Output 9.2(a), we obtain SPSS Output 9.2(c). Notice that the Lowess curve supports the text's suspicion of curvature. Because of the above findings, the investigator used a logarithmic transformation of Y to obtain *ylog*. Based on various diagnostics, the investigator then decided to use *ylog* as the response variable; to use $X1$, $X2$, $X3$, and $X4$ as predictors; and to not include any interaction terms in the linear regression model.

INSERT 9.1

* text Figure 9.2a.
- ✔ Graph
- ✔ Bar
- ✔ Simple
- ✔ Define
- ✔ *res_1*
- ✔ ▶ (to the Y axis)
- ✔ *pre_1*
- ✔ ▶ (to the X axis)
- ✔ OK

* text Figure 9.2b.
- ✔ Analyze
- ✔ Descriptive Statistics
- ✔ Explore
- ✔ *res_1*
- ✔ ▶ (to the Dependent List)
- ✔ Plots
- ✔ Normality Plots with tests
- ✔ Continue
- ✔ OK

* Double click the Normal Q-Q plot is the output viewer and then double click
* on any data point that is not on the diagonal line. Switch the axes and then close
* the Chart Editor.

SPSS Output 9.2

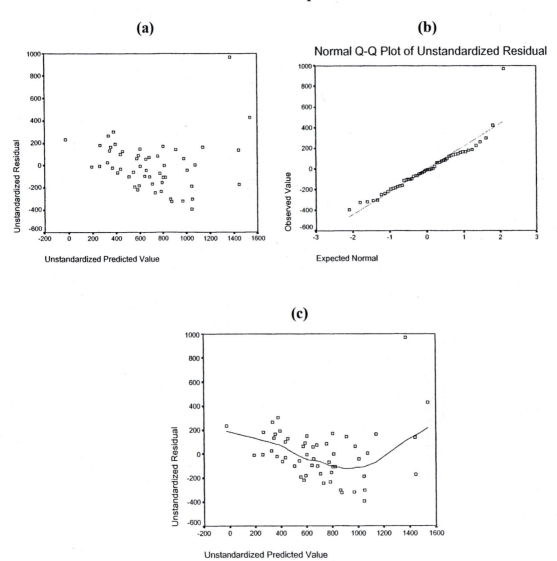

Criteria for Model Selection

The *All-Possible-Regressions Procedure* compares all possible sub-sets of potential predictor variables that could be used to build regression models. Based on various criteria, a small number of regression models are selected for further examination. The number of candidate models, however, increases exponentially as the number of predictor variables increase. A study with only 3 predicator variables has $2^3 = 8$ possible first-order regression models whereas one with 7 predictor variables has $2^7 = 128$. Thus, all-possible-regressions procedures can be used when the number of potential predictor variables is relatively small, but become impractical for use when the number is large.

SPSS does not have available an all-possible-regressions procedure. Using the *Syntax Editor*, however, we can approximate this procedure. The SSE_p, R_p^2, $R_{a,p}^2$, C_p, AIC_p, SBC_p, and

$PRESS_p$ values for all-possible-regression models are presented in Table 9.2, text page 353, for the Surgical Unit example. To begin the approximation of text Table 9.2, we fit a regression model using a dialogue box with *X1* as the only predictor variable and *ylog* as the dependent variable. Note from Insert 9.2 that we do not click OK; instead we click Paste to instruct SPSS to paste the syntax of the current Regression dialogue box into a *Syntax Editor* window. Maximize the SPSS *Syntax Editor* window; it should look like Insert 9.3.

INSERT 9.2

- ✔ Analyze
- ✔ Regression
- ✔ Linear
- ✔ *ylog*
- ✔ ▶ (to the Dependent box)
- ✔ *x1*
- ✔ ▶ (to the Independent box)
- ✔ **Paste**

INSERT 9.3

REGRESSION
/MISSING LISTWISE
/STATISTICS COEFF OUTS R ANOVA
/CRITERIA=PIN(.05) POUT(.10)
/NOORIGIN
/DEPENDENT ylog
 /METHOD=ENTER x1 .

Continuing the approximation, we instruct SPSS to enter and remove each of the 16 possible sub-sets of predictor variables into regression models. (Inserts 9.4 and 9.5) That is, we modify Insert 9.3 to appear as Insert 9.4 by entering *X1* into a regression model and then removing *X1*, entering *X2* and then removing *X2*, etc. Note that Insert 9.4 contains 6 *enter* statements and 6 *remove* statements. This is because SPSS allows only 12 such steps in a *regression* command. Thus, to approximate all 16 sub-sets, we have to break the analysis into 3 separate *regression* commands. To request available selection criteria, type "*selection*" at the end of the "*/STATISTICS*" line. This option will request the *Akaike Information Critrion, Amemiya Prediction Criterion, Mallows' Prediction Criterion* (C_p), and *Schwarz Bayesian Criterion*. Copy the syntax in the *Syntax Editor* (Insert 9.4), paste it twice into the space below, and edit as needed. The *Syntax Editor* should look like Inserts 9.4 and 9.5 combined. Now ✔ *Run* and ✔ *All*. Partial results of this maneuver are shown in SPSS Output 9.3. Notice in the following table the correspondence between text Table 9.2 and SPSS Output 9.3.

Text Table 9.2 heading	SPSS Output 9.3 heading	Comment
SSE_p	Not present – See comment	R_p^2 varies inversely with SSE_p
R_p^2	R Square	
$R_{a,p}^2$	Adjusted R Square	
C_p	Mallows' Prediction Criterion	
AIC_p	Akaike Information Criterion	
SBC_p	Schwarz Bayesian Criterion	
$PRESS_p$	Not present – See comment	Easily calculated in SPSS

INSERT 9.4

```
REGRESSION
/MISSING LISTWISE
/STATISTICS COEFF OUTS R ANOVA (selection)
/CRITERIA=PIN(.05) POUT(.10)
/NOORIGIN
/DEPENDENT ylog
 /METHOD=enter x1
 /METHOD=remove x1
 /METHOD=enter x2
 /METHOD=remove x2
 /METHOD=enter x3
 /METHOD=remove x3
 /METHOD=enter x4
 /METHOD=remove x4
 /METHOD=enter x1 x2
 /METHOD=remove x1 x2
 /METHOD=enter x1 x3
 /METHOD=remove x1 x3.
```

414

Notice in the footnotes the predictor variables associated with each model in SPSS Output 9.3. Model 1 contains $X1$ and the row values are consistent with text Table 9.2 where $X1$ is the only X variable in the model. For Model 2 of SPSS Output 9.3, $R_p^2 = .0$, $AIC_p = -75.703$, $C_p = 151.498$, and $SBC_p = -73.714$. Remember that we entered $X1$ at step 1 and removed $X1$ at step 2. Thus, Model 2 contains no variables and the row values are consistent with those reported in text Table 9.2 when the model contains only an intercept. Now, Model 3 contains $X2$; again the row values are consistent with text Table 9.2 where $X2$ is the only X variable in the model. Model 4 (SPSS Output 9.3) contains no variables and Model 5 contains $X3$. The progression of the models continues for each of the three regression procedures.

SPSS Output 9.4 contains the first of the 3 ANOVA summary tables for this maneuver. Notice that the $SSE = 12.031$ for Model 1 ($X1$ only) is consistent with the SSE_p reported in text Table 9.2 for a model with $X1$ only. Continuing the progression, Model 2 contains no variables and is not of interest. Model 3 contains $X2$ and the SSE is consistent with SSE_p reported in text Table 9.2 for a model with $X2$ only.

SPSS Output 9.3

Model Summary

Model	R	R Square	Adjusted R Square	Std. Error of the Estimate	Selection Criteria			
					Akaike Information Criterion	Amemiya Prediction Criterion	Mallows' Prediction Criterion	Schwarz Bayesian Criterion
1	.246[a]	.061	.043	.48101	-77.079	1.012	141.164	-73.101
2	.000[b]	.000	.000	.49158	-75.703	1.038	151.498	-73.714
3	.470[c]	.221	.206	.43807	-87.178	.839	108.556	-83.200
4	.000[b]	.000	.000	.49158	-75.703	1.038	151.498	-73.714
5	.654[d]	.428	.417	.37549	-103.827	.616	66.489	-99.849
6	.000[b]	.000	.000	.49158	-75.703	1.038	151.498	-73.714
7	.649[e]	.422	.410	.37746	-103.262	.623	67.715	-99.284
8	.000[b]	.000	.000	.49158	-75.703	1.038	151.498	-73.714
9	.513[f]	.263	.234	.43029	-88.162	.824	102.031	-82.195
10	.000[b]	.000	.000	.49158	-75.703	1.038	151.498	-73.714
11	.741[g]	.549	.531	.33668	-114.658	.504	43.852	-108.691
12	.246[a]	.061	.043	.48101	-77.079	1.012	141.164	-73.101

a. Predictors: (Constant), X1

b. Predictor: (constant)

c. Predictors: (Constant), X2

d. Predictors: (Constant), X3

e. Predictors: (Constant), X4

f. Predictors: (Constant), X2, X1

g. Predictors: (Constant), X1, X3

SPSS Output 9.4

ANOVA[h]

Model		Sum of Squares	df	Mean Square	F	Sig.
1	Regression	.776	1	.776	3.355	.073[a]
	Residual	12.031	52	.231		
	Total	12.808	53			
2	Regression	.000	0	.000	.	.[b]
	Residual	12.808	53	.242		
	Total	12.808	53			
3	Regression	2.829	1	2.829	14.74	.000[c]
	Residual	9.979	52	.192		
	Total	12.808	53			
4	Regression	.000	0	.000	.	.[b]
	Residual	12.808	53	.242		
	Total	12.808	53			
5	Regression	5.476	1	5.476	38.84	.000[d]
	Residual	7.332	52	.141		
	Total	12.808	53			
6	Regression	.000	0	.000	.	.[b]
	Residual	12.808	53	.242		
	Total	12.808	53			
7	Regression	5.399	1	5.399	37.89	.000[e]
	Residual	7.409	52	.142		
	Total	12.808	53			
8	Regression	.000	0	.000	.	.[b]
	Residual	12.808	53	.242		
	Total	12.808	53			
9	Regression	3.365	2	1.683	9.087	.000[f]
	Residual	9.443	51	.185		
	Total	12.808	53			
10	Regression	.000	0	.000	.	.[b]
	Residual	12.808	53	.242		
	Total	12.808	53			
11	Regression	7.027	2	3.513	31.00	.000[g]
	Residual	5.781	51	.113		
	Total	12.808	53			
12	Regression	.776	1	.776	3.355	.073[a]
	Residual	12.031	52	.231		
	Total	12.808	53			

a. Predictors: (Constant), X1

b. Predictor: (constant)

c. Predictors: (Constant), X2

d. Predictors: (Constant), X3

e. Predictors: (Constant), X4

f. Predictors: (Constant), X2, X1

g. Predictors: (Constant), X1, X3

h. Dependent Variable: YLOG

Following this progression through the three regression procedures in Inserts 9.4 and 9.5, text Table 9.2 will be produced with the exception of the $PRESS_p$ statistic. Although SPSS does not directly produce the $PRESS_p$ statistic, it is easily calculated for individual regression models. From text page 360, the $PRESS_p$ statistic for a regression model is the sum of the squared deleted residuals. For a model with *X1* only, for example, we regress *ylog* on *X1;* save the deleted residuals (*dre_1* by default) in the active *Date Editor*; and square and sum the deleted residuals. (Insert 9.6) SPSS Output 9.5 contains the sum of the squared deleted residual (*press* = 13.51) which is consistent with the $PRESS_p$ = 13.512 reported in text Table 9.2 for *X1* only.

INSERT 9.6

✔ Analyze
✔ Regression
✔ Linear
✔ *ylog*
✔ ▶ (to the Dependent box)
✔ *x1*
✔ Save
✔ Deleted Residuals
✔ Continue
✔ OK

✔ New
✔ File
✔ Syntax
compute press = dre_1**2 .
execute .
descriptives press
 /stat=sum.
✔ Run
✔ All

SPSS Output 9.5

Descriptive Statistics

	N	Sum
PRESS	54	13.51
Valid N (listwise)	54	

Automatic Search Procedures

SPSS does not have a readily available best subset algorithm for model selection. It does, however, have other automatic search procedures for variable reduction. In the Linear Regression dialogue window, there are five methods of variable selection available: *Enter*, *Stepwise*, *Remove*, *Backward*, and *Forward*. (SPSS Output 9.6)

SPSS Output 9.6

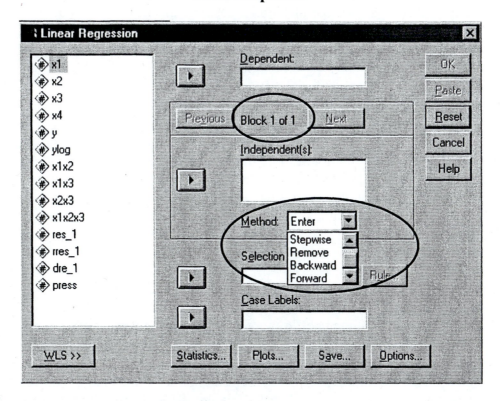

Enter and Remove Methods: The *Enter* and *Remove* methods enter and remove an entire block of variables. The *Enter* method creates a forced entry of all variables in a single step in order of decreasing tolerance. The *Enter* method can be used to control the order of variable entry by using the Block option (SPSS Output 9.6) in the Regression dialogue box. For instance, using the Surgical Unit Example, one could enter *X4* at Block 1 and enter *X1*, *X2*, and *X3* at Block 2. A partial output of the maneuver is shown in SPSS Output 9.7. Notice that Model 1 contains *X4* only and that Model 2 contains *X4* plus *X1*, *X2*, and *X3*. The *Enter* method can also be used to simultaneously enter an entire set of predictor variables in the model. The *Remove* method removes all specified variables in a single step as in Inserts 9.4 and 9.5.

SPSS Output 9.7

Coefficients[a]

Model		Unstandardized Coefficients		Standardized Coefficients	t	Sig.
		B	Std. Error	Beta		
1	(Constant)	5.612	.143		39.381	.000
	X4	.298	.048	.649	6.156	.000
2	(Constant)	3.852	.266		14.467	.000
	X4	.032	.051	.070	.625	.535
	X1	.084	.029	.273	2.902	.006
	X2	.013	.002	.435	5.471	.000
	X3	.016	.002	.676	7.443	.000

a. Dependent Variable: YLOG

Stepwise Selection: The *Stepwise* selection method first selects the best predictor variable (the predictor variable with the largest partial correlation with the response variable). Additional variables are added to the model based on their incremental improvement to the reduction in error sum of squares. Variables are dropped from the model if their test for entry is not significant given the other variables in the model. The default and modifiable α limits for adding and removing a variable are 0.05 and 0.10, respectively.

Using the Stepwise method in SPSS to regress *ylog* on all eight *X* variables from the Surgical Unit Example results in SPSS Output 9.8. From SPSS Output 9.8 – Coefficients table, note that *X3* is entered at step (Model) 1 because *X3* had the highest partial correlation (not shown) with the response variable. From SPSS Output 9.8 – Excluded Variables, we note that *X2* has the highest partial correlation (.642) with the response function of the variables not in the model at step (Model) 1. Thus, *X2* is added to the model at step 2, SPSS Output 9.8 – Coefficients table. Of the variables not in the model at step 2, *X8* has the highest partial correlation (.584) with the response variable and is added to the model at step 3, SPSS Output 9.8 – Coefficients table. Again, of the variables not in the model at step 3, *X1* has the highest partial correlation (.483) with the response variable and is added to the model at step 4, SPSS Output 9.8 – Coefficients table. Beginning with step 2, the search algorithm compares the probability level of the partial correlation of the variables in the model to the α level needed to remove a variable from the model. A variable is removed from the model if the *p*-value associated with the partial correlation is greater than the predetermined α level to remove. In the present example, no variables were removed from the model. Notice that the *p*-value associated with each variable not in the model at step 4 (Model 4 – Excluded Variables, SPSS Output 9.8) is greater than the α level needed to add that variable to the model. Thus, the stepping process terminates with only *X3*, *X2*, *X8*, and *X1* in the final model.

SPSS Output 9.8

Coefficients[a]

Model		Unstandardized Coefficients B	Std. Error	Standardized Coefficients Beta	t	Sig.
1	(Constant)	5.264	.194		27.138	.000
	X3	.015	.002	.654	6.232	.000
2	(Constant)	4.351	.214		20.296	.000
	X3	.015	.002	.665	8.186	.000
	X2	.014	.002	.486	5.975	.000
3	(Constant)	4.291	.176		24.356	.000
	X3	.014	.002	.626	9.326	.000
	X2	.015	.002	.513	7.677	.000
	X8	.429	.084	.342	5.084	.000
4	(Constant)	3.852	.193		19.992	.000
	X3	.015	.001	.668	11.072	.000
	X2	.014	.002	.488	8.196	.000
	X8	.353	.077	.282	4.573	.000
	X1	.073	.019	.239	3.865	.000

a. Dependent Variable: YLOG

SPSS Output 9.8 continued

Excluded Variables[e]

Model		Beta In	t	Sig.	Partial Correlation	Collinearity Statistics Tolerance
1	X1	.352[a]	3.699	.001	.460	.978
	X2	.486[a]	5.975	.000	.642	.999
	X4	.456[a]	4.679	.000	.548	.827
	X5	-.137[a]	-1.310	.196	-.180	1.000
	X6	.143[a]	1.365	.178	.188	.980
	X7	-.071[a]	-.675	.503	-.094	.993
	X8	.300[a]	3.060	.004	.394	.986
2	X1	.311[b]	4.401	.000	.528	.970
	X4	.283[b]	3.108	.003	.402	.683
	X5	-.114[b]	-1.409	.165	-.195	.998
	X6	.082[b]	.987	.328	.138	.964
	X7	-.134[b]	-1.664	.102	-.229	.977
	X8	.342[b]	5.084	.000	.584	.980
3	X1	.239[c]	3.865	.000	.483	.907
	X4	.233[c]	3.101	.003	.405	.671
	X5	-.075[c]	-1.119	.269	-.158	.984
	X6	.106[c]	1.578	.121	.220	.960
	X7	.051[c]	.655	.516	.093	.729
4	X4	.091[d]	.968	.338	.138	.390
	X5	-.078[d]	-1.316	.194	-.187	.984
	X6	.089[d]	1.494	.142	.211	.954
	X7	.050[d]	.715	.478	.103	.729

a. Predictors in the Model: (Constant), X3

b. Predictors in the Model: (Constant), X3, X2

c. Predictors in the Model: (Constant), X3, X2, X8

d. Predictors in the Model: (Constant), X3, X2, X8, X1

e. Dependent Variable: YLOG

Forward Elimination: The *Forward* method begins with no predictor variables in the model. The predictor variable with the largest partial correlation with the response variable is entered in the model. This method continues to add variables with significant ($p<\alpha$ to add) partial correlations. Notice from SPSS Output 9.9 that the progression of predictor variable entry is the same as the *Stepwise* method shown in SPSS Output 9.8. However, the *Forward* method makes no attempt to remove variables from the model. Since the *Stepwise* procedure above did not remove any predictor variables from the model and the *Forward* method makes no attempt to remove variables, the result of the *Stepwise* method (SPSS Output 9.8) and *Forward* method (SPSS Output 9.9) are the same in the present example, although this will not always be true.

SPSS Output 9.9

Coefficients[a]

Model		Unstandardized Coefficients		Standardized Coefficients	t	Sig.
		B	Std. Error	Beta		
1	(Constant)	5.264	.194		27.138	.000
	X3	.015	.002	.654	6.232	.000
2	(Constant)	4.351	.214		20.296	.000
	X3	.015	.002	.665	8.186	.000
	X2	.014	.002	.486	5.975	.000
3	(Constant)	4.291	.176		24.356	.000
	X3	.014	.002	.626	9.326	.000
	X2	.015	.002	.513	7.677	.000
	X8	.429	.084	.342	5.084	.000
4	(Constant)	3.852	.193		19.992	.000
	X3	.015	.001	.668	11.072	.000
	X2	.014	.002	.488	8.196	.000
	X8	.353	.077	.282	4.573	.000
	X1	.073	.019	.239	3.865	.000

a. Dependent Variable: YLOG

Backward Elimination: The *Backward* method begins with all predictor variables in the model. It then removes each predictor variable that does not have a significant ($p > \alpha$ to remove) partial correlation with the response variable. Again, we are using the default and modifiable α limits for adding and removing a variable, 0.05 and 0.10, respectively. From SPSS Output 9.10 we see that at step (Model) 1 all eight *X* variables are entered in the model. Because the probability level ("Sig.") of *X4* is greater than the α needed to remove a variable and is greater than other probability levels of variables in the model, *X4* is removed at step 2. *X7*, *X5*, and *X6* are then removed based on their significance levels at steps 2, 3, and 4, respectively. The final model contains *X1*, *X2*, *X3*, and *X8*.

We have used *Stepwise* selection, *Forward* elimination, and *Backward* elimination to reduce the number of predictor variables in the Surgical Unit example. It should be somewhat reassuring to the researcher that each method yielded the same final model.

SPSS Output 9.10

Coefficients[a]

Model		Unstandardized Coefficients		Standardized Coefficients		
		B	Std. Error	Beta	t	Sig.
1	(Constant)	4.051	.252		16.089	.000
	X1	.069	.025	.223	2.695	.010
	X2	.013	.002	.463	6.909	.000
	X3	.015	.002	.647	8.264	.000
	X4	.008	.047	.017	.172	.865
	X5	-.004	.003	-.081	-1.296	.202
	X6	.084	.061	.086	1.386	.173
	X7	.058	.067	.059	.857	.396
	X8	.388	.088	.310	4.394	.000
2	(Constant)	4.037	.236		17.093	.000
	X1	.071	.019	.233	3.824	.000
	X2	.014	.002	.468	7.896	.000
	X3	.015	.001	.655	10.906	.000
	X5	-.004	.003	-.084	-1.429	.160
	X6	.087	.058	.089	1.505	.139
	X7	.059	.067	.060	.880	.383
	X8	.388	.087	.309	4.439	.000
3	(Constant)	4.054	.235		17.266	.000
	X1	.072	.019	.233	3.837	.000
	X2	.014	.002	.473	8.047	.000
	X3	.015	.001	.654	10.912	.000
	X5	-.003	.003	-.078	-1.342	.186
	X6	.087	.058	.089	1.513	.137
	X8	.351	.076	.280	4.594	.000
4	(Constant)	3.867	.191		20.292	.000
	X1	.071	.019	.232	3.791	.000
	X2	.014	.002	.478	8.073	.000
	X3	.015	.001	.654	10.821	.000
	X6	.087	.058	.089	1.494	.142
	X8	.363	.077	.289	4.740	.000
5	(Constant)	3.852	.193		19.992	.000
	X1	.073	.019	.239	3.865	.000
	X2	.014	.002	.488	8.196	.000
	X3	.015	.001	.668	11.072	.000
	X8	.353	.077	.282	4.573	.000

a. Dependent Variable: YLOG

423

Model Validation: Surgical Unit Example continued

Data File: ch09ta05.txt

Continuing with the Surgical Unit example, the researchers identified three candidate models using the model-selection criteria presented above: SSE_p, R_p^2, $R_{a,p}^2$, C_p, AIC_p, SBC_p, and $PRESS_p$. The researchers now wish to estimate the predictive capability of the three models using the *mean squared prediction error* ($MSPR$) described on text page 370. Model 1, given on text page 373, uses *ylog* as the response variable and *X1*, *X2*, *X3*, and *X8* as predictor variables. In Insert 9.9, we first find the regression model based on Model 1 using the Surgical Unit **training data set** presented in Table 9.1, text page 350. The estimated regression coefficients are given in SPSS Output 9.11. We now open the Surgical Unit **validation data set** presented in Table 9.5, text page 374. After opening ch09ta05.txt and renaming the variables, the first 5 lines of the data file should look like SPSS Output 9.12.

INSERT 9.9

- ✔ Analyze
- ✔ Regression
- ✔ Linear
- ✔ ylog
- ✔ ▶(to the Dependent box)
- ✔ x1
- ✔ ▶(to the Independent box)
- ✔ x2
- ✔ ▶(to the Independent box)
- ✔ x3
- ✔ ▶(to the Independent box)
- ✔ x8
- ✔ ▶(to the Independent box)
- ✔ OK

SPSS Output 9.11

Coefficients[a]

Model		Unstandardized Coefficients		Standardized Coefficients	t	Sig.
		B	Std. Error	Beta		
1	(Constant)	3.852	.193		19.992	.000
	X1	.073	.019	.239	3.865	.000
	X2	.014	.002	.488	8.196	.000
	X3	.015	.001	.668	11.072	.000
	X8	.353	.077	.282	4.573	.000

a. Dependent Variable: YLOG

424

SPSS Output 9.12

	x1	x2	x3	x4	x5	x6	x7	x8	y	ylog
1	7.10	23.0	78.00	1.93	45.0	0	1	0	302.0	5.71
2	4.90	66.0	91.00	3.05	34.0	1	0	0	767.0	6.64
3	6.40	90.0	35.00	1.06	39.0	1	0	1	487.0	6.19
4	5.70	35.0	70.00	2.13	68.0	1	0	0	242.0	5.49
5	6.10	42.0	69.00	2.25	70.0	0	0	1	705.0	6.56

From equation 9.20, text page 370, we now compute $\hat{Y}_i(m1)$, the predicted value of the ith observation in the validation data set using the regression coefficients (SPSS Output 9.11) estimated from the training data set. (Insert 9.10) We then find $devsq=\left(Y_i-\hat{Y}_i\right)^2$, where Y_i is the value of the response variable of the ith observation in the validation data. Finally, we find the $\sum_{i=1}^{n^*}\left(Y_i-\hat{Y}_i\right)^2$ (SPSS Output 9.13). We find by hand calculator $\sum_{i=1}^{n^*}\left(Y_i-\hat{Y}_i\right)^2/n = .07735$.

A note on precision is in order. If in Insert 9.10 we had used the regression coefficients displayed in SPSS Output 9.11 (3 positions to the right of the decimal) to find $\sum_{i=1}^{n^*}\left(Y_i-\hat{Y}_i\right)^2$ and then divided this quantity by 4.18 as displayed in SPSS Output 9.13, we would have found that $MSPR = 0.08259$ for Model 1. This is in disagreement with $MSPR = 0.0773$ reported on text page 373 and is due to the relative magnitude of the numbers involved in the above calculations. That is, because the numbers are relatively small, we require more precise estimates. To gain this precision, double click on the Coefficients table (SPSS Output 9.11) while in the SPSS Viewer. Then double click on the number for which you desire greater precision. SPSS Output 9.14 and 9.15 display the result of this maneuver when attempting to gain more precise regression coefficients and $\sum_{i=1}^{n^*}\left(Y_i-\hat{Y}_i\right)^2$. SPSS Output 9.13 and 9.15 are a result of using 5-digit precision in all calculations and result in $MSPR = .07735$, which is consistent with $MSPR = .0773$ reported on text page 373.

We repeat the above process by estimating regression functions for Models 2 and 3 on text page 373 based on the Surgical Unit training data set and finding $\sum_{i=1}^{n^*}\left(Y_i-\hat{Y}_i\right)^2/n$ when using the validation data set. This will result in $MSPR = 0.0764$ and 0.0794, respectively. From the relative closeness of the three $MSPR$ values, the researchers concluded that the three candidate models performed equally in terms of predictive accuracy. Model 3 was discarded due to reversal of the sign of a regression coefficient from the training data set to the validation data set. Models 1 and 2 preformed equally well in the validation study. The final selection of Model 1 was based on Occam's razor; Model 1 required one less parameter than Model 2.

SPSS Output 9.13

Descriptive Statistics

	N	Sum
DEV	54	4.18
Valid N (listwise)	54	

SPSS Output 9.14

Coefficients[a]

Model		Unstandardized Coefficients		Standardized Coefficients	t	Sig.
		B	Std. Error	Beta		
1	(Constant)	3.85241856	.193		19.992	.000
	X1	.073	.019	.239	3.865	.000
	X2	.014	.002	.488	8.196	.000
	X3	.015	.001	.668	11.072	.000
	X8	.353	.077	.282	4.573	.000

a. Dependent Variable: YLOG

SPSS Output 9.15

Descriptive Statistics

	N	Sum
DEV	54	4.17732685
Valid N (listwise)	54	

Chapter 10 SPSS®

Building the Regression Model II: Diagnostics

This chapter is concerned with diagnostic techniques for identifying inadequacies of a fitted regression model. Graphical methods were used in previous chapters as an aid in deciding whether to use higher-order terms for a predictor variable in the model or whether to add predictor variables that have not been included in the model. Chapter 10 discusses graphs that can provide useful model building information about a predictor variable given that other predictor variables are already in the model. When we fit a regression model to a set of data, some observations may be outlying or extreme relative to most of the data. As shown in Figure 10.5, text page 391, an observaton may contain a *Y* value, one or more *X* values, or both that are outliers. Outlying observations may have too much influence on the estimates of the parameters of the model and, therefore, may require remedial steps. The authors discuss methods for detecting outliers and excessively influential observations. They also discuss remedial steps for dealing with these observations. In Section 10.5, text page 406, the authors continue their discussion of problems created when there is multicollinearity among the predictor variables of a regression model. They present informal methods of detecting multicollinearity problems on text page 407. They then define the variance inflation factor and show how it is used in more formal ways to check for serious multicollinearity among the predictor variables.

The Life Insurance Example

Data File: ch10ta01.txt

Table 10.1, text page 387, presents data from a study of the relationship between amount of insurance carried (*Y*) and annual income (*X1*) and a measure of risk aversion (*X2*). After opening the Life Insurance data file, the first 5 cases of the *Data Editor* should look like SPSS Output 10.1.

SPSS Output 10.1

	x1	x2	y	var
1	45.01	6.0	91 00	
2	57.20	4.0	162 00	
3	26.85	5.0	11 00	
4	66.29	7.0	240 00	
5	40.96	5 0	73 00	

We begin by regressing Y on $X1$ and $X2$ and saving the unstandardized residuals. (Insert 10.1) We then plot $X2$ on the x-axis and the residuals (*res_1*) on the y-axis to produce Figure 10.3 (a), text page 387, (SPSS Output 10.2). Since we will not need *res_1* for the remainder of the problem, we delete this variable from the *Data Editor*. To produce text Figure 10.3 (b), we regress Y on $X2$ and save the unstandardized residuals by default as *res_1*. If we had not deleted *res_1* above, the second residual would be stored as *res_2*. We then regress $X1$ on $X2$ and save the unstandardized residual values by default as *res_2*. We request a scatter plot with *res_1* [$e(Y \mid X_2)$] on the y-axis and *res_2* [$e(X_1 \mid X_2)$] on the x-axis. This produces SPSS Output 10.3.

SPSS Output 10.2

SPSS Output 10.3

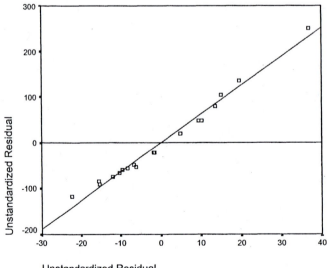

INSERT 10.1	**INSERT 10.1 continued**
✔ Analyze ✔ Regression ✔ Linear ✔ *y* ✔ ► (to the Dependent box) ✔ *x1* ✔ ► (to the Independent box) ✔ *x2* ✔ ► (to the Independent box) ✔ Save ✔ Unstandardized (Residual Values) ✔ Continue ✔ OK ✔ Graphs ✔ Scatter ✔ Simple ✔ Define ✔ *res_1* ✔ ► (to the Y axis box) ✔ *x1* ✔ ► (to the X axis box) ✔ OK * Double click on the scatter plot to open the Chart Editor. ✔ Chart ✔ Reference Line * Add a reference line on the Y-axis at position 0. * Close the Chart Editor. ✔ Analyze ✔ Regression ✔ Linear ✔ *y* ✔ ► (to the Dependent box) ✔ *x2* ✔ ► (to the Independent box) ✔ Save ✔ Unstandardized (Residual Values) ✔ Continue ✔ OK	✔ Analyze ✔ Regression ✔ Linear ✔ *x1* ✔ ► (to the Dependent box) ✔ *x2* ✔ ► (to the Independent box) ✔ Save ✔ Unstandardized (Residual Values) ✔ Continue ✔ OK ✔ Graphs ✔ Scatter ✔ Simple ✔ Define ✔ *res_1* ✔ ► (to the Y axis box) ✔ *res_2* ✔ ► (to the X axis box) ✔ OK * Double click on the scatter plot to open the Chart Editor. ✔ Chart ✔ Options ✔ Fit Options ✔ OK ✔ Chart ✔ Reference Line * Add a reference line on the Y-axis at position 0. * Close the Chart Editor.

The Body Fat Example

Data File: ch07ta01.txt

We use the Body Fat example (Table 7.1, text page 257) to illustrate all regression diagnostics. See Chapter 0, "Working with SPSS," for instructions on opening the Body Fat example and renaming the variables *X1*, *X2*, *X3*, and *Y*. After opening ch07ta01.txt, the first 5 lines in your SPSS *Data Editor* should look like SPSS Output 10.4.

SPSS Output 10.4

body fat example.sav - SPSS Data Editor

File Edit View Data Transform Analyze Graphs Utilities Window Help

1 : x1   19.5

	x1	x2	x3	y	var
1	19.50	43.10	29.10	11.90	
2	24.70	49.80	28.20	22.80	
3	30.70	51.90	37.00	18.70	
4	29.80	54.30	31.10	20.10	
5	19.10	42.20	30.90	12.90	

Added-Variable Plots: We begin by regressing body fat (*Y*) on triceps skinfold thickness (*X1*) and thigh circumference (*X2*) and saving the unstandardized residuals (Insert 10.2). This results in the regression analysis shown in SPSS Output 10.2. The fitted regression function is:

$$\hat{Y} = -19.174 + 0.222X_1 + 0.659X_2$$

INSERT 10.2

✔ Analyze
✔ Regression
✔ Linear
✔ *y*
✔ ▶ (to the Dependent box)
✔ *x1*
✔ ▶ (to the Independent box)
✔ *x2*
✔ ▶ (to the Independent box)
✔ Save
✔ Unstandardized (Residual Values)
✔ Continue
✔ OK

SPSS Output 10.5

ANOVA[b]

Model		Sum of Squares	df	Mean Square	F	Sig.
1	Regression	385.439	2	192.719	29.797	.000[a]
	Residual	109.951	17	6.468		
	Total	495.389	19			

a. Predictors: (Constant), X2, X1

b. Dependent Variable: Y

Coefficients[a]

Model		Unstandardized Coefficients		Standardized Coefficients	t	Sig.
		B	Std. Error	Beta		
1	(Constant)	-19.174	8.361		-2.293	.035
	X1	.222	.303	.219	.733	.474
	X2	.659	.291	.676	2.265	.037

a. Dependent Variable: Y

We now plot the residuals (*res_1*) against *X1* and *X2* (Insert 10.3). This produces Figures 10.4 (a) and (c), text page 389. (SPSS Output 10.6) To produce text Figures 10.4 (b) and (d), we use the regression procedure and request that all partial plots be generated (Insert 10.4). This produces the text Figures 10.4 (b) and (d) without the regression line. To insert the regression line on the charts, we use the *Chart Editor* to request that a linear regression line be fitted through the data points. SPSS Output 10.7 is equivalent to text Figures 10.4 (b) and (d).

INSERT 10.3

✔ Graphs
✔ Scatter
✔ Simple
✔ Define
✔ *res_1*
✔ ▶(to the Y axis box)
✔ *x1*
✔ ▶(to the X axis box)
✔ OK
✔ Graphs
✔ Scatter
✔ Simple
✔ Define
✔ *res_1*
✔ ▶(to the Y axis box)
✔ *x2*
✔ ▶(to the X axis box)
✔ OK

SPSS Output 10.6

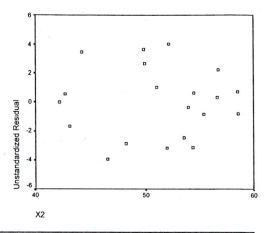

INSERT 10.4

- ✔ Analyze
- ✔ Regression
- ✔ Linear
- ✔ *y*
- ✔ ▶ (to the Dependent box)
- ✔ *x1*
- ✔ ▶ (to the Independent box)
- ✔ *x2*
- ✔ ▶ (to the Independent box)
- ✔ Plots
- ✔ Produce all partial plots
- ✔ Continue
- ✔ OK

* Double click on one of the charts to open the Chart Editor.
- ✔ Chart
- ✔ Options
- ✔ Total (under Fit Line)
- ✔ OK

* Close Chart Editor.
* Repeat the above 4 steps for the second chart.

SPSS Output 10.7

Partial Regression Plot

Dependent Variable: Y

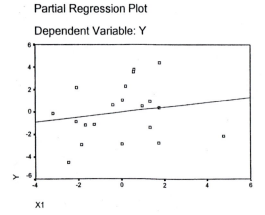

Partial Regression Plot

Dependent Variable: Y

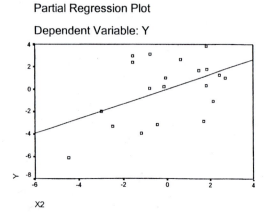

Illustration of Hat Matrix

Data File: ch10ta02.txt

On text page 393, the authors present a small data set to illustrate the relationship between the response variable and the predictor variables. After opening ch10ta02.txt and renaming the variables $X1$, $X2$, and Y, the 4 cases in the *Data Editor* should look like SPSS Output 10.8. In Insert 10.5, we create a new variable named $X0$ that is equal 1 for each of the 4 cases. This variable will be used to create the **X** matrix. We then set matrixes **CON**, **X1**, **X2**, and **Y** to the column variables $X0$, $X1$, $X2$, and Y, respectively, in the *Data Editor*. We create the **X** matrix by concatenating **X0**, **X1**, and **X2**. We then use various text equations to find the **B** (parameter estimates), **H** (hat matrix), **YHAT** (predicted values), and **VARCOVAR** (variance-covariance) matrices. Although the syntax only prints **VARCOVAR**, a *print* statement for any matrix can be added at any location in the matrix program.

SPSS Output 10.8

	y	x1	x2	var
1	301.00	14.0	25.0	
2	327.00	19.0	32.0	
3	246.00	12.0	22.0	
4	187.00	11.0	15.0	

INSERT 10.5	INSERT 10.5 CONTINUED
✔ File ✔ New ✔ Syntax * Write a column of 1's into the Hat Matrix Example. * data data file. compute x0=1. execute. matrix. get con / variables =x0. get x1 / variables = x1. get x2 / variables = x2. * Define the Y matrix. get y /variables=y. * Define the X matrix. compute x = {con, x1, x2}. * Fine the b matrix using text equation 6.25. compute b=inv(t(x)*x)*t(x)*y.	* Find hat matrix (hat) by text equation 10.10. compute hat=x*inv(t(x)*x)*t(x). * Find fitted values of y (yhat) by text equation 10.11. compute yhat=hat*y. * Create a 4x4 idenity (I) matrix. compute I=ident(4,4). * Find variance-covariance matrix using text equation. * 10.13. compute varcovar=574.9*(i-hat). print varcovar. end matrix. execute. ✔ Run ✔ All

433

Formal Diagnostics: The remainder of the diagnostics on text pages 390-410 deals with *residuals*, *deleted residuals*, *leverage values*, *DFFITS*, *DFBETAS*, *Cook's distance measure*, and *variance inflation factors*. To produce these statistics we request the appropriate regression model as before. While defining the regression model we also click *Save* and select the needed available options. (SPSS Output 10.9) For instance, if you select *studentized residuals*, *studentized deleted residuals*, *Cook's distance measure*, *leverage values*, and *DIFF*, the resulting values will be saved in the *Data Editor* as *sre_1*, *sdr_1*, *coo_1*, *lev_1*, and *dff_1*, respectively. SPSS also provides a summary table of residual statistics for use in diagnostics, as in the above Body Fat example. (SPSS Output 10.10)

SPSS Output 10.9

SPSS Output 10.10

Residuals Statistics[a]

	Minimum	Maximum	Mean	Std. Deviation	N
Predicted Value	12.2294	26.3838	20.1950	4.50403	20
Std. Predicted Value	-1.769	1.374	.000	1.000	20
Standard Error of Predicted Value	.56915	1.55098	.95209	.25891	20
Adjusted Predicted Value	11.9443	26.3747	20.2928	4.56721	20
Residual	-3.9469	4.0147	.0000	2.40559	20
Std. Residual	-1.552	1.579	.000	.946	20
Stud. Residual	-1.712	1.661	-.017	1.026	20
Deleted Residual	-5.0567	4.4425	-.0978	2.84958	20
Stud. Deleted Residual	-1.826	1.760	-.018	1.062	20
Mahal. Distance	.002	6.117	1.900	1.622	20
Cook's Distance	.000	.490	.065	.113	20
Centered Leverage Value	.000	.322	.100	.085	20

a. Dependent Variable: Y

Identifying Outlying *Y* Observations – Studentized Deleted Residuals: On text page 396 the researchers wished to examine whether there were outlying *Y* observations when using a regression model with two predictor variables (*X1* and *X2*). In Insert 10.6 we obtain a first order regression model with predictors *X1* and *X2* and request that the *unstandardized* and *studentized deleted residuals* be saved. (Insert 10.6 – Step 1) The *Data Editor* will contain the *unstandardized* and *studentized deleted residuals* (*res_1* and *sdr_1*, respectively, SPSS Output 10.11), consistent with columns 1 and 3 of Table 10.3, text page 397. The researchers now wish to determine if case 13 is an outlier based on the *studentized deleted residual* (text page 397). Using SPSS it is actually just as simple to test for outliers for each of the 20 cases. The appropriate Bonferroni critical value is $t(1-\alpha/2n; n-p-1)$ where $\alpha = 0.10$, $n = 20$, and $p =$ number of parameters in the model (*X1*, *X2*, and β_0) or $t(1-0.10/2*20; 20-3-1) = t(0.9975,16)$. In Insert 10.6 – Step 2, we use the *inverse distribution function* to fine *tvalue* = $t(0.9975;16) = 3.2519$. We then compare the absolute value of the *studentized deleted residual* (*abs(sdr_1)*) to *tvalue*. If the absolute value of the *studentized deleted residual* is greater than *tvalue*, we set *outlier* = 1, otherwise *outlier* = 0. Consistent with text page 398, all data lines in the *Data Editor* with *outlier* = 1 should be considered to be outliers and, conversely, all data lines with *outlier* = 0 should be considered not to be outliers . If we were dealing with a large data file, more than 100 data lines, for example, we could search the entire *Data Editor* using ✔ Data ✔ Select Cases to find all data lines with *outlier* = 1.

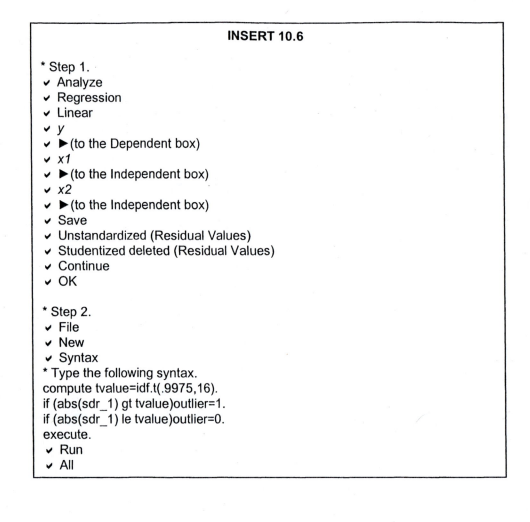

INSERT 10.6

* Step 1.
- ✔ Analyze
- ✔ Regression
- ✔ Linear
- ✔ *y*
- ✔ ▶ (to the Dependent box)
- ✔ *x1*
- ✔ ▶ (to the Independent box)
- ✔ *x2*
- ✔ ▶ (to the Independent box)
- ✔ Save
- ✔ Unstandardized (Residual Values)
- ✔ Studentized deleted (Residual Values)
- ✔ Continue
- ✔ OK

* Step 2.
- ✔ File
- ✔ New
- ✔ Syntax
* Type the following syntax.
compute tvalue=idf.t(.9975,16).
if (abs(sdr_1) gt tvalue)outlier=1.
if (abs(sdr_1) le tvalue)outlier=0.
execute.
- ✔ Run
- ✔ All

SPSS Output 10.11

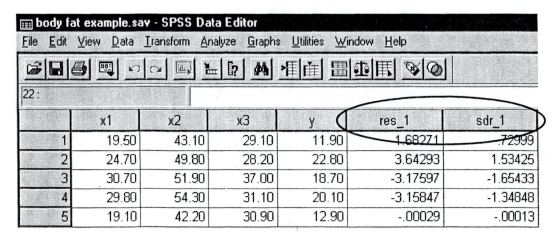

	x1	x2	x3	y	res_1	sdr_1
1	19.50	43.10	29.10	11.90	1.68271	.72999
2	24.70	49.80	28.20	22.80	3.64293	1.53425
3	30.70	51.90	37.00	18.70	-3.17597	-1.65433
4	29.80	54.30	31.10	20.10	-3.15847	-1.34848
5	19.10	42.20	30.90	12.90	-.00029	-.00013

Identifying Outlying *X* Observations - Hat Matrix Leverage Values: To identify potentially outlying cases, the researchers in the Body Fat example plotted triceps skinfold thickness (*X1*) against thigh circumference (*X2*) and identified each line by a case number (text page 399).

436

Notice that the Body Fat data file does not have a variable that represents case number. The "*compute case=$casenum*" statement in Insert 10.7 creates a new variable in the *Data Editor* that is a sequential count of each of the 20 cases. We then request a scatter plot of *X1* against *X2* and that data points be labeled by *case*. (The default value for decimal places in 2. If you produce the scatter plot (SPSS Output 10.12) with this default setting for *case*, the plot will appear cluttered because each case number will be printed with 2 zeros to the right of the decimal. Remedy this by setting the decimal places for *case* to 0 using the *Variable View* tab of the *Data Editor*.) Note that cases 3 and 15 appear to be outliers with respect to the *X* values.

INSERT 10.7	INSERT 10.7 continued
✔ File ✔ New ✔ Syntax * Type the following syntax. compute case=$casenum. execute. ✔ Run ✔ All	✔ Graphs ✔ Scatter ✔ Simple ✔ Define ✔ *x2* ✔ ▶ (to Y axis box) ✔ *x1* ✔ ▶ (to X axis box) ✔ *case* ✔ ▶ (to Label Cases by box) ✔ Options ✔ Display Chart with Case Labels ✔ Continue ✔ OK

SPSS Output 10.12

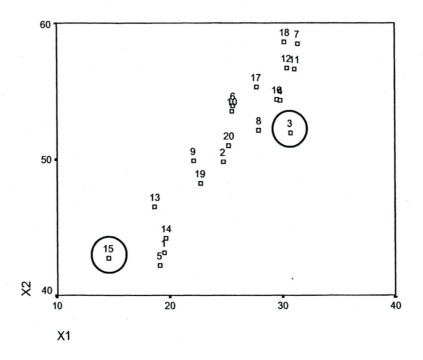

The diagonal element (h_{ii}) of the hat matrix is a measure of the ith case from the center of all X cases. The larger the value of h_{ii} the larger the effect the case has on the corresponding fitted value $(\hat{y}_i)$. Thus, h_{ii} is referred to as the *leverage* of the ith case. In Insert 10.8, we regress Y on *X1* and *X2* and request that leverage values (*lev_1* by default) be saved in the *Data Editor*. Note that SPSS will save **centered leverage values**. The leverage values (h_{ii}) reported in column 2 of Table 10.3, text page 397, are non-centered values. Centered leverages can be found by subtracting $1/n$ from the non-centered leverages, where n is the number of cases. Non-centered leverage values are found by adding $1/n$ to the centered values reported by SPSS. (Centered leverages are multiplied by n-1 to obtain the *Mahalanobis Distance measure*.) Thus, in Insert 10.8 we add 1/20 to *lev_1* and place the result in *nclev* (non-centered leverage values). The values of *nclev* in the *Data Editor* will be identical to the leverage values (h_{ii}) reported in column 2 of text Table 10.3.

The text defines a "large" leverage value as one that is more than twice the magnitude of the mean leverage value, defined as:

$$\bar{h} = \frac{p}{n}$$

where p is the number of regression parameters (including the intercept) and n is the number of cases. So, the non-centered leverage (*nclev*) is considered large in this example if *nclev* > 2*3/20. If so, we set *hilev* = 1, otherwise *hilev* = 0. After executing Insert 10.8 note that case numbers 3 and 15 have high leverage values as indicated by *hilev* = 1 in the *Data Editor*.

INSERT 10.8

✔ Analyze
✔ Regression
✔ Linear
✔ *y*
✔ ▶ (to the Dependent box)
✔ *x1*
✔ ▶ (to the Independent box)
✔ *x2*
✔ ▶ (to the Independent box)
✔ Save
✔ Leverage Values (under Distance)
✔ Continue
✔ OK

✔ File
✔ New
✔ Syntax
* Type the following syntax.
```
compute nclev=lev_1 + 1 / 20.
if (nclev > 2*3/20) hilev = 1.
if (nclev le 2*3/20)hilev = 0.
execute.
```
✔ Run
✔ All

438

Identifying Influential Cases – DFFITS, Cook's Distance, and DFBETAS Measures: The researchers now wish to ascertain whether previously identified outlying cases were also influential cases. In Insert 10.9 we begin by regressing *Y* against *X1* and *X2* and requesting that SPSS save *standardized DFBETA* (*sdb0_1*, *sdb1_1*, and *sdb2_1*, by default), *standardized DFFITS* (*sdf_1*, by default), and *Cook's distance measure* (*coo_1*, by default) in the *Data Editor*. Note that SPSS can generate *standardized* or *non-standardized DFBETAs* and *DFFITS*. The *DFBETAs* and *DFFITS* reported in the Table 10.4, text page 402, are standardized.

INSERT 10.9

- ✔ Analyze
- ✔ Regression
- ✔ Linear
- ✔ *y*
- ✔ ▶ (to the Dependent box)
- ✔ *x1*
- ✔ ▶ (to the Independent box)
- ✔ *x2*
- ✔ ▶ (to the Independent box)
- ✔ Save
- ✔ Standardized DfBeta(s) (under Influence)
- ✔ Standardized DfFit (under Influence)
- ✔ Cook's (under Distance)
- ✔ Continue
- ✔ OK

A *DFFITS* value is judged to indicate an influential case if it exceeds 1 for a small to medium sample and $2\sqrt{p/n}$ for a large sample. In Insert 10.10, we create a new variable, *fitflag*, to indicate if the value of *DFFITS* exceeds $2\sqrt{p/n}$. We set *fitflag* = 1 if *DFFITS* (*sdf_1*) $> 2\sqrt{p/n}$, otherwise *fitflag* = 0. For *Cook's Distance measure* (D_i), the text authors suggest that D_i be compared to the *F* distribution with *df1* = *p* and *df2* = *n–p* degrees of freedom. A case is not considered influential if the corresponding percentile value is less than 10 to 20 percent. However, a case has a major influence on the fitted regression function if the corresponding percentile value is near 50 percent or greater. In Insert 10.10 we use the *cumulative distribution function* for the *F* distribution (*CDF.F*) with *df1* = 3 (parameters) and *df2* = 17 (*n–p*) degrees of freedom to find the percentile value of D_i. We multiply this proportion by 100 to express the value as a percent. The resulting value is saved as a new variable, *percent*. A case that has an absolute *DFBETAS* value greater than 1 for small to medium samples or an absolute *DFBETAS* greater than $2/\sqrt{n}$ for large samples may be considered to be an influential case. In Insert 10.10, we create two new variables, *b1flag* and *b2flag*. We set *b1flag* = 1 or *b2flag* = 1 if the absolute value (*abs*) of *sdb1_1* or *sdb1_2*, respectively, is greater than 0, otherwise *b1flag*=0 and *b2flag*=0.

After executing Insert 10.10, note that all values of *fitflag* = 0, indicating that no *DFFIT* value was greater than $2\sqrt{p/n}$. As reported on text page 404, we also find that the percent value (*percent*) for case 3 is 30.6 percent and that the next largest percent value is for case 13 at 11 percent. Using *DFBETAS*, we find that both *b1flag* = 1 and *b2flag* = 1 for case 3.

If you were working with a large data set, the *flag* variable in Insert 10.10 could be used to mark any case that had a *DFFITS*, *DFBETAS*, or *Cook's Distant measure* that needed further investigation. We use *select cases* to find all cases where *flag*=1 and then use *case summaries* to list the case number of each selected record.

INSERT 10.10	INSERT 10.10 continued

✔ File
✔ New
✔ Syntax
* Type the following syntax.
compute case=$casenum.
compute fitflag=0.
If (sdf_1 > 2*sqrt(3/20))fitflag=1.
compute percent = 100*CDF.F(coo_1,3,17) .
if abs((sdb1_1) > 1) b1flag=1.
if abs((sdb2_1) > 1) b2flag=1.
if (fitflag=1 OR percent > 20 OR b1flag=1 OR b2flag=1)flag=1.
execute.
✔ Run
✔ All
	✔ Data
	✔ Select Cases
	✔ Syntax
	✔ If condition is satisfied
	✔ If (below if condition is satisfied)
	✔ Flag
	✔ ▶
	✔ =
	✔ 1
	✔ Continue
	✔ OK
	✔ Analyze
	✔ Reports
	✔ Case Summaries
	✔ Flag
	✔ ▶ (to Variables box)
	✔ OK

Influence on Inferences: Case 3 was identified as an outlying X observation and all three influence measures identified case 3 as influential. Thus, the researcher fitted regression functions with and without case 3. The researcher then calculated the percent difference between the predicted value of Y ($\hat{Y}_i$) based on the regression function with all 20 cases and the predicted value of Y ($\hat{Y}_{i(3)}$) based on the regression function when case 3 was omitted. From Insert 10.11, we begin this analysis by regressing Y on *X1* and *X2* and saving the *unstandardized predicted values* (*pre_1* by default). We then use the *Select If* function to select cases where case number (*case*) is not equal to 3, and again regress Y on *X1* and *X2*. (See Insert 10.5 if *case* is not in your *Data Editor*.) We do not save the *unstandardized predicted values* for this regression analysis because case 3 will not have a fitted value and we need the fitted values for all 20 cases; this analysis is only to find the parameter estimates for the model without case 3 in the data set. To find $\hat{Y}_{i(3)}$ for all 20 cases, we use the parameter estimates (shown on text page 406) from the regression function with case 3 omitted to compute *pre_2*. At this point, we must turn off (reset) the *Select If* function to use all 20 cases for subsequent analysis. We then find *pcinf*, the absolute value (*abs*) of (($\hat{Y}_{i(3)}$ - $\hat{Y}_i$)/ $\hat{Y}_i$)*100. Finally, we use the *Descriptives* procedure to find the mean of *pcinf* = 3.1039. We can also generate a frequency distribution of *pcinf* by using ✔ Analyze ✔ Descriptives ✔ Frequencies to see that the mean difference for 17 of the 20 cases is less than 5 percent. Based on this direct evidence, the researcher concluded that case 3 did not exert undue influence on the regression function.

INSERT 10.11	INSERT 10.11 continued
✔ Analyze ✔ Regression ✔ Linear ✔ *y* ✔ ► (to the Dependent box) ✔ *x1* ✔ ► (to the Independent box) ✔ *x2* ✔ ► (to the Independent box) ✔ Save ✔ Unstandardized (under Predicted values) ✔ Continue ✔ OK ✔ Data ✔ Select Cases ✔ If condition is satisfied ✔ If (under If condition is satisfied) ✔ case ✔ ► ✔ ✔ 3 ✔ Continue ✔ OK ✔ Analyze ✔ Regression ✔ Linear ✔ *y* ✔ ► (to the Dependent box) ✔ *x1* ✔ ► (to the Independent box) ✔ *x2* ✔ ► (to the Independent box) ✔ OK	✔ Data ✔ Select Cases ✔ Reset ✔ OK ✔ File ✔ New ✔ Syntax * Type the following syntax. compute pre_2=-12.428+.5641*(x1)+.3635*(x2). compute pcinf=(abs((pre_2-pre_1)/pre_1))*100. execute. ✔ Run ✔ All ✔ Analyze ✔ Descriptive Statistics ✔ Descriptives ✔ pcinf ✔ ► (to the Variable box) ✔ OK

Multicollinearity Diagnostics Variance Inflation Factor: The researchers now fitted a regression model with all three predictor variables. From text chapter 7, we noted that triceps skinfold thickness and thigh circumference were highly correlated. We also noted large changes in parameter estimates when a variable was added to the model and that one estimated coefficient was negative when a positive value was expected. Accordingly, the researchers were concerned that there may be *multicollinearity* among the predictor variables. They generated *Variance Inflation Factors* (*VIF*) as a formal test for the presence of *multicollinearity*. Insert 10.12 requests *collinearity diagnostics* and SPSS Output 10.13 contains partial results. The *VIF's* for *X1*, *X2*, and *X3* are identical to those reported on text page 409. SPSS does not report the mean VIF value.

SPSS Output 10.13

Coefficients[a]

Model		Unstandardized Coefficients		Standardized Coefficients	t	Sig.	Collinearity Statistics	
		B	Std. Error	Beta			Tolerance	VIF
1	(Constant)	117.085	99.782		1.173	.258		
	X1	4.334	3.016	4.264	1.437	.170	.001	708.843
	X2	-2.857	2.582	-2.929	-1.106	.285	.002	564.343
	X3	-2.186	1.595	-1.561	-1.370	.190	.010	104.606

a. Dependent Variable: Y

442

Chapter 11 SPSS®

Building the Regression
Model III: Remedial Measures

When we detect inadequacies in a regression model that we are building, we take steps to improve the model so that it is more appropriate for the problem at hand. In earlier chapters, the authors used *remedial measures* such as transformations of Y "to linearize the regression relation, to make the error distributions more nearly normal, or to make the variances of the error terms more nearly equal." Further remedial measures are presented in Chapter 11 to improve model adequacy in the presence of unequal error variances, multicollinearity, and overly influential observations. The use of *weighted least squares* in regression analysis is discussed as an alternative to transformations in building models where the variances of the error terms are unequal. *Ridge regression* is presented as a method for dealing with serious multicollinearity among the predictor variables. *Robust regression* techniques are used to dampen the influence of outlying observations. Two methods of *nonparametric regression* are described: *lowess* and *regression trees*. The method of *bootstrapping* is presented to deal with the problem of estimating the precision of some of the complex estimators discussed in this chapter.

Unequal Error Variances Remedial Measures – Weighted Least Squares: Section 11.1 defines the *generalized multiple regression model*:

$$Y_i = \beta_0 + \beta_1 X_{i1} + \ldots + \beta_{p-1} X_{i,p-1} + \varepsilon_i$$

where

$\beta_0, \beta_1, \ldots, \beta_{p-1}$ are unknown parameters

$X_{i1}, X_{i2}, \ldots, X_{i,p-1}$ are known constants

ε_i are independent $N(0, \sigma_i^2)$

$i = 1, 2, \ldots, n$

The method of *weighted least squares* is frequently used to find estimators of the parameters in a generalized multiple regression model because the resulting estimators are *minimum variance unbiased esimators*. Let

$$w_i = \frac{1}{\sigma_i^2}$$

and

$$\mathbf{W} = \begin{bmatrix} w_1 & 0 & \cdots & 0 \\ 0 & w_2 & \cdots & 0 \\ \vdots & \vdots & \ddots & \vdots \\ 0 & 0 & \cdots & w_n \end{bmatrix}$$

Assume the σ_i^2 and hence the w_i are known. Then the weighted least squares (and maximum likelihood) estimators of the coefficients in the generalized multiple regression model are:

$$\mathbf{b}_W = (\mathbf{X'WX})^{-1}\mathbf{X'WY}$$

and the variance-covariance matrix of these coefficients is:

$$\sigma^2\{\mathbf{b}_W\} = (\mathbf{X'WX})^{-1}$$

The σ_i^2 are unknown in most applications and the authors present methods for dealing with this circumstance.

The Blood Pressure Example

Data File: ch11ta01.txt

A researcher studied the relationship between diastolic blood pressure (*dbp*) and age (*age*). See Chapter 0, "Working with SPSS," for instructions on opening the Blood Pressure example data file and renaming the variables. After opening ch11ta01.txt, the first 5 lines in the SPSS *Data Editor* should look like SPSS Output 11.1.

SPSS Output 11.1

	age	dbp	var	var	var	var
1	27	73.0				
2	21	66.0				
3	22	63.0				
4	24	75.0				
5	25	71.0				

We begin the preliminary analysis of the residuals by fitting an *unweighted least squares regression* model ($Y_i = \beta_0 + \beta_1 X_{i1} + \varepsilon_i$) and saving the *unstandardized residuals (res_1)*. (Insert 11.1) To produce the plots in Figure 11.1 (text page 428), we use the SPSS absolute value function to generate a new variable, *absresid=abs(res_1)*, which is the *absolute value of the unstandardized residual (res_1)*. We can now generate Figure 11.1 using the *Scatter Matrix* procedure. Notice that the first column in SPSS Output 11.2 replicates the three scatter plots shown on text page 428.

INSERT 11.1

- ✔ Analyze
- ✔ Regression
- ✔ Linear
- ✔ *dbp*
- ✔ ▶ (to the Dependent box)
- ✔ *age*
- ✔ ▶ (to the Independent box)
- ✔ Save
- ✔ Unstandardized Residuals
- ✔ Continue
- ✔ OK

- ✔ Transform
- ✔ Compute
- * Type "absresid" in Target Variable box.
- * Scroll down the list of functions.
- ✔ ABS(numexpr)
- ✔ ▲
- ✔ res_1
- ✔ ▶
- ✔ OK

- ✔ Graphs
- ✔ Scatter
- ✔ Matrix
- ✔ Define
- ✔ *age*
- * Hold down the shift key.
- ✔ *absresid*
- ✔ ▶ (to the Matrix Variables)
- ✔ OK

The plot of *age* against the *unstandardized residual (res_1)* suggests that the error variance is not constant. From Figure 11.1c, text page 428, the researcher decided that a linear relation between the error standard deviation and *age* was reasonable. He then estimated the standard deviation function by regressing *absresid* against *age* and saved the *fitted (unstandardized predicted) values*. (Insert 11.2) Notice that SPSS has placed the predicted values (*pre_1*) in the active *Data Editor*. From equation 11.16a, text page 425, we now can compute the weights:

445

SPSS Output 11.2

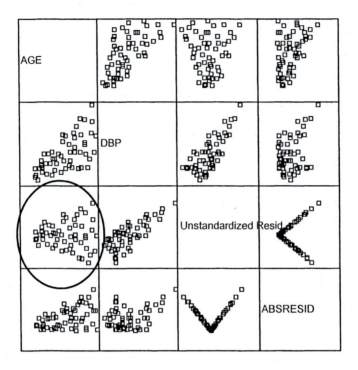

$$w_i = \frac{1}{(\hat{s}_i)^2} \text{ or } w_i = \frac{1}{(pre\_1)^2}.$$

After executing Insert 11.2, the active *Data Editor* should look like SPSS Output 11.3, which is identical to Table 11.1, text page 427.

INSERT 11.2

- ✔ Analyze
- ✔ Regression
- ✔ Linear
- ✔ *absresid*
- ✔ ▶ (to the Dependent box)
- ✔ *age*
- ✔ Save
- ✔ Unstandardized Predicted values
- ✔ Continue
- ✔ OK

- ✔ Transform
- ✔ Compute
- * Type "wt" in Target Variable box.
- * in the "Numeric Express" box type.
- 1 / (pre_1 ** 2)
- ✔ OK

446

SPSS Output 11.3

We can now perform a weighted least squares regression by regressing *dbp* on *age* using *wt* as a weighting variable. (Insert 11.3) Partial output is shown in SPSS Output 11.4. Notice that

$$\hat{Y} = 55.566 + .596\,X$$

and the 95% confidence interval is:

$$0.437 \le \beta_1 \le 0.755$$

consistent with text pages 428-429.

INSERT 11.3

- ✔ Analyze
- ✔ Regression
- ✔ Linear
- ✔ *dbp*
- ✔ ▶ (to the Dependent box)
- ✔ *age*
- ✔ ▶ (to the Independent box)
- ✔ WLS>>
- ✔ *wt*
- ✔ ▶ (to the WLS weight box)
- ✔ Statistics
- ✔ Confidence Intervals
- ✔ Continue
- ✔ OK

SPSS Output 11.4

Coefficients[a,b]

Model		Unstandardized Coefficients		Standardized Coefficients	t	Sig.	95% Confidence Interval for B	
		B	Std. Error	Beta			Lower Bound	Upper Bound
1	(Constant)	55.566	2.521		22.042	.000	50.507	60.624
	AGE	.596	.079	.722	7.526	.000	.437	.755

a. Dependent Variable: DBP

b. Weighted Least Squares Regression - Weighted by WT

Multicollinearity Remedial Measures – Ridge Regression: One approach to estimating regression coefficients in the presence of multicollinearity problems among the predictor variables is to use a method known as *ridge regression*. The idea is to use estimators that have small bias but greater precision than their unbiased competitors. Let $\mathbf{r}_{XX}$ denote the correlation matrix of the X variables in the model of interest and let $\mathbf{r}_{XY}$ denote the vector of coefficients of simple correlation between Y and each X variable. The ridge standardized regression coefficients are:

$$\mathbf{b}^R = (\mathbf{r}_{XX} + c\mathbf{I})^{-1}\mathbf{r}_{XY}$$

The constant c is the amount of bias in the estimators and $\mathbf{I}$ is the $(p-1)$ x $(p-1)$ *identity matrix*. When $c = 0$, $\mathbf{b}^R$ reduces to the standardized least squares estimators. When $c > 0$, the estimators are biased but more precise than ordinary least squares estimators. The strategy is to first obtain estimators based on $c = 0$. Then a small increment is added to c and another set of estimators is obtained. This process is continued for a large number of c values, usually between 0 and 1. Then, we examine the *ridge trace* and *variance inflation factors* $(VIF)_k$ and try to choose the smallest value of c where the coefficients $\mathbf{b}^R$ first become stable and the $(VIF)_k$ are small. This requires judgement but we take the value of $\mathbf{b}^R$ corresponding to the chosen c as the ridge estimate for the problem at hand. (See text page 434).

The Body Fat Example

Data File: ch07ta01.txt

On text page 434, a researcher studied the relationship between the amount of body fat (Y) and triceps skinfold thickness ($X1$), thigh circumference ($X2$), and midarm circumference ($X3$). See Chapter 0, "Working with SPSS," for instructions on opening the Body Fat example data file and renaming the variables. After opening the Body Fat example, the first 5 lines in the SPSS *Data Editor* should look like SPSS Output 11.5.

SPSS Output 11.5

```
body fat example.sav - SPSS Data Editor
File  Edit  View  Data  Transform  Analyze  Graphs  Utilities  Window  Help
```

	x1	x2	x3	y	var
1 : x1			19.5		
1	19.50	43.10	29.10	11.90	
2	24.70	49.80	28.20	22.80	
3	30.70	51.90	37.00	18.70	
4	29.80	54.30	31.10	20.10	
5	19.10	42.20	30.90	12.90	

In text Chapter 7, the researchers noted severe multicollinearity and decided that an appropriate alternative to ordinary least square regression was ridge regression. SPSS does not have a procedure available through a dialogue box (point-and-click) for ridge regression. A macro, however, is available and can be invoked using command syntax in the *Syntax Editor*. The syntax to invoke the macro takes the general form as given in SPSS Output 11.6.

SPSS Output 11.6

```
INCLUDE 'Ridge regression.sps'.
RIDGEREG DEP=varname /ENTER = varlist
[/START={0**}] [/STOP={1**}] [/INC={0.05**}]
{value}      {value}      {value }
[ /K=value] .
```

If you have not moved SPSS program files since the installation of the software, the first command line [*INCLUDE 'Ridge regression.sps'.*] will automatically locate the macro. If the SPSS software is installed on a network drive or has been moved into a different folder, you will have to type the correct file path to connect to the *'Ridge regression.sps'* file. If we get a "file not found" error when invoking the macro, use Windows Explorer© (or equivalent) to find 'Ridge regression.sps'. Insert 11.4 shows an example of a modified '*Include*' statement that indicates the path necessary to connect to the ridge regression macro. (This path will not work on all computers.) We also replace "*varname*" in the *Dep = varname* statement with *y* and "*varlist*" in the *Enter = varlist* statement with *x1 x2 x3* as shown in Insert 11.4. This will generate *R-Square* vs. k (here, k rather than c is used to represent the biasing constant) with the default *START*, *STOP* and *INC* values and plots of parameter estimates vs. the ridge parameter (biasing constant). Partial results (truncated) are shown in SPSS Output 11.7 and are consistent with Tables 11.2 and 11.3, text page 434. The $K = value$ statement can be used to specify a single constant value (biasing constant) with which to produce estimated regression coefficients. Insert 11.5, for instance, requests a *ridge regression* using a *biasing constant* = 0.02. Partial (truncated) results are shown in SPSS Output 11.8 and are consistent with the fitted regression model on text page 435. The *START*, *STOP*, and *INC* commands in SPSS Output 11.6 allow the user to specify the starting and ending constant value (biasing constant) and the value by which the constant will increment.

INSERT 11.4

✔ File
✔ New
✔ Syntax
include 'c:\program files\spss\Ridge regression.sps'.
ridgereg dep=y /ENTER = x1 x2 x3.
✔ Run
✔ OK

SPSS Output 11.7

R-SQUARE AND BETA COEFFICIENTS FOR ESTIMATED VALUES OF K				
K	RSQ	X1	X2	X3
.00000	.80136	4.263705	-2.92870	-1.56142
.05000	.78042	.460460	.439245	-.100508
.10000	.77839	.423354	.448960	-.081246
.15000	.77567	.404876	.443453	-.069952
.20000	.77226	.391425	.434720	-.061290
.25000	.76828	.380223	.425122	-.054086
.30000	.76382	.370323	.415403	-.047887

INSERT 11.5

✔ File
✔ New
✔ Syntax
include 'c:\program files\spss\ridge regression.sps'.
ridgereg dep=y /enter = x1 x2 x3
/K=.02 .
✔ Run
✔ OK

SPSS Output 11.8

```
****** Ridge Regression with k = .02 ******


Mult R      .884191813
RSquare     .781795162
Adj RSqu    .740881755
SE          2.599235292

           ANOVA table
               df        SS        MS
Regress     3.000    387.293    129.098
Residual   16.000    108.096      6.756


        F value            Sig F
    19.10853230          .00001540


--------------Variables in the Equation--------------
                    B        SE(B)         Beta       B/SE(B)
X1          .555353057   .124647201    .546333894    4.455399350
X2          .368144438   .118414502    .377403656    3.108947226
X3         -.191626885   .164356363   -.136871542   -1.165923127
Constant  -7.403425423  6.407173706    .000000000   -1.155490043
```

Table 11.3, text page 434, displays *variance inflation factors* and R^2 for different biasing constants. SPSS Output 11.7 above also displays R^2 for each biasing constant; however, there is no readily available routine in SPSS that will produce *variance inflation factors* for a given biasing constant.

Remedial Measures for Influential Cases - Iteratively Reweighted Least Squares (IRLS) Robust Regression: "For robust regression, weighted least squares is used to reduce the influence of outlying cases by employing weights that vary inversely with the size of the residual. Outlying cases that have large residuals are thereby given smaller weights. The weights are revised as each iteration yields new residuals until the estimation process stabilizes." Two widely used weight functions, the *Huber* and *bisquare weight functions*, are described. These functions are used to dampen the effect of outlying observations.

Mathematics Proficiency Example

Data File: ch11ta04.txt

On text page 441, a researcher studied the relationship between the home environment and aggregate school performance (mathematics proficiency) for 37 states, the District of Columbia, Guam, and the Virgin Islands. The data are given by state and states are the study unit in this example. The average mathematics proficiency score, denoted *Y*, is the dependent variable of

451

interest. The predictor variables are parents (*X1*), home library (*X2*), reading (*X3*), watch TV (*X4*), and absences (*X5*). This example considers only the predictor variable *X2* (home library) which represents the percentage of eighth-grade students who had three or more types of reading materials at home. See Chapter 0, "Working with SPSS," for instructions on opening the Mathematics Proficiency example data file and renaming the variables. After opening the Mathematics Proficiency data file, the first 5 lines in the SPSS *Data Editor* should look like SPSS Output 11.9.

SPSS Output 11.9

	state	y	x1	x2	x3	x4	x5
1	Alabama	252	75	78	34	18	18
2	Arizona	259	75	73	41	12	26
3	Arkansas	256	77	77	28	20	23
4	California	256	78	68	42	11	28
5	Colorado	267	78	85	38	9	25

To produce the scatter plots on text page 442 we first regress *Y* on *X2* and save the residuals. (Insert 11.6) The *unstandardized residuals* are saved in the active *Data Editor* as *res_1*. We then request a *scatter plot matrix* using *res_1*, *X2*, and *Y*. The top and bottom of the middle column in SPSS Output 11.10 correspond to text Figures 11.5 (a) and 11.5 (b) (text page 442), respectively. From the plots, we notice that there are 3 states with outlying *Y* values (mathematics proficiency scores). Also, there are 6 states with low *X2* scores (resources) whose math proficiency scores are above the fitted regression line. Thus, the researchers decided to fit a linear regression function robustly, using *IRLS regression* and the *Huber weight function*.

INSERT 11.6	INSERT 11.6 continued
✔ Analyze	✔ Graphs
✔ Regression	✔ Scatter
✔ Linear	✔ Matrix
✔ *y*	✔ Define
✔ ▶ (to the Dependent box)	✔ *y*
✔ *x2*	* Hold down the **ctl** key.
✔ ▶ (to the Independent box)	✔ *x2*
✔ Save	✔ *res_1*
✔ Unstandardized residuals	✔ ▶ (to the Matrix Variables)
✔ Continue	✔ OK
✔ OK	

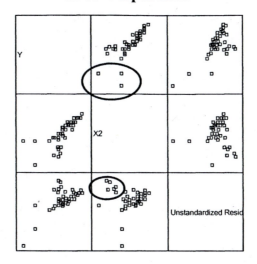

The researchers considered a second order model using *x2* (*homelib*) centered, and its square as the single predictor variable (equation 11.48, text page 443). To diminish the effect of outliers the researchers used *iteratively reweighted least squares* and the *Huber weight function*. We detail each step in the following and in Insert 11.7, although the output for each step is not shown. We begin in Insert 11.7 by centering *x2* (*x2cnt*) and finding the square of the centered variable (*x2cnt2*). We then:

1) Save the unstandardized residuals (*res_1*). This was done for the first order model in Insert 11.6 above . Since we are fitting a second order model, we delete *res_1* from the active *Data Editor* before running the syntax in Insert 11.7. Running Step 1 in Insert 11.7 will then generate *unstandardized residuals* based on the second order model and save them in *res_1*.

2) Find the median value ($median\{e_i\}$) of *res_1* = 0.70629.

3) Compute (name arbitrary) *v1*, the absolute value of res_1 minus the median of the residuals ($|e_i - median\{e_i\}|$).

4) Find the median of ($median\{|e_i - median\{e_i\}|\}$) *v1* = 3.1488.

5) Find the median absolute deviation estimator (*MAD*) = *median of v1 – constant* = 0.6745 (3.1488 / 0.6745) = 4.6683.

6) Compute the scaled residual, $u1 = res\_1 \div mad = res\_1 \div 4.6683$.

7) Use the scaled residual in the computation of the Huber weight (*w*), where *w* = 1 if the absolute value of *u1* ≤ 1.345 and *w* = (1.345 / *absolute value of u1*) if the *absolute value of u1* > 1.345.

8) Regress y on *x2cnt* and *x2cnt2* using w as a weighting variable and save the unstandardized residuals. This will produce the regression model: $\hat{Y} = 259.39 + 1.670\,x_2 + 0.064\,x_2^2$. If the saved residuals from Step 1 above are still in the active *Data Editor*, the residual values for this step will be saved as *res_2*. The saved residual values for Step 8 will be those shown in column 4 of text Table 11.5.

9) Return to Step 2 for the second iteration and use the residuals saved in Step 8 for the next iteration.

INSERT 11.7	INSERT 11.7 continued

* Begin.
* Center x2 and square centered value.
✔ File
✔ New
✔ Syntax
* Type the following.
compute x2cnt = x2-80.4 .
compute x2cnt2=x2cnt**2.
execute .
✔ Run
✔ All
 	
* Step 1.
* Run second order model text equation 11.48.
* and save residuals.
✔ Analyze
✔ Regression
✔ Linear
✔ y
✔ ▶(to the Dependent box)
✔ x2cnt
✔ ▶(to the Independent box)
✔ x2cnt2
✔ ▶(to the Independent box)
✔ Save
✔ Unstandardized residuals
✔ Continue
✔ OK
 	
* Step 2.
✔ Analyze
✔ Descriptive Statistics
✔ Explore
✔ res_1
✔ ▶(to the Dependent box)
✔ OK
 	
* Step 3.
* In the syntax file opened in the Begin step.
* type the following.
compute v1=abs(res_1-.70629).
execute.
* Highlight the above 2 statements only.
✔ [▶] on the tool bar.
	* Step 4.
	✔ Analyze
	✔ Descriptive Statistics
	✔ Explore
	✔ v1
	✔ ▶(to the Dependent box)
	✔ OK
	
	* Steps 5, 6, and 7.
	* In the syntax file opened in the Begin step.
	* type the following.
	compute mad=3.1488/.6745.
	compute u1 = res_1 / mad.
	if (abs(u1) <=1.345) w=1.
	if (abs(u1) > 1.345) w=1.345/abs(u1).
	execute.
	* Highlight the above 5 statements only.
	✔ [▶] on the tool bar.
	
	* Step 8.
	* Run regression using w as a weighting variable.
	* and save residuals as res_2, by default.
	✔ Analyze
	✔ Regression
	✔ Linear
	✔ y
	✔ ▶(to the Dependent box)
	✔ x2cnt
	✔ ▶(to the Independent box)
	✔ x2cnt2
	✔ ▶(to the Independent box)
	✔ Save
	✔ Unstandardized residuals
	✔ Continue
	✔ WLS >>
	✔ w
	✔ ▶(to WLS Weight)
	✔ OK

Nonparametric Regression: There is no readily available procedure in SPSS Base®, SPSS Advanced Models®, or SPSS Regression Models® for performing nonparametric regression. Decision trees are available in SPSS' AnswerTree and Clementine products. These products, however, are not widely available to students through college computing centers.

Remedial Measures for Evaluating precision in Nonstandard Situations – Bootstrapping:
The authors give an overview of the *bootstrap method* on text page 459. The basic idea is as follows. We estimate regression coefficients using some method such as an iterative procedure (that may not provide an estimate of precision). We temporarily view the sample data being analyzed (the original sample) as "the population." We retake a large number of samples (resamples) from the original sample (temporary population). For each resample, we compute regression coefficients using an iterative procedure (that may not provide an estimate of precision). From the estimates gleaned from the resampling, we (using the estimates as data) apply first principles to calculate their standard errors. We consider the calculated standard errors to be estimates of standard errors of the regression coefficients in the original estimation.

The Toluca Company Example

Data File: ch01ta01.dat

Using the Toluca Company example (Table 1.1, text page 19), we found that the parameter estimates for lot size (*lotsize*) using ordinary least squares (linear) regression. (SPSS Output 11.11) Now the authors wish to evaluate the precision of the estimates by the *bootstrap method*. See Chapter 0, "Working with SPSS," for instructions on opening the Toluca Company data file and renaming the variables *lotsize* and *workhrs*. After opening ch01ta01.dat, the first 5 lines in the SPSS *Data Editor* should look like SPSS Output 1.1. To evaluate the precision of the parameter estimates, we use *constrained nonlinear regression (CNLR)*. *CNLR* allows for linear and non-linear constraints on parameters and can compute bootstrap estimates of parameter standard errors and correlations. In Insert 11.9, we begin the procedure by assigning the initial values to the parameters in the *Model Program* statement. The *Model Program* (*Compute* statement) specifies the nonlinear or linear model for the data. We request that predicted values be modeled as: *b0 + b1*lotsize*. We then specify *workhrs* as the dependent variable in the *CNLR* statement and request bootstrap estimates based on 1000 samples. Optionally, you can request (/*OUTFILE* =) that the parameter estimates, *SSE*, and samples sizes for each sample be written to an output file.

SPSS Output 11.11

Coefficients^a

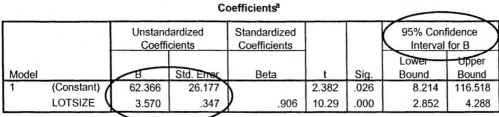

Model		Unstandardized Coefficients B	Unstandardized Coefficients Std. Error	Standardized Coefficients Beta	t	Sig.	95% Confidence Interval for B Lower Bound	95% Confidence Interval for B Upper Bound
1	(Constant)	62.366	26.177		2.382	.026	8.214	116.518
	LOTSIZE	3.570	.347	.906	10.29	.000	2.852	4.288

a. Dependent Variable: WORKHRS

INSERT 11.9

✔ File
✔ New
✔ Syntax
MODEL PROGRAM b0=0 b1=0 .
COMPUTE pred = b0 + b1*lotsize.
CNLR hours
/BOOTSTRAP 1000
/OUTFILE='c:\bootstrap.sav' .
execute.
✔ Run
✔ All

Partial output of the *CNLR* procedure is shown in SPSS Output 11.12. The parameter estimates using linear regression (SPSS Output 11.11) are the same as those generated by specifying a linear equation in the nonlinear regression procedure (*CNLR* – SPSS Output 11.12).

The standard deviation of the 1000 b^*_1 estimates is 0.3733 (listed as "*Std. E*" for *B1* – SPSS Output 11.12) and is relatively close to the estimate ($s\{b_1\}= 0.347$) (listed as "*Std. Error for LOT_SIZE*" – SPSS Output 11.11 and "Asymptotic Std. Error" for B1 – SPSS Output 11.12) based on the original sample. Additionally, the 95% confidence limits ($2.8364 < \beta_1 < 4.2818$) (SPSS Output 11.12) are very close to the confidence limits obtained using the original sample ($2.852 < \beta_1 < 4.288$) (SPSS Output 11.11). To produce the histogram of the 1000 b_1 estimates, simply open the output file specified in Insert 10.9 and request a histogram of *b1*. This result is shown in Output 11.13. The histogram is relatively symmetrical and close to a normal distribution. Based on the above analysis, the parameter estimates for the original sample appear to be relatively precise.

SPSS Output 11.12

Parameter	Estimate	Asymptotic Std. Error	Asymptotic 95 % Confidence Interval Lower	Upper
B0	62.365857908	26.177434151	8.213709530	116.51800629
B1	3.570202034	.346972168	2.852435419	4.287968649

Asymptotic Correlation Matrix of the Parameter Estimates

	B0	B1
B0	1.0000	-.9278
B1	-.9278	1.0000

Bootstrap statistics based on 1000 samples

Parameter	Estimate	Std. E	95% Conf. Bounds Lower	Upper	95% Trimmed Range Lower	Upper
B0	62.3658	29.3921	4.6884	120.0433	3.5152	120.8500
B1	3.5702	.3733	2.8375	4.30289	2.8364	4.2818

Bootstrap Correlation Matrix of the Parameter Estimates

	B0	B1
B0	1.0000	-.9498
B1	-.9498	1.0000

SPSS Output 11.13

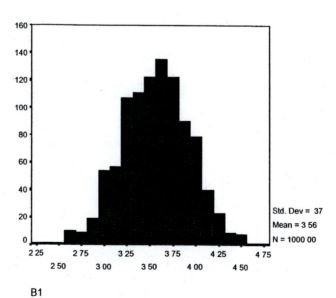

B1

457

Chapter 12 SPSS®

Autocorrelation in Time Series Data

In the context of the generalized multiple regression model, a time series is a set of data collected by observing a random variable and one or more independent variables at each time in a sequence of times. For example, company sales (the dependent variable) and industry sales (the independent variable) could be observed quarterly over a five-year interval. Or, net income (the dependent variable), gross revenues, and labor costs (the independent variables) for a company could be observed monthly over a three-year period. The error terms for regression models for times series data are often correlated and are, therefore, referred to as being *autocorrelated* or *serially correlated*. A generalized multiple regression model in which the error terms are autocorrelated is called an *autoregressive error model*. In this chapter, the authors of the text introduce the concept of *autocorrelation* and associated *autoregressive error models*. They discuss the *Durbin-Watson test for autocorrelation* as a means for detecting *autocorrelation* among error terms of a model. They then discuss remedial measures for dealing with data where *autocorrelation* has been detected.

The Blaisdell Company Example

Data File: ch12ta02.txt

The Blaisdell Company (text page 488) used trade association record of industry sales to predict their own sales. See Chapter 0, "Working with SPSS," for instructions on opening the Blaisdell Company data file and renaming the variables *company* and *industry*. After opening ch12ta02.txt, the first 5 lines in the SPSS *Data Editor* should look like SPSS Output 12.1.

SPSS Output 12.1

	company	industry	var	var
1	20.96	127.30		
2	21.40	130.00		
3	21.96	132.70		
4	21.52	129.40		
5	22.39	135.00		

In Insert 12.1, we begin the analysis by producing a scatter plot of the company and industry sales data. (SPSS Output 12.2) Since the scatter plot suggested that a linear regression model might be appropriate the analyst working with Blaisdell Company fitted an ordinary least squares regression model and saved the unstandardized residuals (*res_1*). To plot the residuals against time, we used the *compute time=$casenum* statement in Insert 12.1 to create a sequential record number for each line in the Blaisdell Company data file. A plot of the residual values against *time* is shown in SPSS Output 12.3.

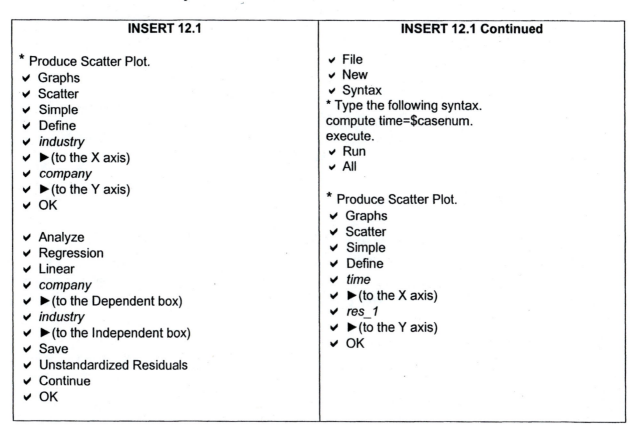

INSERT 12.1	INSERT 12.1 Continued
* Produce Scatter Plot. ✔ Graphs ✔ Scatter ✔ Simple ✔ Define ✔ *industry* ✔ ▶(to the X axis) ✔ *company* ✔ ▶(to the Y axis) ✔ OK ✔ Analyze ✔ Regression ✔ Linear ✔ *company* ✔ ▶(to the Dependent box) ✔ *industry* ✔ ▶(to the Independent box) ✔ Save ✔ Unstandardized Residuals ✔ Continue ✔ OK	✔ File ✔ New ✔ Syntax * Type the following syntax. compute time=$casenum. execute. ✔ Run ✔ All * Produce Scatter Plot. ✔ Graphs ✔ Scatter ✔ Simple ✔ Define ✔ *time* ✔ ▶(to the X axis) ✔ *res_1* ✔ ▶(to the Y axis) ✔ OK

SPSS Output 12.2   **SPSS Output 12.3**

Durbin-Watson Test for Autocorrelation: Since SPSS Output 12.3 indicates a positive autocorrelation in the error terms, the analyst produced the *Durbin-Watson Test for Autocorrelation*. To request the Durbin-Watson test, use the first regression procedure in Insert 12.1 and ✔ Statistics ✔ Durbin-Watson ✔ Continue. Partial output is shown in SPSS Output 12.4. Note that the Durbin-Watson value = 0.735 as reported on text page 488. Using Table B.7, text page 675, we conclude that the error terms are positively autocorrelated.

SPSS Output 12.4

Model Summary^b

Model	R	R Square	Adjusted R Square	Std. Error of the Estimate	Durbin-Watson
1	.999^a	.999	.999	.08606	.735

a. Predictors: (Constant), INDUSTRY

b. Dependent Variable: COMPANY

Cochrane-Orcutt Procedure: On text page 492, the analyst first used the *Cochrane-Orcutt procedure* to estimate the autocorrelation parameter ρ. Column 1 (e_t) of Table 12.3, text page 493, contains the residual values for the regression model fitted in Insert 12.1. Each line in text Table 12.3, column 2 is the residual value of column 1 for the preceding time period. In Insert 12.2 we use SPSS' *Cross-Case operation* that takes the form, *compute new=lag(old)* where *new* is the value of *old* for the previous case. That is, we use [*compute res_m1=lag(res_1)*] to compute a new variable, *res_m1*, that is equal to the residual (*res_1*) of the preceding time period (line) in the data file. This produces text Table 12.3, column 2, e_{t-1}. We then *compute etm1et=res_1*res_m1* which is the residual times the lagged residual. This produces text Table 12.3, column 3, $e_{t-1}e_t$. We then square the lagged residual value [*compute etm1et2=res_m1**2*] to produce text Table 12.3, column 4, e_{t-1}^2. Finally, in SPSS Output 12.5, we find the sum of *etm1et* = 0.0834478 and *etm1et2* = 0.1322127. As before, double click on the table displayed in SPSS Output 12.5 and then double click on the sum for *etm1et2*, for example, to display greater precision (0.13 vs. 0.1322127279868). We now obtain *r*, an estimate of ρ, by equation 12.22, text page 492, where

$$r = 0.0834478/ 0.1322127 = 0.631166$$

INSERT 12.2	INSERT 12.2 Continued
✔ File ✔ New ✔ Syntax * Type the following syntax. compute res_m1=lag(res_1). compute etm1et=res_1*res_m1. compute etm1et2=res_m1**2. execute. ✔ Run ✔ All * Find sum of *etm1et* and *etm1et2*. ✔ Analyze ✔ Descriptive Statistics ✔ Descriptives ✔ *etm1et*	✔ ▶ ✔ *etm1et2* ✔ ▶ ✔ Options ✔ Sum ✔ Continue ✔ OK * Produce columns 3 and 4 of text Table 12.4. ✔ File ✔ New ✔ Syntax compute ypt=company-.631166*lag(company). compute xpt=industry-.631166*lag(industry). execute. ✔ Run ✔ All

SPSS Output 12.5

Descriptive Statistics

	N	Minimum	Maximum	Sum	Mean	Std. Deviation
ETM1ET	19	.00	.02	.08	.0044	.00619
ETM1ET2	19	.00	.03	0.13221272	.0070	.00821
Valid N (listwise)	19					

In Insert 12.2, we use equation 12.18, text page 491, to find $Y_t^{'}$ (*ypt*) and $X_t^{'}$ (*xpt*). This produces the 3rd and 4th columns of Table 12.4, text page 493. To complete the *Cochrane-Orcutt* procedure, we then regress *ytp* on *xpt* and request the Durbin-Watson statistic (syntax not show). Partial results are shown in SPSS Output 12.6. The Durbin-Watson statistic = 1.65 consistent with text page 494. This leads to the conclusion that the autocorrelation of error terms is not significantly different from zero. From SPSS Output 12.6 we note that $b_0^{'}$ = -0.394, $b_1^{'}$ = 0.174, $s\{b_0^{'}\}$ = 0.167, and $s\{b_1^{'}\}$ = 0.003. We can use equation 12.20, text pages 491-492, to transform back to a fitted regression model in terms of the original variables and equation 12.21 to obtain estimated standard deviations of the back-transformed fitted model coefficients.

SPSS Output 12.6

Model Summary[b]

Model	R	R Square	Adjusted R Square	Std. Error of the Estimate	Durbin-Watson
1	.998[a]	.995	.995	.06715	1.650

a. Predictors: (Constant), XPT

b. Dependent Variable: YPT

Coefficients[a]

Model		Unstandardized Coefficients		Standardized Coefficients	t	Sig.
		B	Std. Error	Beta		
1	(Constant)	-.394	.167		-2.357	.031
	XPT	.174	.003	.998	58.767	.000

a. Dependent Variable: YPT

Hildreth-Lu Procedure: The *Hildreth-Lu procedure* uses the value of ρ that minimizes the error sum of squares (*SSE*) for the transformed regression model. As noted in the text, you can repeatedly fit regression models while varying the value of ρ to find the value that minimizes *SSE*. The most efficient method of producing Table 12.5, text page 495, is to use SPSS' *Matrix – End Matrix* procedure to automatically perform the numerical search across a large range of ρ values.

To use Insert 12.3, we must have the Blaisdell Company data file open as shown in SPSS Output 12.1. The other option is to open the Blaisdell Company example in SPSS and then save the file as *blaisdell.sav*, for example, in a user-specified directory. Assume that we saved the Blaisdell Company data file from the SPSS *Data Editor* to a directory on our C: drive named *alrm*. We could remove the asterisk from the first and second *get* statements (un-comment the line) so that Insert 12.3 will read the file into the *Data Editor* for use by the program, and after the program has run and modified the *Data Editor*, reread the Blaisdell Company data file into the *Data Editor*. In the present example, this is preferable to opening the data file in the *Data Editor* as shown in Insert 12.1. This is because the syntax in Insert 12.3 modifies the *Data Editor* such that if we execute the syntax twice without rereading the Blaisdell Company data file back into the *Data Editor*, we will produce incorrect results. Using the un-commented first and second *get* statements in Insert 12.3 assures that the data file used in the analysis will not have been modified from a previous analysis. Note that this requires saving the ch12ta02.txt file from the *Data Editor* as a *.sav format file in a directory indicated on the path of the *get* statements.

In Insert 12.3, we set the maximum number of loops to 100 (the default value in SPSS is 40). We then use the *cross-case operation* to find Y_{t-1} (*ylag*) and X_{t-1} (*xlag*). Since there are 20 lines of data in the file with values for *company* and *industry*, the first line will have a missing value for the lagged variables *ylag* and *xlag*. If we read *company*, *industry*, *ylag*, and *xlag* into matrices and subsequently attempt to use perform arithmetic [e.g., *compute xstep1=industry-(r100*xlag)*]

462

we will get an error due to ***industry*** being a 20x1 matrix and ***xlag*** being a 19x1 matrix. Accordingly, we set *company*, *industry*, and *X0* to a system missing value if *ylag* and *xlag* are missing, as they will be on the first line of the modified data file. We then read the data variables into column vector matrices and instruct SPSS to omit cases with missing values. Thus, all initial column vector matrices will be 19x1.

To reproduce the *Hildreth-Lu* results shown in Table12.5, text page 495, we wish to calculate the *SSE* for a range of ρ values from 0.01 to 1.0 in increments of 0.01. This is possible using the SPSS *loop – end loop* procedure when we are not in *Matrix – End Matrix*. However, when in the matrix program, integers only can be used as an increment value. We loop from *r=1 to 100* (and by default increment by 1) and then compute *r100=r/100* to give us the range of ρ values from 0.01 to 1.0 for calculating 100 regression models using equation 12.17, text page 491. We find $X_t^{'}$ (***xstep1***) and concatenate *X0* (a column vectors of 1's) and ***xstep1*** to form matrix ***xmat***. We find $Y_t^{'}$ (***ystep***) from equation 12.18 (a), text page 491, and use this as our "*Y*" matrix. Finally, we use equations 5.65 and 5.84a, text pages 201 and 204, to find the **b** matrix and **SSE**. The numerical output from this insert is not shown but is consistent with the selected values of ρ and corresponding *SSE* values shown on Table 12.5, text page 495. SPSS Output 12.7 displays the scatter plot of *r* and *SSE* values. Note that the magnitude of *SSE* decreases as the magnitude of *r* increases until *r* = 0.96, at which time the magnitude of *SSE* begins to increase. This is consistent with text Table 12.5.

SPSS Output 12.7

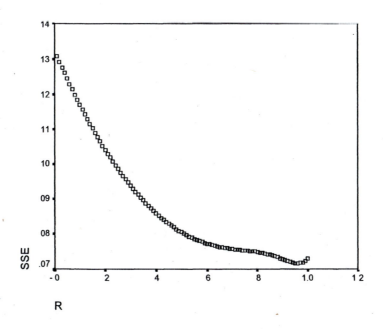

INSERT 12.3

✔ File
✔ New
✔ Syntax

```
* get file='c:\alrm\blaisdell.sav'.
set mxloops=100.
compute x0=1.
compute ylag=lag(company).
compute xlag=lag(industry).
execute.
if sysmis(ylag) company = $sysmis.
execute.
if sysmis(xlag) industry = $sysmis.
execute.
if sysmis(xlag) x0 = $sysmis.
execute.

matrix.
get x0 / variables =x0 / missing = omit / sysmis=omit .
get xlag / variables = xlag / missing = omit / sysmis=omit .
get industry / variables = industry / missing = omit / sysmis=omit .
get ylag / variables=ylag / missing = omit / sysmis=omit .
get company / variables = company / missing = omit / sysmis=omit .
loop r=1 to 100.
compute r100 = r/100.
compute xstep1=industry-(r100*xlag).
compute xmat={x0, xstep1}.
compute ystep1=company-(r100*ylag).
* Find b matrix by text equation 5.65.
compute b=inv(t(xmat)*xmat)*t(xmat)*ystep1.
* Find sse by text equation 5.84a.
compute sse=t(ystep1)*ystep1-t(b)*t(xmat)*ystep1.
* print r100.
* print sse.
save {r100, sse} / outfile=* / variables = r sse.
end loop.
end matrix.
GRAPH
 /SCATTERPLOT(BIVAR)=r WITH sse
 /MISSING=LISTWISE .
EXECUTE.
* get file='c:\alrm\blaisdell.sav'.
```

✔ Run
✔ All

First Difference Procedure: On text page 496, the analyst used the *First Difference procedure* where $\rho = 1.0$ for the transformed model (equation 12.17, text page 491), where $Y_t^{'} = Y_t - Y_{t-1}$ and $X_t^{'} = X_t - X_{t-1}$, and the regression model is based on regression through the origin. In Insert 12.4, we compute $Y_t^{'}$ (*fdyp*) and $X_t^{'}$ (*fdxp*) using the *cross-case operation*. We then regress *fdyp*

464

on *fdxp* and ✔ Option ✔ (Uncheck) Include constant in equation and ✔ Continue (syntax not shown). This results in SPSS Output 12.8 and a regression function where $\hat{Y}' = 0.168X'$. To produce the Durbin-Watson statistic, we run the same regression model as above except we include the intercept term in the model [✔ Option ✔ Include constant in equation, and ✔ Continue (syntax not shown)]. SPSS Output 12.9 shows the Durbin-Watson statistic, which is consistent with text page 497.

```
                              INSERT 12.4


   ✔ File
   ✔ New
   ✔ Syntax
   * Type the following syntax.
   compute fdyp=company-lag(company).
   compute fdxp=industry-lag(industry).
   execute.
   ✔ Run
   ✔ All
```

SPSS Output 12.8

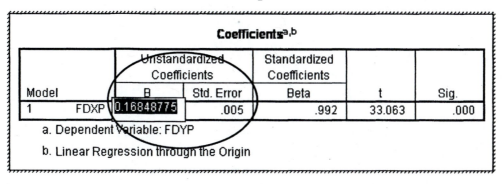

Coefficients[a,b]

Model		Unstandardized Coefficients		Standardized Coefficients	t	Sig.
		B	Std. Error	Beta		
1	FDXP	0.16848775	.005	.992	33.063	.000

a. Dependent Variable: FDYP

b. Linear Regression through the Origin

SPSS Output 12.9

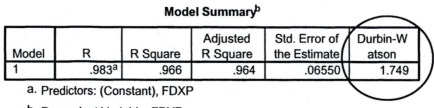

Model Summary[b]

Model	R	R Square	Adjusted R Square	Std. Error of the Estimate	Durbin-Watson
1	.983[a]	.966	.964	.06550	1.749

a. Predictors: (Constant), FDXP

b. Dependent Variable: FDYP

We use equation 12.31, text pages 496-497, to transform the coefficients of the fitted model based on the transformed variables back to a fitted model in terms of the original variables. If in the first regression procedure in Insert 12.1 we had also ✔ Statistics ✔ Descriptives, and ✔

Continue we would have obtained SPSS Output 12.10. We use equation 12.31a and 12.31b, respectively, and SPSS Output 12.8 and 12.10 to find:

$$b_0 = \overline{Y} - b_1' \overline{X}$$

$$b_0 = 24.5690 - 0.168(147.6250) = -0.30349$$

and

$$b_1 = b_1'$$

$$b_1 = 0.16849$$

Thus, the fitted model in terms of the original variables is:

$$\hat{Y} = -.30349 + 0.16849X$$

SPSS Output 12.10

Descriptive Statistics

	Mean	Std. Deviation	N
COMPANY	24.5690	2.41040	20
INDUSTRY	147.6250	13.66520	20

Forecasting with Autocorrelated Error Terms

Forecasting Based on Cochrane-Orcutt Estimates: On text page 500, the analyst forecasts the Blaisdell Company sales for the 21st quarter. The trade association's estimate for this quarter is \$175.3 million. We use the *Cochrane-Orcutt* results presented in Insert 12.2 and SPSS Output 12.6 where:

$$\hat{Y} = -0.3941 + 0.17376X'$$

We transform the model back to the original variables as shown on text page 497, which leads to:

$$\hat{Y} = -1.0685 + 0.17376X$$

Before using Insert 12.5, reread the Blaisdell Example data file to appear as SPSS Output 12.1. In Insert 12.5, we find X_t' (*xpt*) and Y_t' (*ypt*) for subsequent use and set our estimate of ρ (*r*) = 0.631166. We find (*e*) $e_{20} = Y_{20} - \hat{Y}_{20}$ where $Y_{20} = 28.78$ and $\hat{Y}_{20} = -1.0685 + 0.17376 * 171.7$. Using the above regression function, the fitted value (*yhat*) for $\hat{Y}_{21}$ when $X_{21} = 175.3$ is

$-1.0685 + 0.17376*175.3 = 29.392$. We then compute F_{21} (*forcast*) $= \hat{Y}_{21} + re_{20} = 29.40$. We find X'_{n+1} where $X_{n+1} = 175.3$ (X_{21} above), $r = 0.631166$, and $X_{20} = 171.7$. Thus:

$$X'_{n+1} = 175.3 - 0.631166*171.7 = 66.629$$

Using the above numerical results, we find $s\{pred\}$ using equation 2.38, text page 59. Note that in this equation, $MSE = 0.0045097$ (regress *ypt* on *xpt*), $(X_h - \overline{X})^2 = [(66.929 - 56.3186)**2]$, and $\sum(X_i - \overline{X})^2 = 515.8551$. Thus, text equation 2.38a:

$$s^2\{pred\} = MSE\left[1 + \frac{1}{n} + \frac{(X_h - \overline{X})^2}{\sum(X_i - \overline{X})^2}\right]$$

where $n = 19$, $X_h = X'_{n+1}$, $\overline{X} =$ mean of XPT, and $X_i = XPT_i$, becomes:

$$s\{pred\} = \sqrt{0.004509\left[1 + \frac{1}{19} + \frac{(66.929 - 56.3186)^2}{515.8551}\right]}$$

The value of *spred* $= 0.07570$ is consistent with text page 500. Finally, we find *tvalue* $= idf.t(.975,17) = 2.11$ and then compute the lower (*cilo*) and upper (*cihi*) prediction intervals as F_{21} (*forcast*) $= 29.40 \pm 2.11*0.0757$ or $29.24 \leq Y_{21(new)} \leq 29.56$. These values will be contained in your *Data Editor*.

INSERT 12.5

✓ File
✓ New
✓ Syntax
compute ypt=company-.631166*lag(company).
compute xpt=industry-.631166*lag(industry).
execute.
compute r = 0.631166.
compute e = company-(-1.0685+(.17376*industry)).
compute yhat = -1.0685+(.17376*175.3).
compute forecast = yhat+(r*e).

* Use text equation 2.38 to find s{pred} (*spred*).
 * Find mean of xpt=56.3186 using Analyze > Descriptives.
compute xptdif2=(xpt-56.3186)**2.
 * Find sum of xptdif2 = 515.8551 using Analyze > Descriptives and Sum Option.
compute spred=sqrt(0.0045097+ (0.0045097*((1/19)+(((66.929- 56.3186)**2)/515.8551)))).
compute tvalue=idf.t(.975,17).
compute cilo=29.4-(tvalue*spred).
compute cihi=29.4+(tvalue*spred).
exe.
✓ Run
✓ All

Forecasting Based on First Difference Estimates: Before using Insert 12.6, reread the Blaisdell Example data file to appear as SPSS Output 12.1. On text page 501 the authors use the first differences regression function to forecast sales for quarter 21. To find F_{21} we recall that the first part of the expression [(-0.30349 + 0.16849*(175.3)] comes from equation 12.33, text page 497, and from X_{21} = 175.3 above. The latter part of the expression {1.0[28.78 + 0.30349–0.16849*171.70)]} comes from text equation 12.33, the fact that ρ = 1.0 in the *First Difference* model, and X_{20} = 171.70. Our forecasted value for the 21st quarter is F_{21} = 29.39 as shown on text page 501. We find the prediction intervals using equation 4.20, text page 162. We first find X_h^2 (*xh2*), which is the forecasted value (F_{21}) squared. We then find X_i^2 (*fdxp2*) and, subsequently, use *Descriptives* to find the sum of *fdxp2* = 185.42. We find X_{n+1}' (*xnp1*) = X_{21} – (r * X_{20}) (note that X_{20} = *industry*$_{20}$). The MSE = .00482 is from regressing *fdyp* on *fdxp* and requesting that no intercept term be included in the model. The statistic *tvalue* [idf.t(.975,18)] is based on 18 *df*. First, 19 of the original 20 records were used in the analysis because we "lost" a record when we lagged to get *xpt* and *ypt*. (This was also the case for the *Cochrane-Orcutt* procedure above where we used 17 *df* (*n*–2) to find *tvalue*.) We have 18 *df* (*n*–1) here because we estimated only 1 parameter (β_1), i.e., we did not include an intercept term in the model. We then find the 95% prediction intervals for F_{21} = 29.39 as shown on text page 501: $29.24 \leq Y_{21(new)} \leq 29.52$. These values will be contained in your *Data Editor*.

INSERT 12.6

```
✔ File
✔ New
✔ Syntax
* Based on first difference.
compute fdyp=company-lag(company).
compute fdxp=industry-lag(industry).
exe.
compute xh2=29.39**2.
compute fdxp2=fdxp**2.
compute xnp1=175.3-(1.0*171.7).
* compute xnp12=xnp1**2.
exe.
DESCRIPTIVES
  VARIABLES=fdxp2
  /STATISTICS=sum .
compute spred=sqrt(.00482*(1+(12.96/185.42))).
compute tvalue=idf.t(.975,18).
compute cilo=29.39-(tvalue*spred).
compute cihi=29.39+(tvalue*spred).
execute.
✔ Run
✔ All
```

Forecasting Based on Hildreth-Lu Estimates: On text page 501, the authors find the 95 percent prediction interval based on the *Hildreth-Lu* procedure. Before using Insert 12.7, reread the Blaisdell Example data file to appear as SPSS Output 12.1. Similar to the *Cochrane-Orcutt* procedure above, we first find Y_t' (*ytp*) and X_t' (*xpt*) using equation 12.18 (a) and (b), text page 491, and set $r = 0.96$ as shown in Table 12.5, text page 495. We transform the fitted regression model (equation 12.28, text page 496) back to a fitted model in terms of the original variables to obtain: $\hat{Y} = 1.7793 + .16045X$. We use this model to calculate e and *yhat*. Since X_{n+1}' is not given we compute $xnp1 = X_{21} - (r^* X_{20}) = X_{n+1}'$ (note that $X_{20} = industry_{20}$). We use equation 2.38, text page 59, to find $s^2\{pred\}$ (*spred*) where *MSE* is the mean square error from regressing *ypt* on *xpt*. The lower (*cilo*) and upper (*cihi*) prediction intervals are printed on the 20th line of the *Data Editor*.

INSERT 12.7

```
✔ File
✔ New
✔ Syntax
compute r = 0.96.
compute ypt=company-r*lag(company).
compute xpt=industry-r*lag(industry).
execute.

compute e = company-(1.7793+(.16045*industry)).
compute yhat = 1.7793+(.16045*175.3).
compute forecast = yhat+(r*e).
compute xnp1=175.3-(.96*171.7).
* Use text equation 2.38 to find s{pred} (spred).
 * Find mean of xpt=8.1912 using Analyze > Descriptives.
compute xptdif2=(xpt-8.1912)**2.
 * Find sum of xptdif2 = 90.1088 using Analyze > Descriptives and Sum Option.
compute spred=sqrt(0.00422+ (0.00422*((1/19)+(((10.468- 8.1911)**2)/90.1088)))).
compute tvalue=idf.t(.975,17).
compute cilo=forecast-(tvalue*spred).
compute cihi=forecast+(tvalue*spred).
exe.
✔ Run
✔ All
```

Chapter 13 SPSS®

Non Linear Regression

The general linear regression model is:

$$Y_i = \beta_0 + \beta_1 X_{i1} + \beta_2 X_{i2} + ... + \beta_{p-1} X_{i,p-1} + \varepsilon_i$$

In this model, Y_i is a linear function of the $\beta's$ (the parameters). The general linear regression model can also be expressed as:

$$Y_i = f(\mathbf{X}_i, \boldsymbol{\beta}) + \varepsilon_i$$

where $\mathbf{X}_i$ is the vector of predictor variables for the ith subject, $\boldsymbol{\beta}$ is the vector of model parameters, and

$$f(\mathbf{X}_i, \boldsymbol{\beta}) = \beta_0 + \beta_1 X_{i1} + \beta_2 X_{i2} + ... + \beta_{p-1} X_{i,p-1}$$

The nonlinear regression model can be expressed as (text page 511):

$$Y_i = f(\mathbf{X}_i, \boldsymbol{\gamma}) + \varepsilon_i$$

In this representation of the nonlinear regression model, the authors use γ to denote the vector of parameters rather than β as a reminder that in this model $f(\mathbf{X}_i, \boldsymbol{\gamma})$ is a nonlinear function of the parameters.

Estimation of the parameters of a nonlinear regression model is usually based on the method of least squares or the method of maximum likelihood. However, it is usually not possible to find closed form "formulas" for the estimators of the parameters of nonlinear regression models. Instead, iterative search procedures are required. Thus, although the approach to finding estimators is the same as that used for linear regression models, the computations are much more tedious.

The problem reduces to one of finding values of the parameters that maximize (minimize) a nonlinear function of the parameters. Many search procedures have been developed for finding the maxima (minima) of nonlinear functions. SPSS offers two methods for estimating regression parameters and statistics for models that are not linear in their parameters. Constrained nonlinear regression (CNLR) may be used for constrained and unconstrained nonlinear regression. CNLR uses a sequential quadratic programming algorithm. The NLR (nonlinear regression) can only be used for unconstrained problems and uses the Levenberg-Marquardt algorithm. Both CNLR and NLR estimate model parameter values and can compute and save predicted and residual values and derivatives. The CNLR method is the more general and can generate bootstrap estimates of parameter standard errors and correlations.

Severely Injured Patients Example

Data File: ch13ta01.txt

A hospital administrator wanted to predict long-term recovery among a group of severely injured patients (text page 514). The predictor variable used in the regression model was number of days of hospitalized and the response variable was a long-term recovery index measure. See Chapter 0, "Working with SPSS," for instructions on opening the Severely Injured Patient data file and renaming the variables *index* and *days*. After opening ch13ta01.txt, the first 5 lines in the SPSS *Data Editor* should look like SPSS Output 13.1.

SPSS Output 13.1

severely injured patient example.sav - SPSS Data Editor

File Edit View Data Transform Analyze Graphs Utilities Window Help

15 : days   65

	index	days	var	var	var
1	54.0	2.0			
2	50.0	5.0			
3	45.0	7.0			
4	37.0	10.0			
5	35.0	14.0			

The administrator began by producing a scatter plot (Insert 13.1 – SPSS Output 13.2) of the data, which suggested an exponential relationship between number of days hospitalized and long-term recovery. A review of related literature also suggested an exponential relationship. Thus, the administrator explored the appropriateness of a two-parameter nonlinear exponential regression model.

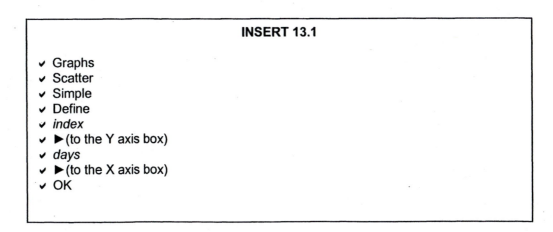

INSERT 13.1

✔ Graphs
✔ Scatter
✔ Simple
✔ Define
✔ *index*
✔ ▶ (to the Y axis box)
✔ *days*
✔ ▶ (to the X axis box)
✔ OK

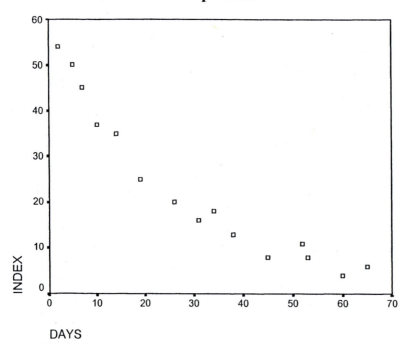

To find the initial starting values $g_0^{(0)}$ and $g_1^{(0)}$ (text page 521), we create a new variable, *logy*, the logarithmic transformation of *index*, and perform an ordinary least squares regression using *logy* as the response variable and *days* as the predictor variable. (Insert 13.2) From SPSS Output 13.3, we find the parameter estimates for this model to be $b_0 = 4.037$ and $b_1 = -0.038$. Using a hand-held calculator, we find $g_0^{(0)} =$ exponential of $b_0 = \exp(4.037) = 56.6646$ and $g_1^{(0)} = b_1 = -0.03797$ (text page 521). We now use the SPSS *Nonlinear Regression* procedure as shown in Insert 13.3 to produce the estimates of the parameters of the nonlinear model and related results. The final least square estimates, including the *MSE*, shown in SPSS Output 13.4 are consistent with Table 13.3, text page 524. The 95% confidence intervals for β_0 and β_1 are also shown in SPSS Output 13.4.

SPSS Output 13.3

Coefficients[a]

Model		Unstandardized Coefficients		Standardized Coefficients		
		B	Std. Error	Beta	t	Sig.
1	(Constant)	4.037	.084		48.002	.000
	DAYS	-.038	.002	-.977	-16.625	.000

a. Dependent Variable: LOGY

SPSS Output 13.4

```
All the derivatives will be calculated numerically.

Iteration  Residual SS            G0            G1

1        58.75436856  56.6640000   -.03700000
1.1      49.48365580  58.5123263   -.03944850
2        49.48365580  58.5123263   -.03944850
2.1      49.45932723  58.6037115   -.03958179
3        49.45932723  58.6037115   -.03958179
3.1      49.45929989  58.6064737   -.03958630
4        49.45929989  58.6064737   -.03958630
4.1      49.45929986  58.6065633   -.03958645


Run stopped after 8 model evaluations and 4 derivative evaluations.
Iterations have been stopped because the relative reduction between
successive residual sums of squares is at most SSCON = 1.000E-08

Nonlinear Regression Summary Statistics    Dependent Variable INDEX

Source              DF   Sum of Squares  Mean Square

Regression           2    12060.54070    6030.27035
Residual            13       49.45930       3.80456
Uncorrected Total   15    12110.00000

(Corrected Total)   14     3943.33333

R squared = 1 - Residual SS / Corrected SS =     .98746

                                    Asymptotic 95 %
                        Asymptotic  Confidence Interval
Parameter   Estimate    Std. Error   Lower        Upper

G0        58.606563279  1.472157894 55.426159508 61.786967050
G1         -.039586448   .001711288  -.043283461  -.035889434

Asymptotic Correlation Matrix of the Parameter Estimates

                G0        G1

G0          1.0000     -.7071
G1          -.7071     1.0000
```

474

On text page 530, the authors generated bootstrap samples to check the appropriateness of large-sample inferences. In Insert 13.4, we generate bootstrap samples for the current data file. By default, the bootstrap option generates $10*p(p+1)/2$ samples where p is the number of parameters. Thus, there are 10 samples generated for each statistic (standard error or correlation) to be calculated. Suppose, however, that you wish to generate 1000 bootstrap samples, as did the authors. We use Insert 13.4 except that we ✔ Paste at the last step as opposed to ✔ OK. In the *Syntax Editor*, we now modify the pasted syntax. Edit the */BOOTSTRAP* statement to read */BOOTSTRAP=1000*. To save the bootstrap estimates for each sample, modify the */OUTFILE* statement to read */OUTFILE='C:\bootstrap.sav'* or indicate a path and file name appropriate for your situation. This results in Insert 13.5. Execution of this edited syntax resulted in SPSS Output 13.5.

INSERT 13.4

✔ Analyze
✔ Regression
✔ Nonlinear
✔ *index*
✔ ▶ (to the Dependent box)
* In the Model Expression box type.
g0 * EXP(g1*days)
✔ Parameters
* Type "g0" in the Name box.
* Type "56.6646" in the Starting Value box.
✔ Add
* Type "g1" in the Name box.
* Type "-0.03797" in the Starting Value box.
✔ Add
✔ Continue
✔ Options
✔ Bootstrap estimates of standard error
✔ Continue
✔ OK

INSERT 13.5

* NonLinear Regression.
MODEL PROGRAM G0=56.664 G1=-.0379 .
COMPUTE PRED_ = g0*exp(g1*days).
CNLR index
 /OUTFILE='C:\bootstrap.sav'
 /PRED PRED_
 /BOOTSTRAP=1000
 /CRITERIA STEPLIMIT 2 ISTEP 1E+20 .

SPSS Output 13.5

```
                                        Asymptotic 95 %
                          Asymptotic    Confidence Interval
     Parameter   Estimate  Std. Error   Lower         Upper

     G0         58.606566138  1.472160332  55.426157099  61.786975176
     G1          -.039586453   .001711294   -.043283479   -.035889427

     Asymptotic Correlation Matrix of the Parameter Estimates

                    G0          G1

     G0          1.0000      -.7071
     G1          -.7071      1.0000

  Bootstrap statistics based on 1000 samples

                                  95% Conf. Bounds      95% Trimmed Range
     Parameter  Estimate  Std. Error   Lower     Upper      Lower      Upper

     G0       58.6065661  1.5067126  55.6498816  61.5632507  55.0486054  60.7722780
     G1        -.0395865   .0017711   -.0430625   -.0361104   -.0429752   -.0361746
```

Notice that $g_0 = 58.6065$ from SPSS Output 13.4; from text page 524, Table 13.3(b); and from SPSS Output 13.5, the mean of the bootstrap sampling distributions. Also, note that $g_1 = -0.3959$ from SPSS Output 13.4; from text page 524, Table 13.3(b); and from SPSS Output 13.5. Additionally, the bootstrap estimates of $s^*\{g_0^*\} = 1.5067$ and $s^*\{g_1^*\} = .00177$ (SPSS Output 13.5) are very close to the large-sample standard deviations given in SPSS Output 13.4 and on text page 524 where $s\{g_0\} = 1.472$ and $s\{g_1\} = .00171$.

On text page 531, Figure 13.4, the authors present the bootstrap sampling distributions of g_0^* and g_1^*. To produce theses distributions, use the *Data Editor* to open the file specified on the */outfile* statement in Insert 13.5. The first line in this file will be the estimates for the original sample. The next 1000 lines will be the estimates for each of the 1000 bootstrap samples. To produce the sampling distributions of the bootstrap samples, delete the first line of the *Data Editor*. You can now ✔ Graph ✔ Histogram and request histograms for g_0^* and g_1^*, separately. Histograms for the current set of bootstrap estimates are shown in SPSS Output 13.6. Of course, the distribution of estimates will change for each bootstrap. The distribution of g_0^* estimates is somewhat skewed to the left. Overall, however, the distribution of both g_0^* and g_1^* are reasonably close to normal. Based on the closeness of the least square estimates to the bootstrap estimates and given

476

the distribution of bootstrap estimates, the authors concluded that the use of large-sample inferences was appropriate.

SPSS Output 13.6

G0

SPSS Output 13.5 continued

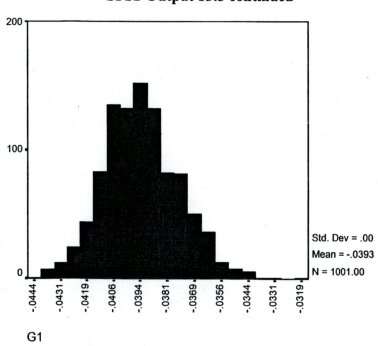

G1

On text page 531 the authors find the 95% confidence interval for γ_1 to be $-0.0433 \le \gamma_1 \le -0.0359$. This confidence interval is found in SPSS Output 13.4 above. The authors now find the 95% confidence interval based on the reflection method (equation 11.59, text page 460). Using our present findings, we have $g_1 = -0.03958$ from SPSS Output 13.4, and $g_1^*(.025) = -0.04306$ and $g_1^*(.975) = -0.03611$ from the bootstrap estimates shown in SPSS Output 13.5. Thus,

$$d_1 = g_1 - g_1^*(.025) = -0.03958 - (-0.04306) = 0.003480$$

$$d_2 = g_1^*(.975) - g_1 = -0.03611 - (-0.03958) = 0.003470$$

$$g_1 - d_2 = -0.03958 - 0.003470 = -0.043050$$

$$g_1 + d_1 = -0.03958 + 0.003480 = -0.036100$$

Previously, we found $-0.0433 \le \gamma_1 \le -0.0359$. Based on the reflection method we find $-0.043050 \le \gamma_1 \le -0.036100$. The confidence intervals are very close, which supports the use of large sample inferences.

Learning Curve Example

Data File: ch13ta04.txt

An electronic products manufacture produces a new product at two different locations: location A ($X1$=1) and location B ($X1$=0). (Text page 533.) The response variable was relative efficiency, a measure related to production costs at each location. See Chapter 0, "Working with SPSS," for instructions on opening the Learning Curve Example data file (Table 13.4, text page 534) and renaming the variables $X1$, $X2$, and Y. After opening ch13ta04.txt, the first 5 lines in the SPSS *Data Editor* should look like SPSS Output 13.6.

SPSS Output 13.6

It was well known that production efficiency of a new product initially increases with time and then levels off. We use the syntax as detailed in SPSS Output 13.7 to produce the scatter plot of relative efficiency (Y) and time ($X2$) with separate symbols for Location A and B (SPSS Output 13.8). The engineers decided to fit an exponential model that used location ($X1$) and the relationship between relative efficiency (Y) and time ($X2$). The selected nonlinear model (equation 13.38, text page 534) was:

$$Y_i = \gamma_0 + \gamma_1 X_{i1} + \gamma_3 \exp(\gamma_2 X_{i2}) + \varepsilon_i$$

On text page 535, the authors detailed the rationale for determining the starting values for parameters: $g_0^{(0)} = 1.025$, $g_1^{(0)} = -0.0459$, $g_2^{(0)} - 0.122$, and $g_3^{(0)} = -0.5$.

SPSS Output 13.7

SPSS Output 13.8

479

To find the fitted regression function for the above model we use ✔ Analyze ✔ Regression ✔ Nonlinear and setup the dialogue box as shown in SPSS Output 13.9. To produce the bootstrap results shown in Table 13.5, text page 535, we also ✔ Options ✔ Bootstrap estimates of standard error ✔ Continue. Finally, ✔ Paste instead of OK, modify the /bootstrap statement to read /bootstrap=1000, and ✔ Run ✔ All. Results of the procedure are shown in SPSS Output 13.10. The nonlinear least squares estimates of the g_k in the first set of estimates are almost identical to the mean $\bar{g}_k^*$ of the respective bootstrap sampling distribution shown in the second set of estimates. Both the nonlinear least squares and the bootstrap estimates of the g_k obtained via SPSS agree with the corresponding estimates reported in the text. Both sets of estimates of the standard deviations of g_0^* and g_1^* are consistent with each other and with the text. The bootstrap estimates of the standard deviations of g_2^* and g_3^*, however, are not in close agreement with the corresponding statistic based on the nonlinear least squares estimates.

SPSS Output 13.9

To produce the histograms on text page 536, we Paste the syntax shown in SPSS Output 13.9 above including a request for bootstrap estimates into the *Syntax Editor*. We modify the /bootstrap statement to indicate /bootstrap=1000 and modify the /outfile statement to indicate the appropriate path as we did in Insert 13.5 above. We then open the file specified in the /outfile statement and ✔ Graph ✔ Histrogram and request histograms for each of the four bootstrap estimates shown in Figure 13.6, text page 536. (SPSS output of these histograms not shown)

SPSS Output 13.10

```
All the derivatives will be calculated numerically.

  Iteration Residual SS        G0           G1           G2           G3

      0.1    .0160356176  1.02500000   -.04590000   -.12200000   -.50000000
      1.1    .0121164281  1.02251428   -.04719754   -.12033423   -.50125049
      2.1    .0061021546  1.01758349   -.03690723   -.13606064   -.55161092
      3.1    .0051054017  1.01772462   -.04638415   -.14369939   -.55737130
      4.1    .0038575425  1.02258114   -.05012288   -.13366241   -.55782249
      5.1    .0032939313  1.01553570   -.04690319   -.13474979   -.55266624
      6.1    .0032926913  1.01558861   -.04726263   -.13482922   -.55249904
      7.1    .0032926829  1.01560015   -.04726789   -.13479238   -.55244318
      8.1    .0032926828  1.01559834   -.04726666   -.13479547   -.55244225


Run stopped after 8 major iterations.
Optimal solution found.


Nonlinear Regression Summary Statistics     Dependent Variable Y

  Source              DF   Sum of Squares  Mean Square

  Regression           4       22.85407       5.71352
  Residual            26     3.292683E-03  1.266416E-04
  Uncorrected Total   30       22.85737

  (Corrected Total)   29         .86673

  R squared = 1 - Residual SS / Corrected SS =     .99620


                                            Asymptotic 95 %
                            Asymptotic    Confidence Interval
  Parameter   Estimate      Std. Error    Lower        Upper

  G0        1.015598343     .003671721   1.008051011  1.023145675
  G1         -.047266663    .004109204   -.055713252   -.038820074
  G2         -.134795470    .004359523   -.143756597   -.125834342
  G3         -.552442252    .008157281   -.569209784   -.535674719

Asymptotic Correlation Matrix of the Parameter Estimates
                  G0        G1        G2        G3

  G0           1.0000    -.5596     .4113    -.1442
  G1           -.5596    1.0000     .0000     .0000
  G2            .4113     .0000    1.0000     .5603
  G3           -.1442     .0000     .5603    1.0000

Bootstrap statistics based on 1000 samples


                                      95% Conf. Bounds    95% Trimmed Range
  Parameter   Estimate   Std. Error   Lower      Upper    Lower      Upper

  G0        1.0155983    .0030804   1.0095535  1.0216432  1.0091062  1.0212429
  G1         -.0472667   .0040116   -.0551387  -.0393946  -.0553678  -.0395930
  G2         -.1347955   .0059994   -.1465683  -.1230226  -.1466684  -.1228470
  G3         -.5524423   .0112183   -.5744564  -.5304281  -.5692589  -.5252973
```

Neural Networks: SPSS Base, Advanced Models, or Regression Models does not offer Neural Network Modeling although SPSS Clementine does.

Chapter 14 SPSS®

Logistic Regression,
Poisson Regression,
And Generalized
Linear Models

In this chapter, the authors consider nonlinear regression models for dependent variables that are categorical. In the simplest case, the dependent variable is binary and has two possible outcomes. Examples of binary outcome categories are success versus failure, disease absent versus disease present, and good performance versus bad performance. At the next level, the dependent variable is multinomial and has more than two possible outcomes. Examples of multinomial outcome categories are complete success, partial success, failure; no disease, minimum disease, moderate disease, severe disease; and performance on an increasing scale of 1 to 5. Lastly, the dependent variable may be a count of the number of events where large counts are rare and thought to be distributed as a Poisson random variable. Examples include counts of the number of accidents at a particular intersection, the number of people with a rare disease, and the number of sales.

One type of nonlinear regression model for categorical random variables is known as the logistic regression model. If the dependent variable is binary, we refer to the model as a logistic regression model whereas, if it is multinomial, we refer to the model as a polytomous or polynomial logistic regression model. If the dependent variable has a Poisson distribution, we refer to the nonlinear regression model as the Poisson regression model. This chapter of the text focuses on the statistical analysis of data based on the logistic model but also gives the essentials for the polytomous logistic regression model and the Poisson regression model.

Linear and nonlinear models considered in the text, including the three models mentioned above, belong to a family of models called *generalized linear models*. The salient feature of generalized linear models is that the initial model formulation is the same for each application with the exception of the specification of a link function. Thus, a unified approach to fitting regression models is provided. A concise description of generalized linear models is given on text pages 623-624.

Simple Logistic Regression

The Programming Task Example

Data File: ch14ta01.txt

An analyst studied the relationship between computer programming experience and success in completing a complex programming task within a specified time period. That is, the response variable was coded $Y=1$ if the task was successfully completed and $Y=0$ if the task was not successfully completed. The predictor variable was the number of months of previous programming experience. See Chapter 0, "Working with SPSS," for instructions on opening the Programming Task example data file (Table 14.1, text page 566) and renaming the variables X, Y, and *FITTED*. After opening ch14ta01.txt, the first 5 lines in the SPSS *Data Editor* should look like SPSS Output 14.1.

SPSS Output 14.1

	x	y	fitted	var
1	14.0	0	31	
2	29 0	0	84	
3	6 0	0	11	
4	25 0	1	73	
5	18 0	1	46	

We begin the preliminary analysis by plotting *fitted* against the X values [Insert 14.1 - SPSS Output 14.2 (a)]. In the second graph, we plot Y against the X values and added a Lowess curve [SPSS Output 14.2 (b)]. The chart exhibits a sigmoidal S-shaped function. Accordingly, the analyst decided to use Logistic Regression.

Continuing in Insert 14.1, we perform a logistic regression using Y as the response variable and X as the single predictor variable. We also request that predicted values based on the regression function be saved to the *Data Editor*, by default as *pre_1*. Actually, the authors included the fitted values in the Programming Task data file. We duplicate the values here to demonstrate that the newly saved *pre_1* variable is equal to the column labeled *fitted* in the *Data Editor*. Finally, we request that the confidence intervals for the odds ratio be generated. Partial regression results are also shown in SPSS Output 14.3. The parameter estimates are consistent with the estimates reported on text page 565. Additionally, the odds ratio (*Exp(B)*=1.175) and 95% confidence interval are displayed and consistent with text page 567.

INSERT 14.1	INSERT 14.1 continued
✔ Graph	✔ Chart
✔ Scatter	✔ Options
✔ Simple	✔ Total (under Fit Line)
✔ Define	✔ Fit Options
✔ fitted	✔ Lowess
► (to the Y axis box)	✔ Continue
✔ X	✔ OK
► (to the X axis box)	* Close the Chart Editor.
✔ OK	✔ Analyze
	✔ Regression
✔ Graph	✔ Binary Logistic
✔ Scatter	✔ y
✔ Simple	✔ ► (to the Dependent box)
✔ Define	✔ x
✔ Y	✔ ► (to the Covariate box)
► (to the Y axis box)	✔ Save
✔ X	✔ Probabilites (under Predicted Values)
► (to the X axis box)	✔ Continue
✔ OK	✔ Options
* Double click the resulting graph to open the Chart Editor.	✔ CI for exp(B)
	✔ Continue
	✔ OK

SPSS Output 14.2

(a)

(b)

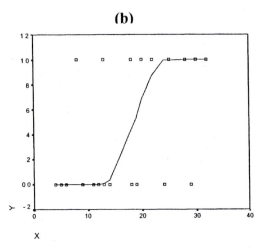

SPSS Output 14.3

Variables in the Equation

		B	S.E.	Wald	df	Sig.	Exp(B)	95.0% C.I.for EXP(B)	
								Lower	Upper
Step 1[a]	X	.161	.065	6.176	1	.013	1.175	1.035	1.335
	Constant	-3.060	1.259	5.903	1	.015	.047		

a. Variable(s) entered on step 1: X.

The Coupon Effectiveness Example

Data File: ch14ta02.txt

Marketing researchers mailed packets containing promotional material and related coupons to 1000 selected homes. Two hundred homes each received one of 5 different coupons that offered price reductions of 5, 10, 15, 20, or 25 dollars. Thus, the predictor variable was the coupon available to the home and the response variable (Y) was whether or not the home redeemed the coupon within a six-month period. See Chapter 0, "Working with SPSS," for instructions on opening the Coupon Effectiveness example data file (Table 14.2, text page 569) and renaming the variables X, N, Y, and *pro*. After opening ch14ta02.txt, the 5 lines in the SPSS *Data Editor* should look like SPSS Output 14.4.

SPSS Output 14.4

	x	n	y	pro
1	5.0	200.00	30.00	.15
2	10.0	200.00	55.00	.28
3	15.0	200.00	70.00	.35
4	20.0	200.00	100.00	.50
5	30.0	200.00	137.00	.69

The data file as shown in Table 14.2, text page 569, is a convenient way to summarize the study outcome. However, SPSS cannot be used to analyze the data in its present form. In Insert 14.2, we present two methods for restructuring the data file so that it can be used by SPSS. In Method 1 the program reads the first line of SPSS Output 14.4 and then writes 2 records (*loop #i=1 to 2*). When *#i*=1 we set *newn=y* and *response*=1. Thus, for the first line of SPSS Output 14.4 we set *newn* = 30 and *y*=1. When *#i*=2 we set *newn* = 200–*y* = 170 and *response* = 0. After each increment of the *loop* statement, we write a record to an output file. We *keep* the value of *x*, *newn*, and *response*, and we rename *newn* to *n* and *response* to *y*. After execution of Insert 14.2, the restructured data file will look like SPSS Output 14.5. The first line indicates that there were 30 (*N*) homes that redeemed (*Y*=1) a \$5 coupon (*X*). The second line indicates that there were 170 (*N*) homes that did not redeem (*Y*=0) a \$5 coupon (*X*). The progression continues such that we have cell counts for each combination of *X* and *Y* values.

In Insert 14.2 (Method 2), we read the input file as shown in SPSS Output 14.4 and write *X* and *Y* values for each of the 1000 observations in the study. Both Method 1 and Method 2 require that the *Data Editor* be as shown in SPSS Output 14.4 before execution of the syntax. Method 2 produces a file structure with which we are most familiar, i.e., a line for each observation. We will use Method 1, however, to introduce the SPSS *weight* statement.

To use the data as shown in SPSS Output 14.5, we first declare *N* to be a weight variable prior to running any statistical procedure. This declaration will be in effect until we open a new data file or turn off the *weight* function. Note that if we save the data file with the *weight* function on, the weight function will remain on when the data file is next used. If *weight* is on, "Weight Cases" will appear in the lower right-hand corner of the *Data Editor*. To turn *weight* off, execute *weight off* in the *Syntax Editor* or ✔ Data ✔ Weight Cases ✔ Reset ✔ OK.

In Insert 14.3, we declare *N* to be a *weight* variable and then request logistic regression using *Y* as the dependent variable and *X* as the single predictor variable. By declaring *N* to be a *weight* variable, SPSS interprets the first line of SPSS Output 14.5 to represent 30 (*N*) cases where *X*=5 and *Y*=1, for example. Insert 14.3 produces the odds ratio = 1.102 as shown on text page 570 (SPSS Output not shown).

INSERT 14.2

```
* METHOD 1 -Table 14.2 as input, write summary data file.
weight off.
LOOP #i = 1 TO 2.
if (#i=1) newn=y.
if (#i=1) response=1.
if (#i=2) newn=200-y.
if (#i=2) response=0.
XSAVE OUTFILE = 'temp.sav' / keep x  newn response / rename newn=n response=y.
END LOOP.
EXE.
GET FILE = 'temp.sav'.
exe.

* METHOD 2 - Table 14.2 as input, write 1000 records.
weight off.
LOOP #i = 1 TO n.
if (#i le y) response=1.
if (#i gt y) response=0.
XSAVE OUTFILE = 'temp.sav' / keep x response / rename response=y.
END LOOP.
EXE.
GET FILE = 'temp.sav'.
weight off.
exe.
```

SPSS Output 14.5

temp.sav - SPSS Data Editor

File Edit View Data Transform Analyze Graphs Utilities W

1 : x   5

	x	n	y	var
1	5.0	30.00	1.00	
2	5.0	170.00	.00	
3	10.0	55.00	1.00	
4	10.0	145.00	.00	
5	15.0	70.00	1.00	
6	15.0	130.00	.00	
7	20.0	100.00	1.00	
8	20.0	100.00	.00	
9	30.0	137.00	1.00	
10	30.0	63.00	.00	

INSERT 14.3	INSERT 14.3 continued
✔ Data ✔ Weight Cases ✔ Weight cases by: ✔ N ✔ ▶ ✔ OK	✔ Analyze ✔ Regression ✔ Binary Logistic ✔ y ✔ ▶ (to the Dependent box) ✔ x ✔ ▶ (to the Covariate box) ✔ OK

Multiple Logistic Regression

The Disease Outbreak Example – Model Building

Data File: ch14ta03.txt and appenc10.txt

Note: Data for the Disease Outbreak example are available in two files: ch14ta03.txt and appenc10.txt. There are differences in the files that we will identify. For all analyses involving the Disease Outbreak example, we must pay close attention to the data file we use, i.e., ch14ta03.txt versus appenc10.txt. We will be unable to match the chapter results if we use the wrong file.

Using ch14ta03.txt, a researcher studied the relationship between disease outbreak ($Y=1$ if disease was present and $Y=0$ if disease was not present) and the individual's age ($X1$), socioeconomic status (represented by indicator variables $X2$ and $X3$), and the sector in which the individual lived ($X4$ coded 0 or 1). See Chapter 0, "Working with SPSS," for instructions on opening the Disease Outbreak example data file (Table 14.3, text page 574) and renaming the variables *case, X1, X2, X3, X4, and Y*. After opening ch14ta03.txt, the first 5 lines in the SPSS *Data Editor* should look like SPSS Output 14.6a.

SPSS Output 14.6 (a)

disease outbreak model building.sav - SPSS Data Editor

File Edit View Data Transform Analyze Graphs Utilities Window Help

1 : case   1

	case	x1	x2	x3	x4	y
1	1.0	33.0	0	0	0	0
2	2.0	35.0	0	0	0	0
3	3.0	6.0	0	0	0	0
4	4.0	60.0	0	0	0	0
5	5.0	18.0	0	1	0	1

Similar to the steps for requesting the logistic regression analysis in the previous example (Insert 14.3), for the Disease Outbreak example we enter Y as the dependent variable and $X1$, $X2$, $X3$, and $X4$ as covariates. Partial results are shown in SPSS Output 14.7(a). The regression function is consistent with equation 14.46, text page 574. The odds ratio [listed under $Exp(B)$] for $X1$=1.03, indicating that, since age is coded in units of years, the risk of disease increases by 1.03 or approximately 3% for each additional year of age. The odds ratio for $X4$=4.83, indicating that individuals living in sector 2 are 4.83 times more likely to have contracted the disease compared to individuals living in sector 1.

As noted above, data file ch14ta03.txt comprises the first 98 cases of a sample of 196 cases used in the Disease Outbreak example. The entire 196 cases are available in the data file appenc10.txt. After opening appenc10.txt and renaming the variables *case*, *age*, *status*, *sector*, *y*, and *other*, the *Data Editor* should look like SPSS Output 14.6(b). In this file, socioeconomic status is represented by one variable (*status*) where *status* = 1 if status is "upper," *status* = 2 if status is "middle," and *status* = 3 if status is "lower." The sector is coded *sector* = 1 if the individual lives in sector 1 and *sector* = 2 if the individual lives in sector 2.

SPSS Output 14.6 (b)

	case	age	status	sector	y	other
1	1.0	33.0	1	1	0	1
2	2.0	35.0	1	1	0	1
3	3.0	6.0	1	1	0	0
4	4.0	60.0	1	1	0	1
5	5.0	18.0	3	1	1	0

appenc10.sav - SPSS Data Editor
File Edit View Data Transform Analyze Graphs Utilities Window Help
1 : case   1

Note that in ch14ta03.txt, two indicator variables ($X2$, $X3$) were used to represent the 3 levels of socioeconomic status. However, SPSS's *Binary Logistic* procedure allows the user to use one variable to represent socioeconomic status (*status*) as done in appenc10.txt. Using this coding scheme we can enter *age*, *status*, and *sector*, as predictor variables and specify *status* as a categorical variable in the *Binary Logistic* dialogue box. For each variable specified as a categorical variable, SPSS will automatically code a set of indicator variables as defined by the user in *Binary Logistic's* Define Categorical Variables dialogue box. We also define the first category (upper) as the reference category. Thus, we replaced $X2$ and $X3$ in the analysis that produced SPSS Output 14.7(a) with *status* and specified the first category (upper) as the reference category. We also replaced $X1$ with *age*, although these two variables are equal, and replaced $X4$ with *sector*. This results in SPSS Output 14.7(b). So, SPSS Output 14.7(a) is a result of using $X1$, $X2$, $X3$, and $X4$ as predictors from the ch14ta03.txt data set. SPSS Output 14.7(b) is a result of using *age*, *status*, and *sector* as predictors from the appenc10.txt data set (and using ✔

Data ✔ Select Cases where *case* < 99). Although the variables used in the two models were coded differently, they contain the same "information." Thus we note the correspondence between the parameter estimates and odds ratios in SPSS Output 14.7 (a) and (b). The only discrepancy in table values is the intercept (*Constant*). This is due to city sector (*X4*) being coded 0 versus 1 in ch14ta03.txt and 1 versus 2 (*sector*) in appenc10.txt. The coding scheme used to produce SPSS Output 14.7(b) also yields an overall test statistic that is indicative of lack of significance for the *status* variable, $p = 0.547$.

SPSS Output 14.7

(a)

Variables in the Equation

		B	S.E.	Wald	df	Sig.	Exp(B)
Step 1[a]	X1	.030	.014	4.854	1	.028	1.030
	X2	.409	.599	.466	1	.495	1.505
	X3	-.305	.604	.255	1	.613	.737
	X4	1.575	.502	9.855	1	.002	4.830
	Constant	-2.313	.643	12.956	1	.000	.099

a. Variable(s) entered on step 1: X1, X2, X3, X4.

(b)

Variables in the Equation

		B	S.E.	Wald	df	Sig.	Exp(B)
Step 1[a]	AGE	.030	.014	4.854	1	.028	1.030
	STATUS			1.206	2	.547	
	STATUS(1)	.305	.604	.255	1	.613	1.357
	STATUS(2)	.714	.654	1.193	1	.275	2.042
	SECTOR	1.575	.502	9.855	1	.002	4.830
	Constant	-4.193	.911	21.194	1	.000	.015

a. Variable(s) entered on step 1: AGE, STATUS, SECTOR.

Polynomial Logistic Regression

The Initial Public Offerings Example

Data File: appenc11.txt

On text page 575, a researcher studies the relationship between whether or not a company was financed by venture capital (*VC*) and the face value (*facval*) of the company. See Chapter 0, "Working with SPSS," for instructions on opening the IPO example data file and renaming the variables *case, VC, FACEVAL, SHARES,* and *X3.* After opening appenc11.txt, the first 5 lines in the SPSS *Data Editor* should look like SPSS Output 14.8.

SPSS Output 14.8

IPO example.sav - SPSS Data Editor

File   Edit   View   Data   Transform   Analyze   Graphs   Utilities   Window   Help

1 : case   1

	case	vc	faceval	shares	x3
1	1.0	0	1200000	3000000	0
2	2.0	0	1454000	1454000	1
3	3.0	0	1500000	300000.0	0
4	4.0	0	1530000	510000.0	0
5	5.0	0	2000000	800000.0	0

In Insert 14.4, we find *LNFACE,* the natural logarithm of *FACEVAL.* We then plot (syntax not shown) *LNFACE* and *VC* and request that a Lowess curve be drawn. As noted in SPSS Output 14.9 (a), there appears to be a mound shaped relationship between the two variables. To produce the first order regression line displayed in Figure 14.9 (a), text page 575, we regress *VC* on *LNFACE* and save the predicted probabilities. We plot the saved predicted probabilities (*pre_1*) against *LNFACE.* It is obvious that the first order regression line displayed in Output 14.9 (b) is not consistent with the mound shaped relationship shown in Output 14.9 (a). Thus, the authors decided to explore a second-order model using *LNFACE* (centered) and *LNFACE* (centered) squared as predictors. Continuing in Insert 14.4, we center LNFACE (*xcnt*), find its square (*xcnt2*), regress *VC* on *xcnt* and *xcnt2*, and save the predicted values. Partial results of this model are shown in 14.10 and are consistent with Table 14.5, text page 576. Additionally, we plotted (syntax not shown) the predicted values (from regressing *VC* on *xcnt* and *xcnt2*) against *xcnt* to obtain the second order logistic curve [Output 14.9 (c)]. Notice that the relationship in Output 14.9 (c) is more consistent with the relationship shown in Output 14.9 (a).

SPSS Output 14.9

(a)   (b)   (c)

✔ File
✔ New
✔ Syntax
* Type the following syntax.
COMPUTE lnface = LN(faceval) .
EXECUTE .
* Find mean of lnface=16.7088, steps not shown.
COMPUTE xcnt = 16.7088 - lnface .
EXECUTE .
COMPUTE xcnt2 = xcnt ** 2 .
EXECUTE .
✔ Run
✔ All

✔ Analyze
✔ Regression
✔ Binary Logistic
✔ vc
✔ ▶(to the Dependent box)
✔ xcnt
✔ ▶(to the Covariate box)
✔ xcnt2
✔ ▶(to the Covariate box)
✔ Save
✔ Probabilities (Under Predicted Values)
✔ Continue
✔ OK

SPSS Output 14.10

Variables in the Equation

		B	S.E.	Wald	df	Sig.	Exp(B)
Step 1^a	XCNT	-.552	.138	15.872	1	.000	.576
	XCNT2	-.862	.140	37.651	1	.000	.423
	Constant	.300	.124	5.874	1	.015	1.350

a. Variable(s) entered on step 1: XCNT, XCNT2.

Inferences about Regression Parameters

The Programming Task Example

On text page 578 the authors wish to test $H_0 : \beta_1 \le 0$ versus $H_a : \beta_1 > 0$. The test for β_1 on SPSS Output 14.3 is a two-sided test. For a one-sided test, we simply divide the probability level (0.013 listed under *sig* and across from X) by 2. This yields the one-sided probability level of

491

0.0065 as noted on text page 579. Also, note that the authors report $z^* = 2.485$ and the square of z is equal to the Wald statistic which is distributed approximately as chi-square distribution with 1 degree of freedom. Thus, the Wald statistic is $X^2 = 2.485^2 = 6.176$ as shown in SPSS Output 14.3.

SPSS does not report the confidence interval for β_1 shown on text page 579. From SPSS Output 14.3, however, we find that $b_1 = 0.161$ and $s\{b_1\} = 0.065$. For a 95% confidence interval, we require $z = 1.96$. The 95% confidence interval is:

$$0.161 \pm 1.96(0.065)$$

or

$$0.034 \leq \beta_1 \leq 0.288.$$

Finally, a logistic model can be specified in SPSS' *Nonlinear Regression*. Bootstrap estimates and confidence intervals for the logistic model can be generated.

The Disease Outbreak Example

Data File: ch14ta03.txt

On text page 581, the researchers now wish to determine if *X1* can be dropped from the model in the Disease Outbreak Example. In Insert 14.5, we use the *block* function that is available in the *Binary Logistic* program. When we use the *block* option in *Binary Logistic*, the results are presented for each block starting with Block 0, which represents an intercept only model. The Omnibus Tests of Model Coefficients table, as shown in SPSS Output 14.11, displays the chi-square test, *df*, and probability level of the test. This table is organized by *step*, *block*, and *model*. If we use the stepwise method, the *step* line will be a test of improvement in the model due to adding the current variable to the model. If we use the *block* option and do not use a stepwise method (*/method=entry*) then the *step* line and *block* line are identical because there is only 1 step per block. The test for *block* in the Omnibus Tests of Model Coefficients table is a test of model improvement for the current block of predictors beyond the predictors previously entered in the model. The test for *block* is analogous to the R^2 Change test that we previously used in the ordinary least squares regression procedure. For any Omnibus Tests of Model Coefficients table, the *model* line is a test of whether the overall model (at the end of the current block) is significantly better then the intercept only model. Thus, the model test is analogous to the test of whether $R^2=0$ at the end of each block in ordinary least squares regression.

We enter *X2*, *X3*, and *X4* at *block* 1 and then enter *X1* at *block* 2. Partial output is shown in SPSS Output 14.11. The test statistic and *sig* (0.023) for *block* 2 are consistent with text page 581. Similarly, we can enter *X1* and *X4* at block 1 and *X2* and *X3* at block 2 to determine if *X2* and *X3* (socioeconomic status) can be dropped from the model (syntax not shown). Partial results are shown in SPSS Output 14.12 and are consistent with text page 581. This is the effect of socioeconomic status and the *p*-value associated with the test is 0.547. If we refer back to SPSS Output 14.7(b) we see that the *p*-value of the partial test for *status* was also 0.547. Finally, we can compute new variables to represent the five possible two-way interactions, e.g., compute *intx1x2 = X1 * X2*. Because *X2* and *X3* are both indicator variables for socioeconomic status, we do not create a term for their interaction. Using the *block* function, we enter all main effects at *block* 1 and all interaction terms at *block* 2 (syntax not shown). This yields the results shown on text page 582.

INSERT 14.5

- ✔ Analyze
- ✔ Regression
- ✔ Binary Logistic
- ✔ Y
- ✔ ▶(to the Dependent box)
- ✔ X1
- ✔ ▶(to the Covariate box)
- ✔ X2
- ✔ ▶(to the Covariate box)
- ✔ X3
- ✔ ▶(to the Covariate box)
- ✔ Next
- ✔ X1
- ✔ ▶(to the Covariate box)
- ✔ OK

SPSS Output 14.11

Block 2: Method = Enter

Omnibus Tests of Model Coefficients

		Chi-square	df	Sig.
Step 1	Step	5.150	1	.023
	Block	5.150	1	.023
	Model	21.263	4	.000

SPSS Output 14.12

Block 2: Method = Enter

Omnibus Tests of Model Coefficients

		Chi-square	df	Sig.
Step 1	Step	1.205	2	.547
	Block	1.205	2	.547
	Model	21.263	4	.000

493

Automatic Model Selection Methods

The Disease Outbreak Example

Data File: appenc10.txt

Best Subsets Procedure. SPSS' *Binary Logistic* does not offer a best subset procedure. Additionally, the AIC_p and SBC_p statistics are not available. The $-2\log_e L(\mathbf{b})$ statistic, Cox and Snell R square, and Nagelkerke r square are standard output for the *Binary Logistic* procedure. Both R squares are pseudo R square measures and tend to be much lower than non-pseudo R squares seen in other regression models.

Stepwise Model Selection. SPSS offers both forward and backward stepwise variable selection. Additionally, for both forward and backward selection the user can specify the statistic used to test for removal of a variable from the model. The Conditional statistic (default method), Wald statistic, and Likelihood ratio statistic are available. The Conditional statistic uses the same formula as the Likelihood ratio statistic. However, the Conditional statistic uses conditional parameter estimates rather than maximum likelihood estimates. The methods generally follow the description of selection procedures described for multiple linear regression in Chapter 9.

From the appenc10.txt data file, we select the first 98 cases and create four new variables to match the coding scheme of ch14ta03.txt (Insert 14.6). That is, socioeconomic status will be represented by two indicator variables: $X2 = 1$ if class is middle, otherwise $X2 = 0$, and $X3=1$ if class is lower, otherwise $X3 = 0$. Thus, upper is the reference class. Also, $X4 = 0$ if the individual lives in sector 1 and $X4=1$ if the individual lives in sector 2. Finally, to use the same variable names as the text, we set $X1=age$.)

We then present the syntax to perform forward stepwise selection using the Wald statistic to test for removal of variables from the model. Partial results are shown in SPSS Output 14.13. At Step 0, before any variables are entered into the model, $X4$ has the lowest probability level of the 4 variables under consideration and, thus, is entered into the model at Step 1 (Variables in the Equation – Step 1). Of the variables not in the model at Step 1, $X1$ has the lowest probability level of the three candidate variables and is entered into the model at Step 2. Of the variables not in the model at Step 2 ($X2$, $X3$) the probability levels are both greater than the probability level required for entering a variable into the model and the stepping process stops.

Although we arrive at the same conclusion as the text, the *constant* values in SPSS Output 14.13 do not match those displayed in Table 14.11, text page 585. In the model specified in Insert 14.7, we used $X1$, $X2$, $X3$, and $X4$ as predictor variables. The text example used *age, status*, and *sector* as predictors. Both sets of predictors contain the same "information" but socioeconomic status and city sector are parameterized differently in the two models. Thus, although we arrive at the same conclusion regarding the regression coefficients, the intercepts differ due to the different parameterization.

INSERT 14.6

- ✔ Data
- ✔ Select Cases
- ✔ If Condition is Satisfied
- ✔ IF (under If Condition is Satisfied
- ✔ "case >= 99" (in the upper right hand corner box).
- ✔ Continue
- ✔ OK

- ✔ File
- ✔ New
- ✔ Syntax

* Type the following syntax.
if (status=2) x2=1.
if (status ne 2)x2=0.
if (status=3) x3=1.
if (status ne 3)x3=0.
if (sector=2) x4=1.
if (sector ne 2)x4=0.
compute x1=age.
exe.

- ✔ Run
- ✔ All

- ✔ Analyze
- ✔ Regression
- ✔ Binary Logistic
- ✔ Y
- ✔ ► (to the Dependent box)
- ✔ X1
- ✔ ► (to the Covariate box)
- ✔ X2
- ✔ ► (to the Covariate box)
- ✔ X3
- ✔ ► (to the Covariate box)
- ✔ X4
- ✔ ▼ (by Method)
- ✔ Forward: Wald
- ✔ ► (to the Covariate box)
- ✔ OK

SPSS Output 14.13

Variables not in the Equation

			Score	df	Sig.
Step 0	Variables	X1	7.580	1	.006
		X2	1.480	1	.224
		X3	3.909	1	.048
		X4	14.780	1	.000
	Overall Statistics		20.407	4	.000

Variables in the Equation

		B	S.E.	Wald	df	Sig.	Exp(B)
Step 1 ^a	X4	1.743	.473	13.594	1	.000	5.717
	Constant	-1.589	.347	20.976	1	.000	.204
Step 2 ^b	X1	.029	.013	4.946	1	.026	1.030
	X4	1.673	.487	11.791	1	.001	5.331
	Constant	-2.335	.511	20.872	1	.000	.097

a. Variable(s) entered on step 1: X4.

b. Variable(s) entered on step 2: X1.

Variables not in the Equation

			Score	df	Sig.
Step 1	Variables	X1	5.239	1	.022
		X2	.664	1	.415
		X3	1.155	1	.283
	Overall Statistics		6.296	3	.098
Step 2	Variables	X2	.968	1	.325
		X3	.733	1	.392
	Overall Statistics		1.221	2	.543

Pearson Chi-Square Goodness of Fit Test: SPSS does not compute the Pearson Chi-Square Goodness of Fit statistic.

Deviance Goodness of Fit Test: As noted on text page 588, the *deviance goodness of fit test* for logistic regression is analogous to the *F lack of fit test* we discussed in previous chapters. We present the steps without the specific syntax. Find –2 log likelihood (1191.973) for the reduced model by regressing Y on X using the Coupon Effectiveness example described above. To find –2 log likelihood for the full model we first compute $j=1$ if $X=5$, $j=2$ if $X=10$, . . . , $j=5$ if $X=30$. Now use *Binary Regression* to regress Y on X and j, and specify j as a categorical covariate. This will result in –2 log likelihood for the full model of 1189.806. The difference in the 2 values is 2.167, consistent with text page 589 where $DEV(X_0,X_1) = 2.16$.

Hosmer-Lemeshow Goodness of Fit Test. On text page 590, the author calculated the Hosmer-Lemeshow goodness of fit test for the Disease Outbreak example (ch14ta03.txt). In this case they based the calculation on 5 classes. SPSS, however, uses approximately 10 classes and the classes are often referred to as deciles of risk. To generate the Hosmer-Lemeshow goodness of fit statistic, request a logistic regression model and ✔ Options ✔ Hosmer-Lemshow goodness-of-fit ✔ Continue. Partial results are found in SPSS Output 14.14. Note that $X^2 = 9.180$ ($p = 0.327$) in SPSS Output 14.14 and the text reports $X^2 = 1.98$ ($p = 0.58$). The discrepancy is due to the test statistics being based on different contingency tables, i.e., 2x5 versus 2x10. The use of 20 cells (2x10) decreases the expected frequencies per cell relative to the use of 10 cells (2x5). However, Hosmer and Lemeshow take a liberal approach to expected values and argue that their method is an accurate assessment of goodness of fit.

SPSS Output 14.14

Hosmer and Lemeshow Test

Step	Chi-square	df	Sig.
1	9.188	8	.327

Contingency Table for Hosmer and Lemeshow Test

		Y = 0		Y = 1		
		Observed	Expected	Observed	Expected	Total
Step 1	1	10	9.214	0	.786	10
	2	9	8.981	1	1.019	10
	3	9	9.489	2	1.511	11
	4	9	8.224	1	1.776	10
	5	7	7.663	3	2.337	10
	6	6	6.909	4	3.091	10
	7	3	6.092	7	3.908	10
	8	8	5.494	3	5.506	11
	9	5	3.684	5	6.316	10
	10	1	1.249	5	4.751	6

Logistic Regression Diagnostics

Logistic Regression Residuals. On text page 591, the authors demonstrate the calculation of various residual values. To request that residual and other values be saved from the logistic procedure, ✔ Options and then select the desired option as shown in SPSS Output 14.15.

SPSS Output 14.15

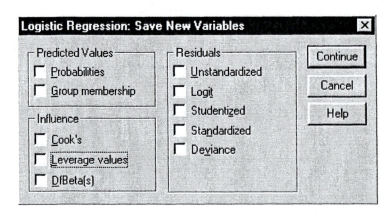

To produce Figure 14.12(d), text page 594, for example, we request that deviance residuals (saved as *dev_1* by default) (text dev_i residuals) and probabilities (*pre_1* by default) (text $\hat{\pi}_i$) be saved. We then (scatter) plot *dev_1* on the Y-axis and *pre_1* on the X-axis. Results are shown in SPSS Output 14.16. We use the *Chart Editor* to add the Lowess curve line to simulate Figure 14.13(c), text page 595.

SPSS Output 14.16

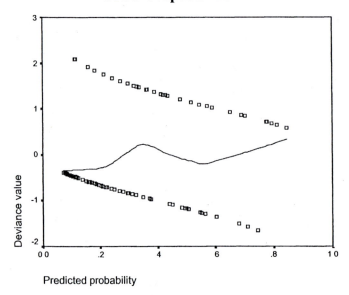

Detection of Influential Observations

Influence on Pearson Chi-Square and the Deviance Statistics. On text page 599, the authors calculate the *delta chi-square statistic* (ΔX_i^2) and the *deviance statistic* (Δdev_i). Here we use appenc10.txt; invoke *Select Cases* as shown in Insert 14.6; and use *age*, *status*, and *sector* as predictors. To calculate these statistics, we first instruct SPSS (syntax not shown) to save the standardized residuals (*zre_1*, text r_{Pi}, Table 14.11, column 1), deviance residuals (*dev_1*, text dev_i, Table 14.11, column 4), and leverage values (*lev_1*, h_{ii}, Table 14.11, column 3). SPSS does not produce the studentized Pearson residual. However, this is given in equation 14.81, text page 592 as:

$$r_{SPi} = \frac{r_{Pi}}{\sqrt{1 - h_{ii}}}$$

or

$$r_{SPi} = \frac{zre\_1}{\sqrt{1 - lev\_1}}$$

In Insert 14.7 we compute the studentized Pearson residual (*rspi*), ΔX_i^2 (*dx2*), and Δdev_i (*ddev*). We also use text equation 14.87, text page 600, to compute D_i (*cook*).

Figures 14.15 (a) and (b), text page 600, can now be produced by plotting *case* on the X-axis and *dx2* and *ddev* on the Y-axis's. Additionally, the above saved and computed values can be used to produce the Figures displayed on text pages 600 and 601.

```
                        INSERT 14.7

✔ File
✔ New
✔ Syntax
* Type the following syntax.
compute rspi=zre_1/(sqrt(1-lev_1)).
compute dx2=rspi**2.
compute ddev=lev_1*(rspi**2)+(dev_1**2).
compute cook=rspi**2*lev_1/(5*(1-lev_1)**2).
exe.
✔ Run
✔ All
```

Inferences about Mean Response

On text page 603, the authors wish to calculate the 95% confidence interval for a new observation. SPSS's *Binary Logistic* procedure does not make the variance-covariance matrix

$[s^2\{b\}$, equation 14.51, text page 578] available to the user. Thus the information to generate this confidence interval is not readily available.

Prediction of a New Observation

The Disease Outbreak Example

Data File: appenc10.txt

We use the first 96 cases of appenc10.txt for this analysis (use *Select Cases* as in Insert 14.6). The authors wish to obtain the best cutoff point for predicting whether the outcome of a new observation will be "1" or "0". If 0.5 is used as the cutoff point, for example, the prediction rule would be: if $\hat{\pi}_h \geq 0.5$, predict the outcome will be "1"; otherwise predict it will be "0". Table 14.12, text page 605, displays the classification table based on text equation 14.95. That is, because 0.316 is the proportion of the diseased individuals in the sample, we use 0.316 as the starting cutoff point.

In the SPSS *Binary Logistic* dialogue window, ✔ Options and then enter the *classification cutoff*. The box allows for only 2 decimal precision and, therefore, will not accommodate 0.316. To remedy the problem, set the *Binary Logistic* dialogue box as needed and then ✔ Paste instead of OK. This will paste the current syntax into the *Syntax Editor* (*Binary Logistic* procedure in Insert 14.8). The /*criteria* statement will indicate *CUT(.5)*, the default cutoff value. Edit the line to read *CUT(.316)* and then execute the syntax. This will produce SPSS Output 14.17. We can produce text Table 14.12 (b) by changing the statement to read *CUT(.326)*.

SPSS Output 14.17

Classification Table[a]

			Predicted		
			Y		Percentage
Observed			0	1	Correct
Step 1	Y	0	49	18	73.1
		1	8	23	74.2
	Overall Percentage				73.5

a. The cut value is .316

There were 8+23=31 (false negatives + true positives) diseased individuals and 49+18=67 (true negatives + false positives) non-diseased individuals. The fitted regression function correctly predicted 23 of the 31 diseased individuals. Thus, the sensitivity is calculated as true positives / (false negatives + true positives) = 23 / 8 + 23 = 0.7419 as reported on text page 606. The regression function's specificity is defined as true negatives / (false positives + true negatives) = 48 / (18 + 48) = 0.727. This is not consistent with text page 607 where the specificity is reported as 47 / 67 = 0.7014. The difference comes from the numerator used to calculate specificity. Table

14.12 (a), text page 605, uses 47 and we determined the number of true negatives to be 49. We assumed that the regression model was to be based on using *age, status, and sector* as predictors. If we use only *age* and *sector* as suggested by the stepwise regression above, the classification table will match Table 14.12, text page 605.

To approximate Figure 14.17, text page 606, we first saved the predicted group membership (✔ Save ✔ Group Membership ✔ Continue) while in the *Binary Logistic* dialogue box and ✔ Paste instead of OK. (Again we use *age, status,* and *sector* as predictors.) In the *Syntax Editor*, edit the */cut* statement to read *CUT(.316)* and execute the syntax as shown in Insert 14.8. This will save the predicted group membership (*pgr_1* by default) based on the cutoff point of 0.316. In Insert 14.8, we then request an ROC curve. We use the *Chart Editor* (steps not shown) to draw a vertical line (*reference line*) at 1-specificity on the *X*-axis and a horizontal line at sensitivity on the *Y*-axis. Results are shown in SPSS Output 14.18.

INSERT 14.8

LOGISTIC REGRESSION VAR=y
 /METHOD=ENTER age status sector
 /SAVE PGROUP
 /CRITERIA PIN(.05) POUT(.10) ITERATE(20) CUT(.316) .
exe.

* Type the following syntax.
roc pgr_1 by y (1)
 /plot = curve
 /print = coordinates.
exe.
 ✔ Run
 ✔ All

SPSS Output 14.18

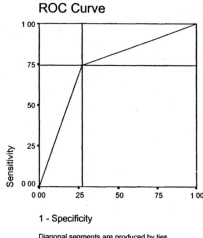

ROC Curve

Sensitivity

1 - Specificity

Diagonal segments are produced by ties

501

Validation of Prediction Error Rate

The Disease Outbreak Example – Validation Data Set

Data File: appenc10.txt

On text page 607, the researchers now wish to use the regression function based on the Model Building data set to classify observations in the Validation data set. After opening appenc10.text and renaming your variables *case*, *age*, *status*, *sector*, *y*, and *other*, the *Data Editor* should look like SPSS Output 14.19.

SPSS Output 14.19

	case	age	status	sector	y	other
1	1.0	33.0	1	1	0	1
2	2.0	35.0	1	1	0	1
3	3.0	6.0	1	1	0	0
4	4.0	60.0	1	1	0	1
5	5.0	18.0	3	1	1	0

In Inert 14.9, we first must compute *X1, X2, X3*, and *X4* so that these values will be contained in the *Data Editor*. We compute the estimated probabilities (*yhat*) for each case using the regression function (equation 14.46, text page 574) based on the model-building data set. We then use prediction rule 14.96 (text page 606) to establish group membership (*newgp*) as *newgp* = 1 if *yhat* ≥ 0.325 and *newgp* = 0 if *yhat* < 0.325. We also select on cases 99 to 196. Finally, we use the *crosstab* procedure to form a 2x2 table of *Y* values (diseased versus non-diseased) by *newgp* values (predicted diseased versus predicted non-diseased). Results are shown in SPSS Output 14.20 and are consistent with text page 608. The off-diagonal percentages indicate that 12 (46.2%) of the 26 diseased individuals were incorrectly classified (prediction error) as non-diseased. Twenty-eight (38.9%) of the 72 non-diseased individuals were incorrectly classified as diseased.

☑ File
☑ New
☑ Syntax
* Type the following syntax.
compute x1=age.
if (status=2) x2=1.
if (status ne 2)x2=0.
if (status=3) x3=1.
if (status ne 3)x3=0.
if (sector=2) x4=1.
if (sector ne 2)x4=0.
compute yhat=(1+exp(2.3129-(.02975*x1)-(.4088*x2)+(.30525*x3)-(1.5747*x4)))**-1.
if (yhat ge .325) newgp=1.
if (yhat lt .325) newgp=0.
exe.
☑ Run
☑ All

☑ Data
☑ Select Cases
☑ If Condition is Satisfied
☑ IF (under If Condition is Satisfied
* Type "case >= 99" (in the upper right hand corner box).
☑ Continue
☑ OK

☑ Analyze
☑ Descriptive Statistics
☑ Crosstabs
☑ Y
☑ ► (to the Row box)
☑ newgp
☑ ► (to the Column box)
☑ Cells
☑ Row
☑ Continue
☑ OK

SPSS Output 14.20

Y * NEWGP Crosstabulation

			NEWGP		Total
			.00	1.00	
Y	0	Count	44	28	72
		% within Y	61.1%	38.9%	100.0%
	1	Count	12	14	26
		% within Y	46.2%	53.8%	100.0%
Total		Count	56	42	98
		% within Y	57.1%	42.9%	100.0%

Polyotomous Logistic Regression for Nominal Response

Pregnancy Duration Example

Data File: ch14ta13.txt

On text page 609, a researcher studied the relationship between gestation period and several predictor variables. Gestation period was classified as less than 36 weeks ($Y=1$), 36 to 37 weeks ($Y=2$), and greater than 37 weeks ($Y=3$). After opening ch14ta13.txt and renaming the variables *case, Y, RC1, RC2, RC3, X1, X2, X3, X4,* and *X5,* the *Data Editor* should look like SPSS Output 14.21. In Insert 14.10, we request SPSS's *Multinomial Logistic* program. We specify *X1* as a covariate; *X2, X3, X4,* and X5 as factors; and *Y* as the dependent variable. Main effects only is the default model in *Multinomial Logistic*. Results are shown in SPSS Output 14.22. Notice that our results are not entirely consistent with Figure 14.18, text page 613. Our odds ratios are generally less than 1 where those in Figure 14.18 are generally greater than 1. Our constants also do not match Figure 14.18. By some hand calculations we could show that our findings are equivalent to those presented in the text. It is easier, however, to re-parameterize our model by executing the *recode* statement in Insert 14.10 and then re-running the *Multinomial Logistic* procedure. That is, we simply reverse the values of *X2, X3, X4,* and *X5* into *x2rev, x3rev, x4rev,* and *x5rev* for use in the *Multinomial Logistic* procedure. We repeat the first *Multinomial Logistic* procedure and use *x2rev, x3rev, x4rev,* and *x5rev* rather than *X2, X3, X4,* and *X5* as independent variables (factors) and *X1* as a covariate. This results in SPSS Output 14.23, which is entirely consistent with text Figure 14.18.

SPSS Output 14.21

SPSS Output 14.22

Parameter Estimates

Y^a		B	Std. Error	Wald	df	Sig.	Exp(B)	95% Confidence Interval for Exp(B)	
								Lower Bound	Upper Bound
1	Intercept	14 987	3 322	20.357	1	.000			
	X1	-.065	018	12.865	1	.000	.937	904	971
	[X2=0]	-2.957	964	9 400	1	002	052	008	344
	[X2=1]	0^b	.		0			.	
	[X3=0]	-2 060	895	5 299	1	021	.127	022	736
	[X3=1]	0^b	.	.	0			.	.
	[X4=0]	-2 043	.710	8 285	1	004	.130	032	521
	[X4=1]	0^b	.	.	0			.	.
	[X5=0]	-2 452	.732	11 239	1	.001	086	021	361
	[X5=1]	0^b	.	.	0	.	.	.	.
2	Intercept	12 057	2 852	17 866	1	.000			
	X1	-.046	.015	9 736	1	002	955	927	983
	[X2=0]	-2.913	858	11 542	1	001	.054	010	292
	[X2=1]	0^b	.	.	0				
	[X3=0]	-1 888	809	5.446	1	020	.151	031	739
	[X3=1]	0^b			0		.	.	.
	[X4=0]	-1 067	.650	2 699	1	.100	344	096	1 229
	[X4=1]	0^b	.		0			.	.
	[X5=0]	-2 230	668	11 143	1	.001	107	029	398
	[X5=1]	0^b	.		0		.		

a The reference category is: 3.

b. This parameter is set to zero because it is redundant

505

SPSS Output 14.23

Parameter Estimates

Y[a]		B	Std. Error	Wald	df	Sig.	Exp(B)	95% Confidence Interval for Exp(B)	
								Lower Bound	Upper Bound
1	Intercept	5 475	2.272	5 809	1	016			
	X1	- 065	018	12 865	1	000	937	904	.971
	[X2REV= 00]	2 957	.964	9 400	1	002	19 241	2 906	127 408
	[X2REV=1.00]	0[b]			0	.	.	.	.
	[X3REV=.00]	2 060	895	5.299	1	021	7 843	1 358	45 304
	[X3REV=1 00]	0[b]	.	.	0	.	.	.	.
	[X4REV= 00]	2 043	710	8.285	1	.004	7 713	1.919	31 001
	[X4REV=1 00]	0[b]			0	.	.	.	.
	[X5REV=.00]	2 452	732	11 239	1	001	11 616	2.769	48 720
	[X5REV=1.00]	0[b]	.	.	0	.	.	.	.
2	Intercept	3 958	1 941	4 158	1	041			
	X1	- 046	.015	9.736	1	002	955	927	983
	[X2REV= 00]	2 913	858	11.542	1	001	18 420	3 430	98 912
	[X2REV=1 00]	0[b]			0	.	.	.	.
	[X3REV=.00]	1 888	809	5 446	1	020	6 603	1 353	32 227
	[X3REV=1 00]	0[b]	.	.	0	.	.	.	.
	[X4REV= 00]	1 067	650	2 699	1	100	2 907	814	10 382
	[X4REV=1.00]	0[b]	.	.	0	.	.	.	.
	[X5REV=.00]	2 230	.668	11.143	1	.001	9.304	2 511	34 470
	[X5REV=1 00]	0[b]			0	.	.	.	.

a. The reference category is: 3

b. This parameter is set to zero because it is redundant.

Polyotomous Logistic Regression for Ordinal Response

Pregnancy Duration Example

Data File: ch14ta13.txt

The steps to perform Polyotomous Logistic Regression for a nominal response completely generalize to the case where there is an ordinal response. Use Insert 14.10 and ✔ *Regression* ✔ *Ordinal* instead of ✔ *Regression* ✔ *Multinomial Logistic*. Results are not shown but are similar to Figure 14.19, text page 618.

Poisson Regression

Miller Lumber Company Example

Data File: ch14ta14.txt

The Miller Lumber Company conducted an in-store customer survey. The researcher counted the number of customers who visited the store from each nearby census tract. The researcher also collected and subsequently retained five (quantitative) predictor variables for use in the Poisson Regression. See Chapter 0, "Working with SPSS," for instructions on opening the Miller Lumber Company data file and renaming the *X1*, *X2*, *X3*, *X4*, *X5*, and *Y*. After opening ch14ta14.txt, we opened the *Syntax Editor* and executed *compute id=$casenum* (syntax not shown) to produce the *ID* variable. After this maneuver, the first 5 lines in the SPSS *Data Editor* should look like SPSS

Output 14.24. Note that Table 14.14, text page 622, appears to indicate that the variables are ordered in the data file as *X1, X2, X3, X4, X5,* and *Y.* By examining the *Data Editor* you will sometimes find that the data file was not structured as expected.

SPSS Output 14.24

	y	x1	x2	x3	x4	x5	id
1	9.0	606.00	41393.00	3.0	3.04	6.32	1.00
2	6.0	641.00	23635.00	18.0	1.95	8.89	2.00
3	28.0	505.00	55475.00	27.0	6.54	2.05	3.00
4	11.0	866.00	64646.00	31.0	1.67	5.81	4.00
5	4.0	599.00	31972.00	7.0	.72	8.11	5.00

There are some complexities in performing Poisson regression in SPSS. The following eight paragraphs of verbatim explanation are used with permission from SPSS and can be found using AnswerNet at spss.com (Resolution number: 16655).

"The easiest way to handle Poisson regression models in current releases of SPSS (Release 6.1 and above) is to use the GENLOG procedure, which does general loglinear and logit modeling. The simplest type of Poisson model for our purposes is one in which the counts are modeled without denominators (i.e., we are modeling counts rather than rates), and all predictors are categorical. Rate models and quantitative predictors introduce further complexities into the process, but they can still be handled."

"If the simplest form of the model is being used, the variables in the data set consist simply of the predictors and a count variable. If rates are to be modeled, an additional variable representing the denominators is added. If quantitative predictors are to be used, a subject ID variable is also added, with a unique value for each case. The file preparation is completed by weighting the data by the count variable (in the dialog boxes, click on Data->Weight Cases, then click on Weight cases by and move the appropriate variable into the Frequency Variable box). The status bar at the bottom of the screen should have "Weight On" in one of the boxes."

"The Poisson option in the GENLOG procedure is the default for Statistics->Loglinear->General. If there are only categorical predictors, these are selected as factors. The count variable is not used (the data are already weighted by this variable). If a rate model is being fitted, the denominator variable is specified as the Cell Structure variable. The model is specified by clicking on the Model button, checking Custom and specifying the desired predictive model (or leaving it as full factorial, if that's the desired model). Continue out of the Model dialog and make any desired specifications in the Options or Save dialogs (printing of parameter estimates is specified in the Options dialog). When finished with these, click OK, or Paste if you want to see the GENLOG syntax that's been created."

"If quantitative predictors are used, the situation will generally be more complicated. The term quantitative predictor here is used to denote a predictor to be treated as is for modeling purposes. That is, you want to use that variable's values directly in the design matrix and produce a single parameter estimate, rather than creating a set of indicator variables to represent the unique levels or categories. Though technically not entirely accurate, the term continuous is commonly used for such a variable."

"The complications arise because GENLOG analyzes data on a cell by cell basis, with cells defined by the combinations of the factor variables. Cell covariates are handled by averaging all values in the same cell defined by the factors specified in the main dialog (on the GENLOG command). Thus, information about individual case values will be lost unless each case is treated as a cell. This is why we have to use the subject ID variable when there are cell covariates: to trick GENLOG into seeing each case as a cell. Note that if you have any quantitative/continuous variables, you must treat all predictors that way (as cell covariates). If you use any factors other than the subject ID variable, the table that GENLOG will construct internally will have as many cells as the product of the number of subjects and the number of levels of those factors, and you will not get the desired results."

"If there are only quantitative variables to be used, specify them as cell covariates and the subject ID variable as the only factor. Then go into the Model dialog box and specify a Custom model that includes the desired predictors and any interactions, but not the subject ID. After requesting any other specifications in other dialogs, click OK or Paste. Since you have a subject ID variable specified as a factor that is not being used in the model, a popup warning will tell you about this. Simply click OK."

"If there are any 0 counts that produce 0 marginals (as any 0 count will with quantitative predictors using the subject ID trick), these should be recoded to a small positive number (e.g., 1E-12). ML estimates will still be good to as many decimals as are printed on the output. 0 marginals will cause the procedure to refuse to run."

"As noted above, if there is a combination of quantitative/continuous and categorical predictors, all predictors must be treated as cell covariates. This means that for categorical factors, you must first dummy or effect code variables to represent the desired contrasts among their levels, and include these dummy variables as cell covariates"

In Insert 14.11, we produce the *ID* variable if not done above. To check for zero counts, we use *Frequencies* to obtain a frequency distribution of *Y*. For the Miller Lumber example we find that 3 of the counts (*Y* values) are zero. As instructed above, if *Y*=0 then we set $Y = 0.00000001$. We continue with the instruction as presented above to produce SPSS Output 14.25. The parameter estimates are consistent with Table 14.15, text page 622. Deviance Residuals can be displayed by checking Residuals under Display in the Options window of the *General Loglinear* window.

INSERT 14.11	INSERT 14.11 continued
✔ File	✔ Analyze
✔ New	✔ Loglinear
✔ Syntax	✔ General
compute id=$casenum.	✔ Poission (under Distribution of Cell Counts)
execute.	✔ x1
✔ Run	✔ ► (to Cell Covariates)
✔ All	✔ x2
	✔ ► (to Cell Covariates)
✔ Analysis	✔ x3
✔ Descriptive Statistics	✔ ► (to Cell Covariates)
✔ Frequencies	✔ x4
✔ y	✔ ► (to Cell Covariates)
✔ ►	✔ x5
✔ OK	✔ ► (to Cell Covariates)
	✔ id
✔ File	✔ ► (Factor(s))
✔ New	✔ Model
✔ Syntax	✔ Custom
if (y=0) y=.00000001.	✔ ▼
exe.	✔ Main effects
✔ Run	✔ x1 x2 x3 x4 x5
✔ All	✔ ► (Under Build Terms)
	✔ Continue
✔ Data	✔ Options
✔ Weight Cases	* Uncheck all options under Display except **Estimates**.
✔ Weight Cases By	* Uncheck all options under Plot.
✔ y	✔ Continue
✔ ►	✔ OK
✔ OK	* Your will get an error: "The following factors are".
	* not used in the Model: id".
	✔ OK

SPSS Output 14.25

- -

                        GENERAL LOGLINEAR ANALYSIS
- -

Parameter Estimates

Parameter	Estimate	SE	Z-value	Asymptotic 95% CI Lower	Upper
1	2.9424	.2072	14.20	2.54	3.35
2	.0006	.0001	4.26	3.272E-04	8.843E-04
3	-1.169E-05	2.112E-06	-5.53	-1.582E-05	-7.547E-06
4	-.0037	.0018	-2.09	-7.219E-03	-2.340E-04
5	.1684	.0258	6.53	.12	.22
6	-.1288	.0162	-7.95	-.16	-.10

- -

Covariance Matrix of Parameter Estimates

Parameter

	1	2	3	4	5	6
1	.0430					
2	-3.70E-06	2.020E-08				
3	-1.40E-07	-1.74E-10	4.459E-12			
4	-9.19E-05	-4.73E-08	5.396E-10	3.175E-06		
5	-.0035	-3.75E-08	-8.01E-09	-6.66E-07	6.640E-04	
6	-.0029	3.097E-09	8.003E-09	2.109E-06	2.530E-04	2.625E-04

- -

Correlation Matrix of Parameter Estimates

Parameter

	1	2	3	4	5	6
1	1.0000					
2	-.1256	1.0000				
3	-.3191	-.5795	1.0000			
4	-.2487	-.1866	.1434	1.0000		
5	-.6503	-.0102	-.1472	-.0145	1.0000	
6	-.8727	.0013	.2339	.0730	.6059	1.0000

Chapter **15** SPSS®

Analysis of Data in Designed Experimental and Observational Studies

In the previous chapters, the authors of the text focused on linear and nonlinear statistical models to investigate the relationship between an observed response vector **Y** and one or more independent variables or predictors arranged in a "design" matrix **X**. These models were called *regression models*. The analysis of regression models typically emphasizes the individual contribution of each independent variable (one of the X's) toward predicting the value of the dependent variable Y. Independent variables are added to or deleted from the regression model, according to their importance, in order to choose an appropriate model for predicting Y given the values of the X's. The analysis of variance in terms of these regression models is an important step in the investigation of a suitable model for a specific problem.

In Chapter 15, the authors give an overview of important types of designed studies and issues involved in the use of various designs. Here, emphasis is on investigating differences among the response means for subjects that are categorized in different groups where the groups of interest are determined by the study design. Again, the analysis of variance is an important approach to investigating these differences. Linear models are formulated for this purpose and these models are referred to as *analysis of variance models*.

The mathematical equation is the same for the regression model and the analysis of variance model, and both can be expressed as

$$\mathbf{Y} = \mathbf{X}\boldsymbol{\beta} + \boldsymbol{\varepsilon}$$

A model of this form is referred to as the *general linear model*. In both the regression model and the analysis of variance model, **Y** is an observed response vector. In the regression model, the first column of **X** is a vector of ones (which is omitted if an intercept term is to be omitted) followed by one or more column vectors, each containing the data for a single independent variable; and **β** is a vector of parameters (intercept and one or more coefficients, one parameter for each column vector of **X**). Typically, the **X** matrix is of full rank implying that there are no linear dependencies among its columns. In the analysis of variance model, the columns of **X** are "indicator" variables that identify the group to which a given response is linked (typically each column of **X** is a variable whose values are 0's, 1's, and −1's). For each specific problem, there are many ways to specify these indicator variables. The following example illustrates the analysis of variance model for data collected in a completely randomized design.

15.1 Single Factor Studies: Fixed Effects

Lipid Study Example

Researchers studied the effect of 4 experimental drug treatments on subsequent changes in lipid concentrations. Twenty patients with a diagnosis of hyperlipidemia participated in the study. Each of four experimental drugs was randomly assigned to five patients. Let y_{ij} denote the change in lipid concentration of the jth patient, $j = 1, 2, \ldots, 5$, treated with the ith experimental drug, $i = 1, 2, \ldots, 4$. The data were arranged for analysis as follows:

Drug A		Drug B		Drug C		Drug D	
Subject	Response	Subject	Response	Subject	Response	Subject	Response
1	$Y_{11}=12$	6	$Y_{21}=7$	11	$Y_{31}=6$	16	$Y_{41}=4$
2	$Y_{12}=9$	7	$Y_{22}=7$	12	$Y_{32}=8$	17	$Y_{42}=3$
3	$Y_{13}=10$	8	$Y_{23}=5$	13	$Y_{33}=2$	18	$Y_{43}=2$
4	$Y_{14}=11$	9	$Y_{24}=6$	14	$Y_{34}=3$	19	$Y_{44}=3$
5	$Y_{15}=8$	10	$Y_{25}=9$	15	$Y_{35}=6$	20	$Y_{45}=4$

We refer to the single classification variable *drug* (treatment) as the *factor* in this study and we refer to the four types of drugs as *levels* of the factor. For the SPSS analysis, we arbitrarily coded the response variable as *y* and the 4 levels of treatment (Drug A, Drug B, Drug C, and Drug D) *drug*=1, *drug*=2, *drug*=3, or *drug*=4, respectively. The 20 observations of *y* and *drug* values are given in SPSS Output 15.1.

SPSS Output 15.1

y	drug	y	drug	y	drug	y	drug
12	1	7	2	6	3	4	4
9	1	7	2	8	3	3	4
10	1	5	2	2	3	2	4
11	1	6	2	3	3	3	4
8	1	9	2	6	3	4	4

We can write the specific form of the general linear model for these data in many different ways, all of which will produce the same numerical values of the relevant test statistics. The different forms of the model are determined by the way we define the indicator variables in the design matrix **X**. We provide here 3 specific models as illustrative examples. In each of these illustrative models, the design matrix **X** has four columns, each defined by values of an indicator variable. We denote the indicator variables as X_0, X_1, X_2, and X_3, respectively.

To analyze the data using SPSS, we can enter the values of the **X** matrix for a given analysis of variance model along with the values for the **Y** vector in the same manner we entered data for the regression models analyzed in previous chapters. Alternatively, we can use SPSS syntax to generate the values of the matrix **X**. We use this latter approach in the examples that follow. Once we have entered the data and have generated or entered the values of the matrix **X**, we can use SPSS' *Regression* procedure to request an (regression) analysis of variance. We can also use

SPSS' *General Linear Model* (*GLM -Univariate*) procedure. Alternatively, we can enter, as part of the data, the group to which each observation in the **Y** vector belongs and specify that this group membership variable is a fixed factor. *GLM* will then automatically generate code for parameterizing an effects model, as defined below.

In SPSS Output 15.1, we see that *drug* has been coded using allocated codes (see text page 321). That is, we have used one variable (*drug*) to code the 4 categories (levels) of the experimental drug. We arbitrarily coded Drug A=1, Drug B=2, Drug C=3, and Drug D=4. As we will see, allocated codes can be very convenient; however, allocated codes can also be misused. The current coding 1, 2, 3, and 4 seems to imply an equal distance between each level of *drug*, an implication that is not tenable. We could have arbitrarily coded Drug A=3, Drug B=1, Drug C=4, and Drug D=2, or, for that matter, we could have coded Drug A=a, Drug B=b, Drug C=c, and Drug D=d (note that we cannot use SPSS' *Regression* procedure if we use alphanumeric coding for the values of indicator variables). Thus, the value of the allocated code is only an arbitrary label to represent a category of *drug*. Given that *drug* is an allocated numeric code, application of SPSS' *Regression* procedure where *y* is specified to be the dependent variable and *drug* the independent variable will produce erroneous results because the SPSS' *Regression* procedure will handle *drug* as a continuous variable as opposed to a categorical variable.

Indicator variables, however, do not necessarily imply order or magnitude of spacing between categories. We will use indicator variables to represent the $c=4$ types (categories) of experimental drugs, and illustrate two effects models (remember there are many choices for effects models) and the cell means model with each specific model parameterization depending on our choice of indicator variables. We also demonstrate the use of allocated codes where the *GLM* automatically assigns values to indicator variables for an analysis of variance effects model.

Effects Model 1

One model can be expressed by defining the indicator variables to have values as follows:

$$X_0 = 1 \text{ (always)} \quad X_1 = \begin{cases} 1 & \text{if } drug = 1 \\ -1 & \text{if } drug = 4 \\ 0 & \text{otherwise} \end{cases} \quad X_2 = \begin{cases} 1 & \text{if } drug = 2 \\ -1 & \text{if } drug = 4 \\ 0 & \text{otherwise} \end{cases} \quad X_3 = \begin{cases} 1 & \text{if } drug = 3 \\ -1 & \text{if } drug = 4 \\ 0 & \text{otherwise} \end{cases}$$

The model can then be expressed in the general linear model (matrix form) $\mathbf{Y} = \mathbf{X\beta} + \varepsilon$ with specific matrices

$$
\begin{bmatrix}
Y_{11} \\
Y_{12} \\
Y_{13} \\
Y_{14} \\
Y_{15} \\
Y_{21} \\
Y_{22} \\
Y_{23} \\
Y_{24} \\
Y_{25} \\
Y_{31} \\
Y_{32} \\
Y_{33} \\
Y_{34} \\
Y_{35} \\
Y_{41} \\
Y_{42} \\
Y_{43} \\
Y_{44} \\
Y_{45}
\end{bmatrix}
=
\begin{bmatrix}
1 & 1 & 0 & 0 \\
1 & 1 & 0 & 0 \\
1 & 1 & 0 & 0 \\
1 & 1 & 0 & 0 \\
1 & 1 & 0 & 0 \\
1 & 0 & 1 & 0 \\
1 & 0 & 1 & 0 \\
1 & 0 & 1 & 0 \\
1 & 0 & 1 & 0 \\
1 & 0 & 1 & 0 \\
1 & 0 & 0 & 1 \\
1 & 0 & 0 & 1 \\
1 & 0 & 0 & 1 \\
1 & 0 & 0 & 1 \\
1 & 0 & 0 & 1 \\
1 & -1 & -1 & -1 \\
1 & -1 & -1 & -1 \\
1 & -1 & -1 & -1 \\
1 & -1 & -1 & -1 \\
1 & -1 & -1 & -1
\end{bmatrix}
\begin{bmatrix}
\mu \\
\tau_1 \\
\tau_2 \\
\tau_3
\end{bmatrix}
+
\begin{bmatrix}
\varepsilon_{11} \\
\varepsilon_{12} \\
\varepsilon_{13} \\
\varepsilon_{14} \\
\varepsilon_{15} \\
\varepsilon_{21} \\
\varepsilon_{22} \\
\varepsilon_{23} \\
\varepsilon_{24} \\
\varepsilon_{25} \\
\varepsilon_{31} \\
\varepsilon_{32} \\
\varepsilon_{33} \\
\varepsilon_{34} \\
\varepsilon_{35} \\
\varepsilon_{41} \\
\varepsilon_{42} \\
\varepsilon_{43} \\
\varepsilon_{44} \\
\varepsilon_{45}
\end{bmatrix}
$$

Thus, because Y_{11} denotes the response for a subject who received Drug A (*drug*=1), the "X variables" for observation Y_{11} are $X_0 = 1$, $X_1 = 1$, $X_2 = 0$, and $X_3 = 0$. These values appear in the first row (line) of the matrix $\mathbf{X}$ shown above. In fact, Y_{12}, Y_{13}, Y_{14}, and Y_{15}, respectively, denote responses for subjects who received Drug A and their X variables are identical to those for Y_{11}. Similarly, Y_{21}, Y_{22}, Y_{23}, Y_{24}, and Y_{25}, respectively, are responses for subjects who received Drug B (*drug* = 2), and the "X variables" for each of these Y's are $X_0 = 1$, $X_1 = 0$, $X_2 = 1$, and $X_3 = 0$. These values appear in rows (lines) 2 through 5 of the matrix $\mathbf{X}$ shown above. Similar coding is displayed in subsequent rows of the matrix $\mathbf{X}$. We see that our choice of the matrix $\mathbf{X}$ is key to our specification of the model.

The analysis of variance model specified above is called an *effects model*. For purposes of discussion here, we shall refer to this model as *Effects Model 1*. In this effects model, we assume the expected values of a random observation from subjects in the four drug groups (cells) are μ_1, μ_2, μ_3, and μ_4, respectively, and the overall expected value is μ. We further assume there is an "effect" for each of the four cells (perhaps the effect is zero) denoted τ_1, τ_2, τ_3, and τ_4, respectively, the effect is the difference between the cell mean and the overall mean, and the sum of the effects is zero so that $\tau_4 = -\tau_1 - \tau_2 - \tau_3$. In this context, the effects for the four cells are as follows:

$$\tau_1 = \mu_1 - \mu$$
$$\tau_2 = \mu_2 - \mu$$
$$\tau_3 = \mu_3 - \mu$$

$$
\begin{aligned}
\tau_4 &= -\tau_1 - \tau_2 - \tau_3 \\
&= -(\mu_1 - \mu) - (\mu_2 - \mu) - (\mu_3 - \mu) \\
&= 3\mu - (\mu_1 + \mu_2 + \mu_3) \\
&= 3\left(\frac{\mu_1 + \mu_2 + \mu_3 + \mu_4}{4}\right) - 4\left(\frac{\mu_1 + \mu_2 + \mu_3}{4}\right) \\
&= 3\left(\frac{\mu_4}{4}\right) + \left(\frac{\mu_4}{4}\right) - \left(\frac{\mu_1 + \mu_2 + \mu_3}{4}\right) + \left(\frac{\mu_4}{4}\right) \\
&= \mu_4 - \mu
\end{aligned}
$$

Thus, once τ_1, τ_2, and τ_3 are known, τ_4 is also known. In fact, once any three of the four effects parameters are known, the fourth is also known. We therefore say there are three *degrees of freedom* for estimating the effects parameters.

Effects Model 2

Another model can be expressed by defining the indicator variables to have values as follows:

$$X_0 = 1 \text{ (always)} \quad X_1 = \begin{cases} 1 & \text{if } drug = 1 \\ 0 & \text{otherwise} \end{cases} \quad X_2 = \begin{cases} 1 & \text{if } drug = 2 \\ 0 & \text{otherwise} \end{cases} \quad X_3 = \begin{cases} 1 & \text{if } drug = 3 \\ 0 & \text{otherwise} \end{cases}$$

As for the previous model, the model associated with these indicator variables is a special case of the general linear model (matrix form) $\mathbf{Y} = \mathbf{X\beta} + \boldsymbol{\varepsilon}$ but here the specific matrices are

$$
\begin{bmatrix}
y_{11} \\
y_{12} \\
y_{13} \\
y_{14} \\
y_{15} \\
y_{21} \\
y_{22} \\
y_{23} \\
y_{24} \\
y_{25} \\
y_{31} \\
y_{32} \\
y_{33} \\
y_{34} \\
y_{35} \\
y_{41} \\
y_{42} \\
y_{43} \\
y_{44} \\
y_{45}
\end{bmatrix}
=
\begin{bmatrix}
1 & 1 & 0 & 0 \\
1 & 1 & 0 & 0 \\
1 & 1 & 0 & 0 \\
1 & 1 & 0 & 0 \\
1 & 1 & 0 & 0 \\
1 & 0 & 1 & 0 \\
1 & 0 & 1 & 0 \\
1 & 0 & 1 & 0 \\
1 & 0 & 1 & 0 \\
1 & 0 & 1 & 0 \\
1 & 0 & 0 & 1 \\
1 & 0 & 0 & 1 \\
1 & 0 & 0 & 1 \\
1 & 0 & 0 & 1 \\
1 & 0 & 0 & 1 \\
1 & 0 & 0 & 0 \\
1 & 0 & 0 & 0 \\
1 & 0 & 0 & 0 \\
1 & 0 & 0 & 0 \\
1 & 0 & 0 & 0
\end{bmatrix}
\begin{bmatrix}
\mu \\
\tau_1 \\
\tau_2 \\
\tau_3
\end{bmatrix}
+
\begin{bmatrix}
\varepsilon_{11} \\
\varepsilon_{12} \\
\varepsilon_{13} \\
\varepsilon_{14} \\
\varepsilon_{15} \\
\varepsilon_{21} \\
\varepsilon_{22} \\
\varepsilon_{23} \\
\varepsilon_{24} \\
\varepsilon_{25} \\
\varepsilon_{31} \\
\varepsilon_{32} \\
\varepsilon_{33} \\
\varepsilon_{34} \\
\varepsilon_{35} \\
\varepsilon_{41} \\
\varepsilon_{42} \\
\varepsilon_{43} \\
\varepsilon_{44} \\
\varepsilon_{45}
\end{bmatrix}
$$

For our discussion here, we shall refer to this model as *Effects Model 2*. In this effects model, we again assume the expected value of a random observation from subjects in the four drug groups (cells) are $\mu_1, \mu_2, \mu_3,$ and μ_4, respectively, and the overall expected value is μ. We further assume there is an "effect" for each of the first three cells (perhaps the effect is zero) denoted $\tau_1, \tau_2,$ and τ_3, respectively, and τ_4, the effect for cell 4, is always equal to 0. The effects for the four cells are as follows:

$$\tau_1 = \mu_1 - \mu_4$$
$$\tau_2 = \mu_2 - \mu_4$$
$$\tau_3 = \mu_3 - \mu_4$$
$$\tau_4 = \mu_4 - \mu_4 = 0$$

Thus, the expected value of a random observation from cell 4 is μ and cell 4 is referred to as the *reference cell*.

Hypothesis to be Tested in Effects Models 1 and 2

Both of the above effects models have four columns in the design matrix and four degrees of freedom for the model. Both have a first column that specifies an overall mean for the response variable (one degree of freedom) and both have three columns that correspond to "effects for the first three cells" of the design (three degrees of freedom, one for each column or effect). In both models we are interested in testing the (global) hypothesis

$$H_0 : \mu_1 = \mu_2 = \mu_3 = \mu_4$$

or, equivalently,

$$H_0 : \tau_1 = \tau_2 = \tau_3 = 0$$

The test statistic for evaluating this hypothesis is a function of the regression sum of squares attributable to adding the indicator variables X_1, X_2, and X_3 to a model that contains only the variable X_0 (i.e., a model that contains no terms other than a term for the overall mean or the reference cell). We denote this added sum of squares as $SS(X_1, X_2, X_3 | X_0)$.

Using SPSS' *Regression* procedure to Analyze Effects Models 1 and 2

In this section, we provide SPSS programs to produce analyses for *Effects Models 1 and 2*. Unless otherwise specified, SPSS automatically creates X_0, a column of ones, so that a parameter corresponding to the overall mean (*Effects Model 1*) or a reference cell (*Effects Model 2*) is included in the model. To represent the $c=4$ experimental drugs, we use SPSS programming syntax to create for each model $c-1=3$ indicator variables (*X1, X2, X3*) that signify the drug effect associated with each response.

We entered the data shown in SPSS Output 15.1 into a SPSS *Data Editor* and named the variables *y* and *drug*. The syntax to parameterize the *Effects Models 1 and 2*, respectively, is shown in Insert 15.1. Note that both models, by default, contain intercept terms so that we do not have to specify explicit code to generate X_0. Regression analyses based on both parameterizations result in identical *Model Summary* and *ANOVA* tables (SPSS Output 15.2). The numerical value of the test statistic for both models is $F = 14.75$ with degrees of freedom = 3 and *p*-value (*Sig*) < 0.0001.

Note that the parameter estimates for the two parameterizations are different (SPSS Output 15.3). For reference, the cell means for the sample data are given by the descriptive statistics shown in SPSS Output 15.4. Note that the intercept for *Effects Model 1* is the overall sample mean 6.25 whereas the intercept for *Effects Model 2* is the sample mean for *drug* = 4. For *Effects Model 1*, the parameter estimates for the indicator variables *X1*, *X2*, and *X3* are equal to the respective difference between the mean of the response variable for each drug category and the overall sample mean. For example, the parameter estimate for *X1* is the difference between the mean response for subjects in the *drug* = 1 group and mean response for all subjects in the four drug categories; i.e., $10.0 - 6.25 = 3.75$.

For the parameter estimates based on *Effects Model 2*, we see that the parameter estimate for *X1*, the indicator variable for *drug*=1, is equal to the mean response for *drug* = 1 minus the mean response for *drug* = 4; i.e., $10.0 - 3.2 = 6.8$.

INSERT 15.1	INSERT 15.1 continued

* Effects Model 1.
✓ File
✓ New
✓ Syntax
if (drug = 1)x1=1.
if (drug = 4)x1=-1.
if (drug ne 1 and drug ne 4)x1=0.
if (drug = 2)x2=1.
if (drug = 4)x2=-1.
if (drug ne 2 and drug ne 4)x2=0.
if (drug = 3)x3=1.
if (drug = 4)x3=-1.
if (drug ne 3 and drug ne 4)x3=0.
exe.
✓ Run
✓ All
✓ Analyze
✓ Regression
✓ Linear
✓ y
✓ ► (to the Dependent box)
✓ x1 x2 x3
✓ ► (to the Independent box)
✓ OK
	* Effects Model 2.
	✓ File
	✓ New
	✓ Syntax
	if (drug = 1)x1=1.
	if (drug ne 1)x1=0.
	if (drug = 2)x2=1.
	if (drug ne 2)x2=0.
	if (drug = 3)x3=1.
	if (drug ne 3)x3=0.
	exe.
	✓ Run
	✓ All
	✓ Analyze
	✓ Regression
	✓ Linear
	✓ y
	✓ ► (to the Dependent box)
	✓ x1 x2 x3
	✓ ► (to the Independent box)
	✓ OK

SPSS Output 15.2

Model Summary

Model	R	R Square	Adjusted R Square	Std. Error of the Estimate
1	.857[a]	.734	.685	1.68819

a. Predictors: (Constant), X3, X2, X1

ANOVA[b]

Model		Sum of Squares	df	Mean Square	F	Sig.
1	Regression	126.150	3	42.050	14.754	.000[a]
	Residual	45.600	16	2.850		
	Total	171.750	19			

a. Predictors: (Constant), X3, X2, X1

b. Dependent Variable: Y

SPSS Output 15.3

Parameter Estimates – Effects Model 1

Coefficients[a]

Model		Unstandardized Coefficients		Standardized Coefficients		
		B	Std. Error	Beta	t	Sig.
1	(Constant)	6.250	.377		16.557	.000
	X1	3.750	.654	.905	5.735	.000
	X2	.550	.654	.133	.841	.413
	X3	-1.250	.654	-.302	-1.912	.074

a. Dependent Variable: Y

Parameter Estimates – Effects Model 2

Coefficients[a]

Model		Unstandardized Coefficients		Standardized Coefficients		
		B	Std. Error	Beta	t	Sig.
1	(Constant)	3.200	.755		4.239	.001
	X1	6.800	1.068	1.005	6.369	.000
	X2	3.600	1.068	.532	3.372	.004
	X3	1.800	1.068	.266	1.686	.111

a. Dependent Variable: Y

SPSS Output 15.4

Descriptive Statistics

Dependent Variable: Y

DRUG	Mean	Std. Deviation	N
1.00	10.0000	1.58114	5
2.00	6.8000	1.48324	5
3.00	5.0000	2.44949	5
4.00	3.2000	.83666	5
Total	6.2500	3.00657	20

519

Cell Means Model

Another analysis of variance model of interest is the *Cell Means Model* or, simply, the *Means Model*, which can be expressed by defining the indicator variables to have values as follows:

$$X_1 = \begin{cases} 1 & \text{if } drug = 1 \\ 0 & \text{otherwise} \end{cases} \qquad X_2 = \begin{cases} 1 & \text{if } drug = 2 \\ 0 & \text{otherwise} \end{cases}$$

$$X_3 = \begin{cases} 1 & \text{if } drug = 3 \\ 0 & \text{otherwise} \end{cases} \qquad X_4 = \begin{cases} 1 & \text{if } drug = 4 \\ 0 & \text{otherwise} \end{cases}$$

Here we have not defined X_0 because in this model we do not wish to have an intercept term. The parameters of this model are simply the means of the 4 drug groups (cells of the design). The model associated with these indicator variables is another special case of the general linear model (matrix form) $\mathbf{Y} = \mathbf{X}\boldsymbol{\beta} + \boldsymbol{\varepsilon}$. The $\mathbf{X}$ matrix has 4 columns, each comprised of values of one of the 4 indicator variables.

As in the previous models, we wish to test the hypothesis

$$H_0 : \mu_1 = \mu_2 = \mu_3 = \mu_4$$

but here we "decompose" the hypothesis into three simultaneous hypotheses of the form

$$H_0 : \begin{cases} \mu_1 - \mu_2 = 0 \\ \mu_2 - \mu_3 = 0 \\ \mu_3 - \mu_4 = 0 \end{cases}$$

This is but one of many ways of specifying the components of the decomposition. Each component of the simultaneous hypotheses is a *contrast* (a linear function of the four means) that is equal to 0. We can write the simultaneous hypothesis in vector-matrix form as follows. First, we write the means in vector form:

$$\boldsymbol{\mu} = \begin{bmatrix} \mu_1 \\ \mu_2 \\ \mu_3 \\ \mu_4 \end{bmatrix}$$

and define a vector of zeros as

$$\mathbf{0} = \begin{bmatrix} 0 \\ 0 \\ 0 \\ 0 \end{bmatrix}$$

Next, we define a contrast matrix **L** as a matrix whose elements are non-negative constants such that the elements in each row of the matrix sum to 0.

The hypothesis can then be written in terms of the *general linear hypothesis* as

$$H_0 : \mathbf{L}\boldsymbol{\mu} = \mathbf{0}$$

or

$$H_0 : \begin{bmatrix} 1 & -1 & 0 & 0 \\ 0 & 1 & -1 & 0 \\ 0 & 0 & 1 & -1 \end{bmatrix} \begin{bmatrix} \mu_1 \\ \mu_2 \\ \mu_3 \\ \mu_4 \end{bmatrix} = \begin{bmatrix} 0 \\ 0 \\ 0 \end{bmatrix}$$

or

$$H_0 : \begin{bmatrix} \mu_1 - \mu_2 \\ \mu_2 - \mu_3 \\ \mu_3 - \mu_4 \end{bmatrix} = \begin{bmatrix} 0 \\ 0 \\ 0 \end{bmatrix}$$

The specific matrices for the *Cell Means Model* are

$$
\begin{bmatrix}
y_{11} \\ y_{12} \\ y_{13} \\ y_{14} \\ y_{15} \\ y_{21} \\ y_{22} \\ y_{23} \\ y_{24} \\ y_{25} \\ y_{31} \\ y_{32} \\ y_{33} \\ y_{34} \\ y_{35} \\ y_{41} \\ y_{42} \\ y_{43} \\ y_{44} \\ y_{45}
\end{bmatrix}
=
\begin{bmatrix}
1 & 0 & 0 & 0 \\
1 & 0 & 0 & 0 \\
1 & 0 & 0 & 0 \\
1 & 0 & 0 & 0 \\
1 & 0 & 0 & 0 \\
0 & 1 & 0 & 0 \\
0 & 1 & 0 & 0 \\
0 & 1 & 0 & 0 \\
0 & 1 & 0 & 0 \\
0 & 1 & 0 & 0 \\
0 & 0 & 1 & 0 \\
0 & 0 & 1 & 0 \\
0 & 0 & 1 & 0 \\
0 & 0 & 1 & 0 \\
0 & 0 & 1 & 0 \\
0 & 0 & 0 & 1 \\
0 & 0 & 0 & 1 \\
0 & 0 & 0 & 1 \\
0 & 0 & 0 & 1 \\
0 & 0 & 0 & 1
\end{bmatrix}
\begin{bmatrix}
\mu_1 \\ \mu_2 \\ \mu_3 \\ \mu_4
\end{bmatrix}
+
\begin{bmatrix}
\varepsilon_{11} \\ \varepsilon_{12} \\ \varepsilon_{13} \\ \varepsilon_{14} \\ \varepsilon_{15} \\ \varepsilon_{21} \\ \varepsilon_{22} \\ \varepsilon_{23} \\ \varepsilon_{24} \\ \varepsilon_{25} \\ \varepsilon_{31} \\ \varepsilon_{32} \\ \varepsilon_{33} \\ \varepsilon_{34} \\ \varepsilon_{35} \\ \varepsilon_{41} \\ \varepsilon_{42} \\ \varepsilon_{43} \\ \varepsilon_{44} \\ \varepsilon_{45}
\end{bmatrix}
$$

Using SPSS' *Regression* procedure to Analyze the Cell Means Model

A direct test of the global hypothesis $H_0 : \mu_1 = \mu_2 = \mu_3 = \mu_4$ in terms of the *Cell Means Model* is readily available in SPSS' *Regression* procedure. In Insert 15.2, we illustrate the SPSS syntax used to generate the indicator variables for the *Cell Means Model*. We specify code for SPSS' *Regression* procedure where y is the dependent variable and *X1*, *X2*, *X3*, and *X4* are independent variables. We further specify that the model will not contain an intercept. Next, we specify a *lmatrix* statement to test the general linear hypothesis: $H_0 : \mu_1 = \mu_2 = \mu_3 = \mu_4$. In the *lmatrix* statement, the code *x1* –1 1 *x2* 1 –1 specifies the hypothesis $\mu_1 - \mu_2 = 0$, x2 –1 1 x3 1 –1 specifies $\mu_2 - \mu_3 = 0$, and x3 –1 1 x4 1 –1 specifies $\mu_3 - \mu_4 = 0$. The fact that the three specified hypotheses are separated by semicolons and listed in a single *lmatrix* statement indicates three hypotheses are to be tested simultaneously yielding a single F value with 3 degrees of freedom. The F value (not shown) produced by this *lmatrix* statement is identical to $F=14.75$ for the *Effects Model 1* and *Effects Model 2* shown in (SPSS Output 15.2).

Using SPSS' *GLM – Univariate* to analyze Effects Model

As an alternative to using the *Regression* procedure to test the hypothesis $H_0 : \mu_1 = \mu_2 = \mu_3 = \mu_4$, we now illustrate the use of SPSS's *General Linear Model* procedure (Insert 15.2 - *Allocated code and GLM*). In Insert 15.2, we specify *GLM - Univariate* where *y* is the dependent variable and *drug* is a fixed factor. That is, we specify that the variable *drug* (allocated code) is a categorical variable; this specification is not directly available in the *Regression* procedure. Execution of Insert 15.2 (*Allocated code and GLM*) results in SPSS Output 15.5. Note that the $R^2=0.734$ from the *Regression* procedure output (SPSS Output 15.2) and that, from the *GLM* output (SPSS Output 15.5), $R^2 = 0.734$. Additionally, the test statistics for the *Regression* procedure ANOVA table are identical to those found in the *GLM* summary table. The parameter estimates produced by the procedure *GLM* (SPSS Output 15.5) are identical to the parameter estimates for the regression analysis based on *Effects Model 2*. Based on the specification that *drug* is a categorical variable (fixed factor), SPSS' *GLM* internally parameterized the model as an *Effects Model 2*. Thus, SPSS' *GLM* eliminates the SPSS program steps of explicitly defining indicator variables for a specific model parameterization by internally providing a "regression formulation" of an analysis of variance effects model. In many subsequent text chapters, the authors present both an analysis of variance and regression approach to chapter problems. Since SPSS's *GLM* is based on a regression formulation that makes the proper adjustments for unbalanced designs, we will present most of the illustrative examples using only *GLM*.

Other Model Parameterizations

We see that there are many ways to specify analysis of variance models for a given set of data. Typically, each specification requires different assumptions about the parameters and therefore imposes different restrictions on these parameters. Estimates of the parameters are not unique because they may be different for different parameterizations of the model even though the data remain the same for the different specifications.

INSERT 15.2	INSERT 15.2 continued

* Cell means model , no intercept via GLM.
if (drug = 1)x1=1.
if (drug ne 1)x1=0.
if (drug = 2)x2=1.
if (drug ne 2)x2=0.
if (drug = 3)x3=1.
if (drug ne 3)x3=0.
if (drug = 4)x4=1.
if (drug ne 4)x4=0.
exe.
✔ Analyze
✔ General Linear Model
✔ Univariate
✔ y
✔ ► (to the Dependent box)
✔ x1 x2 x3 x4
✔ ► (to the Fixed Factor box)
✔ Model
* Uncheck "Include intercept in model".
✔ Continue
✔ Optons
✔ Parameter Estimates
✔ Continue
✔ Paste
	* Your Pasted syntax will appear as.
	* below without the /lmarix statement.
	* Insert the /lmatrix statement and execute.
	UNIANOVA
	 y BY x1 x2 x3 x4
	 /METHOD = SSTYPE(3)
	 /INTERCEPT = EXCLUDE
	 /PRINT = PARAMETER
	 /CRITERIA = ALPHA(.05)
	 /DESIGN = x1 x2 x3 x4
	 /LMATRIX x1 -1 1 x2 1 -1; x2 -1 1 x3 1 -1; x3 -1 1 x4 1 -1.
	exe.
	✔ Run
	✔ All
	
	* Allocated code and GLM.
	✔ Analyze
	✔ General Linear Model
	✔ Univariate
	✔ y
	✔ ► (to the Dependent box)
	✔ drug
	✔ ► (to the Fixed Factor box)
	✔ Optons
	✔ Parameter Estimates
	✔ Continue
	✔ OK

SPSS Output 15.5

GLM Output

Tests of Between-Subjects Effects

Dependent Variable: Y

Source	Type III Sum of Squares	df	Mean Square	F	Sig.
Corrected Model	126.150[a]	3	42.050	14.754	.000
Intercept	781.250	1	781.250	274.123	.000
DRUG	126.150	3	42.050	14.754	.000
Error	45.600	16	2.850		
Total	953.000	20			
Corrected Total	171.750	19			

a. R Squared = .734 (Adjusted R Squared = .685)

Parameter Estimates

Dependent Variable: Y

Parameter	B	Std. Error	t	Sig.	95% Confidence Interval Lower Bound	95% Confidence Interval Upper Bound
Intercept	3.200	.755	4.239	.001	1.600	4.800
[DRUG=1.00]	6.800	1.068	6.369	.000	4.537	9.063
[DRUG=2.00]	3.600	1.068	3.372	.004	1.337	5.863
[DRUG=3.00]	1.800	1.068	1.686	.111	-.463	4.063
[DRUG=4.00]	0[a]	.	.	.	.	.

a. This parameter is set to zero because it is redundant.

15.2 Multifactor Studies: Fixed Effects

Growth Hormone Example

Data File: ch23ta01.txt

On text page 954 the authors present the two-factor Growth Hormone Example that has six cells with unequal sample sizes. A researcher studied the effect of a child's gender (Factor A) and bone development (Factor B) on the rate of hormone-induced growth (Y). We let Y_{ijk}, denote the growth, where $i = 1, 2, 3$ represents the levels of Factor A, $j = 1, 2$ represents the levels of Factor B and $k = 1, 2, \ldots , n_{ij}$ represents the kth subject in the ij^{th} "cell" of the design. The data from text Table 23.1 are:

Data for Growth Hormone Example

Gender (Factor A)	Bone Development (Factor B) Severe (B1)	Bone Development (Factor B) Moderate (B2)	Bone Development (Factor B) Mild (B3)
Male (A1)	$Y_{111}=1.4$ $Y_{112}=2.4$ $Y_{113}=2.2$	$Y_{121}=2.1$ $Y_{122}=1.7$	$Y_{131}=0.7$ $Y_{132}=1.1$
Female (A2)	$Y_{211}=2.4$	$Y_{221}=2.5$ $Y_{222}=1.8$ $Y_{223}=2.0$	$Y_{231}=0.5$ $Y_{232}=0.9$ $Y_{233}=1.3$

Eighteen children, 3 per cell or combination of levels of Factor A and B, began the study. However, four of the children were unable to complete the study. Thus, data for these four children were not available and the resulting treatment sample sizes were unequal. See Chapter 0, "Working with SPSS," for instructions on opening the Growth Hormone Example and renaming the variables *y, gender, bonedev,* and *rep.* After opening ch23ta01.txt, the first 5 lines of the *Data Editor* should look like SPSS Output 15.6.

SPSS Output 15.6

Growth Hormone Example.sav - SPSS Data Editor

File Edit View Data Transform Analyze Graphs Utilities W

1 : y   1.4

	y	gender	bonedev	rep
1	1.40	1	1	1
2	2.40	1	1	2
3	2.20	1	1	3
4	2.10	1	2	1
5	1.70	1	2	2

As in the single factor data discussed above, many analysis of variance models can be specified for this data structure. We shall discuss here only the *Effects Model 1* and the *Cell Means Model*.

Effects Model 1

To formulate an *effects model* (we called this model *Effects Model 1* in the previous section) for this unbalanced design, the authors use the following indicator variables as shown on text page 955:

$$X_1 = \begin{cases} 1 & \text{if gender} = 1 \\ -1 & \text{if gender} = 2 \end{cases} \qquad X_2 = \begin{cases} 1 & \text{if } bonedev = 1 \\ -1 & \text{if } bonedev = 3 \\ 0 & \text{otherwise} \end{cases} \qquad X_3 = \begin{cases} 1 & \text{if } bonedev = 2 \\ -1 & \text{if } bonedev = 3 \\ 0 & \text{otherwise} \end{cases}$$

and

$$X_4 = X_1 * X_2$$

$$X_5 = X_1 * X_3$$

Here, *X1*, *X2*, and *X3* are indicator variables analogous to those defined in the previous example, and *X4* (the product of *X1* and *X2*) and *X5* (the product of *X1* and *X3*) are indicator variables that define effects for interaction between gender and bone development.

In this effects model, we assume the expected values of a random observation from subjects in the six factor combinations (cells) are $\mu_{11}, \mu_{12}, \mu_{21}, \mu_{22}, \mu_{31}$, and μ_{32}, respectively, and the overall expected value is μ. We further assume there is a "main effect" for each level of Factor A, a "main effect" for each level of Factor B, and an effect of interaction at each level of Factor A

526

with each level of Factor B. As shown in Table 23.2, text page 956, the matrix form of this effects model is

$$
\begin{bmatrix}
Y_{111} \\
Y_{112} \\
Y_{113} \\
Y_{121} \\
Y_{122} \\
Y_{131} \\
Y_{132} \\
Y_{211} \\
Y_{221} \\
Y_{222} \\
Y_{223} \\
Y_{231} \\
Y_{232} \\
Y_{233}
\end{bmatrix}
=
\begin{bmatrix}
1 & 1 & 1 & 0 & 1 & 0 \\
1 & 1 & 1 & 0 & 1 & 0 \\
1 & 1 & 1 & 0 & 1 & 0 \\
1 & 1 & 0 & 1 & 0 & 1 \\
1 & 1 & 0 & 1 & 0 & 1 \\
1 & 1 & -1 & -1 & -1 & -1 \\
1 & 1 & -1 & -1 & -1 & -1 \\
1 & -1 & 1 & 0 & -1 & 0 \\
1 & -1 & 0 & 1 & 0 & -1 \\
1 & -1 & 0 & 1 & 0 & -1 \\
1 & -1 & 0 & 1 & 0 & -1 \\
1 & -1 & -1 & -1 & 1 & 1 \\
1 & -1 & -1 & -1 & 1 & 1 \\
1 & -1 & -1 & -1 & 1 & 1
\end{bmatrix}
\begin{bmatrix}
\mu \\
\alpha_1 \\
\beta_1 \\
\beta_2 \\
(\alpha\beta)_{11} \\
(\alpha\beta)_{12}
\end{bmatrix}
+
\begin{bmatrix}
\varepsilon_{111} \\
\varepsilon_{112} \\
\varepsilon_{113} \\
\varepsilon_{121} \\
\varepsilon_{122} \\
\varepsilon_{131} \\
\varepsilon_{132} \\
\varepsilon_{211} \\
\varepsilon_{221} \\
\varepsilon_{222} \\
\varepsilon_{223} \\
\varepsilon_{231} \\
\varepsilon_{232} \\
\varepsilon_{233}
\end{bmatrix}
$$

where μ denotes the overall mean, α_1 denotes the main effect of level A_1 of Factor A, $\alpha_2 = -\alpha_1$ denotes the main effect of level A_2 of Factor A, β_1 denotes the main effect of level B_1 of Factor B, β_2 denotes the main effect of level B_2 of Factor B, $\beta_3 = -\beta_1 - \beta_2$ denotes the main effect of level B_3 of Factor B, $(\alpha\beta)_{ij}$ is the effect of interaction at level A_i of Factor A and level B_j of Factor B, $(\alpha\beta)_{21} = -(\alpha\beta)_{11}$, and $(\alpha\beta)_{13} = -(\alpha\beta)_{11} - (\alpha\beta)_{12}$.

Cell Means Model

The following indicator variables are used for the cell means model for the growth hormone example:

$$
X_1 = \begin{cases} 1 & \text{if gender} = 1 \text{ and bonedev} = 1 \\ 0 & \text{otherwise} \end{cases}
$$

$$
X_2 = \begin{cases} 1 & \text{if gender} = 1 \text{ and bonedev} = 2 \\ 0 & \text{otherwise} \end{cases}
$$

$$
X_3 = \begin{cases} 1 & \text{if gender} = 1 \text{ and bonedev} = 3 \\ 0 & \text{otherwise} \end{cases}
$$

$$X_4 = \begin{cases} 1 \text{ if gender} = 2 \text{ and bonedev} = 1 \\ 0 \text{ otherwise} \end{cases}$$

$$X_5 = \begin{cases} 1 \text{ if gender} = 2 \text{ and bonedev} = 2 \\ 0 \text{ otherwise} \end{cases}$$

$$X_6 = \begin{cases} 1 \text{ if gender} = 2 \text{ and bonedev} = 3 \\ 0 \text{ otherwise} \end{cases}$$

The cell means model can be represented as

$$\begin{bmatrix} Y_{111} \\ Y_{112} \\ Y_{113} \\ Y_{121} \\ Y_{122} \\ Y_{131} \\ Y_{132} \\ Y_{211} \\ Y_{221} \\ Y_{222} \\ Y_{223} \\ Y_{231} \\ Y_{232} \\ Y_{233} \end{bmatrix} = \begin{bmatrix} 1 & 0 & 0 & 0 & 0 & 0 \\ 1 & 0 & 0 & 0 & 0 & 0 \\ 1 & 0 & 0 & 0 & 0 & 0 \\ 0 & 1 & 0 & 0 & 0 & 0 \\ 0 & 1 & 0 & 0 & 0 & 0 \\ 0 & 0 & 1 & 0 & 0 & 0 \\ 0 & 0 & 1 & 0 & 0 & 0 \\ 0 & 0 & 0 & 1 & 0 & 0 \\ 0 & 0 & 0 & 0 & 1 & 0 \\ 0 & 0 & 0 & 0 & 1 & 0 \\ 0 & 0 & 0 & 0 & 1 & 0 \\ 0 & 0 & 0 & 0 & 0 & 1 \\ 0 & 0 & 0 & 0 & 0 & 1 \\ 0 & 0 & 0 & 0 & 0 & 1 \end{bmatrix} \begin{bmatrix} \mu_{11} \\ \mu_{12} \\ \mu_{13} \\ \mu_{21} \\ \mu_{22} \\ \mu_{23} \end{bmatrix} + \begin{bmatrix} \varepsilon_{111} \\ \varepsilon_{112} \\ \varepsilon_{113} \\ \varepsilon_{121} \\ \varepsilon_{122} \\ \varepsilon_{131} \\ \varepsilon_{132} \\ \varepsilon_{211} \\ \varepsilon_{221} \\ \varepsilon_{222} \\ \varepsilon_{223} \\ \varepsilon_{231} \\ \varepsilon_{232} \\ \varepsilon_{233} \end{bmatrix}$$

where μ_{11} represents the mean for the cell in row 1, column 1; μ_{12} represents the mean for the cell in row 1, column 2; and so on.

Hypotheses to be Tested in Two-Factor Model With Interaction

There are three primary hypotheses of interest and they can be expressed in terms of the parameters of the cell means model or the effects model:

1. The means for the 2 levels of Factor A are equal; i.e.,

$$(cell\ means)\ H_0 : \mu_{11} + \mu_{12} + \mu_{13} = \mu_{21} + \mu_{22} + \mu_{23}$$

or, equivalently, the 2 main effects for Factor A are equal to zero; i.e.,

$$(\textit{effects}) \;\; H_0 : \alpha_1 = \alpha_2 = 0$$

2. The means for the 3 levels of Factor B are equal; i.e.,

$$(\textit{cell means}) \, H_0 : \mu_{11} + \mu_{21} = \mu_{12} + \mu_{22} = \mu_{13} + \mu_{23}$$

or, equivalently, the 3 main effects for Factor B are equal to zero; i.e.,

$$(\textit{effects}) \, H_0 : \beta_1 = \beta_2 = \beta_3 = 0$$

3. The difference between the means for the two levels of Factor A is the same for all levels of Factor B; i.e.,

$$(\textit{cell means}) \;\; H_0 : \mu_{11} - \mu_{21} = \mu_{12} - \mu_{22} = \mu_{13} - \mu_{23}$$

or, equivalently, the interaction effects are all equal to zero; i.e.,

$$(\textit{effects}) \;\; H_0 : (\alpha\beta)_{11} = (\alpha\beta)_{21} = \ldots = (\alpha\beta)_{23} = 0$$

Sums of Squares Types I, II, III, and IV

The analysis of variance typically is performed in terms of an effects model such as the one above. In that context, the sum of squared deviations from the overall mean is referred to as the corrected total sum of squares. This "corrected total sum of squares," SSCT is partitioned into a sum of squares due to Factor A (SSA), a sum of squares due to Factor B (SSB), a sum of squares due to interactions between Factor A and Factor B (SSAB), and a residual or "error" sum of squares (SSE). If the number of observations is the same in all cells of the design (equal cell sizes), we can show that

$$\text{SSCT} = \text{SSA} + \text{SSB} + \text{SSAB} + \text{SSE} \quad \text{(provided cell sizes are equal)}$$

However, it is not true in general that this equality is true if the cell sizes are not all equal; i.e.,

$$\text{SSCT} \neq \text{SSA} + \text{SSB} + \text{SSAB} + \text{SSE} \quad \text{(if cell sizes are unequal)}$$

There are different ways to compute SSA, SSB, and SSAB. For the model with terms for Factors A, B, and AB interactions as potential parameters, 4 types of sum of squares are defined as follows:

SS(A) = Type I SSA where Factor A is the only factor in the model (Factor B and AB interactions are not in the model -- they are ignored). Here we are using SS(A) for brevity to denote SS(indicator variables for the levels of A). Similar notation is used in the following discussion.

SS(B) = Type I SSB where Factor B is the only factor in the model (Factor A and AB interactions are not in the model -- they are ignored).

SS(AB) = Type I SSAB where AB interaction terms are the only effects in the model (Factors A and B are not in the model -- they are ignored).

SS(A|B) = Type II SSA, the additional increase in the model sum of squares (reduction in the error sum of squares) achieved by adding Factor A to the model that already has Factor B in the model (AB interactions are not in the model – they are ignored). We say this is the sum of squares for A "adjusted for B."

SS(B|A) = Type II SSB, the additional increase in the model sum of squares (reduction in the error sum of squares) achieved by adding Factor B to the model that already has Factor A in the model (AB interactions are not in the model – they are ignored). We say this is the sum of squares for B "adjusted for A."

SS(AB|A, B) = Type II SSAB, the additional increase in the model sum of squares (reduction in the error sum of squares) achieved by adding all AB interactions to the model that already has Factors A and B in the model We say this is the sum of squares for AB "adjusted for A and B."

SS(A|B, AB) = Type III SSA (= Type IV SSA in this data structure), the additional increase in the model sum of squares (reduction in the error sum of squares) achieved by adding Factor A to the model that already has Factor B and all AB interactions in the model.

SS(B|A, AB) = Type III SSB (= Type IV SSB in this data structure), the additional increase in the model sum of squares (reduction in the error sum of squares) achieved by adding Factor B to the model that already has Factor A and all AB interactions in the model.

SS(AB|A, B) = Type III SSAB (= Type IV SSAB in this data structure), the additional increase in the model sum of squares (reduction in the error sum of squares) achieved by adding all AB interactions to the model that already has Factors A and B in the model.

For the structure considered here, if the cell sizes are all equal, the 4 types of sums of squares are also all equal. If the cell sizes are unequal but proportionate, Type I = Type II and Type III = Type IV for SSA and SSB, and the 4 types are equal for SSAB. Our purpose in analyzing analysis of variance models will be satisfied by using Type III sums of squares for most of the data structures considered in the text. Exceptions, such as data structures where some cells have no observations available for analysis, will be discussed in later chapters.

SPSS Syntax for Analyzing Two Factor Effects Model 1

The authors fitted a Full Model and 3 Reduced Models, as shown in Table 23.3, text page 957. Equation 2.70, text page 73, was used to find the test statistics for the main effects for Factors A and B and the interaction effect. A summary of the study effects is shown in ANOVA Table 23.4, text page 959.

Using the regression approach (text page 953) to perform this two-factor analysis of variance, we parameterize the model as shown on text page 955. (Insert 15.3) We then use these indicator variables in the *Regression* procedure (text equations 23.11, 23.15, 23.17, and 23.18) to fit the full and reduced models shown in Table 23.3, text page 957. We use the strategy of fitting a model that includes all model parameters (full model) and then fitting a model that has deleted terms corresponding to effects to be tested (reduced model). Next we calculate test statistics using (text equation 2.70):

$$F^* = \frac{SSE(R) - SSE(F)}{df_R - df_F} \div \frac{SSE(F)}{df_F}$$

To test the hypothesis that all interaction effects are equal to zero, we fit the Full Model, which contains indicator variables representing the main effects and all possible interaction effects, and find SSE (Residual Sum of Squares) = 1.300 and $df_F = 8$ (SPSS Output 15.7). We then fit the Reduced Model that contains only indicator variables representing the main effects, and find SSE = 1.375 and $df_F = 10$ (SPSS Output 15.8). Thus, to test $H_0 : (\alpha\beta)_{11} = (\alpha\beta)_{12} = 0$ (text equation 23.14a), we calculate

$$F^* = \frac{1.375 - 1.300}{10 - 8} \div \frac{1.300}{8} = 0.23$$

as shown on text page 958. Since this calculated F^* is less than the critical value for $\alpha = 0.05$, we conclude that interaction effects are not statistically significant.

To test the Factor A (*gender*) main effects, we use the output of the Full Model (SPSS Output 15.7) and the output of the reduced model (SPSS Output 15.9) that contains $x2$, $x3$, $x4$, and $x5$ (all effects except $x1$). We then calculate

$$F^* = \frac{1.420 - 1.300}{9 - 8} \div \frac{1.300}{8} = 0.74$$

Similarly, we find F^* for the Factor B (bone development) main effects using SPSS Output 15.7 and 15.10. Table 23.4, text page 959, is a consolidated ANOVA table that contains a summary of the analysis of variance obtained using the regression approach.

We carried out the same analysis (Insert 15.3) using SPSS' *GLM – Univariate* as an alternative to the *Regression* procedure. In specifying *GLM*, we indicate that y (growth) is the dependent variable and *gender* and *bonedev* are fixed factors. Here, *gender* and *bonedev* are variables defined in the input data and in this case are variables whose values are allocated codes. Thus, SPSS will automatically generate indicator variables for an analysis of variance model. To obtain a full factorial model that includes main effects for *gender* and *bonedev* and all possible interactions, we need only specify *gender* and *bonedev* as fixed factors; the default model in *GLM* is full factorial. Also, in SPSS' *GLM*, the *Type III sums of squares* are printed by default. Partial results shown in SPSS Output 15.11 are identical to those shown in text Table 23.4 and to the statistics calculated above using the *Regression* procedure. Thus, we will use *GLM* in subsequent chapters when the authors refer to the regression approach to analysis of variance.

INSERT 15.3	INSERT 15.3 continued
* Regression formulation.	* Reduced Model – equation 23.17.
✓ File	✓ Analyze
✓ New	✓ Regresion
✓ Syntax	✓ Linear
if (gender = 1)x1=1.	✓ y
if (gender = 2)x1=-1.	✓ ▶(to the Dependent box)
if (bonedev = 1)x2=1.	✓ x2 x3 x4 x5
if (bonedev = 3)x2=-1.	✓ ▶(to the Variables box)
if (bonedev ne 1 and bonedev ne 3)x2=0.	✓ OK
if (bonedev = 2)x3=1.	
if (bonedev = 3)x3=-1.	* Reduced Model – equation 23.18.
if (bonedev ne 2 and bonedev ne 3)x3=0.	✓ Analyze
compute x4=x1*x2.	✓ Regresion
compute x5=x1*x3.	✓ Linear
exe.	✓ y
* Full Model – equation 23.11.	✓ ▶(to the Dependent box)
✓ Analyze	✓ x1 x4 x5
✓ Regresion	✓ ▶(to the Variables box)
✓ Linear	✓ OK
✓ y	
✓ ▶(to the Dependent box)	
✓ x1 x2 x3 x4 x5	* GLM approach.
✓ ▶(to the Variables box)	✓ Analyze
✓ OK	✓ General Linear Model
	✓ Univariate
* Reduced Model – equation 23.15	✓ y
✓ Analyze	✓ ▶(to the Dependent box)
✓ Regresion	✓ gender bonedev
✓ Linear	✓ ▶(to the Fixed Factor box)
✓ y	✓ OK
✓ ▶(to the Dependent box)	
✓ x1 x2 x3	
✓ ▶(to the Variables box)	
✓ OK	

SPSS Output 15.7

Full Model – Equation 23.11

ANOVA[b]

Model		Sum of Squares	df	Mean Square	F	Sig.
1	Regression	4.474	5	.895	5.507	.017[a]
	Residual	1.300	8	.163		
	Total	5.774	13			

a. Predictors: (Constant), X5, X1, X3, X4, X2

b. Dependent Variable: Y

SPSS Output 15.8

Reduced Model – Equation 23.15

ANOVA[b]

Model		Sum of Squares	df	Mean Square	F	Sig.
1	Regression	4.399	3	1.466	10.661	.002[a]
	Residual	1.375	10	.138		
	Total	5.774	13			

a. Predictors: (Constant), X3, X1, X2

b. Dependent Variable: Y

SPSS Output 15.9

Reduced Model – Equation 23.17

ANOVA[b]

Model		Sum of Squares	df	Mean Square	F	Sig.
1	Regression	4.354	4	1.089	6.899	.008[a]
	Residual	1.420	9	.158		
	Total	5.774	13			

a. Predictors: (Constant), X5, X2, X3, X4

b. Dependent Variable: Y

SPSS Output 15.10

Reduced Model – Equation 23.18

ANOVA[b]

Model		Sum of Squares	df	Mean Square	F	Sig.
1	Regression	.285	3	.095	.173	.912[a]
	Residual	5.490	10	.549		
	Total	5.774	13			

a. Predictors: (Constant), X5, X1, X4

b. Dependent Variable: Y

SPSS Output 15.11

GLM Model

Tests of Between-Subjects Effects

Dependent Variable: Y

Source	Type III Sum of Squares	df	Mean Square	F	Sig.
Corrected Model	4.474[a]	5	.895	5.507	.017
Intercept	34.680	1	34.680	213.415	.000
GENDER	.120	1	.120	.738	.415
BONEDEV	4.190	2	2.095	12.891	.003
GENDER * BONEDEV	.075	2	.038	.232	.798
Error	1.300	8	.163		
Total	43.560	14			
Corrected Total	5.774	13			

a. R Squared = .775 (Adjusted R Squared = .634)

Chapter 16 SPSS®

Analysis of Single-Factor Studies

The analysis of variance (ANOVA) for a dependent (response) variable of interest is the partitioning of the total sum of squares for the dependent variable into component sums of squares associated with identifiable sources of variation. Once the partitioning is complete, we can use the component sums of squares to test whether variation attributed to some sources is significantly greater than variability attributed to other sources. In this chapter, we are concerned with linear statistical models that are convenient for performing an ANOVA and testing hypotheses about group means for the dependent variable. In this context, we are interested in testing whether variability among group means is significantly greater than the variability among observations within the groups.

Kenton Food Company Example

Data File: ch16ta01.txt

The Kenton Food Company (text page 685) studied the relationship between sales (Y) and the type of package design for a new breakfast cereal. Here, store was the experimental unit. Each of 20 stores was assigned to one package design such that there were 5 stores assigned to each design. One store was unable to fulfill the study requirement and was dropped from the study. After opening the Kenton Food Company data file and renaming the variables Y, *package*, and *store,* the first five lines of the Data Editor should look like SPSS Output 16.1.

SPSS Output 16.1

	y	package	store	var
1	11.0	1	1	
2	17.0	1	2	
3	16.0	1	3	
4	14.0	1	4	
5	15.0	1	5	

We begin the analysis (Insert 16.1) by reproducing the scatter plot in Figure 16.3, text page 686, (SPSS Output 16.2). We then request the *General Linear Model* (*GLM*) procedure where Y is the response variable and *package* is the single independent variable. (Note that when we refer to SPSS *GLM* in this manual, unless otherwise specified, we are referring to *GLM –Univariate*.)

Although Type I, II, III, or IV sum of squares (See Chapter 15 of this manual) can be requested in *GLM*, Type III sum of squares is the default and serves our purpose here. We request descriptive statistics for the 4 levels of *package* and then request the residuals from the fitted model (the residuals are assigned the variable name *res_1* by default). SPSS Output 16.3 is consistent with the decomposition of *SSTO* (text page 692), breakdown of degrees of freedom (text page 693), and the mean sales per store (text page 688). The *Data Editor* will contain the residuals as shown in Table 16.2, text page 689. See the table following SPSS Insert 16.1 for correspondence between the abbreviations used in the text versus terminologies used in SPSS. On text page 699 the authors wish to test that the means (sales) are the same for the four package designs. Consistent with the text, from SPSS Output 16.3 we find the *F*-value for Model is 18.59 and its associated *p*-value is 0.000. Because *package* is the only factor in the study, the Corrected Model *F*-value and the *F*-value for *package* are equal. Based on the *p*-value of 0.000, we conclude that there are significant differences among the sales means for the four package designs.

INSERT 16.1	INSERT 16.1 continued
✔ Graphs ✔ Scatter ✔ Simple ✔ Define ✔ Y ✔ ▶ (to the Y axis) ✔ package ✔ ▶ (to the X axis) ✔ OK	✔ Analyze ✔ General Linear Model ✔ Univariate ✔ Y ✔ ▶ (to the Dependent box) ✔ package ✔ ▶ (to the Fixed Factor box) ✔ Options ✔ Descriptive Statistics ✔ Continue ✔ Save ✔ Unstandardized Residuals ✔ Continue ✔ OK

Text abbreviation	SPSS terminology
SSTR	Sum of Squares – Corrected Model
SSE	Sum of Squares - Error
SSTO	Sum of Squares – Corrected Total
MSTR	Mean Square – Corrected Model
MSE	Mean Square – Error

SPSS Output 16.2

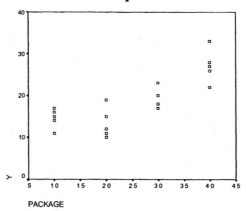

SPSS Output 16.3

Tests of Between-Subjects Effects

Dependent Variable: Y

Source	Type III Sum of Squares	df	Mean Square	F	Sig.
Corrected Model	588.221[a]	3	196.074	18.591	.000
Intercept	6564.812	1	6564.812	622.454	.000
PACKAGE	588.221	3	196.074	18.591	.000
Error	158.200	15	10.547		
Total	7342.000	19			
Corrected Total	746.421	18			

a. R Squared = .788 (Adjusted R Squared = .746)

Descriptive Statistics

Dependent Variable: Y

PACKAGE	Mean	Std. Deviation	N
1	14.600	2.3022	5
2	13.400	3.6469	5
3	19.500	2.6458	4
4	27.200	3.9623	5
Total	18.632	6.4396	19

537

Regression Approach to Single-Factor Analysis of Variance

On text page 704 the authors illustrate the regression approach to a single-factor analysis of variance. In Chapter 15 of this manual we presented the general linear model and discussed the construction of indicator variables for use in the regression approach to analysis of variance. We indicated that *GLM* will generate indicator variables for the regression approach automatically and give the same test statistics as those obtained by our defining indicator variables directly and using SPSS' *Regression* procedure. Here, we give one further example of defining indicator variables and using SPSS' *Regression* procedure in a single factor design. In all subsequent chapters, however, the reader is referred to Chapter 15 of this manual when the text refers to the Regression Approach to ANOVA.

In Insert 16.2, we define indicator variables *X1*, *X2*, and *X3* as shown on text page 707 (referred to in Chapter 15 as *Effects Model 1*). We then perform a regression analysis using *Y* as the response variable and *X1*, *X2*, and *X3* as independent variables. Results are shown in SPSS Output 16.4 and are consistent with the results reported on text page 707, Table 16.4 (c), and the *GLM* output presented in SPSS Output 16.3 where *package* was the single fixed factor in the model. The variable (factor) *package* has values that were specified by allocated coding (see Chapter 15) but *GLM* automatically codes indicator variables to be used in a regression analysis of variance model. We could also define our own choice of indicator variables and specify these as independent variables in the model for *GLM*. This would also result in a Correct Model *F* value of 18.59.

INSERT 16.2	INSERT 16.2 continued
* Regression Approach to Single-Factor Analysis of Variance. ✔ File ✔ New ✔ Syntax * Type the following syntax. RECODE package (1=1) (4=-1) (ELSE=0) INTO x1 . RECODE package (2=1) (4=-1) (ELSE=0) INTO x2 . RECODE package (3=1) (4=-1) (ELSE=0) INTO x3 . exe. ✔ Run ✔ All	✔ Analyze ✔ Regression ✔ Linear ✔ Y ✔ ▶(to the Dependent box) ✔ X1 X2 X3 ✔ ▶(to the Independent box) ✔ OK

SPSS Output 16.4

ANOVA[b]

Model		Sum of Squares	df	Mean Square	F	Sig.
1	Regression	588.221	3	196.074	18.591	.000[a]
	Residual	158.200	15	10.547		
	Total	746.421	18			

a. Predictors: (Constant), X3, X2, X1

b. Dependent Variable: Y

Randomization Tests

SPSS does not have a readily available test for conducting the randomization test presented on text page 712.

Chapter 17 SPSS®

Analysis of Factor Level Effects in Single Factor Studies

In Chapter 16, the authors discussed the analysis of variance for the single-factor ANOVA model. The focus was on an F-test aimed at testing the null hypothesis that the factor level means are all equal; i.e., an F-test aimed at testing

$$H_0 : \mu_1 = \mu_2 = \cdots = \mu_r$$

where r is the number of factor level means. If this hypothesis is rejected, we usually pursue further analyses to investigate the nature of differences among the means. This often involves testing hypotheses and constructing confidence intervals on subsets of the factor level means. When we investigate these sub-hypotheses and confidence intervals, we usually want to use procedures for making simultaneous inferences to preserve the overall significance level at the stated level α for testing hypotheses and the overall confidence level at the stated $100(1-\alpha)\%$ level for constructing multiple interval estimates. In this chapter, the authors present various procedures that are widely used to make simultaneous inferences pertaining to subsets of the factor level means.

Rust Inhibitor Example

Data File: ch17ta02.txt

Researchers tested the effectiveness of four brands of rust inhibitor. Forty experimental units were assigned randomly to the four brands with 10 units assigned to each brand. The response variable was coded so that higher values indicated more rust inhibitor effectiveness. After opening the Rust Inhibitor Example (Table 17.2, text page 735) and renaming the variables Y, *brand*, and *unit*, the first five lines in the *Data Editor* should look like SPSS Output 17.1.

The researcher first wished to determine if there were any significant differences among the response (effectiveness) means for the four rust inhibitors. Here we use the *GLM* procedure where Y is the dependent variable and *brand* is the single fixed factor. Again, *GLM* automatically creates indicator variables suitable for an effects model analysis of variance. Partial results are presented in SPSS Output 17.2 and are consistent with Table 17.2 (b), text page 735. The researchers concluded that there were statistically significant differences among the rust inhibitor means, $F(3, 36) = 866.118, p < 0.000$.

SPSS Output 17.1

```
Rust Inhibitor Example.sav - SPSS Data Editor
File  Edit  View  Data  Transform  Analyze  Graphs  Utilities  W
```

1 : y   43.9

	y	brand	unit	var
1	43.90	1	1.0	
2	39.00	1	2.0	
3	46.70	1	3.0	
4	43.80	1	4.0	
5	44.20	1	5.0	

SPSS Output 17.2

Tests of Between-Subjects Effects

Dependent Variable: Y

Source	Type III Sum of Squares	df	Mean Square	F	Sig.
Corrected Model	15953.466[a]	3	5317.822	866.118	.000
Intercept	145202.500	1	145202.500	23649.258	.000
BRAND	15953.466	3	5317.822	866.118	.000
Error	221.034	36	6.140		
Total	161377.000	40			
Corrected Total	16174.500	39			

a. R Squared = .986 (Adjusted R Squared = .985)

Kenton Food Company Example

Data File: ch16ta01.txt

The Kenton Food Company (text page 686) studied the relationship between sales (*Y*) and the type of package design for a new breakfast cereal. Here, store was the experimental unit. Each of 20 stores was assigned to one package design such that there were 5 stores assigned to each design. One store was unable to fulfill the study requirement and was dropped from the study. After opening the Kenton Food Company data file and renaming the variables *Y*, *package*, and *store*, the first five lines of the *Data Editor* should look like SPSS Output 17.3.

	y	package	store	var
1	11.0	1	1	
2	17.0	1	2	
3	16.0	1	3	
4	14.0	1	4	
5	15.0	1	5	

Kenton Food Company.sav - SPSS Data Editor
File Edit View Data Transform Analyze Graphs Utilities W
1 : y   11

The Line Plot shown in Figure 17.1, text page 736, is not available in SPSS. Text Figure 17.2 (a) can be obtained using ✔ Graphs ✔ Bar. The Main Effect Plot [Figure 17.2 (b), text page 736] can be obtained (output not shown) via *GLM* using the *Plot* option as shown in Insert 17.1.

INSERT 17.1	INSERT 17.1 continued
✔ Analyze ✔ General Linear Model ✔ Univariate ✔ Y ✔ ► (to the Dependent box) ✔ package ✔ ► (to the Fixed Factor box) ✔ Plots	✔ package ✔ ► (to the Horizontal box) ✔ Continue ✔ Options ✔ package ✔ ► (to the Display Means box) ✔ Compare Main Effects ✔ Continue ✔ OK

Review of SPSS Methods for Contrasts and Post Hoc Comparisons

Before continuing the Kenton Food Company Example, we review the some of the methods available in SPSS for Contrasts and Post Hoc comparisons. We will see that there are many ways to request multiple comparisons in SPSS through the use of dialog windows or the *Syntax Editor*. Each method, however, is typically used in different situations or to test different hypotheses. In the *GLM – Univariate – Options* dialog window (SPSS Output 17.4), we can request estimated marginal means. This will produce estimated marginal means (predicted means, not observed means) for the specified factor levels while controlling for any covariates in the model. Multiple comparisons can also be requested and the family α risk can be controlled by use of the *Least Significant Difference* (LSD), *Bonferroni*, or *Sidak* procedures.

Contrasts are used to test for differences among factor levels, and we can specify a contrast for each factor in the model. Using the *GLM – Univariate - Contrast* dialog window (SPSS Output 17.7) we can specify a number of contrast types that are not elsewhere available. For example, *simple* compares each factor level mean to all other factor level means, *deviation* compares the mean of each factor level (except a reference category) to the grand mean, and *polynomial* compares the linear effect, quadratic effect, cubic effect, etc. *Helmert*, *difference*, and *repeated* contrast types are also available. Results include an *F* statistic for each contrast and, for each contrast difference, a "Bonferroni-type" simultaneous confidence interval based on Student's *t* distribution.

The *GLM - Univariate - Post Hoc* dialog window (SPSS Output 17.10) provides approximately 18 multiple comparison methods to control the α risk. Comparisons are made on unadjusted means. Thus, specifying *LSD* (no adjustment) in the *Post Hoc* window, *simple* contrast type in the *Contrast* window, and *confidence interval adjustment – LSD* in the *Option* window will yield the same result if there is no covariate in the model. However, if there is a covariate in the model, the *Post Hoc* dialog box will be grayed out and unavailable. In this case, you can compare the *observed* (unadjusted) means by contrast types available in the *Contrast* dialog box or compare *predicted* (adjusted) means by use of *LSD*, *Bonferroni*, or *Sidak* procedures available in the *Options* dialog box. From each of the three dialog windows, comparisons are for main effects only. Analysis of simple effects, the effect of one factor at one level of another factor as may be of interest in the presence of a factor-by-factor interaction, is not available via drop down menus. This type analysis is available from a *Syntax Editor* and will be discussed in Chapter 19. Finally, contrasts of linear combinations are available only from a *Syntax Editor*; examples are given below.

Estimation and Testing of Factor Level Effects

Kenton Food Company Example Continued

Inferences for a Single Factor Level Mean

On text page 738 the sales manager wishes to estimate the sales mean for package design 1 with a 95% confidence interval. To produce this confidence interval, we request *GLM* (Insert 17.1 above) and click *Options*; this produces SPSS Output 17.4. Under *Estimated Marginal Means*, we move *package* to the *Display Means* box. Partial results are shown in SPSS Output 17.5 and are consistent with the 95% confidence interval reported on text page 738.

SPSS Output 17.4

Univariate: Options

Estimated Marginal Means

Factor(s) and Factor Interactions:
```
(OVERALL)
package
```

Display Means for:
```
package
```

☐ Compare main effects

Confidence interval adjustment:

LSD (none)

Display

☐ Descriptive statistics   ☐ Homogeneity tests
☐ Estimates of effect size   ☐ Spread vs. level plot
☐ Observed power   ☐ Residual plot
☐ Parameter estimates   ☐ Lack of fit
☐ Contrast coefficient matrix   ☐ General estimable function

Significance level: .05   Confidence intervals are 95%

Continue   Cancel   Help

SPSS Output 17.5

Estimates

Dependent Variable: Y

PACKAGE	Mean	Std. Error	95% Confidence Interval	
			Lower Bound	Upper Bound
1	14.600	1.452	11.504	17.696
2	13.400	1.452	10.304	16.496
3	19.500	1.624	16.039	22.961
4	27.200	1.452	24.104	30.296

Inferences for Differences between Two Factor Level Means

On text page 740, the sales manager wishes to estimate the difference between the sales means sales for package designs 3 and 4 using a 95% confidence interval. To produce this confidence interval, we request *GLM* as in Insert 17.1 above. We specify *Compare Main Effects* while in the *GLM - Univariate Dialog* window (SPSS Output 17.4) and accept *LSD* (no adjustment) as the confidence interval adjustment method. Results (not shown) are consistent with $\hat{D} = -7.7$ and the confidence interval reported on text page 740.

Inferences for Contrasts of Factor Level Means

Illustrations of Contrasts: We extend the use of the *lmatrix* statement introduced in Chapter 15 of this manual to specify various custom hypotheses for the contrasts presented on text page 741. As noted in text Chapter 15, linear contrasts (L) are linear functions of factor level means where the contrast coefficients c_i sum to zero. A linear combination of m sample means takes the form:

$$L = c_1 \mu_1 + c_2 \mu_2 + \cdots + c_m \mu_m$$

In SPSS, the *lmatrix* statement is useful for specifying custom hypotheses that otherwise may be not readily available. Upon execution of an *lmatrix* statement, SPSS presents test results for the specified custom hypothesis. We present some specific examples that use the *lmatrix* statement to request test statistics in terms of the following four contrasts (text page 741):

$$\text{Contrast \#1: } L = \mu_1 - \mu_2$$

$$\text{Contrast \#2: } L = \frac{\mu_1 + \mu_2}{2} - \frac{\mu_3 + \mu_4}{2}$$

$$\text{Contrast \#3: } L = \frac{\mu_1 + \mu_3}{2} - \frac{\mu_2 + \mu_4}{2}$$

$$\text{Contrast \#4: } L = \mu_1 - \frac{\mu_1 + \mu_2 + \mu_3 + \mu_4}{4}$$

Contrast #1: The researchers wish to test the hypothesis that the sales means for the two 3-color designs are equal, i.e., the mean for *package*=1 is equal to the mean for *package*=2. Thus, they wish to test the "null" hypothesis

$$H_0 : \mu_1 - \mu_2 = 0$$

If we let $c_1 = 1$, $c_2 = -1$, $c_3 = 0$, and $c_4 = 0$, we see that the left side of the equation for the hypothesis is a contrast L that can be written as

$$L = (1)\mu_1 + (-1)\mu_2 + (0)\mu_3 + (0)\mu_4$$

The corresponding SPSS *lmatrix* statement to test the hypothesis is

/*lmatrix* "Package 1 - Package 2=0" *package* 1 –1 0 0.

The *lmatrix* statement is available only in the *Syntax Editor*. For the current example, we request *GLM* and specify *y* as the dependent variable and *package* as a fixed factor. We paste the syntax into a *Syntax Editor* and add the above *lmatrix* statement. (See Insert 17.2) Execution of this syntax results in SPSS Output 17.6.

Alternatively, we can request *GLM* with *y* as the dependent variable and *package* as the single independent variable (*fixed factor*). We ✔ *Contrasts* while in the *GLM* dialog window and select simple contrasts for *package* with *First* as the reference category and ✔ *Change* as shown in SPSS Output 17.7. This will result in comparisons between the reference group, package design 1, and the other three package designs. Results of the package design 1 versus package design 2 are shown in SPSS Output 17.8. Note that SPSS Outputs 17.6 and 17.8 contain the same information. Thus, both the *lmatrix* statement and the *GLM - Univariate -Contrasts* dialog window can be used to test $H_0 : \mu_1 - \mu_2 = 0$.

SPSS Output 17.6

Contrast Results (K Matrix)[a]

			Dependent Variable
Contrast			Y
L1	Contrast Estimate		-1.200
	Hypothesized Value		0
	Difference (Estimate - Hypothesized)		-1.200
	Std. Error		2.054
	Sig.		.568
	95% Confidence Interval for Difference	Lower Bound	-5.578
		Upper Bound	3.178

a. Based on the user-specified contrast coefficients (L') matrix:
   Package 1 - Package 2=0

SPSS Output 17.7

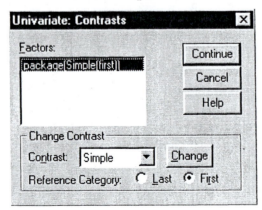

PACKAGE Simple Contrast[a]		Dependent Variable
		Y
Level 2 vs. Level 1	Contrast Estimate	-1.200
	Hypothesized Value	0
	Difference (Estimate - Hypothesized)	-1.200
	Std. Error	2.054
	Sig.	.568
	95% Confidence Interval for Difference	Lower Bound	-5 578
	Upper Bound	3.178

Contrast #4: The researchers wish to test the hypothesis that the sales mean for package design 1 is equal to the overall mean. This contrast represents a combination of factor means and cannot be tested from a dialog window. The overall mean is

$$\mu = \frac{\mu_1 + \mu_2 + \mu_3 + \mu_4}{4}$$

The hypothesis can be expressed as

$$H_0 : \mu_1 = \mu$$

or as

$$H_0 : \mu_1 - \mu = 0$$

or, substituting for μ, as

$$H_0 : \mu_1 - \frac{\mu_1 + \mu_2 + \mu_3 + \mu_4}{4} = 0$$

or, combining terms, as

$$H_0 : \frac{3}{4}\mu_1 - \frac{1}{4}\mu_2 - \frac{1}{4}\mu_3 - \frac{1}{4}\mu_4 = 0$$

Again, we see that the left side of the hypothesis is a contrast. The corresponding SPSS *lmatrix* statement to test the hypothesis is

/lmatrix 'Package 1 - All designs=0' *package* 3/4 –1/4 –1/4 –1/4.

547

We return to the hypothesis expressed as

$$H_0 : \mu_1 - \mu = 0$$

and recall that in the effects model, we define

$$\tau_1 = \mu_1 - \mu$$

as the "effect" of package design 1. Thus, we can also express the hypothesis as

$$H_0 : \tau_1 = 0$$

Suppose we wish to estimate the treatment effect (a contrast) for package design 1; i.e., suppose we wish to estimate

$$\tau_1 = \frac{3\mu_1 - \mu_2 - \mu_3 - \mu_4}{4}$$

This estimate is also obtained by use of the *lmatrix* statement.

/lmatrix 'Package 1 - All designs=0' *package*   3/4 –1/4 –1/4 –1/4.

Note that we prefer to avoid using decimal fractions for the coefficients in *lmatrix* statements because for contrast coefficients like 2/3 –1/3 –1/3, use of 0.6667 –0.3333 –0.3333 does not work; i.e., the sum of the coefficients must be exactly zero in order for the contrast to be estimable (use of 0.6666 –0.3333 –0.3333 does work because the contrast coefficients sum exactly to zero).

Syntax shown in the *lmatrix* statements of Insert 17.2 will produce test statistics and estimates for the 4 contrasts listed above and presented on text page 741. Contrasts of interest in analyzing interactions will be discussed in Chapter 19 of this manual.

Finally, note that the second *lmatrix* statement (Contrast #2) compares the mean response of designs 1 and 2 to the mean response of designs 3 and 4. Partial results are shown in SPSS Output 17.9 and are consistent with text page 743. SPSS does not provide $t^* = -6.23$ as reported on text page 743. To obtain t^*, we use equation 17.26, text page 742, and divide the "Contrast Estimate" $(\hat{L})$ by the "Std. Error" $(s\{\hat{L}\})$ in SPSS Output 17.9 to obtain $t^* = -9.350/1.497 = -6.245$.

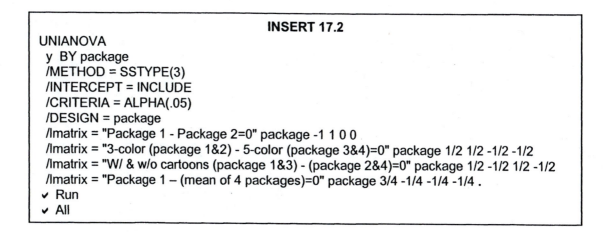

INSERT 17.2

```
UNIANOVA
  y  BY package
  /METHOD = SSTYPE(3)
  /INTERCEPT = INCLUDE
  /CRITERIA = ALPHA(.05)
  /DESIGN = package
  /lmatrix = "Package 1 - Package 2=0" package -1 1 0 0
  /lmatrix = "3-color (package 1&2) - 5-color (package 3&4)=0" package 1/2 1/2 -1/2 -1/2
  /lmatrix = "W/ & w/o cartoons (package 1&3) - (package 2&4)=0" package 1/2 -1/2 1/2 -1/2
  /lmatrix = "Package 1 – (mean of 4 packages)=0" package 3/4 -1/4 -1/4 -1/4 .
  ✔ Run
  ✔ All
```

SPSS Output 17.9

Contrast Results (K Matrix)[a]

Contrast		Dependent Variable Y
L1	Contrast Estimate	-9.350
	Hypothesized Value	0
	Difference (Estimate - Hypothesized)	-9.350
	Std. Error	1.497
	Sig.	.000
	95% Confidence Interval for Difference Lower Bound	-12.541
	Upper Bound	-6.159

a. Based on the user-specified contrast coefficients (L') matrix: 3-color (package 1&2) - 5-color (package 3&4)=0

Simultaneous Inference Procedures

***Tukey* Multiple Comparison Procedure**: SPSS offers approximately 18 options for conducting post hoc analyses that can be accessed by ✔ *Post Hoc* from the *GLM - Univariate* dialog box (SPSS Output 17.10). For example, on text page 748 the authors estimated all pairwise comparisons in the Rust Inhibitor example using the *Tukey* procedure. We request *GLM* with *Y* as the dependent variable and *brand* as the single independent variable (*fixed factor*), and select *Tukey* from the *Post Hoc* menu. Partial results are shown in SPSS Output 17.11. The 95% confidence limits are consistent with those reported in Table 17.3, text page 749. Additionally, the *Homogeneous Subsets* table (SPSS Output 17.12) indicates the difference in the response means between brands A and D are not statistically significant. The adjusted mean for brand B is significantly greater than all other brands. Brand C is significantly greater than brands A and D but significantly less than Brand B. This information is also contained in the *Multiple Comparison* table (SPSS Output 17.11) along with the magnitude of group differences, 95% confidence limits, and probability levels. SPSS makes the proper adjustment in the *Tukey* procedure when there are unequal sample sizes as reported on text page 749-751.

We can mimic Figure 17.4, text page 748, by using ✔ Graphs ✔ Error Bars ✔ Simple. The interval given in equation 17.33, text page 748, is not available, however. The user can select either *confidence interval for mean* (default), *standard error of mean*, or *standard deviation*. In SPSS Output 17.13 we selected *confidence interval for mean* and used the *Chart Editor* to arrange the error bars in ascending order.

SPSS Output 17.10

SPSS Output 17.11

Multiple Comparisons

Dependent Variable: Y

Tukey HSD

(I) BRAND	(J) BRAND	Mean Difference (I-J)	Std. Error	Sig.	95% Confidence Interval Lower Bound	95% Confidence Interval Upper Bound
A	B	-46.3000*	1.10814	.000	-49.2845	-43.3155
	C	-24.8100*	1.10814	.000	-27.7945	-21.8255
	D	2.6700	1.10814	.093	-.3145	5.6545
B	A	46.3000*	1.10814	.000	43.3155	49.2845
	C	21.4900*	1.10814	.000	18.5055	24.4745
	D	48.9700*	1.10814	.000	45.9855	51.9545
C	A	24.8100*	1.10814	.000	21.8255	27.7945
	B	-21.4900*	1.10814	.000	-24.4745	-18.5055
	D	27.4800*	1.10814	.000	24.4955	30.4645
D	A	-2.6700	1.10814	.093	-5.6545	.3145
	B	-48.9700*	1.10814	.000	-51.9545	-45.9855
	C	-27.4800*	1.10814	.000	-30.4645	-24.4955

Based on observed means.

*. The mean difference is significant at the .05 level.

550

Homogeneous Subsets

Y

Tukey HSD[a,b]

BRAND	N	Subset		
		1	2	3
D	10	40.4700		
A	10	43.1400		
C	10		67.9500	
B	10			89.4400
Sig.		.093	1.000	1.000

Means for groups in homogeneous subsets are displayed.
Based on Type III Sum of Squares
The error term is Mean Square(Error) = 6.140.

a. Uses Harmonic Mean Sample Size = 10.000.

b. Alpha = .05.

SPSS Output 17.13

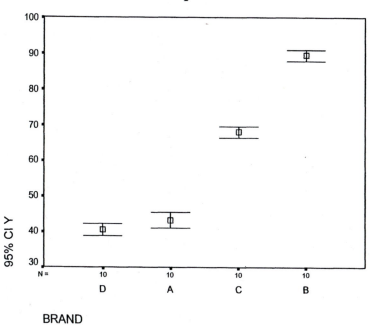

On text page 750, the authors illustrate simultaneous inference procedures for unbalanced designs. Using the Keeton Food Company Example shown above, the researcher wished to compare the performance of the four package designs using the *Tukey* procedure and a family confidence coefficient equal to 90 percent. Since the numbers of observations for the different package designs are unequal, the estimated standard deviations must be calculated for each pairwise comparison. However, SPSS will make the necessary adjustments as shown on text page 751 (text equation 17.30, page 747). Using the Kenton Food Company Example as shown in SPSS Output 17.3, the confidence intervals shown on text page 751 are obtained by specifying the *Tukey* procedure from the *Post Hoc* option and an α=0.1 level from the *Options* option from within the *GLM* procedure.

Scheffe Multiple Comparison Procedure: The researcher in the Kenton Food Company Example used the *Scheffe* procedure and a family confidence coefficient of 90 percent to estimate the four contrasts shown on text page 754. Contrasts L_3 and L_4 are simple pairwise comparisons and can be obtained by specifying the *Scheffe* procedure shown in SPSS Output 17.10. L_1 and L_2 represent linear combinations of factor level means that are not pairwise differences, however, and are not available via the *Post Hoc* dialog box. The L_1 contrast, for example, can only be obtained via the *Syntax Editor*. In fact, the syntax shown in Insert 17.2 (2nd *lmatrix* statement) will produce the L_1 contrast shown in SPSS Output 17.9 but the confidence intervals will not be adjusted. To estimate the *Scheffe* adjusted confidence intervals we use equation 17.43, text page 753. From SPSS Output 17.9 we find $\hat{L}_1 = -9.350$ (Contrast Estimate) and $s\{\hat{L}_1\} = 1.497$ (Std. Error). To find $S = 2.73$ (equation 17.43a, text page 753) as reported on text page 754, we execute the following *compute* statement from a *Syntax Editor*: compute S=sqrt((41)*idf.f(.9,3,15)). We now find that the 90% confidence limits for L_1 using the *Scheffe* procedure are $-9.350 \pm 2.73(1.497)$.

Bonferroni Multiple Comparison Procedure: The researcher in the Kenton Food Company example used the *Bonferroni* procedure and a family confidence coefficient of 97.5 percent to estimate the two contrasts shown on text page 756. If the contrasts were simple pairwise comparisons, we could use the dialog window shown in SPSS Output 17.10. However, since the two contrasts represent linear combinations of factor level means that are not pairwise differences, we must use the *Syntax Editor* as we did for the *Scheffe* procedure above. The steps are identical except that we use equation 17.46, text page 756. Here we must find B by equation 17.46a where g is the number of comparisons. To find $B = 2.84$ as reported on text page 756, we execute the following *compute* statement from a *Syntax Editor*: "compute B=idf.t(1 − (.025/(2*2)),15).". We can now find that the 97.5% confidence limits for L_1 using the *Bonferroni* procedure are $-9.350 \pm 2.84(1.497)$.

Analysis of Means

The Analysis of Means testing procedure presented on text page 758 is not readily available in SPSS.

ANOVA Diagnostics and Remedial Measures

In this chapter, the authors discuss diagnostics and remedial measures to improve the appropriateness of the analysis of variance model. Their discussion begins with analysis of residuals for ANOVA models, procedures that closely parallel the use of residual analysis for regression models. In section 18.3, the authors discuss tests for constancy of error variance. Next, the authors discuss models that employ weighted least squares and transformations as remedial measures for models that have deficiencies identified in the diagnostic process. In section 18.6, the authors describe the effects of departures from the model. The authors conclude the chapter with a discussion of the nonparametric rank F test.

Residual Analysis

Rust Inhibitor Example

Data File: ch17ta02.txt

From text page 734, researchers tested the effectiveness of four brands of rust inhibitor. Forty experimental units were assigned randomly to the four brands with 10 units assigned to each brand. The response variable was coded so that higher values indicated more rust inhibitor effectiveness. After opening the Rust Inhibitor Example (Table 17.2, text page 735) and renaming the variables *Y*, *brand*, and *unit*, the first five lines in the *Data Editor* should look like SPSS Output 17.1.

To produce the residual plots shown in Figure 18.1, text page 777, we use *GLM* to save the residuals (*res_1*, by default) and predicted values (*pre_1*, by default) based on a model where *Y* is the dependent variable and *brand* is the single independent variable (fixed factor). (Insert 18.1) We then plot the residuals on the Y-axis and predicted values on the X-axis and remove the inter frame to produce the plot of residual values against the fitted values. Results are shown in SPSS Output 18.1 and are consistent with text Figure 18.1, residual plot against fitted values. To produce Figure 18.1, normal probability plot (syntax not shown) we use the ✔ Graphs ✔ Q-Q and enter *res_1* as the variable to be plotted. The axes of the resulting plot will be reversed compared to Figure 18.1. To reverse the SPSS graph axes, open the *Chart Editor* as in Insert 18.1 and ✔ Series ✔ Displayed. Results are shown in SPSS Output 18.2 and are consistent with text Figure 18.1. To produce text Figure 18.1, aligned dot plot, (syntax not shown), again use the *Scatter Plot* procedure and enter *brand* on the Y-axis and *res_1* on the X-axis.

INSERT 18.1	INSERT 18.1 continued
✔ Analyze ✔ General Linear Model ✔ Univariate ✔ Y ✔ ► (to the Dependent box) ✔ *brand* ✔ ► (to the Fixed Factor box) ✔ Save ✔ Unstandardized Residuals ✔ Unstandardized Predicted Values ✔ Continue ✔ OK	✔ Graphs ✔ Scatter ✔ Simple ✔ Define ✔ *pre_1* ✔ ► (to the X axis) ✔ *res_1* ✔ ► (to the Y axis) * Double click on the resulting. * scatter plot to open the Chart Editor. ✔ Chart ✔ Inter frame * Close Chart Editor.

SPSS Output 18.1

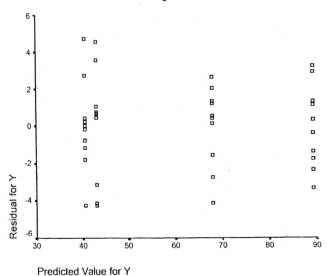

SPSS Output 18.2

Normal Q-Q Plot of Residual for Y

Tests for Constancy of Error Variance

ABT Electronic Example

Data File: ch18ta02.txt

Engineers at the ABT Electronics Corporation evaluated five types of flux used to solder joints. Forty circuit boards were randomly selected and each of the five types of flux was randomly assigned to 8 of the circuit boards. A mechanical device then measured the force required to break the soldered joint. This force, referred to as pull strength by the engineers, was the response variable. After opening the ABT Electronics Example data file (Table 18.2, text page 783) and renaming the variables Y, *flux*, and *board*, the first five lines of the *Data Editor* should look like SPSS Output 18.3.

SPSS Output 18.3

	y	flux	board	var
1	14.87	1	1	
2	16.81	1	2	
3	15.83	1	3	
4	15.47	1	4	
5	13.60	1	5	

ABT Electronics Example.sav - SPSS Data Editor
File Edit View Data Transform Analyze Graphs Utilities W
1 : y   14.87

The researchers plotted the response variable against the flux types in Figure 18.6, text page 784. To reproduce Figure 18.6 (SPSS Output 18.4), we use ✔ Graphs ✔ Scatter and enter Y on the X-axis and *flux* on the Y-axis. (Syntax not shown.) Consistent with the text, flux type 3 has a greater magnitude of variation than the other flux types.

The researchers wished to perform the *Hartley Test*. Since the *Hartley Test* requires approximate normality, the researcher first plotted normal probability plots of residuals for each treatment. In Insert 18.2, we first save the residuals for the ABT Electronic Example. To produce normal probability plots for each treatment, we use ✔ Data ✔ Select Cases as shown in Insert 18.2 to select only one flux type at a time. We then ✔ Graphs ✔ Q-Q and enter *res_1* as the variable to be plotted. The axes of the resulting plot will be reversed compared to the normal probability plot in Figure 18.1. To reverse the SPSS graph axes, open the *Chart Editor* as in Insert 18.1 and ✔ Series ✔ Displayed.

The researchers then performed a formal test of normality of error terms that was discussed in text Chapter 3. Computational details for the *Correlation Test for Normality*, the correlation between the ordered residuals and their expected value under normality, were presented in Chapter 3 of this manual. In Insert 18.2, we obtain *MSE*=2.109 from the *GLM* model where Y is the dependent variable and *flux* in the independent variable (fixed factor), and we save the residuals (*res_1*, by default). Remember, if we have previously saved residuals in the *Data Editor*, by default as *res_1*, a subsequent save of residuals will be under the name *res_2* if *res_1* has not been deleted for the *Data Editor*. We then rank the residuals and place the rank in a variable named *rres_1*, by default. We use equation 3.6, text page 111, to find the expected value (*ev*) of the error terms. Finally, we correlate *ev* with *res_1*. The resulting correlation is 0.982 and is consistent with text page 783. Since our obtained correlation is greater than the critical value in text Table B.6, we conclude that the error terms among *flux* type 1 are normally distributed. To perform the same operation for *flux* type 2, delete *rres_1* from the *Data Editor*, begin at the *Data - Select Cases* statement of Insert 18.2, and modify the syntax to select *flux* = 2.

INSERT 18.2	INSERT 18.2 continued
✔ Analyze ✔ General Linear Model ✔ Univariate ✔ Y ✔ ► (to the Dependent box) ✔ flux ✔ ► (to the Fixed Factor box) ✔ Save ✔ Unstandardized Residuals ✔ Continue ✔ OK ✔ Data ✔ Select Cases ✔ If condition is satisfied ✔ IF (under If condition is satisfied) ✔ flux ✔ ► ✔ = 1 ✔ Continue ✔ OK ✔ Graphs ✔ Q-Q ✔ res_1 ✔ ► ✔ Variables ✔ OK	* *Correlation Test for Normality.* ✔ Transform ✔ Rank Cases ✔ res_1 ✔ ► ✔ Variables ✔ OK ✔ File ✔ New ✔ Syntax * Type the following syntax. compute ev=sqrt(2.109)* Probit ((rres_1-.375)/(8+.25)). exe. ✔ Run ✔ ALL ✔ Analyze ✔ Correlate ✔ Bivariate ✔ res_1 ✔ ► ✔ Variables ✔ ev ✔ ► ✔ Variables ✔ OK

SPSS Output 18.4

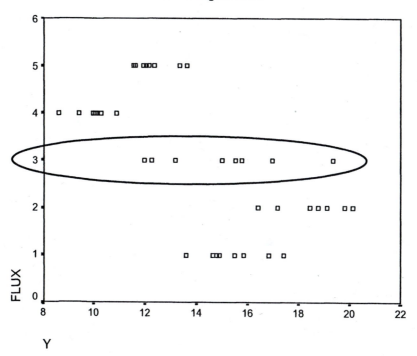

Y

To formally test for constancy of error variance, we conduct a *Hartley Test* as described on text page 782. This test is based on the ratio of the largest factor level variance to the smallest factor level variance. In Insert 18.3, we request the variance of each factor level in the ABT Electronics Example. Results are shown in SPSS Output 18.5. We now find $H = 6.183 / 0.592 = 10.44$. Since $H = 10.44 >$ the critical value we conclude that the variances of the five factor levels are not all equal.

INSERT 18.3	INSERT 18.3 continued
✔ Analyze	✔ ▶(to the Independent box)
✔ Compare Means	✔ Options
✔ Means	✔ Variance
✔ Y	✔ ▶(to the Cell Statistics)
✔ ▶(to the Dependent box)	✔ Continue
✔ flux	✔ OK

SPSS Output 18.5

Report

Y

FLUX	Mean	N	Std. Deviation	Variance
1	15.4200	8	1.23714	1.531
2	18.5275	8	1.25297	1.570
3	15.0037	8	2.48664	6.183
4	9.7412	8	.81660	.667
5	12.3400	8	.76942	.592
Total	14.2065	40	3.31048	10.959

On text page 784, the researchers in the ABT Electronics Example also performed a *Brown-Forsythe* test for constancy of error variance. This test is based on the absolute deviation of each *Y* value from its respective factor level median. In this application it is desirable to have SPSS perform summary calculations and retain the values for subsequent calculations. In Insert 18.4, we use the *aggregate* function to find and retain the median of *Y* for each value of *flux*. Using the ABT Electronics data file as shown in SPSS Output 18.3, we specify that our *aggregate* results be placed in a file name *temp.sav* and that the median of *Y* for each value of *flux* (/break=flux) be calculated and placed in a variable named *median* [/median=median(y)]. Using the *match file* function, we specify that the summary data of the *aggregate* function be placed in the active *Data Editor* (/file=*). That is, *temp.sav* will contain five median values, one for each level of *flux*. The *match* function will add the factor level median to each *Y* value in the corresponding factor level for the 40 records of the ABT Electronics data file by matching the values of *flux* in *temp.sav* and the *Data Editor*. We then compute the absolute value of the deviation (*absdev*) of each *Y* value from its respective factor level median. Finally, we perform an ANOVA where *absdev* is the dependent variable and *flux* is the single independent variable. Results are shown in SPSS Output 18.6 where $F_{BF}^{*} = 2.936$, $p = 0.034$, consistent with text page 785.

INSERT 18.4	INSERT 18.4 continued
✔ File	✔ Analyze
✔ New	✔ General Linear Model
✔ Syntax	✔ Univariate
* Type the following syntax.	✔ absdev
aggregate	✔ ►(to the Dependent box)
/outfile='temp.sav'	✔ flux
/break=flux	✔ ►(to the Fixed Factor box)
/median=median(y).	✔ OK
match files /file=*	
/table='temp.sav'	
/by flux.	
compute absdev=abs(y-median).	
exe.	
✔ Run	
✔ All	

SPSS Output 18.6

Tests of Between-Subjects Effects

Dependent Variable: ABSDEV

Source	Type III Sum of Squares	df	Mean Square	F	Sig.
Corrected Model	9.348[a]	4	2.337	2.936	.034
Intercept	38.652	1	38.652	48.556	.000
FLUX	9.348	4	2.337	2.936	.034
Error	27.861	35	.796		
Total	75.860	40			
Corrected Total	37.208	39			

a. R Squared = .251 (Adjusted R Squared = .166)

Weighted Least Squares

ABT Electronics Example

Continuing with the ABT Electronics Example on text page 787, because there is evidence that the error variances are not constant across *flux* levels, we use weighted least squares regression as a remedial measure. We begin with the data file as shown in SPSS Output 18.3. In Insert 18.5, we use the *aggregate* function to find the standard deviation (variance is not an option) of Y for each level of *flux*. We use the *match file* function to add the standard deviation to each line of the *Data Editor* based on the value of *flux*. We use the coding presented on text page 787 to create *X1* though *X5*, use equation 18.14 (text page 787) to compute the weight (w_{ij}), and set $X=1$ for all lines in the *Data Editor*. After executing Insert 18.5, we use SPSS's linear regression procedure (steps and output not shown) where Y is the dependent variable; *X1*, *X2*, *X3*, *X4*, and *X5* are independent variables; *wt* is the *WLS Weight Variable*; and in the *Linear Regression Options* dialog box we uncheck *Include Constant in Equation*. This produces Figure 18.7 (a), text page 788. To produce Figure 18.7 (b), we use SPSS's linear regression procedure where Y is the dependent variable, X is the independent variable, *wt* is the *WLS Weight Variable*, and in the *Linear Regression Options* dialog box we uncheck *Include Constant in Equation*. We can now use equation 18.15, text page 787, to solve for $F_W^* = 81.05$, as shown on text page 789.

INSERT 18.5	INSERT 18.5 continued
✔ File	recode flux (1=1) (else=0) into x1 .
✔ New	recode flux (2=1) (else=0) into x2 .
✔ Syntax	recode flux (3=1) (else=0) into x3 .
aggregate	recode flux (4=1) (else=0) into x4 .
/outfile='temp.sav'	recode flux (5=1) (else=0) into x5 .
/break=flux	compute wt=1/sd**2.
/sd=sd(y).	compute x=1.
match files /file=*	exe.
/table='temp.sav'	✔ Run
/by flux.	✔ All

Box-Cox Procedure

Servo-Data, Inc. Example

Data File: ch18ta05.txt

The Servo-Data, Inc., wished to study the relationship between location of mainframe computer installations and the amount of time between computer failures, the response variable. After opening Table 18.5, text page 774, and renaming the variables *Y, location,* and *interval*, the first 5 lines of the *Data Editor* should look like SPSS Output 18.7.

SPSS Output 18.7

Servo-Data Inc.sav - SPSS Data Editor

File Edit View Data Transform Analyze Graphs Utilities W

1 : y   4.41

	y	location	interval	var
1	4.41	1	1	
2	100.65	1	2	
3	14.45	1	3	
4	47.13	1	4	
5	85.21	1	5	

Here we use the Box-Cox procedure to identify a power transformation of the type Y^λ that may be helpful in correcting for non-constancy of error variance and lack of normality. We presented syntax for the Box-Cox transformation in Chapter 3 of this manual. The independent variable was continuous in the example of Chapter 3. In the present example independent variables represent three levels of a single factor. Here, we have modified the syntax from Chapter 3 to accommodate the use of indicator variables to represent levels of a factor in the ANOVA model rather than directly using one or more continuous variables in the regression model.

The syntax in Insert 18.6 requires that the Servo-Data data file be opened as shown in SPSS Output 18.7. Note that the syntax will overwrite the active *Data Editor*; save the contents of the *Data Editor* as needed. This procedure uses a range of λ values starting at λ (*start*) = - 1 and incrementing (*incremen*) by a value of 0.1 for 21 iterations (*noiter*). The syntax will list the values of λ and *SSE* (consistent with Table 18.6, text page 792), and plot *SSE* as a function of λ (not shown). The start, increment, and iterations values can be varied to specify choices suitable for different data sets.

INSERT 18.6	INSERT 18.6 continued

✔ File
✔ New
✔ Syntax
if (location = 1) x1 = 1.
if (location = 1) x2 = 0.
if (location = 2) x1 = 0.
if (location = 2) x2 = 1.
if (location = 3) x1 = -1.
if (location = 3) x2 = -1.
exe.
matrix.
get x1 / variables = x1.
get x2 / variables = x2.
get y / variables = y.
 	
compute start = -1.
compute noiter = 21.
compute incremen = 0.1.
 	
compute n=nrow(y).
compute x = {make(n,1,1),x1,x2}.
compute hat = x*inv(t(x)*x)*t(x).
compute lambda = {make(noiter,1,1)}.
compute lambda(1,1)=start.
loop i = 2 to noiter.
   compute lambda(i,1)=lambda(i-1,1) + incremen.
end loop.
	compute sse={make(noiter,1,0)}.
	loop i = 1 to noiter.
	  compute lamb = lambda(i).
	  compute k2 = exp((1/n)&*({make(1,n,1)}*ln(y))).
	  compute k1 = 1/(lamb*k2**(lamb-1)).
	  do if (lamb > -.00000001 and lamb < .00000001).
	  compute w=k2*ln(y).
	  else.
	  compute w = k1*(y&**lamb-{make(n,1,1)}).
	  end if.
	  compute e=(ident(n) - hat)*w.
	  compute sse(i)=t(e)*e.
	end loop.
	compute newm={lambda,sse}.
	  print newm / format "f10.1".
	  save newm / outfile=*/variables=lambda sse.
	end matrix.
	graph
	  /scatterplot(bivar)=lambda with sse
	  /missing=listwise
	  /title= 'Plot of Box-Cox for Servo-Data Ex.'.
	  execute.
	✔ Run
	✔ All

Nonparametric Rank *F* Test

Servo-Data, Inc. Example

Data File: ch18ta05.txt

On text page 796, the authors present the nonparametric rank *F* test as an alternative to performing transformations of *Y* in the presence of non-normality or non-constancy of error variances. Servo-Data, Inc. wished to compare the length of time between computer failures (*Y*) during 5 failure intervals (*interval*) at three different locations (*location*). After opening the

Servo-Data Example (Table 18.5, text page 791) and renaming the variables *Y, location,* and *interval,* the first five lines in the *Data Editor* should look like SPSS Output 18.7.

Initial examination of the data indicates the presence of non-normality or non-constancy of error variances. On text page 796, the researchers performed the nonparametric rank *F* test and presented the *Kruskal-Wallis* test. In Insert 18.5 we rank the dependent variable (*Y*) and place the ranks by default into a variable named *ry*. Results (not shown) of the *GLM* procedure using *ry* as the dependent variable are F_R^*=2.898, *p*=0.094, consistent with text page 796. Results of the *Kruskal-Wallis* test are X_{KW}^2=4.560, *p*=0.102.

Multiple Pairwise Testing Procedure: On text page 797, the authors now wish to perform multiple pairwise testing following a significant rank *F* test or *Kruskal-Wallis* test. The last *GLM* procedure in Insert 18.5 produces the three desired confidence intervals and associated test statistics.

INSERT 18.5	INSERT 18.5 continued
✔ Transform ✔ Rank Cases ✔ Y ► (to the Variables box) ✔ OK ✔ Analyze ✔ General Linear Model ✔ Univariate ✔ *ry* ✔ ► (to the Dependent box) ✔ *location* ✔ ► (to the Fixed Factor box) ✔ OK ✔ Analyze ✔ Nonparametric tests ✔ K independent samples ✔ Kruskal-Wallis H ✔ Y ✔ ► (to the Test Variable list) ✔ *location* ✔ ► (to the Grouping Variable box) ✔ Define Range * 1 (in the Minimum box) * 3 (in the Maximum box) ✔ Continue ✔ OK	✔ Analyze ✔ General Linear Model ✔ Univariate ✔ *ry* ✔ ► (to the Dependent box) ✔ *location* ✔ ► (to the Fixed Factor box) ✔ Post Hoc ✔ *location* ✔ ► (to the Post Hoc tests for) ✔ *location* ✔ Bonferroni ✔ Continue ✔ Opitons * Type "0.1" in Significance Level box. ✔ Continue ✔ OK

Chapter 19 SPSS®

Two-Factor Studies with Equal Sample Size

In this chapter, the authors discuss two-factor studies with equal sample size. The typical model for these studies includes terms for estimating and testing hypotheses relevant to investigating the main effects of the two factors and possible interaction between the two factors. If the interactions are not statistically significant, we can focus the analysis directly on main effects. On the other hand, if they are significant, we must investigate differences among the means for the levels of each factor separately at each level of the other factor.

Castle Bakery Company Example

Data File: ch19ta07.txt

On text page 833, researchers studied the effect of shelf display height (bottom, middle, top) and width (regular, wide) on the number of cases (Y) of Italian bread sold during the study period. After opening text Table 19.7, text page 833, and renaming the variables Y, *height*, *width*, and *rep*, the first 5 lines in the *Data Editor* should look like SPSS Output 19.1.

SPSS Output 19.1

The researcher first plotted the estimated treatment means, Figure 19.8, text page 836. In Insert 19.1 we use the *Plot* option from within *GLM* to reproduce this figure as shown in SPSS Output 19.2. Inspection of the graph suggests that the middle display height may be associated with more sales than the bottom and top display heights. Additionally, there appears to be little difference in sales means between the wide and regular display widths. The researchers now wished to formally test the effects of display height and width. We have already used the *GLM* procedure where we specified Y as the dependent variable and *height* and *width* as the independent variables (fixed factors). The *Model* option in *GLM* allows the user to specify which interaction terms are to be included in the model. The default in *GLM* is a full factorial model that includes all possible main effects of the factors together with all possible interactions among the factors. Thus, in the present example, main effects for *height* and *weight* and the interaction effect of *height* and *weight* are included in the model by default. We also ✔ Options ✔ Descriptive Statistics. Results are shown in SPSS Outputs 19.3 and 19.4, and are consistent with Table 19.9 and Figure 19.9, text page 842. On text page 845, the researchers test for an interaction effect between *height* and *width*. From SPSS Output 19.3, we see that for the *height*width* interaction term, $F(2, 6)=1.161$, $p=0.375$. Thus, we conclude that the interaction between display height and display width is not statistically significant. Since we failed to find significant interaction between the two factors, we tested hypotheses about the main effects of *height* and *width*. For display height, we find $F(2, 6)=74.71$, $p<0.000$ and conclude that the means for the three levels of *height* are not all equal. For display width we find $F(2, 6)=1.161$, $p=0.323$ and conclude that the means for the two levels of *width* are not significantly different. These findings are consistent with the analysis of main effects reported on text page 845-846.

INSERT 19.1	INSERT 19.1 continued
✔ Analyze ✔ General Linear Model ✔ Univariate ✔ Y ✔ ▶(to the Dependent box) ✔ *height width* ✔ ▶(to the Fixed Effects box) ✔ Plots ✔ *height*	✔ ▶(to the Horizontal box) ✔ *width* ✔ ▶(to the Separate Lines box) ✔ Add ✔ Continue ✔ Options ✔ Descriptive Statistics ✔ Continue ✔ OK

SPSS Output 19.2

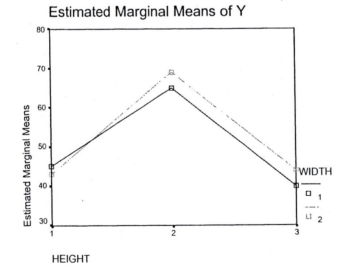

564

SPSS Output 19.3

Tests of Between-Subjects Effects

Dependent Variable: Y

Source	Type III Sum of Squares	df	Mean Square	F	Sig.
Corrected Model	1580.000[a]	5	316.000	30.581	.000
Intercept	31212.000	1	31212.000	3020.516	.000
HEIGHT	1544.000	2	772.000	74.710	.000
WIDTH	12.000	1	12.000	1.161	.323
HEIGHT * WIDTH	24.000	2	12.000	1.161	.375
Error	62.000	6	10.333		
Total	32854.000	12			
Corrected Total	1642.000	11			

a. R Squared = .962 (Adjusted R Squared = .931)

SPSS Output 19.4

Descriptive Statistics

Dependent Variable: Y

HEIGHT	WIDTH	Mean	Std. Deviation	N
1	1	45.000	2.8284	2
	2	43.000	4.2426	2
	Total	44.000	3.1623	4
2	1	65.000	4.2426	2
	2	69.000	2.8284	2
	Total	67.000	3.7417	4
3	1	40.000	1.4142	2
	2	44.000	2.8284	2
	Total	42.000	2.9439	4
Total	1	50.000	12.0665	6
	2	52.000	13.4313	6
	Total	51.000	12.2177	12

On text page 843, the authors plot the residuals against the predicted values [Figure 19.10 (a), text page 843] and present a normality plot of the residuals [Figure 19.10 (b)]. The syntax to reproduce Figures 19.10 (a) and (b) is presented in Insert 19.2 (output not shown). The syntax to find the coefficient of correlation between the ordered residuals and their expected values under normality was presented in Chapter 18 of this manual and is not repeated here.

INSERT 19.2	INSERT 19.2 continued
✔ Analyze	* Produce Figure 19.10 (b).
✔ General Linear Model	✔ Graphs
✔ Univariate	✔ Q-Q
✔ Y	✔ *res_1*
✔ ► (to the Dependent box)	✔ ► (to the Variables box)
✔ *height width*	✔ OK
✔ ► (to the Fixed Effects box)	* Double click on output to open Chart Editor.
✔ Save	* Click Series – Displayed to reverse axes.
✔ Unstandardized Residuals	
✔ Unstandardized Predicted Values	* Produce Figure 19.12 (a).
✔ Continue	✔ Graphs
✔ OK	✔ Bar
* Produce Figure 19.10 (a).	✔ Simple
✔ Graphs	✔ Define
✔ Scatter	✔ Other summary function
✔ Simple	✔ Y
✔ Define	✔ ► (to the Variable box)
✔ *res_1*	✔ *height*
✔ ► (to the Y axis box)	✔ ► (to the Category Axis box)
✔ *pre_1*	✔ OK
✔ ► (to the X axis box)	
✔ OK	

Analyses of Factor Effects when Factors do not Interact

Estimates Based on Treatment Means

Pairwise Comparisons of Factor Level Means: Since SPSS Output 19.2 and the formal analysis shown in SPSS Output 19.3 failed to detect a significant interaction effect, the authors plotted bar graphs of the estimated *height* and *width* factor level means. In Insert 19.2 we produce Figure 19.12 (a), text page 853 (output not shown). To produce Figure 19.12 (b), replace *height* with *width* in the *Category Axis*.

On text page 853, the authors test all pairwise comparisons among the shelf height means using the *Tukey* procedure and a family significance level of $\alpha = 0.05$. Additionally, they wish to estimate the differences in sales means between the middle shelf height and the other two heights. For this analysis, we set *GLM* as in Insert 19.1 (without the *Plot* option) and also use the *Post Hoc* option to specify a *Tukey* post hoc test for *height*. Results are shown in SPSS Output 19.5 and 19.6. From the Homogeneous Subsets Table, we see that the middle shelf height (*height*=2) had a significantly higher sales mean $\left(\bar{Y}_{2.} = 67\right)$ than the bottom $\left(\bar{Y}_{1.} = 44\right)$ or top $\left(\bar{Y}_{3..} = 42\right)$ shelf height. No other comparisons were statistically significant. This is also seen in SPSS Output 19.5 along with the 95% confidence intervals for the differences between the middle shelf height and the bottom and top shelf heights. Both SPSS Output 19.5 and 19.6 are consistent with text page 854-855.

SPSS Output 19.5

Multiple Comparisons

Dependent Variable: Y

Tukey HSD

(I) HEIGHT	(J) HEIGHT	Mean Difference (I-J)	Std. Error	Sig.	95% Confidence Interval	
					Lower Bound	Upper Bound
1	2	-23.000*	2.2730	.000	-29.974	-16.026
	3	2.000	2.2730	.671	-4.974	8.974
2	1	23.000*	2.2730	.000	16.026	29.974
	3	25.000*	2.2730	.000	18.026	31.974
3	1	-2.000	2.2730	.671	-8.974	4.974
	2	-25.000*	2.2730	.000	-31.974	-18.026

Based on observed means.

*. The mean difference is significant at the .05 level.

SPSS Output 19.6

Homogeneous Subsets

Y

Tukey HSD[a,b]

HEIGHT	N	Subset	
		1	2
3	4	42.000	
1	4	44.000	
2	4		67.000
Sig.		.671	1.000

Means for groups in homogeneous subsets are displayed.
Based on Type III Sum of Squares
The error term is Mean Square(Error) = 10.333.

a. Uses Harmonic Mean Sample Size = 4.000.

b. Alpha = .05.

On text page 855, the authors wish to estimate the sales means for the middle and top shelf heights for the regular display width only. The estimate will be made using the *Bonferroni* procedure to construct a 90% family confidence interval ($\alpha = 0.1$). We could use "*compute t=idf.t(1- (alpha/(2*g)),6)*", where $g=2$, from a *Syntax Editor* to find $t=2.447$ and perform the calculations as shown on text page 855. Alternatively, we can use the *GLM* procedure as shown in Insert 19.1 and use the *Options* specification to request estimated marginal means for the *height*width* interaction. SPSS will print (output not shown) the estimated marginal means for each of the six cells and also the 95% (by default) confidence intervals. However, these confidence intervals are not adjusted using a *Bonferroni* approach. That is, each interval essentially assumes that there is $g=1$ group for which the confidence interval is being constructed. Thus, requesting *GLM* estimated marginal means and confidence intervals with $\alpha = 0.1$ will not match the intervals on text page 855, which are based on $g=2$. SPSS does not allow us to specify $g=2$ in the calculation of the interval, but we can still produce the intervals shown on text page 855 by specifying $\alpha = 0.1/2 = 0.05$ (✔ *GLM* ✔ Options - Significance Level $= 0.05$). Results are shown in SPSS Output 19.7 and are consistent with text page 855.

SPSS Output 19.7

HEIGHT * WIDTH

Dependent Variable: Y

HEIGHT	WIDTH	Mean	Std. Error	95% Confidence Interval	
				Lower Bound	Upper Bound
1	1	45.000	2.273	39.438	50.562
	2	43.000	2.273	37.438	48.562
2	1	65.000	2.273	59.438	70.562
	2	69.000	2.273	63.438	74.562
3	1	40.000	2.273	34.438	45.562
	2	44.000	2.273	38.438	49.562

Analysis of Factor Effect when Interactions are Important

On text page 856, a researcher at a junior college studied the effect of teaching method (Abstract versus Standard) and student's quantitative ability (Excellent vs Good vs Moderate) on the acquisition of mathematical knowledge. The data file for this example is not available, so we will present the syntax only for analyzing the Mathematics Learning Example. We let *Y* represent the response variable and *method* and *ability* represent the two independent variables. We begin by using *GLM* and the *Plot* option to produce Figures 19.13 (a) and (b), text page 859.

On text page 859, the authors investigated analyzing the response in terms of the logarithmic and square root transformations. To investigate the square root transformation, we compute a new variable named *ysqrt* (Insert 19.3), which is the square root of *Y*, the response variable [*compute ysqrt=sqrt*(y).], and repeat the preceding *GLM* using *ysqrt* as the response variable. To investigate the logarithmic transformation, we create another variable arbitrarily named *ylog10* [*compute ylog10 = LG10*(*y*)], which is the base 10 logarithm of *Y* and then repeat the preceding *GLM* using *ylog10* as the response variable.

INSERT 19.3	INSERT 19.3 continued
✔ Analyze ✔ General Linear Model ✔ Univariate ✔ Y ✔ ► (to the Dependent box) ✔ *method ability* ✔ ► (to the Fixed Effects box) * Request Figures 19.13 (a) and (b). ✔ Plots ✔ *ability* ✔ ► (to the Horizontal axis box) ✔ *method* ✔ ► (to the Separate Lines box) ✔ Add ✔ *method* ✔ ► (to the Horizontal axis box)	✔ *ability* ✔ ► (to the Separate Lines box) ✔ Add ✔ Continue ✔ OK * Square root transformation of Y. ✔ File ✔ New ✔ Syntax compute ysqrt=sqrt(y). exe. ✔ Run ✔ All * Repeat above GLM model except replace. * Y with *ysqrt* as the dependent variable.

The researcher next wished to investigate the nature of the interaction effects shown in Figure 19.13, text page 859. Specifically, the researcher wished to estimate the difference between the learning means of the two teaching methods separately for each of the three levels of quantitative ability. We use a *Bonferroni* multiple comparison procedure with a 95% confidence coefficient for this. In Insert 19.4 we specify a *GLM* model with *Y* as the dependent variable and *method* and *ability* as two fixed factors. In SPSS the default specification of the model is a full factorial model that includes all main effects and all interactions for the specified factors. We request estimated marginal means for the *model*ability* interaction, and then Paste the syntax into a *Syntax Editor*. We then add "*compare (method)*" to the */EMMEANS* line of the pasted syntax so that the edited line appears as shown in Insert 19.4 – Edited, Pasted Syntax. Execution of this syntax results in a *Pairwise Comparison* table (not shown) that compares the abstract method of instruction to the standard method of instruction separately at each of the three levels of *ability*. We could have added "*compare (method) adj(bonferroni)*" to the */EMMEANS* line but this would result in *Bonferroni* adjusted confidence intervals for differences between the abstract and standard *method* within each level of *ability*. *Method* has 2 levels (abstract and standard) within each level of *ability* so this specification for a *Bonferroni* adjustment would have no effect. Additionally, the family of confidence intervals given on text page 860 is for differences in *method* of instruction for each of the 3 levels of *ability*, not for difference between *ability* levels for each level of *method*. To produce the *Bonferroni* adjusted confidence intervals for differences in *method* of instruction for each of the 3 levels of *ability*, we specified $\alpha = 0.05 / 3 = .016666$ in Insert 19.4. This produces simultaneous 95 percent confidence intervals for the family of three differences in *method* of instruction.

INSERT 19.4	INSERT 19.4 continued

✔ Analyze
✔ General Linear Model
✔ Univariate
✔ Y
✔ ▶(to the Dependent box)
✔ *method ability*
✔ ▶(to the Fixed Effects box)
✔ Options
✔ *method*ability*
✔ ▶(to the Display Means box)
* Type ".016666" in Significance Level.
✔ Continue
✔ Paste
	* Edited, Pasted syntax.
	UNIANOVA
	  y BY method ability
	  /METHOD = SSTYPE(3)
	  /INTERCEPT = INCLUDE
	  /EMMEANS = TABLES(method*ability) compare (method)
	  /CRITERIA = ALPHA(.016666)
	  /DESIGN = method ability method*ability.
	✔ Run
	✔ All

Testing Custom Hypotheses and Estimating Custom Functions (text page 860).

In this section, we further illustrate use of the *lmatrix* statements (introduced in Chapter 15 and also discussed in Chapter 17 of this manual) to test custom hypotheses about the means and estimate custom functions of the means. We choose applications from the hypothetical Mathematics Learning Example.

First, suppose that *ability* is the <u>only independent variable</u> in our model and that we are interested in comparing students with excellent quantitative ability (*ability*=1) to students with moderate quantitative ability (*ability*=3). There are three means for the three levels of *ability* (μ_1, μ_2, μ_3). We can express the null hypothesis for this comparison as

$$H_0 : \mu_1 - \mu_3 = 0$$

If we let $c_1 = 1$, $c_2 = 0$, $c_3 = -1$ then

$$L = (1)(\mu_1) + (0)(\mu_2) + (-1)(\mu_3)$$

The corresponding *lmatrix* statement to test this hypothesis ($H_0 : \mu_1 - \mu_3 = 0$) is

/lmatrix "Ability 1 - Ability 3=0" ability 1 0 –1.

If we wished to compare the mean of students with excellent *ability* level (*ability*=1) to the average of the means of the students at *ability* levels 2 and 3, then:

$$H_0 : \mu_1 - \frac{\mu_2 + \mu_3}{2} = 0$$

If we let $c_1 = 1$, $c_2 = -0.5$, $c_3 = -0.5$ then

$$L = (1)(\mu_1) + (-0.5)(\mu_2) + (-0.5)(\mu_3)$$

The corresponding *lmatrix* statement becomes

/lmatrix "Ability 1 – 0.5(Ability 2 & 3)" ability 1 –0.5 –0.5.

Now suppose that the model contains <u>both</u> *method* and *ability*, and the interaction between *method* and *ability*. There are now six "population" means associated with the combinations of levels of *method* and *ability* and we denote these cell means as follows:

	ability=1	*ability*=2	*ability*=3
method=1	μ_{11}	μ_{12}	μ_{13}
method=2	μ_{21}	μ_{22}	μ_{23}

Again, assume that we are interested in comparing students with excellent quantitative ability (*ability*=1) to students with moderate quantitative ability (*ability*=3). SPSS requires that we specify contrast coefficients for each factor (unless the coefficients are zero) and interaction in the model. Thus, in the present example, we must specify coefficients for *ability* and the *method**ability* interaction. (We will see that the coefficients for *method* are zero.) Given that there are 6 population means, we can state the hypothesis as

$$H_0 : (\mu_{11} + \mu_{21}) - (\mu_{13} + \mu_{23}) = 0$$

or

$$H_0 : (1)\mu_{11} + (0)\mu_{12} + (-1)\mu_{13} + (1)\mu_{21} + (0)\mu_{22} + (-1)\mu_{23} = 0$$

We can rewrite the terms as follows and then sum the coefficients by "rows" and "columns" to get marginal coefficients for *method* and *ability* as shown:

method coefficients

$$1\mu_{11} + 0\mu_{12} - 1\mu_{13} \qquad (1 + 0 - 1 = 0)$$

$$1\mu_{21} + 0\mu_{22} - 1\mu_{23} \qquad (1 + 0 - 1 = 0)$$

ability coefficients   2   0   –2

Thus, our *method* coefficients are 0 0, our *ability* coefficients are 2 0 -2, and our *method*ability* coefficients are 1 0 –1 1 0 –1. The *lmatrix* statement for comparing the mean where *ability*=1 to the mean where *ability*=3 when the model contains both *method* and *ability*, and the *method*ability* interaction becomes:

/*lmatrix* "*Ability* 1 - *Ability* 3=0"
ability 2 0 –2
*method*ability* 1 0 –1 1 0 –1.

When specifying coefficients for one factor effect and one interaction effect, the sum of positive and negative coefficients for the single factor must both equal the sum of positive and negative coefficients for the interaction. This is insured if we add the interaction row and column coefficients to obtain the factor coefficients.

Finally, on text page 860 the authors wish to test the difference in learning between the standard and abstract methods for students with moderate quantitative ability (*ability*=3) versus students with good quantitative ability (*ability*=2). This is an interaction contrast between *method* and two levels of *ability*. They estimate the single contrast:

$$L = (\mu_{23} - \mu_{13}) - (\mu_{22} - \mu_{12})$$

which can be rewritten as:

$$L = \mu_{23} - \mu_{13} - \mu_{22} + \mu_{12}$$

We can rewrite the terms as:

$$0\mu_{11} + 1\mu_{12} - 1\mu_{13}$$

$$0\mu_{21} - 1\mu_{22} + 1\mu_{23}$$

Note that interaction contrasts require only coefficients for the interaction cells; coefficients for main effects are not required. This leads to a set of contrasts in the following *lmatrix* statement.

/*lmatrix* "(M2A3-M1A3)-(M2A2-M1A2)=0"
*ability*method* 0 1 –1 0 –1 1.

Lmatrix statements are not available via dialog windows. Thus, to test the hypothesis $[L = (\mu_{23} - \mu_{13}) - (\mu_{22} - \mu_{12})]$, we use the *GLM - Univariate* dialog window as shown in Insert 19.5. However, we paste the syntax into a *Syntax Editor*. We then add the *lmatrix* statement to the syntax as shown in the *Pasted, Edited Syntax* section of Insert 19.5.

INSERT 19.5	INSERT 19.5 continued
✔ Analyze	* Edited, Pasted syntax.
✔ General Linear Model	UNIANOVA
✔ Univariate	y BY method ability
✔ Y	/METHOD = SSTYPE(3)
✔ ▶(to the Dependent box)	/INTERCEPT = INCLUDE
✔ *method ability*	/CRITERIA = ALPHA(.05)
✔ ▶(to the Fixed Effects box)	/DESIGN = method ability method*ability
✔ Paste	/lmatrix " (M2A3-M1A3)-(M2A2+M1A2)=0"
	ability*method 0 1 −1 0 −1 1.
	✔ Run
	✔ All

Chapter 20 SPSS®

Two-Factor Studies – One Case per Cell

In Chapter 19, the authors discuss two-factor studies in which there are an equal number ($n > 1$) of subjects at each combination of levels of the two factors. They refer to each combination of levels of the two factors as a "cell." In Chapter 20, they consider two factor studies in which there is one subject per cell for every cell. When there is only one subject per cell, we cannot estimate the error variance σ^2 and, therefore, we must use Tukey's test for additivity to test for interaction between the two factors.

Insurance Premium Example

Data File: ch20ta02.txt

An insurance analyst studied insurance premiums of six cities of different sizes and from two different regions of the state. There was only one observation per cell for each of the six combinations of the two factors: city size (3 levels) and region (2 levels). After opening the Insurance Premium Example [Table 20.2(a), text page 882] and renaming the variables Y, *city*, and *region*, the *Data Editor* should look like SPSS Output 20.1.

SPSS Output 20.1

	y	city	region	var
1	140.00	1	1	
2	100.00	1	2	
3	210.00	2	1	
4	180.00	2	2	
5	220.00	3	1	
6	200.00	3	2	

In Insert 20.1, we begin the analysis by producing text Figure 20.1, text page 883. (Output not shown.) As noted by the authors, the lines are only moderately lacking in parallelism and there could be a slight interaction between region and city size. Accordingly, the analyst calculated the *Tukey* test for interaction, referred to as the *Tukey Test for Additivity*, on text page 886. This test is not readily available in SPSS but may be obtained by the syntax shown in Insert 20.2. With the Insurance Premium data file open as shown in SPSS Output 20.1, we use the *aggregate* function to find $\bar{Y}$ values for each level of *city* ($\bar{Y}_i$) and *region* ($\bar{Y}_{.j}$) and the overall mean $\bar{Y}$. We then find *SSA*, *SSB*, *SSAB*[*], and *SS*rem[*] by equations on text page 886-887 and finally find F^* by text equation 20.11. Results are shown in SPSS Output 20.2 and are consistent with calculations presented on text page 888. Since $F^* = 6.75$ is less than the specified $F(.90; 1, 1)=39.9$, the authors concluded that there was no significant interaction between *city* and *region* and proceeded with the no-interaction model (equation 20.1, text page 881).

INSERT 20.1	INSERT 20.1 continued
✔ Graphs ✔ Line ✔ Multiple ✔ Summaries for groups of cases ✔ Define ✔ Other summary function ✔ Y	✔ ▶(to the Variable box) ✔ region ✔ ▶(to the Category axis box) ✔ city ✔ ▶(to the Define Lines by box) ✔ OK

INSERT 20.2	INSERT 20.2
✔ File ✔ New ✔ Syntax compute constant=1. SORT CASES by city. AGGREGATE outfile='city.sav' / presorted / break=city /citymean=mean(y). MATCH FILES file=* / table='city.sav' / by city. SORT CASES by region . AGGREGATE outfile='region.sav' / presorted / break=region /regmean=mean(y). MATCH FILES file=* / table='region.sav' / by region. AGGREGATE outfile='all.sav' / presorted / break=constant /ymean=mean(y). MATCH FILES file=* / table='all.sav' / by constant. compute t=(y-ymean)**2. compute a=(citymean-ymean)**2. compute b=(regmean-ymean)**2. compute c=(citymean-ymean)*(regmean-ymean)*y.	aggregate /outfile='temp4.sav' /break=constant /sst=sum(t) /ssa=sum(a) /ssb=sum(b) /x=sum(c). match files /file=* /table='temp4.sav' /by constant. compute dfa=2. compute dfb=3. compute ssab=(x**2)/((ssa/dfa)*(ssb/dfb)). compute ssrem=sst-ssa-ssb-ssab. compute f=(ssab/1)/(ssrem/(dfa*dfb-dfa-dfb)). SUMMARIZE /Title='Tukey Test for Additivity' /TABLES=ssa ssb sst ssab ssrem f /FORMAT=VALIDLIST NOCASENUM TOTAL LIMIT=1 /MISSING=VARIABLE /CELLS=COUNT . exe. ✔ Run ✔ All

SPSS Output 20.2

Tukey Test for Additivity[a]

		SSA	SSB	SST	SSAB	SSREM	F
1		9300.00	1350.00	10750.00	87.10	12.90	6.75
Total	N	1	1	1	1	1	1

a. Limited to first 1 cases.

575

In Insert 20.3, we produce the no-interaction model using the *GLM* procedure. Since SPSS will produce an interaction term by default when two or more factors are in the model, we use the *Model* option to specify that the model will contain main-effects only (no-interaction term). Results shown in SPSS Output 20.3 are consistent with Table 20.2 (b), text page 882 and text pages 883-884, and indicate that there are significant main-effects for *city* [$F(2, 2)=93.0$, $p=0.011$] and for *region* [$F(1, 2)=27.0$, $p=0.035$].

INSERT 20.3	INSERT 20.3 continued
✔ Analyze ✔ General Linear Model ✔ Univariate ✔ Y ✔ ▶(to the Dependent box) ✔ city ✔ ▶(to the Fixed Factor box) ✔ region ✔ ▶(to the Fixed Factor box)	✔ Model ✔ Custom ✔ ▼ ✔ Main Effects ✔ city(F) ✔ region(F) ✔ ▶(under Build Terms) ✔ Continue ✔ OK

SPSS Output 20.3

Tests of Between-Subjects Effects

Dependent Variable: Y

Source	Type III Sum of Squares	df	Mean Square	F	Sig.
Corrected Model	10650.000ª	3	3550.000	71.000	.014
Intercept	183750.000	1	183750.000	3675.000	.000
CITY	9300.000	2	4650.000	93.000	.011
REGION	1350.000	1	1350.000	27.000	.035
Error	100.000	2	50.000		
Total	194500.000	6			
Corrected Total	10750.000	5			

a. R Squared = .991 (Adjusted R Squared = .977)

On text page 884, the authors estimate the treatment means by text equation 20.5. In Insert 20.4, we again use the *aggregate* function to find $\overline{Y}$ values for each level of *city* ($\overline{Y}_i$) and *region* ($\overline{Y}_{.j}$) and the overall mean $\overline{Y}$. We then use text equation 20.5 to find *muhat* ($\hat{\mu}_{ij}$). Execution of Insert 20.4 will result in the *Data Editor* as shown in SPSS Output 20.4. Finally, on text page 885 the authors parameterize an effects model and we can use the estimates obtained on fitting this model to find the confidence intervals for the treatment means. In Insert 20.5 we parameterize the model as shown on text page 885 and in the regression procedure specify that predicted values and their prediction intervals be saved to the *Data Editor*. Execution of Insert 20.5 (with the *Data Editor* as shown in SPSS Output 20.1) results in SPSS Output 20.5. The 95% upper and lower confidence limits are saved as *lmci_1* and *umci_1*, respectively. Notice that *muhat* calculated in Insert 20.4 is equal to the predicted value (*pre_1*) saved by the syntax in Insert 20.5.

	INSERT 20.4	INSERT 20.4

INSERT 20.4 (left column)

```
✔ File
✔ New
✔ Syntax
compute constant=1.
SORT CASES BY
  city (A) .
aggregate
 /outfile='city.sav'
 /break=city
 /citymean=mean(y).
match files /file=*
 /table='city.sav'
 /by city.
SORT CASES BY
  region (A) .
aggregate
 /outfile='region.sav'
 /break=region
 /regmean=mean(y).
```

INSERT 20.4

```
match files /file=*
 /table='region.sav'
 /by region.
aggregate
 /outfile='all.sav'
 /break=constant
 /ymean=mean(y).
match files /file=*
 /table='all.sav'
 /by constant
 /drop=constant.
compute muhat=citymean+regmean-ymean.
exe.
✔ Run
✔ All
```

SPSS Output 20.4

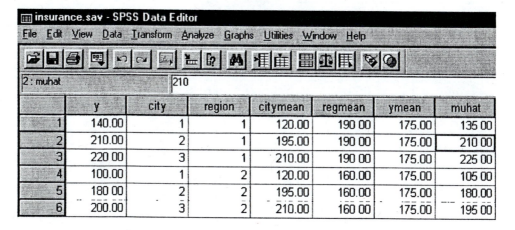

insurance.sav - SPSS Data Editor

File Edit View Data Transform Analyze Graphs Utilities Window Help

2 : muhat   210

	y	city	region	citymean	regmean	ymean	muhat
1	140.00	1	1	120.00	190 00	175.00	135 00
2	210.00	2	1	195.00	190 00	175.00	210 00
3	220 00	3	1	210.00	190 00	175.00	225 00
4	100.00	1	2	120.00	160.00	175.00	105 00
5	180 00	2	2	195.00	160.00	175.00	180.00
6	200.00	3	2	210.00	160 00	175.00	195 00

INSERT 20.5	INSERT 20.5 continued

✔ File
✔ New
✔ Syntax
if (city = 1) x1 = 1.
if (city = 2) x1 = 0.
if (city = 3) x1 = -1.
if (city = 1) x2 = 0.
if (city = 2) x2 = 1.
if (city = 3) x2 = -1.
if (region = 1) x3 = 1.
if (region = 2) x3 = -1.
exe.
	✔ Run
	✔ All
	✔ Analyze
	✔ Regression
	✔ Linear
	✔ Y
	✔ ▶ (to the Dependent box)
	✔ *x1 x2 x3*
	✔ ▶ (to the Independent box)
	✔ Save
	✔ Unstandardized (Predicted Values)
	✔ Mean (Prediction Intervals)
	✔ Continue
	✔ OK

SPSS Output 20.5

insurance.sav - SPSS Data Editor

File Edit View Data Transform Analyze Graphs Utilities Window Help

1 : muhat   135

	muhat	x1	x2	x3	pre_1	lmci_1	umci_1
1	135.00	1.00	.00	1.00	135.00	110.16	159.84
2	210.00	.00	1.00	1.00	210.00	185.16	234.84
3	225.00	-1.00	-1.00	1.00	225.00	200.16	249.84
4	105.00	1.00	.00	-1.00	105.00	80.16	129.84
5	180.00	.00	1.00	-1.00	180.00	155.16	204.84
6	195.00	-1.00	-1.00	-1.00	195.00	170.16	219.84

Chapter 21 SPSS®

Randomized Complete Block Designs

The authors present randomized block designs in Chapter 21. They state that "A randomized block design is a restricted randomization design in which the experimental units are first sorted into homogeneous groups, called *blocks*, and the treatments are then assigned at random within the blocks." With effective blocking, we can obtain a more precise estimate of error variance and, hence, more efficient tests of hypotheses about the treatment factor which is usually our primary goal. The simplest randomized block designs have one treatment factor (with multiple levels) in addition to the blocking factor and are thus called two factor studies.

When each level of treatment is included exactly once in each block, we call the design a *randomized complete block design*. The randomized complete block design is a two-factor study with one subject per cell. We usually assume there is no block by treatment interaction in the analysis of data collected using a randomized complete block design. If we include n > 1 subjects per cell in a randomized block design, we call the design a *generalized randomized block design*. We can test for block by treatment interaction in generalized randomized block designs.

Risk Premium Example

Data File: ch21ta01.txt

On text page 895, investigators studied the relationship between three methods of quantifying risk premium and subsequent confidence in the method. Fifteen executives were studied with age of executive used as a blocking variable. Five blocks (age groups) were used; block 1 comprised the three oldest executives, block 2 comprised the next three oldest executives, and so on. The three methods were randomly assigned to the three executives separately within each block. Thus, the design is a *randomized complete block design*. After opening the Risk Premium Example (Table 21.1, text page 896) and renaming the variables *Y*, *block*, and *method*, the first 5 lines of the *Data Editor* should look like SPSS Output 21.1.

SPSS Output 21.1

	y	block	method	var
1	1.0	1	1	
2	5.0	1	2	
3	8.0	1	3	
4	2.0	2	1	
5	8.0	2	2	

How to Randomize

The 15 executives were grouped into five blocks according to age. Within each block, we assigned a "tag" number (1,2,3) to each executive so that none of the executives within a block have the same tag number. This step of the randomization process was done manually but could be automated, a step that would be especially convenient for large samples.

On text page 895, the authors indicate that random permutations are used to assign "treatments" to experimental units within each block. That is, there are six permutations of the three treatment methods. The six permutations are "CWU", "CUW", "WCU", "WUC", "UCW", and "UWC". In Insert 21.1, we first generate a data file with six lines, each with a random number between 0 and 1000 from a uniform distribution. We assign one of the six permutations to each of the six lines, assign a rank to the line based on the value of the random number, and sort the file based on the rank variable (*rrandom*). Each execution of Insert 21.1 will yield different results. Output from one execution is shown in SPSS Output 21.2. The third permutation (WCU) has been assigned to block 1, the fifth permutation (UCW) has been assigned to block 2, and so on. Starting with block 1, the youngest (or oldest) group of three executives, assign method W to the executive numbered 1, method C to the executive numbered 2, and method U to the executive numbered 3. We proceed to block 2, the next youngest (oldest) age group, and assign executive numbered 1 to method U, executive numbered 2 to method C, and method W to the executive numbered 3. We continue in this fashion until the treatment assignment is complete for all age groups. Thus, we will have used random permutations to assign treatments to experimental units within each block. Note that the forth permutation (WUC) was assigned to block 6 and will not be used because the first five will determine the 15 required assignments for the subjects in the 5 blocks used in the study. If the number of executives were 33, for instance, we would assign the 18 youngest (oldest) executives based on the first execution of program and then assign the final 15 executives based on a second execution of the program.

SPSS Output 21.2

	block	order$	perm
1	1	WCU	3
2	2	UCW	5
3	3	UWC	6
4	4	CUW	2
5	5	CWU	1
6	6	WUC	4

INSERT 21.1	INSERT 21.1 continued

* Create 6 lines each with a random.
* number between 0 and 1000.
✓ File
✓ New
✓ Syntax
INPUT PROGRAM.
LOOP perm = 1 to 6.
compute #rannum=trunc(uniform(1000)) .
compute random=#rannum.
END CASE.
END LOOP.
END FILE.
END INPUT PROGRAM.
* Assign permutations to the six lines.
string order$(a3).
if (perm=1) order$="CWU".
if (perm=2) order$="CUW".
	if (perm=3) order$="WCU".
	if (perm=4) order$="WUC".
	if (perm=5) order$="UCW".
	if (perm=6) order$="UWC".
	* Find rank based on the value of the random
	number.
	rank variables=random/print=no.
	sort cases rrandom.
	Format rrandom(f2.0).
	format random (f3.0).
	format perm (f1.0).
	xsave outfile= 'temp.sav'/keep rrandom order$
	perm
	/rename = (rrandom=block).
	Exe.
	Get file = 'temp.sav'.
	exe.
	✓ Run
	✓ All

In Insert 21.2, we use *GLM* to produce the ANOVA table shown in Table 21.3, text page 899. Note that we enter *block* and *method* as fixed factors and then specify a model that contains main effects only. For subsequent use, we request pairwise comparisons using the *Tukey* procedure. (Output not shown.) The syntax to calculate the *Tukey Test for Additivity* (text page 903) was presented in Chapter 20 of this manual and is generalizable to the current problem. We also present syntax to produce the graphs as shown in text Figure 21.5 (a) and (b).

Analysis of Treatment Effects: On text page 905, the researcher used the *Tukey* procedure to obtain all pairwise comparisons with a 95% family confidence coefficient. This syntax was presented in Insert 21.2 above. Partial results are shown in SPSS Output 21.3 and are consistent with the results presented on text page 905. For completeness, in Insert 21.3 we show the syntax for using each of the procedures given on text page 904, equations 21.9 a – d.

SPSS Output 21.3

Multiple Comparisons

Dependent Variable: Y

Tukey HSD

(I) METHOD	(J) METHOD	Mean Difference (I-J)	Std. Error	Sig.	95% Confidence Interval Lower Bound	95% Confidence Interval Upper Bound
1	2	-4.200*	1.0924	.012	-7.321	-1.079
	3	-9.000*	1.0924	.000	-12.121	-5.879
2	1	4.200*	1.0924	.012	1.079	7.321
	3	-4.800*	1.0924	.006	-7.921	-1.679
3	1	9.000*	1.0924	.000	5.879	12.121
	2	4.800*	1.0924	.006	1.679	7.921

Based on observed means.

*. The mean difference is significant at the .05 level.

581

INSERT 21.2	INSERT 21.2
✔ Analyze ✔ General Linear Model ✔ Univariate ✔ Y ✔ ► (to the Dependent box) ✔ *block method* ✔ ► (to the Fixed Factor box) ✔ Model ✔ Custom ✔ ▼ ✔ Main Effects ✔ *block*(F) ✔ *method*(F) ✔ ► (under Build Terms) ✔ Continue ✔ Save ✔ Unstandardized – Residuals ✔ Unstandardized – Predicted Values ✔ Continue ✔ Post Hoc ✔ *method* ✔ ► (to Post Hoc test for: box) ✔ Tukey ✔ Continue ✔ OK	* Produce text Figure 21.3 using Risk Premium. ✔ Graphs ✔ Scatter ✔ Simple ✔ Define ✔ *Block* ✔ ► (to the Y axis) ✔ *res_1* ✔ ► (to the X axis) ✔ OK * Produce text Figure 21.5(a) using Risk Premium. ✔ Graphs ✔ Scatter ✔ Simple ✔ Define ✔ *res_1* ✔ ► (to the Y axis) ✔ *pre_1* ✔ ► (to the X axis) ✔ OK * Produce text Figure 21.5(b) using Risk Premium. ✔ Graphs ✔ Q-Q ✔ *res_1* ✔ ► (to Variables box) ✔ OK * Double click on chart to open Chart Editor. * for reversing axes to match text Figure 21.5(b).

INSERT 27.3

```
compute n=5.
compute r=3.
compute alpha=.05.
compute g=3.
exe.
* Single comparison - equation 27.9a.
compute t=IDF.T((1-(alpha/2)), (n-1)*(r-1)).
exe.
* Tukey comparison -  equation 27.9b.
compute T = (1/sqrt(2))*IDF.SRANGE((1-alpha),r,((n-1)*(r-1))) .
exe.
* Scheffe procedure - equation 27.9c.
compute S2=(r-1)*IDF.F((1-alpha),(r-1),(n-1)*(r-1)).
exe.
* Bonferroni procedure - equation 27.9d.
compute B=IDF.T((1-(alpha/2*g)), (n-1)*(r-1)).
exe.
```

Generalized Randomized Block Design: In the previous *randomized complete block design*, we assumed there was no *block* by *method* interaction and executed a model that included only main effects. However, use of the additive model (main effects only) will decrease the power of the test for treatment effects if the block effect is fixed and there is interaction between the block and treatment effects. The *generalized randomized block design* allows for investigation of the block by treatment interaction even when the block effects are fixed as in the example presented in Table 21.4, text page 907. For this analysis, we simply use *GLM* and enter the variables *distraction* and *gender* as fixed factors. Remember that the default model in *GLM* is full factorial, i.e., all main effects and all possible interactions. Results of this analysis will be consistent with Figure 21.6, text page 908.

Note that text Figure 21.6 displays Type I sum of squares. (Sums of square Types I, II, III, and IV are discussed in Chapter 15 of this manual). Type I and Type III sums of squares yield identical results when the design is balanced (cells have equal sample sizes) as in the present example. However, Type III sum of squares should be used when the design is unbalanced.

Chapter 22 SPSS®

Analysis of Covariance

We learned in previous chapters that we may reduce the error variance by using randomized block designs. The impact is narrower confidence intervals and greater sensitivity in tests of hypotheses relevant to the factor(s) of primary interest. In this chapter, the authors present the *analysis of covariance* as an additional method for reducing error variance. A covariance model includes the features of an ANOVA model and also includes one or more quantitative variables as "covariates." The idea is to account for the variability in the response variable that can be attributed to a linear regression type of relationship with the covariate(s). Once this variability has been quantified, we can "remove" it from the estimate of error variance; otherwise, it is pooled with the estimate of error variance.

We must exercise caution when we perform an analysis of covariance because the analysis is based on the rather strong assumption of parallelism or constancy of slopes. To see how the assumption works, consider a single factor study with a single covariate. The authors illustrate the models for analysis of covariance in text equations 22.1 – 22.7. The expected response for a specific subject depends not only on the treatment (level of the factor) the subject receives but also the value of the covariate for that subject. The analysis of covariance model specifies separate regression lines all with the same slope (coefficient for the covariate) for the treatments. The difference between the means of any two treatments is the same for all values of the covariate because the regression lines are parallel (they have the same slopes). If the analysis of covariance model is specified as

$$Y_{ij} = \mu_Y + \tau_i + \gamma\left(X_{ij} - \mu_X\right) + \varepsilon_{ij}$$

then $\tau_i - \tau_j$ measures the difference between the response mean with treatment i and the response mean with treatment j for any value of the covariate X. Thus, we can use unbiased estimators of $\tau_i - \tau_j$ to investigate differences between response means for the ith and j^{th} treatments. We can show that the residual mean square is the appropriate estimate of error variance.

Because the assumption of parallelism is so important in the analysis of covariance, it usually is desirable to conduct a formal test of this assumption. An example is given in the text and SPSS syntax for that example is given in the following section.

Single Factor Covariance Analysis

Cracker Promotion Example

Data File: ch22ta01.txt

On text page 926, a company studied the effect of three sales promotions on the number of cases of crackers sold. The number of cases sold in the study period is coded Y, the sales promotion/treatment is arbitrarily coded t, and number of cases sold in the period preceding the study period is coded x. Thus, Y is the response variable, t is a factor, and x is a covariate or concomitant variable. After opening the Cracker Promotion Example (Table 22.1, text page 926) and renaming the variables Y, x, t, and *store*, the first five lines of the *Data Editor* should look like SPSS Output 22.1.

SPSS Output 22.1

To develop the full regression model on text page 926 (equation 22.13), we create indicator variables ($i1$, $i2$) for the treatment variable (t) as shown on text page 926. Additionally, we create a new variable, *x_center*, which is the covariate (x) centered by subtracting the overall mean $\overline{X} = 25$ from the original value of the covariate x. Finally, to subsequently test for parallel slopes, we create two new variables, $i1x$ and $i2x$ where $i1x=i1*x\_center$ and $i2x=i2*x\_center$. (Insert 22.1)

The authors begin the analysis by generating a symbolic scatter plot of Y and X, various residual plots, and the *Correlation Test for Normality* (text pages 927-928). The computational details of the *Correlation Test for Normality* are presented in Chapters 3 and 18 of this manual. The syntax for the various text plots and the *Correlation Test for Normality* is given without comment in Insert 22.1.

The Full Model can now be obtained using the *Regression* procedure to regress Y on *x_center*, $i1$, and $i2$. (Insert 22.1) SPSS Output 22.1 and 22.2 are partial output of the above full model solution and is consistent with Table 22.3, text page 928.

INSERT 22.1	INSERT 22.1 continued

INSERT 22.1

- ✔ File
- ✔ New
- ✔ Syntax

```
if (t =  1) i1 = 1 .
if (t =  3) i1 = -1.
if (t =  2) i1 = 0 .
if (t =  2) i2= 1 .
if (t =  3) i2= -1.
if (t =  1) i2= 0 .
compute x_center=x-25.
compute i1x=i1*x_center.
compute i2x=i2*x_center.
exe .
```

- ✔ Run
- ✔ All

* Text Figure 22.5.
- ✔ Graphs
- ✔ Scatter
- ✔ Simple
- ✔ Define
- ✔ Y
- ✔ ► (to the Y-axis box)
- ✔ x
- ✔ ► (to the X-axis box)
- ✔ t
- ✔ ► (to the Set Markers by box)
- ✔ OK

* Save residuals.
- ✔ Analyze
- ✔ Regression
- ✔ Linear
- ✔ Y
- ✔ ► (to the Dependent box)
- ✔ x_center i1 i2
- ✔ ► (to the Independent box)
- ✔ Save
- ✔ Unstandardized Residuals
- ✔ Continue
- ✔ OK

* Text Figure 22.6 (a).
- ✔ Graphs
- ✔ Scatter
- ✔ Simple
- ✔ Define
- ✔ t
- ✔ ► (to the Y-axis box)
- ✔ res_1
- ✔ ► (to the X-axis box)
- ✔ OK

INSERT 22.1 continued

* Text Figure 22.6 (b).
- ✔ Graphs
- ✔ Q-Q
- ✔ res_1
- ✔ ►
- ✔ OK
* Double click on chart output to open the.
* Chart Editor – reverse the chart axes.

* *Correlation Test for Normality.*
* Residuals must have been saved as in.
* this Insert above.

- ✔ Transform
- ✔ Rank Cases
- ✔ res_1
- ✔ ► (to the Variables box)
- ✔ OK

- ✔ File
- ✔ New
- ✔ Syntax

```
compute ev=sqrt(3.506)*probit((rres_1-.375)/(15+.25)).
exe.
```

- ✔ Run
- ✔ All

- ✔ Analyze
- ✔ Correlate
- ✔ Bivariate
- ✔ ev
- ✔ ►
- ✔ res_1
- ✔ ►
- ✔ OK

* Full Model.
- ✔ Analyze
- ✔ Regression
- ✔ Linear
- ✔ Y
- ✔ ► (to the Dependent box)
- ✔ x_center i1 i2
- ✔ ► (to the Independent box)
- ✔ Statistics
- ✔ Covariance Matrix
- ✔ Continue
- ✔ OK

SPSS Output 22.1

ANOVA[b]

Model		Sum of Squares	df	Mean Square	F	Sig.
1	Regression	607.829	3	202.610	57.781	.000[a]
	Residual	38.571	11	3.506		
	Total	646.400	14			

a. Predictors: (Constant), X_CENTER, I2, I1

b. Dependent Variable: Y

SPSS Output 22.2

Coefficients[a]

Model		Unstandardized Coefficients		Standardized Coefficients		
		B	Std. Error	Beta	t	Sig.
1	(Constant)	33.800	.483		69.908	.000
	X_CENTER	.899	.103	.671	8.759	.000
	I1	6.017	.708	.748	8.496	.000
	I2	.942	.699	.117	1.348	.205

a. Dependent Variable: Y

Test for Treatment Effects

To test treatment effects, we use the reduced model shown in equation 22.15, text page 929. Again, we use the *Regression* procedure with *x_center* as the only independent variable. This yields SPSS Output 22.3, which is consistent with Table 22.4, text page 929. We can now calculate the partial F^* value from SPSS Output 22.1 and 22.3, as shown on text page 929:

$$F^* = \frac{SSE(R) - SSE(F)}{(n_T - 2) - [n_T - (r+1)]} \div \frac{SSE(F)}{n_T - (r+1)}$$

$$F^* = \frac{455.722 - 38.571}{13 - 11} \div \frac{38.571}{11} = 59.5$$

SPSS Output 22.3

ANOVA[b]

Model		Sum of Squares	df	Mean Square	F	Sig.
1	Regression	190.678	1	190.678	5.439	.036[a]
	Residual	455.722	13	35.056		
	Total	646.400	14			

a. Predictors: (Constant), X_CENTER

b. Dependent Variable: Y

Alternatively, we can use the *GLM* procedure to test for treatment effects. (Insert 22.2) We enter *t* as a fixed factor and *x_center* as a covariate. Insert 22.2 results in SPSS Output 22.4; the calculated *F* value for *t* is 59.483 consistent with the *F** value calculated above. This indicates that, controlling for the number of cases sold in the preceding period, there are significant differences in the number of cases of crackers sold among the treatment groups.

INSERT 22.2	INSERT 22.2 continued
✔ Analyze ✔ General Linear Model ✔ Univariate ✔ Y ✔ ▶ (to the Dependent box)	✔ *t* ✔ ▶ (to the Fixed factor box) ✔ *x_center* ✔ ▶ (to the Covariate box) ✔ OK

SPSS Output 22.4

Tests of Between-Subjects Effects

Dependent Variable: Y

Source	Type III Sum of Squares	df	Mean Square	F	Sig.
Corrected Model	607.829[a]	3	202.610	57.781	.000
Intercept	17136.600	1	17136.600	4887.120	.000
X_CENTER	269.029	1	269.029	76.723	.000
T	417.151	2	208.575	59.483	.000
Error	38.571	11	3.506		
Total	17783.000	15			
Corrected Total	646.400	14			

a. R Squared = .940 (Adjusted R Squared = .924)

Using the SPSS *Regression* procedure, yet another solution is to enter *x_center* at block 1, *i1* and *i2* at block 2 and check the *R squared change* box using the *Statistics* option. (Insert 22.3) This maneuver results in an *F change statistic* of 59.483 (SPSS Output 22.5) when *i1* and *i2* are added to a model that previously contained a constant and *x_center*. The interpretation is the same as obtained with the *General Linear Model*.

INSERT 22.3	INSERT 22.3 continued
✔ Analyze ✔ Regression ✔ Linear ✔ *y* ✔ ▶ (to the Dependent box) ✔ *x_center* ✔ ▶ (to the Independent box) ✔ Next	✔ *i1* ✔ ▶ (to the Independent box) ✔ *i2* ✔ ▶ (to the Independent box) ✔ Statistics ✔ R square change ✔ Continue ✔ OK

SPSS Output 22.5

Model Summary

Model	R Square Change	Change Statistics			
		F Change	df1	df2	Sig. F Change
1	.295[a]	5.439	1	13	.036
2	.645[b]	59.483	2	11	.000

a. Predictors: (Constant), X_CENTER

b. Predictors: (Constant), X_CENTER, I2, I1

Estimation of Treatment Effects

To obtain the estimated treatment effects and adjusted estimated treatment effects shown on text page 930 - 932, we use the *GLM* procedure. (Insert 22.4) This procedure results in SPSS Output 22.6 and 22.7. Note that the comparison of $\tau_1 - \tau_2 = 5.075$ presented on text page 930, for instance, is found below in SPSS Output 22.6 along with the Bonferroni adjusted 95 percent confidence interval. Also note that when a covariate is in the model, the *LSD*, *Bonferroni* and *Sidak* methods are the only options available for comparing main effects in SPSS. SPSS Output 22.7 displays the adjusted estimated treatment means reported on text page 932. From SPSS Output 22.6 we see there was a significant difference ($p = 0.005$) in the estimated means of Treatment 1 versus Treatment 2. Also, the adjusted means of Treatment 1 and Treatment 2 were 39.817 and 34.742, respectively. Thus, Treatment 1 resulted in significantly more cracker sales on average than Treatment 2. Differences between means for Treatment 1 versus Treatment 3 and Treatment 2 versus Treatment 3 were also significantly significant.

INSERT 22.4	INSERT 22.4 continued
✔ Analyze ✔ General Linear Model ✔ Univariate ✔ *y* ✔ ► (to the Dependent box) ✔ *t* ✔ ► (to the Fixed Factors box) ✔ *x* ✔ ► (to the Covariate box)	✔ Options ✔ *t* ✔ ► ✔ Compare main effects ✔ ▼ (under confidence interval adjustment) ✔ Bonferroni ✔ Continue ✔ OK

SPSS Output 22.6

Pairwise Comparisons

Dependent Variable: Y

(I) T	(J) T	Mean Difference (I-J)	Std. Error	Sig.[a]	95% Confidence Interval for Difference[a]	
					Lower Bound	Upper Bound
1	2	5.075*	1.229	.005	1.610	8.541
	3	12.977*	1.206	.000	9.577	16.377
2	1	-5.075*	1.229	.005	-8.541	-1.610
	3	7.901*	1.189	.000	4.549	11.254
3	1	-12.977*	1.206	.000	-16.377	-9.577
	2	-7.901*	1.189	.000	-11.254	-4.549

Based on estimated marginal means

*. The mean difference is significant at the .05 level.

a. Adjustment for multiple comparisons: Bonferroni.

SPSS Output 22.7

Estimates

Dependent Variable: Y

T	Mean	Std. Error	95% Confidence Interval	
			Lower Bound	Upper Bound
1	39.817[a]	.858	37.930	41.705
2	34.742[a]	.850	32.872	36.612
3	26.841[a]	.838	24.995	28.686

Adjusted Means

a. Evaluated at covariates appeared in the model: X = 25.00.

Test for Parallel Slopes

The usual ANOVA assumptions apply to Analysis of Covariance, and SPSS solutions for testing these assumptions were presented in Chapter 18 of this manual. An additional assumption of Covariance is that the slopes of regression lines for the different treatments are equal (text page 932). This is referred to in the text as Constancy of Slopes. To obtain the general linear model (equation 22.23, text page 932), we regress Y on x_center, $i1$, $i2$, $i1x$, and $i2x$. (Insert 22.5)

In SPSS Output 22.8 below, we produced text Table 22.5 including the SSE=31.521 and in SPSS Output 22.1 above we have $SSE(R)$=38.571, quantities needed to calculate the F^*=1.01 as shown on text page 933.

590

INSERT 22.5	INSERT 22.5 continued
✔ Analyze ✔ Regression ✔ Linear ✔ y ✔ ▶(to the Dependent box) ✔ x_center ✔ ▶(to the Independent box)	✔ i1 ✔ ▶(to the Independent box) ✔ i2 ✔ ▶(to the Independent box) ✔ i1x ✔ ▶(to the Independent box) ✔ i2x ✔ OK

SPSS Output 22.8

ANOVA[b]

Model		Sum of Squares	df	Mean Square	F	Sig.
1	Regression	614.879	5	122.976	35.113	.000[a]
	Residual	31.521	9	3.502		
	Total	646.400	14			

a. Predictors: (Constant), X, I2X, I1, I2, I1X

b. Dependent Variable: Y

Alternatively, we can use the *GLM* procedure to test for interaction between the covariate and the factor. (Insert 22.6) We create a model that includes a term for interaction between t (factor) and x (covariate). From SPSS Output 22.9, we see that the $t*x$ interaction term has an obtained F value of 1.007. This is the same, within rounding error, of the obtained value ($F*=1.01$) reported on text page 933. Both the *Regression* procedure and *GLM* procedure yield an $F=1.007$, $p=0.403$, a result that suggests the assumption of equal treatment slopes is tenable in this example.

INSERT 22.6	INSERT 22.6 continued
✔ Analyze ✔ General Linear Model ✔ Univariate ✔ Y ✔ ▶(to the Dependent box) ✔ t ✔ ▶(to the Fixed Factors box) ✔ x_center ✔ ▶(to the Covariate box) ✔ Model	✔ Custom ✔ t(F) ✔ ▶ ✔ x_center(C) ✔ ▶ ✔ t(F) ✔ x_center(C) ✔ ▶ ✔ Continue ✔ OK

SPSS Output 22.9

Tests of Between-Subjects Effects

Dependent Variable: Y

Source	Type III Sum of Squares	df	Mean Square	F	Sig.
Corrected Model	614.879[a]	5	122.976	35.113	.000
Intercept	15328.055	1	15328.055	4376.549	.000
T	393.052	2	196.526	56.113	.000
X_CENTER	243.141	1	243.141	69.423	.000
T * X_CENTER	7.050	2	3.525	1.007	.403
Error	31.521	9	3.502		
Total	17783.000	15			
Corrected Total	646.400	14			

a. R Squared = .951 (Adjusted R Squared = .924)

Covariance for Two-Factor Studies and Randomized Complete Block Designs

The authors present a two-factor covariance example. The syntax presented for the previous one-factor covariance study generalizes completely to two-factor studies. Additional syntax for this example will not be presented.

Chapter 23 SPSS®

Two-Factor Studies Unequal Sample Sizes

As stated in Chapter 16 of this manual, the analysis of variance (ANOVA) for a dependent (response) variable of interest is the partitioning of the total sum of squares for the dependent variable into component sums of squares associated with identifiable sources of variation. Once the partitioning is complete, we can use the component sums of squares to test whether variability attributed to some sources is significantly greater than variability attributed to other sources. In two-factor studies, if the sample sizes are equal in all cells (the number of subjects is the same for all combinations of levels of the two factors), the components of the ANOVA decomposition are said to be orthogonal and the sum of the component sums of squares is equal to the corrected total sum of squares. On the other hand, if the sample sizes are unequal, the components are *not* orthogonal and the sum of the component sums of squares is *not* equal to the corrected total sum of squares. The regression approach to ANOVA for two-factor studies with unequal sample sizes is to compute sequential sums of squares for each component (Factor 1, Factor 2, and Factor 1 by Factor 2 interaction) as if all the model effects for each component in turn are the last to be added to the regression model. This procedure produces respective component sum of squares for Factor 1, Factor 2, and Factor 1 by Factor 2 interaction that are adjusted in a sense for all the other component effects having been entered in the model. The sums of squares relative to this procedure are referred to as the Type III sums of squares. The four types of sums of squares that are available in SPSS *GLM* are discussed in Chapter 15. In SPSS, the *GLM* procedure uses an underlying regression approach and prints analysis of variance tables based on Type III sums of squares. Thus, we can use the *Regression* procedure and write SPSS code to define independent variables directly to produce the ANOVA, but it is easier to use the *GLM* procedure because *GLM* requires less code (See Chapter 15 for additional discussion).

Growth Hormone Example

Data File: ch23ta01.txt

A researcher studied the effect of a child's bone development and gender on the rate of hormone-induced growth (Y). Eighteen children, 3 per factor combination, began the investigation. However, four of the children were unable to complete the study. Thus, data for these four children were not available and the resulting sample sizes for the cells (factor combinations) were unequal. After opening the Growth Hormone Example (Table 23.1, text page 954) and renaming the variables Y, *gender*, *bonedev*, and *rep*, the first 5 lines of the *Data Editor* should look like SPSS Output 23.1.

SPSS Output 23.1

	y	gender	bonedev	rep	var
1	1.40	1	1	1	
2	2.40	1	1	2	
3	2.20	1	1	3	
4	2.10	1	2	1	
5	1.70	1	2	2	

We begin the analysis of the Growth Hormone Example by reproducing Figure 23.1, text page 955. (Insert 23.1 - Output not shown) Results indicate that a child's bone development may be related to hormone-induced growth rate and that there may be interaction between gender and bone development. On text page 953, the authors analyze the regression model to investigate these effects. The regression model was used because of the unequal sample sizes. However, as we discussed in Chapter 15 of this manual, the *GLM* procedure uses a regression approach and prints results based on Type III sums of squares. Thus, the *GLM* procedure provides the analysis of interest when the within cell sample sizes are unequal. We present all solutions in this chapter using the *GLM* procedure.

INSERT 23.1	INSERT 23.1 continued
✔ Analyze ✔ General Linear Model ✔ Univariate ✔ Y ✔ ►(to the Dependent box) ✔ gender bonedev ✔ ►(to the Fixed Factor box) ✔ Plots ✔ bonedev ✔ ►(to the Horizontal box)	✔ gender ✔ ►(to the Separate Lines box) ✔ Continue ✔ Options ✔ bonedev ✔ ►(to the Display Means box) ✔ Compare Main effects ✔ ▼(under Confidence Interval Adjustment) ✔ Bonferroni * Enter ".1" in the Significance Level box. ✔ Continue ✔ OK

To produce ANOVA Table 23.4, text page 959, we use the *GLM* procedure and specify *Y* as the dependent variable and *gender* and *bonedev* as fixed factors. (Insert 23.1) Results are shown in SPSS Output 23.2 and are consistent with text Table 23.4. Neither the *gender* by *bonedev* interaction nor the *gender* main effect was statistically significant. However, there were significant differences among the means for the three levels of *bondev* ($p=0.003$). The authors now investigate the nature of the differences among the levels of *bonedev* by performing pairwise comparisons using the *Tukey* procedure and a 90% family confidence coefficient. For the current problem, we should not use the *Post Hoc* option in SPSS from within the *GLM* procedure to generate pairwise comparisons based on observed factor level means because we have unequal sample sizes. Instead, as shown in Insert 23.1, we use the *Options* option to generate pairwise comparisons based on estimated marginal factor level means. However, the *LSD*, *Bonferroni*, and *Sidak* are the only options available in SPSS for pairwise comparisons between estimated marginal means. Requesting *Bonferroni* for pairwise comparisons of levels of *bonedev* and an overall significance significance level of 0.10 results in SPSS Output 23.3. As noted in the text, the confidence intervals for the *Bonferroni* procedure are wider than those reported on text page 963 for the *Tukey* procedure. However, SPSS Output 23.3 gives the point estimate (Mean Difference) for the difference in *bonedev* levels and the estimated standard deviation (Std. Error) for each pairwise comparison. To calculate the intervals reported on text page 963, we need only to find T, which can be found by executing "*compute T = (1/sqrt(2))*IDF.SRANGE(.9,3,8).*" from a *Syntax Editor*.

SPSS Output 23.2

Tests of Between-Subjects Effects

Dependent Variable: Y

Source	Type III Sum of Squares	df	Mean Square	F	Sig.
Corrected Model	4.474[a]	5	.895	5.507	.017
Intercept	34.680	1	34.680	213.415	.000
GENDER	.120	1	.120	.738	.415
BONEDEV	4.190	2	2.095	12.891	.003
GENDER * BONEDEV	.075	2	.038	.232	.798
Error	1.300	8	.163		
Total	43.560	14			
Corrected Total	5.774	13			

a. R Squared = .775 (Adjusted R Squared = .634)

SPSS Output 23.3

Pairwise Comparisons

Dependent Variable: Y

(I) BONEDEV	(J) BONEDEV	Mean Difference (I-J)	Std. Error	Sig.[a]	90% Confidence Interval for Difference[a]	
					Lower Bound	Upper Bound
1	2	.200	.297	1.000	-.561	.961
	3	1.300*	.297	.007	.539	2.061
2	1	-.200	.297	1.000	-.961	.561
	3	1.100*	.260	.009	.432	1.768
3	1	-1.300*	.297	.007	-2.061	-.539
	2	-1.100*	.260	.009	-1.768	-.432

Based on estimated marginal means

*. The mean difference is significant at the .1 level.

a. Adjustment for multiple comparisons: Bonferroni.

Single Degree Of Freedom Test

On text page 964, the authors wish to determine whether children with mildly depressed bone development experience, on average, a significant increase in growth rate during the study period. Thus, we want to test if the increase in growth rate for children with *bonedev* (level 3) = 0 regardless of the child's gender; i.e., we want to test if the growth rate mean is ≤ 0 for children with level 3 bone development regardless of the child's gender. This is the union of two possibilities: *bonedev* = 3 given *gender* = 1 and *bonedev* = 3 given *gender* = 2. We can express the hypothesis as

$$H_o : 0\mu_{11} + 0\mu_{12} + .5\mu_{13} + 0\mu_{21} + 0\mu_{22} + .5\mu_{23} = 0$$

We can rewrite the terms as shown below and then sum the coefficients for *gender* and for *bonedev*:

	gender coefficients
$0\mu_{11} + 0\mu_{12} + .5\mu_{13}$	$(0 + 0 + .5 = .5)$
$0\mu_{21} + 0\mu_{22} + .5\mu_{23}$	$(0 + 0 + .5 = .5)$

bonedev coefficients $\qquad\overline{\;\;0\;\;}\quad\overline{\;\;0\;\;}\quad\overline{\;\;1\;\;}$

Thus, the *gender* coefficients are .5 .5, the *bonedev* coefficients are 0 0 1, and the *gender*bonedev* coefficients are 0 0 .5 0 0 .5 (the coefficients in H_o:). Finally, since we are comparing one group to zero (as opposed to comparing two groups to each other), we must include a coefficient for the intercept term.

We specify the *GLM* model shown in Insert 23.1 (without the *Plots* and *Options* options) and paste the syntax into a *Syntax Editor*. We edit the syntax to add the *lmatrix* statement as shown in Insert 23.2. Execution of this syntax results in SPSS Output 23.4, which is consistent with text page 964, where $t^* = 4.89$. From SPSS Output 23.4, we obtain $t^* = 4.89$ by *Difference (Estimate - Hypothesized) / Std. Error* = 0.9/0.184 = 4.89. The *p*-value in SPSS Output 23.4 is *Sig* = 0.0012 corresponding to a two-sided test. (To see more precision in the probability level of SPSS Output 23.4, double click on the *Contrast Results* table and then double click on 0.001 while in the SPSS Output Viewer.) We divide this *p*-value by 2 to get the *p*-value for the one-sided test; i.e., $p(t > + 4.89) = 0.0006$.

INSERT 23.2

UNIANOVA
 y BY gender bonedev
 /METHOD = SSTYPE(3)
 /INTERCEPT = INCLUDE
 /CRITERIA = ALPHA(.05)
 /DESIGN = gender bonedev gender*bonedev
 /lmatrix "bonedev level 3 = 0" intercept 1
                                   gender .5 .5
                                   bonedev 0 0 1
                                   gender*bonedev 0 0 .5 0 0 .5.

SPSS Output 23.4

Contrast Results (K Matrix)[a]

Contrast		Dependent Variable Y
L1	Contrast Estimate	.900
	Hypothesized Value	0
	Difference (Estimate - Hypothesized)	.900
	Std. Error	.184
	Sig.	.001
	95% Confidence Interval for Difference Lower Bound	.476
	Upper Bound	1.324

a. Based on the user-specified contrast coefficients (L') matrix:
   bonedev level 3 = 0

Test Results

Dependent Variable: Y

Source	Sum of Squares	df	Mean Square	F	Sig.
Contrast	3.888	1	3.888	23.926	.001
Error	1.300	8	.163		

Empty Cells in Two-Factor Studies

Data File: ch23ta06.txt

Missing Observations in Randomized Complete Block Designs: On text page 968 the authors present a data set that contains 3 treatments and 3 blocks, where the observation for block 1, treatment 1 is missing. After opening ch23ta06.txt and renaming the variables *y*, *block*, and *tx*, the first lines of the *Data Editor* should look like as SPSS Output 23.5.

SPSS Output 23.5

	y	block	tx	var
1	10.0	1	2	
2	9.0	1	3	
3	11.0	2	1	
4	10.0	2	2	
5	7.0	2	3	

Table 23.7 rcbd missing values.sav - SPSS Data Editor

File Edit View Data Transform Analyze Graphs Utilities W

1 : y   10

In Insert 23.3 we specify the *GLM* procedure where *y* is the response variable and *block* and *tx* are fixed factors. We specify a model that includes main effects but does not include interaction effects. We further specify adjusted means and confidence intervals for *tx*. Results (not shown) are consistent with all statistics presented on text page 970.

INSERT 23.3	INSERT 23.3 continued
✔ Analyze ✔ General Linear Model ✔ Univariate ✔ Y ✔ ▶ (to the Dependent box) ✔ block tx ✔ ▶ (to the Fixed Factor box) ✔ Model ✔ Custom ✔ ▼ (under Build Terms)	✔ Main Effects ✔ block ✔ tx ✔ ▶ (under Build Terms) ✔ Continue ✔ Options ✔ tx ✔ ▶ (to the Display Means box) ✔ Compare Main effects ✔ ▼ (under Confidence Interval Adjustment) ✔ LSD ✔ Continue ✔ OK

ANOVA Inferences When Treatment Means Are of Unequal Importance

Tests for Factor Main Effects by Use of Equivalent Regression Models

In the Growth Hormone example (text page 972), the authors indicate that females receive growth hormone treatment twice as often as males and that the 2:1 ratio is consistent across each level of bone development. The authors present a regression formulation to test the effect of bone development while adjusting the analysis for the unequal importance of treatment means. Again, we use the *GLM* procedure to test the null hypothesis, which can be stated by equation 23.37a, text page 972 as:

$$H_0 : \begin{cases} \dfrac{2\mu_{11} + \mu_{21}}{3} - \dfrac{2\mu_{12} + \mu_{22}}{3} = 0 \\[4mm] \dfrac{2\mu_{11} + \mu_{21}}{3} - \dfrac{2\mu_{13} + \mu_{23}}{3} = 0 \end{cases}$$

If we multiply through by 3, the first half of the above can be rewritten as:

$$2\mu_{11} + 1\mu_{21} - 2\mu_{12} - 1\mu_{22} = 0$$

Rearranged, the left side of this equation can be written as:

$$2\mu_{11} - 2\mu_{12} + 0\mu_{13}$$
$$1\mu_{21} - 1\mu_{22} + 0\mu_{23}$$

Thus, the contrast coefficients for *gender*bonedev* are 2 –2 0 1 –1 0, or rearranged:

$$2 \;\text{–}2\; 0$$
$$1 \;\text{–}1\; 0$$

To find the coefficients for *gender*, we sum each of the two rows to find:

$$0 \; 0$$

To find the coefficients for *bonedev*, we sum each of the three columns to find:

$$3 \;\text{–}3\; 0$$

Since both coefficients for *gender* are zeros, we can omit the *gender* specification from the *lmatrix* statement. We specify the *GLM* model shown in Insert 23.1 and paste the syntax into a *Syntax Editor*. We edit the syntax to add the *lmatrix* statement as shown in Insert 23.4 to specify the syntax for the first half of H_0 as shown in lines 1 and 2 of the *lmatrix* statement; i.e.,

    bonedev 3 -3 0
    gender*bonedev 2 -2 0 1 -1 0;

We then repeat the above algorithm to find the contrast coefficients for the second half of H_0, which are *bonedev* 3 0 –3 and *gender*bonedev* 2 0 –2 1 0 –1. We complete the syntax for H_0 in lines 3 and 4 of the *lmatrix* statement; i.e.,

    bonedev 3 0 -3
    gender*bonedev 2 0 -2 1 0 -1.

Since the both halves of H_0 are specified in one contrast statement (separated by a semicolon), the resulting test statistic will be based on a simultaneous test of both halves of H_0. Execution of this syntax results in the SAS Output 23.6, which is consistent with text page 974.

INSERT 23.4

```
UNIANOVA
 y  BY gender bonedev
 /METHOD = SSTYPE(3)
 /INTERCEPT = INCLUDE
 /CRITERIA = ALPHA(.05)
 /DESIGN = gender bonedev gender*bonedev
 /lmatrix "page 972-974 example" bonedev 3 -3 0
                    gender*bonedev 2 -2 0 1 -1 0;
                    bonedev 3 0 -3
                    gender*bonedev 2 0 -2 1 0 -1.
```

SPSS Output 23.6

Test Results

Dependent Variable: Y

Source	Sum of Squares	df	Mean Square	F	Sig.
Contrast	3.454	2	1.727	10.629	.006
Error	1.300	8	.163		

Tests for Factor Effects when Weights are Proportional to Sample Sizes

In the Growth Hormone study, assume that the treatment sample sizes are proportional to the treatment means. We wish to study the relationship between *gender* and the weighted means for the response "change in rate of growth." This is stated on text page 979 as:

$$H_0 : \frac{3}{7}\mu_{11} + \frac{2}{7}\mu_{12} + \frac{2}{7}\mu_{13} = \frac{1}{7}\mu_{21} + \frac{3}{7}\mu_{22} + \frac{3}{7}\mu_{23}$$

and can be rewritten as:

$$H_0 : \frac{3}{7}\mu_{11} + \frac{2}{7}\mu_{12} + \frac{2}{7}\mu_{13} - \frac{1}{7}\mu_{21} - \frac{3}{7}\mu_{22} - \frac{3}{7}\mu_{23} = 0$$

Rearranged, the left side of the equation of the hypothesis can be expressed as:

$$\frac{3}{7}\mu_{11} + \frac{2}{7}\mu_{12} + \frac{2}{7}\mu_{13}$$

$$-\frac{1}{7}\mu_{21} - \frac{3}{7}\mu_{22} - \frac{3}{7}\mu_{23}$$

Multiply through by 7:

$$3\mu_{11} + 2\mu_{12} + 2\mu_{13}$$

Thus, the *gender*bonedev* interaction coefficients are:

$$\begin{matrix} 3 & 2 & 2 \\ -1 & -3 & -3 \end{matrix}$$

To find the coefficients for *gender*, we sum each of the two rows to find:

$$7 \quad -7$$

To find the coefficients for *bonedev*, we sum each of the three columns to find:

$$2 \quad -1 \quad -1$$

Again, we specify the *GLM* model as shown in Insert 23.1 and paste the syntax into a *Syntax Editor*. We edit the syntax to add the *lmatrix* statement as shown in Insert 23.5. Execution of this syntax (output not shown) results in the F^* value shown on text page 979.

INSERT 23.5

```
UNIANOVA
 y  BY gender bonedev
 /METHOD = SSTYPE(3)
 /INTERCEPT = INCLUDE
 /CRITERIA = ALPHA(.05)
 /DESIGN = gender bonedev gender*bonedev
 /lmatrix "text page 979 contrast"
         gender 7 –7
         bonedev 2 –1 –1
         gender*bonedev 3 2 2 –1 –3 –3.
```

Chapter 24 SPSS®

Multifactor Studies

In this chapter, the authors discuss studies with three or more factors. This presentation is a generalization of the discussion for two factor studies. The primary difference between studies with two factors and those with three or more factors is that the additional factors create more main effects and more possibilities for interactions, and ordinarily we must consider these additional effects in the analysis. Consider, for example, a four-factor study with factors denoted by A, B, C, and D. There are four main effects (A, B, C, D), six two factor interactions (AB, AC, AD, BC, BD, CD), four three factor interactions (ABC, ABD, ACD, BCD), and one four factor interaction (ABCD). Unless we have prior knowledge that some of these effects are not present, we typically include all of them in the model and in significance tests associated with the analysis of variance. The analysis can be cumbersome but is relatively straightforward.

Stress Test Example

Data File: ch24ta04.txt

A researcher studied the relationship between exercise tolerance (Y) and gender, body fat, and smoking history. After opening the Stress Test Example (Table 24.4 (a), text page 1004) and renaming the variables Y, *gender*, *fat*, *smoke*, and *rep*, the first 5 lines of the *Data Editor* should look like SPSS Output 24.1.

SPSS Output 24.1

To produce the estimated treatment and factor level means presented in Table 24.4 (b), text page 1004, we use the *Options* option from within the *GLM* dialog window as shown in Insert 24.1. The plots shown in Figure 24.5 (a) and (b), text page 1007, can be generated via the *Plots* option from within a *GLM* dialogue window. To generate Figure 24.6 (a), for example, ✔ Plot while in the *GLM* dialog window, set up the *Profile Plot* window as shown in SPSS Output 24.2, and ✔ Add. Add other plots as needed, ✔ Continue, and ✔ OK. Partial results are shown in SPSS Output 24.3.

INSERT 24.1	INSERT 24.1 continued
✔ Analyze ✔ General Linear Model ✔ Univariate ✔ Y ✔ ►(to the Dependent box) ✔ *gender fat smoke* ✔ ►(to the Fixed Factor box) ✔ Save ✔ Unstandardized Residuals ✔ Continue ✔ Options ✔ *gender*fat*smoke* ✔ ►(to Display Means for box) ✔ Continue ✔ Plots ✔ *fat* ✔ ►(to Horizontal Axis) ✔ *smoke* ✔ ►(to Separate Lines) ✔ *gender* ✔ ►(to Separate Plots) ✔ Continue ✔ OK	* Text Figure 24.6, page 1007. ✔ Graphs ✔ Q-Q ✔ *res_1* ✔ ►(to the Variables box) ✔ OK * Double click on the resulting. * Q-Q plot to open the Chart Editor. * Reverse axes. * Close Chart Editor.

SPSS Output 24.2

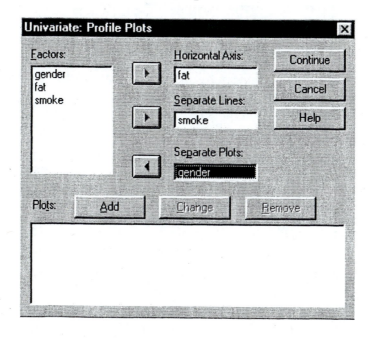

603

Estimated Marginal Means of Y

At GENDER = 1

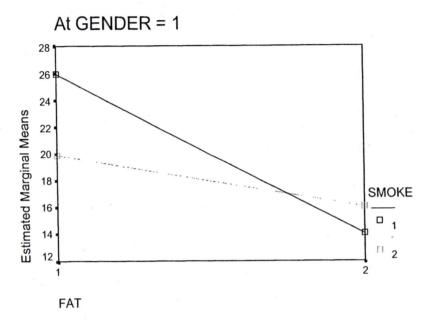

FAT

Residual Analysis: To produce the normal probability plot of residuals and the correlation between the ordered residuals and their expected values under normality, as reported on text page 1006, we first specify the *GLM* procedure where *Y* is the dependent variable and *gender*, *fat*, and *smoke* are Fixed Factors, and request that the unstandardized residual values (*res_1*) be saved to the *Data Editor*. (Insert 24.1) The normal probability plot of residuals (Figure 24.6, text page 1007) can be reproduced using the *Q-Q* Plot procedure as shown in Insert 24.1. The correlation coefficient between the ordered residuals and their expected values under normality can be calculated as discussed in Chapter 18 of this manual.

For the Stress Test Example (text page 1011), there are 3 main effects for factors (*gender*, *fat*, *smoking*), 3 two-factor interactions (*gender* by *fat*, *gender* by *smoking*, *fat* by *smoking*), and 1 three-factor interaction (*gender* by *fat* by *smoking*) for a total of 7 potential tests. The researchers tested for these 7 factor effects and used the *Kimball* inequality (equation 24.25, text page 1010) to control the family level of significance at 0.10. This resulted in a $\alpha_i = 0.015$ being used to determine statistical significance of each of the 7 tests while maintaining the family level of significance at a level that does not exceed 0.10. We use the *GLM* dialog window by ✔ Analyze ✔ General Linear Model ✔ Univariate and enter *Y* as the dependent variable and *gender*, *fat*, and *smoke* as Fixed Factors. This results in SPSS Output 24.4. To test for the three-factor interaction, we note that $F(1, 16)=0.20$, $p=0.66$. For $\alpha_i = 0.015$ we require $F^* > 7.42$ or $p < 0.015$. Thus, the authors concluded that the three-factor interaction is not statistically significant. To test the two-factor interactions, we inspect the *F* values as discussed on text page 1012, or we can use the probability level (Sig.) for each two-factor interaction to determine significance. From SPSS Output 24.4 we find that the probability levels of the *gender*fat* ($p=0.244$) and *gender*smoke* ($p=0.292$) interactions are both greater than the Kimball inequality

$\alpha_i = 0.015$. Thus, we conclude that the *gender*fat* and *gender*smoke* interactions are not statistically significant. The probability level of the *fat*smoke* interaction ($p=0.013$) is less than the required alpha level (0.015), so we conclude that there is significant *fat*smoke* interaction. Main effects for *fat* and *smoke* were not tested because each interacted with another factor. The researchers did test the main effect for *gender*, $F(1, 16)=18.915$, $p < 0.000$, and concluded that *gender* is statistically significant.

SPSS Output 24.4

Tests of Between-Subjects Effects

Dependent Variable: Y

Source	Type III Sum of Squares	df	Mean Square	F	Sig.
Corrected Model	588.583[a]	7	84.083	9.007	.000
Intercept	6353.760	1	6353.760	680.608	.000
GENDER	176.584	1	176.584	18.915	.000
FAT	242.570	1	242.570	25.984	.000
SMOKE	70.384	1	70.384	7.539	.014
GENDER * FAT	13.650	1	13.650	1.462	.244
GENDER * SMOKE	11.070	1	11.070	1.186	.292
FAT * SMOKE	72.454	1	72.454	7.761	.013
GENDER * FAT * SMOKE	1.870	1	1.870	.200	.660
Error	149.367	16	9.335		
Total	7091.710	24			
Corrected Total	737.950	23			

a. R Squared = .798 (Adjusted R Squared = .709)

On text page 1018, the researchers wish to test separately for persons with low and high body fat, the difference in exercise tolerance for light smokers and heavy smokers. These effects are sometimes called the *simple effects* of smoking. This test is available via the *GLM* procedure but only from a *Syntax Editor*. The researchers also wish to test the main effect for *gender* in the same analysis. Thus, there are three planned comparisons, and the researchers wish to use the *Bonferroni* method to construct 3 confidence intervals with a 95% family confidence coefficient.

We set up the *GLM* dialog window as indicated in Insert 24.2 and *Paste* into the *Syntax Editor*. The *Syntax Editor* will look like Insert 24.3 – *Pasted Syntax*. Edit this syntax by adding "*COMPARE* (*smoke*) *ADJ*(*lsd*)" to the */EMMEANS = TABLES*(*fat*smoke*) line so that the edited syntax looks like Insert 24.3 – *Edited Syntax*. This instructs SPSS to compare light and heavy smokers (*smoke*) at each level of *fat*. The */EMMEANS = TABLES*(*gender*) line specifies that the estimated marginal means of the two levels of *gender* be compared. To produce the *Bonferroni* adjusted 95% confidence intervals, we set the alpha level to $\alpha = 0.05/3 = 0.01666$. That is, specifying *ADJ*(*BONFERRONI*) instead of *ADJ*(*lsd*) (*lsd* is equivalent to no adjustment) will not simultaneously adjust for each of the three comparisons. Execution ($\checkmark$ Run $\checkmark$ All) of the edited syntax results in SPSS Output 24.5. This output indicates a 98.3334% [100(1-0.01666)%] confidence interval for each comparison. The family confidence interval is $100[1 - (3)(0.01666)] = 95\%$. Thus, the confidence intervals are consistent with those reported on text page 1018.

On text page 1019, the authors note that regression analysis can be used to analyze multifactor studies with unequal cell sizes. As we discussed in Chapter 15 of this manual, *GLM* uses a regression based approach and thus we can use *GLM* to analyze multifactor studies with unequal cell sizes. However, we must be careful that the analysis of variance and associated contrasts are based on Type III sums of squares.

INSERT 24.2

- ✔ Analyze
- ✔ General Linear Model
- ✔ Univariate
- ✔ Y
- ✔ ► (to the Dependent box)
- ✔ *fat gender smoke*
- ✔ ► (to the Fixed Factor box)
- ✔ Options
- ✔ *fat*smoke*
- ✔ ► (to the Display Means for box)
- ✔ *gender*
- ✔ ► (to the Display Means for box)
- ✔ Compare Main Effects
- ✔ Continue
- ✔ Paste

INSERT 24.3	INSERT 24.3 continued

* PASTED SYNTAX.
 	
UNIANOVA
  y BY gender fat smoke
  /METHOD = SSTYPE(3)
  /INTERCEPT = INCLUDE
  /EMMEANS = TABLES(fat*smoke)
  /EMMEANS = TABLES(gender) COMPARE
    ADJ(LSD)
  /CRITERIA = ALPHA(.05)
  /DESIGN = gender fat smoke gender*fat
    gender*smoke fat*smoke gender*fat*smoke .
	* EDITED SYNTAX.
	
	UNIANOVA
	  y BY gender fat smoke
	  /METHOD = SSTYPE(3)
	  /INTERCEPT = INCLUDE
	  /EMMEANS = TABLES(fat*smoke) COMPARE
	    (smoke) ADJ(lsd)
	  /EMMEANS = TABLES(gender) COMPARE
	    ADJ(LSD)
	  /CRITERIA = ALPHA(.01666)
	  /DESIGN = gender fat smoke gender*fat
	    gender*smoke fat*smoke gender*fat*smoke .

SPSS Output 24.5

Pairwise Comparisons

Dependent Variable: Y

FAT	(I) SMOKE	(J) SMOKE	Mean Difference (I-J)	Std. Error	Sig.[a]	98.3334% Confidence Interval for Difference[a]	
						Lower Bound	Upper Bound
1	1	2	6.900*	1.764	.00	2.185	11.615
	2	1	-6.900*	1.764	.001	-11.615	-2.185
2	1	2	-.050	1.764	.978	-4.765	4.665
	2	1	.050	1.764	.978	-4.665	4.765

Based on estimated marginal means

*. The mean difference is significant at the .016666 level.

a. Adjustment for multiple comparisons: Least Significant Difference (equivalent to no adjustments).

Pairwise Comparisons

Dependent Variable: Y

(I) GENDER	(J) GENDER	Mean Difference (I-J)	Std. Error	Sig.[a]	98.3334% Confidence Interval for Difference[a]	
					Lower Bound	Upper Bound
1	2	5.425*	1.247	.000	2.091	8.759
2	1	-5.425*	1.247	.000	-8.759	-2.091

Based on estimated marginal means

*. The mean difference is significant at the .016666 level.

a. Adjustment for multiple comparisons: Least Significant Difference (equivalent to no adjustments).

Chapter 25 SPSS®

Random and Mixed-Effects Models

In previous discussion of ANOVA models, the authors restricted attention to methods for models in which all factors were fixed effects factors. The ANOVA model in which the factor levels for all factors are considered fixed is called model I or the *fixed effects model*. In model I studies, the factor levels included in the study are the only ones of interest relative to the inferences made in the conclusions. In some studies, the factor levels are a sample from "a larger population of potential factor levels" and the researcher wishes that relevant conclusions pertain to that larger population. The effects for such factors are called random effects and the ANOVA model with all random effects (the levels of every factor included in the model is a sample from some larger population) is referred to as model II or the *random effects model*. The ANOVA model that includes some fixed effects factors and some random effects factors, is called model III, or a *mixed effects model* or simply a *mixed model*.

Example of Single-Factor Study Model II: Factor Effects Random

Apex Enterprises Example

Data File: ch25ta01.txt

Apex Enterprises studied personnel officer evaluation ratings of potential employees. Five of the company's personnel officers were randomly selected, and four job applicants were randomly assigned to each of the five officers. Thus, each officer rated four job applicants. After opening the Apex Enterprises Example (Table 25.1, text page 1036) and renaming the variables *Y*, *officer*, and *candidate*, the first 5 lines of the *Data Editor* should look like SPSS Output 25.1.

SPSS Output 25.1

	y	officer	candidat	var
1	76.0	1	1	
2	65.0	1	2	
3	85.0	1	3	
4	74.0	1	4	
5	59.0	2	1	

We begin the Apex Enterprises analysis by generating ANOVA Table 25.2 (text page 1037) using SPSS' *GLM* procedure. (Insert 25.1) Because the five officers are perceived as a random sample from a very large "population" of officers, we refer to the factor *officer* as a random factor. The twenty candidates also are viewed as a random sample from a very large "population" of candidates, and we use ANOVA model II (all factors are random). The ratings of candidates by each officer are assumed to follow a normal distribution with mean μ_i and variance σ^2 (the variance for each officer is the same), i = 1, 2, ... , ∞ . The variability among the μ_i is denoted σ_μ^2 .

Test of hypothesis $\sigma_\mu^2 = 0$

To carry out the test of the null hypothesis that $\sigma_\mu^2 = 0$, we specify that *officer* is a random factor in the *GLM* procedure. (Insert 25.1) Partial results are shown in SPSS Output 25.2. Consistent with text page 1037, we conclude that the means for officers in the population (of officers) are not all equal, or $\sigma_\mu^2 > 0$, $F(4, 15)=5.389$, $p=0.007$.

INSERT 25.1	INSERT 25.1 continued
✔ Analyze ✔ General Linear Model ✔ Univariate ✔ Y ✔ ▶(to the Dependent box) ✔ officer ✔ ▶(to the **Random** Factor box) ✔ OK ✔ Analyze ✔ Mixed Models ✔ Linear ✔ Continue ✔ Y ✔ ▶(to the Dependent Variable box) ✔ officer ✔ ▶(to the Factor box)	✔ Random ✔ officer ✔ Add ✔ Continue ✔ Statistics ✔ Parameter Estimates ✔ Tests of Covariance Parameters ✔ Covariances of Parameter Estimates * Type "90" in Confidence Interval box. ✔ Continue ✔ EM Means ✔ ovarall ✔ ▶(to the Display Means box) ✔ Continue ✔ OK

Estimation of μ

To construct confidence intervals for functions of σ^2 and σ_μ^2 and carry out additional analyses illustrated in the Apex Enterprises Example, we use SPSS' *Mixed Models* procedure in Insert 25.1. Note that the *Estimation* option can be used to specify the estimation method [*restricted maximum likelihood* (REML) or *maximum likelihood* (ML)] for the covariance parameters. The default method is *REML*.

From text page 1039, we estimate the mean rating (μ.) of all personnel officers with a 90% confidence interval. This is accomplished by the *EM Means* option. That is, we specify that SPSS estimate the overall mean of Y (μ.) and construct 90% confidence limits. From SPSS Output 25.3, *Estimate of Fixed Effects* table, the estimate is $\hat{\mu}.=71.45$. The confidence limits ($61.97 \leq \mu. \leq 80.92$) are consistent with text page 1039.

SPSS Output 25.2
GLM

Tests of Between-Subjects Effects

Dependent Variable: Y

Source		Type III Sum of Squares	df	Mean Square	F	Sig.
Intercept	Hypothesis	102102.050	1	102102.050	258.535	.000
	Error	1579.700	4	394.925[a]		
OFFICER	Hypothesis	1579.700	4	394.925	5.389	.007
	Error	1099.250	15	73.283[b]		

a. MS(OFFICER)

b. MS(Error)

SPSS Output 25.3
Mixed Models

Estimates of Fixed Effects[a]

Parameter	Estimate	Std. Error	df	t	Sig.	90% Confidence Interval	
						Lower Bound	Upper Bound
Intercept	71.45000	4.4436753	4	16.079	.000	61.9767651	80.9232349

a. Dependent Variable: Y.

Estimates of Covariance Parameters[a]

Parameter		Estimate	Std. Error	Wald Z	Sig.	90% Confidence Interval	
						Lower Bound	Upper Bound
Residual		73.28333	26.75929	2.739	.006	40.1939941	133.6131695
OFFICER	Variance	80.41042	70.13333	1.147	.252	19.1540743	337.5696999

a. Dependent Variable: Y.

Covariance Matrix for Estimates of Covariance Parameters[a]

Parameter		Residual	OFFICER Variance
Residual		716.0596	-179.015
OFFICER	Variance	-179.015	4918.684

a. Dependent Variable: Y.

Estimation of $\left(\sigma_{\mu}^2 + \sigma^2\right)$ **and** $\sigma_{\mu}^2 / \left(\sigma_{\mu}^2 + \sigma^2\right)$

From text page 1042, we estimate $\left(\sigma_{\mu}^2 + \sigma^2\right)$ and $\sigma_{\mu}^2 / \left(\sigma_{\mu}^2 + \sigma^2\right)$ with 90% confidence intervals. From text equation 25.23 we find that an estimate of σ^2 is $\hat{\sigma}_{\mu}^2 = s_{\mu}^2 = 80.4$, which was generated by *Mixed Models* procedure in Insert 25.1 and is given in SPSS Output 25.3. An estimate of σ^2 is given by *MSE*=73.28 (equation 25.6, text page 1035) and is shown in SPSS Output 25.2. In Insert 25.2 we use equation 25.18, text page 1040, to calculate confidence intervals for $\left(\sigma_{\mu}^2 + \sigma^2\right)$ and $\sigma_{\mu}^2 / \left(\sigma_{\mu}^2 + \sigma^2\right)$ as shown on text page 1040-1041. The lower and upper limits of $\left(\sigma_{\mu}^2 + \sigma^2\right)$ are stored in variables named *l* and *u*. The corresponding limits for $\sigma_{\mu}^2 / \left(\sigma_{\mu}^2 + \sigma^2\right)$ are stored in *lstar* and *ustar*.

INSERT 25.2	INSERT 25.2 continued
✔ File ✔ Syntax ✔ New * Use text equation 25.18. formats l u lstar ustar (f6.4). compute n=4. compute r=5. compute mstr=394.925. compute mse=73.28333. compute alpha=0.05.	compute fl=idf.f(1-alpha,r-1,r*(n-1)). compute fu=idf.f(alpha,r-1,r*(n-1)). compute l=1/n*((mstr/mse)*(1/fl)-1). compute u=1/n*((mstr/mse)*(1/fu)-1). compute lstar=l/(1+l). compute ustar=u/(1+u). summarize /tables=l u lstar ustar. exe. ✔ Run ✔ All

Estimation of σ^2

On text page 1042, the authors estimate σ^2 with a 90% confidence interval. In Insert 25.1, *Mixed Models* procedure, we requested that the asymptotic covariance matrix of the covariance parameters be displayed and that 90% confidence limits be computed to estimate the parameters. The Wald Z value in the *Estimates of Covariance Parameters* table is the estimate of the parameter divided by its standard error. From the SPSS Output 25.3, *Estimate of Covariance Parameters* table, we see that a 90% confidence interval is calculated to be $40.19 \le \sigma^2 \le 133.61$, which is not consistent the confidence interval by text equation 25.21 reported on text page 1042.

Point and Interval estimation of σ_{μ}^2

The authors next estimate σ_{μ}^2. As noted above, $\hat{\sigma}_{\mu}^2 = s_{\mu}^2 = 80.4$ as shown in SPSS Output 25.3, *Estimates of Covariance Parameter* table, in the row labeled *officer* and column labeled *estimate*. Next, the authors wish to estimate σ_{μ}^2 using a 90% confidence interval. They note that exact interval estimates are not possible, but that several approximations are available. Note that this interval ($19.15 \le \sigma_{\mu}^2 \le 337.56$, SPSS Output 25.3) is not consistent with the interval

$(30.9 \le \sigma_\mu^2 \le 685.2)$ presented on text page 1044. The approximate interval estimate of σ_μ^2 given on text page 1044 can be computed on a hand calculator and is not detailed here.

On text page 1045 the authors present an improved procedure for computing approximate confidence intervals for σ_μ^2 based on a modified large sample (*MLS*) procedure. In Insert 25.3, we use the computational formulas presented in Table 25.3, text page 1045, to estimate a confidence interval for σ_μ^2 based on the *MLS* procedure. The lower and upper limits for σ_μ^2 are given by *cl90l* and *cl90u*, respectively. The lower and upper limits for σ_μ are given by *sqrt90l* and *sqrt90u*, respectively.

INSERT 25.3

```
✔ File
✔ Syntax
✔ New
formats cl90l cl90u sqrt90l sqrt90u (f8.4).
compute n=4.
compute c1=1/n.
compute c2=-1/n.
* ms1=mstr.
compute ms1=394.925.
*ms2=mse.
compute ms2=73.28333.
compute lhat=(ms1-ms2)/n.
compute f1=idf.f(.95,4,9999).
compute f2=idf.f(.95,15,9999).
compute f3=idf.f(.95,9999,4).
compute f4=idf.f(.95,9999,15).
compute f5=idf.f(.95,4,15).
compute f6=idf.f(.95,15,4).
compute g1=1-(1/f1).
compute g2=1-(1/f2).
compute g3=((f5-1)**2-(g1*f5)**2-(f4-1)**2)/f5.
compute g4=f6*(((f6-1)/f6)**2-(((f3-1)/f6)**2)-g2**2).
compute hl=(((g1*c1*ms1)**2)+(((f4-1)*c2*ms2)**2)-g3*c1*c2*ms1*ms2)**.5.
compute hu=(((f3-1)*c1*ms1)**2+((g2*c2*ms2)**2)-(g4*c1*c2*ms1*ms2))**.5.
compute cl90l=lhat-hl.
compute cl90u=lhat+hu.
compute sqrt90l=sqrt(cl90l).
compute sqrt90u=sqrt(cl90u).
summarize
  /tables=cl90l cl90u sqrt90l sqrt90u.
✔ Run
✔ All
```

If candidate rating means for personnel officers are equal for all personnel officers in the population, we expect the variance component for *officer* to be small. We therefore wish to test the null hypothesis that this variance component is equal to 0. From the Wald Z-score and corresponding two-tailed probability (*Sig*=0.252) in SPSS Output 25.3, we would conclude that the variance component for *officer* is not significantly greater than 0. However, the Wald Z can be unreliable when used with small samples, and contrary to this conclusion, results of the *GLM* procedure presented above suggest that the rating means are not equal for all officers in the population, or that $\sigma_\mu^2 > 0$. Additionally, the *intraclass correlation* defined by equation 25.3, page 1034, is $\sigma_\mu^2/\left(\sigma_\mu^2 + \sigma^2\right)$=80.4/80.4+73.28=0.5229. Thus, about 52% of the total variability among individual candidate ratings can be attributed to variability among rating means for officers. If the variance component for *officer* is 0, the variability among candidate ratings is due solely to differences among candidates and none is due to differences among means for officers in the population. Using equations 25.18, text page 1040, we find that the 90% (and 95%, not shown) confidence limits for $\sigma_\mu^2/\left(\sigma_\mu^2 + \sigma^2\right)$ do not include 0. This finding leads us to reject the hypothesis that the proportion $\sigma_\mu^2/\left(\sigma_\mu^2 + \sigma^2\right)$ (of the total variance of candidate ratings accounted for by variance among means for officers) is 0. As alternative tests of the hypothesis that σ_μ^2=0, we used the *Satterthwaite* procedure (text page1043), the *MLS* procedure (text page 1045), and the SPSS approximation shown in SPSS Output 25.2. None of the three sets of 90% confidence limits included 0. Thus, we are led to reject the hypothesis that the variance component for *officer* is 0 by any of the three procedures. (Note that 95% intervals are narrower than their 90% counterparts so that the corresponding three sets of 95% confidence necessarily do not include 0).

In summary, the Wald Z test, which can be unreliable when used with small samples, fails to reject the hypothesis $\sigma_\mu^2 = 0$. However, the *GLM* procedure, the *intraclass correlation coefficient* confidence interval, and the three methods of interval estimation of σ_μ^2 all led to the conclusion that there are significant differences among candidate rating means for officers.

ANOVA Models II and III with Unequal Sample Sizes

Sheffield Food Company Example

Data File: ch25ta12.txt

The Sheffield Food Company studied the reliability of two methods of determining the milk fat content of yogurt. Each method was to be used at 4 laboratories to determine the milk fat content of 12 samples of yogurt that had a known fat content. "Method of measurement" was considered to be a fixed factor with 2 levels: a propriety method of the Sheffield Food Company and a governmental method. "Laboratory" was considered to be a random factor with 4 levels; i.e., 4 laboratories. Due to technical problems, each laboratory was unable to establish a fat content for some samples by use of the governmental method. Thus, an ANOVA *Mixed Model* (model III) for unequal sample sizes is appropriate. After opening the Sheffield Food Company Example (Table 24.12, text page 1071) and renaming the variables *Y* (fat content), *method* (method of measurement), *lab* (laboratory), and *rep*, the first 5 lines of the *Data Editor* should look like SPSS Output 25.4.

SPSS Output 25.4

	y	method	lab	rep	var
1	5.19	1	1	1	
2	5.09	1	1	2	
3	4.09	1	2	1	
4	3.99	1	2	2	
5	3.75	1	2	3	

Sheffield Foods Company.sav - SPSS Data Editor

File Edit View Data Transform Analyze Graphs Utilities Window Help

1 : y   5.19

On text page 1075, the researchers obtained the maximum likelihood estimates of the parameters and standard deviations of the maximum likelihood estimators. In Insert 25.4 we request a mixed model analysis where the method of estimation is maximum likelihood (*ml*) and the parameter estimates are printed. Partial results are shown in SPSS Output 25.5. Fixed effects estimated parameters ($\hat{\mu} = 3.0612$ and $\hat{\alpha}_1 = 1.2657$) and estimated variances of the estimators for the parameters are found in the *Estimates of Fixed Effects* table listed under *Estimate* and *Standard Error*. Estimates of the variance component parameters ($\hat{\sigma}^2 = 0.023$ is listed as *Residual Estimate*, $\hat{\sigma}_\beta^2 = 0.0544$ is listed as *lab Estimate*, and $\hat{\sigma}_{\alpha\beta}^2 = 0.0857$ is listed as *lab*measure Estimate*) and estimated variances of the estimators of these parameters are found in the *Estimates* of *Covariance Parameters* table.

Note that the text shows parameter estimates $\hat{\mu}_{..} = 3.694$ and $\hat{\alpha}_1 = 0.633$. If these were the only effects in the model, the predicted value of *Y* given *method*=1 would be $3.694 + 0.633 = 4.327$ and given *method*=2 would be $3.694 - 0.633 = 3.061$. SPSS shows parameter estimates $\hat{\mu}_{..} = 3.0612$ and $\hat{\alpha}_1 = 1.2657$. The apparent discrepancy is due to a difference in the way the text parameterized the model and SPSS' internal parameterization. However, from the *Estimates of Fixed Effects* table we see that if *method*=1 the predicted value would be $3.0612 + 1.2657 = 4.3269$ and if *method*=2 the predicted value would be $3.0612 + 0 = 3.0612$, which are both consistent with text page 1075.

On text page 1075, the authors first examine the *method*lab* interaction. From SPSS Output 25.4, we see that the Wald z=1.321, p=0.186, which indicates that the *method*lab* interaction effects are not statistically significant. In the absence of bootstrapping, the effect of *method* would then be examined in SPSS Output 25.5. In the *Type III Test of Fixed Effects* table we see that *F*=35.17, p=0.004, indicating a significant difference in fat content when controlling for the random factor, *lab*.

INSERT 25.4	INSERT 25.4 continued
✔ Analyze ✔ Mixed Models ✔ Linear ✔ Continue ✔ Y ✔ ►(to the Dependent Variable box) ✔ *method lab* ✔ ►(to the Factor box) ✔ Fixed ✔ *method* ✔ Add ✔ Continue ✔ Random ✔ *lab*	✔ Add ✔ ▼ (select Interaction) * Hold down ctl key. ✔ *method lab* (release ctl key) ✔ Add ✔ Continue ✔ Estimation ✔ Maximum Likelihood ✔ Continue ✔ Statistics ✔ Parameter Estimates ✔ Tests of Covariance Parameters ✔ Covariances of Parameter Estimates ✔ Continue ✔ OK

SPSS Output 25.5

Type III Tests of Fixed Effects[a]

Source	Numerator df	Denominator df	F	Sig.
Intercept	1	3.947	545.918	.000
METHOD	1	3.949	35.174	.004

a. Dependent Variable: Y.

Estimates of Fixed Effects[b]

Parameter	Estimate	Std. Error	df	t	Sig.	95% Confidence Interval	
						Lower Bound	Upper Bound
Intercept	3.0612500	.1897507	6.609	16.1	.000	2.6071284	3.5153716
[METHOD=1]	1.2657975	.2134286	3.949	5.931	.004	.6702099	1.8613852
[METHOD=2]	0[a]	0	.	.	.	.	.

a. This parameter is set to zero because it is redundant.

b. Dependent Variable: Y.

Estimates of Covariance Parameters[a]

Parameter		Estimate	Std. Error	Wald Z	Sig.	95% Confidence Interval	
						Lower Bound	Upper Bound
Residual		.0232542	.0059431	3.913	.000	.0140916	.0383745
LAB	Variance	.0544393	.0771863	.705	.481	.0033810	.8765585
METHOD * LAB	Variance	.0857062	.0648563	1.321	.186	.0194484	.3776944

a. Dependent Variable: Y.

The bootstrap method described on text page 1076 is not readily available in SPSS.

Chapter 26 SPSS®

Nested Designs, Subsampling and Partially Nested Designs

In previous chapters when two or more factors were involved in an experiment, the factors were *crossed* in the sense that every level of each factor occurred with all levels of every other factor. This was the situation in randomized complete block designs and in full factorial experiments where we investigated interactions among factors. In Chapter 26, the authors discuss *nested factors*. We say factor B is nested within factor A if each level of factor A contains different levels of factor B. We may encounter many variations in nested and crossed factors. For example, we could have factor A crossed with factor B and factor C nested within all the combinations of levels of A and B. Further, we could have factor C nested within factor B where factor B is itself nested within factor A. Closely related to the concept of nested factors is the notion of *subsampling*. Subsampling occurs when more than one observation is made on the response variable of interest for each (primary) study unit. The authors give an example in which batches of flour mix (primary study unit) are randomly assigned to treatment. Three loaves of bread (subsamples) from each batch of flour mix are then observed for each treatment. The authors refer to situations in which some factors are crossed and others are nested as *partially nested*, *partially hierarchical*, or *cross-nested designs*. Variations in the use of crossed and/or nested factors and subsampling lead to different considerations in the statistical analysis of relevant data.

Training School Example

Data File: ch26ta01.txt

A manufacturing company operates a training school in each of three districts. Each school has two instructors. Because each school has its own set of two instructors, we say that instructors are nested within schools. The company wished to investigate the effect of training school and instructors on student learning. Classes were formed at each training school and randomly assigned to one of the two instructors within the school. After opening the Training School Example (Table 26.1, text page 1089) and renaming the variables *Y*, *school*, *instruct*, and *session* the *Data Editor* should look like SPSS Output 26.1.

SPSS Output 26.1

Training School Example.sav - SPSS Data Editor

File Edit View Data Transform Analyze Graphs Utilities Window Help

1 : y | 25

	y	school	instruct	session	var
1	25.0	1	1	1	
2	29.0	1	1	2	
3	14.0	1	2	1	
4	11.0	1	2	2	
5	11.0	2	1	1	

On text page 1095, the authors viewed both *school* and *instruct* as fixed factors. The results shown in text Table 26.4, page 1097, are available in SPSS but only through the *Syntax Editor*. In Insert 26.1, we begin the analysis by setting up the *GLM* dialog window with *Y* as the dependent variable and *school* and *instruct* as fixed factors, and pasting the syntax into a *Syntax Editor*. This results in the *Pasted* syntax in Insert 26.1. We then edit the pasted */Design* statement to read "*/DESIGN = school instruct(school)*." as shown in the *Edited Syntax - /Design* statement. This specifies that we wish to test for a school effect and an instructor within school effect. Execution of the *Edited* syntax results in SPSS Output 26.2. This output is consistent with Table 26.4, text page 1097. To test for factor effects in this nested two-factor study, we refer to SPSS Output 26.2. From these results, we find $F(2, 6)=11.179$, $p=0.009$, and conclude that there are significant differences among learning score means for *school*. The results of the test of equal learning score means for instructors within schools is $F(3, 6)=27.024$, $p=0.001$, so we conclude differences between instructors are significant in at least one school.

SPSS Output 26.2

Tests of Between-Subjects Effects

Dependent Variable: Y

Source	Type III Sum of Squares	df	Mean Square	F	Sig.
Corrected Model	724.000[a]	5	144.800	20.686	.001
Intercept	2700.000	1	2700.000	385.714	.000
SCHOOL	156.500	2	78.250	11.179	.009
SCHOOL(INSTRUCT)	567.500	3	189.167	27.024	.001
Error	42.000	6	7.000		
Total	3466.000	12			
Corrected Total	766.000	11			

a. R Squared = .945 (Adjusted R Squared = .899)

617

INSERT 26.1	INSERT 26.1 continued

✔ Analyze
✔ General Linear Model
✔ Univariate
✔ Y
✔ ► (to the Dependent Variable box)
✔ *school instruct*
✔ ► (to the Fixed Factor box)
✔ Paste
 	
* *Pasted* syntax.
UNIANOVA
  y BY school instruct
  /METHOD = SSTYPE(3)
  /INTERCEPT = INCLUDE
  /CRITERIA = ALPHA(.05)
  /DESIGN = school instruct school*instruct .
	* *Edited* syntax.
	UNIANOVA
	  y BY school instruct
	  /METHOD = SSTYPE(3)
	  /INTERCEPT = INCLUDE
	  /CRITERIA = ALPHA(.05)
	  /DESIGN = school instruct(school) .

Estimation of Factor Level Means $\mu_{i.}$

On text page 1101, the authors wish to estimate the response mean for the Atlanta school with a 95% confidence interval. To find this estimated marginal mean, request the *GLM* procedure where *Y* is the dependent variable, *school* and *instruct* are fixed factors, and use the *Options* option to specify estimated marginal means for *school*. Results (not shown) are consistent with text page 1101.

On text page 1101, the authors performed pairwise comparisons of the learning score means for the three schools using the *Tukey* test and a 90% confidence interval. To specify the *Tukey* test and associated confidence intervals, request the *GLM* procedure where *Y* is the dependent variable, *school* and *instruct* are fixed factors, use the *Post Hoc* option to specify a *Tukey* post hoc for *school*, and use the *Options* option to set "Significance level" to 0.1. Results (not shown) are consistent with text page 1101.

Estimation of Treatment Means μ_{ij}

On text page 1102, the authors compare the learning score means of the two instructors in each of the three schools using the *Bonferroni* procedure and a 90% confidence interval. To specify the *Bonferroni* test and associated confidence intervals, request the *GLM* procedure where *Y* is the dependent variable, *school* and *instruct* are fixed factors, use the *Options* option to specify estimated marginal means for *school*instruct*, use the *Options* option to set "Significance level" to $(1-0.9)/3 = .03333$, and Paste the syntax. Edit the pasted syntax by adding "*COMPARE (instruct) ADJ(LSD)*" to the "*/EMMEANS = TABLES(school*instruct)*" line. The edited line will read, "*/EMMEANS = TABLES(school*instruct) COMPARE (instruct) ADJ(LSD)*". Execution of the edited syntax yields results (not shown) consistent with text page 1102.

On text page 1103, the authors estimate the overall mean with a 95% confidence interval. Here we specify the *GLM* procedure where *Y* is the dependent variable; *school* and *instruct* are fixed factors; and use the *Options* option to set "Significance level" to 0.05 and to display estimated marginal means for the overall mean (*OVERALL*). Results (not shown) are consistent with text page 1103.

Unbalanced Nested Two-Factor Designs

On text page 1104 the authors present an unbalanced nested two-factor design and use the regression approach for analyzing the data. As we discussed in Chapter 15 of this manual, SPSS' *GLM* procedure is a regression-based approach and can be used with unbalanced data as shown in Table 26.6 (a), text page 1105, without recoding the data as shown in Table 26.6 (b). Thus, execution of the syntax described in Insert 26.1, while the data from text Table 26.6 (a) are in the *Data Editor*, will result in the analysis of variance table shown in Table 26.7, text page 1106.

Subsampling in Single-Factor Study with Completely Randomized Design

Bread Crustiness Example

Data File: ch26ta09.txt

On text page 1109, researchers studied the relationship between three levels of oven temperature and a measure of bread crustiness (the response). There were two experimental units (batches of flour mix) randomly assigned to each treatment, and three subsamples were selected from each batch. After opening the Bread Crustiness Example data file and renaming the variables *Y*, *temp*, *batch*, and *obser,* the first five lines of the *Data Editor* should look like SPSS Output 26.3.

SPSS Output 26.3

	y	temp	batch	obser
1	4.00	1.00	1.00	1.00
2	7.00	1.00	1.00	2.00
3	5.00	1.00	1.00	3.00
4	12.00	1.00	2.00	1.00
5	8.00	1.00	2.00	2.00

We begin the analysis by pasting the syntax from the initial steps shown in Insert 26.2. We edit the */Design* statement of the pasted syntax to indicate that our model has *temp* and *batch(temp)* as effects. Execution the edited syntax will result in SPSS Output 26.4. Notice that the *SS, df,* and *MS* terms are consistent with Table 26.10, text page 1110. However, the test statistic (F=45.085) for the hypothesis that all *temp* effects are equal to zero is not consistent with F^*=7.21 as reported on text page 1109. This is because SPSS uses the error mean square (2.611) as the denominator for the test statistic by default instead of the batch within temperature mean square

[*MeanSquare* for *batch(temp)*=16.33 in SPSS Output 26.4] as shown in equation 26.38a, text page 1108. To specify syntax for a test that uses the mean square for *batch(temp)* in its denominator, we use the *Test* subcommand from within *GLM* (available only via the *Syntax Editor*) to test a (numerator) mean square for a specified factor against a specified denominator mean square. That is, we add the /*Test* subcommand [/*Test* = *temp vs batch(temp)*] as shown in Insert 26.2 - * *Edited syntax with* /*Test statement*, to request a test for temperature effects (*temp*) using the means square for batches within temperature setting as the denominator mean square [*batch(temp)*] in the *F*-test. This results in SPSS Output 26.5, which is consistent with the *F**=7.21 reported on text page 1109. We use the error mean square (2.61) as the denominator for the tests statistic for evaluating *batch* differences. The value of the resulting test statistic is shown in SPSS Output 26.4 as *F*=6.225 for the effect of *batch(temp)*, which is consistent with text page 1110.

INSERT 26.2	INSERT 26.2 continued
✔ Analyze ✔ General Linear Model ✔ Univariate ✔ Y ✔ ► (to the Dependent Variable box) ✔ *temp batch* ✔ ► (to the Fixed Factor box) ✔ Paste	* *Edited* syntax. UNIANOVA y BY temp batch /METHOD = SSTYPE(3) /INTERCEPT = INCLUDE /CRITERIA = ALPHA(.05) /DESIGN = temp batch(temp) .
* *Pasted* syntax. UNIANOVA y BY temp batch /METHOD = SSTYPE(3) /INTERCEPT = INCLUDE /CRITERIA = ALPHA(.05) /DESIGN = temp batch temp*batch .	* *Edited* syntax with *Test* statement. UNIANOVA y BY temp batch /METHOD = SSTYPE(3) /INTERCEPT = INCLUDE /CRITERIA = ALPHA(.05) /DESIGN = temp batch(temp) /Test = temp vs batch(temp) .

SPSS Output 26.4

Tests of Between-Subjects Effects

Dependent Variable: Y

Source	Type III Sum of Squares	df	Mean Square	F	Sig.
Corrected Model	284.444[a]	5	56.889	21.787	.000
Intercept	2544.222	1	2544.222	974.383	.000
TEMP	235.444	2	117.722	45.085	.000
BATCH(TEMP)	49.000	3	16.333	6.255	.008
Error	31.333	12	2.611		
Total	2860.000	18			
Corrected Total	315.778	17			

a. R Squared = .901 (Adjusted R Squared = .859)

Custom Hypothesis Tests

Test Results

Dependent Variable: Y

Source	Sum of Squares	df	Mean Square	F	Sig.
Contrast	235.444	2	117.722	7.207	.071
Error[a]	49.000	3	16.333		

a. BATCH(TEMP)

On text page 1111, the authors wish to find the 95% confidence interval for bread baked at the low temperature and to estimate the difference in means for the measure of crustiness for breads baked at low versus high temperatures. The calculations are performed easily on a hand calculator and are not detailed here.

On text page 1112 the authors wish to estimate σ^2, the variance component for variability among response means for batches within temperatures, with a 95% confidence interval. [See Chapter 25 (Random and Fixed Effects Models) of this manual for example syntax.]

Three-Factor Partially Nested Designs

Group Decision Making Example

Data File: ch26ta12.txt

On text page 1115 the authors present a partially nested design with three factors: A, B, and C. Factors A and B and factors B and C are crossed. Factor C is nested within factor A. After opening the Group Decision Making data file and renaming the variables Y, a, b, c, and k, the first 5 cases of the *Data Editor* should look like SPSS Output 26.6.

SPSS Output 26.6

Group Decision Making Example.sav - SPSS Data Editor

File Edit View Data Transform Analyze Graphs Utilities Window Help

1 : y   16

	y	a	b	c	k
1	16.0	1	1	1	1
2	20.0	1	1	1	2
3	14.0	1	1	2	1
4	19.0	1	1	2	2
5	7.0	2	1	1	1

As above, we use *GLM* and enter *Y* as the dependent variable and *a*, *b*, and *c* as fixed factors, and paste the syntax to the *Syntax Editor*. (Insert 26.3) We use the rationale described under *Development of Model*, text page 1114, and the model shown in equation 26.48, text page 1115, to specify an edited */Design* statement. Thus, our edited */Design* statement contains the same factors as presented in text Table 26.11. To test for the effect of nationality as shown on text page 1117, we add the */Test* subcommand to indicate that we wish to test the effect of *a* while using the mean square for *c* nested within *a* [*c(a)*] as the denominator. The result of this custom test is $F^*=1681.00$, $p=0.001$, consistent with text page 1118. Continuing in Insert 26.3, we use equation 26.50 and 26.50a (text page 1118) to estimate the difference between response means for the U.S. and foreign teams. The resulting lower (*lhatlo*) and upper (*lhathi*) confidence limits will be written to each line of the *Data Editor*.

INSERT 26.3	INSERT 26.3 continued
✔ Analyze ✔ General Linear Model ✔ Univariate ✔ Y ✔ ▶ (to the Dependent Variable box) ✔ *a b c* ✔ ▶ (to the Fixed Factor box) ✔ Paste * *Pasted* syntax. UNIANOVA y BY a b c /METHOD = SSTYPE(3) /INTERCEPT = INCLUDE /CRITERIA = ALPHA(.05) /DESIGN = a b c a*b a*c b*c a*b*c .	* *Edited* syntax. UNIANOVA y BY a b c /METHOD = SSTYPE(3) /INTERCEPT = INCLUDE /CRITERIA = ALPHA(.05) /DESIGN = a b c(a) a*b b*c(a) /test = a vs c(a) . * Type the following syntax. compute lhat=20.25-10.00. compute t=idf.t(1-(.05/2),(2-1)*2). compute lhatlo=lhat-t*sqrt((2*.25)/8). compute lhathi=lhat+t*sqrt((2*.25)/8). exe. ✔ Run ✔ All

Chapter *27* SPSS®

Repeated Measures and Related Designs

In this chapter, the authors take up studies in which the response variable is observed repeatedly, perhaps under different experimental conditions. In a weight loss study, for example, subjects may be weighed weekly during a 6 week study period to assess possible changes in weight across time. In this context, "subject" is considered to be a block and the individual subjects are considered to be a random sample from a large population of subjects. Thus, "subject" may be viewed as a random factor (blocks random). SPSS and other software packages provide many options for analyzing repeated measures data. For example, if the subjects compose a single group of subjects of interest, we can analyze the data following the steps used for analyzing a randomized complete block design where subjects are regarded as blocks (See text Figure 27.1). If there are multiple groups, we can use the analysis of variance for split plot designs. These methods are univariate approaches to the analysis of multivariate data because repeated measures data are inherently multivariate data. Of course, multivariate analysis of variance can also be performed. There are advantages to using univariate approaches if they are appropriate but the univariate methods require the covariance matrix (for the inherently multivariate data structure) to have the property of sphericity relative to the hypothesis being tested. Mauchley's test for sphericity is useful for checking whether the property is plausible. On the other hand, the sphericity assumption for the covariance matrix is not required for multivariate analysis. SPSS' *GLM – Repeated* procedure is useful for analyzing repeated measures data, and we provide an overview of *GLM - Repeated* in this chapter.

Single-Factor Experiments with Repeated Measures on All Treatments

Wine-Judging Example

Data File: ch27ta02.txt

In the Wine-Judging example, six judges rated the overall excellence of four wine types. After opening the Wine-Judging Example (Table 27.2, text page 1132) and renaming the variables *Y*, *judge*, and *wine*, the first 5 lines of the *Data Editor* should look like SPSS Output 27.1.

SPSS Output 27.1

Wine Judging Example.sav - SPSS Data Editor

File Edit View Data Transform Analyze Graphs Utilities W

1 : y   20

	y	judge	wine	var
1	20.0	1	1	
2	24.0	1	2	
3	28.0	1	3	
4	28.0	1	4	
5	15.0	2	1	

The researchers considered the six judges a random sample of judges from a population of potential judges; thus, they considered the effects associated with *judge* to be random. They considered effects associated with *wine* to be fixed because the four wines were the only wines of interest. From Figure 27.2, text page 1133, the researchers concluded that there did not appear to be significant interaction between *judge* and *wine*; thus an additive model was adopted. A single-factor repeated measures analysis was performed to test for differences in the response variable (*Y*) among the 4 levels of *wine*. There are at least two approaches to this analysis. Given the file structure of SPSS Output 27.1, we first use SPSS' *GLM – Univariate* procedure. In Insert 27.1 we enter *wine* as a fixed factor and *judge* as a random factor. To obtain the model as reported in Figure 27.3, text page 1133, we must define the model using the *Model* option from within the *GLM – Univariate* dialog window. To obtain the *Tukey* procedure and the 95% family confidence intervals, we use the *Post Hoc* dialog window. Results are shown in SPSS Output 27.2 and are consistent with the ANOVA Table presented on text page 1133 (Figure 27.3) and the pairwise comparisons shown on text page 1137.

INSERT 27.1	INSERT 27.1 continued
✔ Analyze	✔ Main Effects
✔ General Linear Model	✔ *wine*(F)
✔ Univariate	✔ *judge*(R)
✔ Y	✔ ► (under Build Terms)
✔ ► (to the Dependent box)	✔ Continue
✔ *wine*	✔ Post Hoc
✔ ► (to the Fixed Factor box)	✔ *wine*
✔ *judge*	✔ ►
✔ ► (to the Random Factor box)	✔ *Tukey*
✔ Model	✔ Continue
✔ Custom	✔ OK
✔ ▼	

SPSS Output 27.2

GLM – Univariate

Tests of Between-Subjects Effects

Dependent Variable: Y

Source		Type III Sum of Squares	df	Mean Square	F	Sig.
Intercept	Hypothesis	13442.667	1	13442.667	387.769	.000
	Error	173.333	5	34.667[a]		
WINE	Hypothesis	184.000	3	61.333	57.500	.000
	Error	16.000	15	1.067[b]		
JUDGE	Hypothesis	173.333	5	34.667	32.500	.000
	Error	16.000	15	1.067[b]		

a. MS(JUDGE)

b. MS(Error)

Multiple Comparisons

Dependent Variable: Y

Tukey HSD

(I) WINE	(J) WINE	Mean Difference (I-J)	Std. Error	Sig.	95% Confidence Interval	
					Lower Bound	Upper Bound
1	2	-2.000*	.5963	.020	-3.719	-.281
	3	-6.667*	.5963	.000	-8.385	-4.948
	4	-6.000*	.5963	.000	-7.719	-4.281
2	1	2.000*	.5963	.020	.281	3.719
	3	-4.667*	.5963	.000	-6.385	-2.948
	4	-4.000*	.5963	.000	-5.719	-2.281
3	1	6.667*	.5963	.000	4.948	8.385
	2	4.667*	.5963	.000	2.948	6.385
	4	.667	.5963	.684	-1.052	2.385
4	1	6.000*	.5963	.000	4.281	7.719
	2	4.000*	.5963	.000	2.281	5.719
	3	-.667	.5963	.684	-2.385	1.052

Based on observed means.

*. The mean difference is significant at the .05 level.

Introduction to SPSS' *GLM – Repeated* Procedure

In SPSS, the *GLM – Repeated* procedure provides many useful features for the analysis of repeated measures. Unlike the *GLM – Univariate* procedure, *GLM – Repeated* requires that the repeated measurements for each observation be recorded on the same line of the input file. This may require rearranging the data in the input data file or using SPSS programming code to create a data set that contains the rearranged data.

In the Wine-Judging Example, we rearrange the data as follows so that each line of data contains the judge number and scores for the four wines assigned by one judge:

SPSS Output 27.3

	judge	score1	score2	score3	score4
1	1	20.00	24.00	28.00	28.00
2	2	15.00	18.00	23.00	24.00
3	3	18.00	19.00	24.00	23.00
4	4	26.00	26.00	30.00	30.00
5	5	22.00	24.00	28.00	26.00
6	6	19.00	21.00	27.00	25.00

Wine Judging wide file example.sav - SPSS Data Editor

Given this latter file structure, we illustrate the syntax to use *GLM – Repeated* for the analysis of the Wine-Judging Example. In Insert 27.2 we request *GLM – Repeated* and arbitrarily assign the factor name *wine* to label the factor for the repeated measures. We specify *score1*, *score2*, *score3*, and *score4* as the four levels of the within-subject factor, *wine*. In *GLM - Repeated*, post hoc tests are not available for a within-subject factor. Instead, we use the *Option* dialog window to request pairwise comparisons for the 4 levels of the within subject variable. By this method, however, *LSD* (no adjustment), *Bonferroni*, and *Sidak* are the only options available. In Insert 27.2, we request the *Bonferroni* procedure (results not shown); the authors used the *Tukey* procedure on text page 1137. The method used for making pairwise comparisons from within the *GLM – Repeated Measures* procedure is not equivalent to the pairwise comparisons made using the *GLM – Univariate* approach in Insert 27.1 and reported on text page 1137. The *GLM – Repeated Measures* procedure uses separate error terms for each comparison, and each contrast is equivalent to a paired t-test. For a *Bonferroni* correction, for example, the p value of each comparison (paired t-test) is multiplied by the number (g) of comparisons. This method is also valid but more conservative than the *GLM – Univariate* approach and the method reported by the text. By default, *GLM – Repeated* displays the *Mauchly* test for the hypothesis of sphericity of the covariance matrix and the *Greenhouse-Geisser* epsilon and the *Huynh-Feldt* epsilon for use if Mauchley's test suggests the assumption of sphericity is not tenable.

Partial results of Insert 27.2 are shown in SPSS Output 27.4. From the table labeled *Mauchly's Test of Sphericity*, we conclude that the assumption of Sphericity is tenable, *Mauchly's W* = 0.352, $X^2 = 3.89$, $p = 0.577$. Here, the X^2 statistic has a distribution that is approximately that of chi-square with 5 degrees of freedom. Because the assumption of Sphericity is tenable, we base the test for equality of taste score means for wines on the unadjusted *F* test, and disregard the Greenhouse-Geisser and Huynh-Feldt adjustments. Note that the methods shown in Insert 27.1 and 27.2 both yield an $F=57.5$ for testing the hypothesis that the rating means for the four wine types are equal, consistent with text page 1133.

INSERT 27.2	INSERT 27.2 continued
✓ Analyze	✓ ▶(to the Within Subjects variable box)
✓ General Linear Model	✓ Options
✓ Repeated Measures	✓ score
* Type "wine" in the Within Subject Factor box.	✓ ▶(to the Display Means for: box)
* Type "4" in the Number of Levels box.	✓ ▼ (under Confidence Interval Adjustment)
✓ Add	✓ Bonferroni
✓ Define	✓ Continue
✓ score1 score2 score3 score4	✓ OK

SPSS Output 27.4

GLM – Repeated Measures

Multivariate Tests[b]

Effect		Value	F	Hypothesis df	Error df	Sig.
WINE	Pillai's Trace	.977	42.200[a]	3.000	3.000	.006
	Wilks' Lambda	.023	42.200[a]	3.000	3.000	.006
	Hotelling's Trace	42.200	42.200[a]	3.000	3.000	.006
	Roy's Largest Root	42.200	42.200[a]	3.000	3.000	.006

a. Exact statistic

b.

Design: Intercept
Within Subjects Design: WINE

Mauchly's Test of Sphericity[b]

Measure: MEASURE_1

Within Subjects Effect	Mauchly's W	Approx. Chi-Square	df	Sig.	Epsilon[a]		
					Greenhouse-Geisser	Huynh-Feldt	Lower-bound
WINE	.352	3.891	5	.577	.604	.927	.333

Tests the null hypothesis that the error covariance matrix of the orthonormalized transformed dependent variables is proportional to an identity matrix.

a. May be used to adjust the degrees of freedom for the averaged tests of significance. Corrected tests are displayed in the Tests of Within-Subjects Effects table.

b.

Design: Intercept
Within Subjects Design: WINE

SPSS Output 27.4 continued

Tests of Within-Subjects Effects

Measure: MEASURE_1

Source		Type III Sum of Squares	df	Mean Square	F	Sig.
WINE	Sphericity Assumed	184.000	3	61.333	57.500	.000
	Greenhouse-Geisser	184.000	1.811	101.583	57.500	.000
	Huynh-Feldt	184.000	2.781	66.162	57.500	.000
	Lower-bound	184.000	1.000	184.000	57.500	.001
Error(WINE)	Sphericity Assumed	16.000	15	1.067		
	Greenhouse-Geisser	16.000	9.057	1.767		
	Huynh-Feldt	16.000	13.905	1.151		
	Lower-bound	16.000	5.000	3.200		

At times it is advantageous to work with either *GLM – Univariate* or *GLM – Repeated Measures* but the data file is not structured as needed for the desired procedure. For instance, assume that we wish to use the *GLM – Repeated Measures* procedure but 1000 data records have been entered in the format shown in SPSS Output 27.1. This format is not compatible with *GLM – Repeated Measures*. The syntax shown in Insert 27.3 - Method 1 will convert the data file as shown in SPSS Output 27.1 to the structure as shown in SPSS Output 27.3, which is compatible with *GLM – Repeated Measures*. The syntax shown in Insert 27.3 - Methods 2 and 3 will each convert the data file as shown in SPSS Output 27.3 to the structure as shown in SPSS Output 27.1, which is compatible with *GLM – Univariate*.

```
                              INSERT 27.3

* METHOD 1 - One measurement per line to multiple measurements per line.
* Restructure Output 27.1 to Output 27.3.
* Data Editor must be as shown in SPSS Output 27.1.
sort cases by judge (A) wine (A) .
compute record=1.
if judge=lag(judge) record=lag(record)+1.
vector y (4).
compute y(record)=y.
aggregate outfile *
 /break judge
 /score1 to score4 = max(y1 to y4).
exe.


* METHOD 2 - Multiple measurements per line to one measurement per line.
* Restructure Output 27.3 to Output 27.1.
* Data Editor must be as shown in SPSS Output 27.3.
vector score = score1 to score4.
loop wine=1 to 4.
compute y=score(wine).
format judge wine (f1.0).
xsave outfile = 'temp' / keep y judge wine.
end loop.
exe.
get file 'temp'.


* METHOD 3 - Multiple measurements per line to one measurement per line.
* Restructure Output 27.3 to Output 27.1.
* Data Editor must be as shown in SPSS Output 27.3.
compute record=1.
format record (f1.0).
save outfile =  'score1.sav' / keep = score1 judge record / rename score1=y record=wine.
compute record=2.
save outfile =  'score2.sav' / keep = score2 judge record / rename score2=y record=wine.
compute record=3.
save outfile =  'score3.sav' / keep = score3 judge record / rename score3=y record=wine.
compute record=4.
save outfile =  'score4.sav' / keep = score4 judge record / rename score4=y record=wine.
add files file='score1.sav'/file='score2.sav'/file='score3.sav'/file='score4.sav'
/by judge.
exe.
```

Ranked Data: Coffee Sweetener Example

Data File: ch27ta04.txt

In Table 27.4, text page 1138, the authors present the results of six subjects' ranking of coffee sweeteners. The data are arranged in ch27ta04.txt in the following order: *Y, subject,* and *sweetener*. Additionally, the ratings have already been ranked within each subject so that *Y* represents a rank variable. Here we simply specify a main-effects only *GLM - Univariate* model where the rank (Y) is the dependent variable and *subject* and *sweetener* are fixed factors (syntax not shown). This will result in $F_R^* = 7.50$ for *sweetener* as reported on text page 1138. The pairwise comparisons reported on text page 1139 can be calculated on a hand calculator except for text equation 27.9a. To find $B = z(1 - \alpha / 2g) = 2.326$ execute the following statement from a *Syntax Editor*: "*compute B=probit*(1-0.2/(2*10))).".

Two-Factor Experiments with Repeated Measures on One Factor: Analysis of Factor Effects without Interaction

Athletic Shoes Sales Example

Data File: ch27ta07.txt

Market researchers selected 10 test markets (*market*) to study the effects of two advertising campaigns (*campaign*). The outcome measure was athletic shoes sales (Y) and data were collected for three 2-week periods (*period*). After opening the Athletic Shoe Example (Table 27.7, text page 1146) and renaming the variables Y, *market*, *campaign*, and *period*, the first 5 lines of the *Data Editor* should look like SPSS Output 27.5.

SPSS Output 27.5

	y	market	campaign	period	var
1	958.00	1	1	1	
2	1005.00	2	1	1	
3	351.00	3	1	1	
4	549.00	4	1	1	
5	730.00	5	1	1	

The researchers first visually inspected the relationship between *campaign* and *period*. The steps to reproduce Figure 27.6, text page 1146, are given in Insert 27.4. Based on this figure and other diagnostics, they concluded that a repeated measures model was appropriate. *Campaign* and *period* were considered fixed factors. Levels of *market* were considered a random sample from a population of potential markets and, thus, *market* was considered to be a random factor. Additionally, *market* was nested within *campaign* because 5 test markets are assigned to the first advertising campaign and 5 different test markets are assigned to the second campaign. In Insert 27.5 we specify the appropriate model and request a *Tukey* procedure with a 99% confidence interval as shown on text page 1148. However, since the syntax for nesting a factor within another cannot be done in the *GLM –Univariate* dialog window, we paste the syntax into a

Syntax Editor. This produces the *Pasted Syntax* in Insert 27.6. Edit the *Pasted Syntax - /Design* statement by changing *market* to *market(campaign)*. This indicates that *market* is to be nested within *campaign*. Execution of the *Edited Syntax* results in SPSS Output 27.6. This output is consistent with Figure 27.7, text page 1147, and the confidence intervals shown on text page 1148.

INSERT 27.4	INSERT 27.4
* Use ✔ *Data* ✔ *Select Cases* to select only cases. * where *campaign = 1*. ✔ Graphs ✔ Line ✔ Define ✔ Y ✔ Other summary function	✔ ▶(to Change Summary) ✔ *period* ✔ ▶(to Category Axis:) ✔ *market* ✔ ▶(to Define Line by:) ✔ OK * Use ✔ *Data* ✔ *Select Cases* to select only cases. * where *campaign = 2* – repeat above steps.

INSERT 27.5	INSERT 27.5
✔ Analyze ✔ General Linear Model ✔ Univariate ✔ Y ✔ ▶(to the Dependent box) ✔ *campaign period* ✔ ▶(to the Fixed Factor box) ✔ *market* ✔ ▶(to the Random Factor box) ✔ Model ✔ Custom ✔ ▼ ✔ Main Effects ✔ *campaign*(F) ✔ *period*(F) ✔ *market*(R)	✔ ▶(under Build Terms) ✔ ▼ ✔ All 2-way ✔ *campaign*(F) ✔ *period*(F) ✔ ▶(under Build Terms) ✔ Continue ✔ Post Hoc ✔ *period* ✔ ▶ ✔ Tukey ✔ Continue ✔ Options * Change"Significance Level" to ".01" . ✔ Continue ✔ Paste

INSERT 27.6	INSERT 27.6

* **Pasted syntax**.
UNIANOVA
  y BY campaign period market
  /RANDOM = market
  /METHOD = SSTYPE(3)
  /INTERCEPT = INCLUDE
  /POSTHOC = period (TUKEY)
  /CRITERIA = ALPHA(.01)
  /DESIGN = campaign period market
campaign*period.
	* **Edited syntax** .
	UNIANOVA
	  y BY campaign period market
	  /RANDOM = market
	  /METHOD = SSTYPE(3)
	  /INTERCEPT = INCLUDE
	  /POSTHOC = period (TUKEY)
	  /CRITERIA = ALPHA(.01)
	  /DESIGN = campaign period market(campaign)
	campaign*period.

Tests of Between-Subjects Effects

Dependent Variable: Y

Source		Type III Sum of Squares	df	Mean Square	F	Sig.
Intercept	Hypothesis	13248136.5	1	13248136.53	57.799	.000
	Error	1833680.933	8	229210.117[a]		
CAMPAIGN	Hypothesis	168150.533	1	168150.533	.734	.417
	Error	1833680.933	8	229210.117[a]		
PERIOD	Hypothesis	67073.067	2	33536.533	93.686	.000
	Error	5727.467	16	357.967[b]		
MARKET(CAMPAIGN)	Hypothesis	1833680.933	8	229210.117	640.311	.000
	Error	5727.467	16	357.967[b]		
CAMPAIGN * PERIOD	Hypothesis	391.467	2	195.733	.547	.589
	Error	5727.467	16	357.967[b]		

a. MS(MARKET(CAMPAIGN))

b. MS(Error)

Multiple Comparisons

Dependent Variable: Y

Tukey HSD

(I) PERIOD	(J) PERIOD	Mean Difference (I-J)	Std. Error	Sig.	99% Confidence Interval	
					Lower Bound	Upper Bound
1	2	-80.4000*	8.46128	.000	-109.0321	-51.7679
	3	32.0000*	8.46128	.004	3.3679	60.6321
2	1	80.4000*	8.46128	.000	51.7679	109.0321
	3	112.4000*	8.46128	.000	83.7679	141.0321
3	1	-32.0000*	8.46128	.004	-60.6321	-3.3679
	2	-112.4000*	8.46128	.000	-141.0321	-83.7679

Based on observed means.

*. The mean difference is significant at the .01 level.

As noted above, there are advantages to using univariate approaches (Insert 27.5) but the univariate methods require the covariance matrix to have the property of sphericity relative to the hypothesis being tested. Mauchley's test for sphericity is useful for testing this assumption but is not available from the syntax in Insert 27.5. To obtain Mauchley's test for sphericity, we use *GLM - Repeated*. *GLM - Repeated*, however, requires that the data file be structured as multiple (repeated) measurements per line, which is not the structure shown in SPSS Output 27.5 (text Table 27.7). In Insert 27.6, we read the data file shown in Table 27.5 and use the logic of syntax in Insert 27.3 to convert the file to multiple measurements per line. After executing Insert 27.6, the first five lines of the *Data Editor* will look like SPSS Output 27.7. We then specify *GLM - Repeated* where *sales1*, *sales2*, and *sales3* represent the three levels of the within-subject factor and *campaign* is a between-subjects factor. We also specify *period* as the label of the three levels of shoe sales. Partial output of this *GLM - Repeated* procedure is shown in SPSS Output 27.8. Notice that the *F* values for *campaign*, *period*, and *campaign*period* in SPSS Output 27.8 are consistent with SPSS Output 27.6 above and text Figure 27.7. However, from the table labeled *Mauchly's Test of Sphericity* in SPSS Output 27.8, we find that the assumption of sphericity is rejected, $X^2 = 7.97$, $p = 0.0186$. Given that the sphericity assumption is not supported, we can adjust the univariate tests using the methods of Greenhouse and Geisser or Huynh and Feldt. For example, the adjusted *Greenhouse-Geisser* and *Huynh-Feldt* probability level for the *period*campaign* interaction are *p*=0.508 and *p*=0.539, respectively.

INSERT 27.6	INSERT 27.6
✔ File ✔ New ✔ Syntax * METHOD 1 - One measurement per line to multiple measurements per line. * Restructure Output 27.1 to Output 27.3. * Data Editor must be as shown in SPSS Output 27.1. sort cases by campaign (A) market (A) period (A). compute record=1. if market=lag(market) record=lag(record)+1. vector y (3). compute y(record)=y. aggregate outfile * /break campaign market /sales1 to sales3 = max(y1 to y3). exe. ✔ Run ✔ All	✔ Analyze ✔ General Linear Model ✔ **Repeated Measures** * Type "period" in Within Subject Name box. * Type "3" in Number of Levels box. ✔ Add ✔ Define * While depressing CTL key. ✔ *sales1 sales2 sales3* ✔ ▶(to the Within Subject variables box) ✔ *campaign* ✔ ▶(to the Between Subjects Factor box) ✔ OK

SPSS Output 27.7

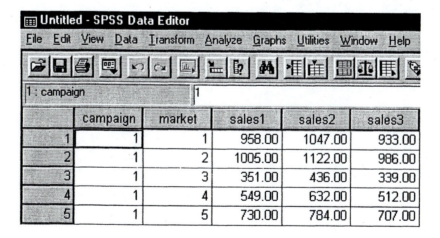

SPSS Output 27.8

Multivariate Tests[b]

Effect		Value	F	Hypothesis df	Error df	Sig.
PERIOD	Pillai's Trace	.931	47.279[a]	2.000	7.000	.000
	Wilks' Lambda	.069	47.279[a]	2.000	7.000	.000
	Hotelling's Trace	13.508	47.279[a]	2.000	7.000	.000
	Roy's Largest Root	13.508	47.279[a]	2.000	7.000	.000
PERIOD * CAMPAIGN	Pillai's Trace	.424	2.576[a]	2.000	7.000	.145
	Wilks' Lambda	.576	2.576[a]	2.000	7.000	.145
	Hotelling's Trace	.736	2.576[a]	2.000	7.000	.145
	Roy's Largest Root	.736	2.576[a]	2.000	7.000	.145

a. Exact statistic

b.
  Design: Intercept+CAMPAIGN
  Within Subjects Design: PERIOD

Mauchly's Test of Sphericity[b]

Measure: MEASURE_1

Within Subjects Effect	Mauchly's W	Approx. Chi-Square	df	Sig.	Epsilon[a] Greenhouse-Geisser	Huynh-Feldt	Lower-bound
PERIOD	.320	7.973	2	.019	.595	.727	.500

Tests the null hypothesis that the error covariance matrix of the orthonormalized transformed dependent variables is proportional to an identity matrix.

a. May be used to adjust the degrees of freedom for the averaged tests of significance. Corrected tests are displayed in the Tests of Within-Subjects Effects table.

b.
  Design: Intercept+CAMPAIGN
  Within Subjects Design: PERIOD

Tests of Within-Subjects Effects

Measure: MEASURE_1

Source		Type III Sum of Squares	df	Mean Square	F	Sig.
PERIOD	Sphericity Assumed	67073.067	2	33536.533	93.686	.000
	Greenhouse-Geisser	67073.067	1.191	56337.012	93.686	.000
	Huynh-Feldt	67073.067	1.455	46107.817	93.686	.000
	Lower-bound	67073.067	1.000	67073.067	93.686	.000
PERIOD * CAMPAIGN	Sphericity Assumed	391.467	2	195.733	.547	.589
	Greenhouse-Geisser	391.467	1.191	328.807	.547	.508
	Huynh-Feldt	391.467	1.455	269.105	.547	.539
	Lower-bound	391.467	1.000	391.467	.547	.481
Error(PERIOD)	Sphericity Assumed	5727.467	16	357.967		
	Greenhouse-Geisser	5727.467	9.525	601.337		
	Huynh-Feldt	5727.467	11.638	492.152		
	Lower-bound	5727.467	8.000	715.933		

Tests of Between-Subjects Effects

Measure: MEASURE_1

Transformed Variable: Average

Source	Type III Sum of Squares	df	Mean Square	F	Sig.
Intercept	13248136.5	1	13248136.53	57.799	.000
CAMPAIGN	168150.533	1	168150.533	.734	.417
Error	1833680.933	8	229210.117		

The *Greenhouse-Geisser* adjustment is conservative, especially for small samples; the *Huynh-Feldt* adjustment is more liberal than the *Greenhouse-Geisser* adjustment. When we do not reject the assumption of sphericity and the p-value of the test is large, say $p > 0.15$, we would quote the p-value for the unadjusted F test (in this case for testing *campaign*period* and *campaign*); if the sphericity p-value is modestly large, say $0.15 \leq p < 0.05$, we would quote the p-values based on the *Huynh-Feldt* adjustment; if the sphericity p-value is small, say $0.05 \leq p < 0.01$, we would quote the p-values based on the *Greenhouse-Geisser* adjustment; and if the sphericity p-value is very small, say $p \leq 0.01$, we would use multivariate tests. The multivariate tests are not discussed in the text and are usually presented in a separate course on multivariate analysis. We point out here that the multivariate tests make no assumptions regarding the within-subject covariance matrix and hence they are valid for all covariance structures. But the univariate tests are more powerful provided the covariance matrix for the repeated measures has the property of sphericity or "near spherecity." *Wilks' Lambda, Pillai's Trace, Hotelling-Lawley Trace,* and *Roy's Greatest Root* are also displayed in SPSS Output 27.8. The *F* values for these four multivariate tests are identical in many situations including the present example but that is not always the case. None of the four is uniformly superior to the others and SPSS prints all four test results so the analyst can choose differently for different situations.

Two-Factor Experiments with Repeated Measures on Both Factors

Blood Flow Example

Data File: ch27ta12.txt

A researcher studied the effects of drug A (levels = A_1 and A_2) and drug B (levels = B_1 and B_2) on blood flow in 12 human subjects. Each subject received each of the four treatments (A_1B_1, A_1B_2, A_2B_1, A_2B_2) in a random order over several days. The half-life of each drug was such that there was no carryover effect. The 12 subjects were considered a random sample from a larger population of potential subjects; thus *subject* was considered a random factor and drug *A* and drug *B* were fixed factors. After opening the Blood Flow Example (Table 27.12, text page 1158) and renaming the variables *Y*, *subject*, *a*, and *b*, the first 5 lines of the *Data Editor* should look like SPSS Output 27.9.

SPSS Output 27.9

	y	subject	a	b	var
1	2.0	1.0	1	1	
2	-1.0	2.0	1	1	
3	.0	3.0	1	1	
4	3.0	4.0	1	1	
5	1.0	5.0	1	1	

To produce the test statistics given in Figure 27.11, text page 1159, we specify *GLM – Univariate* where *Y* is the dependent variable, *A* and *B* are fixed factors, *subject* is a random factor, and paste the syntax into a *Syntax Editor*. (Insert 27.7) The default full model will contain all possible interactions including an unwanted *a*b*subject* interaction as shown in Insert 27.7 - *Pasted Syntax*. Thus, in the *Edited Syntax* of Insert 27.9 we have deleted this interaction from the */DESIGN* statement. Execution of the *Edited Syntax* will result in SPSS Output 27.10 and is consistent with Figure 27.11, text page 1159. (Note: You may also use the *GLM – Univariate* dialog window, *Model* option, to specify a custom model containing the effects shown in SPSS Output 27.10).

<table>
<tr><td colspan="2" align="center">INSERT 27.7</td><td colspan="2" align="center">INSERT 27.7 continued</td></tr>
</table>

INSERT 27.7

✔ Analyze
✔ General Linear Model
✔ Univariate
✔ Y
✔ ► (to the Dependent box)
✔ a b
✔ ► (to the Fixed Factor box)
✔ subject
✔ ► (to the Random Factor box)
✔ Paste

```
*  Pasted Syntax.
UNIANOVA
  y  BY a b subject
  /RANDOM = subject
  /METHOD = SSTYPE(3)
  /INTERCEPT = INCLUDE
  /CRITERIA = ALPHA(.05)
  /DESIGN = a b subject a*b a*subject b*subject
a*b*subject .
```

INSERT 27.7 continued

```
*  Edited Syntax.
UNIANOVA
  y  BY a b subject
  /RANDOM = subject
  /METHOD = SSTYPE(3)
  /INTERCEPT = INCLUDE
  /CRITERIA = ALPHA(.05)
  /DESIGN = a b subject a*b a*subject b*subject.
```

SPSS Output 27.10

Tests of Between-Subjects Effects

Dependent Variable: Y

Source		Type III Sum of Squares	df	Mean Square	F	Sig.
Intercept	Hypothesis	5808.000	1	5808.000	247.149	.000
	Error	258.500	11	23.500[a]		
A	Hypothesis	1587.000	1	1587.000	775.867	.000
	Error	22.500	11	2.045[b]		
B	Hypothesis	2028.000	1	2028.000	524.894	.000
	Error	42.500	11	3.864[c]		
SUBJECT	Hypothesis	258.500	11	23.500	4.924	.005
	Error	58.614	12.281	4.773[d]		
A * B	Hypothesis	147.000	1	147.000	129.360	.000
	Error	12.500	11	1.136[e]		
A * SUBJECT	Hypothesis	22.500	11	2.045	1.800	.172
	Error	12.500	11	1.136[e]		
B * SUBJECT	Hypothesis	42.500	11	3.864	3.400	.027
	Error	12.500	11	1.136[e]		

a. MS(SUBJECT)

b. MS(A * SUBJECT)

c. MS(B * SUBJECT)

d. MS(A * SUBJECT) + MS(B * SUBJECT) - MS(Error)

e. MS(Error)

Note that for the $A*B$ interaction, $F=129.360$, $p<0.000$. The syntax shown in Insert 27.8 will reproduce text Figure 27.12, which shows the interaction plot for the present example. Given the significant interaction effect and the results of text Figure 27.12, the authors proceeded to make 5 pairwise comparisons to study the nature of the interaction. These comparisons are most easily made using a hand calculator. *MSABS* [*MS(Error*=1.136)] is taken from SPSS Output 27.10 and *B* is found be executing "*compute bon=idf.t*(1-(.05/(2*5)),11)." from a *Syntax Editor*. The *compute* statement uses *bon* instead of *B* as the use of *B* will overwrite the *b* values in the *Data Editor* (SPSS Output 27.9).

INSERT 27.8

```
*  Reproduce Figure 27.12, text page 1160.
✔ Graphs
✔ Scatter
✔ Simple
✔ Define
✔ Y
✔ ▶ (to Y axis box)
✔ a
✔ ▶ (to X axis box)
✔ b
✔ ▶ (to Set Markers by: box)
*  Double click on graph in Output Viewer.
✔ Chart
✔ Options
✔ Sub-group
✔ Fit Options
✔ Linear Regression
✔ Continue
✔ OK
```

Split-Plot Designs

On text page 1162 the authors describe Split-Plot Designs. For the layout shown in text Figure 27.13 (text page 1163), assume that the response variable is bushels of vegetables produced per split-plot treatment as shown in the following reproduction of Figure 27.13. To analyze this data set, we use the variable names *a*, *b*, and *field* to represent the factors irrigation method, fertilizer type, and field, respectively, and the variable name *Y* to represent the response variable as shown in SPSS Output 27.11. We then use ✔ Analyze ✔ General Linear Model ✔ Univariate and enter *Y* as the dependent variable, *a* and *b* as fixed factors, and *field* as a random factor. We use the *Model* option to specify a model that contains main effects for *a*, *b*, and *field* and a two-way interaction between *a* and *b*. After pasting this syntax into a *Syntax Editor*, we edit the /*Design* statement to indicate that *field* in nested within *a* [*field(a)*] as noted on text page 1163 and shown in Insert 27.9. Execution of Insert 27.9 (output not shown) indicates that neither the two-way interaction nor the main effect for fertilizer type is statistically significant. However, we do find a significant main effect for irrigation method [$F(1, 2) = 225.00. p = 0.004$].

In Insert 27.9, we also show the syntax for a repeated measures approach to this Split-Plot Example using *GLM – Repeated*. This is the syntax pasted from the *GLM – Repeated* dialog window. For this procedure, we rearranged the data file as shown in SPSS Output 27.10. The sample sizes within irrigation methods are too small in this example to support Mauchly's test of sphericity. Although we do not show the results, the computed values of the test statistics are the same for the two programs shown in Insert 27.9.

Fields

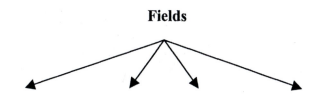

	Field 1	Field 2	Field 3	Field 4
Split Plot	A_2B_2 Fertilizer 2	A_1B_1 Fertilizer 1	A_1B_2 Fertilizer 2	A_2B_1 Fertilizer 1
	Y = 6 bushels	Y = 6 bushels	Y = 4 bushels	Y = 7 bushels
Split Plot	A_2B_1 Fertilizer 1	A_1B_2 Fertilizer 2	A_1B_1 Fertilizer 1	A_2B_2 Fertilizer 2
	Y = 9 bushels	Y = 2 bushels	Y = 3 bushels	Y = 8 bushels

Irrigation method (A) A_2 A_1 A_1 A_2

Whole-Plot Treatments

SPSS Output 27.11

	a	b	field	y
1	2	2	1	6
2	2	1	1	9
3	1	1	2	6
4	1	2	2	2
5	1	2	3	4
6	1	1	3	3
7	2	1	4	7
8	2	2	4	8

INSERT 27.9	INSERT 27.9

* GLM – Univariate.
UNIANOVA
  y BY a b field
  /RANDOM = field
  /METHOD = SSTYPE(3)
  /INTERCEPT = INCLUDE
  /PRINT = DESCRIPTIVE
  /CRITERIA = ALPHA(.05)
  /DESIGN = a b field(a) a*b .
	* GLM – Repeated.
	GLM
	  yb1 yb2 BY a
	  /WSFACTOR = fertiliz 2 Polynomial
	  /METHOD = SSTYPE(3)
	  /CRITERIA = ALPHA(.05)
	  /WSDESIGN = fertiliz
	  /DESIGN = a .

SPSS Output 27.12

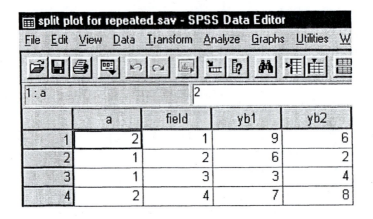

Chapter 28 SPSS®

Latin Square, Balanced Incomplete Block, and Related Designs

In some randomized block designs it may be impossible to use all treatments in every block. Suppose, for example, we wished to investigate the effects of 4 treatments using a randomized block design but there are only 3 experimental units available per block. We can use a *balanced incomplete block design* in which every pair of treatments is used the same number of times in the experiment. We can represent the experimental layout as follows:

Block	Treatment			
1	A	_	C	D
2	_	B	C	D
3	A	B	C	_
4	A	B	_	D

Note that the design is balanced because every pair of treatments (AB, AC, AD, BC, BD, and CD) is used twice in the experiment. We would randomly assign the treatments separately within each block as usual. The number of blocks required for balancing depends upon the number of treatments that can be used in each block (i.e., upon the number of experimental units available per block).

In some experiments, we wish to block on more than one factor. For example, we might wish to block on gender (Male, Female) and socio-economic status (Low, Medium, High). We could create 6 blocks (Male-Low, Male-Medium, Male-High, Female-Low, Female-Medium, Female-High). If there are 4 treatments we can represent the experimental layout as follows:

Block	Treatment			
1	A	B	C	D
2	A	B	C	D
3	A	B	C	D
4	A	B	C	D
5	A	B	C	D
6	A	B	C	D

Again, we would randomly assign the treatments separately within each block as usual. In this layout, every treatment is used exactly once in every block so the design is a randomized complete block design. Moreover, every treatment is used in every block and the 6 blocks use every combination of the levels of the two blocking factors. We say that we have made full use of the blocking factors.

641

The number of experimental units required to make full use of multiple blocking factors in a randomized complete block design is sometimes too large and we may want to use a randomized incomplete block design. A design in which each treatment appears once and only once in each row (blocking factor 1) and once and only once in each column (blocking variable 2) is called a *Latin Square design*. Latin squares designs are a special type of incomplete block designs that may be useful when we have two blocking factors. However, use of a Latin square design is possible only when the number of levels of both blocking factors equals the number of levels of the treatment factor. An example of a 4x4 Latin square follows:

Block		Block Factor 2		
Factor 1	1	2	3	4
1	A	B	C	D
2	D	A	B	C
3	C	D	A	B
4	B	C	D	A

In this chapter the authors discuss balanced incomplete block designs including the Latin square design and other variations. The steps required for using SPSS to analyze data collected in these designs are the same as those used for previously discussed designs.

Balanced Incomplete Block Designs

Food Product Taste-Testing Example

Data File: ch28ta02.txt

Researchers wished to test consumer preference of five breakfast cereals. However, previous research has demonstrated that consumers are not able to discriminate among more than 3 cereals. Thus, the 10 consumers each rated three of the five cereals on a 10-point scale. This experiment represents a balanced incomplete block design with five treatments (cereals) and block size of three. After opening the Food Product Taste-Testing Example (Table 28.2, text page 1178) and renaming the variables i, j, y, $z1$, $z2$, $z3$, $z4$, $z5$, $z6$, $z7$, $z8$, $z9$, $x1$, $x2$, $x3$, and $x4$, the first 5 lines of the *Data Editor* should look like SPSS Output 28.1.

SPSS Output 28.1

Food Product Taste Testing Example.sav - SPSS Data Editor

File Edit View Data Transform Analyze Graphs Utilities Window Help

1 : i   1

	i	j	y	z1	z2	z3	z4	z5	z6	z7	z8	z9	x1	x2	x3	x4
1	1	1	6	1	0	0	0	0	0	0	0	0	1	0	0	0
2	1	2	6	1	0	0	0	0	0	0	0	0	0	1	0	0
3	1	3	8	1	0	0	0	0	0	0	0	0	0	0	1	0
4	2	1	3	0	1	0	0	0	0	0	0	0	1	0	0	0
5	2	2	7	0	1	0	0	0	0	0	0	0	0	1	0	0

In Table 28.2 (SPSS Output 28.1), i and j are allocated codes that represent block and treatment, respectively. The "z" and "x" variables are indicator variables (see text page 1178) that indicate the block and treatment combination in which each response was observed. The authors begin the analysis of this balanced incomplete block design by presenting a regression approach. As we discussed in Chapter 15 of this manual, we use the alternative regression based *GLM* procedure and allocated codes.

In Insert 28.1, we specify the *GLM* procedure where y is the dependent variable and i and j are fixed factors; we also specify that the model is a main effects only model. Results shown in SPSS Output 28.2 are consistent with the F statistics shown on text page 1179. On text page 1180-1181 the authors present the least squares estimates of the five treatment means and 10 pairwise comparisons of treatment means based on the *Tukey* procedure. Note that the comparisons are based on least squares means and that in SPSS the only methods of adjustment available for pairwise comparisons of least squares means (estimated marginal means) are *LSD*, *Bonferroni*, and *Sidak*. Thus, to find the *Tukey* based confidence intervals shown on text 1181, we specify estimated marginal means for j and a *LSD* confidence interval adjustment method in Insert 28.1. From the output (not shown) we find the estimated cell means, $s\{\hat{D}\}=0.568$, and $T=3.06$ (equation 28.11a, text page 1180) by execution of the following syntax from the *Syntax Editor*: "*compute $T = (1/sqrt(2))*IDF.SRANGE(.95,5,16)$.*". The 10 confidence intervals can then be found by hand calculator as $\hat{D} \pm Ts\{\hat{D}\}$.

INSERT 28.1	INSERT 28.1
✔ Analyze	✔ *i*(F)
✔ General Linear Model	✔ j(F)
✔ Univariate	✔ ▶ (under Build Terms)
✔ Y	✔ Continue
✔ ▶ (to the Dependent box)	✔ Options
✔ *I j*	✔ *j*
✔ ▶ (to the Fixed Factor box)	✔ ▶ (under Display Means for)
✔ Model	✔ Compare Main Effects
✔ Custom	✔ Continue
✔ ▼ (under Build Terms)	✔ OK
✔ Main Effects	

Tests of Between-Subjects Effects

Dependent Variable: Y

Source	Type III Sum of Squares	df	Mean Square	F	Sig.
Corrected Model	97.278[a]	13	7.483	9.289	.000
Intercept	1140.833	1	1140.833	1416.207	.000
I	40.278	9	4.475	5.556	.001
J	50.444	4	12.611	15.655	.000
Error	12.889	16	.806		
Total	1251.000	30			
Corrected Total	110.167	29			

a. R Squared = .883 (Adjusted R Squared = .788)

Latin Square Designs

Background Music Example

Data File: ch28ta04.txt

Investigators studied the relationship between various types of background music and productivity of bank tellers. Day of week and week of study were blocking variables. After opening the Background Music Example (Table 28.4, text page 1187) and renaming the variables *Y*, *week*, *day*, and *trt*, the first 5 lines of the *Data Editor* should look like SPSS Output 28.3.

SPSS Output 28.3

	y	week	day	trt
1	18.0	1	1	4
2	13.0	2	1	3
3	7.0	3	1	1
4	17.0	4	1	5
5	21.0	5	1	2

Background Music Example.sav - SPSS Data Editor

File   Edit   View   Data   Transform   Analyze   Graphs   Utilities   W

1 : y   18

We begin by producing all indices needed to perform the diagnostic and inferential analyses described on text page 1191. The researchers analyzed residuals by various plots, and performed the *Bonferroni* outlier test and *Tukey's* test of additivity. The *Bonferroni* outlier test and the *Tukey* test for additivity were discussed in Chapters 10 and 20, respectively, of this manual. For the Latin Square design, as illustrated in Table 28.4, text page 1187, we use *week*, *day*, and *trt* as fixed factors, and assume that there are no interactions involving these three variables. While specifying this model in Insert 28.2, we request that pairwise comparisons be made between the different types of background music (*trt*) and that 90% confidence intervals be constructed. Finally, we also request that the predicted values and residuals be saved (by default, as *pre_1* and *res_1*, respectively.) To produce Figure 30.1 (a), text page 1216, simply ✔ Graph ✔ Scatter, and enter *pre_1* on the X-axis and *res_1* on the Y-axis. For Figure 30.1 (b), use ✔ Graph ✔ Q-Q and enter *res_1* as the variable to plot, and then use the *Chart Editor* to reverse the displayed axes. Partial results of Insert 28.2 are shown in SPSS Output 28.4. Notice that $F=10.58$ for *trt*, and this is consistent with the value reported for treatment effects on text page 1192. The confidence intervals (not shown) from the *Tukey* specification indicate three homogenous subgroups (SPSS Output 28.4 – Homogenous Subsets) also consistent with results on text page 1192.

INSERT 28.2	INSERT 28.2
✔ Analyze ✔ General Linear Model ✔ Univariate ✔ Y ✔ ▶ (to the Dependent box) ✔ *week day trt* ✔ ▶ (to the Fixed Factor box) ✔ Model ✔ Custom ✔ ▼ ✔ Main Effects ✔ *week*(F) ✔ *day*(F) ✔ *trt*(F) ✔ ▶ (under Build Terms)	✔ Continue ✔ Post Hoc ✔ *trt* ✔ ▶ ✔ *Tukey* ✔ Continue ✔ Options * Type ".1" in the Significance Level box. ✔ Continue ✔ Save ✔ Unstandardized – Predicted Values ✔ Unstandardized – Residual Values ✔ Continue ✔ OK

SPSS Output 28.4

Tests of Between-Subjects Effects

Dependent Variable: Y

Source	Type III Sum of Squares	df	Mean Square	F	Sig.
Corrected Model	1223.600[a]	12	101.967	6.495	.001
Intercept	10609.000	1	10609.000	675.732	.000
WEEK	82.000	4	20.500	1.306	.323
DAY	477.200	4	119.300	7.599	.003
TRT	664.400	4	166.100	10.580	.001
Error	188.400	12	15.700		
Total	12021.000	25			
Corrected Total	1412.000	24			

a. R Squared = .867 (Adjusted R Squared = .733)

Homogeneous Subsets

Y

Tukey HSD[a,b]

TRT	N	Subset 1	Subset 2	Subset 3
1	5	11.400		
3	5		19.600	
5	5		21.600	21.600
4	5		23.800	23.800
2	5			26.600
Sig.		1.000	.482	.324

Means for groups in homogeneous subsets are displayed.
Based on Type III Sum of Squares
The error term is Mean Square(Error) = 15.700.

    a. Uses Harmonic Mean Sample Size = 5.000.

    b. Alpha = .1.

Additional Replications with Latin Square Designs

Retraining Program Experiment

Data File: ch28ta08.txt

Researchers studied the relationship between three different reward methods and achievement. Age and IQ were used as blocking factors and there were 2 replications per cell as shown in Table 28.8, text page 1197. After opening the Retraining Program Experiment and renaming the variables *Y*, *iq*, *age*, and *trt*, the first 5 lines of the *Data Editor* should look like SPSS Output 28.5.

SPSS Output 28.5

	Retraining Program Experiment.sav - SPSS Data Editor

File Edit View Data Transform Analyze Graphs Utilities W

1 : y   19

	y	iq	age	trt
1	19.0	1	1	2
2	16.0	1	1	2
3	24.0	2	1	3
4	22.0	2	1	3
5	10.0	3	1	1

For this analysis, we ✔ Analyze ✔ General Linear Model ✔ Univariate. We enter Y as the dependent variable; *iq*, *age*, and *trt* as fixed factors; and specify a model that contains main effects only for the 3 independent variables. Additionally, we use *Options* from within *GLM* to specify *Lack of Fit*. Results are not shown but are consistent with Table 28.8(b) and the Lack of Fit $F^*=2.05$ reported on text page 1196.

Replications in Repeated Measures Studies

Apple Sales Example

Data File: ch28ta11.txt

Researchers used a Latin Square crossover design to study the effect of 3 different displays on apple sales. There were six stores in the study; two were randomly assigned to each of the treatment order patterns. After opening the Apple Sales Example and renaming the variables Y, *pattern*, *order*, *display*, and *stores*, the first 5 lines of the *Data Editor* should look like SPSS Output 28.6.

SPSS Output 28.6

Apple Sales Example.sav - SPSS Data Editor

	y	pattern	order	display	stores
1	9.0	1	1	2	1
2	4.0	1	1	2	2
3	12.0	2	1	1	1
4	13.0	2	1	1	2
5	7.0	3	1	3	1

For this analysis, we ✔ Analyze ✔ General Linear Model ✔ Univariate. We enter Y as the dependent variable; *pattern*, *order*, *display*, and *stores* as fixed factors; specify a model that contains main effects only for the 4 independent variables; and paste the syntax into the *Syntax Editor*. We then edit the */Design* statement [*/DESIGN = pattern order display stores.*] to indicate that *stores* are nested within *pattern* [*/DESIGN = pattern order display stores(pattern).*] Results are not shown but are consistent with Table 28.11 (b) and the treatment (*display*) $F^*=37.18$ reported on text page 1200.

Chapter 29 SPSS®

Exploratory Experiments: Two-Level Factorial and Fractional Factorial Designs

In this chapter, the authors discuss strategies for using exploratory experiments aimed at investigating a large number of factors that may be related to the response outcome. By including a large number of factors in the early stages of inquiry, we may be able to identify the most important factors and focus on these in future experiments. When we investigate multiple factors, the size of a full factorial experiment may become prohibitively large. However, we may be able to carefully select a subset of all the possible combinations of levels of the factors and run the experiment using only this *fraction* of the full factorial study. Using a *fractional factorial* combination of factor levels, we can study a large number of factors in a single experiment with a relatively small number of experimental subjects. To see how we might use a fractional factorial study, consider an experiment with three factors denoted A, B, and C, each with two levels denoted A_1, A_2, B_1, B_2, and C_1, C_2, respectively. In the full factorial, there are $2^3 =$ eight possible combinations of levels of the factors:

$$A_1B_1C_1$$
$$A_2B_1C_1$$
$$A_1B_2C_1$$
$$A_2B_2C_1$$
$$A_1B_1C_2$$
$$A_2B_1C_2$$
$$A_1B_2C_2$$
$$A_2B_2C_2$$

Thus, we say there are 8 factor combinations or 8 treatments, and a minimum of 8 experimental subjects are required if we are to run a full factorial experiment (subjects are randomly assigned to the 8 treatments with one subject per treatment). An analysis of variance *effects model* for the 2^3 full factorial study is given in equation 29.2 of the text. We can arrange the X variables for the model as follows:

Treatment	X_1	X_2	X_3
1	−1	−1	−1
2	1	−1	−1
3	−1	1	−1
4	1	1	−1
5	−1	−1	1
6	1	−1	1
7	−1	1	1
8	1	1	1

A one-half fraction of the treatment combinations is:

$$A_2B_1C_1$$
$$A_1B_2C_1$$
$$A_1B_1C_2$$
$$A_2B_2C_2$$

An analysis of variance effects model for this fractional factorial study is

$$Y_i = \beta_0 X_{i0} + \beta_1 X_{i1} + \beta_2 X_{i2} + \beta_3 X_{i3} + \varepsilon_i$$

where:

ε_i are independent $N(0, \sigma^2)$

$X_0 \equiv 0$

$X_1 = \begin{cases} -1 \text{ if observation is from level } A_1 \text{ of factor A} \\ 1 \text{ if observation is from level } A_2 \text{ of factor A} \end{cases}$

$X_2 = \begin{cases} -1 \text{ if observation is from level } B_1 \text{ of factor B} \\ 1 \text{ if observation is from level } B_2 \text{ of factor B} \end{cases}$

$X_3 = \begin{cases} -1 \text{ if observation is from level } C_1 \text{ of factor C} \\ 1 \text{ if observation is from level } C_2 \text{ of factor C} \end{cases}$

but only the indicated combinations of levels of A, B, and C are used. We can arrange the X variables for the model as follows:

Treatment	X_1	X_2	X_3
1	1	−1	−1
2	−1	1	−1
3	−1	−1	1
4	1	1	1

In this example, we can estimate 7 effects using the full factorial study: the 3 main effects of A, B, and C; the 3 two-factor interaction effects AB, AC, BC; and the three factor interaction ABC. In the fractional factorial, we can estimate only the 3 main effects. Nevertheless, fractional factorial studies can be very useful especially in exploratory investigations.

Stress Test Example

Data File: ch24ta04.txt

In the Stress Test Example researchers studied the effects of gender, body fat, and smoking history on exercise tolerance. After opening the Stress Test Example (Table 24.4 (a), text page 1004) and renaming the variables *Y*, *gender*, *fat*, *smoke*, and *rep*, the first 5 lines of the *Data Editor* should look like SPSS Output 24.1.

The authors present further aspects of the analysis on text page 1215 in terms of the effects model defined by the design matrix **X** shown in Table 29.1, text page 1213. We obtain the results shown in Figure 29.1, text page 1215, by executing the syntax given below in Insert 29.1. We use a series of *if* statements to recode the variables *gender*, *fat*, and *smoking*, and subsequently produce the design matrix shown in Table 29.1. We also create variables to represent all possible interactions between *gender*, *fat*, and *smoking*. The results shown in SPSS Output 29.2 are consistent with those presented in Figure 29.1, text page 1215. We obtain the pooled sum of squares for the three main effects from SPSS Output 29.2 by adding the individual sums for *gender*, *fat*, and *smoking*, i.e., Sum of Squares (main effects) = 176.5837500 + 242.570 + 70.383 = 489.537. Similarly, we find Sum of Squares (2-way interactions) = 13.650 + 11.070 + 72.453 = 97.174. These results are consistent with text page 1215.

INSERT 29.1	INSERT 29.1 continued

✔ File
✔ New
✔ Syntax
if (gender = 1) gender=-1.
if (gender = 2) gender=1.
if (fat=1) fat=-1.
if (fat=2) fat=1.
if (smoke = 1)smoke=-1.
if (smoke = 2)smoke=1.
compute gxf=gender*fat.
compute gxs=gender*smoke.
compute fxs=fat*smoke.
compute gxfxs=gender*fat*smoke.
exe.
✔ Run
✔ All
	✔ Analyze
	✔ Regression
	✔ Linear
	✔ *y*
	✔ ▶(to the Dependent box)
	✔ *gender fat smoke gxf gxs fxs gxfxs*
	✔ ▶(to the Independents box)
	✔ OK

SPSS Output 29.1

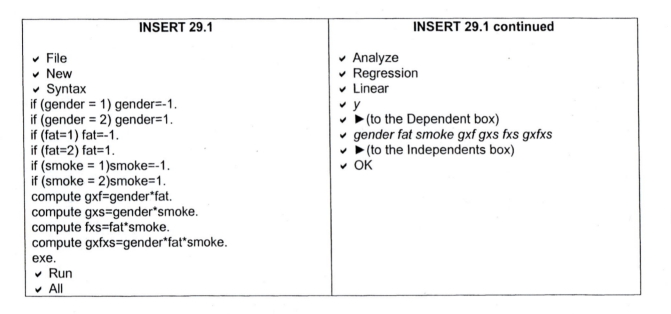

650

SPSS Output 29.2

Tests of Between-Subjects Effects

Dependent Variable: Y

Source	Type III Sum of Squares	df	Mean Square	F	Sig.
Corrected Model	588.583[a]	7	84.083	9.007	.000
Intercept	6353.760	1	6353.760	680.608	.000
GENDER	176.584	1	176.584	18.915	.000
FAT	242.570	1	242.570	25.984	.000
SMOKE	70.384	1	70.384	7.539	.014
GXF	13.650	1	13.650	1.462	.244
GXS	11.070	1	11.070	1.186	.292
FXS	72.454	1	72.454	7.761	.013
GXFXS	1.870	1	1.870	.200	.660
Error	149.367	16	9.335		
Total	7091.710	24			
Corrected Total	737.950	23			

a. R Squared = .798 (Adjusted R Squared = .709)

Parameter Estimates

Dependent Variable: Y

Parameter	B	Std. Error	t	Sig.	95% Confidence Interval	
					Lower Bound	Upper Bound
Intercept	16.271	.624	26.088	.000	14.949	17.593
GENDER	-2.713	.624	-4.349	.000	-4.035	-1.390
FAT	-3.179	.624	-5.097	.000	-4.501	-1.857
SMOKE	-1.713	.624	-2.746	.014	-3.035	-.390
GXF	.754	.624	1.209	.244	-.568	2.076
GXS	-.679	.624	-1.089	.292	-2.001	.643
FXS	1.738	.624	2.786	.013	.415	3.060
GXFXS	-.279	.624	-.448	.660	-1.601	1.043

Pecos Foods Corporation Example

Data File: ch29ta02.txt

The Pecos Food Corporation conducted a study to investigate the effects of process temperature ($x1$), an antimicrobial agent ($x2$), moisture level ($x3$), and acidity ($x4$) on the microbial growth in a fruit bar (y). The four factors were studied at high and low levels as defined on text page 1216. The response (y) is the natural logarithm of the microbial count. After opening the Pecos Foods Corporation Example (Table 29.2, text page 1217) and renaming the variables y, $x0$, $x1$, $x2$, $x3$, $x4$, $x12$, $x13$, $x14$, $x23$, $x24$, $x34$, $x123$, $x124$, $x134$, $x234$, and $x1234$, the first 5 lines of the *Data Editor* should look like SPSS Output 29.3.

SPSS Output 29.3

Pecos Foods Corp Example.sav - SPSS Data Editor

File Edit View Data Transform Analyze Graphs Utilities Window Help

1 : y   5.55

	y	x0	x1	x2	x3	x4	x12	x13	x14	x23	x24	x34	x123	x124	x134	x234	x1234
1	5.55	1	-1	-1	-1	-1	1	1	1	1	1	1	-1	-1	-1	-1	1
2	4.47	1	1	-1	-1	-1	-1	-1	-1	1	1	1	1	1	1	-1	-1
3	5.19	1	-1	1	-1	-1	-1	1	1	-1	-1	1	1	1	-1	1	-1
4	5.32	1	1	1	-1	-1	1	-1	-1	-1	-1	1	-1	-1	1	1	1
5	10.54	1	-1	-1	1	-1	1	-1	1	-1	1	-1	1	-1	1	1	-1

In Insert 29.2 (Full Model Analysis), we first obtain the results shown in Figure 29.2, text page 1217 by regressing y on $x1$ through $x1234$ as shown in SPSS Output 29.3. Partial results shown in SPSS Output 29.4 are consistent with text Figure 29.2. The researchers decided that all three-factor and four-factor interactions were unimportant and dropped these terms from the previous model. In Insert 29.2 (Reduced Model Analysis) we produce Figure 29.3, text page 1219. A parameter estimate table is shown in SPSS Output 29.5. We can now find the percent contribution to the sum of squares for each factor using equation 29.16 and results from SPSS Output 29.4 and 29.5. From text page 1220 we find the percent contribution of $x3$:

$$\frac{n_T b_3^2}{SSTO}(100) = \frac{16(1.403)^2}{91.628}(100) = 3\%$$

INSERT 29.2	INSERT 29.2 continued
* Produce Figure 29.2. *** Full Model Analysis. ✔ Analyze ✔ General Linear Model ✔ Univariate ✔ y ✔ ►(to the Dependent box) ✔ x1 x2 x3 x4 x12 x13 x14 x23 x24 x34 x123 x124 x134 x234 x1234 ✔ ►(to the Covariate box) ✔ Options ✔ Parameter Estimates ✔ Continue ✔ OK	* Produce Figure 29.3. *** Reduced Model Analysis. ✔ Analyze ✔ General Linear Model ✔ Univariate ✔ y ✔ ►(to the Dependent box) ✔ x1 x2 x3 x4 x12 x13 x14 x23 x24 x34 ✔ ►(to the Covariate box) ✔ Options ✔ Parameter Estimates ✔ Continue ✔ OK

SPSS Output 29.4
Full Model Analysis
(Truncated Table)
Tests of Between-Subjects Effects

Dependent Variable: Y

Source	Type III Sum of Squares	df	Mean Square	F	Sig.
Corrected Model	91.628[a]	15	6.109	.	.
Intercept	726.976	1	726.976	.	.
X1	.248	1	.248	.	.
X2	25.025	1	25.025	.	.
X3	31.500	1	31.500	.	.
X4	.146	1	.146	.	.
X12	.273	1	.273	.	.

(Truncated Table)

Parameter Estimates

Dependent Variable: Y

Parameter	B	Std. Error	t	Sig.	95% Confidence Interval	
					Lower Bound	Upper Bound
Intercept	6.741	.	.	.	.	.
X1	-.124	.	.	.	.	.
X2	-1.251	.	.	.	.	.
X3	1.403	.	.	.	.	.
X4	.096	.	.	.	.	.
X12	-.131	.	.	.	.	.

SPSS Output 29.5
Reduced Model Analysis

Parameter Estimates

Dependent Variable: Y

Parameter	B	Std. Error	t	Sig.	95% Confidence Interval	
					Lower Bound	Upper Bound
Intercept	6.741	.167	40.283	.000	6.310	7.171
X1	-.124	.167	-.743	.491	-.555	.306
X2	-1.251	.167	-7.474	.001	-1.681	-.820
X3	1.403	.167	8.385	.000	.973	1.833
X4	.096	.167	.571	.592	-.335	.526
X12	-.131	.167	-.781	.470	-.561	.300
X13	.048	.167	.288	.785	-.382	.478
X14	-.179	.167	-1.072	.333	-.610	.251
X23	-1.396	.167	-8.340	.000	-1.826	-.965
X24	.134	.167	.803	.458	-.296	.565
X34	-.109	.167	-.654	.542	-.540	.321

Lack of Fit. On text page 1223, the authors posit a scenario in which four replicate observations are made at the center point of the 2^4 factorial combinations of treatment levels used in the Pecos Food Corporation Example. The hypothetical data for the center point are appended to the original data set (ch29ta02.txt) to provide a total of 20 lines of data. The **last** five lines of the appended *Data Editor* are shown below. To obtain the lack of fit test, we use the Full Model Analysis of Insert 29.2 above and also ✔ Options ✔ Lack of Fit ✔ Continue. The results are shown in SPSS Output 29.6.

16	4.93	1	1	1	1	1	1	1	1	1	1	1	1	1	1	1	1
17	7.23	0	0	0	0	0	0	0	0	0	0	0	0	0	0	0	0
18	7.89	0	0	0	0	0	0	0	0	0	0	0	0	0	0	0	0
19	7.80	0	0	0	0	0	0	0	0	0	0	0	0	0	0	0	0
20	7.39	0	0	0	0	0	0	0	0	0	0	0	0	0	0	0	0

SPSS Output 29.6

Lack of Fit Tests

Dependent Variable: Y

Source	Sum of Squares	df	Mean Square	F	Sig.
Lack of Fit	2.241	1	2.241	22.184	.018
Pure Error	.303	3	.101		

The Iowa Aluminum Corporation Example

Data File: ch29ta07.txt

The Iowa Aluminum Corporation manufactures sheet aluminum from recycled aluminum beverage containers (text page 1233). Six factors that might affect the quality of the product were considered:

1. coolant temperature ($x1$)
2. percentage of oil in the coolant ($x2$)
3. volume 1 of coolant ($x3$)
4. volume 2 of coolant ($x4$)
5. volume 3 of coolant ($x5$)
6. strip speed ($x6$)

Low and high levels for each of these six factors were used in an experiment with the goal to improve the quality of the aluminum. The response variable was a surface impurity score. Only 20 experimental units were available for the study so $2^6 = 64$ factorial combinations of treatments (a full factorial) could not be investigated. Instead, the company conducted a study using a one-quarter fractional factorial plan with an additional four observations made at the center point. The design matrix and the observed data are shown in Table 29.7. After opening the Iowa Aluminum Corporation Example and renaming the variables x1, x2, x3, x4, x5, x6, and y, the first 5 lines of the *Data Editor* should look like SPSS Output 29.7.

SPSS Output 29.7

	x1	x2	x3	x4	x5	x6	y
1	-1	-1	-1	-1	-1	-1	4
2	1	-1	-1	-1	1	-1	6
3	-1	1	-1	-1	1	1	7
4	1	1	-1	-1	-1	1	2
5	-1	-1	1	-1	1	1	3

Iowa Aluminum.sav - SPSS Data Editor
File Edit View Data Transform Analyze Graphs Utilities Window Help
1 : x1 -1

In Insert 29.4, the first *GLM* produces (output not shown) the initial factorial model as shown in Figure 29.9, text page 1237. From Figure 29.9, the researchers identified active effects for x2, x5, x6, and the interaction between x1 and x3. We fitted a regression model based on these four effects and produced the *lack of fit* test for the model. Partial results of this analysis are shown in SPSS Output 29.8 and are consistent with the *lack of fit F*=0.04* reported on text page 1235 and Figure 29.10, text page 1238.

SPSS Output 29.8

Lack of Fit Tests

Dependent Variable: Y

Source	Sum of Squares	df	Mean Square	F	Sig.
Lack of Fit	.200	4	.050	.044	.996
Pure Error	12.500	11	1.136		

INSERT 29.4	INSERT 29.4 continued
* Produce Figure 29.9. *** Initial Model. ✔ Analyze ✔ General Linear Model ✔ Univariate ✔ *y* ✔ ▶(to the Dependent box) ✔ *x1 x2 x3 x4 x5 x6* ✔ ▶(to the Covariate box) ✔ Model ✔ Custom * Specify a Custom Model. * with the following terms:. * *x1 x2 x3 x4 x5 x6 x1*x2* * *x1*x3 x1*x4 x1*x5 x1*x6* * *x2*x4 x2*x6 x1*x2*x4 x1*x2*x6.* ✔ Continue ✔ Options ✔ Parameter Estimates ✔ Continue ✔ OK	* Produce Figure 29.10,. * model with active effects and lof; ✔ File ✔ New ✔ Syntax compute x13=x1*x3. exe. ✔ Run ✔ All ✔ Analyze ✔ General Linear Model ✔ Univariate ✔ *y* ✔ ▶(to the Dependent box) ✔ *x2 x5 x6 x13* ✔ ▶(to the Covariate box) ✔ Options ✔ Parameter Estimates ✔ Lack of Fit ✔ Continue ✔ OK

The Caramel Example

Data File: ch29ta10.txt

On text page 1248, researchers wished to study the relationship between three recipe ingredients and the plasticity of caramel. Plasticity measured on a scale of 1 to 100, where 100 indicated complete plasticity; the target value was 70. The three ingredients investigated were brown sugar ($x1$), sweetened condensed milk ($x2$), and light corn syrup ($x3$). An experiment was run using a full factorial 2^3 with four replicates for each treatment combination. Text Table 29.10 contains the coded values for the three ingredients ($x1 - x3$) and the interaction between the three ingredients ($x12 - x123$), the replicates ($y1 - y4$), the sample variances ($s2$), the logarithms of the sample variances ($logs2$), and estimated weights (w). After opening the Caramel Example (Table 29.10, text page 1248) and renaming the variables $x1$, $x2$, $x3$, $x12$, $x13$, $x23$, $x123$, $y1$, $y2$, $y3$, $y4$, $s2$, $logs2$, and w, the first 5 lines of the *Data Editor* should look like SPSS Output 29.9.

The analyst fitted the dispersion model shown in text equation 29.40 as a first step in the analysis. That is, the researchers regressed *logs2* on the coded values of the three ingredients and all possible interaction combinations. In the first *GLM* of Insert 29.5 we specify *logs2* as the dependent variable and all *x* variables in SPSS Output 29.9 as independent variables. Results are not shown but the parameter estimates are consistent with Figure 29.13(a), text page 1249. We also saved the coefficient statistics including the parameter estimates for subsequent use in the normal probability plot as shown in Figure 29.13(b). After opening the file that contains the saved coefficient statistics, the *Data Editor* will look like SPSS Output 29.10. The parameter estimates appear on the row labeled *EST* under *rowtype_*. There are eight parameters, one for the intercept (*p1*) and a parameter for each of the seven independent variables (*p2* to *p8*). We use the

Select If syntax of Insert 29.5 to select only records that contain *EST* in the *rowtype_* column. All records that do not contain *EST* are deleted from the *Data Editor*. We then read the one remaining record that contains the parameter estimates and write to a new file one record for each of the seven non-intercept parameter estimates (*loop z=2 to 8*). Finally, we use the *Q-Q* procedure to create SPSS Output 29.11(a), which is equivalent to Figure 29.13(b). The syntax for saving and restructuring the coefficient statistics may be helpful when dealing with large numbers of independent variables. For most situations, however, it is more expedient to enter the parameter estimates manually into a *Data Editor*.

SPSS Output 29.9

	x1	x2	x3	x12	x13	x23	x123	y1	y2	y3	y4	s2	logs2	w
1	-1	-1	-1	1	1	1	-1	42	65	70	73	197.67	5.2870	.0102
2	1	-1	-1	-1	-1	1	1	50	52	55	63	32.670	3.4860	.0322
3	-1	1	-1	-1	1	-1	1	61	70	78	79	70.000	4.2480	.0102
4	1	1	-1	1	-1	-1	-1	48	51	55	60	27.000	3.2960	.0322
5	-1	-1	1	1	-1	-1	1	65	74	74	77	27.000	3.2960	.0322

From the above analysis the researchers identified one nonzero dispersion effect and decided to use weighted least squares regression (estimated variance function based on equation 29.44) for estimation of parameters in the location effects model. (See Chapters 11 of this manual and the text for additional computational details of weighted least squares regression.) In Insert 29.6, we restructure the data file as shown in SPSS Output 29.9. The restructured file will contain 4 records for each record in SPSS Output 29.9. Each of the 4 new records will contain one of the *y* values (*y1 – y4*) from the original file. Using the restructured file, we specify *y* as the dependent variable, all *x* variables in SPSS Output 29.9 as independent variables, and *w* as the weight variable. Resulting parameter estimates (not shown) are consistent with Figure 29.14(a). SPSS Output 29.11(b) is consistent with the Figure 29.14(b). We created SPSS Output 29.11(b) by entering the parameter estimates manually into the *Data Editor* and using the *Q-Q* procedure.

INSERT 29.5	INSERT 29.5 continued
* Produce Figure 29.13(a). ✔ Analyze ✔ General Linear Model ✔ Univariate ✔ *logs2* ✔ ►(to the Dependent box) ✔ *x1 x2 x3 x12 x13 x23 x123* ✔ ►(to the Covariate box) ✔ Options ✔ Parameter Estimates ✔ Continue ✔ Save ✔ Coefficient Statistics ✔ File * Indicate an arbitrary path & file name. ✔ Continue ✔ OK * Produce Figure 29.13(b). ✔ File ✔ Open ✔ Data * Indicate path & file name that contains. * the Coefficient Statistics.	✔ File ✔ New ✔ Syntax FILTER OFF. USE ALL. SELECT IF(rowtype_ = "EST "). EXECUTE . * METHOD 2 - Multiple measurements per line to one measurement per line. vector parm = p1 to p8. loop z=2 to 8. compute parm=parm(z). format parm (f6.4). xsave outfile = 'temp' / keep parm. end loop. exe. get file 'temp'. exe. ✔ Run ✔ All ✔ Graphs ✔ Q-Q ✔ y ✔ ►(to Variable box) ✔ OK * Use Chart Editor to reverse axes.

Output 29.10

Caramel Coefficients.sav - SPSS Data Editor

File Edit View Data Transform Analyze Graphs Utilities Window Help

1 : rowvar_   LOGS2

	rowvar_	colvar_	rowtype_	varname_	p1	p2	p3	p4	p5	p6	p7	p8
1	LOGS2	LOGS2	COV	P1	00	.000	.000	000	000	.000	.000	.000
2	LOGS2	LOGS2	COV	P2	.00	.000	.000	.000	000	.000	.000	.000
3	LOGS2	LOGS2	COV	P3	00	.000	.000	.000	000	.000	.000	.000
4	LOGS2	LOGS2	COV	P4	00	.000	.000	.000	.000	.000	.000	.000
5	LOGS2	LOGS2	COV	P5	00	.000	.000	000	000	.000	.000	.000
6	LOGS2	LOGS2	COV	P6	.00	.000	.000	.000	000	.000	.000	.000
7	LOGS2	LOGS2	COV	P7	00	.000	.000	.000	.000	.000	.000	.000
8	LOGS2	LOGS2	COV	P8	.00	.000	.000	.000	000	.000	.000	.000
9	LOGS2	LOGS2	EST		4 01	-.113	-.237	- 070	-.069	.575	.070	-.281
10	LOGS2	LOGS2	SE		00	.000	.000	.000	.000	.000	.000	.000
11	LOGS2	LOGS2	SIG		.	.	.	.	.	.		
12	LOGS2	LOGS2	DFE		00	.000	.000	000	.000	.000	.000	.000

INSERT 29.6	INSERT 29.6 continued
✔ File	* Produce Figure 29.14(a).
✔ New	✔ Analyze
✔ Syntax	✔ General Linear Model
* METHOD 2 - Multiple measurements per line	✔ Univariate
to one measurement per line.	✔ *y*
vector y = y1 to y4.	✔ ▶ (to the Dependent box)
loop z=1 to 4.	✔ *x1 x2 x3 x12 x13 x23 x123*
compute y=y(z).	✔ ▶ (to the Covariate box)
format y (f2.0).	✔ *w*
xsave outfile = 'temp' / drop y1 to y4 z.	✔ ▶ (to the WLS Weight box)
end loop.	✔ Options
exe.	✔ Parameter Estimates
get file 'temp'.	✔ Continue
exe.	✔ OK
✔ Run	
✔ All	

SPSS Output 29.11

(a) Normal Q-Q Plot of PARM

(b) Normal Q-Q Plot of PARM

Clutch Slave Cylinder Example

Data File: ch29ta12.txt

An automotive company conducted research to identify a clutch slave cylinder design that minimized fluid leakage. The response variable was fluid leakage; the five control factors were body inner diameter ($X1$), body outer diameter ($X2$), seal inner diameter ($X3$), seal outer diameter ($X4$), and seal design ($X5$); and the two noise factors were temperature and load. After opening the Clutch Slave Cylinder Example (Table 29.12, text page 1252) and renaming the variables *x1*, *x2*, *x3*, *x4*, *x5*, *y1*, *y2*, *y3*, *y4*, *logs2*, and *w*, the first 5 lines of the *Data Editor* should look like SPSS Output 29.12.

659

SPSS Output 29.12

	x1	x2	x3	x4	x5	y1	y2	y3	y4	logs2	w
1	-1	-1	-1	-1	-1	.8	.4	.0	.0	-1.920	1.245
2	1	-1	-1	1	-1	3.2	.0	.0	.0	.940	.195
3	-1	1	-1	1	-1	.0	.0	.0	2.4	.365	1.245
4	1	1	-1	-1	-1	5.8	0	.0	2.8	2.036	.195
5	-1	-1	1	1	-1	0	3.0	.0	2.4	.912	1.245

In Insert 29.7, we estimate the dispersion model by regressing *logs2* on the first dispersion effect from each of the 16 pairs shown in equation 29.46, text page 1253. Results are consistent with Figure 29.15(a) (not shown) and (b) [SPSS Output 29.13(a)]. From the plot, the researchers found active dispersion effects for *x5* and *x15*. In the second *GLM*, we eliminate the inactive effects and estimate the subset dispersion model. Partial results in SPSS Output 29.14 are consistent with equation 29.48, test page 1254.

SPSS Output 29.13

(a)

Normal Q-Q Plot of PARM2

(b)

Normal Q-Q Plot of PARM

SPSS Output 29.14

Parameter Estimates

Dependent Variable: LOGS2

Parameter	B	Std. Error	t	Sig.	95% Confidence Interval	
					Lower Bound	Upper Bound
Intercept	2.241	.221	10.146	.000	1.764	2.718
X5	1.534	.221	6.945	.000	1.057	2.011
X15	-.926	.221	-4.192	.001	-1.403	-.449

INSERT 29.7	INSERT 29.7 continued
✔ File ✔ New ✔ Syntax compute x12 = x1*x2. compute x13 = x1*x3. compute x14 = x1*x4. compute x15 = x1*x5. compute x25 = x2*x5. compute x35 = x3*x5. compute x45 = x4*x5. compute x125 = x1*x2*x5. compute x135 = x1*x3*x5. compute x145 = x1*x4*x5. exe. ✔ Run ✔ All * Produce Figure 29.15. ✔ Analyze ✔ General Linear Model ✔ Univariate ✔ *logs2* ✔ ▶(to the Dependent box) ✔ *x1 x2 x3 x4 x5 x12* *x13 x14 x15 x25 x35 x45* *x125 x135 x145* ✔ ▶(to the Covariate box) ✔ Options ✔ Parameter Estimates ✔ Continue ✔ OK * Produce equation 29.48. ✔ Analyze ✔ General Linear Model ✔ Univariate ✔ *logs2* ✔ ▶(to the Dependent box) ✔ *x5 x15* ✔ ▶(to the Covariate box) ✔ Options ✔ Parameter Estimates ✔ Continue ✔ OK	* Produce Figure 29.16. * METHOD 2 - Multiple measurements per line to one measurement per line. vector y = y1 to y4. loop z=1 to 4. compute y=y(z). format y (f2.0). xsave outfile = 'temp' / drop y1 to y4 z. end loop. exe. get file 'temp'. exe. ✔ Analyze ✔ General Linear Model ✔ Univariate ✔ *y* ✔ ▶(to the Dependent box) ✔ *x1 x2 x3 x4 x5 x12* *x13 x14 x15 x25 x35 x45* *x125 x135 x145* ✔ ▶(to the Covariate box) ✔ Options ✔ Parameter Estimates ✔ Continue ✔ OK * Produce equation 29.49. ✔ Analyze ✔ General Linear Model ✔ Univariate ✔ *y* ✔ ▶(to the Dependent box) ✔ *x5* ✔ ▶(to the Covariate box) ✔ Options ✔ Parameter Estimates ✔ Continue ✔ OK

The researchers elected to fit a weighted least squares regression model to estimate the location model. In Insert 29.6 we restructure the original data file (ch29ta12.txt, shown in SPSS Output 29.12). The restructured file will contain 4 records for each record in SPSS Output 29.12. Each of the 4 new records will contain one of the y values ($y1 - y4$) from the original file. Using the new file, we specify y as the dependent variable and $x1$, $x2$, $x3$, $x4$, $x5$, $x12$, $x13$, $x14$, $x15$, $x25$, *x35*, *x45*, *x125*, *x135*, and *x145* as independent variables. Resulting parameter estimates and normal probability plot (not shown) are consistent with Figure 29.16(a) & (b). Both Figure 29.16 (a) and (b) indicate that *x15* (β_{15}) is the only active location effect. Thus, in the last *GLM* of Insert 29.9 we specify *y* as the dependent variable and *x5* as an independent variable to produce equation 29.49, text page 1254.

Response Surface Methodology

The goal of *response surface* techniques is to determine the levels of the factors under investigation that produce an optimum response. The methods involve choosing wisely the levels of factors to include in an experiment, fitting linear regression models, and then estimating the combination of factor levels that produces the optimum response. Sometimes the optimum response is not found in the range of the levels chosen for initial experimentation but the results from that experiment point toward a range for additional experimentation. In the regression model, the dependent variable is the response y and the independent variables are a function of the levels of the factors. The independent variables typically are linear and quadratic terms representing levels of the factors. Thus, the regression model is usually a first or second-order model and the predicted values lie on the surface of the curve described by the fitted model. In this chapter, the authors discuss the design and analysis of experiments using response surface methods in studies where the goal is to find the combination of levels of quantitative factors that produce the best quantitative response.

Analysis of Response Surface Experiments

SPSS has no readily available way to analyze Response Surface Experiments.